1 MONTH OF
FREE
READING

at

www.ForgottenBooks.com

By purchasing this book you are
eligible for one month membership to
ForgottenBooks.com, giving you
unlimited access to our entire
collection of over 1,000,000 titles via
our web site and mobile apps.

To claim your free month visit:

www.forgottenbooks.com/free861520

ISBN 978-0-266-53077-0
PIBN 10861520

CYCLOPEDIA

OF

Eminent and Representative Men

OF THE

Carolinas of the Nineteenth Century,

WITH A

BRIEF HISTORICAL INTRODUCTION ON SOUTH CAROLINA BY GENERAL
EDWARD McCRADY, Jr., AND ON NORTH CAROLINA
BY HON. SAMUEL A. ASHE.

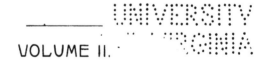

VOLUME II.

MADISON, WIS.:
BRANT & FULLER.
1892.

AND

F
268
.C99
1892

~~958185~~

v.2

Democrat Printing Co., Madison, Wis.
Bindery of W. B Conkey, Chicago, Ill.

PREFACE.

In presenting this Cyclopedia of Eminent and Representative men of the Carolinas to their subscribers, the publishers beg leave to make a few brief remarks touching its compilation. Of the excellent historical sketches by S. A. Ashe, Esq., of North Carolina, and by Gen. Edward McCrady, Jr., of South Carolina, but little need be said, as they sufficiently recommend themselves. But it is only proper to say that these gentlemen are in no respect responsible for the biographical sketches contained within the covers of the work. The publishers are indebted for these, in a measure, to such works as Wheeler's Reminiscences of North Carolina, O'Neall's Bench and Bar, of South Carolina, Dowd's Prominent Living North Carolinians, the works of ex-Governor Perry, of South Carolina, Smith's Western North Carolina, Appleton's Encyclopedia, and, more than all, to the labors of the force of able writers employed for the purpose by the publishers.

That there may be some defects in the work, as there are in all works, it would be useless to deny, but the publishers feel warranted in saying that they have fully kept up to their contract with their subscribers, and may with pardonable pride point to the excellent typography and attractive binding of the work.

INDEX.

HISTORICAL SKETCH OF NORTH CAROLINA.

BY S. A. ASHE.

ONNECTED with the biographies of men whose lives illustrate the annals of a state, it is desirable to present a succint account of the influences which have evolved their characteristics and moulded them, as it were, into harmony with their surroundings. Nor will this be difficult in regard to the men of North Carolina, for more than a century has passed since the population of that state has received accessions from abroad, and her people are sons and daughters of the soil, native and to the manner born as their forefathers were before them.

Although the first English settlement made in the New World was upon Roanoke Island, within the limits of North Carolina, that memorable event exerted no influence upon the citizens of the state, since the colony located there ended in disaster and was entirely lost to history. Nearly three-quarters of a century elapsed after Raleigh's ill-fated attempt at settlement had become a tradition before a permanent lodgment was made in the primeval wilderness of Carolina.

When the English had become well established at Jamestown, the planters began to extend their possessions to the southward, following, according to the needs of those days, the margins of the water courses. Soon the outskirts of the plantations were pressed well up the Nansemond river, until at length, about the year 1650, adventurous spirits, passing down the waters of the Chowan, made settlements along the fertile shores of Albemarle sound.

Doubtless many of the pioneers in this movement to the southward were native born Virginians, men bred in the forests of the New World and accustomed to the hardships of life on the frontiers of civilization, inured to its dangers, and imbued with the spirit of personal independence that invariably accompanies such a residence.

Familiar with the Indians on the borders of the great sound, who had habitually traded with the English, the settlers found no difficulty in securing their good-will. They purchased titles to the lands they desired and established, from the first, friendly relations with the native tribes, who, continuing to occupy the neighboring forests, supplied them with provisions and even aided in the preparation of their fields. Thus happily the foundations of the Albemarle colony were not stained with blood nor laid in wrong and outrage,

B—2

but in peace and good-will the new comers made their homes in the wilderness, receiving help and encouragement from the aborigines of the country.

In 1663, King Charles by way of recompensing some gentlemen who had been chiefly instrumental in restoring him to the throne, granted them the territory lying between Virginia and Florida, which his father had formerly granted to Sir Robert Heath, and which was called Carolina. Under the terms of his charter, those grantees became owners and rulers of the whole of Carolina with power to establish governments and courts and to make laws and regulations, and they are known to history as "Lords Proprietors."

To induce a speedy settlement of this magnificent domain, the Proprietors offered concessions that the people settling there should have an assembly "to be by them chosen out of themselves," to make their own laws; and granted freedom and liberty of conscience in all religious or spiritual things. The Proprietors, however, were to select their own governor, who was to hold for three years, and each Proprietor had a representative, called his deputy, in the governor's council.

William Drummond, then a resident of Virginia, a Scotchman of education and of fine character, was the first governor of Albemarle, and an assembly was held about the close of the year 1664. The terms under which the settlers were to take up and hold land were not so favorable in some respects as those to which they had been accustomed in Virginia, and the assembly petitioned for a change, which was granted by the Lords Proprietors in what was called "The Great Deed of Grant," dated May 1, 1668.

Another settlement having been made further to the south, leaving a vast wilderness intervening, the one became known as South and the other as North Carolina; and as Charleston being admirably located for trade, rapidly grew, the Proprietors paid more attention to the southern settlement than to Albemarle. And so for a period of sixty years North Carolina continued under the dominion of the Lords Proprietors, their heirs and those who as purchasers succeeded to their legal rights under the broad terms of Charles' grant, yielding them, however, but small pecuniary returns and exciting so little interest that her affairs were generally neglected by her proprietary rulers.

The people led quiet lives in the forest, making their own laws in an assembly of their own choosing and enjoying liberty of conscience and all the natural rights of men living in a state of absolute freedom. It was in those early days that Nathaniel Bacon, calling the people of Virginia to his standard, rallied them against the arbitrary government of Berkeley, in which bold movement he had the countenance of William Drummond who had been the first governor of Albemarle. When Bacon's flag went down in disaster, and his watchcry of "Carolina" ceased to be heard, and Drummond had paid the penalty with his life, many of their supporters came to the Albemarle and found refuge in the wilderness from the heavy hand of Berkeley's tyranny. The spirit of liberty which imbued the hearts of Bacon's followers was thus transplanted to the infant colony of Carolina where it was fostered and treasured and where it expanded with advancing years.

The handful of scattered settlers grew in numbers slowly but surely as the new lands attracted more and more the attention of friends in the other colonies and in England. There were constant accessions; but the region was difficult to reach, and the country to be occupied was broad and extensive. The people lived in their clearings, often remote from each other. With their plantations in the depths of the forests, separated by miles of intervening woods, they found no necessity for those laws and regulations which obtain in a complex civilization, but led a life of natural freedom, but little restrained by civil codes. \ There were no ministers of the gospel among them, and so, as early as 1669, the assembly passed an act "Forasmuch as there may be divers people that are minded to be joyned together in the holy state of Wedlock, and for that there is noe minister as yet in this County by whom the said partyes may be joyned in Wedlock according to the rites and customs of our native country, the Kingdom of England, that none may be hindered from this soe necessary a worke for the promotion of mankind and settlement of this county, it is enacted and be it enacted by the Palatine and Lords Proprietors of Carolina by and with the advice and consent of the Present Grand Assembly and authority thereof that any two persons desiring to be joyned in the holy state of matrimony, taking three or four of their neighbors along with them, and repairing to the Governor or any one of the Council, before him declaring that they doe joyne together in the holy state of Wedlock and doe accept one the other for man and wife; and the said governor or councellor before whom such act is performed, giving certificate thereof, and the said certificate being registered in the Secretary's office or by the register of the Precinct or in such other office as shall hereafter for that use be provided. It shall be deemed a lawful marriage and the partyes violating this marriage shall be punishable as they had been married by a minister according to the rites and customs of England."

In like manner the other institutions and mode of life of the settlers were in large measure the outgrowth of their isolated situation. They had neither silver nor gold; but their surplus products were valuable in the markets of the world, and their accounts were kept in "tobacco" and were payable in tobacco; while there were established rates at which other articles, including skins and furs, were to be received in payment of all debts—even the quitrents due for the land to the Lords Proprietors.

Left largely to themselves, government rested lightly on these men of Carolina, and they passed their days in the peaceful enjoyment of their secluded homes, self reliant, courageous, nurturing a spirit of independence, revelling to the fullest in the sweets of unrestrained liberty. Occasionally some governor, hastening to be rich, would seek by fraud or peculation to prosper at their expense, or some customs officer would attempt to enforce British regulations in regard to tobacco, or the provisions of the odious Navigation laws that restrained trading with New England and forbade it with the Spanish colonies in the West Indies. On such occasions the people of Albemarle would show that they were neither respecters of persons nor loyal submissionists to the will of parliament. They had a disposition to live under their own regulations and they manifested their purpose in ways that admitted of no misconstruction. The people would make the lives of their customs house officers intolerable, while the assembly would try offending governors and depose them, banish them for a time from the settlement and exclude them from ever holding office again in the colony. Indeed, according to the narration of Gov. Burrington, fifty years later, they seized one of their early governors and "clapped him into a log house without a roof," and presumably without food or drink, until he should submit himself to their authority.

To use the words of the immortal Bancroft — Vol. I, p. 158 —"The planters of Albemarle were men who had been led to a choice of their residence from a hatred of restraint and had lost themselves among the woods in search of independence. Are there any who doubt man's capacity for self-government; let them study the history of North Carolina; its inhabitants were restless and turbulent in their imperfect submission to a government imposed upon them from abroad; the administration of the colony was firm, humane and tranquil when they were left to take care of themselves. Any government but one of their own institution was oppressive." And again the same historian pays this noble tribute to those people: "The planters of North Carolina recovered tranquillity as soon as they escaped the misrule from abroad; and sure of amnesty, esteemed themselves the happiest people on earth. They loved the pure air and clear skies of their summer land. True there was no fixed minister in the land until 1703; no church erected till 1705; no separate building for a court house till 1722; no printing press till 1754. Careless of religious sects, or colleges, or lawyers, or absolute laws, the early settlers enjoyed liberty of conscience and personal independence; freedom of the forest and of the river. The children of nature listened to the inspiration of nature. From almost every plantation they enjoyed a noble prospect of spacious rivers, pleasant meadows enameled with flowers; of primeval forests where the loftiest branches of the tulip tree or the magnolia were wrapped in jasimines and honeysuckle. * * * North Carolina was settled by the freest of the free; by men to whom the restraints of the other colonies were too severe. They were not so much caged in the woods as scattered in lonely granges. Their was neither city nor township; there was hardly even a hamlet or one house within sight of another; nor were there roads, except as the paths from house to house were distinguished by notches in the trees. But the settlers were gentle in their tempers, of serene minds, enemies to violence and bloodshed. Not all the successive revolutions had kindled vindictive passions;

freedom, entire freedom was enjoyed without anxiety or without guaranties; the charities of life were scattered at their feet, like the flowers on their meadows, and the spirit of humanity maintained its influence in the Arcadia, as royalist writers will have it "'of rogues and rebels' in the paradise of Quakers."

At length the Lords Proprietors ceased sending governors to Albemarle and the president of the council acted as governor, the inhabitants of the colony thus administering its affairs entirely. And so under the wise and patriotic sway of Major Alexander Lillington, of Thomas Harvey and Henderson Walker, tranquillity reigned for a happy period.

Taking a view of the colony about the close of the seventeenth century, we find that there had been considerable progress made in settlement, although still there was not a village to be seen. There were landings where vessels lay while trading with the people, and country stores where products were bartered; and the people led easy lives, basking in their health-giving sunlight.

Among the chief men in the colony were Thomas Harvey, Alexander Lillington, Henderson Walker, John Porter, Samuel Swann, and a little later Thomas Pollock, William Glover, Edward Moseley and Maurice Moore.

Major Lillington is said to have come to Albemarle from the Barbadoes, where one of his name was member ofthe Royal council and an officer of the army. He early attained influence in his new home and was probably the most powerful man in the colony. His family intermarried with Walker, Moseley, Swann and Porter and the connection exercised a controlling influence on the destiny of the colony for many years.

The Harveys had long been settled in Virginia, where at an early date Sir John Harvey was Governor; later John Harvey was president of the council of North Carolina and acted as governor; and toward the close of the century Thomas Harvey, presumably his son, held the same position. From him came the Harveys of Harvey Neck, always cultured, respected and influential; and in the person of John Harvey, speaker of the assembly at the beginning of the Revolution, contributing one of the greatest figures that has played upon our stage of action.

John Porter had been a member of the Virginia assembly as early as 1663, as burgess for lower Norfolk, but was then expelled "because he was well affected to the Quakers." He had long been settled on the Albemarle and was a merchant trading with Boston and had amassed wealth.

Colonel Swann was a descendant of William Swann, who was an alderman of the city of Jamestown and settled Swann's Point, immediately across the river from Jamestown, dying there in 1638. Colonel Swann's first wife was Sarah Drummond, a daughter of the first governor of Albemarle, and whose mother was so devoted to the cause of Bacon; and he next married a daughter of Major Lillington. He was the collector of customs for Albemarle, being a crown

officer and also a member of the council. He was a strict churchman as were the others mentioned, unless Porter was not.

The administration of public affairs by their own inhabitants, with
such eminent satisfaction, created an indisposition for a change in
the system; but now a change was made and it was attended with
most unhappy results.

Liberty of conscience being secured to the settlers in Carolina,
and the Quakers having met with unfriendly legislation in Virginia,
some of that faith early came to Albemarle. In 1672 William Edmundson visited that region, and the celebrated George Fox followed
closely in his footsteps, while Edmundson made a second visitation
four years later. By their ministrations the seeds of their faith were
planted, and in the absence of other regular forms of worship, the
attractive tenets of the gentle Fox took firm root in the settlement.
Indeed, as if to secure such immigrants, the Lords Proprietors in
their instructions given to Peter Carteret, governor of Albemarle in
1670, directed: "You are to cause all persons chosen (to the
assembly and as deputies or members of the council) to swear allegiance to our soveriegn lord the King, and fidelity and submission to
the Proprietors and the form of government established by them;
but in case any man for religion's sake be not free to swear, then
shall he subscribe the same in a Book for that case provided, which
shall be deemed the same with swearing." With such inducements —
liberty of conscience, the right to hold office, and to affirm instead of
swearing — offered to the Quakers who were treated with marked intolerance elsewhere, many were drawn to the quiet shores of the
Albemarle; and later John Archdale, a Quaker, became one of the
Lords Proprietors and governor of Carolina, and his daughter with
her husband, Emanuel Low, settled in Perquimans and their example
and influence tended to the propagation of the new doctrine. And
so the Quakers prospered in Albemarle. But the year 1700, which
was proclaimed by the Papal See as a year of jubilee, witnessed a revival of religious enthusiasm in Europe and brought trouble even to
this distant settlement. Henderson Walker wrote that for near fifty
years they had been settled there "without priest or altar," but in
1701 the legislature passed an act to establish vestries and erect
church buildings and support ministers of the church of England;
and in the same year the Quakers began to hold quarterly meetings.
And Granville, who was then Palatine, the oldest and administrative
officer among the Proprietors, being an intolerant churchman, proposed an aggressive course in regard to religious matters. Gov.
Johnston was appointed governor of the whole of Carolina with instructions to appoint a deputy governor for Albemarle, and he sent
there Maj. Daniel in that capacity, who thus succeeded Henderson
Walker. The new governor supported by Glover, Pollock and a
majority of the council disregarded the custom, which had obtained
in the colony from the beginning, of allowing the Quakers to hold
office upon affirmation, and required all persons to make oath in regular form before qualifying. This was a virtual exclusion of about

one-half the colony from participation in the government, and it led to turmoil and confusion that lasted till the spring of 1711. During this period Edward Moseley and Thomas Pollock became prominent actors in public matters—the former espousing the cause of the Quakers or of popular right, and the latter favoring the change proposed to be made in the government. Both were churchmen; both men of mark, of capacity, of superior education; and each became a leader of his side. John Ashe, having been sent by the dissenters of South Carolina to represent their grievances to the Crown, young Edmund Porter joined him on behalf of the Quakers and dissenters of Albemarle, and as a result of this mission Maj. Daniel was displaced as governor and Col. Carey was sent by Gov. Johnston to succeed him. Carey, however, agreeably to Lord Granville's views, started out on the same course as Daniel, and this led John Porter himself to go to England where he obtained a commission authorizing him to settle the government, together with new appointments of councilmen, and an order removing Carey from his office. On Porter s return William Glover was chosen president of the council until an assembly should be convened, but he, backed by Col. Pollock, continued the same course as formerly, which led to Porter's defection and the gathering of all the dissenters around Carey, who made terms with them. By an agreement an assembly was elected under the joint order of each faction to decide between the contending governors. This body was favorable to the Quakers, admitted them to seats, elected Moseley speaker and decided for Carey. Glover refused to submit and with Col. Pollock and others fled to Virginia. At length Edward Hyde, a cousin of the Queen, who was intended for governor, but whose commission had not reached him, arrived in Virginia and was invited by all parties to assume the administration. Hyde soon however sided against Carey and Moseley and Porter, caused them to be arrested and, urged on by Pollock and Glover, proposed to visit them with severe punishment; but having escaped, Carey embodied a force and offered to try the arbitrament of arms. The affair ended, however, without bloodshed and the Lords Proprietors forbade any further proceedings.

Hardly had this episode ended before the Indians struck a blow at the colony that threatened to extirpate it. Notwithstanding the commotions that had occurred since 1704, the colony continued to receive considerable accessions and its confines were extended well to the westward and southward along the Tar. Some Huguenots settled on the Pamlico and DeGraffenried in 1710, led a body of Swiss to the Neuse, making a lodgment at New Berne. The Indians had been on most friendly terms with the whites, but seeing their lands encroached on, and noticing the dissensions of the colonists, in September, 1711, they seized DeGraffenried and Lawson, the surveyor, who were ascending the Neuse, and immediately began a massacre along the Tar and Pamlico that cut off almost the whole of the lower settlement. Had it not been for the friendly help of South Carolina, whose assembly dispatched aid under Col. Barnwell, and later, another force under

Col. James Moore and his brother, Maurice Moore, the entire settlement would doubtless have been destroyed. After various vicissitudes and a most harrowing experience, the Indian fort on Contentnea creek was taken by Col. Moore, the greatest battle being fought that had yet taken place on American soil, and the power of the Tuscaroras was broken. Soon afterward that fierce tribe removed to New York, and although desultory hostilities continued until 1718, yet the great danger was over when in the summer of 1714, Charles Eden reached the colony to succeed Gov. Hyde, who had died two years before. A new assembly met in 1715, when the clouds that had settled over the colony were passing away. Moseley was chosen speaker; provision was made for paying the paper money issued because of the Indian war, the first issue being in 1712. Quakers were excluded from office and from testifying in criminal cases and from serving on juries, but otherwise were tolerated and were allowed to affirm instead of making oath. Other dissenters enjoyed all rights of citizenship, but the Church of England was established by law. The entire body of the laws was revised and re-enacted, and the value of commodities to be received in payment of quitrents was fixed by legislative enactment. The assembly in token of its disapprobation of methods employed by Col. Pollock, who, as president of the council, had conducted the war, resolved, "That the impressing of the inhabitants, or their property, under pretence of its being for the public service, without authority from the assembly, was unwarrantable, a great infringement of the liberty of the subject and very much weakened the government by causing many to leave it." While this was but a mild manifestation of the old spirit of the colony, yet it was a protest against the action of Col. Pollock during the war, and embodied the feeling of speaker Moseley and of the people towards the administration. During the succeeding administration this divergence of sentiment took a different form. With Gov. Eden, came over from England, Tobias Knight, to be secretary of the colony, and the instructions were that all records should be open to public inspection. Teach, an acknowledged pirate, the notorious Blackbeard, was a friend of Tobias Knight, having illicit dealings with him, and Moseley and Maurice Moore, who had at heart the fair fame of the colony, forced their way into the secretary's office and held possession some hours, examining papers to obtain evidence of the complicity of Knight with the pirate. This led to an open rupture with Eden; but Moseley so far succeeded that Knight resigned and soon died, while Teach was attacked by British war vessels and killed. In 1722, Gov. Eden died, and George Burrington was appointed his successor with the approbation of the Crown, which now claimed the right to disapprove of such appointments in the colonies. Upon his arrival in 1724, President Pollock, Chief Justice Christopher Gale and Secretary John Lovick, who were also deputies of Lords Proprietors, sought to obtain a dominant influence over the new administration, but Burrington was more complaisant with Moseley and Moore and Ashe and those who represented the popular party. There had been an inhibition of the

Lords Proprietors against any settlement on the Cape Fear, but Burrington explored that region and opened it up for entry, and he so far ingratiated himself with the people, that representations were made by the disappointed faction to the Proprietors that Burrington was preparing to follow the example of James Moore in South Carolina, and by a popular revolution, throw off their power and hold the province directly from the Crown. This information led to his immediate displacement, and in 1725, Sir Richard Everard succeeded him. Sir Richard on his first coming not unnaturally gave ear to the deputies of the Lords Proprietors who had procured the deposition of his predecessor, but in 1728 the Crown bargained for the purchase of North Carolina and for a time the colony was left to its own control. During that period, Sir Richard cast off his old advisers and sought the favor of Moseley and the people; and at the assembly of 1729, he agreed to a law for the issue of a large amount of paper currency, a part of which was to be lent to the planters themselves, and to various regulations as to the payment of quitrents, a matter of popular concern, for no lands were held in the colony in fee simple but each land owner had to pay an annual quitrent to the Proprietors which by custom was payable in commodities; and in consequence of his complaisance, the assembly did what it had never done before — made to the governor a present of five hundred pounds.

It was 1731 before Burrington, who now came as the first colonial governor representing the Crown, reappeared in the colony and took the oaths of office at Edenton. He had caused some of his former friends to be put in the council or upper house, and on his arrival showed signal favor to the leaders of the faction which had formerly opposed him. and apparently sought to sustain his administration with strong influences; but unhappily for him his instructions were to assert prerogatives of the Crown that were in derogation of the rights of the assembly under the charter and as the government had been administered from the beginning of the colony. A conflict was at once precipitated, and the assembly under Moseley, and the council itself led by John Baptista Ashe withstood him to the utmost,— so indeed that "not a single act was passed required by the King's instructions or proposed by the governor." He claimed for the Crown the right to create new precincts, entitled to representation in the assembly; but the assembly denied the right and would not admit the members. He denied the right of the old precincts of Albemarle to five members, the new ones being allowed only two; but the assembly maintained that the representation should remain as it always had been. He insisted that the rents should be paid in money, and at certain points or in produce at such values as he might declare. The assembly insisted that the people should pay their rents on their farms; and in certain commodities at the values ascertained by the assembly of 1715. He insisted on fixing the fees of the officers and what should be the relative value of the colonial paper currency and sterling; but the assembly denied these demands and fixed these values itself. He undertook to appoint the public treasurers — but the assembly elected them and declared that it held the purse strings.

Such were some of the causes of difference between the assembly and the Crown, arising at the outset of Burrington's administration and continuing for many years under the colonial governors. It was the assertion of prerogative on the one side and the steady maintenance of chartered rights and traditional freedom on the other. Moseley, who had sided with popular rights in 1708, in later years strengthened by his family connections, continued until his death at the head of the popular party, and constantly and firmly maintained the chartered rights of the people.

It is to be said to Burrington's credit, however, that though he was at points with the assembly, and was in violent personal antagonism with many of the most prominent inhabitants, he addressed himself with assiduity to promoting the material prosperity of the colony, and it was his proud boast that the colony had made most rapid advances under his active administration and unremitting efforts for its development. In 1734 he was relieved by the appearance in the colony of Gov. Gabriel Johnston, who for the next eighteen years represented the Crown in North Carolina. During Johnston's administration, the same contentions that had marked his predecessor's term were continued, and though Johnston was a more adroit manager, yet the conflict at times was accompanied with disturbances of a very violent nature.

As North Carolina was now a dependency of the Crown, steps were taken to assimilate the government to that of Great Britain. The precincts were changed to counties; provost marshals gave place to sheriffs, the council was called the upper house, and the governor, representing the Crown, claimed the right to erect counties and to do other acts by virtue of prerogative. The assembly made firm and strong resistance to such of those demands as were in derogation of its rights. The King had purchased but seven out of the eight shares of Carolina, and the eighth, Lord Granville's, was in 1744, set apart to him next to Virginia, the line running near Bath, Washington, Smithfield and the southern line of Chatham county. The inhabitants north of that line were Granville's tenants, to the south, the King's. The old counties, claiming five members each, lay in Granville's territory, and Edenton, where the assembly had habitually met was also in his domains. Gov. Johnston desired to have the capital in the King's territory and to curtail the undue power of the inhabitants in Granville's half of the province, for the dividing line cut the colony nearly into equal parts. With this view, Johnston knowing that the northern members could not conveniently attend, in 1746, called the assembly to meet at Wilmington in November. The northern members remained away. No quorum was present according to the old rule; but as the quorum of the British house of commons was forty out of a membership of 400, it was considered that fifteen might well be a quorum of the assembly. The few

southern members present passed two bills — one fixing representation which allowed to each county two members and no more, thus
depriving the northern counties of their preponderating influence in
the assembly, and another establishing the seat of government at
New Berne where the records of the courts were to be kept.

The northern counties declined to recognize the validity of these
acts, and insisted on their right to their old representation, which
being denied, they abstained from recognizing the government.
They closed their court houses, would pay no taxes nor participate in
the administration of affairs. At length the southern counties followed their example in the matter of taxes; and for several years
prior to Gov. Johnston's death in 1752, no public revenues were collected, and his salary was far in arrears. At last, after his death, the
Crown officers at London determined that fifteen members did not
constitute a quorum, and that the two acts were nullities, and so the
northern counties won their cause and retained their five members
until the adoption of the constitution in 1776.

But although there were constant conflicts between the assembly
and Gov. Johnston, and though the northern counties were in a state
of revolt for several years, yet during his term of office the material
progress of the country was great; its population increased from fifty
to about ninety thousand, and streams of immigration set in, which
exercised an important influence upon the province and the characteristics of the people.

About 1725 a lodgment had been made on the Cape Fear by the
Moores with their friends from South Carolina, and Moseley, Swann,
Porter, Ashe, Harnett and others from the Albemarle, which eventually came to be the seat of much wealth, refinement and culture.
Here, later, came some Irish and also some Welchmen who located
on the Northeast river; while some Highlanders dispersed themselves along the waters of the Northwest branch, the fore-runners of
a very important movement. In the meantime many inhabitants
from lower South Carolina, claiming the Pee Dee as the boundary,
pushed up the banks of that stream, among them being some of
the Huguenots, while Virginians crossed the northern border in considerable numbers.

When Charles Edward, the grandson of James II, in 1745, made a
descent on Scotland, many who had followed the flag of his father
and grandfather, rallied to his standard. The Duke of Cumberland,
however, met him on the fatal field of Culloden, where the hopes of
the Scottish people were entirely destroyed. A considerable number
of prisoners were executed, but others were pardoned on condition
of their emigrating. A number came to the Cape Fear, and after
that a stream of Highlanders steadily flowed to the upper waters of
that river, until all that region was taken up by Scotchmen, and there
for a century the Gælic language was heard around the humble
hearth as well as in the pulpit. Equally important were the accessions from Pennsylvania — these were Germans and Scotch-Irish.
They came down the "great road" to Winchester, thence down the

valley, and crossed the Blue Ridge on the banks of the Staunton
river, and then, either by the Moravian settlement at Salem, or the
"Old Red House" in Caswell, pursued their way to their settlements
in Carolina.   These streams, beginning in Johnston's administration,
continued until the western portion of the province was fairly well
occupied.   Side by side the new-comers located their sequestered
homes in the wilderness.   Different in racial characteristics, they still
had in common, thrift, energy, piety and an appreciation of the advantages of education and a spirit deeply imbued with a love of personal liberty.   The Germans brought with them their teachers and
their preachers, and the Scotch-Irish, their pastors, who soon established in their several charges schools and academies whose influence
was widely felt by succeeding generations.

It was in 1605 that the earls of Tyrconnel and Tyrone having re-
belled, King James confiscated their estates in Ulster and started
those settlements of English and of Scotch that supplanted the old
Irish tenantry.   The Scotch greatly increased in their new home,
and when, after several generations, their right to maintain their
Presbyterian faith without interference was denied, they measurably
dispersed throughout the settlements of the New World.   Those
coming to Carolina made a most important addition to the population.   From them have sprung numbers of illustrious sons who have
added to the glory and fame of the commonwealth.   And thus it
came about that while the peaceful Quaker flourished on the Albemarle, and the church of England was fostered in the east, the west
was settled largely by men of the Presbyterian and Lutheran faiths, and
the active Baptists disseminated themselves throughout the whole.

The settlers coming from Pennsylvania had perhaps been diverted
to the southward by the Indians who held the country west of the
Alleghanies and whose depredations somewhat later even checked
the movement to Carolina, but on peace being restored the tide of
immigration set in again and continued without interruption until the
Revolutionary war.   Then it ceased, and for more than a century
North Carolina has received no accessions from abroad, her population being only natural increase, descendents of English, Irish, Scotch,
French, Swiss and Welsh, in greater or less admixture of blood,
made more sturdy by a residence in the wilderness, and more patriotic by memories of their glorious ancestry.

On the death of Gov. Johnston in 1752, first Rice and then Rowan
succeeded to the administration as president of the council, but in
October, 1754, Arthur Dobbs, the new governor, arrived.   He found
the colony making preparations to aid Virginia in driving back the
French and Indians, who were threatening an invasion of that province.   In January of that year Gov. Dinwiddie of Virginia had solicited help and the assembly had promptly responded by voting £12,000
to equip a regiment of 750 men, of which James Innis, who had commanded a North Carolina battalion at Carthagena, was appointed
colonel.   Caleb Grainger was lieutenant colonel and Robert Rowan,
major.   Among the other officers were Thomas Arbuthnot, Hugh

Waddell, Thomas McManus, Edmund Vail and Moses John DeRosset. While Col. Innis was organizing his regiment and preparing to transport it to Virginia, he sent John Ashe as his aide to Gov. Dinwiddie, who, on June 4th, conferred on Innis the appointment of commander-in-chief of the entire expedition. The North Carolina regiment reached Winchester, but the Virginia assembly having failed to make any provision for the sustenance of the men, and the supplies brought from Carolina being exhausted, the regiment on September 1, returned home, leaving Col. Innis in Virginia preparing for a new campaign. In October the Crown appointed Gov. Sharpe, of Maryland, to be commander-in-chief, and Col. Innis was designated as "Campmaster-General." He remained at Fort Cumberland making treaties with the Indians and organizing the forces and constructing works of defense until a year later, when he returned to Carolina.

Early in 1755 a company under Capt. Ed. Brice Dobbs, a son of the governor, and a British army officer, was sent to Virginia to take part in Braddock's campaign, and the next year three new companies, commanded by Caleb Grainger, Thomas Arbuthnot and Thomas McManus, were ordered to New York, where Capt. Brice's company joined them, and Brice was appointed major of the North Carolina battalion. Capt. Hugh Waddell had a command on the western confines of the colony and built Fort Dobbs in 1755. In 1758, with these companies, he marched with Gen. Forbes against Fort Duquesne and won great credit as an Indian fighter and scout. In 1759 he was promoted to be colonel and was again in charge of the North Carolina frontier, and later in that year he commanded the North Carolina contingent sent under Gov. Lyttleton against the Cherokees. While our troops were being trained to war by these various expeditions in different parts of America, our people on the western frontier were harassed by a local Indian warfare and were learning valuable experience that was to stand them in good stead in after years. It was in such a school that Gen Howe, Gen. Moore and many other patriot leaders obtained the skill that distinguished them when the Revolutionary struggle came on.

The differences between the people and the governor, who represented the prerogatives of the Crown, continued without abatement under Dobbs' administration, there being several new sources of trouble developed. One was the appointment of the judges who formerly had been sent to the province from England, but now the assembly sought to procure the appointment of natives. Because of this and other points of difference the law establishing courts and providing for the judges was enacted every two years " only temporarily." Another matter that caused the governor much concern was the determination of the assembly to have its own agent in London to represent the affairs of the colony to the board of trade, and other officers of the Crown, and to parliament. The representations of these agents often were entirely antagonistic to the views and projects of the governor, and annoyed him greatly. He claimed the right to make the appointment, but the assembly exercised it, and appointed to conduct the correspondence, Samuel Swann, who on the retirement of his uncle Edward Moseley, had succeeded him as the popular leader and as speaker of the assembly. Associated with him were his two nephews, George Moore and John Ashe, and John Starkey who was particularly obnoxious to the governor because of his alleged republicanism. Of Starkey, the governor wrote that he had won public confidence "by his capacity and diligence and in some measure from his garb and seeming humility, by wearing shoe-strings, a plain coat and having a bald head," but the governor rated him as "the most designing man in the province; that he was a professed violent republican, in every instance taking from His Majesty's prerogative, and adding to the power of the assembly." Indeed Gov. Dobbs frequently declared "that the spirit of republicanism was rife in the colony and that it was much stronger here than in any other;" and he declared that, "as burdensome as the administration was, the republican leaders had offered to make it pleasant and agreeable, if he would only permit the republican junto to absorb his powers." His divergence from the assembly was so great that in April, 1760, the house sitting, as it were, as a grand inquisition went into secret session and made presentment of the grievances which the people suffered by means of the governor's conduct. This presentment was to be laid before the King by the agent of the colony at London. In the meantime progress was made in giving shape to the government, and the right of the people to rule themselves after the fashion of Englishmen at home was firmly engrafted upon the system. The assembly asserted and maintained its right to hold the purse; it elected its own treasurers; imposed its own taxes, and spent the public money in its own way. Whatever aid the colony rendered the Crown was to be freely given by the assembly, and the bill was to originate in the lower house. As there could be no taxation in the colony except by a law passed by the assembly, contributions to the coffers of the King were made by appropriations and were called "aids to the King." The amount of these aids also came to be a source of disagreement with the governor. Because of the expenses of the French and Indian wars, parliament in 1765 undertook to levy taxes on the American colonies. The resistance to this measure, the stamp act, in North Carolina was quite as determined as elsewhere. John Ashe, who had succeeded Samuel Swann as speaker, told Governor Tryon that the law would be resisted unto death. Associations were formed called Sons of Liberty, and papers were signed binding the subscribers to sacrifice their lives and fortunes to maintain the liberties of the people. When the stamp masters were appointed they were forced to resign. The stamps were not distributed, but as Gov. Tryon sought to prevent the entire nullification of the law and would not ignore it, no courts were held and no public business transacted. The affairs of the colony were indeed at a stand-still, as little could be done without the use of stamped paper and the people would not use it. In January, 1766, two vessels arrived in Cape Fear river whose clearances were not on stamped paper, and they were seized for that reason by the customs house officers and held by two British ships of war then in the harbor. Thereupon the people embodied and under the direction of John Ashe, Thomas Lloyd and Alexander Lillington, and led by Gen. Waddell, Gen. Moore and accompanied by Cornelius Harnett and others, marched to Brunswick where Gov. Tryon lived, took from his residence Col. Pennington, the comptroller of the province, and made him and all the officers of the province swear that they would not execute the law, and forced the ships of war to surrender the detained vessels. The obnoxious act was soon afterwards repealed.

The people of North Carolina had long suffered for the want of a sufficient currency. In 1712 there had been an issue of paper money; and later other issues were made. After the King purchased the province, still further laws were passed relative to the currency, but finally parliament prohibited the colonies from issuing more paper money. The effect of this was to deprive the people of a needed supply of circulation and the settlements in the west were great sufferers thereby. At certain points in the east products could be stored in warehouses convenient for shipment, and notes given by the inspectors for their value served as local currency. But there were no shipping points west of Fayetteville, and no warehouses inland, and the people in the interior could not obtain currency to pay their taxes. They hauled their produce more than a hundred miles through the wilderness to Fayetteville and there had to dispose of it for "one-half trade" in order to obtain some cash to pay the sheriff. This together with an oppressive system of administration in the back country, where the counties were extensive, and some of the officers corrupt, led to an association for a reform of abuses and to correct grievances, called the Regulation. But eventually the association refused to pay taxes and disturbances ensued that finally terminated in the battle of Alamance in 1771. Nearly the entire population at the west was enlisted on the side of the Regulation, which, originally a laudable movement of the people to redress their grievances, subsequently took the form of disorder, leading to its forcible suppression by the eastern part of the King's domain, for the Albemarle counties rendered the government but little assistance. But despite the disorders that attended it, and its luckless termination, the Regulation Association was a bold manifestation of the spirit of manly freedom which characterized the independent people of western Carolina. Upon its suppression many of those engaged in it plunged into the wilderness and made settlements across the mountains.

In the meantime great streams of population continued to flow into the Piedmont region of the province, as before chiefly Germans and Scotch-Irish, and the country was occupied. Schools were taught, religion was preached and material progress and development made, and the people enjoyed repose until the groundswell of the coming revolution disturbed the quiet of the colony.

The old question of the exclusive right of the assembly to tax the people, again came to the front in 1774, and although the province

had been racked and torn by internal dissensions, although the
western half was at points with the east for suppressing the rising of
1771, yet the assembly boldly took advanced ground in maintaining
the ancient privileges and rights of the commonwealth. A sturdy
spirit of independence prevailed among the entire people. Speaker
Harvey, learning that Gov. Martin would postpone the meeting of
the assembly to prevent that body from sending delegates to the
Continental congress, declared that the people themselves would
call an assembly; and after consultation, the committee of safety at
Wilmington issued a call for the election of a body which is known as
the first provincial congress. It met in New Berne, August 1774, and it
is said was the first legislative body of a revolutionary character chosen
by the people of any colony. It was composed of the first men in the
colony and its resolves had all the force of law throughout the province. Other congresses followed in the same manner, and associations were formed as in the stamp act troubles; and committees of
safety under the resolves of congress, supplanted the regular authority of the colonial government. Gov. Martin finding that British
power had vanished, hastily fled from his palace in New Berne to
shipping in the lower Cape Fear where he devised measures for the
subjugation of the people. A large British force was expected to
join him in the Cape Fear, and he caused the Highlanders and those
Regulators who now adhered to the royal cause, to be embodied with
the view of co-operating with the expected army. The British
standard was erected first in Moore county and then at Campbellton,
now Fayetteville—but the patriots had not been idle. Steps had
been taken to organize the militia in the various sections of the province and Gen. James Moore, after a brilliant campaign, cut off the
insurgents at Moore's Creek, and utterly routed them. And when
the British regiments with a hundred sail arrived in the harbor,
Gen. Ashe had 7,000 Carolinians ready to contest the field with them.
In April 1776, while the tremendous force of invasion was yet in the
Cape Fear, the North Carolina congress defiantly took the fatal
plunge and authorized their delegates in the Continental Congress to
concur in declaring independence and in forming foreign alliances;
the earliest action of this kind taken by any colony.

Reviewing in detail the Revolutionary proceedings in North Carolina, one observes that there was not a single defection among the
leading men of the province; and from the very beginning those
who had held public place remained together and acted as a single
man. In nearly every community there were association papers and
strong resolves for a maintenance of the people's rights; and in
Mecklenburg, where the Scotch-Irish dominated, the patriotic ardor of
the people was unbounded. There in May, 1775, they adopted the
first declaration of independence and assumed an attitude that has won
imperishable renown for the immortal patriots of Mecklenburg and
added luster to the name of Carolina. The spirit of republicanism,
of which Gov. Johnston so bitterly complained twenty years before,
now found full scope for play, and without a shock the old order of

things passed away and free republican institutions were established in the land. The direction of affairs was in wise hands. Hard indeed would it be to find in any legislative body men of superior parts to those who formed the provincial congress of North Carolina, or men of greater wisdom or loftier character. North Carolina then possessed a galaxy of statesmen of whom any state might justly be proud: Harvey, Ashe, Howe, Moore, Harnett, Hooper, Caswell, Johnston, Avery, Jones, Person, Nash, Buncombe, Martin, Burke, and a host of others, whose names sparkle as brilliants in the rays of the noonday sun. With devotion they entered upon the struggle that was to last seven weary years, and during which trying vicissitudes befell the people. Many perished, all suffered. The fortunes of thousands were dissipated, and when peace came, the sun of independence rose upon a land of impoverished families, of widows and orphans bereft of their natural support, of ruined men, whose constitutions had been shattered in the protracted contest, and homes once bright with thrift and energy, now desolate. But those years of trial had also been years of activity, and the fortitude, the endurance, the exertions of the patriots left an indelible impress upon the characteristics of the people. The courage of North Carolinians had been displayed in a hundred encounters, conspicuously at Charleston, Brandywine and Germantown, where Nash fell, at Valley Forge, where the troops suffered so grievously, at Charleston again, when the entire North Carolina continental line was captured, at King's Mountain, Cowpens, Guilford Court House and Eutaw Springs, and in other battles made glorious by the libation of American blood.

In those years population had extended further into the interior, and the barriers of the mountains were crossed and the good lands of eastern Tennessee occupied. The war being over the energy and activity developed in its progress were now diverted into other channels, and measures were taken to lay on solid foundations the prosperity and happiness of the people. Schools were fostered; highways constructed, trade and commerce again established, and agriculture advanced. The genius of the people did not draw them to manufactures, nor was their situation favorable for such enterprises.

There were no large towns, no aggregations of wealth ready to be associated in great undertakings. The planters resided upon their estates where they cultivated hospitality and enjoyed the abundant fruits of their agricultural labors.

At an early day the stalwart democracy of some of the leaders led to their separation from those who possessed greater conservatism. Thomas Person, Willie Jones, Samuel Ashe, Samuel Spencer, Richard Caswell and others were the advocates of ultra democratic principles of government; while Samuel Johnson, James Iredell, Hay, McClaine, Hooper, Davie and others were more conservative. When the proposition was made to adopt the proposed constitution of the United States, the latter advocated it; but the former, determined to obtain amendments affording greater guarantees of popular freedom, were

B—3

successful in preventing its immediate ratification. A year later,
amendments being then assured, the instrument was ratified. Such
were the lines on which parties were formed in North Carolina.
Naturally the advocates of advanced democratic principles ranged
themselves as followers of Jefferson, while the other party became
adherents of the Federal leaders. Such lines of division largely continued until all parties ceased to exist in the presence of the great
crisis of 1860. In the intervening years North Carolina produced
many statesmen deserving to rank high among their contemporaries.
James Iredell and Alfred Moore adorned the supreme court bench of
the United States. William R. Davie, Nathaniel Macon, Samuel
Johnston, Spaight, the elder, John Stanly, David Stone, Montford
Stokes and Benjamin Hawkins illustrate the statesmen of the earlier
period. In 1819 the assembly employed an English engineer, named
Fulton, to improve our rivers and cut canals. Later they employed
the first state geologist ever engaged by any state to make known our
mineral resources; and when railroads came into successful operation,
the idea of utilizing them was quickly seized on, and many were
speedily projected and much activity displayed in devising means for
their construction. The state became largely interested in the road
from Raleigh to the Roanoke river, which was opened in 1835 with
imposing ceremonies. The same year a great internal improvement
convention was held at which a state policy was established, of running the lines from east to west. The people of Wilmington desiring also a north and south line, subscribed to that enterprise a large
sum, said to be four times the value of the entire real estate of the
town. When that road was finished to Weldon, it was the longest in
the world, and remained so for many years.

The democratic party disapproved of state aid to such enterprises,
and plans for such development were thus arrested. Indeed, when
in 1849 a great effort was made to charter the North Carolina road
from Goldsboro through the interior towns to Charlotte, although
the act was drawn by a democratic leader, William S. Ashe, and supported by James C. Dobbin of that party, yet when Calvin Graves,
the speaker of the senate gave the casting vote for it, his democratic
constituents were so displeased that they never again brought him
forward for office. Such influences tended to retard internal development, and remote counties were long without trade facilities.
During three quarters of a century there was peace, and the progress
that attended it. Schools were established and religion flourished,
all denominations sharing in the advance, but the Methodists and
the Baptists making the greatest headway; hamlets sprung up at the
county seats, wealth became diffused throughout the state, and the
agricultural resources of the various sections were developed and
substantial progress was made in refinement and culture.

From an early period it had been the happy fortune of the people
to have courts of great respectability, the judges being men of blameless lives, of good repute and unusual learning. The first determination of any court to disregard a legislative enactment because of its

unconstitutionality was by NorthC arolina judges—who set bounds to the hitherto unlimited exercise of power by the legislature—Judge Ashe saying, "As God said unto the waters: Thus far and no farther!" Legislation was conservative, and the administration of justice inspired the greatest confidence among the people. The supreme bench was adorned by men eminent for their virtue and learning, and Taylor, Henderson, Hall, Gaston, Daniel, Ruffin, Nash, Pearson, Battle, Manly, and their associates gave to the court a reputation surpassed by none in the Union; and there was fostered a respect for the law and a spirit of submission to authority which have been characteristic of North Carolinians.

The state finances were well administered, without scandal and with scrupulous exactness, and the fame of the people became established for their honest and upright dealing. The condition of society partook of these characteristics, and while the people were unpretentious, they were known abroad for their honesty, their virtue and their hospitality. Many of our statesmen achieved national fame. Branch, Gaston, J. J. McKay, Strange, Iredell the younger, Swain, the Shepherds, Archibald Henderson, Graham, Badger, Haywood, Branch, Owen, Bragg, Dobbin, Morehead, Mangum, Clingman, and a galaxy of brilliant stars in the political firmament added luster to the name of North Carolina.

Although North Carolina had soon after the adoption of the Federal constitution taken steps to prevent the importation of negroes, not only from abroad but from any other state, yet in the progress of time the system of slavery became strongly engrafted on her social structure, and the agitation of the slavery question excited her people greatly. Periodically this agitation stirred the people and animated them to maintain with steadfastness the right to manage their own domestic, local concerns in their own way. At length when it was declared that an "irrepressible conflict" had arisen, and that the "Union could not exist half slave and half free," it came to be regarded that the limitations of the Federal constitution were no longer to be observed, and that the abolition party would seek to abolish slavery. This led South Carolina and other commonwealths to the south to withdraw from the Union. The question of holding a convention for the purpose of withdrawing was submitted to the people of North Carolina in the spring of 1861, but so conservative were they and so attached to the Union, that they separated themselves from their southern brethren, and refused to call the convention. The difference between the votes was, however, small — only about 250 in the poll of the entire state. Such was the situation, when in April, 1861, Fort Sumter was bombarded, and President Lincoln called on North Carolina to furnish her quota of troops to coerce the seceding states. These events changed the aspect of affairs in North Carolina instantaneously. All differences ceased. Union men, who, like George E. Badger, did not hold to the right of secession, united now in the declaration that North Carolinians must needs share the fortunes of their southern kindred. Then amid the excitement of that period came the rapid preparation for the inevitable conflict — the marshaling of troops, the formation of armies, the strenuous endeavors to equip and train our citizen soldiery and make defense of our unprotected coast. Never was there a finer display of patriotic ardor; never did peaceable ploughboys more quickly assume the character of veteran soldiers. It was as if a common inspiration possessed the souls of all the people and animated them to die, if need be, in defense of their traditional liberties. During the four years of strife that followed, the people of North Carolina bore themselves with un· paralleled heroism. No nobler spectacle of human devotion has ever been presented in the annals of mankind. Her regiments were kept well filled and their prowess, their endurance and constancy were unsurpassed. In the great struggle between the contending armies before Richmond, her losses were greater than those of any other state; and so indeed it was in all the battles where Lee commanded. At Gettysburg, our trained veterans illustrated still more conspicuously their native heroism; if their losses were great on the first and second days of that grand encounter and their bravery peerless, yet on the third day they blazoned the pages of history in colors even more brilliant with the gallantry of their magnificent charge under the chivalrous Pettigrew. Never indeed have any Anglo-Saxons displayed higher qualities than the North Carolina forces from Great Bethel to Appomatox — never was greater heroism found united with a finer modesty — or splendid bravery with greater resolution, fortitude and endurance.   .

With a voting population of 112,000, North Carolina sent to the army 125,000 soldiers. Strenuous efforts were made to provide food for the soldiers and the poor, and while salt works were erected along the sea coast, vast quantities of cards were imported for the women to use at home, and other supplies were brought through the blockade. The few factories in the state were pushed to their full capacity, and new enterprises were started to aid the government. Powder mills were erected, furnaces were built in the Deep river section, and the mines at Egypt supplied coal for steamships, and every known resource was utilized. The period was of the greatest mental activity as well as one developing physical force. A leaf in the life of the people was turned and the quiet and peace that had reigned for generations gave place to unremitting action, enlarging the intelligence of the people, and quickening the energies of their life. It was accompanied, however, by straits and hardships, suffering and mourning, the separation of husbands and fathers from their families and the pall of death that fell upon every household. What awful experiences were crowded into four years of heroic and grand sacrifice — how trying the vicissitudes, how calamitous the dire result!

But from the activities and energies of the war, from the calamities and sufferings, from the poverty and despair, there issued influences that made their impress deep upon the character of the people. When the final catastrophe was realized, the men of Carolina who had been veterans in the immortal army, now of a different type from the quiet countrymen of the previous decade, turned with a resolute purpose to the future, and began to solve the great problem pressing upon them. New ideas possessed them, a greater activity, more resolution, as they began the work of rebuilding their homes and creating prosperity in their desolate fields.

The reconstruction of the state was accompanied by a sharp conflict in ideas, which culminated in 1870, when the whites gained the ascendency and in an orderly proceeding impeached the governor of the state and deposed him from office. From the day when the Anglo-Saxons so asserted the majesty of their sovereignty, quiet has reigned throughout the borders of Carolina, and the watchword has been progress and the development of our resources and the advancement of the religious, social, educational and material interests of the people.

The newspapers, the chief instrumentality for the dissemination of information, largely increased in numbers, in power and influence, and by their progressive spirit have led in the work of popular enlightenment.

A diversification of industries has been enjoined; manufactures have been fostered, mines and forest wealth developed and agriculture greatly improved. Railroad building has been energetically promoted. banks established, facilities for trade enlarged, and public schools have been put on a satisfactory basis. General prosperity has blessed the people. The country has worn a smiling face, while the towns have increased in size and importance. Asheville has attained a marvelous growth. Winston is a leading seat of tobacco manufacturing, and Durham's fame is world-wide. Wilmington, Raleigh, Charlotte and many other towns are sharing in the new life, while on the streams are dotted manufacturing establishments that tell of the energy and skill of the present race of North Carolinians.

It is the high purpose of these pages to perpetuate the names and services of those men who have wrought these industrial changes. The career of jurists, statesmen and military heroes find their appropriate place in historical works, where but scant space is allotted to the business men of the country. The former render important services but at last it is the men engaged in business who build up a state. It is these who develop resources, create wealth, build towns, construct railroads, furnish employment to the workingmen and lead on in the march of progress and prosperity, and it is likewise these toilers in diversified industries whose wealth supports the schools and churches of the state, disseminating intelligence and learning and religion, improving the morals of the people, and crowning the enlightenment of the commonwealth with examples of virtue and high moral character. They are indeed more than the supporting pillars, for they constitute the state itself.

Eminent and Representative North Carolinians.

JAMES IREDELL.

James Iredell, a distinguished jurist, was born in Lowes, England, October 5, 1750. When he had arrived at the age of seventeen years, he emigrated to Edenton, N. C., where he was afterward appointed deputy collector of the port. Here he made the acquaintance of Miss Johnston, sister of Samuel Jonhston, governor and United States senator, and in 1773, Mr. Iredell and Miss Johnston were united in marriage. He read law in the office of his brother-in-law (who afterward was chief justice of the superior court of North Carolina), and was admitted to practice in 1775. His reputation as a jurist, which then had its beginning, is well known to the profession. He held the office of collector of customs from 1774, till the Revolutionary war practically put an end, for the time, to that office. Taking a lively interest in the cause of the independence of the colonies he did not desire a commission under the British government and at once resigned the office when hostilities were about to commence. He had at that time a prospective interest in a large property in the West Indies, owned by a loyal uncle, and this he also relinquished for the cause of the colonists. In December, 1777, he was elected judge of the superior court of North Carolina, but, after holding the office less than a year, he resigned. He was appointed attorney-general of the state in 1779, but resigned that office within a short period. In politics as has before been intimated, he was an ardent whig, and his counsels in the cause of that party became of great value to its leaders in their struggles for independence.

In 1787 Mr. Iredell was appointed a commissioner to revise and codify the laws of the state, and "Iredell's Revisal," the publication of which began in 1789, was completed in 1791, and published in full at Edenton, the same year. At the convention which was held at Hillsborough, in 1788, to discuss the proposed federal constitution, Judge Iredell was a delegate, and was the leader of the federal party in that body. He urged the adoption of the constitution with great force and earnestness, but the majority was against him, and he failed to accomplish his purpose. In 1790 President Washington appointed Mr. Iredell one of the justices of the supreme court of the United States, and he was the author of several dissenting opinions in important cases brought before that high tribunal. In one of these — Wilson vs. Daniels — in which the jurisdiction of the court on a writ of error was at issue, his opinion was subsequently concurred in by the court. Many of his opinions, holdings and addresses, upon legal topics, were published, and held in great esteem, by members of the profession, in all the principal northern cities. At the present day, they are often cited, and held as good authority. At his death he left, nearly ready for the press, an elaborate treatise on pleading, but up to a recent date, it had not been published. Judge Iredell died at Edenton, October 20, 1799, but his memory will be perpetuated, not only by his descendants and by his published works, but by the county which took its name in honor of its illustrious resident.

JAMES IREDELL, JR.,

was born at Edenton, Chowan county, N. C., November 2, 1788. He was the son of Judge James Iredell, a sketch of whose career will be found in this volume. James, the subject of this sketch, received a liberal education, graduating from Princeton college with honor, when only eighteen years of age. He studied law and entered into practice and not only became prominent in the legal profession but also in politics. In 1812 at the opening of hostilities between this country and England. Mr. Iredell raised a company of volunteers of which he was chosen captain. His company was detailed to Craney Island, Va., near Norfolk, where he rendered very effective service in the defense of that point against the attacks of the British forces. At the close of his military service, he returned to Edenton and resumed the practice of his profession, laying the foundation for a distinguished and brilliant career as a lawyer and a judge.

In 1816, Mr. Iredell was elected a member of the state legislature, as the representative of his native city. The next year he was elected speaker of the house, holding that position during the sessions of 1817 and 1818. He was elected to the legislature many times afterward. He was appointed judge of the superior courts of law and equity in March, 1819, but resigned in the following May. In 1827 he was elected governor of North Carolina, and the next year was called to represent that state in the senate of the United States. He was the successor in that body of Nathaniel Macon, and was himself succeeded by Hon. W. P. Mangum. At the expiration of his senatorial term, Judge Iredell again returned to his law practice in Edenton. He was appointed a reporter of the supreme court decisions, and Iredell's Reports are to this day to be found in every well-regulated public and private law library. Few law reports are more frequently cited as authority in the courts, or oftener alluded to in law books, than Iredell.

In the three great departments of government, the legislative, the executive and the judicial, Mr. Iredell was a most distinguished personage. In private life he was greatly esteemed and beloved. Even while holding high official stations he did not forget nor neglect the amenities of social acquaintanceship, and in all polite circles of society he was the object of attraction and admiration. He was an honor and an ornament to his profession, and in the private walks of life was a most pleasant companion and an agreeable and entertaining conversationalist. Judge Iredell married Miss Treadwell, daughter of Samuel Treadwell, of Edenton, and they had a large and very interesting family of children. He died in his native city, April 13, 1853, deeply lamented by all his fellow citizens.

THOMAS RUFFIN,

the eldest child of his parents, was born at Newington, the residence of his maternal grandfather, Thomas Roane, in the county of King and Queen, in Virginia, on the 17th of November, 1787. Among the most eminent characters in American annals he takes appropriate rank. Whether we consider the virtues that adorn character, the learning that entitles the jurist to fame, or the benefits that an eminent citizen confers on his generation, the subject of this sketch is equally deserving of our admiration. His father, Sterling Ruffin, was a planter of Essex county, Va., who transferred his residence, in 1807, to North Carolina, settling in Rockingham county, and dying in the county of Caswell. His mother, Alice Roane, was of a family much distinguished in Virginia by the public service of many of its members, and was herself first cousin of Spencer Roane, a chief justice of that state, of more than usual prominence and distinction. His early boyhood was passed on the paternal homestead in Essex, and in attendance on the schools of the vicinity. Thence, at a suitable age, he was sent to a classical academy in Warrenton, N. C., under the instruction of Mr. Marcus George, a celebrated instructor, and from the Warrenton academy young Ruffin was transferred to the College of Nassau Hall, at Princeton, N. J. He entered the freshman class at Princeton, and graduated at the commencement in 1805, graduating with honors.

Returning home with his bachelor degree, Mr. Ruffin, soon afterward entered the law office of David Robertson, Esq., of Petersburg, as a student of law, and continued there, through the years 1806 and 1807. In the latter year, his father changed his home to North Carolina, and the son followed, a willing emigrant, for it was in North Carolina, he had received his first training for useful life, and here was the home of most of his early friends, with whom he confidently hoped to renew his association. On his arrival in North Carolina, he pursued his further study of the law, under the direction of the Hon. A. D. Murphey, until his admission to the bar, in 1808. Early in 1809, he established his home in the town of Hillsborough, and on the 7th of December, in that year, he was united in marriage,

with Miss Anne Kirkland, eldest daughter of William Kirkland, of that place, who was a prominent merchant and leading citizen. The twenty years next ensuing, during which his residence was continually in Hillsborough, comprehend his career at the bar, and on the bench of the superior courts. In 1813, 1815 and 1816, he served as a member of the legislature, in the house of commons for his town, under the old state constitution, and filled the office of speaker of the house, at the last mentioned session, when first elected a judge, upon the resignation of that office, by Judge Duncan Cameron. He was also a candidate of the electoral ticket, in favor of William H. Crawford for President of the United States, in 1824, but his aspirations, tastes and interests, inclined him not to political honors, but to a steady adherence to the profession, to which his life was devoted. He remained on the superior court bench only two years, and resigned to the legislature of 1818, and immediately returned to the practice. The wants of an increasing family, and an unfortunate involvement, by suretyship, forbade his continuance in a situation of no better income than the salary which was its compensation. For forty-three weeks in the year, he had his engagements in court, and despite of all conditions of the weather or other impediments to traveling, in the then state of the country, rarely failed to fulfill them. He held the appointment of reporter of the decisions of the supreme court for one or two terms, but relinquished it from the engrossment of his time, by his practice.

In the summer of 1825, upon the resignation of Judge Badger, Mr. Ruffin again accepted the appointment of a judge of the superior courts. His recent successes had relieved him of embarrassment, and supplied him a competent fortune. His health, which had never been very robust, demanded relaxation and rest, and his duties to his family, now quite numerous in his estimation, required more of his presence at home than was consistent with the very active life he was leading. He therefore relinquished his great emoluments at the bar for the inadequate salary then paid to a judge, and virtually closed his career as an advocate. By the bar and the public he was welcomed back on the circuits, and for the three following years he administered the law with such universal admiration and acceptance, both on the part of the profession and the people, that he was generally designated by the public approbation for the succession to the bench of the supreme court whenever a vacancy should occur. The reputation he had established by this time, however, did not merely assign him capabilities as a lawyer, but ascribed to him every qualification of a thorough business man, and in the autumn of 1828, he was prevailed on to take the management of the old State bank of North Carolina, the affairs of the institution being greatly embarrassed, and within twelve months devoted to the office of president of the bank, with his characteristic energy, mastering the affairs of the bank with a true talent for finance, making available its assets and providing for its liabilities, and inspiring confidence by the general faith in his abilities and high purpose to do right, he effectually redeemed the institution and restored it to solvency.

At this period in his life, also, another place of high political eminence was at his choice; but was promptly declined. It was the nomination to the United States senate. He was earnestly solicited to accept a candidacy for this position with every assurance of success. But his desire was, as he himself expressed it among his friends, "after the labor and attention he had bestowed upon his profession, to go down to posterity as a lawyer," preferring to be known merely as a jurist. Irrespective, therefore, of his domestic interests, and the care and attention due to his family, of which no man ever had a truer or warmer conception, he could not be diverted from his chosen line of life by the attractions of even the highest political distinction. During his administration of the affairs of the bank, in 1829, his services were still demanded by clients in the higher courts, and his reputation at the bar suffered no eclipse. He was elected a judge of the supreme court at the session of the legislature, in the autumn of 1829, and in 1833, upon the demise of Chief-Justice Henderson, he was elevated to the chief-justiceship. Here he won imperishable fame. His decisions illumine the annals of jurisprudence. When in the zenith of his reputation in 1852, he resigned his high position and retired, as he supposed, forever, from the professional employments he had so long and with so much renown pursued. But on the death of his successor and friend, Chief-Justice Nash, in December, 1858, he was called by the almost unanimous vote of the general assembly, then in session, to fill the vacancy, and he sat again upon the supreme court bench until the autumn of 1859, when failing health rendered his labors irksome, and he took his final leave of judicial life.

Judge Ruffin's decisions form within themselves a complete treatise on the principles of equity, then a branch of jurisprudence which had not been reduced to harmony and system. As a chancellor he has had no superior, either in England or America; while his common law decisions have been quoted with approbation in Westminster Hall. His opinion in Hoke vs. Henderson is itself a monument to his fame, that will endure as long as learning and clear reasoning and cogent argument are appreciated by the legal profession. Indeed it may be claimed for this eminent jurist not only that he has had no equal in North Carolina, but no superior in the United States. His nature was ardent, and his manner of speech earnest and often vehement in tone and gesticulation. Though versed in belles lettres, and with tastes to relish eloquent declamation, it was a field into which he did not often, if at all, adventure. His reliance was upon logic, not upon rhetoric; and even his illustrations were drawn from things practical rather than the ideal. Analyzing and thoroughly comprehending his cause, he held it up plainly to the view of others, and with a searching and incisive criticism exposed and dissipated the weak points in that of his adversary; and all this, in a vigorous, terse and manly

English, every word of which told.   As a counselor, his opinions were
not the result of cramming for an occasion, or a fortunate authority,
but the well considered reflections of a gifted mind imbued with law
as a science, and he explored to their sources, the principles involved
in the subjects examined, and made them his own.   This full development of his forensic character does not appear to have been manifest
until after his return to the bar subsequent to his first service on the
bench.   But from this period till his second retirement, in 1825, he
had hardly a rival in the bar of the supreme court of the state or the
circuit court of the United States, except Archibald Henderson and
William Gaston, and he had command of the practice in all the state
courts he attended.   His style of writing was elevated and worthy of
the themes he discussed.   His language was well selected, and he
exhibited a critical acquaintance with English philology.   A marked
characteristic in his writings, as it was also in his conversation, was
the frequent, dexterous, and strikingly appropriate use he made of the
brief words of our language, usually of Saxon derivation.   Considering how thoroughly he had mastered the systems prevailing in England and the United States. the fullness of his knowledge in kindred
studies and the facility with which he labored and wrote, it is to be
regretted that he did not betake himself to professional authorship.

There are other aspects of Mr. Ruffin's character than that of a
lawyer and judge.   At an early period he became the proprietor of
an estate on Dan river, in Rockingham county, on which he established a plantation at once, and gave personal direction to its
profitable cultivation, from that time until his death.   Carrying
his family to Raleigh for a sojourn of twelve months upon assuming the presidency of the State bank, as has already been stated,
he removed thence to Haw river, in Alamance county, in 1830, and
there under his own eye carried on the operations of a planter with
success until 1866, when the results of the war deprived him of laborers, and he sold the estate and removed again to Hillsborough. From
early life he appeared to have conceived a fondness for agriculture,
including horticulture. Here on his plantation for thirty-five years,
in the recess of his courts, he found recreation in farm pursuits and
rearing of domestic animals.   He was one of the most progressive
and successful farmers of the state, and it was no empty compliment
to a great jurist and leading citizen, when the Agricultural society of
North Carolina, in 1854, elected him to its presidency after his retirement from the bench, and in this position he continued for six years,
when declining health demanded his retirement.   In that capacity he
rendered the people of the state a service hardly inferior to that connected with his administration of justice.   His home on Haw river
was a seat of culture and refinement, and of bounteous hospitality.
There purity and affection were united with elegance and learning.

When no longer the chief-justice, Judge Ruffin, being appointed
a magistrate, presided over the court of Alamance county, and gave
direction to the local concerns of his neighbors, managing county
matters with the same acumen that distinguished his administration

of the affairs of the State bank. As grand and lofty as was his part in
life, he performed these simple duties of magistrate with scrupulous
exactness. His character may be illustrated by a saying of his own:
" Next to the sin of disobeying a commandment of the bible, it is a sin
to violate the law of the state." In the winter of 1860–1861, he was
appointed by the state one of the peace commission to prevent, if
possible, the anticipated rupture of the Union, and in that body he
urged compromise, concession and conciliation. At Washington, D. C.,
where the commission met, he met once more his early friend, Gen.
Winfield Scott, with whom he was a fellow student of law at Petersburg, and urged upon him that there should be peace, but the pleading of this illustrious patriot was unheeded by the victorious partisans
of the incoming administration. In May of 1861, he was elected a
member of the secession convention, and was firm and ardent in his
efforts for southern independence. Surviving the calamities of war,
which with its close found his farm desolate in consequence of an
army encampment, and its system of labor being abolished, he felt
unequal to the enterprise of its resuscitation and culture, and therefore disposed of the estate and again took up his abode in Hillsborough, as already stated, and on the 15th of January, 1870, after
an illness of but four days, though he had been an invalid from an
affection of the lungs for a year or more, he breathed his last, in
the eighty-third year of his age. His end was resigned and peaceful, and in the consolation of an enlightened and humble Christian
faith. For more than forty years a communicant in the Protestant Episcopal church, he was one of its most active members
in the state, and more than once represented the diocese in the
triennial conventions of the union. He was, too, of a most high
appreciation of high education, and was until superseded by the
changes made in 1868, the oldest trustee of the university of the
state, and always one of the most efficient and active members of the
board.

The venerable companion of his life, a bride when not yet fifteen,
a wife for more than sixty years survived him a short time and passed
away. She bore her husband several daughters and sons. Among
the daughters is the widow of the late Paul C. Cameron; among the
sons, there was William K. Ruffin, who possessed a mind of great
powers, whose native capacity, indeed, was of the highest order, and
whose acquirements in jurisprudence were considered, by those who
knew him, as very extraordinary. Another son, Peter Browne Ruffin,
has long been treasurer of the North Carolina Railroad company,
and has maintained an enviable fame as a business man and a gentleman of high integrity and spotless character. Of the fourth son,
Thomas Ruffin, mention is made elsewhere in these pages. Sterling
Ruffin, another son, is a respected citizen of Hillsborough, and the
youngest son, Dr. John Ruffin, is a resident of Wilson, N. C. In every
relation of life, Chief-Justice Ruffin was exemplary, a tender, affectionate husband, a solicitous, loving father, a kind, steadfast friend,
prudent in business, of unblemished character and integrity, and the

object of esteem and veneration throughout the state, and his example and course in all things will be cherished in the recollection of his friends, and may well be commended to the imitation of our youth.

GEORGE E. BADGER.

George Edmund Badger was born in Newbern, N. C., April 13, 1795. His father was a native of Connecticut, consequently when the son was fitted for college he naturally sent him to Yale. From this institution young Badger graduated in 1815. He turned his attention to the study of law, his preceptor being John Stanly, a relative of the family. He had but just arrived at the legal age of manhood when he was elected a member of the state legislature, and was only twenty-five years of age when he was elected a judge of the superior courts of law and equity — one of the youngest, if not the youngest, judge ever called to sit on the bench. He resigned his seat, however, in 1825, and opened a law office in Raleigh, where he pursued the practice of his profession with signal success. He was a whig in politics, and, in March, 1841, was appointed by President Harrison secretary of the navy, under the then whig national administration. But when Mr. Tyler, who became president on the death of Gen. Harrison, showed his enmity to the United States bank by vetoing the bills rechartering that institution, Mr. Badger resigned his position in the cabinet. In 1846 he was elected United States senator, a position which he held until 1855. He was nominated as one of the justices of the United States supreme court by President Fillmore, but the nomination failed to be confirmed by the senate. At the close of his senatorial term he retired from public life and devoted himself to the practice of his profession. Mr. Badger was a member of the convention which passed the ordinance of secession in May, 1861, and signed his name to that instrument. He was opposed to the measure, however, in the beginning, and used all the powers of his eloquence in favor of the preservation of the Union. After the adoption of the ordinance, he was known as a member of the conservative party. He died of paralysis at Raleigh, May 11, 1866.

In the United States senate, Mr. Badger was regarded as one of its most able and eloquent debaters. He was quick at repartee and pungent and forcible in argumentation. His powers of analysis were remarkable, and no man on the floor of the senate could more plainly discriminate between the true and fallacious in debate. He he had a fine sense of humor, and however dry or abtruse might be the subject under discussion, he would invest it with an interest that at once arrested the attention of his audience. As has been stated in this sketch, Mr. Badger resigned his seat in President Tyler's cabinet, in consequence of the action of that functionary in vetoing the bills to re-establish the United States bank. This was one of the great issues involved in the presidential election of 1840, and most of the whig statesmen of that day were in favor of a national bank. Mr. Badger was strongly committed to that measure, but he did not act hastily when he found the president inimical to the bank.   One bill had been vetoed, and another, supposed to avoid all of Mr. Tyler's constitutional objections, had been passed and shared the same fate of the former.   Mr. Badger looked upon this as an abandonment on the part of the president of his former pledges, and he believed he could no longer consistently hold a seat in his cabinet.   In giving his reasons for withdrawing he used the following plain and forcible language:

"It was only from the newspapers, from rumor, from hearsay, that I learned he (the president) had denied the constitutionality of the proposed institution, and had made the most solemn asseverations that he would never approve a measure which I knew was suggested by himself, and which had been, at his own instance, introduced into congress.   It is scarcely necessary to say that I have not supposed, and do not now suppose, that a difference, merely between the president and his cabinet, either as to the constitutionality or the expediency of a bank, necessarily interposes any obstacles to a full and cordial co-operation between them, in the general conduct of his administration; and, therefore, deeply as I regretted the veto of the first bill I did not feel myself at liberty to retire on that account from my situation.   But the facts attending the initiation and disapproval of the last bill made a case totally different from that — one, it is believed, without a parallel in the history of our cabinets; presenting, to say nothing more, a measure embraced and then repudiated — efforts prompted, and then disowned — services rendered, and then treated with scorn or neglect.   Such a case required, in my judgment, upon considerations private and public, that the official relations existing between the president and myself should be immediately dissolved."

But Mr. Badger did not go out alone.   Mr. Ewing, secretary of the treasury, and Mr. Bell, secretary of war, for the same reasons, stated in equally strong language, joined the secretary of the navy in retiring from the cabinet.   Mr. Webster, secretary of state, had also designed to retire, but was prevailed upon to remain.   Yet even he remained under the expressed conviction that the president would finally approve of the measure, for he declared, "notwithstanding what has passed, I have confidence that the president will co-operate with the legislature in overcoming all difficulties in the attainment of these objects; and it is to the union of the whig party, by which I mean the whole party, the whig president, the whig congress and the whig people, that I look for a realization of our wishes."   But in thus remaining in the cabinet, it is certain that Mr. Webster was not looked upon by his party as having exercised the same degree of consistency and true fealty to his party as was the case with Mr. Badger and the other cabinet officers that joined him in retiring.

RICHMOND MUNFORD PEARSON

was born in June, 1805, in Rowan county the fourth son of Col. Richmond Pearson.   His grandfather, Richmond Pearson, was a native of Dinwiddie county, Va. He was an officer in the Revolutionary war, and a man of marked courage. He died in 1819. He had been a successful merchant, but had failed at the close of the Revolutionary war, owing to the sudden fall in prices. The subject of this sketch, at the time of his father's failure, was a child of seven years of age, and would have been unable to receive a liberal education but for the kindness of his elder brother, the Hon. Joseph Pearson, member of congress from North Carolina for fifteen successive years. He received his early education under John Mushat, one of the most successful instructors of his day, and at Washington, D. C., spending his boyhood at Brentwood, the residence of his elder brother. He entered the University of North Carolina in 1815, and graduated thence with the highest honors of his class in 1823, delivering the Latin salutatory. Among his classmates were Gov. William A. Graham, Hon. Robert B. Gilliam and Daniel W. Courts. Choosing the law as his profession, he entered the office of Judge Henderson, and having completed his course, received his license in 1826. He commenced the practice of his profession at Salisbury, N. C., and his rise was at once rapid and marked, his early career giving evidence of the great abilities by which he was afterward so eminently distinguished. In 1829 he represented his native county in the legislature, and served three terms, and in 1836 was elected a judge of the superior court, and in 1849 was elected a member of the supreme bench.

Upon the death of Chief-Justice Nash, in 1858, he was chosen chief justice. During his term as chief justice he took a very bold stand in support of the integrity of the writ of *habeas corpus*, and would not countenance the idea of its suspension, in spite of the strong pressure brought to bear, and by his independent and almost defiant attitude on this question, rendered himself exceedingly unpopular. He was a candidate for the constitutional convention in 1865, but was defeated by Mr. Haynes. He was appointed provisional chief justice by the military authority in 1865, and when the civil authority was restored was again elected to that office which he held until his death, in January, 1878. Elected a judge when he was but thirty years old he presided over the courts of North Carolina for more than forty years. It is said on good authority that after the death of Chief-Justice Chase, that the commission of Judge Pearson, as chief justice of the United States had been made out and signed by President Grant, but learning that Judge Pearson was sixty-eight years of age, he appointed Justice Waite.

Judge Pearson was the greatest master of the common law the state has ever produced, among the many honored names which have stood in the front rank of American jurists. He had a wondrous grasp of intellect and unequaled reasoning powers, added to a phenomenal memory. The facility with which he seized the strong points of a case was remarkable, and his views were logical, plain and forceful. He was a modern high priest of Coke upon Littleton, and he was such a master of the law as a science, that his opinions stand high in England, where his decisions have been many times quoted in Westminster Hall. The young disciples of the law who made Richmond Hill their home felt to him as a father, and his communion with them in the classic shades of that famous retreat was like the converse of Plato to the aspiring Grecian youths in the groves of the Lyceum. As a man he was distinguished for his honesty of purpose, unbending integrity, inflexible idea of justice, and conscientious devotion to what he considered to be his duty. While to the eyes of the world he seemed somewhat cold and austere, to those who knew him intimately he was a genial, generous, warm-hearted man. He was twice married: first, June 12, 1832, to Margaret M. Williams, daughter of United States Senator John Williams, of Tennessee, and niece of Hugh L. White, also United States senator from Tennessee, and whig candidate for the presidency in 1836; and second, in 1859, to the widow of Gen. John Gray Bynum, and daughter of Charles McDowell, of Morganton, N. C.

RICHMOND PEARSON

was the son of Chief-Justice Pearson, and was born at Richmond Hill, the family seat, in Yadkin county, January 26, 1852. The most of his life was spent amid the familiar scenes of his childhood until he entered Princeton college, at the early age of seventeen. At college his conduct was excellent and his progress most rapid. He rapidly developed those qualities of mental acquisition and retention so essential to broad and comprehensive scholarship. He was fond of the occult sciences and a devotee to classic literature. He early became familiar with all the choicest productions of the great English masters in prose and verse. He was one of those few men whose boundless reading found expression in a full and polished vocabulary. In private life he was a fascinating conversationalist, which is the re sult of natural fluency, large information and good breeding. He graduated in 1872, and took up the study of law under his eminent father, and was admitted to the bar a couple of years later. He was married in 1882, to Miss Gabrielle Thomas, of Richmond, Va. Mr. Pearson has done much in the way of public improvements about Asheville, where he has made his home since his marriage. He has represented his county in the legislature upon two occasions, in 1875 and 1877.

THOMAS C. FULLER,

of Raleigh, one of the justices of the court of private land claims, recently established by the congress of the United States, is a native of the town of Fayetteville, in the state of North Carolina. He was prepared for college by John B. Bobbitt, of Louisburg, N. C., and at an early age entered the University of North Carolina. In 1850 he returned to Fayetteville and engaged in mercantile pursuits and manufacturing. But his talents drew him to the bar — at that time the favorite road to fame and fortune in North Carolina. In 1855 he became a student under Richmond M. Pearson, chief-justice of North Carolina, whose law school was so justly famous, and the next year began the practice of his profession at Fayetteville, quickly attaining by his merits a lucrative business. Although a union whig in principle and ardently devoted to the Union, when the war came on Mr. Fuller did not hesitate to take up arms for the south. In April, 1861, he enlisted as a private in Company F, First regiment of North Carolina volunteers, commanded by Col. D. H. Hill, known as the Bethel regiment, because it was engaged with such credit to itself in the first battle of the war, at Big Bethel in Virginia. When his term of enlistment expired Mr. Fuller, together with Col. J. B. Star, of Fayetteville, organized a battery of light artillery, of which Col. Star was captain and Mr. Fuller was first lieutenant, and he continued in active service with the company until November, 1863, when he was elected to the congress of the Confederate States. During the subsequent period of the war he remained in the Confederate congress, and although the youngest member of the body he was far from being the least influential or the least useful, and his counsel was freely sought by men of greater years. At the close of the war he resumed the practice of the law at Fayetteville, and at the first election in 1865 he was chosen by the Cape Fear district to the congress of the United States, but the house of representatives refused to admit the state to representation. At the succeeding election he was again a candidate, but his opponent was awarded the certificate by the military officers under whose supervision the election was held.

In the presidential election of 1872, Col. Fuller, as a district presidential elector, made an extensive canvass and warmly urged the election of Horace Greeley, as a peace offering on the part of the south, and as indicating the purpose of Confederate soldiers to fully accept the results of the war; and wherever his voice was heard, the Greeley ticket received an excellent vote. Since that time, Col. Fuller, though taking an active part in politics, has never been a candidate for any position until his name was presented to President Harrison in connection with the high office he now holds. His practice in the circuit court of the United States being large, he determined to move to Raleigh, as a more convenient location, and in March, 1873, he did so, and entered into partnership with Hon. A. L. Merrimon, then United States senator and the present chief-justice of North Carolina and Capt. S. A. Ashe, under the name of Merrimon, Fuller & Ashe. This firm was at once recognized as one of the strongest at the bar within the limits of the state, and its extensive business gave full scope to Col. Fuller's fine abilities and claimed his exclusive attention. The partnership continued until 1879, when Capt. Ashe withdrew to enter the fields of journalism. Col. Fuller and Judge Merrimon, however, remained together, and eventually the latter was appointed to the supreme court bench, and the former associated himself with George H. Snow, Esq., under the name of Fuller & Snow. Congress having passed the act establishing the court of private land claims, to

B—4

pass upon titles based on Mexican grants in the territory acquired
from Mexico, on June 10, 1891, President Harrison, at the instance of
Senator Ransom, and upon the recommendation of the bar of North
Carolina, appointed Col. Fuller a justice of that court, and on June 13,
Judge Fuller took the oath of office in the circuit court of the United
States, before Judge Seymour. Col. Fuller's grandfather was Bar-
tholomew Fuller, a Baptist minister, who was born in what is now
Franklin county, N. C., in 1756, and after a life of devoted ministerial
labor, died in 1827. His father, Thomas, was born in Franklin county,
in 1800, and in 1825, married Catherine Raboteau, a daughter of John
Raboteau, of Huguenot descent. To them were born, Sarah, wife of
R. H. Blount, of Durham; Bartholomew Fuller, who died in 1884, and
the subject of this sketch. In 1856, Col. Fuller married Miss Caroline D. Whitehead, daughter of Williamson Whitehead, Esq., of Fayetteville; of their children, W. W. Fuller, of Durham; Kate, wife of
J. F. Hill, Esq.; Frank L. Fuller, Mattie, Janet and Jones Fuller,
survive.

Col. Fuller is a gentleman of fine address and distinguished presence, gifted as a raconteur and to a rare degree master of the art of
pleasing. Social by nature, considerate of others, with a most affectionate disposition and full of the milk of human kindness, he is a
general favorite and warmly admired for his personal qualities. Indeed, in him seem to be commingled the best characteristics of his
French and English blood. No man is more constant in his friendships or more unselfish in his devotion to his friends. He warmly
espouses their cause and is ever ready to make any personal sacrifice
in their behalf. And thus it is that the names of his friends throughout the state is legion, and among them are men of all parties, colors
and creeds. Indeed, it has been said with truth that the appointment
of no other person to the high office President Harrison has conferred
upon him would have given such general satisfaction and such genuine pleasure to the people of the state without regard to race or
political affiliations. As a lawyer Judge Fuller has had a most distinguished career. His powers as an advocate are superb. He can
move a jury to pity or arouse their indignation, or awaken anger, and
sway them largely at his will. Some of his addresses will long be
remembered because of their invective and his arraignment of false
witnesses or interested parties, and no suitor or witness whom he has
once excoriated ever willingly submits to the ordeal a second time.
In his practice, it has been a peculiarity with him to take no notes of
the proceedings. No matter how involved the case, how many witnesses are examined, how many days the trial is protracted, he makes
no memoranda, but always as bland as a May morning and apparently
unmoved in the most trying crisis of the case, he mentally arranges
his proofs and considers his strong points, and at the end of a tedious
trial often astonishes both court and jury with his perfect mastery of
every point in the case and of all the evidence that bears upon it. It
has been said that he has never appeared against a man for his
life, while he has defended hundreds charged with capital crimes,

and many without compensation, and almost invariably with success. But as distinguished as Judge Fuller is as an advocate, he takes equal rank in the profession for his sound learning and discriminating judgment as a counselor. He was a diligent student of the common law under the learned Chief-Justice Pearson, one of the greatest common law lawyers of this century, either in America or Europe; and but few practitioners are more conversant with the underlying principles of our jurisprudence than Judge Fuller. Gifted with quick perceptions and possessing a logical mind, admirably poised, deeply imbued with the philosophy of the law, and skilled in the application of its principles to the facts of any case, he is admirably qualified for high judicial station and will adorn the bench to which he has been so worthily appointed.

WILLIE PERSON MANGUM,

a distinguished United States senator, was born in Orange county, N. C., in 1792. He entered North Carolina university and graduated from that institution in 1815. He studied law and was admitted to the bar in 1817, and very soon made his mark in the profession. He was chosen to the North Carolina house of commons the next year, and had only been in the practice of his profession two years before he was chosen a judge of the superior court. In the political division of that day, Mr. Mangum was a whig, and in 1823 he was elected a member of congress by the whig party of his district. He served one term and was re-elected, but before the completion of his second term he resigned to again accept a place on the bench of the superior court. In 1831 he was elected to the United States senate, taking his seat in that body December 5, 1831. Near the end of his six years' term he resigned his seat in obedience to the instructions of the North Carolina legislature, the politics of which had changed during his incumbency in the senate. He was offered the nomination for congress in 1837, but declined.

At the presidential election in 1836 the vote of the South Carolina electors was cast for Mr. Mangum for president. When the whig party was again in the ascendency in the state, and Bedford Brown had resigned his seat in the United States senate, Mr. Mangum was chosen to succeed him. He served this time from December 9, 1840, to March 3, 1853, and both in the senate and in the house he was one of the foremost leaders of the whig side. On the death of President William Henry Harrison, and the accession of Mr. Tyler to the presidency, and after the resignation of Samuel L. Southard, Senator Mangum was elected president *pro tem.* of the senate, serving the remainder of Mr. Southard's term, and the next session of congress entire. At the close of this term he retired from public life, seeking, after so long and conspicuous an official career, the quiet of his home at Red Mountain.

Mr. Mangum was joined in marriage with Miss Cain, of Orange, and they had an only son who lost his life at the first battle of Bull

Run, July 21, 1861. This sad event is said to have hastened the death of the father, who was already the victim of nervous prostration. Senator Mangum died at his home September 14, 1861. Few public men in the south have filled so long and so brilliant a public career.

ROBERT STRANGE, JR.,

was born in Fayetteville, N. C., July 27, 1823. He was the second son of Hon. Robert Strange, once a judge of the superior court, and subsequently a United States senator. Robert, Jr., graduated from the North Carolina university in 1840, studied law and was admitted to practice. Shortly after his admission to the bar, he removed to Wilmington, and was soon called to take a prominent position in public life. In 1852 he was elected to the state legislature to represent the county of New Hanover, and took a leading and influential part in the legislation of that session. He was afterward chosen state solicitor, for the duties of which office he developed a high capacity. His knowledge of law was profound, and to a naturally bright intellect he had added the culture of a finished education and a rigid discipline of mind. He was noted for the accuracy of his knowledge and for the versatility of his talents. He held an exalted position in the estimation of his professional associates, and, whether upon the bench or at the bar, his opinions carried with them great weight. He was a safe counselor, at once inspiring the confidence of his clients, and as an advocate, he had few if any superiors. In whatever position he was placed, his integrity and honesty of pur- pose were never questioned.

In the walks of private life, Mr. Strange was gentle and unostentatious; he had a large circle of friends, of which he was the admired center. His sense of honor was high and he was incapable of doing an ungentlemanly act, or of harboring an unworthy thought. No man could be more loyal to his friends, and as for enemies he had none. His moral and religious instincts were of an exalted kind. His life was pure and Christian-like, and he had before him, the bright and flattering prospect of a most distinguished career. But his death was premature. While arguing a case in court, apparently in the full vigor of manhood, his eloquent voice was hushed, and he was suddenly called to a higher tribunal than any earthly court. He died in the very zenith of his useful life, January 24, 1877. Mr. Strange was twice married; first, to Sarah Caroline, daughter of Thomas H. Wright. Of this marriage, three sons were born, Thomas Wright, Rev. Robert, and Joseph Huske Strange. His second wife was Bettie Andrews, by whom he had two daughters, Caroline Wright and Jane Hawkins Strange.

JAMES EDWARD SHEPHERD,

an associate justice of the supreme court of North Carolina, was born near Suffolk, in Nansemond county, Va,, on the 26th of July, 1847.

JAMES E. SHEPHERD, Judge Supreme Court.

His parents were Thomas and Ann Eliza (Browne) Shepherd; both being of Virginian birth, and English lineage. They had several children, of whom the following reached maturity: William S., deceased; Elizabeth, deceased; James E. and Frances S. When Judge Shepherd was only two years of age, he lost his mother in death, and his father's death followed in 1859. Soon thereafter he came to North Carolina, along with his older brother, William S. Shepherd, settling at Murfreesboro, where he continued his home till the war came on, when at the age of fourteen he enlisted in the Confederate army, but being too young for other service, he was made "marker," and as such continued for twelve months, when he was detailed military telegraph operator, in which capacity he did both field and station work till the close of the war. His position was no sinecure, and he distinguished himself by his activity, skill and devotion to duty. When the close of the war came, he began life again, under adverse and discouraging circumstances. His brother, Lieut. William S. Shepherd, of the First North Carolina regiment of state troops, having fallen at the battle of Sharpsburg, while leading his company, a brother's counsel was lost. He had, before the war, attended the neighboring high school, and had thus secured a fair education, but having lost all of his pecuniary means he was unable to enter college, and in order to support himself and at the same time prosecute his studies, he took charge of the telegraph office at Wilson, N. C., during several years that followed, in which he diligently continued his several studies and finally commenced the study of the law. He afterward entered the State university, where under the direction of Hon. William H. Battle, a justice of the supreme court, he was prepared for the bar, and he was admitted to practice in 1869, and opening an office in Wilson, began the practice of his chosen profession at that place, but in 1871 he moved to Washington, N. C., and formed a copartnership with Major Thomas Sparrow in the practice of law.

In 1872, Judge Shepherd was most happily married to Elizabeth B., eldest daughter of Mr. Silvester T. Brown, of Washington, N. C. Two sons have blessed the happy union — James E. (deceased) and Silvester B. Shepherd. The career of Judge Shepherd from the early practice of his profession was a series of steady successes, and he soon rose to high rank at the bar. In 1875, he was elected to the constitutional convention of the state by a large majority, and took an active part in the work of that body, being a member of the committee on the judiciary, and chairman of the committee on municipal corporations. Though he was the youngest member, he wielded a strong influence in the convention. The legislature had authorized the organization of inferior courts in the several counties of the state, and he was elected as the first chairman of the inferior court of Beaufort county in 1876. This was the beginning of his judicial career, which has since been continuous, and by successive and gradual stages has culminated so happily to the state. In the summer of 1882, he was nominated for judge of the superior court for the first district, and Judge Eure, the incumbent resigning, he was appointed by Gov. Jarvis to fill the unexpired term, and rode the Asheville circuit. At the ensuing election in November he was elected by the people, and served on the superior court bench with such acceptability that in 1888 he was nominated to one of the new places recently created on the supreme court, and was elected an associate justice, taking his seat January 1, 1889. On the bench Judge Shepherd has exhibited not only fine legal ability and sound, discriminating judgment, but a moderation and courtesy that have rendered him extremely popular. He has taken high rank among the jurists of the state, and his opinions have received much commendation among the members of the bar. In the summer vacation of the court, he lectures to the students in the law department of the University of North Carolina, and his work in this field is regarded as most excellent.

For many years Judge Shepherd was chairman of the democratic executive committee of Beaufort county, and for a number of years he was an efficient member of the congressional committee of his district. He is a member of the Masonic order, and is largely imbued with the spirit of charity, and he is of the Protestant Episcopal church faith, and leads the life of a consistent Christian. Affable, kind and considerate of others, he is noted for his gentle bearing, while his sincerity and singleness of purpose have gained him a high place in public estimation. He is singularly modest in manner, and is unostentatious in character. His success in life has been phenomenal, and due to his superior endowments enforced with firm will and worthy ambition. The mental and moral fibre of his nature was hardened and invigorated in the school of adversity. Early in life he was left an orphan and to face unaided the vicissitudes of youth, but having character, persistence and courage he surmounted such obstacles as fell in his way to a bright and successful career. The profession of law was the dream of his ambitious youth, and he is entirely free of political ambition. In his chosen profession his career has been a marked success, and his elevation to the supreme court bench was a fitting rounding of a career distinguished for learning, ability and integrity.

WILLIAM LAWRENCE SAUNDERS

was born in Raleigh, N. C., July 30, 1835. He entered the North Carolina university, from which he graduated in 1854. He then began the study of law, under the direction of Judge Battle, and was admitted to the bar in 1856. When the Civil war began, he was residing at Salisbury, and, in April, 1861, volunteered, enlisting in the Rowan rifle guards, under Capt. Frank McNeely. The guards were ordered to Fort Johnston, but in June of the same year Mr. Saunders was chosen lieutenant of the Rowan artillery, then stationed near Weldon, and went immediately to join the army in Virginia. He was chosen captain, in 1862, of a company of infantry which had been enlisted in Salisbury, as a part of the Forty-sixth North Carolina regiment, and afterward joined Walker's brigade, and, later on, Cook's brigade. The brigade participated in many of the hardest-fought battles, and Capt. Saunders was successively raised in rank, first, to major of his regiment, then to lieutenant-colonel, then to colonel. At the battle of Fredericksburg Col. Saunders received a wound in the right cheek, and again, in the battle of the Wilderness, in 1864, he received a shot in the face, which passed out on the right of the back of the neck, being a very narrow escape from a fatal wound.

In 1864 Col. Saunders was united in marriage with Miss Florida Call Cotton, who departed this life in 1865. In 1870, and again in 1872, Col. Saunders was chosen secretary of the state senate, in which office he fully demonstrated his fitness for the discharge of its duties. He entered the journalistic field in 1872, becoming one of the editors of the Wilmington *Journal*, and his accession to that post was the means of strengthening the democratic party in a very marked degree. In November, 1876, he established the *Observer*, at Raleigh, to which city he had removed, but within a few years the cares of editorship began to tell upon his constitution, and by the advice of his physician, in 1879, he quit the arduous duties of journalism. Almost immediately he was appointed secretary of state, by Gov. Jarvis, the incumbent of that office, Maj. Engelhard, having died, and Col. Saunders continued to hold the office up to the time of his death, in 1890, he having for many years been an invalid. But in spite of ill health and the pressure of official duties, he found time to devote to authorship, and up to the date of his death he had been engaged in writing a history of the colonial government of North Carolina, several volumes of which he had completed. Col. Saunders was a man of broad views and of a character above reproach. His position as a state officer and as an editor gave him a very wide acquaintanceship throughout the state, and the high consideration in which he was held by his fellow citizens was co-extensive with his acquaintanceship. Both in public and private life he established an enviable reputation, and his memory will be perpetuated through the invaluable historic work he has left behind, for the writing of which he had unusual facilities and was endowed with mental abilities which peculiarly fitted him for such a task.

RICHARD HENRY BATTLE,

lawyer, was born in Louisburg, N. C., December 3, 1835. He was educated at the University of North Carolina, at Chapel Hill, from which he graduated with honors in 1854. After his graduation, he served four years as a tutor of Greek and mathematics in the university, and then in December, 1858, commenced the practice of law in Wadesboro, N. C. In November, 1858, Mr. Battle was joined in marriage with Miss Anna Ruffin Ashe, daughter of Hon. Thomas S. Ashe, late justice of the supreme court of North Carolina, and to them were born ten children, six of whom now survive. Their names are Lucy P., Louis J., Carolina B., Edmund S., Rosa H. and William K. Battle. Mrs. Battle died in 1883. In 1861 Mr. Battle was appointed clerk and master in equity, and served as such until February, 1862, when he enlisted in Company I, Forty-third regiment of North Carolina troops, as first lieutenant. He served with that rank until the summer of the same year, when he was appointed quartermaster of the regiment and served as such until September. His health then failing, he resigned his commission and became private secretary of United States Senator Vance, who was elected governor of North Carolina in 1862. Mr. Battle returned to Raleigh in 1862, and in 1864 was appointed auditor of the state. He was re-elected to that office by the legislature, in 1865, and served until the war was ended. While in the army he was in the seven days' fight around Richmond. When peace was restored he began again the practice of law at Raleigh, and has followed up his practice ever since. In 1886 he was appointed by Gov. Scales, judge of the superior court, which appointment he declined. He was a candidate, in 1875, for delegate to the constitutional convention, to represent Wake county, but was defeated by his republican opponent. In 1880 he was a candidate for the state senate from Wake county, and reduced the republican majority, averaging 300, to sixty. Mr. Battle has been several times chosen as a delegate to the democratic state conventions, was a member of the state executive committee from 1870 to 1888, and served for the last four years of that time as chairman of the committee.

DANIEL G. FOWLE

first saw the light in Washington, N. C., March 3, 1831. Until his fourteenth year he attended the Washington academy, but at that time became a student in the excellent school known as the "Oaks," taught by William G. Bingham. He was graduated from Princeton college in the class of 1851, and after a six months' vacation, entered the law school, then under the direction of Chief-Justice R. M. Pearson, at Richmond Hill, N. C. After two years he completed the course and was admitted to practice in the superior courts December 31, 1853. At this time Mr. Fowle took up his residence at Raleigh and became the assistant of the late Col. H. C. Jones, who was then reporter of the supreme court. May 9, 1854, he opened a law office at Raleigh. The first year's success was not flattering, his receipts for the entire year being but $64. From that time, however, he rapidly rose in his profession. On the 15th of April, 1856, he was so fortunate as to form a marriage alliance with Miss Ellen Brent Pearson, the second daughter of the late Chief-Justice Pearson, of the North Carolina supreme court. He was a strong Union man, and opposed secession so long as it seemed wise, after which he volunteered in the cause of his people, becoming a member of the Raleigh rifles, afterward assigned to the Fourteenth regiment, North Carolina troops. Before the expiration of a week he was made a lieutenant, and soon after was elected major and ordered to report to Col. William Johnson, at Raleigh, to assist in organizing the commissary department.

In August, 1861, he obtained leave to resign for the purpose of organizing a regiment for active service. He was largely instrumental in raising several companies, which, with others, were organized as the Thirty-first regiment state troops, and Major Fowle was elected lieutenant colonel. This regiment was ordered to Fort Hill and Col. Fowle was placed in command. They remained there until December, 1861, when the regiment was sent to Roanoke Island, and while it was on its way there, Col. Fowle, on the 6th of February, 1862, was ordered to Raleigh, and was on the Sound when the Federal fleet made its appearance. Col. Fowle made his escape with his men and returned to Roanoke Island, where a council of war was held, and our subject was deputized by Col. Short, commandant of the post, to conduct the negotiations for the surrender of the 2,300 troops on Roanoke Island to the 9,000 Federal force. The surrender was successfully carried out, and a few days later they were paroled, with the understanding that they were not to assume active hostilities again during the war.

In October, 1862, Col. Fowle was elected to the state legislature from Wake county, and at the end of the session Gov. Vance tendered him the office of adjutant-general with the rank of major-general, which he accepted and held until the fall of 1863, when he resigned and again became a candidate for the legislature. He was easily elected, and presided over the last hour of the Confederate legislature, acting as speaker *pro tem*. While a member of that august body he introduced the famous *habeas corpus* resolutions, taking the ground that the suspension of the *habeas corpus* gave no right to arrest except upon warrant issued upon an affidavit. This point was sustained and is now a well established principle of law. In August, 1866, he was appointed a provisional judge by Gov. Holden, and in January, 1866, was elected judge of the superior court of North Carolina by the legislature, serving until November, 1867, when he was nominated as a delegate to the constitutional convention which was held in Raleigh in 1868. He was defeated for that honor, but two years later, or a little more, was nominated by the democratic party for the state senate and lowered the usual republican majority by 1,000 votes, although he was not successful in gaining the election. In 1876 Mr. Fowle was elected an elector at large on the Tilden and Hendricks ticket, and in 1880 was barely defeated for the nomination for governor of the state. He stumped the state for the national democratic ticket in that year, and again in 1884 spoke throughout the state for Cleveland. In 1888 he was nominated for governor, and in the ensuing campaign made a thorough canvass of the state. When the ballots were counted at the close of the contest Judge Fowle was found to be elected. By this time he had become very popular all through the state, having stumped it twice, and his public record having been long, honorable and above reproach. His term of office as governor does not expire until 1892. His whole political course has been conservative, yet loyal to the principles held by the party which he espoused on entering man's estate. He has never been a mere party worker as such, but has striven to ennoble and strengthen the whole people of his native commonwealth. In her hour of adversity he remained true, and when the time came to drop the old and take up with new methods, at a time when the state was plunged in trouble and peril by reason of the unforeseen perils of reconstruction, this man was found above the clouds of personal care. That was thrown aside and the people's cause championed. It is to such men that North Carolina owes its prosperity and very existence to-day. He has long been held in respect and esteem by his native state, where he is regarded as a man of great talent and culture. He brought to his life work a mind keenly alive to the needs of the day. Educated in one of the most thorough and proudest colleges in the land, he was eminently fitted to take his place in the dangerous scenes that followed.

Col. Fowle has made many notable speeches as a public man, and his name is sufficient to draw immense audiences from the people. In 1877 he was selected to deliver the annual address at Wake Forest college, and also at the University of North Carolina. In the same year he was requested to repeat his address at Davidson college, which he did. In June, 1877, the degree of LL. D. was conferred upon him by Wake Forest college, and a little later Davidson college gave him the same degree. In 1890 he was honored with the same degree from the University of North Carolina, and subsequently his *alma mater*, proud old Princeton, bestowed that laurel on her honored son. Gov. Fowle's first wife died December 13, 1862, leaving two children, viz.: Margaret P., wife of Philip H. Andrews, and Martha, wife of David B. Avera. He was again married on the 30th of January, 1867, Miss Mary E. Haywood, daughter of Dr. Thadeus Haywood, becoming his wife. This latter union has resulted in the birth of four children, as follows: Helen W., Mary E., Daniel G., Jr., and one now deceased. Mrs. Fowle died April 14, 1886. Gov. Fowle is the son of Samuel Richardson Fowle, who was born at Woburn, Mass., in February, 1797. In 1817 he removed to North Carolina and founded the southern branch of this old American family. He was a merchant at Washington, N. C., during the greater part of his life, and died there January 12, 1877. He married Martha B. Marsh, daughter of Daniel G. Marsh, and to them ten children were born, of whom seven are now living, Daniel G. being the fourth child. The mother passed away in 1843. William Fowle, the grandfather of our subject, was a native of Massachusetts. The first member of the Fowle family to come to America was George, who was born in 1610. He came from England in 1633, and settled in Massachusetts.

E. G. READE.

Edwin Goodwin Reade, LL. D., was born at Mt. Tirzah, Person county, N. C., on the 13th day of November, 1812. He is the second of three sons of Robert R. Reade and Judith A. Reade, *nee* Gooch. He was but a prattling child when his father died, leaving but

a meager estate for the support of his widow and family. Hence in early life young Reade found it necessary to aid his mother in gaining a support for the family and did work on the farm, in the carriage, and blacksmith shop, and in the tanyard, and being ambitious, and of determined mind, and desirous of obtaining a liberal education and of leading a professinal life, he started out at the age of eighteen, to secure an education by his own exertions. His mother was well educated for her day, and thereby was enabled to give her sons at home the rudiments of education, which together with that of the country schools was all the early education they had. Our subject's first academical training was at the academy of George Morrow, in Orange county, where he made rapid progress. Next, he entered the academy of Alexander Wilson, D. D., at Spring Grove, in Granville county, as an assistant teacher, remaining here until he was prepared for college. Instead of entering college, he began the study of law at the home of his mother in 1833, reading the law books of Benjamin Sumner, a retired lawyer, who was kind enough to loan them, and to occasionaly examine him. He secured license to practice in 1835, and was admitted to the bar, but a preliminary event in his life may well be mentioned here: It was his becoming a candidate for the legislature, and solely for the purpose of forming acquaintance with the public and practicing public speaking.

At the June term of court, when candidates were accustomed to declare themselves, the democrats nominated two candidates for the commons and one for the senate, and who made speeches from the court bench; and when they had finished, Mr. Reade, who had communicated his intention to but one other man in the county, went upon the court bench and declared himself a whig candidate, in a well-prepared and well-delivered speech, arraigning the administration of President Jackson — an apparent folly and error, if done with a serious view to election, for in the previous election there were but eleven anti-Jackson votes in the county. This very much surprised the democrats, who, fearing the ability of young Reade as a speaker, withdrew one of their candidates, neither of whom was gifted in speech, and substituted in his place James M. Williamson, who was a college graduate, and a law student at Greensboro, under his brother-in-law Judge Dick, the elder. The young men proved themselves good speakers and able canvassers, and made an able and interesting canvass; and many of the voters asserted that they would vote for both of the "boys" as an honor to their country. They did so, and Reade was defeated by only one hundred votes. He had accomplished his purpose, in becoming well and favorably known, and soon he took prominence among public men and in public affairs. In 1855, without his knowledge or solicitation, the whig-American party nominated him for congress in opposition to Hon. John Kerr, the then incumbent, and after a spirited and able contest, Mr. Reade was elected, receiving a handsome majority in his own county, then more than two to one democratic. Congress was not congenial to his nature, and the day of the expiration of his term he issued a card declining to enter the race for a second term. For awhile he continued the practice of his profession in the superior court, and quit to accept an appointment as a magistrate, and as chief justice of the county court. He presided without compensation for a number of years, with great acceptability, much satisfaction, and great benefit to the county, the effect of which is manifest to this day. In 1863, he was elected judge of the superior court, and served to the close of the war, at which time all offices were vacated, but being appointed to the superior court by the governor, served till 1866, when, by the legislature, he was elected to the supreme court, which now was composed of Chief-Justice Richmond Pearson, and Associate-Justices Battle and Reade.

In 1868, the new state constitution was adopted, and the election of judges to the supreme court, was delegated to the people. Judge Reade was nominated by both the democratic and republican parties, and was elected, and served with honor and distinction on the supreme bench till 1878, when his term expired. Judge Reade had accumulated an ordinary fortune, and had invested all of it in the Raleigh National bank, and at the close of his term on the supreme bench, in 1878, he was elected president of this bank, whose stock at this time was worth about 75 cents on the dollar, and of course the bank was not in the best of condition. By Judge Reade's assiduity and acquirements, and financial management, the bank prospered, and the stock was soon restored to par, and when its charter expired, its stock was at a premium. The bank was re-chartered, under the name of the National bank of Raleigh, and Judge Reade elected its president, which position he has since held, marking his course as a financier, a success. After leaving congress, Judge Reade took but little part in politics. He was of the old line whig school; and when the question of secession was proposed, at the approach of the Civil war, he opposed the measure. He was elected to the first state convention, which was to pass upon the measure, but which was voted down before the time for the convention to convene. When the second state covention was called, and secession seemed inevitable, he refused to become a candidate. He accepted, however, the ordinance of secession, and did his duty to the state. Before he took his seat on the superior court bench, to which he had been elected in 1863, as observed above, he was appointed by Gov. Vance, a senator in the Confederate congress, to fill the vacancy caused by the resignation of Hon. George Davis, and at the expiration of his term, he took his seat on the superior court bench.

At the close of the war he was almost unanimously elected a delegate to the state convention called to form a new constitution and to return to the Union. In the election there were but fifteen votes against him, and without the least expectation, he was elected president of the convention. He was elected by acclamation, after an informal ballot, without nomination, had been cast, and several members voted for, and Mr. Reade having the largest vote, was then elected by acclamation. On taking his seat he delivered an address, that received high compliment, both north and south and in congress, as manifesting the prevailing patriotic sentiment. During and since his services on the bench, he has taken no part in politics, not even voting, and although twice nominated for congress, he declined the honor. On the incoming of President Lincoln's administration, Hon. John A. Gilmer, then in congress from North Carolina, wrote to Mr. Reade, at the instance of Mr. Seward, to know whether he would accept a seat in President Lincoln's cabinet. Mr. Reade answered that he would not accept a seat in any cabinet, but he strongly urged Mr. Gilmer to accept. As a speaker, Judge Reade is clear, logical and pursuasive, and though without any special gifts of oratory, he speaks with such logic and simplicity, as give eloquence and fervor to his speech, which convinces and converts. It is said of him, when in the prime of his life, he never had his superior in the history of the state as an advocate before a jury. He was a diligent and faithful judge, of clear opinion and of cogent argument, and always having the courage of his convictions. In some of the most important and troublesome questions that have ever come before the supreme court, Judge Reade has written the opinion always in singularly clear English. He sat on the supreme bench at a time when political warfare in the north was bitter and unscrupulous, and he left the bench with the highest regard and esteem of both the bar and the people. He is a man of universal knowledge, and of a naturally strong legal mind. In 1865, the University of North Carolina conferred upon him the degree of LL. D.

As a writer, Judge Reade has attained distinction. In 1855 he wrote "Pickle Rod Letters," in favor of temperance. He wrote a "Vindication of the Legal Profession," against the assault of the Rev. William Hooper, D. D., LL. D., and has delivered several addresses of consequence and merit. He delivered the address before the bar association of North Carolina, at Asheville, in 1884, and before the same at Raleigh, at the close of his term as president of the association in 1886, and several of his more important addresses have been published in pamphlet and are models of their kind. He has been twice happily married. His first wife was Emily A. L. Moore, of the family of Gen. Moore, of Revolutionary fame, and of the family of Bishop Moore, of the Episcopal church. She died early in 1871, and in the latter part of the same year, he married Mrs. Mary E. Parmele, widow of Benjamin J. Parmele. Judge Reade is a communicant of the Presbyterian church, which he joined in early life, and of which he has been an active member ever since, and a ruling elder for more than thirty years. His character and disposition have been that of a man of simple faith and strict probity. He is plain, and unostentatious, conscientious and straightforward, and few lives are more radiant with good deeds than is his. He has done much to aid the distressed and his charities have been many, but in a quiet and unpretending manner. By reason of his own efforts and force of energy and predominating will-power, he has arisen from an humble station in life to one of distinction, eminence and wealth, and his course may challenge inquiry and would doubtless repay it. Such is a brief outline of the life of one whose name in the history of his time will appear among the most honored and revered.

JOHN W. HINSDALE,

son of Samuel Johnston Hinsdale, of Fayetteville, N. C., was born February 4, 1843. He was educated in Fayetteville. Later on he entered the University of North Carolina, where he won first distinction in his classes. After three years' study at Chapel Hill, he joined the Confederate army at the age of eighteen, serving on the staff of his uncle, Lt.-Gen. T. H. Holmes. When Gen Pettigrew was promoted and assigned to the command of a brigade, young Hinsdale became his adjutant-general, and as such participated in the battle of Seven Pines. Afterward he served as Gen. Pender's adjutant-general, in the seven days' fight around Richmond. When Gen. Holmes was transferred to the command of the Trans-Mississippi department he was accompanied by young Hinsdale, as one of his adjutant-generals. During the last years of the war he was colonel of the Seventy-second North Carolina regiment, otherwise known as the Third regiment of junior reserves, which he commanded in the battles of Kinston and Bentonsville, N. C., and surrendered with Gen. J. E. Johnston's army, at High Point, N. C. He was, perhaps, the youngest colonel commanding a regiment in the service. After the war he entered the Columbia college law school, in New York, diligently acquired a fundamental knowledge of the rules of the science, and was admitted to the bar in that state in 1866. He was in the same year admitted to the practice in North Carolina, and later in the United States supreme court, where he has sucessfully conducted a goodly number of important cases. The colonel first began practice in Fayetteville, but about 1875 removed to Raleigh, from which center his clientage was greatly increased, and in North Carolina, without invidious comparisons, we may well say that he stands easily first as one of the ablest attorneys and most learned counselors of our state. Of late years he has become an authority and given his attention more particularly to railroad, insurance and corporation cases. He has been for many years attorney for the Raleigh & Gaston railroad company, and for a number of insurance companies. In 1878 he published an annotated edition of Winston's North Carolina reports, thus adding to his reputation of a sound and discriminating lawyer. Col. Hinsdale may be said to be a thorough progressive man. In his extensive law library of 4,000 volumes are to be found, the best and latest publications, and his office is thoroughly equipped in every respect for speedy and accurate work. Although an indefatigable worker, the colonel enjoys society, and is never happier than when surrounded by his friends at his hospitable board. An ardent democrat, he has never sought political preferment, but confining his energies closely to his profession, he has attained an honorable and enviable position throughout the state. He is a member of the

Yours Truly
Jno. W. Hinsdale.

Episcopal church, and married in 1869, a daughter of Major John Devereux, and a granddaughter of the Hon. T. P. Devereux.

HON. WILLIAM HORN BATTLE

was born in Edgecombe county, N. C., October 17, 1802; died at Chapel Hill, N. C., March 14, 1879. He was the eldest of six sons of Joel Battle, one of the earliest cotton manufacturers of the state. He was descended on both sides from ancestors who took an active and honorable part in the Revolutionary war. At the age of sixteen, Mr. Battle entered North Carolina university, at Chapel Hill, and at the end of two years, graduated with honor, being appointed to deliver the validictory oration. On leaving the university, he began the study of law in the office of Chief-Justice Henduren, one of the profoundest and most distinguished jurists in North Carolina. Here he read law for more than three years, and so proficient did he become that he was awarded license to practice in all the state courts without an examination, a singular departure from a long established rule. On the 1st of June, 1825, Mr. Battle was joined in marriage with Miss Lucy M. Plummer, daughter of Kemp Plummer, a distinguished lawyer. She was an estimable and highly cultivated lady and moved in the best society circles. In January, 1827, Mr. Battle settled in the practice of his profession at Louisburg, but the first years of his professional career were not the most promising, and he delighted to attribute his subsequent success to the charming qualities of his wife. He was elected to the North Carolina house of commons, as the representative of Franklin county, in 1833-4. In the latter year he was associated with Thomas P. Devereux, as supreme court reporter, and reported the decisions of that court from December, 1834, to December, 1839, inclusive. In 1835, he assisted Gov. Iredell and Judge Nash in preparing the revised statutes of the state, and to him alone was entrusted the work of superintending the printing of the volume in Boston. It was a work that reflected great credit upon all parties concerned in its production.

Mr. Battle removed to Raleigh in 1839, and, the same year, was chosen a delegate to the national convention which nominated William Henry Harrison to the presidency. He was a whig in politics, but was not a partisan, and when elevated to the judiciary, he abandoned politics altogether. When Judge Toomer withdrew from the superior court bench, in August, 1840, Mr. Battle was appointed in his place by Gov. Dudley, and in the following winter he was elected by the legislature one of the judges of the superior court. In 1843 he removed to Chapel Hill to superintend the collegiate education of his sons, and in 1845 was elected by the trustees of the university to the professorship of law in that institution. He held this position until 1868, when he returned to Raleigh and associated himself with his sons, Kemp P., and R. H. Battle, Jr., in the practice of law. On the death of Judge Daniel, in May, 1848, Gov. Graham appointed Mr. Battle a justice of the supreme court of the state, but the legislature failed to confirm the appointment, although the same body, a few days later, without opposition, elected him a superior court judge to fill the vacancy created by the resignation of Hon. Augustus Moore. The reasons for this seeming inconsistency in the action of the legislature were given in a letter to him, requesting his acceptance, in which all the members joined, and in which they said: "The preference of another to you for a still higher judicial station was owing principally to your residing in a county where there are already three judges, a governor and a senator in congress." This and other considerations induced him to accept the position, but three years later, in 1852, he was called to the supreme bench, and continued to preside in that court as one of the associate justices until the inauguration of the re-constructed state government in 1868.

In 1872-73, Judge Battle was again appointed as sole reviser of the statutes of North Carolina — a task involving too great labor and responsiblity to impose upon a single individual. But his singular qualification for such a work was amply illustrated in "Battle's Revisal," which, though unjustly criticised in some quarters, would, with proper assistance have received the commendation which was bestowed upon the revised statutes and revised code by the bar. During the last year of Judge Battle's residence in Raleigh, he was president of the Raleigh National bank. In the spring of 1874 he lost his wife, a blow which caused infinite grief, but he was cared for by his eldest son, Kemp, with whom he afterward removed to Chapel Hill, where he magnanimously took up the work of restoring the university to its former excellent standing. Judge Battle was the father of ten children, eight of whom reached their majority — six sons and two daughters. Two sons, Junius and W. Lewis, lost their lives on the battle field, and but three sons now survive, Kemp, William and Richard. During Judge Battle's career as court reporter, his name appears during forty-two years, in fifty-six volumes of reports, and his opinions as a justice of the supreme bench are recorded in twenty-one volumes of the supreme court reports — a proud memorial of his rare qualities as a lawyer and jurist.

THEODORE F. DAVIDSON.

Among the first of that hardy race of Scotch-Irish, coming from Pennsylvania to Mecklenburg county, N. C., whose descendants have contributed so greatly to the upbuilding of the state were the parents of William Davidson, who came with his parents from Pennsylvania, his native state, to North Carolina as early as 1748. During the Revolution William Davidson was zealous and active in the cause of independence, and was a major of militia, rendering efficient service during the protracted struggle for the independence of the colonies. He was a whig, and being in the prime of life, of substantial property, high standing and influence, he played a prominent part during the Revolutionary period. He represented Rutherford county in the general assembly of 1791, and was active in promoting the passage of the law creating the county of Buncombe at that session. He resided in that part of Rutherford which was incorporated in the new county, and the latter was, in pursuance of its organic act, organized at his house in 1792. He was made a member of the first court for Buncombe county, and for several years thereafter represented that county in the senate. He died in the year 1800. One of his sons, William Mitchell Davidson, was born in the year 1773, in the territory then embraced in Burke, but now in McDowell county. He married Elizabeth Vance, a daughter of Capt. David Vance, of the Continental troops in the Revolutionary war, who rendered brilliant service at the battles of Brandywine, Monmouth, Ramsuer's Mills, Kings Mountain, Cowpens, and many other minor engagements. After the Revolutionary war Capt. Vance removed to Buncombe county, and was the first clerk of the court of that county, holding the office till his death, which occurred several years after going into the office. Among his descendants are United States senator Z. B. Vance and Gen. R. B. Vance. Unto the marriage of William Mitchell Davidson and Elizabeth Vance were born nine children, Allen T. Davidson being among them. The father settled on Jonathan's creek in Haywood county, and here he reared his family; and here he became a large and successful farmer and stock raiser. He died in 1843, but his wife survived him several years, dying in 1861.

Allen T. Davidson, above mentioned, was born in Haywood county, N. C., May 9, 1819. He received his education at the common schools in his native county, and at the Waynesville academy; afterward studied law, and practiced in the western counties. For many years he was president of the Miners & Planters' bank, at Murphy, N. C., and was otherwise largely interested in the development of western North Carolina. He was director in various railroad companies, and filled with credit to himself, many responsible places of trust. He was solicitor of Cherokee county, and during the time of the Confederacy, he represented his district in the Confederate congress. He was married in 1842, to Adeline Howell, and to them were born eight children, of whom six survive, viz: Theodore F. Davidson; Wilbur S. Davidson, of Beaumont, Tex.; Ella H., wife of T. S. Morrison, of Asheville, N. C.; Robert V. Davidson, of Galveston, Tex.; Betty, widow of William S. Childs; and Addie, wife of W. B. Williamson, of Asheville, N. C.

Theodore F. Davidson, who is now the distinguished attorney-general of North Carolina, was born in Haywood county, N. C., March 30, 1845. He was prepared for college at Asheville, by Col. Stephen Lee, a cousin of Gen. Robert E. Lee, and had been appointed a naval cadet, at Annapolis, when the breaking out of hostilities between the sections of the Union, changed the course of his life. Responding with alacrity to the call of his state, he, on April 16, 1861, being just sixteen years of age, enlisted as a private in the Buncombe rifles, W. W. McDowell, captain, that being the first company organized in the state, west of the Blue Ridge. This company was assigned to the First North Carolina regiment, and was disbanded at the end of six months, its term of enlistment. However, young Davidson, at once enlisted in Company C, of the Thirty-ninth regiment, Col. David Coleman, commanding the regiment, serving with the western army. He was made sergeant-major, and held that position till after the battle of Murfreesboro, when he was commissioned as aide to Gen. Robert B. Vance, who was assigned the command of the military district of western North Carolina. Subsequently he served as assistant adjutant-general, on the staff of his brigade, successively commanded by Col. John B. Palmer and Gen. James G. Martin, which post he held until the close of the war. He participated with gallantry and heroism, in the campaigns of Chickamauga, Cumberland Gap, Kentucky, and East Tennessee. A portion of the brigade to which he belonged, about May 1, 1865, fired the last hostile guns in the great drama of the war, east of the Mississippi River.

As soon as peace was restored, young Davidson resumed his studies, under the direction of his old preceptor, Col. Lee, and toward the close of the year 1865, he began the study of the law under Judge J. L. Bailey, at Asheville, and two years later was admitted to the bar. In 1868 he entered into partnership with his father, in the practice of the law, and, on the dissolution of that partnership, upon the retirement of his father, in 1882, he became a partner of Col. James G. Martin, of Asheville. In 1867, Mr. Davidson was elected solicitor for Clay county, and he retained that office until it was abolished by the constitution in 1868. He opposed the adoption of that constitution with all his powers, and early took an active part in the political contests of that time. In 1872, his talents for organization and his zeal, led to his selection for the arduous post of chairman of the democratic executive committee for Buncombe county, the exacting duties of which position he acceptably discharged for a period of ten years. At the same time he was also chairman of the democratic congressional executive committee for the ninth district. In 1878 the people of Buncombe county called upon him to represent them in the state senate, the district being then composed of Buncombe and Madison; and two years later he was re-elected to the same position. At the first session, he was assigned to the chairmanship of the important committee on corporations, Western North Carolina being at that time, largely interested in the extension of railroad construction; and at the succeeding session he was chairman of the judiciary committee, and the recognized leader of the body. In 1879 he was appointed director, for the state at large, of the Western North Carolina railroad, whose completion was of such vast importance to the western counties; and in 1881 he was made director of the Western North Carolina insane asylum, the act, establishing that institution, having been zealously and ably advocated by him.

In 1882 Mr. Davidson was appointed judge of the criminal court of Buncombe, called the "Inferior court," which position he filled with great acceptability and credit to himself until June, 1884, when the state democratic convention, recognizing his excellent talents, his purity of character and sound learning, nominated him for attorney-general. He was elected together with the rest of the democratic state ticket by a handsome majority, after a warm campaign, in which he made an able and extensive canvass of the state, winning many encomiums for the excellency of his political addresses. At the end of his term, so satisfactorily had he discharged his duties as attorney-general and reporter of the supreme court's decisions, that there was no opposition to his re-nomination by the state democratic convention, and he was again chosen for a four years' term by an increased popular majority. As attorney-general Mr. Davidson has largely increased the high reputation he has so long enjoyed as a safe and learned jurist, and he has so conducted the affairs of his office as to enhance the respect and confidence with which he has ever been regarded. In 1866 Mr. Davidson was happily married to Miss Sarah Katherine Alexander, a daughter of Capt. A. M. Alexander, of French Broad, near Asheville, of whom, however, he was bereaved in July of 1887.

J. N. HOLDING

is one of the active, progressive business men of Raleigh. A man of sound judgment and indefatigable in enterprise he is making his mark in the capital city of the state. Mr. Holding was born at Wake Forest, November 4, 1857, and received his education there, graduating in 1880. He chose the law as his profession and after reading law a year at Raleigh he entered a law school at Greensboro and was admitted to the bar in 1882. Shortly afterward he formed a partnership with W. H. Pace, Esq., which at once brought him into full practice and which still continues, Mr. Holding becoming each year more and more esteemed as a lawyer worthy of trust and public confidence. In May, 1889, Mr. Holding was happily married to Miss Maggie M. Askew, daughter of William F. Askew, Esq. (deceased), a resident of Falls of Neuse, and to them has been born a son, Arthur Newton. In addition to his law practice, Mr. Holding is engaged in business enterprises. He is half owner of the Raleigh Paper company, and of the paper mills known as the Askew Paper mills, at Falls of Neuse, near Raleigh. He is a stockholder in the Raleigh Cotton factory, and in the Land Improvement company; and in the Acid-phosphate company, and also in the North Carolina Wagon company, of which he is also a director and the attorney. Mr. Holding is likewise the attorney for the city of Raleigh. With a clear and discriminating judgment and full of energy, he has not hesitated to embark in new enterprises calculated to promote the prosperity of the community in which he lives, and his progressive activity is appreciated by his friends.

Mr. Holding has a strong political influence in Wake county, being one of the leaders of the democratic party, who has never sought office and whose zeal is based only on a desire to promote good government., He has been chairman of the county committee and has represented his county frequently in the district and state conventions. He is a

man of enlarged sympathies and is an active member of the Odd
Fellows, and is assistant superintendent of the Baptist Sunday-
school, of which church he is a consistent and useful member. The
father of the subject of this sketch was Mr. Willie Holding, who was
born in Wake county, in 1830, and was educated in the common
schools of Wake. He is a farmer, who stands deservedly high in his
community. In 1856 he married Miss Nancy C. Pace, daughter of
Solomon and Eliza Pace, and to them were born six sons: J. N.
Holding, Henry G., William W., Thomas E., Otto K. and Solomon P.
Holding. In 1887, the mother of Mr. I. N. Holding, died at the age
of fifty years. The father of Mr. Solomon Holding was Isam Holding,
who was born in Wake county in 1795, where he resided during his
life. He was a large land owner, being possessed of between five and
six thousand acres of land in Wake and Franklin counties. He was
a successful planter and a man of ample means. He died in Wake
county in 1870, at the age of seventy-five years.

DAVID MILLER CARTER

was born in Fairfield, Hyde county, N. C., January 12, 1830. He
was of Revolutionary lineage, being a descendant of Capt. Peter
Carter, of Virginia, who rendered efficient service in the war for independence, and in after life removed to the fertile and attractive
shores of Pamlico Sound, where his family have ever since held high
social position. David Carter, a son of the Revolutionary hero, was
a man of intelligence, education, high character and influence. For
twenty years he presided over the county court of Hyde county, and
administered the affairs of the county with credit to himself and advantage to the people. He served as a representative in the house
of commons for nine years consecutively, and in 1816 was returned to
the state senate. His son, David Carter, the father of the subject of
this sketch, was born in Hyde county, in 1801, and, like his father,
was possessed of large estates. He devoted himself chiefly to the
development of his properties, and was much engaged in constructing
canals in the swamps. Although exerting strong influence, only once
did he accept political preference. In 1846 he represented his district
in the senate. He married Sallie Lindsay Spencer, a daughter of
Peleg Spencer, an influential planter of the same county, by whom he
had eight children. He died in 1862, and his wife survived him six
years. The eldest child of this union was David Miller Carter, who
was born in 1830, and reared amid affluence in a region noted for its
wealth and generous hospitality. At an early age he was put to
school at the celebrated Lovejoy academy, at Raleigh, and after
being thoroughly prepared for college, entered the University of
North Carolina in 1847, where he graduated with distinction in 1851.
He remained at Chapel Hill, studying law with Judge Battle, and in
January, 1852, obtained his county court license. A year later, having
received his superior court license, he formed a partnership with

Judge Richard S. Donnell, an eminent lawyer at Washington, N. C., and at once entered upon a leading practice. He was chosen solicitor for the county of Hyde, and, although residing at Washington, held that office for many years.

Hardly had Mr. Carter entered upon the duties of this position before he was called on to prosecute Rev. G. W. Carrowan for the murder of a schoolmaster named Lassater. Carrowan was a man of great influence, a minister who had been much esteemed and who wielded, by virtue of his superior mental capacity and strong will and self-assertion, a sort of despotic power over the people in a wide scope of territory. The victim had been waylaid and shot from the bush, and the circumstances implicating Carrowan were not generally known. It required unusual nerve in a young lawyer to start such a prosecution, but young Carter was equal to his duty. Edward J. Warren, of Washington, was employed to assist, and on the the trial the evidence was so adroitly made manifest as to secure the conviction of the accused. As soon as the verdict was announced, Carrowan drew a pistol, and quickly shooting Mr. Warren, blew his own brains out. Carter was fortunately out of the room, and happily though the ball was directed at Warren's heart, his watch saved his life. Though not tall, Col. Carter was a man of large frame and capable of great endurance. His mind was comprehensive and his disposition studious. His logic was severe and he brought to the consideration of any subject of discussion rare analytical powers and a fine intelligence. So equipped, he soon took high rank even among the gifted men who then adorned the bar of the Pamlico region. In politics he was a whig and devoted to the Union of the states. Early in 1861, the question of having a constitutional convention to withdraw from the Union was submitted to the people, who at the same time chose delegates to represent them if the convention should be called; while a majority of the voters decided against the convention, Col. Carter was elected as the delegate from Hyde. The war quickly came on, and disregarding his Union proclivities, he volunteered as a soldier, and on May 16, 1861, was commissioned captain of Company E, of the Fourth North Carolina regiment, state troops, Col. George B. Anderson commanding. The regiment at once went to the front, and Capt. Carter shared all the vicissitudes of its arduous toils. At the battle of Seven Pines, May 31, 1862, his regiment suffered heavily, and he himself received wounds that were deemed at the time necessarily mortal. On that day the Fourth regiment carried into action 678 men, and lost in killed seventy-seven, of whom two were captains, and wounded 286, of whom there were five captains—a total loss of 363, or more than fifty per cent.

It was months before Capt. Carter recovered sufficiently to permit his return to duty; but he won his promotion and was commissioned lieutenant-colonel, and in December was appointed a military judge on the corps court of Jackson's corps; and later was appointed presiding judge of the Third army corps (A. P. Hill's). However, in August, 1862, he was elected a member of the assembly, and he discharged the duties of legislator in the trying times of the war with fidelity. After the failure of Lee at Gettysburg, and the fall of Vicksburg, he perceived that the defeat of the Confederate cause was inevitable, and he then began to be a zealous advocate for peace. In the assembly, he took an active part in discussing questions pertaining to the enforcement of the Confederate conscript law, earnestly urging that the privilege of the writ of *habeas corpus* should be maintained. In January, 1865, he was sent as a member of the assembly, together with Hon. John Pool, Hon. Samuel J. Person, and Col. E. D. Hall, on a secret mission to President Davis, for the purpose of urging some accommodation with the United States. After the war had closed he returned to Washington, and in 1866, formed a partnership with Judge E. J. Warren, which continued until Judge Warren's death. In 1867 he served his people acceptably in the senate, and in 1872 was nominated for congress by the democrats, but the district being largely republican failed of election. Two years later he removed to Raleigh, where he at once took the position his wealth, capacity and character commanded. He was then in the full meridian of his fine powers; and though there were more learned technical lawyers at the bar, it was generally conceded that in breadth of intellect, and comprehensive views and strength and power, he had few equals and no superior in the state. He was a man of more than ordinary culture, literary in his tastes and gifted as a conversationalist.

Mr. Carter's large landed interests in the low lands of Hyde that were to be developed by canalling much engaged his attention; but he was a director of the Raleigh National bank, a director of the Home Insurance company, a trustee of the university, and a member of the executive committee; chairman of the board to build the governor's mansion — and, what occupied him more than any other public employment, was president of the board of directors of the state penitentiary. This appointment opened to him a large field for the useful exercise of his great talents, and he made himself master of every detail of the vast work committed to his supervision and displayed at all points his fine capacity and intelligence.

Col. Carter, was in April, 1858, married to Isabella Perry, daughter of David B. Perry, Esq., a wealthy planter, of Beaufort county, and had by her four children, of whom David M., and Sallie Lindlay Carter alone survive. His first wife dying in 1866, Col. Carter in May, 1868, married Mrs. Harriet Armistead Benbury (a daughter of Joseph Ryan, Esq., of Bertie county, and a step-daughter of Hon. David Outlaw), the widow of Capt. John Benbury, of Edenton, and has by her three children of whom two survive — Laura Carter and Francis Spencer Carter. Col. Carter became very corpulent after the war, and toward the end of his life suffered from heart trouble, of which disease he expired at Baltimore, in January. 1879. Mrs. Carter survived him eight years, and died May 3, 1887.

CHARLES MANLY BUSBEE.

Among the younger North Carolinians who have attained distinction, none has occupied a more notable field than Charles Manly Busbee, an eloquent speaker, a wise and safe counselor and a learned lawyer, and at the head of the great order of Odd Fellows in America. Mr. Busbee's ancestors were among the pioneer settlers in Wake county, N. C., and•his grandfather, Johnson Busbee, for thirty years, presided over the county court of Wake and directed the local concerns of the county. Perrin Busbee, the father of the subject of this sketch, was one of the leaders of Wake county when she was prolific of great men. He was a profound lawyer, a ready debater, and the idol of his political party. Genial in his disposition, kindly in his sympathies, generous in his nature, and gifted with an inexhaustible fund of wit and humor, he was popular with all classes of his fellow citizens irrespective of party affiliations, and his memory is held in high esteem by the people of the county. Unhappily he died before he had even reached middle life, but he left sons to perpetuate his name. His wife was the lovely and talented daughter of James F. Taylor, Esq., who had been attorney-general of the state, whose father, Philip Taylor, was a captain in the war of the Revolution. While each of the sons has won success in his chosen field, the eldest, Charles Manly Busbee, has attained a most distinguished position. He was born in Raleigh, October 23, 1845, and was educated at the Raleigh academy, and entered Hampden-Sidney college, Virginia. But while still in the junior class he left his studies and entered the Confederate army as a private soldier, being then in his eighteenth year. After a short service in the ranks he was promoted to sergeant-major of the Fifth North Carolina infantry, and gallantly served in that famous regiment. He was in the battle of the Wilderness, and at the bloody battle of Spottsylvania Court House. May 12, he was captured and confined at Fort Delaware and Fort Pulaski. During his captivity he was subjected to one of the most savage ordeals of the war. The Confederate authorities had assigned quarters to Federal prisoners in the city of Charleston, and in that part of the city within the reach of the Federal artillery. To retaliate, the Federal government selected 500 Confederate prisoners and exposed them on Morris's Island to the fire of the Confederate batteries on Sullivan's Island, and Mr. Busbee was one of the victims so chosen. He was placed in front of the Federal redoubts, immediately under the fire of the Confederate batteries, and was exposed to death by disease and by the shells of his own friends. In December, however, he was paroled, and in the following March was exchanged. He returned at once to his regiment then in the trenches before Petersburg, and shared their sufferings in the final days of the war. He was constantly under fire there and during the retreat to Appomatox, where he was surrendered.

After the war Mr. Busbee attended the University of North Carolina for half a session, and then addressed himself to the study of the law, obtaining his license to practice in 1867. He was reading clerk of the North Carolina senate in the winter of 1866–7, and in May, 1867, was elected county solicitor for Wake county, which office he filled until it was abolished in 1868. Mr. Busbee has met with gratifying success in his business, and has for ten years been a member of the well-known law firm of Reade, Busbee & Busbee. Mr. Busbee was a member of the state executive committee of the democratic party, and has always been influential in party councils. He was the leader of the ticket, being candidate for the state senate in 1874, when for the first time the county gave a majority for the democratic party, and in the memorable campaign of 1884 he was brought forward for the house and was triumphantly elected, leading his ticket. In 1886 he was appointed one of the three commissioners to refund the debt of the state in regard to the construction bonds of the North Carolina railroad, a delicate duty he well discharged. In 1870 Mr. Busbee joined the Independent Order of Odd Fellows, and is a member of Mantio lodge, No. 8, of the city of Raleigh. In 1874 he was elected a representative to the sovereign grand lodge, and he served continuously in that national legislature of the order until 1888, when he was elected deputy grand sire. At the session of 1890 he was elected grand sire, the highest office known to the order. Mr. Busbee has successfully discharged all the duties of his exalted position, and has won the admiration of the million members of the fraternity. When he was in the height of his usefulness he suffered a severe illness, and from all over the United States there came words of affectionate interest, and throughout North Carolina a tender solicitude was manifested that amply illustrated the great esteem in which he is held by his people. In his religious affiliations Mr. Busbee is an Episcopalian, and for many years has been a vestryman of Christ church, Raleigh. His character is indeed well rounded, and he is a fine specimen of a North Carolina gentleman—one who resides in a family homestead where the lustre of departed virtue is reflected in the present worth of the occupants. He resides in a dwelling-house occupied for more than three-quarters of a century by his family, and where at one time four generations were gathered around the hearth. On July 28, 1868, Mr. Busbee led to the altar Miss Lydia L. Littlejohn, of Oxford, an ornament of her sex, who died in 1887, leaving the following children: James L. Busbee, Perrin, Louisa T., Sophy D., Isabel B. and Christine. On January 21, 1891, Mr. Busbee was again married, to Miss Florence Eleanor Cooper, a lovely daughter of Harvey Cooper, Esq., of Kentucky, and niece of Mrs. Vance, the wife of Senator Vance.

WILLIAM RUFFIN COX

was born March 11, 1832, in Scotland Neck, Halifax county, N. C. His family is of English extraction, his paternal grandfather, baptized in Old St. Paul's cathedral, London, having belonged to the English

navy, though afterward, during the Revolutionary war, he was in the American merchant service, in which he was captured by the British. His father, Thomas Cox, was a native of Chowan county, N. C., and a prominent merchant, having been a partner in the firm of Martlain, Cox & Co., Plymouth, N. C., and Devereux, Clark & Co., of Philadelphia, houses largely engaged in exporting to and importing from the West Indies, owning the vessels employed in their trade. Thomas Cox was also a member of the senate of North Carolina, from Washington county, and a leading advocate of the building of the first railroads in the state. It may be added that the late Mrs. Gen. John H. Winder, of Baltimore, was a sister of Thomas Cox. The wife of Thomas Cox, whose maiden name was Olivia Norfleet, was a daughter of Marmaduke Norfleet, a well known planter in the eastern portion of North Carolina, and she was a sister of Mrs. Weldon N. Edwards, of Warren county. In 1825 Thomas Cox removed to Halifax county, N. C., and there died in 1836. His widow afterward removed to Nashville, Tenn., where her death occurred years afterward. William Ruffin Cox, their son, received his first scholastic training at the Vine Hill academy in his native county. After going to Tennessee, with his widowed mother, he was placed in school near Nashville, and was prepared for college. In 1846 he entered Franklin college, from which he graduated with distinction in 1850. Choosing the law for his profession, he attended the Lebanon, Tenn., law school, at which he graduated in 1852, having as preceptors, Judges Green, Carruthers and Ridley, and as fellow-students Gen. Bate, now United States senator from Tennessee, Judge McHenry and Judge East, both of whom have been members of the supreme court of Tennessee.

Going to the Nashville bar, Mr. Cox formed an advantageous partnership with the Hon. John G. Ferguson, an experienced and accomplished lawyer, with whom he continued to practice during his residence in that state. In 1857, Mr. Cox returned to North Carolina, and relinquished the practice of his profession to engage in agriculture, settling in Edgecombe county. In 1859, he removed to Raleigh, and the following year was nominated by the democrats as a candidate for the house of commons, on the ticket with E. G. Haywood and Henry Mordecai, opposing the Hon. Sion H. Rogers, Hon. Kemp P. Battle, and J. P. H. Russ, who after a spirited contest, were elected by a small majority. Upon the outbreak of hostilities between the states of the Union in 1861, he, having contributed to the equipment of an artillery company, was employed in recruiting a company of infantry, when Gov. Ellis tendered him a commission as major of the Second regiment of North Carolina troops, of which the gallant C. C. Few was colonel, Judge W. P. Bynun lieutenant-colonel, Judge W. T. Faircloth, quartermaster, and Judge Hilliard commissary. On the death of his colonel at Sharpsburg (Antietam), he became lieutenant-colonel following the promotion of Judge Bynun, and, on the resignation of the colonelcy by that gentleman for the purpose of accepting the office of solicitor, to which he had been elected after the battle of Fredericksburg, Mr. Cox came into full command of the regiment, at the head of which, and of the brigade, which he commanded later, he participated in the various battles of Stonewall Jackson's corps. In the battle of Chancellorsville, he was shot down, being wounded in three places, and leaving half of his men killed or wounded on the field. Brigadier-General Stephen D. Ramseur, in his report of the Chancellorsville campaign, said: "And last though not least, the manly and chivalrous Cox of the Second North Carolina, the accomplished gentleman, splendid soldier, and warm friend, who, though wounded five times, remained with his regiment until exhausted. In common with the entire command, I regret his temporary absence from the field, where he loves to be." Disabled by his wounds, he could not follow Gen. Lee's army to Gettysburg, but on its way back from Pennsylvania rejoined it, finding that in the meantime, he had been recommended by his superior officers for promotion, and being, in fact, promoted shortly afterward to the rank of brigadier-general. After the battle of Spottsylvania court house, he was placed in command of Ramseur's brigade, composed of the Second, Fourth, Fourteenth and Thirtieth regiments, with part of the First and Third of Stuarts' brigade, and attached to Gen. Ewell's corps, a position which he held till the close of the war, the celebrated brigade maintaining its full prestige under his leadership. In the battle of the 12th of May, at the close of a gallant charge, he had the honor to receive on the field, with the other officers of the brigade, the thanks of Gen. Lee. His brigade on the death of Gen. Jackson, served with Gen. Ewell, Jackson's successor, until it was detached from the army of northern Virginia, and made what is known as the Valley campaign, participating in numerous battles with varied success, under Generals Early and Gordon, but always against overwhelming numbers. Returning from this campaign, he joined Gen. Lee in front of Richmond, where he again had the good fortune to win the acknowledgments of that noble chieftain, lighting his sad heart with a gleam of sunshine even amid the fast gathering clouds of overwhelming disaster. The incident has been well told by Senator Z. B. Vance in a public address, and may be fitly given here in his words:

"During the retreat from Petersburg to that memorable spot which witnessed the final scenes of that once splendid army of northern Virginia, when everything was in the utmost confusion, the soldiers straggling hopelessly along, thousands deliberately leaving for their homes, and the demoralization increasing every moment, and the flushed and swarming enemy pressing them closely, a stand was made to save the trains, upon which all depended. Some artillery was placed in position, and Gen. Lee, sitting on his horse on a commanding knoll, sent his staff to rally the stragglers, mixed in hopeless, inextricable confusion, behind a certain line, when presently an orderly column comes in view, a small but entire brigade, its commander at its head, and files promptly along its appointed position. A smile of momentary joy passed over the distressed features of the general as

he calls out to an aide, ' What troops are those?' 'Cox's North Carolina brigade,' was the reply. Then it was that taking off his hat, and
bowing his head with Godly courtesy and kindly feeling, he said,
'God bless gallant old North Carolina.' "

It was in accordance with the fitness of things that the brigade
whose gallantry drew forth this invocation should have made, as it
did make, the last charge in the last battle at Appomatox, its commander still at its head. Unfortunately the written testimony borne
by his superior officers to the valor and efficiency of his brigade was
destroyed amidst the general confusion and disorder that prevailed
at the close of the war, but its deeds are imprinted in the hearts of
those whom it served, and will not grow dim while they live. As for
himself, the deeds of Gen. Cox are in part recorded on his person,
which bears the marks of no less than eleven wounds received in
battle.

When the war ended Gen. Cox resumed the practice of his profession at Raleigh, and, not long afterward, was elected president of
the Chatham railroad. In the early days of reconstruction, most of
his friends being bound, he kept aloof from politics; but at the first
election under the constitution adopted in 1868, he consented to stand
for the office of solicitor of the metropolitan district, though without
expectation that he would be elected, as the district was republican
by about four thousand majority. Nevertheless, he was elected by
twenty-seven majority; holding the office for six years, and justifying,
by the ability and fidelity with which he performed its duties, alike
the choice of his friends and the trust of his opponents. In 1873 he
was made chairman of the state educational association, which position he held during that year and the two following ones, being instrumental, as chairman of the executive committee, in establishing the
North Carolina Journal of Education, a monthly devoted principally
to the cause of common-school education, and having on its list of
contributors the best literary talent of the state. Established at a
critical time in the history of public education in North Carolina, this
periodical, it can be hardly doubted, exerted a decisive influence in
favor of the cause. His services in this relation afford not the least
of his many titles to the grateful esteem of the people.

On the 20th of May, 1875, the one hundredth anniversary of the
Mecklenburg Declaration of Independence was celebrated at Charlotte, N. C., in the presence of 30,000 people, who were addressed by
Hon. Thomas A. Hendricks, of Indiana, Gov. Walker, of Virginia,
Gov. Graham, of North Carolina, and other able and distinguished
gentlemen. Gen. Cox also delivered an address which was remarkable for the broad and lofty patriotism that pervaded it, and in
which he thus described the spirit and requirements of the people of
North Carolina, who, in this respect, may be said to have represented
the people of all the other states of the south: " North Carolina
has always been attached to the principles upon which the government is founded. But give her the rights guaranteed her by law,
secure her local self-government and liberty, and she will be found as

true and loyal as any in the most favored portions of the country. We have no war to make upon the government, but will hold up to merited condemnation any party which through corrupt and partisan ends may seek to array section against section." On the occasion of a banquet given at the Yarborough house, Raleigh, in honor of the second annual meeting of the cotton states congress, held in that city in July, 1875, he presided, and welcomed the guests, declaring with emphasis that the true purpose of such conventions was the development of the resources of the states and the promotion of the welfare of the citizens by a national and comprehensive policy. He, indeed, lost no fit opportunity to reinforce the national sentiments of the people. When the chairmanship of the democratic state executive committee became vacant by the death of Hon. D. M. Barringer, Gen. Cox was elected to that office, which he filled with marked vigor and ability, contributing largely by his rare powers of organization and unsleeping vigilance, and scarcely less by his personal character and acknowledged patriotism, to the success of his party in the campaign of 1876. His name, at this period, was brought forward by the people of his district in connection with the nomination for the governorship of the state, but he declined to compete for the honor, in opposition to Hon. Z. B. Vance. He was chosen a delegate from the state at large to the democratic national convention at St. Louis, in 1876, as he had been chosen a delegate from the state at large to the convention which nominated Seymour and Blair, in 1868, though he declined to attend the St. Louis convention.

On the 31st of January, 1877, Mr. Cox was appointed by Gov. Vance, judge of the Sixth judicial district of North Carolina, comprising the central portion of the state, an office which he held until he resigned to canvass for a seat in congress, not desiring to connect the office of judgeship with politics. He made an efficient judge, and filled the position with credit to himself and to the satisfaction of the public. His dignity and urbanity of deportment, and his intellectual culture marked his service on the bench, and during his judgeship he rendered several able decisions, among them one of more than local interest, and which, although contrary to the rulings of two of his associates on the superior court bench, was, upon appeal to the supreme court of the state, sustained in terms peculiarly complimentary to his judicial capacity. The case referred to was that of the State vs. J. F. Hoskins et al., in which he sustained the constitutionality of the act of congress upon which the Federal courts base their claim to remove to the circuit court of the United States for examination the cases of revenue officers charged with criminal offenses by the state. As mentioned above, Gen. Cox, on nearing his judicial term of office resigned to canvass for congress; subsequently he was elected to the forty-seventh congress, and re-elected to the forty-eighth, and to the forty-ninth congress, receiving on each occasion increased majorities. For six years he ably represented the Fourth congressional district in congress. In the forty-seventh congress he served on the committee on pensions; and on a select committee to investigate charges against an officer of the house. In the forty-eighth congress he served on the committees on foreign affairs and militia; in the forty-ninth congress he was chairman of the committee on civil service reform, and a member of the committee on foreign affairs. In addition to attending to the work pertaining to these committees, the *Congressional Record* shows he took active part in the discussion of measures not connected with the committees on which he served; indeed, in the short session of the forty-ninth congress he addressed the house in speeches on such measures not less than seven times. He spoke on such subjects as classification and compensation of public officers; corruption in public office; civil service commission; American labor and Chinese immigration; inter-state commerce; diplomatic and consular service; wrongs to American fishermen; and the preparation and submission of reports, all received his earnest thought and consideration.

A few extracts from some of the speeches he made while in congress may fitly be given here, as they embody those patriotic sentiments and conservative views which Mr. Cox has ever held and advocated. In the house he spoke, on June 9, 1886, in reference to civil service, and in that speech, "Let us Stand by our Pledge," Mr. Cox said: "Talk about it being aristocratic to appoint men on account of merit instead of political influence; why, sir, it is the very genius and essence of democracy. It brings the offices within the reach of the people, and says to the tenant of the humblest hamlet, qualify yourself to serve your country, and if you have merit you shall be rewarded without respect to influence or power. There is in the treasury department to-day a chief of a division who, but a short time ago, was an obscure village boy. He was selected by a competitive examination, entered at the lowest grade, rose, and by his merit was appointed to his present position without extraneous influence or patronage, for indeed, neither of his senators had ever heard of him." On American Labor and Chinese Immigration, Mr. Cox said in congress: "It is the part of statesmanship to foster and cherish the laboring and wage-earning persons of our native population, 'man the worker, man the brother.' The poor should feel that in the halls of congress they have friends and protectors, Knights of Labor if you please, instead of those who are neglectful of their interest. True statesmanship points the duty we owe to this class of our citizens, and bids throw around them every protection which the law can secure. They should be made to feel that instead of submitting to the restrictions and exactions of protective organizations, whose rules are often arbitrary, that through their representatives in congress, they can secure every redress the laws of the land can guarantee to them. No one will deny that the laborers in this country, through the organization of capital, are exposed to many grievances. They have escaped the abuses of the old world merely to have others to fasten upon them in the new, yet, we are not Utopian enough to suppose that mere legislation will prove a panacea for all such evils, the thews and sinews of government are its revenues. Let the grant

of supplies be coupled with the securing of prerogatives. With hon
est and capable men at the helm they may rest at ease. The power
is in the ballot and not in the bullet."

On the reduction of tariff Mr. Cox made an able speech in congress, and made use of these words, taken from the *Congressional
Record:* "This cry against pauper labor on the part of high pro-
tectionists is but the song of the siren. And, if necessary to effect
their purpose, they are ready to renew their war upon all foreigners.
What is pauper labor? As Mr. Lincoln would say, 'I desire to speak
to plain people,' and doing so insist the term itself is an insult to the
laborers of this country. Labor is capital, as much so as manufactures, and one, though poor, should not be arraigned as a pauper,
simply because he fails to possess that wealth which gives him immunity
from toil. The principles of the democratic party compel it to oppose
its encroachment upon the constitution, high protective tariff and
class legislation; to discountenance partisanism; to maintain the
rights of the poor against the aggressive power, and preserve the
polls from military usurpation. All tariff should be levied in a spirit
of equity, caution and compromise, so that the great interests of agriculture, manufacture and commerce be equally preserved, and an
intelligent ballot, cast by an intelligent freeman, is the right preservation of those rights. What democracy has most to fear is a persuasive eloquence of the purchasing power, wielded by a corrupt party
or privileged classes."

Gen. Cox is an intellectual and able speaker; and in his public
addresses has pronounced much sound doctrine, and expressed
both high and moral culture and noble sentiment. He is frequently called upon to deliver public addresses, and one of
his most noted of recent date was on the life and character of
Maj.-Gen. Stephen D. Ramseur, before the Ladies Memorial association, of Raleigh, N. C., May 10, 1891, when among other things he
said:

"In the late war, and by the chronicles of that war, we were denounced as rebels and traitors, as if the promoters of such epithets
were ignorant of the fact that in our Revolutionary war Hancock,
Adams and their compeers were denounced as rebels and traitors,
while Washington and Franklin broke their oath of allegiance to join
this despised class. Indeed, the very chimney-sweeps in the streets
of London are said to have spoken of our rebellious ancestors as their
subjects in America. Therefore, with a conscience void of offense,
while we would not and should not forget our hallowed memories of
comradeship and of common suffering, we cherish them alone as
memories, and seek no willows upon which to hang our harps, no
rivers by which to sit down and weep while we sing the songs of long
ago."

Gen. Cox holds a position in the hearts of the people of North
Carolina, that might be coveted by any man; he has been intimately
connected with the history of the state for over thirty years, and has
all that time worked zealously to advance her interests. Upon retir-

I am &c Jr. truly,
A. S. Merrimon.

ing from congress, he turned his attention chiefly to agriculture, in which he has become prominent and very successful. In fact he has always been interested in this pursuit, and his operations as an agriculturist have been and are observed and appreciated throughout the state. In the advancement of agriculture he has borne an influential part, having been a member of the executive committee of the state agricultural society, and often delivered addresses before such associations. Nor has he wholly passed over financial affairs, as is evidenced by the fact, among others, that he was a director of the National bank, of Raleigh. In addition to his prominence in so many spheres of secular activity, he is a zealous churchman, having been for many years a member and vestryman of Christ church, Raleigh, a regular attendant at the dioceasan conventions, and a joint trustee with others over the property of the diocese. He married, in 1857, Miss P. B. Battle, daughter of James S. Battle, who was a planter and manufacturer, of Edgecombe county, of whom, however, he was bereaved in 1880. One son, P. B. Cox, survives her. In 1883 Mr. Cox married Miss Fannie Augusta Lyman, daughter of Right Reverend Theodore B. Lyman, of Raleigh. She died August 21, 1885, leaving two surviving sons.

AUGUSTUS SUMMERFIELD MERRIMON,

chief-justice of North Carolina, was born on the 15th of September, 1830, at Cherryfields, in the present county of Transylvania, N. C., then constituting a part of the county of Buncombe. His father was Branch H. Merrimon, of whose family history, previous to his leaving Virginia, little is known. He was born in Dinwiddie county, in that state, removing to Tennessee in early life; a youth without large advantages, but subdued by good influences, engaging in the ministry, in which duty he served in the Holston conference in the Methodist Episcopal church, for sixty years; a man of earnest piety, strong natural powers, with considerable culture; he was an effective and eloquent preacher. In the course of his ministerial service, he was sent to Buncombe county, N. C., where he married Mary E., daughter of William and Sarah Paxton, a lady of great excellence, who did much in after life to mould the character of her son, the subject of this sketch. William was of good family, brother of Judge Paxton, of the superior courts of North Carolina. Sarah Grace, his wife, was a McDowell, of the Revolutionary stock of the McDowells of Virginia and North Carolina. Soon after his marriage, Branch H. Merrimon, removed to Mills River, in Henderson, also then a part of Buncombe county, where he added to his ministerial duties, the avocations of merchant and farmer. Subsequently he removed to the farm now occupied by Charles McDowell, on the road between Hendersonville and Asheville, and afterward to Hooper's creek, in Henderson county. There he devoted himself, earnestly and almost exclusively, to farm life and its incidental works, in which was included

the operation of a saw mill, in connection with which, the career of
his subsequently distinguished son was largely guided and influenced.

Augustus S. Merrimon began in this rural, industrious and secluded
life, the development of those characteristics which controlled and
shaped his after life. Biography has an end more noble and more
useful than to amuse or astonish, or to unduly exalt the subject of it.
It is to stimulate by example, to encourage by the picture of bravely
fought adversity, by the illustration of the honors that crown patient
conflict with untoward conditions. And all these seemed to oppose
with concentrated forces the onward progress of the subject of this
sketch. His father's circumstances denied him the advantages of the
higher schools; the exactions of a life of daily toil restricted his efforts at self-improvement. Yet, like the missionary Livingston, compelled in his boyhood to the daily drudgery at the blacksmiths' forge,
yet contriving to store up during the process of manual labor, an as-
tonishing stock of knowledge, by keeping his book laid up on the
heaving bellows constantly before his eye; so did the young Merrimon, following the plow, succeed in committing to memory, and understanding well, the book he still preserves and cherishes as the key
that opened up his book of knowledge, Towne's Analysis, reading it
by snatches as he trudged along in the soft furrows; or as he watched
the saw slowly and methodically notching its way through the leis-
urely traveling log, acquiring a thorough mastery of some standard
works, and even an intelligent knowledge of Blackstone, long before
that light of legal science was taken up seriously as his professional
guide. His appetite for knowledge was constantly whetted, as its
value became more largely recognized; and he was gratified when at
last his father sent him to Asheville to the school of Mr. James Norwood, a teacher in his day of high repute, and for whom his former
pupil still retains profound respect and warm affection. At this school
young Merrimon needed no spur to excellence except his ambition,
and the conviction of his absolute dependence on his own exertions.
He was an eager and apt pupil, rapidly surpassing in the English
branches of learning (he attempted none other) all his fellow students, and receiving from his teacher the written expression of his
judgment, that he was the best English scholar he had ever had.
Compelled by the exhaustion of means to suspend his regular school
studies at the end of eight months, he received the striking tribute
to his proficiencies of being chosen by his teacher as his assistant in
the school in those branches in which he excelled, and in such capacity he remained with Mr. Norwood six months longer. After he had
detached himself altogether from the school, he was anxious to go to
the University of North Carolina. His poverty forbade; and then he
began earnestly to study law, the ultimate object of all his hopes and
plans. With the study of law he read closely history and general
literature, and thoroughly familiarized himself with the history of the
feudal system, so intimately connected with the validity of the English common law. He wasted not an hour; his defects in education
demanded incessant application to correct and overcome them. In

twelve months, he applied for and obtained license to practice in the county courts of the state, and in twelve months more, to practice in the superior courts; and then his professional life began.

In viewing the early part of a career, afteward so brilliant and distinguished, one of those contrasts in past and after conditions presents itself, apparently designed by Providence as encouragement to the oppressed, yet courageous hewer-out of his own fortune; a dark, gloomy back-ground against which the achievements of after years stand out in lustrous relief; a contrast, not of humiliation, but of honor, as the fulfillment of the promise to patience, hope, toil and manly courage. Mr. Merrimon was practically self-dependent, he was without money; not so absolutely without friends, however, that he did not find some willing to wait for the rise in his fortunes, which, to their prophetic eye, his intense ambition, his indomitable industry, his irreproachable character, seemed to assure. Yet these secured for him only the bare means for bodily sustenance; for all else, his was a life of labor, of hardship, of privation, to which, in the after time of prosperity he might refer with gratitude as the agencies to the training which enabled him to achieve so much; and also with pride that to himself mainly he owed the power that enabled him to put them so far behind him. Mr. Merrimon was soon made county attorney for Buncombe and other western counties. He soon entered upon an encouraging practice at the bar, for suitors of both political parties perceived his studiousness, his careful preparation of his cases, and his fidelity to his clients. He entered early into the spirit of politics without becoming a professional politician. Yet his adaptation to politics as well as to law was readily admitted by his countrymen; and in 1860, he was elected to the house of commons, defeating his able and popular opponent, David Coleman, by twenty-eight votes. This was for the session immediately preceding the war; Ellis, a democrat, was governor. Mr. Merrimon was a whig. Party spirit was intensely heated, the immediately agitating question being the recognition of the certainty of approaching civil war. As a test of the question, a bill introduced into the house at the instance of Gov. Ellis, asked anticipatory provision of $300,000 for the purpose of purchasing arms and munitions of war. The sessions of the legislature at that time began in the month of November, and the advocates of the bill urged its passage before the coming of the Christmas holidays. The legislature of 1860-1 contained many men of ability and some of great distinction, and many able speeches were made for and against the bill. Mr. Merrimon opposed it and in debate contributed largely to the delay of its passage until after the holidays. The war was approaching and the excitement in the legislature increased with the progress of the session, and in February Mr. Merrimon made a powerful argument against the doctrine of secession to a crowded and excited house.

About this time a general election was ordered to ascertain the voice of the people on the question of secession, and the popular vote was decided in its opposition to the call of a convention. But when

Mr. Lincoln issued his proclamation calling upon North Carolina to furnish its quota of troops to aid in suppressing the insurgent states, a convention was at once called and the state passed the ordinance of secession, and joined in the movement against the Federal government. Mr. Merrimon soon volunteered in the "Rough and Ready Guard." Its members were chiefly from the county of Buncombe, and up to the secession of the state, had mostly been Union men. While the company was drilling in camp at Raleigh, Gov. Ellis commissioned Mr. Merrimon as captain on Col. William Johnson's staff, in the commissary department, and he engaged at once actively in his new duties, serving usefully at Weldon, Ocracoke, Fort Macon and elsewhere. This department was soon merged in that of the Confederate states; and in the same year Mr. Merrimon was appointed by Judge French, solicitor for the Eighth judicial district, and at the end of his *pro tem.* term he was unanimously elected to the same office, which he held to the close of the war. Mr. Merrimon's sincere convictions made him a Union man, not in sympathies nor in action, but in judgment. He never hoped for the success of the southern cause, but his sympathies bound him to his own people. During the course of the long struggle, his effort was to aid in preserving law and order and so much respect for civil authority as was possible during the existence of active hostilities. He had occasion to exert such influences powerfully and usefully at the very outset of the war. A portion of the people of Madison county, of strong Union sentiments, bitterly hostile to secession and its advocates, made an inroad upon Marshall, the county seat of Madison, the citizens of which mostly favored the southern cause, and committed many acts of violence and plundering stores of supplies. This flagrant outrage was bitterly resented by the people of the adjoining county of Buncombe; and a body of armed men to the number of 1,000 or more, under the lead of popular and prominent men, hurried at once into Madison to capture and punish the marauders. The justices of the peace were about to open a term of the county court. The Buncombe people were intent upon their violent purpose. Solicitor Merrimon would not consent to ignore or disregard the civil power. A violent contention arose between the opposing opinions. That of Mr. Merrimon prevailed, that state's warrants be issued for the arrest of the offending parties, and that the sheriff of Madison, if he chose, might summon as many of the Buncombe militia as he saw fit to act as a civil posse. This course was pursued, the warrants were served as far as the offenders could be reached, and the civil power was vindicated, and military ardor was appeased by its application to the service of legal civil process. But Mr. Merrimon's triumph was achieved at much personal risk, because it was alleged among some of the Buncombe soldiers that he had advised the issue of the warrants to screen his Union friends from just military punishment. Violent opposition to his counsel and personal injury to himself were threatened and imminent. But prudent counsel prevailed and the law was suffered to take its regular course,

When the war closed, Mr. Johnson, then president of the United

States, issued his proclamation for an election of delegates to the state convention to be held in the city of Raleigh. This was in 1865. Mr. Merrimon was a candidate for the convention, but was defeated by a small majority by Rev. Dr. Stewart. The canvass and the elections also were conducted under the shadow of bayonets. The irregular, insubordinate violent body, known as "Kirk's Men," were everywhere present, fully armed, and breathing out vengeance against Mr. Merrimon, for as solicitor, it had fallen to his duty to prosecute a number of them. His life was often in jeopardy; but he passed through the trial without bodily harm. At the session of the legislature which followed the sitting of the convention, Mr. Merrimon was elected judge of the Eighth judicial district, and David Coleman was made solicitor of the same district. The history of his brief judicial career, if fully set forth, would be a valuable contribution to the history of a remarkable, turbulent period. It afforded admirable illustration of the firmness, the judgment and the patriotism of Judge Merrimon. The war was nominally over, the armies had disbanded and the soldiers had returned to their homes. But if it was not war, it certainly was not peace. In the war, and in some localities, neighbor had fought against neighbor, and besides the wounds of battle, indelible injury had been inflicted by the men of both sides on the homes and families of each other. They all returned home to find that the civil law was almost in abeyance, and each man became a law unto himself, with assumed right and duty to avenge past wrongs. Men brought home with them their side-arms or readily procured them. In some localities, communities were arrayed against each other like hostile camps, and whenever the men of opposite sides met, there was frequently sure to be blood-shed and death. It was chaos until the arm of the civil law should resume its sway. The opening of the courts seemed to promise the renewal of war rather than the restoration of peace, for the court-grounds were seen to be filled with armed men waiting and eager for collision with each other. At the opening of the court in Clay county, at the first term after the war, there was no grand jury to which to entrust the inquisition into crime or violence — no magistrates to draw a grand jury, and only a sheriff as a nucleus around which order might form. There were hundreds of armed men waiting for pretext for collision. Judge Merrimon, with quick judgment, saw the danger, and with prompt decision, adopted his line of action. He suggested to the magistrates appointed by Gov. Holden (but who had not yet qualified), to be sworn in, after which jurors were drawn and summoned and a grand jury drawn, sworn and charged. On the first day of the term, a dangerous outbreak took place in which sixty to eighty persons were engaged. The judge at once directed the sheriff to summon and swear sixty trusty and resolute men of both parties or factions, to see that they were well armed, and to instruct them to shoot without hesitation the first man guilty of violence with intent to create general disturbance. The knowledge of this preparation calmed the turbulent element, and the court was held without the incident of a single act of further disorder. The same course of action secured quiet in the county of Cherokee, where danger was still more imminent. This statement is made at some length, because it marked an important era in the history of the state. It was then that the voice of war was finally hushed, appeal to violence no longer made, and when the normal reverence for law began to be resumed. And it was mainly because a man of courage, firmness and judgment represented the law in its peaceful majesty.

This was in the spring of 1866, when Judge Merrimon rode the western circuit. In the fall of that year he rode the Wake circuit, in many of the counties of which violence and disorder had been rife. Firmness of action pursued in one circuit produced like happy results in the other. While holding court in Johnston county, he received military orders from Gen. Sickles to suspend proceedings in a case before the court, in which indictments had been found against a large body of men charged with outrageous and causeless riot. Judge Merrimon refused to obey the order, but as the case was continued on affidavit, there was, therefore, no open conflict of authority. A similar order having been issued to another county, where Judge Merrimon was engaged in holding court, he determined to resign his seat on the bench, not finding himself able to resist a power then so overwhelming, and he tendered his resignation to Gov. Worth. The governor, however, persuaded him to withhold it until after the trial of the celebrated "Johnson will case", which was to be heard in Chowan county. Of this case, it is only possible to say here, that it was, perhaps, the most important civil case ever tried in North Carolina. It involved the validity of bequests amounting to over one million dollars, and there was the largest and the most brilliant array of legal talent ever present at one time, engaged in one case at the North Carolina bar. The trial lasted four weeks, and resulted in establishing the will; and then Judge Merrimon's resignation took effect. He subsequently opened his law office in Raleigh, removing from Asheville, his former residence, with the chief view to the important business of the federal courts. His first partner in the law was Mr. Samuel F. Phillips, afterward United States solicitor general. Subsequently the firm (to anticipate somewhat) was Merrimon, Fuller & Ashe, and after the withdrawal of the latter to engage in journalism Merrimon & Fuller.

Judge Merrimon had taken much interest in public affairs, and since the war much of his efforts were directed, in conjunction with that of others, to the restoration and security of good government. To that end, he identified himself with the democratic party, and was a member (and part of the time chairman) of its executive committee. That committee in 1868 nominated him as the democratic candidate for governor, but he declined the nomination. He was also nominated for associate justice of the supreme court. The election was practically decided by Gen. Canby, and Mr. Holden was declared governor. Meanwhile Judge Merrimon was an active and able contributor to the press, arousing the people to a sense of the dangers which threatened their liberties. In the violation of those liberties which attended the course of the "Kirk war" he was especially severe in his denunciation of those who were its chief instruments, and exhibited his usual courage and decision in defending the rights of the people. He was of the first to make application for writs of *habeas corpus* in the cases of those citizens seized and held by Kirk under the orders of the governor, and participated largely in the struggle for the restoration of free government. In 1871, in the election for delegates to a state convention to be called by a majority of the votes of the people of the state, Judge Merrimon, with D. M. Barringer, Ex-Gov. Thomas Bragg and Green Alford, was a candidate for delegate from the county of Wake, and was defeated. But he was much in the eyes and minds of men for his able and persistent maintenance of law and liberty. He had made many able speeches when and where required, and was regarded as the most available candidate the democratic party could present for governor; and at the convention held in Greensboro in 1872, he was nominated by acclamation. His opponent was Tod R. Caldwell, of Burke county. The campaign was an arduous and also a very able one. Mr. Merrimon spoke in most of the counties of the state, and the people, eager for instruction in the newly revived principles of law, order and liberty, heard him with avidity and received impressions of lasting endurance. He was defeated nominally. He was believed to have been fairly elected, and a contest was proposed but abandoned, because the executive committee of his party thought it unadvisable.

At the legislature of 1872 his name was presented as a candidate for the senatorial nomination. Zebulon B. Vance was also a candidate. The latter had been elected to the senate at the session of 1870, but had been denied his seat, and was now again a candidate. The conflict was a warm one between the two gentlemen, ending after a few days contest in the withdrawal of both. The next week, however, the friends of Mr. Vance again introduced his name into the caucus. Eighteen friends of Mr. Merrimon indignantly withdrew from the caucus, and on the same day his name was presented in open session of the legislature, and those eighteen friends were joined by the republicans and Mr. Merrimon was elected. It is just to him to say that, though at the time he was bitterly assailed for apparent conflict with his political associates, the whole transaction occurred without his knowledge or procurement. It was only upon the advice of judicious and honorable men, whose fidelity to the democratic party was above reproach, that he accepted the nomination. His fidelity to his party long since effaced all suspicion of his party integrity and only some few traces of personal bitterness remain.

His service of six years in the senate was honorable to himself, to his party and to his state. He was an indefatigable student; he familiarized himself with the important questions of the day; he was as watchful there as he had been in less exalted stations, for liberty and the supremacy of the law, and was thoroughly well informed on questions of finance; he spoke ably and frequently upon a bill for

the expansion of the currency, favoring an increased issue of green-
backs to the extent of $50,000,000. Congress passed the bill with
which he was largely identified, but it was vetoed by President Grant.
In so brief a resume of his senatorial career, it is impossible to more
than refer to his speeches on the Louisiana question, the southern
questions—many of them—the Japan refunding bill, the Thurman
bill in respect to the Pacific railroad companies and others, indicating wide range of information and strong powers of argument. He
was an active member of the committee on the postoffice, on post
roads, on privileges and elections, on claims, on rules, on the District
of Columbia, and also of the committee to visit South Carolina to
investigate its presidential election affairs, etc. His senatorial term
expired March 4, 1879, and he continued to pursue his practice at
the bar until 1883, when he was appointed by Gov. Jarvis associate
justice of the supreme court upon the resignation of Associate-Justice
Ruffin. This position he held until the death of Chief-Justice Smith.
The vacancy was filled by Gov. Fowle, who appointed Judge Merrimon, and at the next democratic convention he was unanimously
nominated as the candidate for chief-justice and elected by a majority of upwards of forty thousand votes, and this was the crowning
honor of his life.

As Chief-Justice Merrimon is still living, and in the full, enjoyment
of his mental powers, eulogy of him as a jurist would hardly be in good
taste. Great respect for the profession of the law, faithfulness to
his clients and indomitable industry characterized him while at the
bar; and these qualities, added to decided natural ability, great self-
reliance, a well deserved character for high personal integrity, a
ready command of language, insured his success as a counselor and
advocate, and entitled him to the promotion he has received from the
executive and the people in his profession. While on the superior
court bench, his administration of the duties of that difficult office
was unanimously admitted to be admirable. Punctual, prompt,
quick and decided, but ever just and courteous, he inspired the officers of court, litigants, jurors and by-standers with proper respect for
the law and him who so well administered it. Like qualities he exhibits still, when occasion demands, in the dignified court of appeals
in which he so well presides. The labors of the court are great, and
his industry is quite equal to his full share of them. His able opinions, to be found in a score of volumes of the supreme court reports
of North Carolina, beginning with the eighty-ninth, already published
—and, it is hoped in many more cases to be decided in the future—
are and will be a lasting monument, *aere perennius*, to his strong sense
of justice, his powers as a logician and his wide legal learning.

At the age of twenty-two, he married Margaret J. Baird, daughter
of Israel Baird, of Buncombe county. Mr. Baird was a member of
that large and influential family so closely associated with the character and progress of his county. His wife was of the prominent Pennsylvania family of Tates, which family also has been and is now
usefully prominent in western North Carolina. Mrs. Merrimon was

JOS. J. DAVIS, Judge Supreme Court.

beautiful in person, her beauty enlightened by great loveliness of character, culture and intelligence. Her devotion to her husband, her cheerful endurance of sacrifice through his struggles, her faith, her hope, her courage, made her a noble help-meet for him who had set out to conquer the difficulties of life and continually to grasp its highest rewards. She lives to enjoy the conquests achieved over fortune with pride in welcoming the honors that have come to her husband. Judge Merrimon lives in the enjoyment of vigorous health, the fruit of regular systematic habits from boyhood, of the most rigid temperance in all things, of the most perfect abstinence from all the usually condoned weaknesses of youth, of the absolute avoidance of all those habits which custom has made so well nigh universal. He has always been a close and careful student of his profession, and an ardent reader of the purest literature, and thus has largely supplied his early deficiencies in education. He is clear, chaste and strong as a writer, and luminous, animated and effective as a speaker. In this last characteristic, in his warmth and impetuosity in debate, he gives striking illustration of the conquest he has achieved over himself. His warmth betrays the existence of strong internal fires. The subjugation of all the passions which lead to evil prove the mastery he has gained over them. He has reached his aim in life by the most rigid and unrelaxed self-discipline.

JOSEPH J. DAVIS.

On the 13th day of April, 1828, in Franklin county, N. C., was born Judge Joseph J. Davis. His youth was spent amid the scenes of plantation life, and his early scholastic training was at the Male academy of Louisburg, under Mr. John B. Bobbitt, an educator of considerable repute in his day. After receiving a thorough academical education at the Louisburg male academy, he attended for one year the well known Wake Forest college, and subsequently entered the University of North Carolina, where, in 1850, he received the degree of bachelor of laws. Being admitted to the bar in June of 1850, he located at Oxford, N. C., and began the practice of his chosen profession. However, he continued here less than three years, then located at Louisburg, in his native county. Mr. Davis soon rose to high rank as a lawyer, and was conducting a good practice when the Civil war came on. In 1862 he became captain of Company G, Forty-seventh regiment, North Carolina troops. The company had been raised in his own county and the county of Granville, mainly by his effort and by those of his first lieutenant, Dr. P. P. Peace, and he was made its captain, and remained as such till the battle of Gettysburg, when, upon July 3, when in the charge made by Gen. Pettigrew, he was captured and made a prisoner of war, and afterward confined first, at Fort Delaware, and later at Johnson's Island; and just a short time before the close of hostilities he was paroled, but soon the war closed, and again Mr. Davis took up the practice of his profession at Louisburg. He was soon called into public life, being elected as a democrat to the house of commons from Franklin county. He had been a whig and union man before the war, but since has faithfully co-operated with the democratic party. He was elected to the legislature in 1866, and after serving one term withdrew from public life, to give his time and attention to the exclusive practice of his profession, continuing actively engaged till 1874, when the democratic party made him its candidate for congress from the "Metropolitan" or Fourth district. The district was republican by a fair majority, and Mr. Davis entered the race against this majority and a strong opponent, but after a spirited and ably contested campaign, he was elected, as he was also re-elected in 1876 and 1878. He served six years in congress with credit to himself and to the satisfaction of the people; evidence of which is manifest in the fact of his re-electons.

Declining to enter the race for a fourth term in congress, Mr. Davis retired again to private life and to the practice of law. As a legislator, his record bears evidence of faithful, honest and able service, and his course in congress was marked for its fidelity to principle, and sincerity of purpose, and in the halls of legislation and in congress, as well as at the bar, or in the social or business world, Mr. Davis has proven himself the honest man, the cultured gentleman, and the learned scholar that he is. He had gained the esteem and confidence of the people; he had distinguished himself at the bar as an able and profound lawyer, and by his pleasant disposition, genial character and noble principles, he had become a popular, well-known and influential man, and in 1887, when by the death of Judge Thomas S. Ashe, a vacancy on the supreme court bench was occasioned, Gov. Scales, in his wise choice, selected Mr. Davis as the fittest man for the vacancy, appointing him to the exalted position. The people were well pleased with the elevation of Mr. Davis to this judgeship, and at their regular election in 1888, voiced their confidence in his fitness for the position by electing him for a term of eight years. This was a well deserved promotion, and since sitting on the bench of this high tribunal, Judge Davis has justified the most sanguine hopes of his friends, and his judgeship has been characterized as one of learning, wisdom and purity. As a jurist, he is profound, exact, and sincere, and his urbanity of character praiseworthy; and among members of the bar he sustains their highest esteem and respect; and among his brother members of the supreme court he seems to enjoy happy relations, and among whom he presents a pleasing and striking appearance on the bench, as he bears himself with dignity, and wears an expression of nobility and intelligence.

Judge Davis has continued his fixed residence at Louisburg, where he is especially honored and esteemed In social circles, he sustains prominence as a man of culture and moral and religious principle, and throughout his course he has been a faithful Episcopalian in church faith. He has twice been happily married. In October, 1852, he wedded Catherine Shaw, of Louisburg, a daughter of Robert J. Shaw, a merchant. To them were born five children, of which four survive. In 1881, his first wife died, and in 1883, he married for a second wife Louisa Kittrell, of Oxford, a daughter of Benjamin Kittrell, of Granville county. Judge Davis comes of an old and respected North Carolina family. It is not remembered, whether his paternal grandfather, William Davis, was born in North Carolina or not, but he was of Welsh lineage; a farmer by occupation, and participated in the Revolution for American Independence. The judge's father, Jonathan Davis, was a native of Franklin county, N. C., where he lived a long and useful life as a planter. He was born in 1769, and died in 1842. He married Mary Butler, by whom he had eleven children of whom Judge Davis is the youngest but one, and that one died in infancy. Mary Butler was born in King William county, Va., but when an infant was brought to North Carolina, by her parents, of whom it is said that they were of English ancestry. She was a granddaughter of Rev. John Pomphret, an early and powerful Presbyterian minister of Virginia, and from whom descends a long line of descendants. And such is a brief outline of the life and a mention of the family history of one of North Carolina's honored sons, who has attained to distinction as a man of legal and general learning, and gained a gratifying place in the affection and esteem of his countrymen, and to his good name, excellent character, and life achievements our pen cannot do justice.

WILLIAM NATHAN HARRELL SMITH

was born September 24, 1812, in Murfreesboro, Hertford county, N. C. His father was William L. Smith, a native of Lyme, Conn., and after having studied medicine removed to Hertford county, N. C., where he married and died, his death occurring in 1813. The subject of this sketch was a half-brother of the Rev. Dr. James Murdock, D. D., the distinguished ecclesiastical historian, orientalist and philosopher, who was accustomed each Sabbath, at least in his later years, to read a chapter of the Bible in seven different tongues. Our subject received his preliminary scholastic training in Murfreesboro, N. C., Kingston, R. I., Colchester, Conn., at which last place he was prepared for college. In 1830 he entered Yale college, and graduated in 1834. Such distinguished characters as Morrison R. Waite, chief justice of the United States, William M. Evarts, secretary of state, and Edward Pierrepont, once minister to Great Britain, were freshmen in Mr. Smith's senior year in Yale college. From the academical department of Yale, Mr. Smith was passed to the law department, where under the instructions of Judge David S. Daggett and Prof. Hitchcock, he was qualified for the bar. After a visit of some six months in Texas, he began the practice of his profession in Hertford, his native county. He rose rapidly at the bar and was soon to enter public life. In 1840 he was elected to the house of commons as representative from Hertford county; and in the year 1848, was elected to represent the Hertford district in the state senate, and during his service in this body he was chosen by the legislature, state solicitor for the superior court of the First judicial district, comprising the northeastern portion of the state. This office he held for two consecutive terms of four years each, the second term expiring in 1857, in which year he was nominated by the whigs of his district, for congress, and was defeated by a small majority, which, however, he overcame at the next election, in 1859, and took his seat in the house of congress just as the sectional conflict was about to merge into Civil war.

At once Mr. Smith became a prominent figure in the parliamentary struggles of the period. During the long and exciting strife, consuming a period of eight weeks, which preceded the organization of the house, Mr. Smith was nominated for the speakership by the southern whigs, in opposition to John Sherman, nominated by the republicans, and Thomas S. Bocock, the democratic nominee. Some of the more moderate republicans known as " The People's Party," having signified their intention to vote for Mr. Smith, a tacit agreement was made by which a majority of the democrats were to transfer their votes from Bocock to Mr. Smith, who would have been elected speaker, but Mr. Smith refusing to pledge himself to Mr. E. Joy Morris, of Pennsylvania, one of the certain republicans above alluded to, to constitute the committee on ways and means in the interest of protection, the republicans, with the honorable exception of Mr. Milliard, of Pennsylvania, withheld their votes, and Mr. Sherman having withdrawn, Mr. Pennington, of New Jersey, was finally elected speaker. Mr. Smith held his seat in congress till the close of the session, being present at the inauguration of President Lincoln, in March, 1861. He was a member of the Confederate congress during its existence, being elected to the Provisional congress, in July, 1861, and subsequently to the first and second permanent Confederate congresses, representing the First electoral district of North Carolina. During the course of this congressional service, Mr. Smith was closely associated with such able, discreet and enlightened statesmen as ex-Gov. William A. Graham, a member of the Confederate senate from North Carolina, and John Baldwin, a Confederate representative from Virginia. On the 18th of March, 1865, the second permanent Confederate congress adjourned, to be followed in less than one month by the memorable scene at Appomatox C. H., and after which Mr. Smith, for a time, employed himself with his private affairs, but before the close of 1865, he was elected to the house of commons of North Carolina, and here zealously promoted the reconstruction of the state government under the plan of President Johnson.

In 1868, during the exciting presidential campaign of this year, the action of the judges of the supreme court of North Carolina, called forth a solemn protest from the bar against judicial interference in political affairs, which was signed by one hundred and fifty members of the bar, including B. F. Moore, Ex-Gov. Thomas Bragg, and E. Graham Haywood, three of its most prominent members. This protest was treated by Chief-Justice Pearson as contempt of court, and argument was heard thereon at length. Mr. W. N. H. Smith was associated with Ex-Judge Battle, Ex-Judge Fowle, Ex-

Judge S. J. Person, and Ex-Judge Barnes for the defense, and in an able speech bore eloquent testimony to Mr. Moore's consistent support of the dignity and prerogatives of the judicial tribunals of the county, and succeeded in obtaining a motion to discharge the rule on payment of costs. In March, 1870, Mr. Smith removed to Norfolk, Va., still retaining, however, his practice in the courts of North Carolina. While residing in Norfolk, it was in the winter of 1870, that Gov. W. W. Holden was impeached for misdemeanor in office, and tried before the senate of the state, sitting as a high court of impeachment, presided over by the chief-justice, the trial being protracted over many weeks. Mr. Smith, although a political opponent, was selected by Gov. Holden, as one of his counsel, and made the closing argument in his defense, vindicating his official conduct with masterly power. Two years were spent in Norfolk, and then Mr. Smith returned to North Carolina, settling at Raleigh, where he formed a law partnership with George N. Strong, under the firm name of Smith & Strong, which continued till the elevation of his partner to the bench. In 1873 Mr. Smith's political disabilities were removed by a special act of congress, there being only one other person in the state to whom the act applied, Mr. Burton Craige, a former member, like himself, of the Federal and Confederate congresses. In 1874 Mr. Smith received from the Wake Forest college of North Carolina, the degree of LL.D., and on the 24th of June, of the same year, it being the fortieth anniversary of his class, there was held a general meeting of the Yale alumni, and here Mr. Smith made a touching speech to only twenty-five present, out of the original sixty-five who graduated in the class with him, and many of whom he had never met since they parted, forty years before.

January 12, 1878, Mr. Smith was appointed by Gov. Vance, chief-justice of the supreme court of North Carolina, to fill the vacancy caused by the death of Chief-Justice Pearson, thus receiving the unusual honor of being elevated at once from the bar to the head of the bench. The appointment, wholly unsought by him, was approved alike by the bar and the public, to whom his abilities as a lawyer and his traits as a man, pointed him out as the fit person for the place. To a legal mind of a high order, enriched by wide and varied learning the fruit of unremitting study, he added the rare faculty of seizing the points of a case at a glance, and the power, yet more rare perhaps of maintaining his intellectual balance in the presence of all snares and under all surprises. He was besides, a writer noted for the perspicuity and purity of his style, and a cogent, logical and strong speaker, and especially he excelled in the argument of cases in the courts of last resorts, where his practice had perhaps exceeded that of any other lawyer in the state. He was a pleasant and courteous gentleman, scrupulously just, and possessed singular purity of character. He was ever conservative in principle, and his patriotism and zealous devotion to the great principles of constitutional liberty were undoubted. His death occurred November 14, 1889, while still on the supreme bench as chief-justice. He married, January, 1839,

Mary O. Wise, daughter of William B. Wise, who was a merchant of Murfreesboro, N. C. This marriage gave issue to two sons, who are now surviving, the eldest, William W. Smith, is a prominent insurance agent; and the youngest, E. Chambers Smith, who is a representative member of the bar, and chairman of the state democratic executive committee. They both reside at Raleigh, N. C.

DUNCAN CAMERON.

Indeed but very few men of North Carolina were better known and more highly appreciated as an advocate, judge, statesman and financier, than Duncan Cameron, born in Prince Edward county, Va., in 1777, and dying in North Carolina in 1853. The Cameron family was ancient and highly respected. There were four brothers (two of them ministers), who came to America from Scotland. Rev. John Cameron, one of these brothers was the father of Duncan Cameron, our subject. He was a native of the highlands of Scotland, a lineal descendant of Sir Ewan Cameron, chief of the Clan Cameron, the Lochiel whom Macaulay portrays as " a man in personal qualities unrivaled among the Celtic princes; a gracious master, a trusty ally, a terrible enemy; a man with countenance and bearing singularly noble; a courtier with manners that would have graced the levees of Louis the XIV, to whom he bore in contenance a striking resemblance, though greatly exceeding him in stature; in courage and skill, in the use of weapons without an equal, a mighty hunter, with his own hands killing the last wolf of the savage bands that, up to that period, had wandered through the British islands; a fierce soldier, but a wise and prudent statesman, and though unlearned, a liberal patron of letters. His high qualities, if fortune had placed him in the English parliament or the French court, would have made him one of the foremost men of his age." Such was the man, the progenitor of the Rev. John Cameron, who emigrated to Virginia during colonial times, and married Ann Owen, daughter of Col. Thomas Nash, elder brother of Gov. Abner Nash and Gen. Francis Nash, both distinguished in North Carolina Revolutionary annals. There were born of this union four sons and two daughters, all, with the exception of one daughter, Jean, wife of the Rev. Andrew Syme, D. D., long time rector of Blandford church, Petersburg, Va., removing to North Carolina and becoming prominent in social, political and professional life, inheriting the father's virtue, piety and abilities. The eldest son, Duncan, the subject of this mention, came to North Carolina before he became of age; studied law under Paul Carrington, of Virginia, and was soon (in 1798) admitted to the bar of North Carolina. He first settled at Martinsville, then the county seat of Guilford, but subsequently removed to Hillsboro, where he soon became a successful and prominent practitioner. In 1803 he married Rebecca, the only daughter of Richard Bennehan, a wealthy merchant and planter in the northeast corner of the present county of Durham, then a portion of Orange. By his marriage with Miss

Bennehan Judge Cameron had two sons and six daughters. Of his children, his older son and all his daughters, except Margaret, who married Mr. George W. Mordecai, of Raleigh, a lawyer and banker, died unmarried after reaching maturity, and Mrs. Mordecai dying without issue. The only living descendants of Duncan Cameron are the children of his younger son, the late Paul C. Cameron.

The career of Judge Duncan Cameron is part of the history of his time. In his relations to his state and to society, to politics, to law, to finance, to education, to measures of internal improvement, he was always conspicuous. His reputation was early made, and though of rapid rise, was of enduring stability. For every position in life in which he was placed, he proved his eminent fitness. By his assiduity and acquirements, he soon attained fame and fortune. In 1800 he was appointed clerk of the court of conference (then the court of last jurisdiction), and prepared and published the reports of cases decided in that court. It was entitled, "Reports of Cases Determined by the Judges of the Superior Courts of Law and Equity of the State of North Carolina, at their meeting on the 10th of June, 1800, held pursuant to an act of assembly for settling questions of law and equity arising in the circuit." In 1806,-'7,-'12 and '13' he represented Orange county in the house of commons. In 1814, he was elected judge of the superior court, vice Edward Harris, deceased, and after presiding with satisfaction to the bar and country, he resigned this position in 1816. In 1819, 1822 and 1823, he was in the senate of the state legislature. His course in the legislature was marked by dignity, urbanity and patriotism; especially in the exciting periods of war with England (the war of 1812), was he a leading and unflinching advocate for its prosecution. He was the devoted friend of internal improvement, and of all schemes to develop the state, with which subject no one was more familiar. He served as a member of the board of internal improvement, and in his judgment and opinion the people placed full confidence and respect. He was chairman of the committee to build the present state capitol of North Carolina. For years he presided over the largest banking institution in the state, "The Bank of the State of North Carolina," whose affairs he conducted with unparalleled skill and success from 1829 to 1849. He directed the affairs of this bank with singular wisdom, fidelity and great financial ability, and was succeeded by his son-in-law, Mr. George W. Mordecai. As a financier, he was unrivaled, not only because of the clearness of his judgment, but also the integrity of his character and the proverbial caution of the race from which he came. In private life he was a sincere and unshrinking friend, a kind neighbor, just and charitable, and throughout the long career of his life he was a Christian, sincere and benevolent. He was the founder of Christ church at Raleigh, and was chairman of the building committee that built the church.

Soon after his marriage Judge Cameron selected a fine site for a dwelling about a mile and a half from Stagville, and there erected the commodious dwelling in which his large family was reared, and which yet remains in perfect preservation, after the lapse of three-quarters of a century. He tested or inspected every plank or piece of timber that entered into its construction, and inexorably rejected whatever was faulty or defective. In the construction of this dwelling, the careful prudent characteristics of Judge Cameron were strikingly displayed, and to-day the building stands as sound as when it came from the hands of the builders, and though of wood it has gone without material intermediate change or repair. Taste and judgment were exhibited in the selection of the site, on the margin of the broad valleys or bottoms, which distinguish the confluence of the Eno, Flat and Little rivers, uniting not far below Fairntosh (the name given Judge Cameron's residence), and here form the Neuse. The land had originally been densely set with massive forests of oak, hickory and other "hard-wood" trees, indicative of great strength and depth of soil, and here along the broad bottoms of the rivers above named, swept luxuriant fields covered with the wealth of the crops of wheat, corn, cotton and other products, all responding generously to good land tilled with care and intelligent system. The taste and judgment which guided in the selection of the site, also controlled in the adornment of the domain, and sturdy oaks with massive trunks and wide-spreading boughs, standing in stately parks, or over-shadowing the road sides in long extending avenues, gave it a baronial aspect more characteristic of English than American scenery. On this magnificent estate, comprising many large plantations, worked by a great and constantly increasing body of slaves, were exhibited the best of agricultural skill, the most admirable foresight, the most sagaciously economical administration of vast and various occupations, joined with the most humane consideration for the vast body of workers, and also the most watchful care for the comfort of those who had passed the age of active work, and the judicious provision and care for those who had not reached that period. A wise economy was observed in all the affairs of the several plantations, in their several parts and in the aggregate. Looms converted into clothing for the slaves, the wool clipped from the flocks, or the cotton picked from the fields, all the products of the estate, all the work of its own trained and skilled labor. Shoe-makers, wagon-makers, blacksmiths, artisans of many kinds, combined to make the operations of the large plantations self-sustaining. The cultivated fields supplied the breadstuffs, the large herds of hogs and cattle provided the meats, the cotton fields and the sheep folds furnished the material which domestic skill converted into clothing. The sick were carefully tended in well equipped hospitals under care of skillful physicians, or nursed through their sickness by the females of the white family, nor was the care of the souls of the slaves neglected, for divine services were regularly held in the neat chapel on the Fairntosh farm, or in other places of public worship on one of the plantations. It was patriarchal life on a grand scale, in which one great family was combined, where the interest of the master and servant manifested its mutuality, where the hard hand of the master was restrained by the joint influences of humanity and interest, and where the slave bent cheerfully to a burden he could not feel as oppression. Slavery was divested of its sterner features, as master and slave regarded each other with mutual good-will and affection. Judge Cameron found it necessary to extend his investments to other states to provide employment for the growing number of his slaves, and established large cotton plantations in Alabama and Mississippi, and continued an active and close attention to his vast agricultural interests, till in old age, when his son, Paul C. Cameron, assumed the management of the vast and varied interests.

Thus we have reviewed the career of Judge Cameron, as related to his agricultural associations and achievements, but it must not be forgotton that Judge Cameron was a warm friend of education, and did much to supply the educational needs of the people. In the decay of the old Episcopal school for boys, establised at Raleigh, in 1833, upon the sale of the property, Judge Cameron became the purchaser, and by his wish, and under his direction, St. Mary's school for girls, became the successor of the Episcopal school for boys, and is to-day a prosperous and popular school for the education of girls, and to this property, upon the death of Judge Cameron, succeeded his son, Paul C. Cameron, whose heirs upon his death, in turn succeeded to it. He was for a number of years, an active and faithful trustee of the University of North Carolina. Judge Cameron may justly be classed among the eminent and great men of his day; and had we space, there are countless other achievements and events of his life that might enlist interest, and appear worthy of consideration. As a lawyer, he was the equal of any of his time; he had an excellent logical mind, and was profound as a jurist, and was an able judge. As an advocate, his name is conspicuous in many of the important cases of his day. Particularly was he prominent, as the leading counsel for the defense, in the great suit of Earl Granville, in the circuit court of the United States, involving the title to nearly the whole of the northern half of the states of North Carolina and Tennessee. Mr. Cameron gained the suit in the lower court, and the noble Earl, whose counsel was William Gaston, appealed to the supreme court of the United States, but the suit, in consequence, probably, of the war of 1812, was discontinued.

As a citizen, Judge Cameron was of the progressive order. He was a man of keen and scrutinizing observation, and a student of political economy, and his learning, and his universal and farseeing judgment, enabled him to be the statesman he was; in the halls of legislature, he excelled; on the bench as a judge, or before the bar as an advocate, he was of power and influence; in speech, he couched his thoughts and propositions in simple and effective language, and from the rostrum as a speaker, he was possessed of eloquence and grace, and of a strong persuasive power. He was a ready speaker, and went to the point. As a man, he was universally esteemed, and when death came to him, at the advanced age of seventy-six years, an honored grave opened to receive him, and into its bosom, sank the remains of one, whose life was pure, noble, useful and exemplary;

and though now, his race is run, and Judge Duncan Cameron is no more, he lives yet, in affectionate remembrance, as a good man, a profound lawyer, an able judge, a skilled financier, honest and worthy citizen, a Christian gentleman.

THOMAS RUFFIN.

The fourth son of Chief-Justice Ruffin was Thomas Ruffin, who like his illustrious father wore the ermine on the supreme bench of North Carolina with distinguished ability. He was born in 1824, and after an excellent preparatory education, entered the University of North Carolina, in 1840, graduating with honors in 1844. Coming early to the bar, he located first in Rockingham county, where he formed a partnership with Judge Dillard, cementing a friendship that lasted through life. Their business was extensive and lucrative. In 1854 Judge Ruffin was elected solicitor of the superior court, and was recognized as one of the most efficient of the law officers of the state. Subsequently he removed to Graham, and resided there at the breaking out of the war. He entered but little into politics, but served one term in the assembly, and was a strong democrat in principle. On the fall of Fort Sumter he immediately volunteered; and on May 3, 1861, was commissioned captain of Company E, Thirteenth regiment, North Carolina troops. In October, 1861, on the death of Judge Dick, he was appointed judge of the superior court, and held the courts of the eastern circuit for one term. But he considered that his place was at the front, and in the fall of that year resigned his commission and was appointed lieutenant-colonel of his regiment. At the battle of South Mountain, which was one of the most stubborn encounters of the war, he was severely wounded, and in March, 1863, he resigned his commission in the army, but was soon afterward appointed a member of the corps court for the western army. He was on the field a man of decided capacity and fearless courage, and always manifested great calmness in positions of difficulty and danger. He was kind to his soldiers, and dilligent in securing them all possible comforts, and with sympathetic actions and words he soothed the sufferings of the sick and wounded.

After the war Judge Ruffin returned to his profession with renewed vigor. At the bar he was honest, laborious, learned, able and self-reliant. He was a splendid advocate, often truly eloquent. language was pure and forcible, and his argument convincing while his bearing commanded the admiration of the court and suitors. As an orator he was more like Cæsar than Cicero, more like Fox than Burke. He was formidable in debate, and fertile in intellectual resources. He was again associated with Judge Dillard, until the latter was elevated to the supreme court bench, and on the resignation of Judge Dillard, February 11, 1881, the eyes of the state at once turned to Judge Ruffin as the most worthy successor. Gov. Jarvis appointed him to the vacancy with the concurrence of the entire state. On the supreme court bench, he was accorded the high consideration which his learning and ability merited. His opinions were always strong. The public was fond of comparing him with his great father, and many thought him the equal in some respect of the eminent chief-justice. But his health failed him and on September 23, 1883, he retired from the bench and resumed the practice, associating himself with Maj. John W. Graham, at Hillsboro, N. C. His health was however precarious, and he was not as active in the practice as he had formerly been, and on May 23, 1889, he passed away, universally lamented by the people of the state. In early life Judge Ruffin married Miss Mary Cain, of Hillsboro, and left an interesting family surviving him, consisting of three sons and a daughter and widow.

GOV. ABNER NASH

was born in Prince Edward county, Va., August 8, 1716. He removed with his parents at an early age to Newbern, N. C., where he received his early educational training. He entered the law and was admitted to the bar while yet a young man, and practiced his profession successfully throughout the state. His first experience in public life was upon the occasion of his being chosen a delegate to the first provincial congress which met in North Carolina in 1774, and previous to the Revolution, and during its continuance was faithful, brave and earnest in the patriot cause. In 1775 he was a member of the provincial council, and also a member of the council and committee that framed the state constitution, as well as first speaker of the house of commons that assembled in North Carolina in 1776, and speaker of the senate in 1779. In the latter part of 1779 he was elected governor of the state, which office he held until 1781. During his administration North Carolina passed through the gloomiest period of the Revolutionary war, and being a man of mild temper and failing health, Gov. Nash could not have been equal to the situation, yet all his official actions bore the stamp of a strong will, a clear mind and a good heart. His first assembly in April, 1780, made Gen. Richard Casswell commander of all the militia of the state, although by the constitution the governor was commander-in-chief, and later on the same body appointed a board of war to manage military operations, which was another encroachment upon the governor's prerogative. Gov. Nash was a man of fine natural ability and large acquirements, a thorough Christian gentleman. His death, which occurred while on a visit to the city of Philadelphia, on the 2d of December, 1786, was deeply mourned throughout the state.

RICHARD HENDERSON.

Some philosopher has said that adversity scourges some men into greatness. Thus it was with the subject of our sketch, and the manner in which he rose. from the utmost obscurity and poverty to a national reputation is almost a satire upon those educational institutions of which Col. Ingersoll speaks as being a place where " diamonds are

B—7

dulled and brickbats are polished." Richard Henderson was born in Hanover county, Va., 1734. His parents were very poor, and he grew to manhood before he learned to read and write. While quite a lad he was appointed a constable, and when he had learned to write was made an under-sheriff. He removed to North Carolina in 1762, and having devoted several years to the study of the law, during which time he frequently read ten hours a day he was admitted to the bar. And so remarkable was his success at the bar, and so wonderful was his legal information, that in 1769 he was appointed associate judge of the superior court.

In 1770 the populace, which had been aroused by the unjust system of taxation, broke into the court room where Judge Henderson was presiding and compelled him to leave the bench. He was again elected to the bench but refused to serve, and a few years later he, as the president of the Transylvania Land company, negotiated with the Cherokee Indians for all that territory lying between the Cumberland mountains and the Cumberland river and the Kentucky river, and situated south of the Ohio, which was transferred to the company, by which Henderson and his associates became the proprietors of a tract of land larger than the present state of Kentucky. The country was named Transylvania. Mr. Henderson was speaker of the first legislature, and among its members were Daniel Boone, Richard Calloway, Thomas Slaughter, John Floyd and James Harrod. This purchase was shortly afterward annulled by the state of Virginia as an infringement of its chartered rights, but to compensate the families, the state granted them a tract of land twelve miles square on the Ohio, below the mouth of Greene river. A few years later Mr. Henderson removed to Tennessee, where he practiced law successfully for several years, but returned to North Carolina in 1780, where he settled on his large plantation and engaged in farming. He died January 30, 1785.

HON. ALFRED MOORE WADDELL,

of Wilmington, was born in Hillsboro, Orange county, N. C., September 16, 1834. After receiving a rudimentary education, he was prepared for college by William Bingham, Sr., whose school was then located at Hillsboro, and at the Caldwell institute, from which, in 1850, he entered Chapel Hill, and was graduated in 1853. •Having chosen the profession of the law, he was admitted to the bar in his twenty-first year, soon after which he removed to Wilmington, and entered into practice. In July, 1860, he purchased the *Wilmington Herald*, the leading whig paper of the Cape Fear section, which he edited until sometime in 1861. He was opposed to secession, believing that the south could secure the rights for which she was contending by remaining in the Union, and he fought the secession movement with all his ability. But when North Carolina decided to secede with her sister states, like a loyal son, he cast aside his own opinions, joined his fortunes with his native state, and, in 1861, entered the Confederate army. For awhile he was adjutant, afterward lieutenant-colonel of the Third cavalry, Forty-first North Carolina regiment. He served until 1864 with that command, when his health failing him, he was compelled to resign. When the war closed he returned to Wilmington, and entered into partnership with his father, Hon. Hugh Waddell, in the practice of law. This firm soon secured a large and lucrative business.

The year 1870 was a memorable one in North Carolina's history. The republicans had complete control of the state, and were determined to remain in power at all hazards. Kirk and his hirelings were overrunning a large part of the state, the civil law was "exhausted," and drumhead courts-martial were in vogue. The outlook at this time was indeed gloomy, congressional elections were approaching, and the nominee of the democratic conventions in the Third district had refused to encounter what was supposed to be sure defeat. The executive committee was at its wits' ends; as only seventeen days would elapse before election, and Oliver H. Dockery, the sitting member, was the republican candidate, and had been for several days busily at work in canvassing his district. At an opportune moment the committee looked to Col. Waddell, urging him to accept the nomination and fight the forlorn hope. Obeying this call of duty and seeing the dire extremities of his party, he accepted the nomination, and at once went forth to meet his political opponent, Dockery, who was a persuasive man on the stump, not only so, but he was personally popular in the district, and backed by his father's prestige, who had long held large power in that part of North Carolina. Their coming together in debate was eagerly looked forward to, by some with apprehension, for Col. Waddell was wholly, or almost without experience as a stump speaker, while Dockery was a giant in debate and a shrewd politician. But with all his ability, Dockery was overwhelmed and vanquished at the beginning, and as meeting succeeded meeting, it became clearly evident that Waddell was more than a match for his opponent, for he proved himself ready and fearless in debate with fertile resources. This proved to be the beginning of the end, for Col. Waddell was elected by a large majority, and the district which Dockery had carried by 2,000 majority, was redeemed. He took his seat in 1871, which he retained until 1879, continuously.

Colonel Waddell's maiden speech in the house was made in April, 1872, on the condition of the south. He was at that time one of the five democrats composing the minority of the special committee of thirteen designated as the "Ku Klux committee." The house received this speech with attention, for it was a manly and eloquent defense of his people from the slanders venomously poured upon them. He was placed early one the postoffice committee, and in 1877 he was made its chairman, and occupied this position through the balance of his service in congress. In January, 1876, he delivered a speech which attracted much attention. Northern and southern papers united in words of praise of this speech. In 1878 he was re-nominated, but was not re-elected. Many things compassed his defeat, namely, it was an off-year in politics, and the democrats over-estimated their strength. In addition Waddell had a severe attack of sickness and was unable to prosecute a personal canvass until late in the cam· paign. In 1880 Col. Waddell was a candidate at large to the national democratic convention which convened in Cincinnati and nominated Hancock. After the convention Waddell canvassed for the ticket in New England, New York and Pennsylvania. In 1882 he went to Charlotte and took editorial charge of the *Charlotte Journal*, afterward the *Journal-Observer*. Upon sundering his connection with this paper he went to Wilmington and resumed his law practice, in which he is still engaged. Col. Waddell is a vigorous thinker, a fine belles-letters scholar, a pulished writer and eloquent speaker. He is also a brilliant conversationalist. At the re-union of the army of northern Virginia, in Richmond, he delivered the annual address, which was highly praised. All in all he is a most genial and gifted gentleman.

EDWARD S. LATIMER,

of Wilmington, can be said to be a self-made man. He started in life with little money and few friends, but endowed with that faculty of indomitable will and energy which conquers all things. He was born in Wilmington, September 21, 1837. His parents were natives of Connecticut, and when our subject was thirteen years of age, re-moved with him to Wilmington. He was educated in the common schools of his time, and while yet in his youth he entered a dry goods store where he learned the business, and later on in life embarked in the same business for himself. At the breaking out of the war he entered the Confederate service as a member of a company of home guards. He was all through the four years of that great struggle and took part in many important and disastrous engagements. After the war he engaged in no business for several years, but about 1878 he entered Columbia law school and graduated in due time with high honor from that institution. In 1881 he formed a partnership with ex-Lieut-Gov. Steadman, for the practice of the law and in 1885, he was made president of the W. D. & C. railway, which important and lucrative office he now holds.

WILLIAM B. MEARES.

The subject of this sketch was born on the 8th of December, 1787; at Spring Garden, county of New Hanover, and state of North Carolina. He was educated at Bingham's school and the University of North Carolina. He read law in the office of that eminent statesman and jurist, the Hon. William Gaston, who never ceased through long years of close friendship and observation, only ending with his death, to entertain and frequently express the highest opinion of the moral and intellectual endowments of his former pupil. Indeed, on one occasion when Mr. Meares had been defeated by one vote for the position of United States senator, he publicly declared that he was the fittest man then living in the state to represent her in that distinguished body. Mr. Meares possessed to an eminent degree the moral, mental and physical qualifications which constitute a leader among men. He was gifted to an extraordinary degree with moral courage, frankness and honesty of purpose, was bold in the expression of his opinions, and looked with contempt upon those seekers of public honors who were mere followers in the wake of public opinion. His intellectual characteristics were chiefly those of great logical power; quickness of preception and a wonderful power of concentration. He was thus enabled to acquire the immense amount of general knowledge which he possessed in a remarkably short space of time, and being a self-reliant and independent thinker, when he had arrived at a conclusion he adhered to it with the greatest tenacity. His physical vigor and energy, like his mental, was most extraordinary. In person he was very handsome, and was possessed of elegant manners and such was his conversational powers that his companionship was greatly sought after by his acquaintances. He became prominent in early life and soon became a leading and successful practitioner of the laws in his section of the state. His first entrance into public life was as a representative in the legislature for the town of Wilmington, in the year 1818. He afterward represented the county of New Hanover as senator, in the legislatures of 1828-30-32. He was also a leading and influential member of the convention which was called in the year 1835 for the purpose of amending the constitution, and which has ever since been regarded as the ablest body of men ever assembled together in the history of the state. This was his last appearance in a legislative body. His reputation as a great legislative debater and political leader had become co-extensive with the state, and he withdrew from the political arena and also from the further practice of the legal profession. The latter part of his life was devoted to rice planting, and the other branches of agriculture. In this vocation he evinced great energy and judgment. He adopted the improved and scientific methods of farming, and his efforts were crowned with great success. He was a man emphatically of progressive ideas, and throughout his career he was an ardent advocate and supporter of the state university as well as of an efficient system of public schools throughout the state. His opinion was that the inheritance of a fortune would blight and ruin the prospects of almost all young men, and that a boy should be properly reared and given a liberal education and then be thrown on his own resources. He died in the prime of life leaving nine children, eight of whom were sons, and of so much more importance in his judgment were the advantages of the " higher " education over the mere possession of money, that he provided in his " will " that his estate should be held together until his youngest became of age, and he enjoined upon his " executors " to expend the last dollar of his estate, if it should be necessary, in order to give to each of his sons a collegiate education. He was an earnest and zealous advocate of the construction of railroads and other works of internal improvement, and it was truly said of him at his death that he had lived more than fifty years in advance of his people.

These were the characteristics which adorned the man and which were accorded to him with marked unanimity by the distinguished men and intelligent portion of society of his day and generation. It was perfectly natural that with such mental and physical endowments he should have wielded a powerful personal influence and that, at the same time his progressive views should have called forth the opposition of the narrow-minded anti-progressive portion of the public. It was not his fortune to have received the highest honors either of his profession or in the political arena, but in this country the distribution of public honors does not ordinarily depend upon the merits of the recipient, but is most apt to be the result of mere chance or the combination of fortuitous circumstances. Unlike most of our distinguished men, he was pre-eminently practical and useful, and when he died his loss was deeply felt in the political, professional, social and business circles of the Cape Fear section of the state. He died at the comparatively early age of fifty-three years and eleven months.

JOSEPH A. HILL.

This eminent son of North Carolina was born at Hilton, the former residence of Cornelius Harnett, about a mile north of Wilmington, N. C., in the year 1800. He was the son of Hon. William Hill, member of congress from 1799 to 1803, and grandson of John Ashe, of Revolutionary memory. He was named after his first cousin, Joseph Alston, subsequently governor of South Carolina and the husband of Theodosia, daughter of Aaron Burr. He was graduated at Yale college and trained for the law at the celebrated Litchfield law school. He represented the town of Wilmington in the legislatures of 1826, 1827 and 1830, and the county of New Hanover in 1823 and 1824. He had no pretentions to beauty but his face was lit by the brilliancy of his eye and the fascination of his smile, his gesticulation was graceful and his voice full, rich and flexible. He had no rival of his years as a debater and orator, and no superior of any age in North Carolina. The late distinguished Judge Gaston, of the supreme court of North Carolina, pronounced him the most brilliant man of his age he had ever met and Gaston was certainly a competent judge. His talents were versatile and he could, as occasion demanded, convince, convulse with laughter or move to tears. His style was chaste, not disdaining ornament but using it simply by way of illustration, and yet his oratory was often fervid. His speeches on Fisher's resolution, on the bank bill, on the tariff or nullification, sustain what is claimed for him. His letters to the late Gavin Hogg, a distinguished citizen of Raleigh, long since deceased, have been pronounced by competent authority the finest efforts of controversial writing yet produced in North Carolina.

In the internal improvement convention at Raleigh, in 1833, Mr. Hill met in debate the ablest men in the state. The journals show that he triumphed in carrying all the resolutions he submitted, and tradition reports that so splendid was his exhibition of ability that his claim to leadership was generally, if not universally, conceded. With a genius equal to the highest occasion and loftiest efforts, his amiability and bonhomie disarmed the envy his brilliancy excited. Unselfish and unassuming he alone was unconscious of the superiority universally conceded him. In social life without pretense, distinguished for his playful humor, his satire which left no sting in the wound, his fund of anecdote, his joyous vivacity and his delightful abandon, he was the center of attraction always. Without phariseeism, gay and debonair his society was sought by a people distinguished for politeness and hospitality and somewhat given to conviviality. Because a social pet it must not be supposed that he gave entirely to society what nature designated for nobler uses. He did not neglect the duties of his profession, which involved labor and study, but was so close an observer and diligent a student in his private hours that his advice was asked by the old and grave, who valued his wisdom and learning as much as the more volatile pleasantry and fun. He came to the bar with a mind probably better disciplined than that of any other man who had preceded him in North Carolina. Thus prepared, thus skilled in dialectics, and with a genius of the highest order, it is no wonder, though he died at the early age of thirty-five years, that he left behind him a fame co-extensive with the state. His friends believe that he was equal to any effort, and regret that he did not live long enough to display his powers upon a stage worthy of his extraordinary strength. He died without issue in the summer of 1835, and his ashes repose in the family burying ground at Hilton where he was born, around which place a historic interest attaches as having been in Revolutionary times the home of Cornelius Harnett, the representative man in those days of the Cape Fear section.

HON. GEORGE DAVIS.

This distinguished gentleman, one of the first of North Carolinians in character and talents, is the third son of the late Thomas F. Davis, one of the most prominent citizens of Wilmington, and the head of a family distinguished in the annals of the Cape Fear section for intelligence and virtue. The subject of this notice is a native of Wilmington, and was born in that city in the year 1820. His early education was obtained in the best schools then existing in the state, and he was so apt to learn and so well prepared that he entered the university of the state the youngest among all of the students, and graduated with the highest honors of his class. Adopting the profession of the law, he soon became a prominent leader at the bar, and acquired a large and lucrative practice which has suffered no diminution during a long and varied career, but, on the contrary, has increased with advancing years. He early embarked upon the stormy sea of politics, and was a leader of the old whig party. His speeches on the hustings during the campaigns in which he was engaged, and the many addresses made before crowded assemblies were marked by great intellectual vigor, and were so beautified and adorned by the graces of oratory, that they never failed to convince and to delight. Though in a helpless minority politically, he could always be found in the front of the fight, inspiring his followers with enthusiasm by his impassioned eloquence, his powerful invective and his wonderful fertility of resource, and commanding the respect and extorting the admiration even of his opponents by his chivalric bearing, his generous courtesy, and his high toned sense of honor. He was always more than equal to every demand upon his powers, and soon established a reputation as an orator and jurist co-extensive with the state; and so, when troublous times approached, and men's hearts were failing them from fear, they instinctively turned to him with the most abounding faith in his integrity, his patriotism, and his ability to guide and direct them in the right way.

And thus it happened in 1861, without action on his part and even without his knowledge, that such a thing was contemplated, Mr. Davis was appointed by the state of North Carolina one of its commissioners to the peace congress which met that year in Washington city. He attended its sessions and labored earnestly with others to effect a settlement of the difficulties which convulsed the country, but his efforts were vain, fanaticism rode rampant over truth and justice, and reason seemed dethroned in the minds of the northern majority, the congress accomplished nothing. Upon his return home from Washington an immense meeting of citizens was held, before whom he appeared to give an account of his stewardship, and did so in a speech so clear in its statements, so convincing in argument, and so pathetically eloquent, that the vast assemblage, in which were many who had clung to the hope of a peaceful solution of all difficulties and were opposed to any hasty movement on the part of the south, gave utterance, as with one voice, " well done thou good and faithful servant." Again, in 1862, he was elected to the high position of a senator in the congress of the Confederate states by the legislature of North Carolina, and this, like his first appointment, came to him unsolicited and unexpectedly. He served out the term to which he had been elected with distinguished ability, and at its termination the legislature, again without his knowledge, unanimously presented his name to President Davis for a position in his cabinet, who tendered him the attorney-generalship, which he accepted and held until the collapse of the Confederacy.

At the termination of hostilities Mr. Davis returned to his home in Wilmington, and resumed the practice of his profession, applying himself closely to it, and abstaining, as far as he was permitted to do so by the public, from active participation in politics. In 1877 Gov. Vance voluntarily tendered him the position of chief-justice of the supreme court of North Carolina, made vacant by the death of that able jurist, Chief-Justice Pearson, which he declined as he has other positions of honor and trust offered him time and again, and there has never been a time since the war that he could not have gone to congress from the Wilmington district if he would have accepted the nomination. His is the only case the writer can recall in which so many honorable positions have sought the man and not man the position, and it is the best illustration of his character that can be given. He would not turn upon his heel for any office that required personal solicitation, and would shrink with disgust from the manner in which preferment is now sought and obtained, for he was born at a time and raised among men who had not learned the art of rising to distinction by pandering to the base passions of the multitude or practising the wiles of the demagogue. No man in North Carolina stands higher than he, for he is known of all men to be able, pure and incorruptible, whose aspirations are all of the highest, who is an accomplished orator, a profound jurist, and a noble specimen of that highest type of true manhood, a Christian gentleman. Mr. Davis, though now advanced in years, is still engaged in the practice of his profession, but confines himself principally to office duties, and seldom appears at the bar except in important cases. His powers have suffered no dimunition from age, and he is *facile princeps* at the bar, and like Saul among his brethren, towers above all competitors. He has been twice married and is again a widower, but with children and grandchildren around him to brighten his home and administer to his comfort.

JUDGE OLIVER P. MEARES,

judge of the criminal circuit of New Hanover and Mecklenburg counties, was born in the city of Wilmington, on February 24, 1828. He is the son of William B. Meares, notice of whom will appear in this work. He was prepared for college at the Bingham school and Caldwell institute, and completed his education at the University of North Carolina, graduating in 1848. He then commenced the study of law under Judge Battle, of the university law school, and remained with him about one year. In 1850 he was licensed to practice, and from that time until the breaking out of the war, he followed his profession in his native city. He was an old line whig, and took an active part in the campaign of 1852, as a political speaker, and in 1856 was an electoral candidate on the Fillmore ticket, and was an active and distinguished speaker in the campaign of 1860. After the election of Lincoln he became a secessionist, and in April, 1861, he entered the military service, as captain of a company which was organized in Wilmington, and afterward became part of the Eighteenth North Carolina regiment, in which regiment he rose to the rank of lieutenant-colonel, and served until the re-organization of the same, at the expiration of one year. In January, 1867, he was elected by the legislature to the office of judge of the criminal court of New Hanover county, which position he held until the adoption of the new constitution, in July, 1868. He again entered the practice of the law, and also took an active part in the campaigns of 1868, 1870, 1872 and

1876, as a democratic speaker and leader. In 1877 he was re-elected to the bench by the legislature, and served eight years. In 1885 he was elected judge of the criminal circuit, of New Hanover and Mecklenburg counties, and is serving as such at the present time. In 1851 Judge Meares was married to Miss Ann Eliza, the daughter of Dr. Thomas H. Wright, of this city, and the granddaughter of Judge Wright, who was a native of Wilmington. This union has been blessed with several children, who have all reached maturity. Judge Meares has devoted his life to his profession, and is an able, fearless judge and a terror to evil doers. He is one of the most candid of men, a man of strong convictions and force of character, who will do what he believes to be right, even should the heavens fall.

WILLIAM GASTON

was of distinguished Huguenot descent. He was born in Newbern, September 19, 1778. He was the son of Alexander Gaston, one of the most eminent physicians of the state, who was murdered by the tories in the presence of his family. The tragic death of his father left its terrible imprint on the mind of the son, in the way of an ineffaceable melancholy which age and vicissitude could not quite shake off. He commenced his education at Georgetown (D. C.) college, and graduated from Princeton with distinguished honors. He studied law at Newbern, where he was admitted to the bar, and a few years later attained great distinction in his profession. In 1779 he was elected to the state senate from Craven county, in 1808 to the house of delegates, over which body he was chosen to preside. He was a member of congress from 1813 to 1815, and his speech in that body in opposition to the loan bill which proposed to place $25,000,000 at the disposal of the executive for the conquest of Canada during the war with Great Britain, was a master-piece of eloquence and was widely read and greatly admired. He was judge of the supreme court from 1834 till his death, and some of the best statutes of the state are the result of his judicial genius. In 1835 he was a member of the state constitutional convention, and suggested and elaborated nearly all the reforms in the new constitution. He was offered, but declined, the United States senatorship in 1840. He died in Raleigh, January 23, 1844.

JOHN LOUIS TAYLOR.

This eminent jurist was born in London, Eng., in March, 1769. His father having died at an early age, young Taylor was brought to this country by his brother, at the age of twelve years. He was for two years at William and Mary college, and at the age of fourteen years removed to North Carolina, where he studied law and was admitted to practice at Fayetteville, which latter place he represented in the legislature in 1792–4. He removed to Newbern in 1796, and in 1798 he was elected a judge of the superior court. In 1808 he was chosen by his colleagues as president of the supreme court, which, at that time, consisted of periodical conventions of the judges of the superior courts at Raleigh. When a new and separate tribunal was instituted as a court of last resort, in 1818, he was appointed chief-justice, which he held until his death. In 1817 he accomplished the colossal task of revising the statutory laws of the state. The work was completed and published in 1821, and a continuation appeared by the same author in 1825. Such a feat as this for a man already well along in the journey of life, encumbered with the cares of high judicial office, bespeaks a wonderful power of mental and physical energy. Among his other published works, which stand high in the common law to this day, may be mentioned: "Cases in Law and Equity of the State of North Carolina," "The North Carolina Law Repository," two volumes, "Charge to the Grand Jury at Edgecombe, Exhibiting the Criminal Law," and a work on "Executors and Administrators."

COL. E. C. YELLOWLEY.

Soon after the termination of the Revolutionary war between the American colonies and the mother country Capt. Edward Yellowley emigrated from England, and coming to America, settled at Williamston in Martin county, N. C. He raised a large family, and among his children was the subject of this sketch, Edward Clements Yellowley, who was born on the 22d day of October, 1821. He received a good preparatory education under Mr. J. M. Lovejoy, who was well known for many years as one of the best educators in the South, and entering the University of North Carolina at Chapel Hill took the regular course, graduating with the degree of A. B., in the class of 1844. He chose the law as his profession and, having obtained his license to practice, settled at Greenville in Pitt county. Here a good practice speedily rewarded his efforts and he was forging well ahead in his profession when in 1847, he became involved in a personal difficulty with Mr. H. F. Harris, who was then representing Pitt county in the legislature of the state. The difficulty like so many in which public men of this country have been engaged in the days when the Code was considered the proper resort for gentlemen to settle their affairs of honor, grew out of political differences and was of such a character that Mr. Harris saw proper to demand satisfaction by sending a challenge to fight a duel. Though averse to duelling, the challenge, which was borne by Mr. Harris' friend, Henry Dimock, Esq., was promptly accepted by Mr. Yellowley and the preliminary arrangements made for him by his friend, Mr. F. B. Satterthwaite. Friends exerted themselves to settle the difficulty amicably and prevent the meeting, but their efforts were of no avail. The duel was delayed for a time by the interference of the authorities, the principals being arrested just as they arrived at the place of meeting first agreed upon which was in Northampton county, N. C. A few days afterward the principals with their friends went to Norfolk, Va.,

Mr. Yellowley and his friends stopping at Keeling's Hotel, Mr. Harris and his friends at Walter's Hotel. There the final arrangements were made for the duel, which took place in the state of Virginia, at the half-way house between Portsmouth, Va., and Elizabeth City, N. C., in the Dismal swamp canal on Friday the 1st day of October, 1847, between the hours of five and six o'clock A. M. Dr. W. J. Blow appeared on the field as the second of Mr. Yellowley, and M. B. Smith, Esq., as the second of Mr. Harris. Pistols were the weapons used. At the first fire Mr. Yellowley discharged his weapon in the air and was shot through the hat by his opponent; seeing that nothing would satisfy Mr. Harris but his blood, at the second fire he took deliberate aim and shot his enemy through the heart, killing him instantly. In this affair so trying to a young man just beginning his public career, Mr. Yellowley behaved with the utmost coolness, and exhibited that calm, unflinching courage which characterized his course through life. Kind, charitable and generous, with a heart as gentle as a woman's, ready at any time to help a friend or forgive an enemy, high bred and chivalrous, a gentleman in the true acceptation of the term there was no such thing as fear in his make up, and, although in this lamentable affair he only defended his life, he regretted the difficulty and its melancholy termination all his days. So profound was his regret he never alluded to the matter at any time. During a residence in his family of eighteen years the writer of this — his nephew — mentioned the subject to him but once and then was bidden never to refer to it again.

In the year 1850 or thereabouts, Mr. Yellowley was elected clerk of the superior court and afterward solicitor for the county court; in both capacities he served with credit to himself and satisfaction to his constituents. In politics he was an old line whig, and as such, voted in 1860, for Bell and Everett, for the Union and the enforcement of the laws. Although in feeling and sentiment opposed to the secession of the southern states from the Union, when Mr. Lincoln had been elected, the efforts made looking to pacification and peace had proven fruitless, and the southern leaders could obtain no guarantees for the protection of their rights and the preservation of the sovereignty of the states, he became an advocate of secession and urged the people in the spring of 1861, to vote in favor of the proposition to hold a convention. Immediately after the secession of the state he raised a military company by his own exertions, offered his services to the governor, received his commission as captain and was assigned to the Eighth regiment, which rendezvoused at Warrenton, with H. M. Shaw as colonel commanding. He remained in active service throughout the war. In 1862 he became major of the Eighth regiment, and was afterward appointed lieutenant-colonel of the Sixty-eighth regiment, of which he was in immediate command until the end of the war, the colonel, William J. Hinton, being captured by the enemy and never having been exchanged. He fought in many battles and took part in the last engagement of the war, at Bentonsville, between Gen. J. E. Johnston and Gen. Sherman.

In 1863, at the urgent solicitation of his friends Mr. Yellowley consented to become a candidate for a seat in the Confederate congress against the Hon. R. R. Bridgers. Being in active service he was unable to make a canvass of the district; notwithstanding this however, he received a considerable majority of the votes, but owing to some alleged informality Mr. Bridgers received the certificate of election. At the end of the war he resumed the practice of law. In 1866 he was elected a member of the general assembly of North Carolina from Pitt. This was the first legislature which assembled after the termination of the war and it was burdened with grave responsibilities and confronted by serious difficulties. In the deliberations of that body he was a conspicuous figure, maintaining by his course the calm, conservative sentiment characteristic of the old whigs. Under the circumstances prevailing at that trying time, he did not think a reckless, defiant course was advisable, but considered it best to accept in good faith the facts of the situation then existing and adjust the troubles besetting the south on the lines fixed by the result of the war. Conservative in his opinions and in common with a large element of the people regretting that the whig party no longer existed, he became an ardent and zealous supporter of the democratic party, and took an active part in shaping the events which led to the final discomfiture and rout of the carpet-bag and negro regime. As a lawyer he had a large and lucrative practice and accumulated a handsome fortune. The contemporary of E. J. Warren, Henry Gilliam, F. B. Satterthwaite and David M. Carter, he was prominent among the distinguished men who maintained the prestige and added lustre and distinction to the bar of eastern Carolina. In 1885, at the age of sixty-three, he died suddenly at Asheville. North Carolina, where he had gone to recuperate his health.

THOMAS JORDAN JARVIS

was born in Currituck county, on the 18th of January, 1836. His father, Rev. B. H. Jarvis, was a native of the same county, a minister of the Methodist Episcopal church, who devoted his life to zealous work in his honored calling and was a successful and able preacher of the Word. His mother was Elizabeth Daly, of Camden county, N. C. His father's circumstances being very poor, the subject of this sketch did not enjoy the advantages of early education, but being determined to improve himself, he set to work, and with the aid of friends, entered Randolph-Macon college, January, 1855, and with money earned by teaching at intervals, and assistance furnished by Mr. John Sanderson, he finally completed his course there, graduating in 1860. The indomitable will displayed by him in pursuing his purpose to obtain an education well illustrates the stamina of the man, and the self-denial he practiced in accomplishing success so early in life exemplifies the strong qualities that have distinguished him throughout his career. On graduating, he began to teach a school in Pasquotank county, where he was engaged until June, 1861, when

he entered the Confederate army. He enlisted first in the Seventeenth North Carolina regiment, and afterward in the Eighth North
Carolina troops, where as captain of a company, he displayed a
heroism, fortitude and endurance not surpassed by any of his comrades in arms. He was an excellent soldier, cool, resolute, and unflinching in the presence of danger. Passing through many perils
and exposed to many trying vicissitudes he escaped unharmed until
on the 14th of May, 1864, at Drury's Bluff, he received a wound that
disabled him, and since then his right arm has hung useless at his
side.

When the war was over, and the future was still involved in doubt
and obscurity, Mr. Jarvis courageously applied himself to business,
and opened a small store in Tyrrell county, at the same time studying law. In the fall of that year, a state convention was called, and
his friends in Currituck county brought him forward as a candidate
for election to that body. He was elected and then began a public
career alike honorable to himself and useful to the people of his native state. The following year he obtained his license to practice
law and entered with zeal upon that as his business in life, but his intelligent appreciation of the importance of the grave questions then
challenging public attention led him to take a deep interest in political movements.

In 1868 he was elected as a democrat to the legislature from Tyr-
rel county, and in the fall made an extensive canvass as district
elector on the Seymour and Blair ticket. When the legislature met
in November, he allied himself with John W. Graham. Plato Durham, James L. Robinson and the few other democrats of that body
in strenuous opposition to the measures of the republican majority.
They were but a handful, but most gallantly did they throw themselves into the breach. They stood steadfast, immovable in their devotion to the interests of North Carolina, and the state soon became
filled with the fame of these young men, who, having served with
honor on the field of battle, now by their wisdom and prudence and
stern integrity, won for themselves leadership in public affairs. Their
triumph in establishing the Bragg-Phillips investigating committee,
and in repealing the special tax laws was complete and the people
loved to do them honor. To their action was largely due those
events which culminated in the defeat of the republicans in 1870, the
impeachment of Gov. Holden, and the pacification of the state at
that early date and the subsequent era of quiet, harmony and prosperity. When the new assembly met Capt. Jarvis was tendered the
speaker's chair, and from being one of a half-a-dozen in the minority,
he became the chief director of state legislation. The democrat-con-
servative party was then in a form itive condition and Speaker Jarvis
exercised great influence in welding the fragments of the old parties
into a solid organization In 1872, he moved to the county of Pitt,
and formed a law partnership with Col. David M. Carter, one of the
strongest intellects of the state, and that fall canvassed the state as
an elector on the Greeley ticket. He was elected a member of the

constitutional convention of 1875, and to his address and prudence was chiefly due the power of the democrats to control that body which was evenly divided between the parties. The next year he was nominated by the state convention for the office of lieutenant-governor, and made an exhaustive canvass of the state, and upon Gov. Vance's election to the United States senate, in February, 1879, he succeeded to the executive chair, to which position he was re-elected for a full term in 1880.

During the six years in which Mr. Jarvis was governor, he impressed himself more thoroughly on the activities of the people than any other governor of the state. He was wise and prudent in council, and bold and progressive in action. He deemed it a function of the executive office to give direction to public measures, and he met the responsibilities of his position with zeal and patriotism. He shrunk from the discharge of no duty; and regarding that the governor was in some measure the head of the political party that had elected him, he largely participated in every campaign, giving a detailed account of his stewardship, and challenging the most thorough scrutiny into every act of his administration, whose cleanness and integrity commended itself to public confidence. He knew no favorite section, but sought to promote the welfare of every portion of the state. While warmly advocating the new system of county government for the east, he used every means to advance the construction of the Western North Carolina railroad, and eventually, when it became necessary to do so, he convened the legislature in special session and disposed of that road in order that it might be speedily finished. Under his wise administration the industries of the state greatly advanced, and party bitterness rapidly disappeared. Indeed it may be asserted that no state can boast a more splendid administration than that of Gov. Jarvis, one during which, considering the impoverished condition of the people, more has been done for the advancement of education, for the promotion of beneficent public purposes, and the establishment of industrial progress and prosperity.

On the retirement of Gov. Jarvis from the executive office, he was appointed by President Cleveland United States minister to Brazil, which post he resigned soon after the election of President Harrison. Abroad he deported himself as a worthy representative of his country, and he maintained a high position at the court to which he was accredited. Since his returned he has resumed the practice of the law at Greenville, N. C., and still enjoys the confidence and warm regard of the people of his native state. Gov. Jarvis has ever been an industrious and laborious worker. He has a mind capable of comprehending the details of the most intricate subject, and he fully masters whatever engages his attention. As a speaker he is clear, bold, comprehensive; forcible in the use of language, and convincing in argument. He has, we believe, spoken in every county in the state, and as a popular orator he is unsurpassed among our public men. Gov. Jarvis, in 1874, was married to Miss Mary Woodson, the accomplished daughter of John Woodson, of Virginia, who is greatly admired and esteemed by a large circle of friends throughout North Carolina. He has not allowed public matters to overshadow concerns of higher import, and he is an humble, active and consistent member of the Methodist Episcopal church, south.

ALLISON C. ZOLLICOFFER

was born in Halifax county, N. C., April 24, 1854. He received a thorough preliminary schooling and then entered Wake Forest college, remaining until 1878. At this time he commenced his legal studies with W. H. Day, of Weldon, N. C., and one year subsequent was admitted to the bar. He then formed a copartnership with his former preceptor, Mr. Day, and they continued together until January, 1891. In January, 1882, Mr. Zollicoffer removed to Henderson, and looked after the interests of the business there, while Mr. Day remained at Weldon. In 1884 Mr. Zollicoffer was united in marriage to Miss Tempie B. Perry, a daughter of Dr. A. S. Perry, of Franklin county, N. C., and to them have been born four children, two of whom are living, named Augustus A. and Jeremiah P. The paternal grandfather of these children was J. B. Zollicoffer. He was a native of Halifax county, N. C., where he was born in 1819. He was a farmer and horticulturist, and held an honorable position in the community. He married Miss Mary A. Hawkins, daughter of Ambrose Hawkins, who bore him eight children, four of whom survive, viz.: Dr. A. R. Zollicoffer, of Weldon, N. C.; Dr. D. B. Zollicoffer, of Gareysburg, N. C.; A. C. Zollicoffer, of Henderson, N. C., and M. E. Zollicoffer, of Portsmouth, Va. The father died in 1885, and the mother in 1876. J. B. Zollicoffer was the son of J. H. Zollicoffer, who was also a native of Halifax county. He was a farmer during the whole of his active career, and a man of influence and ability. His demise occurred in 1824. Allison C. Zollicoffer, the subject of this sketch, has won distinction and honor at the bar. He is a lawyer of no mean ability, and stands in the front ranks of his profession in the state.

ANDREW J. HARRIS,

one of the ablest among the younger members of the Vance county bar, was born about four miles southeast of Oxford, in Granville county, N. C., October 28, 1861. He was given ample opportunity for obtaining a thorough preliminary schooling, and in 1884 was graduated from the university of North Carolina, with the degree of Ph. D. He began his legal studies with Messrs. Dick & Dillon, prominent attorneys of Greensboro, N. C., and in October, 1885, was admitted to the bar. At this time he took up his residence in Henderson and opened a law office, where he has since practiced. Mr. Harris was married November 7, 1888, to Miss Lee Mitchell, a daughter of the Hon. W. L. Mitchell, of Granville county, N. C. One daughter, Anne, is the issue of this marriage. Mr. Harris is the son of Benjamin F. Harris, who was born in Granville county, N. C., in 1812. He was an extensive agriculturist and carried on several stores and mills in connection with his farming interests. He was married in 1850, to Miss Anne E., daughter of Samuel Rogers, of Warren county, N. C., and five children blessed their union, four of whom survive the parents, viz.: George B., Samuel R., Fletcher R. and Andrew J. Harris. Benjamin F. Harris died in 1875. He was the son of George W. Harris, who was a Virginian, having been born in the last century. He came to North Carolina with his parents in early boyhood. They settled in Granville county, where the son subsequently became a leading farmer and mill owner.

BEVERLY CAMERON COBB,

a prominent attorney of Lincolnton, N. C., is the eldest son of Joseph C. and Margaret E. Cobb. He was born in Lincolnton, August 17, 1848. He attended the schools of his native county until his sixteenth year, when he entered the high school at Mebanesville, where he remained during 1865 and 1866. In 1869 he entered the law school of Judge Pearson, at Richmond Hill, N. C., and was admitted to practice in June, 1870. He entered into partnership, in 1871, with Judge Schenck, and began the practice of his profession at Dallas, N. C. This firm continued until 1874, when Judge Schenck was called to the bench, and Mr. Cobb succeeded him in the entire business of the firm, and removed to Lincolnton, where he has ever since been engaged in successful practice. He is a staunch democrat, and has been an active politician ever since he came to the years of manhood. In 1876 he was elected by his party to represent Lincoln county in the state legislature. He was re-elected in 1878, and was one of the most active and efficient members of the house; he had several of the most important chairmanships in the gift of the presiding officer, and did excellent work in the committees. At the Chicago national convention in 1884, which nominated Grover Cleveland, he was a delegate from his congressional district. Mr. Cobb has served one term as mayor of Lincolnton. He is a member of the Masonic fraternity. In his religious views Mr. Cobb is identified with the Episcopal church, having been a vestryman in that church for the past ten years. In January, 1880, Mr. Cobb was united in marriage with Miss Jane, daughter of Hon. V. A. McBee, of Lincolnton, but his married life was of brief duration, Mrs. Cobb's untimely death occurring in New York city, in 1881. Mr. Cobb has an extensive practice from which he derives an ample income, and he enjoys the respect of his professional brethren as well as of the community where he is so widely and favorably known.

HON. CHARLES M. COOKE.

Of the many honored names of North Carolina, none deserves more than the Hon. Charles M. Cooke. Born in Franklin county, on

B—8

the 10th of March, 1844, and, since reaching manhood, he has been actively and prominently identified with the best movements of his native state. Having received an excellent preliminary schooling at the Louisburg academy, the ardent student was pursuing the sophomore studies at Wake-Forest college when his people called upon him to take up arms in defense of his native state. In the winter of 1861 he enlisted in Company I, Fifty-fifth North Carolina regiment, as a private, was soon made lieutenant of Company I, and the captain of the company being captured at Gettysburg, he was placed in command of the company, and discharged the duties of that rank faithfully and well until June, 1864, when he was assigned to duty as adjutant of the regiment, and he held that rank at the close of the war, having participated in the following battles: Little Washington, N. C., second battle of Cold Harbor, Wilderness, Spottsylvania, Bristol Station, Hanover C. H., Davis's Farm, Va., and all the engagements around Petersburg. He was grievously wounded at Petersburg, March 31, 1865, and was confined in a Richmond hospital at the time of the evacuation of that city. He was paroled by the Federal government after Lee's surrender, and immediately returned to Franklin county, to his father's farm. He resumed his studies of the law, and was admitted to practice in the county courts in January, 1867, and in the superior and supreme courts in January, 1868. In 1874 he was elected to the state senate, and served one term. In 1877 he was appointed solicitor of the Sixth judicial district, known as the Raleigh district, by Gov. Z. B. Vance, and he held that office until 1878, when he declined further service. In 1878 Mr. Cooke was sent to the house of representatives, and held the chairmanship of the judiciary committee. Two years later he was re-elected a member of that body, and was chosen speaker of the house. Gov. Jarvis appointed him in March, 1879, as a member of the board of internal improvements, and he filled that office till August, 1880, when he resigned upon his re-election to the general assembly. Four years subsequent Gov. Scales appointed him a director of the state prison, and four years later Mr. Cooke resigned the honor to become a candidate for the house of representatives. Having been elected to that position, he declined to be a candidate for the speakership, and was appointed chairman of the committee on internal improvements, and also of the house branch of the committee on railroad commission. In 1872 he was a delegate to the democratic national convention. For a number of years he has been the president of the board of trustees of Wake-Forest college, and he is also a trustee of the University of North Carolina.

In February, 1868, Mr. Cooke, was so fortunate as to form a marriage alliance with Miss Bettie Person, daughter of Weldon E. Person, of Salabusha county, Miss., and to them nine children, seven of whom survive, have been born, viz.: Percy, Charles M., Jr., Francis N., Frederick K., Wilbur C., Edwin W. and Lizzie K. Cooke. Mr. Cooke is a member of the Blue Lodge Masons, having held the chair of W. M. of Clinton lodge, No. 124. He is active and consistent in church work, having for many years been a communicant of the Missionary Baptist denomination. Capt. Jones Cooke, father of Hon. C. M. Cooke, was born in Franklin county, N. C., in 1786. He held many important public positions and was a man of much prominence and influence. For several years chairman of the county court and charter sessions, he served as a loyal and efficient captain in the patriotic army during the war of 1812. He was thrice married, his last marriage being to Miss Jane A. Kingsbury, daughter of Darius Kingsbury, of Litchfield, Conn. She was the granddaughter of Esther Mather, who was of the Cotton Mather family. Their marriage was solemnized in August, 1841, and resulted in the birth of five children, named: Josephine, Charles M., Belle, Dr. W. J. (deceased in 1888); and Eudora F., wife of James N. Tisdale, of Selma, N. C. The father of these children died in 1872, and the mother in 1880. Capt. Jones Cooke was the son of Thomas Cooke, a Virginian, having been born in Gloucester, in 1700. He died in 1801, aged one hundred and one years. In his early manhood he removed to Franklin county, N. C. By his second wife, Belle Congers, he had several children. Six of her brothers were soldiers in the Revolutionary war, all having served with valor.

THOMAS BRAGG,

a distinguished North Carolinian, was born in Warren county, N. C., November 9, 1810. He was the son of Thomas and Margaret Bragg, and brother of the celebrated Gen. Braxton Bragg. He had an academic education, first attending the academy at Warrenton under the instruction of George W., afterward Bishop Freeman, then at the military academy at Middletown, Conn., under the tutorship of Capt. Alden Partridge, a noted instructor of the sciences, especially of the military. Here young Bragg spent about three years. He studied law under John Hall, a judge of the supreme court of North Carolina, and was admitted to the bar. He opened a law office at Jackson, N. C., and there carried on a most successful practice. In 1842 he was elected a member of the lower house of the legislature, and in that body was appointed chairman of the judiciary committee, the real post of honor in the house. He was one of the leading and most influential members. In politics he was a democrat and was nominated by that party and elected governor of the state in 1854; he was re-elected in 1856 over one of the most popular men in the state, Hon. John A. Gilmer. He was chosen a United States senator in 1858, for the regular term of six years, but on the opening of the Civil war in 1861, resigned with other senators of the southern states. When the Confederate government removed from Montgomery to Richmond, in 1862, the attorney-generalship of the Confederate states was tendered to Gov. Bragg by President Davis, and was accepted. He discharged the duties of this responsible position with distinguished ability until 1863. He then returned to the practice of his profession. During the troublous times which succeeded the Civil war, Gov. Bragg was among the foremost statesmen of North Carolina to engage in the work of reducing the conflicting elements to unison and bringing order out of confusion.

In 1871 Gov. Bragg and several other distinguished North Carolinians addressed a letter to Judge Bond, of the United States district court, in relation to the prosecution of the secret organization known as the Ku Klux. The letter was in the nature of a petition, asking Judge Bond to continue the trial of the persons charged as belonging to this secret organization to the next term of the court, declaring that such continuance " would enable us to enlist all law-loving citizens of the state to make an energetic and effectual effort for the restoration of good order." The letter concluded: " In presenting these considerations to your honor, we declare that it is our duty and purpose to exert all the influence we possess, and all the means in our power to absolutely suppress the organization, and to secure a lasting and permanent peace to the state. The laws of the country must and shall be vindicated. We are satisfied and give the assurance that the people of North Carolina will unite in averting and forever obliterating an evil which can bring nothing but calamity to the state. In the name of a just and honorable people, and by all the considerations which appeal to good men, we solemnly protest that these violations of law and public justice must and shall cease."

This very reasonable and patriotic appeal received a prompt reply from Judge Bond, in which he declared his inability to comply therewith. The subsequent proceedings against the organization are a matter of public and voluminous record. Mr. Bragg took an active and conspicuous part in the impeachment trial of Gov. W. W. Holden before the state senate, " for high crimes and misdemeanors." This trial resulted in an order that Gov. Holden " be removed from the office of governor, and disqualified to hold any office of trust, honor or profit under the state of North Carolina." Governors W. A. Graham and Thomas Bragg, and Judge A. S. Merrimon were selected by the managers as counsel for the prosecution of the impeachment, and an abler or more learned counsel could not have been found in the state. But the labor and anxiety of this trial proved too much for Gov. Bragg's constitution, and he retired from it with health permanently impaired and with physical powers completely exhausted, yet in the full and vigorous possession of his intellectual powers. He died January 21, 1872, at Raleigh, attended by the ministrations of a devoted and deeply afflicted family, and mourned by a whole community of sympathizing neighbors and friends.

THEODORE F. KLUTTZ,

a citizen of Salisbury, N. C., a son of Caleb Kluttz, was born in the city of his present residence, October 4, 1848. The father was of German lineage, and was for many years sheriff of Rowan county. He married Elizabeth Moose, who was of Swiss descent. The subject of this sketch was left by his parents with only moderate means of support and even this narrow estate was swept away by the ravages of the Civil war, and at an early stage in his life he was obliged to provide for himself; but his native energy and self-reliance stood him in good stead of a patrimony. At the age of sixteen he became a clerk in the drug establishment of Henderson & Enniss, in Salisbury. Here he spent several years and when he arrived at his majority he purchased the interest of Mr. Enniss in the concern and the firm became Theodore F. Kluttz & Co., under which name it still exists. After having accumulated a comfortable fortune, Mr. Kluttz, in 1880, resolved to indulge in his life-long desire to enter the legal profession and began study under Hon. James M. McCorkle, one of the foremost members of the Salisbury bar, with whom after he was admitted to the practice he formed a law partnership. On the death of his partner, Mr. Kluttz began practice by himself, and by his indomitable energy and studious habits has drawn around him a large clientage and fairly earned the confidence and esteem of his professional brethren and of the courts in which he and they practice. In the argument of cases at the bar, Mr. Kluttz is a very effective advocate, and never fails to give satisfaction to his numerous clients who repose the most implicit coufidence in his legal skill and judgment. Though he is almost exclusively confined to his law practice, he yet retains a large interest in his drug establishment which he entrusts mostly to the care and direction of his excellent junior partner, Mr. C. R. Barker.

In the midst of his business engagements Mr. Kluttz does not neglect to lend a helping hand to the material development of the city and county in which he resides. He holds the office of vice-president of the Yadkin railroad company; president of the Salisbury chamber of commerce; of the Rowan Knitting company; the Chestnut Hill cemetery association, and the Salisbury Building & Loan association. He is a director in the North Carolina railroad company, the Salisbury cotton mills, the Connelly Springs company, the Salisbury water works company, the North Carolina Steel & Iron company, and other industrial companies in all of which he commands the confidence and respect of his various business associates. His fine judgment and correct habits make him an efficient helper in any business enterprise, and no citizen of Salisbury has done more to promote its progress and prosperity than he. In 1873 Mr. Kluttz was united in marriage with Miss Sallie Caldwell, whose family name stands pre-eminent in the historic annals of North Carolina. This happy union has been blessed by the advent of six bright children to cheer and gladden their handsome residence, where good will and hospitality reign supreme. Mr. Kluttz has taken little part in politics, but in 1880 was one of the presidential electors for the state on the Hancock ticket. He is a member of the Presbyterian church in Salisbury, and is one of the deacons of that church. He is yet in the prime of his useful life and can reasonably look forward to still greater and more satisfactory accomplishments.

HON. DAVID FRANKLIN CALDWELL,

one of the best known and most distinguished citizens of Rowan county, and one of the ablest judges of the superior court of North Carolina, was born in Iredell county, then a part of Rowan county, in March, 1791. He died at Salisbury, April 4, 1867. More than a century ago, there resided in Rowan county, a substantial citizen, of Scotch-Irish stock, so many of whom peopled that part of North Carolina, named Andrew Caldwell. In his young manhood he wedded Ruth, the second daughter of Hon. William Sharpe. Andrew Caldwell was a leading man of his time, and he was called to represent his fellow citizens in the state legislature. He was the father of a number of children, among whom there were three sons who became widely known. They were, Hon. D. F. Caldwell, Hon. Joseph P. Caldwell, of Iredell, and Dr. Elane Caldwell, of Lincolnton. Hon. David F. Caldwell, was educated at the university at Chapel Hill, and though completing a thorough literary course in that institution, he never graduated, because of financial inability. He studied law with the Hon. Archibald Henderson, of Salisbury, and early set out in public life, as a member of the house of commons, from Iredell county. The date of his first election was 1816, and he served thereafter for several years with distinguished ability. The first two years of his practice in the legal profession were spent in Statesville, and then he located in Salisbury, where he ever after continued to reside. In the years 1829-30-31, he represented Rowan county in the state senate, and was president of that body in 1829. After his legislative career was ended, he resumed the practice of his profession, and for several years thereafter, pursued it with great success. In the year 1844, he was appointed judge of the superior court of North Carolina, which position he ably filled for about fourteen years. He presided on the bench with rare dignity, grace, discrimination and impartiality. When he had reached the age of sixty-eight years, he felt it his duty to resign, being unwilling to remain upon the judicial bench, when there could be the slightest suspicion that his mental powers could be impaired in the smallest degree by his advanced age. In 1859 he became president of the Branch bank of North Carolina, at Salisbury, remaining as such, until the collapse of the bank, consequent upon the Civil war, and after which he retired from the incumbency of any public calling. Aside from the rare excellencies, which characterized Judge Caldwell, while presiding upon the bench, he was very popular as a private citizen. He was kind, gentle, polite, and was beloved and honored by all who were privileged to be associated with him. His cultured intellect and refined manners were a passport for him in the best society. Judge Caldwell was twice married. In 1819, he was married to Miss Fannie M. Alexander, by whom he had four sons and two daughters. His second wife was Mrs. Rebecca M. Troy, *nee* Nesbit, by whom he had no children.

HON. CHARLES PRICE,

of Salisbury, one of the ablest and best known politicians of North Carolina, is a native of Warren county, and was born July 26, 1846. He is the son of John M. and Martha (Reynolds) Price, the former of whom was born in Wake county, N. C. His ancestors were of English origin, and settled at an early day in Raleigh, but subsequently removed to Missouri. Mr. Price's mother was born and reared in Warren county, and was of Scotch extraction. She was the mother of eight sons and two daughters. The father was by occupation a merchant and manufacturer, and for years conducted an extensive business in the manufacture of all kinds of carriages at Warrenton. He was a whig in politics and naturally opposed to the secession movement, but when the war came he promptly volunteered in the Confederate service, but the infirmities of old age soon interposed to relieve him from this service. His death followed close upon the end of the war. Mr. Price's mother survived his father many years, reaching the ripe old age of seventy-four, universally respected and beloved by all who knew her. She and her husband were lifelong members of the Episcopal church. Hon. Charles Price was brought up in the town of Warrenton until reaching the age of seventeen. He attended school there until April, 1864, when he entered the Confederate army, serving one year as captain of the First regiment of junior reserves. He surrendered with Gen. Johnston's army at Greensboro, and returning to the parental home, again set out in his educational course. For about a year he was under the instruction of Mr. W. H. Thompson, from whom he received thorough training in the elementary branches. He then began the study of law at Richmond Hill, under Chief-Justice Pearson, continuing for about a year. He was admitted to the bar in June, 1868, being the last candidate examined under the provision of the old constitutional law of the state. In 1870 Mr. Price located in Davie county and began the practice of his profession. He very soon drew around him a circle of friends who were ready to promote his advancement both professionally and politically, and in 1872 he was nominated for the state senate from Davie and Rowan counties. He was elected and served in 1872 and 1873-4. In 1875 he was chosen a member from Davie county to the constitutional convention, in which he took an active part. In 1876 he was nominated by the democratic party for the lower house of the legislature, and was elected without opposition. He was elected speaker of that body for the session of 1876-7, being at that time the youngest member who had ever been honored with that distinction.

At the close of the session during which he had presided over the house in 1877, Mr. Price retired from legislative life, and located in Salisbury in the active practice of the law. He has risen to the foremost rank of his profession, and has probably the largest practice of any lawyer in the state. He has been an attorney for the Richmond & Danville R. R. Co. since 1883, being assistant counsel with Hon.

David Schenck, of Greensboro, who acts as the railroad attorney for the state. His work as counsel has mainly consisted in the trial of cases for damages for injuries to person and property, and in this direction he has made a most admirable record. He is also counsel for the Charleston, Cincinnati & Chicago R. R. Co. In June, 1889, he was appointed by President Harrison to the office of United States district attorney, for the western district of North Carolina, a position which he still holds. In his young days, Mr. Price imbibed the principles of the Jeffersonian democracy, and holding a sincere belief in those principles up to the year 1882, he was identified with the democratic party. Having been convinced of the hurtful tendencies of those principles when carried to their ultimate extent, and believing that the principles of the republican party were safer and more conservative of the integrity of our government, he abandoned the democratic party and has since joined his political fortunes with the republican party. In that year he made a canvass in the interest of the republican party, and in 1884, being acquainted with Hon. James G. Blaine and regarding him as one of the foremost statesmen of the age, supported him for president, canvassing portions of the state in behalf of the republican ticket. He also supported Mr. Harrison for president in 1888. During his legislative career, Mr. Price took an active part for the furtherance of internal improvements, in the interests of which he has taken an advanced position in contrast with some of the public men and leaders in his section. He is of the progressive type, his fine classical and legal education bringing him to take broader views in a material as well as a social sense. Mr. Price has been twice married. In 1871 he was wedded to Miss Annie Hobson, a niece of Gov. John M. Morehead. She died in 1876, leaving him a son, Augustus Hobson Price. In 1878 he married for his second wife, Miss Mary Roberts, of Mobile, Ala. Mrs. Price is gifted with a rare intellect and fine executive ability and has been selected as one of the two lady managers of the World's Fair from North Carolina, at the Columbian exposition to be held in Chicago, in 1893. She is also vice-president of the ladies' board of managers from the six states of Virginia, West Virginia, Maryland, Delaware, North and South Carolina.

HON. BURTON CRAIGE.

Among the distinguished men whose names have given lustre to the pages of biographical history, none deserves a more prominent place that Hon. Burton Craige, an eminent and widely known statesman of North Carolina. He was born in Rowan county, March 13, 1811, at the family residence on the south fork of the Yadkin, a few miles above the point of junction of the two rivers. He was the youngest son of David Craige, Jr., and Mary Foster, his three elder brothers being named respectively Robert Newton, Samuel and John Craige. The ancestors of the Craige family in North Carolina came directly from Scotland without sojourning for a time, as many did, in the northern states. They were adherents of Prince Charles in his efforts to regain the throne of his father, and after the fatal battle of Culloden, April 16, 1746, they deemed it expedient to seek safety in America. The name of Craige in the Scottish dialect signifies a sharp, high rock, and was probably given to the family or was assumed by them because their hall or castle was situated upon some high rock, thus securing safety to life and property in the days of violence and lawlessness. The early days of Burton Craige were spent upon the farm, and his primary education was received in the schools in the neighborhood of his home. After attending a classical school in Salisbury under the preceptorship of Rev. Jonathan Otis Freeman, he entered the University of North Carolina where he was graduated in 1829. Returning to his native county for about three years he edited the *Western Carolinian*, and studied law with David F. Caldwell as his preceptor. He was admitted to the bar in 1832, and in the same year was elected to the legislature from what was known as the Salisbury borough. His public career from this took its rise. After the borough system was abolished, in 1834, Mr. Craige was elected to the assembly from the county of Rowan.

In 1836, Mr. Craige was united in marriage with Elizabeth P., a daughter of Col. James Erwin, of Burke county, and a great-granddaughter of Gen. Mathew Locke, of Rowan. In the same year, being in feeble health, Mr. Craige visited Europe. Regaining his health he returned home and resumed an active practice of his chosen profession. He rose rapidly in his practice and for many years maintained an extensive law business. He was endowed with a taste for legal studies and never ceased to be a student. Possessed of the qualities of clearness, accuracy and rare powers of analysis, his expressed opinions were to be regarded as authority on legal points. As a public speaker he was instructive, entertaining and eloquent. His style was clear, forcible, logical and gracefully ornamented with the brightest rhetorical flowers. In his manners he was simple, familiar and engaging. He possessed a remarkable memory both of names and faces, and never failed to recognize an acquaintance however humble in circumstances or personality. These were characteristics and qualities which well fitted him for a politician. He had become widely known and was surrounded by hosts of friends and admirers, and in 1853 was elected to congress from the Mecklenburg district, and from thence he served in four successive sessions of that body, his last term finding him in congress at the breaking out of the Civil war. In this struggle he was in sympathy with the south, and he resigned his seat in the national house of representatives and cast his lot with those people who had delighted to honor him with their suffrages. When the convention of North Carolina was called in 1861, to determine what course the state should pursue, Mr. Craige was sent to voice the sentiments of Rowan county, and on the 20th day of May he offered the ordinance of secession, which was adopted and placed North Carolina along with other states of the south which had resolved to with 'draw from their allegiance to the Federal government. This convention also chose as representatives in the Confederate congress from North Carolina, Burton Craige, W. N. H. Smith, Thomas Ruffin, T. D. McDowell, A. W. Venable, J. M. Morehead, R. C. Puryear and A. T. Davidson, a cluster of distinguished men. His services in the Confederate congress put a period to the official career of Mr. Craige, and he retired to private life. When the flag upon which were emblazoned the "stars and bars" was furled he felt that his political life was closed, and he declined to take any further part in national affairs, and he refused to apply for the removal of his political disabilities. He now began to devote himself exclusively to the practice of his profession which he continued until his death. In the study of history and in recounting the deeds of former days, he sought repose in the bosom of his family from the turmoil and strife of public affairs. On the 30th of December, 1875, while attending the Carbarrus court, he died at the house of his son-in-law, Mr. A. B. Young. Thus left its earthly tenement, a noble spirit, the spirit of a true patriot, a distinguished lawyer, an eminent statesman and a beloved and honored citizen.

JOSEPH CARTER ABBOTT,

journalist and senator, was born in Concord, N. H., July 15, 1825. His education was acquired under private instruction, preceded by a course at Phillips Andover academy. He studied law in his native town, and was admitted to the bar in 1852. He was for five years editor of the Manchester *Daily American*, and afterward of the Boston *Atlas and Bee*. During this time, from 1855 to 1861, he held the commission of adjutant-general of New Hampshire, and thoroughly re-organized the state militia. He was a frequent contributor of magazine literature, particularly upon historical topics. In the settlement of the boundary question between New Hampshire and Canada he acted as one of the commissioners on the part of his native state. He rendered effective service on the breaking out of the Civil war, in raising and organizing Union troops, and was finally chosen lieutenant-colonel of the Seventh regiment of New Hampshire volunteer infantry. He was a gallant officer, and distinguished himself for his bravery, especially at the storming of Fort Fisher, in North Carolina, July 23, 1863. He was promoted to the colonelcy by his regiment, and held the command of that regiment till the summer of 1864, when he was raised to the rank of brevet-brigadier-general, and was put in command of a brigade. After the war he took up his residence at Wilmington, N. C., and, in 1867, was elected a member of the state constitutional convention. The following year he was elected a member of the legislature, and by that body was chosen a United States senator for a partial term, ending in 1871. He was extensively engaged in agriculture as well as manufactures, carrying on a prosperous and profitable business. He was appointed collector of the port at Wilmington, under President U. S. Grant, and afterward inspector of ports, by President R. B. Hayes. He died at his home in Wilmington, October 8, 1882.

WALTER H. NEAL.

One of Richmond county's most eminent young lawyers is Walter H. Neal, who was born in Franklin county, N. C., February 19, 1859. He received his education under the tutelage of his father. For two years he was engaged as a book-keeper for Mr. W. S. Clark, in Tarboro, and during that time spent his nights in reading law. In 1878 he became connected with the Rockingham public high school as a teacher, and after filling that position satisfactorily for one year he entered the law office of J. T. LeGrand, and was admitted to the bar in the June term of 1880. Taking up his residence at Laurenburg, he has since continued to practice there with success. December 18, 1884, he was married to Miss Emma Gill, daughter of W. A. and L. M. Gill, of Laurenburg, and their home has been blessed by the birth of two children, named Walter H. and Fanny Louise. Mr. and Mrs. Neal are members of the Methodist Episcopal church, south, and he is a trustee of the church at Laurenburg, and is also a member of the K. of P., being past grand chancellor of the lodge. The parents of Mr. Neal are Prof. George W. and Fanny P. (Hart) Neal, natives of North Carolina. Prof. Neal is professor of Greek in the Newbern high school, and is recognized as one of the leading educators of the state. Both himself and wife are earnest communicants of the Methodist Episcopal church, south. Their six children are Fanny N., wife of John H. Bell, who is a clerk in the pension department at Washington, D. C. (and their five children are: David, Neal, Lissette, Laura and Imogen); Walter H., Thomas, deceased, Lizzie, Benjamin, a member of the firm of L. H. Cutler & Co., of New bern, and John.

HON. THOMAS C. GUTHRIE.

The present encumbent of the office of mayor of Rockingam, Richmond county, N. C., is the Hon. Thomas C. Guthrie, who was born in Franklin county, N. C., February 9, 1865. He is the son of the Rev. T. W. Guthrie, one of the leading clergymen of the Methodist Episcopal church, south. Mr. Guthrie, senior, was educated in the common schools of his native town, and when but eight years of age united with the Methodist Episcopal church. In 1851 he joined the North Carolina conference, and has filled various appointments, having been stationed at Wilmington, Salisbury, Fayetteville, Rockingham, and other places in the state. In 1883 he was made presiding elder of the Charlotte district, and in 1887 was appointed presiding elder of the Wilmington district, and at present holds the same office in the Shelby district. His ministerial labors extend over a period of forty years, during which time he has accomplished much for good, and has won for himself a widespread reputation as an orator. In early manhood Miss Emily P. Robbins became his wife, and has borne him four children, viz.: Mattie B., wife of E. J. Gibsen; Henry, Hattie and Thomas C. The latter was educated in private schools at Rockingham, and was graduated from the law department of the Vanderbilt university in 1887, with the degree of B. L. His office experience was obtained with the Hon. Franklin McNeill. Mr. Guthrie was granted a license for the practice of law at the September term of the supreme court in 1887, and began the active practice of his profession at Rockingham. In February, 1888, he formed a partnership with Messrs. Burwell and Walker, and this firm still exists. In May, 1889, Mr. Guthrie was elected mayor of Rockingham, and was re-elected to that office in the following May. In 1890 he purchased the printing office of the *Rocket*, and assumed the editorial charge of that journal, which he continued until his rapidly increasing practice compelled him to dispose of it some time subsequent. December 18, 1890, Mr. Guthrie was very happily married to Miss Rusie Wilson, daughter of the late Dr. N. H. D. Wilson, an eminent clergyman of the Methodist Episcopal church, south. This gentleman excels as a lawyer, and is rapidly rising to the front ranks of his profession in the state, and no further evidence of his popularity in the community is needed than his continued election to the office of mayor of the city.

HON. FRANKLIN McNEILL.

One of Richmond county's most prominent citizens is the Hon. Franklin McNeill, solicitor of the Seventh judicial district, and a leading attorney. He was born in Richmond county, N. C., January 4, 1850, the son of John and Elizabeth (Buchanan) McNeill, both parents being natives of North Carolina. John McNeill was a planter, and a man of prominence in the community. For several years he had charge of the county schools, and before the late war was a major of militia. Himself and wife were active and devout communicants of the Presbyterian church, in which he was an elder. His demise occurred in August. 1879, at the age of seventy-eight years; his wife surviving him until April, 1885, when she too went to rest, aged seventy-four. By a former marriage Mr. McNeill had three children, all of whom are living. The mother of these children was Catherine (McCoy) McNeill. She died in 1835. The Hon. Franklin McNeill was the youngest of four children born to the second union. His preliminary schooling was obtained in the schools of the county in which he was born, and later he attended the Davidson college, where he remained two years, after which he was a student in the law department of the University of Virginia one year. His law course was completed in the excellent law school of Chief-Justice Pearson, at Richmond Hill. His admission to the bar in J   , 1873, was immediately followed by his removal to Maxton, Robeson county, N. C., where he remained in practice alone until January, 1877, when Mr. Thomas McNeill, a cousin, became his law partner the firm existing until 1882, in which year Mr. Franklin McNeill took up his residence at Rockingham. In 1886 he began a four years' term as state solicitor, and in 1890 was re-elected to that office. Mr. McNeill was married to Miss Jennie E. Elliot, daughter of Col. Alexander Elliot, of Cumberland county, N. C., in August, 1882. Both himself and wife are consistent members of the Presbyterian church, in which he is an elder, and he is also a prominent member of the Knights of Pythias. His career has been marked by much ability, and a strict adherence to the principles of right and justice. None has a fairer reputation as a man of integrity than he, and his continued retention of the prominent office he now holds is ample proof of his popularity with the people.

HON. JAMES T. LeGRAND,

of Richmond county, N. C., is descended on both the paternal and maternal sides from old and influential southern families. He is a native of Richmond county, having first seen the light there April 4, 1849. In 1870 he was graduated from Trinity college, as valedictorian of his class. He began the study of law under the tutelage of the late Chief-Justice Pearson, at Richmond Hill, N. C., and was admitted to the bar in 1877. Immediately thereafter he began the practice of his chosen profession at Rockingham. A staunch democrat, he was elected, the first of his party since the war from his district, and served in the state senate in 1874–5, and again in 1888–89. He has been a member of every state democratic convention since 1870, and was a delegate to the democratic national convention at Chicago which nominated Grover Cleveland for the presidency, and his support was given that candidate. Mr. LeGrand is a prominent Knight of Honor, having been grand dictator for the state of North Carolina, and for the past two years a delegate to the supreme lodge of the order. The happiest event of his life was his marriage to Miss Rebecca Wilson, daughter of the late Dr. N. H. D. Wilson, a leading clergyman of the Methodist Episcopal church, south, in October, 1877. Five children have blessed this marriage, named: Pattie, Mary, Rebecca, James T., Jr., and Nathan Wilson LeGrand. Mr. LeGrand has won a reputation as a lawyer in his state that is not excelled by any. He is also largely interested in agriculture, and is the second largest planter in the county. James and Martha (Leak) LeGrand were his parents, and both were natives of North Carolina. James was an extensive planter and a leading merchant. For several years he served as a member of the state legislature, being an old line whig in politics. His death occurred in 1853, when he was in his fifty-third year, and the mother survived until 1883, when she too went to rest, having reached the advanced age of seventy-nine years. There were six children born to this union, James T. being the youngest. Both parents were active and devout members of the Methodist Episcopal church.

HON. WILLIAM E. CLARKE,

attorney-at-law and postmaster of Newbern, was born in Raleigh, N. C., on the 7th of March, 1850, the son of William J. and Mary Byard (Devereaux) Clarke. The father was a native of Raleigh, and was graduated from Chapel Hill university with high honors. He studied for the law, and rose to eminence in the profession. He served as auditor of his native state; was a captain in the Twelfth regiment, United States army, Company K, during the Mexican war, and was promoted to the rank of major by brevet, for his bravery and for saving the artillery at the national bridge. During the Civil war he was colonel of the Twenty-fourth North Carolina regiment during the entire war, acting as brigadier general at the last. He was wounded in the thigh in the Mexican war, and at Drury's Bluff, during the Civil war, received a painful wound in the left shoulder. In 1855 Col. Clarke went to Texas, where he practiced his profession. He was elected to the presidency of the San Antonio & Mexican Gulf railroad, being the first to hold that office, and negotiated for the purchase of the first iron for that road. On the breaking out of the Civil war he returned home, and entered the Confederate service, as above mentioned. After the close of hostilities he took up his residence in Raleigh, and remained there until his removal to Newbern, some two or three years later. He was principal of the Newbern academy for some time, and later was appointed judge of the criminal court, by Gov. Holden, to fill the unexpired term of C. R. Thomas, who had been elected to congress. Col. Clarke held the judgeship for three years. He was a staunch republican, and a devout communicant of the Episcopal church. Mary Devereaux Clarke was the daughter of the Hon. Theodore P. Devereaux, of Halifax county, N. C. He was the author of "Devereaux's Reports of North Carolina," and a lawyer of much ability and prominence, as well as being a large and wealthy planter.

The maternal grandfather was Thomas Pollock, one of the earliest settlers of Newbern. Mrs. Clarke was a woman of great literary ability and attainments. Under the *nom de plume* of "Tenella" she contributed to many of the leading papers and periodicals of the day. Her first production was "Wood Notes." During the late war she wrote "Mosses from a Rolling Stone," and subsequently "Clytie and Zenobia, or the Lily and the Palm." These widely known works were published by E. P. Dutton & Co., of New York. She also wrote sketches of celebrated men in North Carolina. She was an earnest Christian woman, and a loyal member of the Episcopal church. Her death was mourned wherever her name was known. Of the four children born to these parents, all are living, their names being: Francis, president of the deaf and dumb asylum at Little Rock, Ark., and for many years in the New York city deaf and dumb asylum; William E.; Mary Devereaux Clarke, wife of George Moulton, of Newbern, and Thomas Pollock Clarke, a prominent banker of Little Rock, Ark. William E. Clarke was reared in Raleigh, and after sufficient preliminary preparation entered Davidson college, but was prevented from graduating by the breaking out of the war. At the age of fifteen he entered the quartermaster's department at Raleigh, and gave his services to the cause he loved until the end. After peace was declared Mr. Clarke taught in the Newbern academy for two years, after which he went to New York city, and was there engaged in teaching in the deaf and dumb asylum, remaining there for three years. He was graduated from Columbia college's law department in 1873, and immediately engaged in the practice of law at Newbern. As a politician he is a leader in the republican party, having been a member of the legislature for two terms, and of the state senate four years. In 1889 President Harrison appointed him postmaster of Newbern. He is a member of St. John's lodge, A. F. & A. M., and the Newbern B. & L. association, and of the Interstate B. & L. association, of Wilmington, in which he is a local director. February 23, 1886, Miss Elizabeth Howerton, daughter of Dr. William H. Howerton, ex-secretary of state, and for many years proprietor of the Warm Springs hotel, became his wife, and they have three children, viz.: Elizabeth, Mary Byard and William Edwards. Both Mr. and Mrs. Clarke are communicants of the Episcopal church.

FREDERICK C. ROBERTS,

secretary and treasurer of the Atlantic & North Carolina railroad company, is a native of Newbern, having first seen the light there on the 15th of January, 1836. He is the son of John M., and Mary E., (Jones) Roberts; the mother a native of Craven county, and the father of Edenton, Chowan county, N. C. The latter removed to Norfolk, and in 1816 came to Newbern. He early became identified with the old State bank, of which he was cashier for many years; subsequently becoming the cashier of the bank of North Carolina. He was a prominent whig and a devout member of the Episcopal church, being for many years a vestryman. His demise occurred in 1862, his wife surviving him until 1874. Their children are: Rev. John J. Roberts, of New York city; Rev. Stephen C. Roberts, of Chestertown, Md.; Mrs. L. L. Chester, of Englewood, N. J.; Frederick C.; George H., cashier of the National bank of Newbern, and Edward B., agent for the Old Dominion steamship company. Mr. Frederick Roberts was educated in the Newbern schools and later graduated from the University of North Carolina. In 1855 he was given a diploma at Princeton college, and then became a student in Judge Pearson's law school in Yadkin county, N. C. In 1857 he completed his legal studies and was duly licensed to practice in the county courts and in 1858 was admitted to practice in the superior courts of the state. He was actively and successfully engaged in his profession at Newbern until 1879. In 1861 he joined the Confederate army as a member of Company A, Fifth North Carolina cavalry, enlisting as a lieutenant. He was subsequently promoted to the captaincy of his company and participated in the battles around Newbern, Goldsboro, and in various skirmishes in North Carolina and along the Virginia line. Receiving his honorable discharge from the service in 1863, on account of physical disability, he returned to his home. In 1879, Mr. Roberts was elected to the position he now holds, and has since been identified with the Atlantic & North Carolina railroad company. After the war being one of the stockholders in the Newbern Bank of Commerce he was made a director in that institution, and also attorney for the same. A prominent democrat, he was clerk and master in equity of the Craven courts from 1858 to 1868; has served as town commissioner for several years, and at present is a trustee of the Newbern academy, having held that office for twenty-five years. Mr. Roberts is a member of St. John's lodge, No. 13, A. F. & A. M., and also of the Eureka chapter of Royal Arch Masons. As a lawyer he excelled, and as a business man he is prudent, keen, and of undoubted integrity and ability.

HON. AUGUSTUS S. SEYMOUR,

judge of the United States district court for the eastern district of North Carolina, is a native of New York state, having been born in the city of Ithaca, on the 30th of November, 1836, son of Hezekiah C. Seymour, state engineer of New York in 1850, and a prominent contractor and builder of many railroads, also chief engineer of the N. Y., L. E. & W. railroad. His mother was Mary (Sherrill) Seymour. Judge Seymour was graduated from Hamilton college in 1857, and one year later was admitted to the bar. He began the practice of his chosen profession in New York city, but in 1864 removed to North Carolina and located at New Berne, and was admitted to the bar of North Carolina in 1866, at the first term of the superior court after the war. In May, 1868, he was elected a member of the house of representatives, and in the fall of the same year was appointed judge of the criminal court of Newbern. This office he resigned, and was re-elected to the legislature in the fall of 1868. In 1870 he was elected to the constitutional convention, and two years later, served as state senator, and in 1874 was elected judge of the superior court. His appointment to the office of judge of the district court of the United States, by President Arthur, in 1881, met with universal favor. Previous to this, however, Judge Seymour had served as chairman of the judiciary committee, in 1867, and in the same year was elected attorney of the city of Newbern. He has ever been a staunch republican, and has rendered his party efficient service. He is a member of the Masons and several college societies. In 1863 he married Miss Nancy O. Barton, daughter of the Rev. John Barton, a prominent Presbyterian clergyman, of New York. They have two children living, viz.: Mrs. Cornelia Welsh, of Manchester, Eng., and John Barton Seymour. Judge Seymour is the author of "Seymour's Sixth and Seventh Digests of North Carolina Reports."

HON. GEORGE GREEN

was born in Craven county, N. C., July 17, 1823. His parents were John and Charlotte (Harrison) Green, the former being a native of this state, and the latter of England. The father was an extensive planter and owned many slaves. He was a prominent member of the whig party. Our subject was reared on the homestead farm and was educated in the public schools of his native county, and later in the excellent private school taught by Robert G. Moore. In 1846 he was licensed to practice law, and has since been engaged in active practice. He is the oldest living member of the Newbern bar and holds a very high position among the attorneys of the county. Soon after his admission to the bar he was elected attorney for Jones county, and later held the same office in Craven county. In 1854 he was sent to the state legislature, being a member of the secession committee of that session, and in 1861, was one of the signers of the declaration of secession. In 1867 he was appointed by the state legislature, criminal judge of Craven county, and discharged the duties of that office for two years, until the reconstruction act. He was then elected to the state senate, and was subsequently elected attorney for Craven county. In 1889 he was appointed clerk of the United States district court for the eastern district of North Carolina. For ten years he was attorney for the Atlantic & North Carolina railroad company, of which he was a director and organizer. He was a director and attorney of the state bank of Newbern for some time, and is a prominent member of the Masonic order, having taken the thirty-second degree. In 1855 he married Miss Lizzie Watkins, daughter of Beckton Watkins, of Craven county, and two children have been born to them: George, ex-state senator and member of the legislature; and Mary, wife of Hamilton C. Chambers. Judge Green and his wife are communicants of the Episcopal church. James Green, his great-uncle, was secretary of the first convention for forming the constitution of North Carolina.

POU & POU.

The prominent law firm of Pou & Pou, of Johnson county, N. C., is composed of men who are leaders in their profession and influential and active in political affairs. It is composed of J. H. Pou and Edward W. Pou, Jr. The Hon. Edward W. Pou was born in Orangeburg, S. C., October 26, 1830, the son of Joseph and Eliza M. (Felder) Pou, both natives of Orangeburg. Joseph Pou was an able and eminent attorney. He removed to Talbotton, Ga., where he spent the remainder of his life, dying there in 1888, at the advanced age of ninety years. Mr. Edward W. Pou was graduated from the University of Georgia, in 1851, and began the practice of law at Talbotton, where he continued for seven years, after which he retired and turned his attention to agriculture. In 1874 he resumed his profession, having removed to Smithfield, N. C., in 1867. In 1868 he was a member of the house of representatives, and was chairman of the committee on privilege and election. During the Civil war he served in the Confederate army three months, being compelled to resign at the expiration of that period on account of ill-health. He held the commission of first lieutenant in Cable's Georgia legion. Mr. Pou has been twice married, first to Miss Lucy Carter, of Talbotton, Ga., in 1853. She died in 1858, leaving one child, Arthur Pou, a civil engineer of Talbotton. In 1859, Mr. Pou was again married, Miss Annie Maria Smith, of Alabama, becoming his wife. Their three children are: James H., Edward W., Jr., and Martha T. Pou. The eldest son, James H., was born in Alabama, July 21, 1861. His scholastic training was obtained at Smithfield, N. C. Having read law under the direction of his father, he was admitted to the bar in 1885. In 1884 he was elected to the house of representatives of the state, and in 1886-8 was elected to the state senate, being the youngest member of the senate by several years. In 1890 Mr. Pou declined further nomination to the senate. For the past twelve years he has been extensively interested in agriculture, which he has carried on in addition to his large law practice. In 1889 his marriage to Miss Annie Walker, daughter of Samuel Walker, of Randolph county, N. C., was happily solemnized, and one child, Edith Walker, has been born to their union. Both Mr. and Mrs. Pou are active members of the Presbyterian church, and he is also a prominent member of the I. O. O. F., and like his father, is a staunch democrat.

Edward W. Pou, Jr., first saw the light in Macon county, Ala., where he was born September 9, 1863. He entered the University of North Carolina, and remained in that institution through his junior year. For the succeeding eight months Mr. Pou was engaged in teaching school in Johnston county, and then began the study of the law under the direction of his father, and was admitted to practice in October, 1885. Since his admission to the bar Mr. Pou has been associated with his brother in the practice of the law under the firm name of Pou & Pou. His political career is peculiar on account of his youth at the time of his first election to office. In 1886 he was chairman of the democratic executive committee of Johnston county, an office he held for two terms. He was a presidential elector in 1888, and in 1890 he was elected solicitor of the Fourth district, and he is the incumbent of that position at the present time. Mr. Pou is a member of the Masonic fraternity, and also of the I. O. O. F., and the Alpha Tau Omega college society. Miss Carrie Horton Ihrie, daughter of Col. R. R. Ihrie, of Pittsborough, N. C., became his wife in 1887, and Edward Felder Pou is their offspring. Mrs. Pou is a granddaughter of the Hon. John H. Hughton, who for several terms was a member of congress from Newbern district. Mr. Edward W. Pou, Jr., ranks among the best lawyers of the state, and is esteemed as a man of intelligence and prominence, and of the strictest integrity.

HON. HARRY W. STUBBS,

one of North Carolina's leading lawyers, was born in Williamston, N. C., February 16, 1860. He is a son of J   R. and Mary Ella (Williams) Stubbs, the former a native of Beaufort county, N. C., and the mother of Martin county, N. C. Jesse R. Stubbs gained a thorough scholastic training by his own efforts at the Washington academy and prepared for the practice of law. He was a member of the house of commons of the state from Beaufort county, and later represented Martin and Washington counties in the state senate. Immediately after the war he was elected to the United States congress from the First North Carolina district, but was not seated. He was a man of great ability, and a brilliant orator. He first affiliated with the whig party, but later became a staunch democrat. His death occurred in September, 1870. Mr. Stubbs was one of the original stockholders in the Williamston & Tarboro railroad company, and was the first president of the company. His wife died in 1864. She was a daughter of Harry Williams, Esq., one of the earliest citizens of Williamston. Two children were born to Jesse and Mary Stubbs, Harry W. and Jessie, wife of D. D. Simmons, of Williamston. The subject of this biographical mention was given exceptional educational advantages, having been a student of the Hornor school at Oxford, and later spending three years in the Hillboro academy, he was graduated from the University of North Carolina, and took up the study of law under the direction of Mr. James E. Moore, and completed his course with Dick & Dillard of Greensboro, N. C. He was admitted to the bar in January, 1881, and began the active practice of his profession in Williamston, in October, 1885, at that time having become associated with Mr. James E. Moore. In 1889 he was elected to the state senate from the Second senatorial district on the democratic ticket, and for two years he held the office of solicitor of the inferior court of Martin county, and at one time was mayor of Williamston. His first marriage was in 1882, when Miss Della B. Lanier became his wife. One year later her death occurred. In 1888 he married Miss Carrie L. Siterson, and one child, Jesse R., has been born to them. Mr. Stubbs is a prominent Royal Arch Mason, and also a member of the I. O. O. F. As a lawyer he excels, being keen and well read.

HON. JAMES E. MOORE.

The bar of eastern North Carolina has no more able member than Hon. James E. Moore. Mr. Moore is a native of Martin county, and first saw the light there January 30, 1841. He was one of five children born to Clayton and Elizabeth S. (Smithwick) Moore, both natives of Martin county, N. C. The father obtained an academic education and was then ordained a minister in the Primitive Baptist church. During the war he served in the Confederate army as a member of the home guards. His life was spent in his honored calling and in agriculture, his demise occurring in 1881, and that of his wife three years later. The son, James E., was prepared for college in the Williamston academy, and in 1862 was graduated from the University of North Carolina, and at the same time was admitted to the bar. He put aside all other interests and offered his services to the cause of the south, as a member of Company K, Third North Carolina cavalry. Enlisting as a private he was subsequently promoted to the rank of lieutenant of his company for honorable conduct, and at the close of the war held the commission of provost-marshal of the brigade. Mr. Moore was taken prisoner while on picket duty and confined in a Federal prison for ten days at Plymouth. In May, 1864, his regiment was attached to the army of northern Virginia, and he participated with his command in all the important engagements in which that army fought. At the close of the war he began the practice of his profession at Williamston, and in 1865 and 1866 was a member of the house of commons of North Carolina from Martin county. He was the representative of Martin and Beaufort counties in the state senate in 1866-7, and served on the judiciary committee in each branch of the legislature. After leaving the senate Mr. Moore formed a partnership with Judge Biggs of Tarboro, and continued with him for one year, after which he returned to Williamston, and has since resided and practiced in that city. Mr. Harry Stubbs became associated with him in 1885, and this connection has since existed. Mr. Moore is one of the most prominent leaders of the democratic party in eastern North Carolina, and is recognized throughout the state as one of its ablest lawyers. He has served as mayor of Williamston, and was a director in the Williamston & Tarboro railroad company, and his firm is now attorney for the Atlantic Coast line. As an agriculturist Mr. Moore has also made a success, and now operates an extensive plantation. One of the happiest events of his life was his marriage, in 1870, to Miss Jane S. Sykes, of Martin county, N. C. This cultured home has been blessed by the birth of six children, their names being, Bettie, Jennie, Mattie, James E., Jr., Clayton and Maurice Sheppard. Mr. Moore is a member of the board of trustees of the Primitive Baptist church, and also of the Williamston academy.

HON. HARRY SKINNER.

One of the most prominent lawyers and political leaders of the state of North Carolina is the Hon. Harry Skinner, the descendant of a family noted for its many able men, many of whom have held high positions in government. Mr. Skinner is a native of Perquimans county, N. C., where he was born on the 25th of May, 1855, the son of James C. and Elmira (Ward) Skinner, both North Carolinians by birth. The Hon. James C. Skinner was the direct descendant of an old Welsh family, three of its members having settled in Perquimans county, N. C., early in the history of that section of the country.

Harry Skinner.

James C. Skinner was a man of great force of character and of brilliant mind. He was at one time a large slaveholder and land owner, and was prominent in public affairs, having held the office of clerk of the county court from 1850 until 1868. In 1870-2 he represented the first senatorial district in the state senate, and was a member of that body during the impeachment trial of Gov. W. W. Holden. His father was the Hon. Harry Skinner, a native of Chowan county, N. C. While a resident of that county he represented it in the state legislature, and after his removal to Perquimans county was a member of the state senate from the first senatorial district for many years. He was a son of the Hon. John Skinner, who also served as a distinguished member of the state legislature, his terms as representative and senator extending over a long period. Harry Skinner, the grandfather of our subject, was very active in church work, and built and presented a church to the society, which is now known as the Skinner Methodist Episcopal church, in Chowan county, he having been the founder of the same.

From this very brief mention of his immediate antecedents it will be seen that Col. Skinner comes of a line well calculated to produce eminent men, men of brains and affairs. Mr. Skinner's boyhood was spent in his native county, and his scholastic training was obtained at the Hertford academy, where he remained until 1874. In the latter year he entered the University of Kentucky, at Lexington, and was graduated from the excellent law department of that noted institution in June, 1875, with the degree of B. L. In August of the same year he removed to Greenville, and there continued his law studies under the tutelage of Maj. L. C. Latham. At the January term of the supreme court, in 1876, Mr. Skinner was licensed to practice, and immediately thereafter formed a partnership for the practice of his profession with his former preceptor, Maj. Latham, and this firm has since continued, being recognized at the present time as one of the distinguished connections in the state. Mr. Skinner's rise to the front ranks of the bar was rapid, and in some respects phenomenal. At the start he exhibited superior abilities as a political leader, and soon found his place in the democratic party, in which he is now considered one of the leaders of eastern North Carolina. He has served as chairman of the county democratic executive committee for four years, has been a member of the state executive committee of that organization for the past eight years, and a member of the democratic congressional committee since 1880, having been chairman for two years. In 1881 he was elected town commissioner of Greenville by an unanimous vote, and in the preceding year was appointed aide-de-camp to Gov. Jarvis, with the rank of colonel, and held that position during the remainder of the administration. His name was very prominently mentioned to represent the First congressional district in the United States congress in 1890, but was not brought before the convention. But in the same year he was nominated by the county committee of Pitt county for a seat in the house of representatives of the state, and was elected by a majority of 1,076 votes, he having made his canvass upon the sub-treasury plan, and the reasonable demands of the farmers' alliance.

As a political writer, Mr. Skinner has gained more than a local reputation, his productions having been published in some of the leading papers of the nation. In 1886 he wrote an article, entitled, "A Landed Basis for our National Bank Issue," embodying the same ideas as are now embraced in the "Stamford" bill. In January, 1887, Mr. Skinner represented Pitt county in the first farmers' convention held in the state, and there introduced a resolution, having for its purpose the awakening of the interest of the assembly in a plan for financial relief, and advocating that farming in North Carolina could not be made successful under the present ruinous credit system, nor profitable after paying the present rate of interest on money hired to cultivate crops. This able effort was followed by an article which was first published in the *Progressive Farmer*, taking the ground that with the same assistance the government gives to the manufacturing interests of the country, if extended with the same ratio to the cotton planter, they could dictate and command the price of cotton. Placing the protection given the manufacturer at forty-three per cent., the same protection would give to the planter at least 14 cents per pound for his cotton, without injustice to anyone. In other words, the article demanded that the protection be not for a class, but be extended to the producer as well as the manufacturer. The planter's protection was to be gained by a warehouse system, and it said that the present sub-treasury bill had its origin in this suggestion. The article attracted widespread interest, and was reproduced in full as the leading editorial in *Frank Leslie's Illustrated Newspaper* for November 30, 1889, under the heading of "The Hope of the South." Subsequently it was read on the floor of the St. Louis convention at the time the sub-treasury idea was first formulated by the alliance. Since then Mr. Skinner has advocated the latter measure, and has taken a very active and prominent part in securing the proper legislation.

While a member of the legislature Mr. Skinner served as chairman of the committee on internal improvements; was a member of the judiciary, educational and insane asylum committees, and was chairman of the house branch of the committee on redistricting the state. He advocated the reduction of legal interest to a six per cent. rate; and introduced a bill to prevent the sale of land under mortgage or other execution, that did not bring fifty per cent. of the tax value; and also supported the bill providing for an industrial training school for girls. He voted for the appropriation to the southern soldiers' home, and also for the appropriation for completing the gubernatorial mansion for the Columbian exposition. His vote and influence were cast for the extension of the A. & N. C. R. R., and for the railroad commission bill; but he voted against the acceptance of the proposition of the Wilmington & Weldon railroad. He was the father of the bill establishing an orphan's court, and also of a bill to prescribe other duties for the railroad commissioners, and presented a bill providing for the appointing of a committee to codify the laws upon corporations, and to make suggestions to the following legislature, whereby they might be relieved from the great bulk of private legislation. One of his most popular acts as a legislator was his introduction of a bill prohibiting the dredging for oysters in eastern North Carolina; but he did not favor the "Mann" bill. The firm of Skinner & Latham is largely interested in real estate in Greenville, and has done much to advance the prosperity of the town. In addition to his extensive law practice, Mr. Skinner also gives much attention to agriculture, and has made a marked success in that work. As a staunch friend to public education, he has proven himself a man of broad and liberal mind, and his name will be perpetuated in the Greenville female institute, as a man of charitable and progressive nature, he having furnished one third of the funds necessary for the erection of the building. He is a member of the Masonic fraternity, Royal Arch Chapter, and is also a member of the I. O. O. F., the Knights of Honor, and the Legion of Honor. In 1878 he was so fortunate as to form a marriage alliance with Miss Lottie Monteiro, daughter of Mr. A. A. and P. C. Monteiro, of Richmond, Va. April 12, 1888, Mrs. Skinner died, leaving four children, viz.: Lovinia, Ella Monteiro, Lottie and Harry, Jr. She was a lady of rare refinement and of beautiful Christian character, and her death was a sad blow, not only to the husband and children, but to the community at large.

DAVID S. REID.

David Settle Reid, governor, was born in Rockingham county, N. C., April 19, 1813. He had only an academic education, but studied law, was admitted to the bar and began the practice of his profession, in 1834. He soon took up politics, and was elected in 1835, to the state senate to represent his native county. He proved to be a most sagacious and useful legislator, was elected senator for four successive terms. He was then, in 1843, elected a member of congress, and was re-elected in 1845. In 1848, he was put in nomination for governor, by the democratic state convention, but was defeated by Charles Manly, who made a strong canvass, and was elected by a large majority. Mr. Reid had also made a lively canvass and his political friends had great confidence in his success, but 1848 was not a democratic year. At the next convention, Mr. Reid was nominated, but against his written protest, that under no circumstances would he take another nomination. This time, however, he was elected. He was then elected to the United States senate, to succeed Hon. Willie P. Mangum, holding the office from December 4, 1854, to March 3, 1859. In the senate he was chairman of the committee on patents, on the patent-office and on commerce. He was a delegate to the peace congress at Washington, in February, 1861, as a conservative democrat. After the secession of the state, he was chosen a member of the Confederate congress, in which he served with signal ability. When the war was over he retired to his farm in

Rockingham county, devoting himself to his agricultural interests, and to the practice of his profession. For unaffected simplicity of character, for personal integrity, and purity of life, for consistency in his public acts, Gov. Reid stands, pre-eminent in the estimation of his fellow citizens. He married Henrietta, daughter of Judge Thomas Settle, Sr.

JUDGE THOMAS B. WOMACK

was born in Chatham county, February 12, 1855. His parents are John A. and Rebecca (Brown) Womack, both natives of North Carolina. The father still lives, an honored resident of Chatham. He is widely known and as widely respected. Though taking but little interest in politics, he was, in 1872, a candidate for secretary of state on the Merrimon ticket, but was defeated by less than 1,500 majority. He has been chairman of the board of justices of his county since its organization in 1876. He was a member of the house of representatives in 1870, that body being the first democratic house elected after the war. He served his constituents with signal ability and faithfulness. Mr. Womack is especially prominent in the Presbyterian church, having been a ruling elder for more than forty years. Several times he has been chosen a commissioner to the general assembly. His wife is a devoted member of the same church. Her father was John Bright Brown, a son of Gen. Thomas Brown, of Revolutionary renown. Judge Womack, the subject of this sketch, is the eldest of a family of three surviving children. He received an academic education and read law under the tutelage of Hon. John Manning, LL. D., at present professor of law at the University of North Carolina. He was admitted to the bar at the June term of the supreme court in 1876, and at once began the practice at Pittsboro. The first office to which he was elected was that of solicitor of the inferior court of Chatham county, in 1878. He was twice re-elected, resigning his position during his third term to serve as state senator, to which he was elected in 1882. In 1885 he was a member of the house of representatives, and served his constituents in an able and satisfactory manner. During the administration of Gov. Scales, he was appointed as proxy for the state to represent its stock in the Atlantic & North Carolina railroad.

Judge Womack was chief clerk of the house of representatives for the session of 1889, which position he resigned to become a director of the North Carolina insane asylum. This latter office he resigned January 20, 1890, having been appointed judge of the superior court by Gov. Fowle, to fill the unexpired term of Judge Gilmer, resigned. Upon the expiration of that term Judge Womack located at Pittsboro, and has since been engaged in the practice of the law and in the preparation of a complete civil digest of the decisions of the supreme court of North Carolina, a work for which he is admirably qualified, and upon which he has been engaged for several years. He is in the foremost rank of the legal profession of the state, and takes an active part in every enterprise which looks to the development and prosperity of the community at large. He was married, November 30, 1881, to Miss Susie, daughter of Capt. John W. and Sarah A. Taylor, of Chatham county. Judge Womack is a member of and ruling elder in the Presbyterian church, and a member of the board of regents of the South Atlantic university.

HON. JOHN M. MORING,

a prominent citizen and attorney of Chatham county, was born March 11, 1841, in the county where he now resides. His parents were Alfred and Elizabeth M. Moring, nee O'Kelly, and both parents were natives of Chatham county. The father is still living at the advanced age of seventy-eight years, and though retired from active life, he is not forgotten by his fellow citizens, but retains an honored place in their respect and esteem. When in business he was both a merchant and a farmer. He resides at Raleigh and is an active member and a deacon of the Christian church, to the work of which he has given over fifty years of his life. His wife was also a very devout member of the same church, and her death occurred in 1873, at the age of sixty-one years. These parents had a family of nine children, five of whom are still living, the subject of this sketch being the eldest of the survivors. Mr. Moring was educated at Grosham college and at the North Carolina university. He was matriculated at the former institution in 1860, and in 1861, enlisted in Company G, Seventh North Carolina infantry. He took part in the battle of Hanover C. H., and was present in all the engagements of the army of northern Virginia, under Lee, until the battles around Petersburg, in the spring of 1865. In the summer of 1862, he was detailed to serve on the signal corps attached to Gen. A. P. Hill's light division, and served in that capacity until November, 1864, when he rejoined his regiment and surrendered with Gen. Johnston's army at Greensboro, the regiment having been detailed from Gen. Lee's army in March, 1865. He was one of the fortunate few who was never wounded, nor taken prisoner, nor confined in the hospital by sickness, being blessed with good health throughout the entire war.

When peace came, Mr. Moring returned to his farm for a year or two, and in 1867 read law. In 1868 he was licensed to practice in all the courts in the state. He opened a law office in Pittsboro at once, and has been in the practice since with good success. In 1872, Mr. Moring was elected to the general assembly as a member of the house of representatives, and served in that body four consecutive terms. At each successive election his majority was increased, and at his last term, in 1879, he was chosen speaker of the house, holding that position two years. September 15, 1868, Mr. Moring was married to Miss Emma, daughter of Chesley F. Fawcetts, of Alamance county. They have had a family of five children: Alberta, teacher of art in Elon college, and giving a high degree of satisfaction; Lelia, of the home circle; Bessie, teacher of stenography and type-writing in Elon college, in which she performs good service; John T., deceased at the age of one year; Augustus M., a bright boy of twelve summers. Both parents and their three daughters are members of the Christian church. Mr. Moring is a member of the Masonic order, also of the Royal Arch chapter. He has been W. M. of the lodge for several years, and his standing both among his fraternal associates and among the citizens at large is in the front rank.

HON. HENRY A. BOND

is the oldest living merchant in Edenton and one of its most honored citizens. He was born in that town on the 17th of August, 1811. He was reared and educated in his native place, and early entered mercantile life there. In 1835 he and his brother, Samuel, engaged in business together on a borrowed capital of $4,000, but two years later the firm was dissolved, Mr. Henry Bond continuing alone. Although severe reverses have come, the name of Henry Bond has never been in a court of bankruptcy. During the late war over $50,000 were lost by him, but he kept on undaunted and succeeded. He has been quite an extensive vessel owner, and is now largely interested in real estate. Formerly a whig, but now a staunch democrat, Mr. Bond has been active in politics, and has held the offices of justice of the peace of the county, mayor of Edenton, and since the war has been a United States commissioner. For many years he served as a member of the town council, and for the past ten years has been treasurer of Edenton. In early days he was captain of the volunteer fire department, and in all these various capacities has shown himself to be a man of unusual ability and of the strictest integrity. Mr. Bond was married in 1836 to Miss Mary Manning, daughter of Joseph and Sarah Manning, of Chowan county. She died in 1840, and some time later he was again married, Miss Margaret G. Manning, a sister of his first wife, becoming his wife. Their five children are: Henry A. Bond, of Edenton, a member of the state legislature in 1887–88 and 1889–90; John C. Bond, member of the firm of Bond & Jones, of Edenton, formerly he was clerk of the superior court; Millard F. Bond, Southern Express and Western Union telegraph agent at Edenton; Mary, wife of F. F. White, of Edenton, and Lela, wife of John M. Jones, of the same place. Mrs. Bond died in 1862, and in November, 1863 Mr. Bond espoused as his third wife Ann Eliza McDowell. Mr. Bond has been a devout member of the Baptist church for many years, and has been treasurer of the Edenton church for more than twenty years. He died June 17, 1891.

HON. THOMAS H. BATTLE.

One of the oldest and most distinguished families of North Carolina is the Battle connection. The Hon. Thomas H. Battle, one of the leading lawyers and financiers of the state, was born at Raleigh, N. C., August 2, 1860. He was educated in Raleigh under the direction of J. N. Lovejoy and Dr. J. M. Atkinson, and in 1880 was graduated from the University of North Carolina. For one year after leaving college he taught as a private tutor, and then spent six months in Europe. Returning home Mr. Battle entered the law department of the university at Chapel Hill, and in October, 1882, was admitted to the bar. In the following December he went to Tarboro, and soon after was elected solicitor of the inferior court of Edgecombe county, retaining that office for three years. His removal to Rocky Mount took place in March, 1884, and since that time Mr. Battle has become very intimately connected with some of the leading industries of that thriving city. He organized the bank of Rock Mount in January, 1889, the greater portion of the stock being held by himself and one other gentleman, and has since had the management of that bank as vice-president. For several years he has been prominently identified with the Rocky Mount Yarn mills as a director, and for the past three years has served as president of the same, the concern having prospered greatly under his able management. In addition to these extensive interests, Mr. Battle also operates a very large plantation in Edgecombe county, where he raises cotton largely, and also conducts an extensive dairy. In December, 1886, he was elected mayor of Rocky Mount, an office he has since held to the entire satisfaction of the people. As a democrat he is earnest and active, and holds a high place in the councils of his party. In November, 1887, Mr. Battle was so fortunate as to form a marriage alliance with Miss Betty Davis, of Wilson, N. C., and one child, Kemp Davis, was born to the union. This most estimable lady was called to her eternal rest in April, 1890. She was a woman of rare culture and refinement, and lived a life beautiful for its Christian simplicity and charity. Mr. Battle is a communicant of the Episcopal church, as was his wife, and was formerly vestryman and treasurer of the church at Rocky Mount.

The Hon. Kemp Battle, father of the above, was born in Franklin county, N. C., and received his educational training at the University of North Carolina, at Chapel Hill. In 1850 he was admitted to the bar. During the Civil war he was president of the Chatham railroad, and was state treasurer under Gov. Worth's administration. In 1876 he was elected president of the University of North Carolina, and only recently resigned to accept the chair of history in that institution. Mr. Battle is very prominent in public affairs as a democrat, and is one of the ablest and most influential men in the state. By his marriage to Patty Battle these children have been born, their names being: Nellie, who married Dr. Lewis, of Raleigh, and is now dead; Hon. Thomas H., Kemp, Jr., M. D., of Raleigh, of the United States marine hospital service; H. B. Battle, Ph. D., director of the agricultural experiment station and state chemist; graduated from University of North Carolina with degree of Ph. D., and W. J. Battle, A. B., Ph. D., now at Harvard college, where he holds a fellowship. The first of this family to settle in Rocky Mount was Elisha Battle, a native of Virginia, whence he came in 1742. He was born of English parentage, the family seat being in Yorkshire, England.

Elisha Battle was a member of the state senate during the Revolution, and was a member of the commission appointed to adopt the constitution. He was a Primitive Baptist, and the first moderator of the Kehukee association. The extensive acreage which he purchased f   ı Lord Granville on the Tar river, is still in the possession of the faomily.

JONATHAN WORTH

was a native of Guilford county, N. C., born November 18, 1802. He was the son of Dr. David Worth. He was educated in the English branches at the "old field schools," and afterward attended the Greensboro academy where he remained for over two years, and made extraordinary proficiency in his studies. The means of his father being limited, he was unable to enter the higher institutions of learning, but engaged in teaching in a neighboring county. In connection with this occupation he studied law under the instruction of Hon. A. D. Murphey, one of the most distinguished and erudite lawyers in the state. In January, 1825, he was admitted to the bar, and soon thereafter began the practice of his profession at Asheboro, Randolph county. Notwithstanding his fine academic training and and his extensive law reading he was of a reserved, diffident, and retiring nature, and his contemporaries in the profession with less of legal learning but more boldness and push, outstripped him in amount of business. He was able in counsel, but shrank from arguing his cases at the bar, and consequently lost many a profitable client. Failing, as many of his profession do, for the want of self-assertion and assurance, he determined to turn his attention to politics, and sought a nomination to the state legislature; he was successful both before the nominating convention and at the polls. He was re-nominated and again made a successful canvass.

At his second term Mr. Worth distinguished himself as the author of a set of resolutions strongly denunciatory of Mr. Calhoun's nullification doctrines. The introduction of these resolutions was the signal for an earnest, long-continued and bitter debate in which Mr. Worth took a prominent part. The debate ended in the adoption of the resolutions by a large majority. His success in this contest gave him prestige in his profession. He retired from official life and devoted himself to his law practice, with results quite the opposite of his first experience. His clientage at once became large and remunerative. But he had not quite lost his penchant for politics, and in the great political revolution of 1840, he united his fortunes with the winning party and rode in upon the popular wave. He was elected to the senate by an overwhelming majority. Here he was appointed chairman of the joint committee on education, and formulated a bill for the establishment and support of public schools, which at that time won him great popularity. In 1841 he made an unsuccessful canvass for representative in congress in opposition to Hon. Abram Rencher, who though a whig, was accused by Mr. Worth of defection in his fealty

to Henry Clay.   Mr. Worth again returned to the practice of his profession, in which he continued until 1858, when he was again elected
to the state senate and was re-elected in 1860.   At the latter session
he was a strong opponent of the secession movement, voting against
the bill to submit the question of calling a convention to a popular
vote; he did not cease his opposition when the bill was passed, but
made a strenuous effort to defeat the measure before the people.
When the convention was called he declined to be a candidate for
delegate.   After the ordinance of secession was adopted, like other
Union men in the south, he gave in his adhesion to the Confederate
government and was elected to the lower house of the state legislature, which position he held until the end of the war.

   Under the provisional state government he was appointed treasurer, but soon resigned to make the canvass for governor of the state.
He was elected by a large majority, and re-elected by an increased
majority, continuing as the chief magistrate until July, 1868.   At that
date the reconstruction act which legislated Gov. Worth out of office,
took effect, but he did not yield his position without entering a
strong protest in which he denied the constitutionality of the act
and the power of congress to remove a state executive.   He returned
to private citizenship once more, and, on the 5th of September,
1869, at Raleigh, his eventful life came to a close.   Gov. Worth was
one of the ablest lawyers in the state; he was an excellent financier,
a legislator of rare resources and excellent judgment, and as chief
executive was one of the most distinguished ever called to that position in North Carolina.   In his private relations the same high principles governed him which characterized his public career.   His wife,
whose maiden name was Martila Daniel, whom he married in 1824,
and one son and five daughters, survived him at his death.

HON. CYRUS WILEY GRANDY,

one of the most prominent lawyers of Pasquotank county, N. C., was
born in Cameron county, N. C., on the 29th of June, 1831.   He was
educated in the county schools, at the high school of Oxford, N. C.,
and was graduated from William and Mary college in Virginia, July 4,
1855.   Three years later he began the practice of his profession at
Elizabeth City, where he had taken up his residence in 1851.   In
1865–67 he served as register of deeds of the county.   In 1861 he enlisted in Company G, Seventeenth North Carolina regiment, C. S. A.,
as a private, but in 1862 raised a company which was attached to the
Sixty-eighth North Carolina regiment, and during the rest of the war
Mr. Grandy served as captain of that company.   For many years he
served as chairman of the board of county commissioners of Pasquotank county, and in 1872 was elected to the state senate, serving for
two years.   He was a member of the judiciary committee in the
senate, and rendered distinguished aid to that committee.   Mr.
Grandy was elected attorney for the First judicial district of North
Carolina, in 1878, and retained that office until 1882.   Before the

organization of the republican party he was a whig, and then affiliated himself with the republican party, which he left in 1880, and has since been an independent. His marriage to Miss Florence L. Glover, daughter of William Glover of this county, was solemnized January 11, 1859, and has resulted in the birth of seven children, their names being: Lessells, who is in the pension department at Washington, D. C.; Cecelia, wife of J. J. Baxter, of Memphis, Tenn.; S. M. Grandy, of Denver, Col.—the latter gentleman has visited every country on the globe; Charles R., a member of the government geological survey, now stationed in Florida; Susan, Kate and Harry, who reside at home. Mr. Grandy is associated in the practice of the law with Mr. E. F. Aydlett, and this is the leading law firm of the city, both being eminent jurists. Mr. Grandy is largely interested in agriculture, and is a progressive and influential citizen. He is a communicant of the Episcopal church, and a prominent Mason.

HON. J. W. ALBERTSON.

Among the many distinguished gentlemen who have won prominence at the bar of Pasquotank county, N. C., we find the name of Hon. Johnathan W. Albertson. Mr. Albertson is a native of Perquimans county, N. C., where he first saw the light on the 9th of September, 1826, the son of Anthony B. and Rebecca (White) Albertson, who were both born in that county. Elias T. Albertson, the grandfather of our subject, was of Dutch parentage, his family having emigrated from Amsterdam to America, in 1669, and settled in Long Island. Later they removed to Pennsylvania, but finally settled in the south. They were prominent and enterprising men of the Quaker faith. Elias Albertson was a merchant, and came to Perquimans county after his marriage. Gen. Washington appointed him collector of the port of Newbegun, in Pasquotank county. Anthony B. Albertson, his son, was a planter, and lived and died in Perquimans county. He was a Quaker. The maternal ancestors of our subject on the paternal side were of Irish nationality, and were driven from their native land by the persecutions of the Quakers. Settling in Virginia, they were finally forced to seek a home elsewhere on account of the continued persecution of the Quakers, and settled in Perquimans county, N. C. The Hon. J. W. Albertson, of whom we will now write, was reared in Perquimans county, and remained there until 1879. His education was obtained in Belvedere academy, and completed in Guilford college. Having taken up the study of the law, he was admitted to the bar in 1849, and began active practice in Perquimans county, N. C., in the First judicial district. For many years he was solicitor of Perquimans county, and of the First judicial district and before the war represented that county in the legislature of the state. In 1872 he was appointed judge of the superior court for the First district, and in 1875, was a member of the constitutional convention. Three years later he was appointed United States district attorney for the eastern district of North Carolina, and was also appointed a member of the committee from North Carolina to the centennial of 1876, at Philadelphia.

Mr. Albertson removed to Elizabeth City in 1882, and has since conducted an extensive practice there. He is a Royal Arch Mason and also a Knight Templar. In 1855 Miss Catharine F. B. Pescud — daughter of Edward Pescud, editor of the *Old Dominion*, at Petersburg, Va., who served as a colonel in the war of 1812 — became his wife. Mrs. Albertson is also a granddaughter of Peter Francisco, of Revolutionary fame. Six children have been born to this happy union: Jonathan W., Jr., who is associated in the practice of law with his father; Marceline P.; Robert B., of Seattle, Wash., where he is practicing law; Rebecca; Thomas E., druggist of Port Townsend, Wash.; and Catherine S. Albertson. The entire family are communicants of the Episcopal church, in which the father is a senior warden. Mr. Albertson is recognized throughout the state as one of its ablest lawyers and most eminent citizens. On the side of his mother's maternal progenitors, he is a descendant of the Winslows, of Plymouth Rock or Massachusetts.

EDWIN F. AYDLETT.

A leading attorney of eastern North Carolina is Edwin F. Aydlett, of Elizabeth City. His birth took place in Camden county, N. C., on the 14th of May, 1857, and his parents, Abner and Clotilda (Lamb) Aydlett, were both natives of that county. Abner Aydlett served as sheriff of the county for several years, and was a prominent and successful planter. Mr. Edwin F. Aydlett was graduated from Wake-Forest college in June, 1879. Having read law in Elizabeth City for one year, he then completed his legal training in Judge Strong's law school, and was admitted to the bar in January, 1881, and began practice in Camden. In December, 1881, he came to Elizabeth City, and formed a partnership with Mr. C. W. Grandy, and this firm has since practiced at that place. While a resident of Camden county Mr. Aydlett was elected county superintendent of schools, but resigned from the office. For three terms he has been city attorney of Elizabeth City, and at present he is a member of the board of town commissioners, and is active and prominent in democratic politics in that section of the country. Mr. Aydlett is a stockholder in the Elizabeth City Fair association, and any movement, having for its object the advancement of the industries of the community or the uplifting of the people, finds in him a firm friend. In 1883 he was most happily married to Miss Henrietta Briggs, and two children. Henrietta N. and Evelyn L., are the result of their union. Mrs. Aydlett is a daughter of Thomas H. Briggs, Esq. Both Mr. and Mrs. Aydlett are communicants of the Baptist church, of which he is treasurer, and are held in the highest esteem throughout the community.

STEPHEN W. ISLER,

a leading lawyer of Goldsboro, N. C., is a native of Jones county, N. C., where he was born on the 18th of October, 1839, the son of Simmons Isler, who was likewise a native of that county, as was his father, William S. Isler. The family is of German extraction the founder of the American branch of the family having come to this country in colonial days. They first settled in Newbern, having accompanied the Baron de Groffeneice to America. The records show that Christian Isler was a juror in Jones county in 1763; other than this no correct statement of the family's history prior to the Revolution is at hand. A maternal ancestor of our subject was a Miss Williams, sister of Gov. Williams. William Isler owned 4,000 acres of land in Jones county (then Craven county), which were divided between his children. His father was an officer in the Revolution. His family consisted of Simmons, Mrs. Consul Wooten, Mrs. Rebecca Herring, E. B. Isler and Mrs. William Ford. Simmons Isler was a farmer by occupation. He was twice married, first to Miss Becton, of Jones county, who bore him three children, viz.: Col. John W. Isler, of Wayne county, Mrs. Susan Dawson, of Pitt county, and Mrs. John Shade Wooden, of Wayne county. His second marriage was to Mrs. Barbara Lane, widow of Ezekiel Lane, of New Hanover county, and a daughter of Stephen Miller, of Duplin county, a state senator from that county. Four children resulted from this union: George M. (deceased); Stephen W., Simmons H., a prominent Presbyterian clergyman of Goldsboro, and William R. (deceased). The father lived and died in Jones county, was a large land owner and slaveholder, and was held in the highest esteem throughout the county. He commanded a militia regiment during the " Nat." Turner insurrection. He was related to William Henry Harrison, and on one occasion entertained the Harrison party at his plantation, and while Gov. Mosely, of Florida, was a candidate for governor of North Carolina, Mrs. Mosely and Mrs. Isler were intimate friends, and Mrs. Mosely asked Mrs. Isler if she gave a dinner in honor of the elder Harrison, and was answered in the affirmative and informed that Gen. Harrison was a relative of her husband, whereupon Mrs. Mosely replied: " I will not speak to my own brother should he vote against Gov. Mosely." It was considered that the Harrison party opposed Mosely. Stephen W. Isler, our immediate subject, was reared in J county, and was educated in an academy in Virginia, which he left to enter college at Chapel Hill, from which he was graduated. Subsequently he entered Harvard college, and was graduated from the law department of that famous institution, in 1860. Two years later he entered the Confederate service as a member of the Sixteenth North Carolina cavalry, Deering's brigade, and served through the war. In 1866 he began the practice of his chosen profession at Goldsboro, and was soon elected solicitor for Greene county, which

Yours truly
W. T. Faircloth

office he held until the reconstruction act of 1867 went into force. Since that time he has practiced in the state and United States courts, having distinguished himself as a man of great ability. Mr. Isler is a member of the Royal Arch Chapter of the Masonic fraternity, and of the Harvard law association, of Cambridge, Mass. His political faith is founded upon the tenets of the republican party. Brought up in the faith of the Presbyterian church, he has ever clung to its doctrines.

HON. WILLIAM TURNER FAIRCLOTH

was born January 8, 1829, on Otter creek, in Edgecombe county, N. C. His father, William Faircloth, and his mother, Susan Edwards, had five children, of whom he was the oldest. His ancestors were English, and they came to North Carolina from the eastern shores of Maryland and Virginia. His father was an agriculturist, and the subject of this sketch bore his hand to the plow until he was eighteen years of age. Having attended the common schools and an academy, and having had other preparatory instruction, in June, 1850, he entered Wake Forest college, where he completed the college course in June, 1854, standing with the head of his class. His means being limited, he taught school during vacation and thus earned the money to pay the principal part of his college expenses. In July, 1854, he entered the law school of Chief-Justice Pearson at Richmond Hill, N. C., and on January 1, 1856, was licensed to practice in all the state courts, and located at Snow Hill, Greene county, N. C., and in a few weeks was elected county solicitor by the county court. He was still then in debt for necessary expenses at college and at the law school, which he soon discharged with the first fruits of his practice. In May, 1856, he located in Goldsboro, N. C., and has resided there ever since in the pursuit of his profession with slight interruptions. Politically he was a Henry Clay whig, and was opposed to the doctrine of secession, but after his state seceded, he volunteered as a private in Company C, Second North Carolina state troops, commanded by Col. C. C. Tew, and was on duty in the army of northern Virginia until its surrender at Appomatox C. H. in April, 1865, when he retired with the rank of captain of cavalry, and resumed his professional work. In August, 1865, he was elected by the people of his county (Wayne) as a delegate to the provisional state convention which convened October 2, 1865. In the fall of 1865, he represented his county in the first legislature after the war, which convened November 27, 1865. During this legislature he was elected solicitor of the Third judicial district of North Carolina, and held the office until displaced in the reconstruction of the state in 1868.

On January 10, 1867, Mr. Faircloth married Evelyn, the oldest living daughter of the late Council Wooten, of Mosely Hall (now La Grange), in Lenoir county, N. C. He followed his profession closely, but in 1875, he was again sent by his county as a delegate to the state constitutional convention, which assembled in Raleigh, Sep-

B— 10

tember 6, 1875, and on November 18, 1875, he was appointed and commissioned a justice of the supreme court of North Carolina, and remained on the bench until the term of the court expired. The other members were Chief-Justice Pearson, Justices Reade, Rodman and Bynum. Judge Faircloth is an ardent friend of the cause of education. He is now (1891) a trustee of the university at Chapel Hill, N. C.; of Wake Forest college, of the Baptist female university at Raleigh, and of the Baptist orphanage at Thomasville, N. C. At different times he has been a director in the W. & W. railroad, and A. & N. C. railroad, and in the North Carolina insane asylum. In 1884 he canvassed the state from "Cherokee to Currituck" as the republican nominee for lieutenant-governor, and in 1888 was on the republican ticket for justice of the supreme court. He has been extensively identified with various important enterprises looking toward the development of the state's resources. He is one of the original stockholders of the Goldsboro Furniture factory; is a third owner of the Hotel Gregory, and has erected several fine brick buildings in Goldsboro. He is among the largest stockholders in the Bank of Wayne, and has other interests of like importance. Originally an old time Henry Clay whig, Judge Faircloth is now a staunch national republican, and is recognized as one of its ablest leaders in the state. As a lawyer he excels and he has reaped the reward of a successful practitioner. He and his family are communicants of the Missionary Baptist church, and he is highly esteemed for purity of character and an upright walk in life.

HON. CURTIS HOOKS BROGDEN,

ex-governor of North Carolina, was born in Wayne county, N. C., on the 6th of December, 1816. His father, Pierce Brogden, was of English descent, and also a native of North Carolina. He married a Miss Amy Beard, who came of Irish parentage, but was a North Carolinian by birth. Pierce Brogden was a blacksmith by trade, and also carried on a small farm. He was a soldier in the war of 1812 and a man of ability and great integrity. His father was Thomas Brogden, a native of North Carolina and a soldier in the Revolution. He married a Miss Pierce, of Maryland. Curtis H. Brogden, the subject of this biographical mention, was reared on his father's farm and attended the common schools. Having chosen the law as his life vocation, he was admitted to the bar in 1845. For many years he presided as a justice of the Wayne county court. In 1838 he was elected by almost a unanimous vote to represent Wayne county in the house of commons. He was the choice of the people as their representative in one branch or the other of the general assembly until 1856, in the house from 1838 to 1852, and in the state senate thereafter to 1856, the year he was elected comptroller of North Carolina, and for ten years was the incumbent of that office; his term of office having extended from January 1, 1857, to January 1, 1867, In 1868 he was elected to the state senate, and again in 1870. Two years later he was the successful candidate of the republican party for lieutenant governor, and presided over the senate until 1874, when, on the death of Gov. Todd R. Caldwell, he succeed to the executive office of the state, which he held until January, 1877. Previous to this, however, in 1868, Gov. Brogden was an elector and presided over the electoral college which cast the vote of the state for Grant and Colfax.

In 1869 Mr. Brogden was appointed by President Grant, collector of internal revenue, for the Second district of North Carolina which he declined. He has held the principal offices in the state militia from captain to major-general, has served as a trustee of the state university, and has filled several local offices, such as town commissioner, railroad director, etc. In 1876, while governor of the state, he was elected to the forty-fifth congress, receiving 21,060 votes against 11,874 cast for Col. Wharton J. Green, democrat. In 1886 he yielded to the urgent solicitations of his friends, without regard to party, and ran for a seat in the house of representatives, and was elected by a majority of 479 votes. Gov. Brogden is extensively interested in agriculture, and is probably the largest land owner in Wayne county. He now owns the homestead which was occupied by his grandfather, and left by him to his father, who in turn bequeathed it to his son. Mr. Brogden was unalterably opposed to secession, and has been identified with the republican party since 1862. He was offered the colonelcy of the Twenty-sixth North Carolina regiment, but declined. He was a member of the senate that conducted the famous impeachment of W. W. Holden, and made an able speech on that occasion. It is but just to say that few men have done more for the advancement of the various different interests of the state than this man.

J. L. PATTERSON.

Few families have held a higher place in the confidence and esteem of the people of the proud old state of North Carolina than the Patterson connection. The first member of this family to settle in the new world came from the north of Ireland early in the eighteenth century, somewhere about the year 1700 or 1701. He first settled in Pennsylvania, then removed to Virginia. The Hon. Samuel F. Patterson is the first of the name to whom we will refer. He was born in Rockbridge county, Va., in 1799, and when but a lad came to North Carolina, settling in Wilkesboro, where he resided until about 1835, when he removed to Raleigh, having been elected treasurer of the state, in which office he served two years, when he returned to Wilkesboro. In 1840 he was elected president of the Raleigh & Gaston railroad, and served in that responsible position for several years, when he resigned, in 1845, and removed to Caldwell county, to take charge of his father-in-law's, Gen. Jones, estate. He was the first man to hold the office of grand master of the Masonic order in the state. He was trustee of the University of North Carolina for many years. Several times he ably represented Caldwell county in the state legislature. His demise occurred in 1874. The Hon. Rufus L. Patterson, a son of the Hon. Samuel F., was born in Caldwell county, N. C., in 1830. He was graduated from the University of North Carolina in 1851, and subsequently became a manufacturer in Caldwell and Forsyth counties, and later embarked in mercantile life at Salem. He represented Caldwell and Forsyth counties, and was a member of both the constitutional conventions of 1861 and 1865. He was a trustee of the state university for an extended period, and was a man of great ability and worth. His death occurred in 1879. He was twice married, the first time in 1852, to Miss Louise M. Morehead, a daughter of Gov. John M. Morehead, of Greensboro, N. C., and four children were born to them, two of whom still survive him, namely, Caroline F., wife of A. L. Coble, of Statesville, N. C., and J. L. Patterson, of Winston, N. C. The mother of these children died in May, 1862, and the father was again married in 1864, Miss Mary E. Fries, daughter of Francis Fries, of Salem, N. C., becoming his wife. This latter union resulted in the birth of six children, named as follows: Francis F., Samuel F., Andrew H., Rufus L., John L. and Edmund V.

Jesse Lindsay Patterson, the particular subject of this sketch, and the son of the first marriage of Rufus L. Patterson, was born May 16, 1858. Having been thoroughly prepared for college at Finley high school in Caldwell county, N. C. Mr. Patterson entered Davidson college, in Mecklenburg county, N. C., and was graduated therefrom in 1878. He then commenced the study of law under Judge J. H. Dillard and Judge Robert P. Dick, of Greensboro, N. C., and was admitted to the bar in 1881, after which he immediately located in Winston, N. C., and embarked in the practice of his chosen profession. In 1882 we find him serving as county solicitor of Forsyth county, which office he held for two years. He is the attorney for the Peoples' National bank of Winston, N. C., and extensively interested in several land and improvement companies. In 1888 he was most happily united in marriage to Miss Lucy B. Patterson, a daughter, of W. H. Patterson, of Philadelphia, and a granddaughter of Gen. Robert Patterson. As a lawyer Mr. Patterson excels, and although but just in the flush of his manhood he is already reckoned among the leaders at the bar of the county.

ASA BIGGS,

lawyer and senator, was born in Williamstown, Martin county, N. C., February 4, 1811. He was educated in the schools of the county, and afterward attended a classical school, in which he attained great proficiency. He studied law and was admitted to the bar in 1831. He entered the political arena, as a member of the constitutional convention, which met in 1835, to amend the old colonial constitution, adopted in 1767. In 1840 he was elected a member of the state legislature, by the democrats of his legislative district. He at once took a prominent position in that body, and was distinguished as the friend of the internal improvement of the state. He was elected for another term in 1842, and in 1844, was chosen a member of the state senate. In 1844 he made a canvass for member of congress, against Hon. David Outlaw, and was successful, but on his re-nomination in 1846, he was defeated by his former opponent. In 1850 he was appointed a member of the commission to revise and codify the laws of North Carolina, his associates on the commission being Messrs. B. F. Moore and R. M. Saunders. For this duty he was amply equipped and the code was completed and went into effect in 1854. In that year Mr. Biggs was again elected to the state senate, in which body he was the recognized leader of the democratic side of the house. Though the whigs were in the majority in the senate, they failed to carry a bill, providing for a state convention, to revise the state constitution, and to the forcible speeches of Mr. Biggs in opposition to the measure, its defeat is chiefly attributed. By this same legislature, Mr. Biggs was elected to the United States senate, where he served his state with distinction for four years. He then resigned, to accept the appointment of United States district judge, to fill the vacancy occasioned by the death of Judge Potter. He held this office till the breaking out of the Civil war in 1861. He was one of the members of the state convention, which passed the ordinance of secession, and was appointed to a judgeship under the Confederate government. He accepted the position, holding it until the close of the war. He then returned to the practice of law, which he pursued with success, until 1869. He then removed to Norfolk, Va., where he engaged in the commission business, as a partner in the firm of Kedar, Biggs & Company.

In 1870 Judge Biggs formed a law partnership at Norfolk with Judge W. N. H. Smith, which firm continued to do business until the latter gentleman was made chief-justice of the supreme court of North Carolina, and removed to Raleigh. Judge Biggs died at Norfolk, March 6, 1878. As a public speaker he did not shine for his brilliant eloquence or his fine-spun rhetortic. He was plain, yet forcible and direct, tenacious of his purpose, but never obstinate if convinced of his error. He was modest in his demeanor, unostentatious, but always gentlemanly and refined. He was conciliatory towards his opponents, appealing to their reason, judgment and common sense as the best method of convincing them. No purer statesman ever had a place in the halls of legislation, no fairer man ever expounded the law from the bench or bar, and no private citizen led a more exemplary life. In his family relations he was provident, kind and affectionate. He was a religious man, and belonged to that strait sect known as Primitive Baptist, in which faith he lived and died.

HON. JOHN H. DILLARD.

To be ranked among the great lawyers of North Carolina one must be possessed of superior abilities indeed, for few states have produced more eminent jurists than she. The Hon. John H. Dillard who for many years has figured prominently in the courts of North Carolina, was born in Rockingham county, N. C., November 29, 1819. His preliminary schooling was obtained at the Patrick Henry academy in Virginia, and later in Samuel Smith's school in Rockingham county, N. C. Entering the University of North Carolina, his course was cut short there after eighteen months by the failure of his health. Subsequently health was restored, and Mr. Dillard then matriculated in William and Mary college in 1839, and was graduated from the law department of that institution with the degree of B. L., in 1840. He then went to Richmond, Va., where he was admitted to the bar, and immediately afterward located at Patrick Court House, now Stewart, Va., and remained there for five years, a portion of which time he held the office of commonwealth attorney. In 1846 Rockingham Court House, N. C., became the scene of his labors, and from 1848 until 1870 he was associated in the practice of his profession with the late Judge Ruffin, who at one time sat on the bench of the supreme court of the state. Mr. Dillard removed to Greensboro, N. C., in 1868, and has since made that city his home. For a number of years he served as county attorney in Rockingham county, and also held the office of clerk and master to the court of equity of that county, his term of service extending until 1862, when he resigned. In 1878 he was elevated to the supreme court of North Carolina, and entered upon his high judicial duties January 1, 1879. His resignation from the bench in 1881 was accepted with the most sincere sorrow by the people, but was rendered necessary, owing to the distinguished gentleman's failing health.

During the dark days of 1862, Judge Dillard organized a company in Rockingham county, of which he was elected captain, the command being assigned to the Forty-fifth regiment, North Carolina volunteer infantry, and he served at the head of his company until February, 1863. On the 13th of January, 1846, Miss Ann I. Martin, a daughter of Col. Joseph Martin, of Henry county, Va., became his wife. The children of this union are: Lucy, wife of John T. Pannill, of Reidsville, N. C.; Thomas Ruffin Dillard, of Guilford county, N. C.; Anna, wife of E. F. Hall, of Reidsville, John H. Dillard, Jr., of Murphy, N. C., Drury C. Dillard, of Greensboro, N. C., and two others now dead. The family are communicants of the Presbyterian church, and Judge Dillard is a member of the Masonic fraternity. As a lawyer he excels. Possessed of a mind of rare strength and symmetry, well stored with the thrifty study of years, this man has achieved much in his calling. After an extended period of service as a judge in the highest court of the state, he left the bench with ermine unspotted. When incapacitated from active work by disease, he was too proud to enjoy the emoluments of an office whose duties he could not discharge with the best of his energies. Judge Dillard is the son of James Dillard, who was born in Henry county, Va., in 1780. All his active years were spent as a planter and tobacco manufacturer. He died in 1859. His marriage to Lucy Moorman, daughter of Henry Moorman, of Lynchburg, Va., was solmnized, and the

happy union resulted in the birth of ten children, only three of whom
survive. They are: Lucy, widow of George L. Aiken, of Leeksville,
N. C., John Dillard and James P. Dillard. James Dillard was a son
of John Dillard. He too was a Virginian, and also a planter. He
served in the Revolutionary war as a patriot soldier.

HON. JOHN A. GILMER

was born in Greensboro, N. C., April 22, 1838. He was graduated
from the University of North Carolina in 1858, and then began the
study of law under the tutelage of his father, Hon. John A. Gilmer.
In 1859 he entered the University of Virginia, and completed the law
course there in 1860. At this time Mr. Gilmer became associated
with his father in the practice of his profession, and the partnership
then formed existed until the death of his distinguished sire, in 1868.
The declaration of war between north and south found our subject a
member of the Guilford Grays, and he accompanied that company to
Fort Macon, N. C., in April, 1861, where several independent companies, among which was the Guilford Grays, were organized into the
Ninth, later the Twenty-seventh regiment of North Carolina state
troops. Mr. Gilmer held the rank of sergeant at this time, but later,
in the year 1861, was promoted to adjutant of the regiment. In 1862
he was made major, and was in command at the battle of Newbern.
At the battle of Sharpsburg he was made a lieutenant-colonel for
gallant conduct, and subsequently was promoted to the rank of colonel, with which office he left the army at the close of the war. In
the battle of Fredericksburg, Col. Gilmer was wounded, and at Bris-
ton Station he was again wounded, this time most grievously, and he
is still a sufferer from that injury. As soon as he was able to leave
the hospital he reported for duty, and was placed in the invalid corps,
and assigned to duty at Salisbury, where he served until attacked by
a malignant fever which entirely incapacitated him for further military duty. In 1864 he returned to Greensboro and resumed the practice of law. Two years later Gov. Worth appointed him adjutant
general of North Carolina, and he held that office for one year. In
the convention which met at Raleigh in 1868 he was a delegate, but
was counted out by Gen. Canby, at Charleston, S. C.

During the sessions of the state senate, in 1871-2, Mr. Gilmer represented his district with ability, and to the satisfaction of his constituents. He was not a candidate for public office again until 1879, and
in that year was appointed judge of the superior court of the Fifth
judicial district, and until January, 1891, when he resigned to attend
to his important law practice; he served with faithfulness and integrity. Judge Gilmer was a delegate to the national convention which
met at New York city, in 1868, and has frequently been a delegate to
state conventions. He is considered an able financier as well as a
lawyer, and is a stockholder in the National bank of Greensboro, the
North Carolina railroad company, and is interested in any movement

that promises renewed industry in his city and state. On the 14th of July, 1864, he consummated one of the happiest acts of his life by his marriage to Miss Sallie L. Lindsay, a daughter of Jesse H. Lindsay, late of Greensboro, and who at the time of his death was the president of the National bank of Greensboro. Three children have been born to this most fortunate union, named: Ellison L., Julia P., wife of Samuel W. Dick, of Greensboro; and John A. Gilmer, Jr. The Hon. John Adams Gilmer, father of Judge Gilmer, was born in Guilford county, N. C., in 1805. He was licensed to practice and was a lawyer of wide reputation. For several years he held the office of county attorney of his native county, and from 1845 to 1850, represented his district in the state senate. In 1858 he was elected to congress, and again in 1860. He was the whig candidate for governor of North Carolina in 1856, but was defeated by Thos. Bragg. In 1861 he served as a delegate to the convention which met at Raleigh, and resulted in the secession of the state from the union, and was elected to the Confederate state congress; and in 1861, was a member of the peace convention. His marriage to Juliana Paisley, daughter of Rev. Wm. D. Paisley, a pioneer clergyman of the Presbyterian church of North Carolina, and a man greatly beloved in the state, was solemnized in 1835, and resulted in the birth of six children, named: Mary, (died in 1858), wife of Col. Charles E. Shober; William, died at the age of six years; John A., of Greensboro, N. C.; Fanny M., wife of Capt. A. G. Brenizer, of Charlotte, N. C.; Hattie P. (deceased), wife of Peter H. Adams, and Julia, wife of S. J. Perry, of Charlotte, N. C. The mother of these children died in November, 1865.

John Adams Gilmer was the son of Mr. Gilmer, a Pennsylvanian by birth, where he was born in 1775. In his early manhood he came to North Carolina and settled in Guilford county, where he was engaged in agriculture the greater part of his life. His demise occurred in 1850. He served for many years as a captain in the state militia, and was a man of intelligence and integrity. Judge Gilmer is descended from an old and influential family on the maternal side, as well as on the paternal. But before going further we will pause to state that Capt. Arthur Forbis, who served as a captain in the patriot army of 1776, was a brother of the paternal grandmother of our subject. Gen. Alexander Nebane was the maternal great-grandfather, and his distinguished service as a general in the Revolutionary army is a matter of national history. Judge Gilmer's mother's uncle was Col. William Paisley, also of Revolutionary fame. In this brief sketch it will be seen that our subject comes of families who have been connected very prominently with the establishment and growth of this nation. From time to time their members have distinguished themselves on the battle-field and at the bar, while many have lived peaceful lives as honorable gentlemen, tillers of the soil. It is of such material that the backbone of this nation is formed, and so long as families of like worth remain true to the names they bear all will be well.

HON. DARIUS H. STARBUCK

was born in Guilford county, N. C., in 1818, and died in 1887. He was graduated from New Garden, now Guilford, college, and then began the study of law with John A. Gilmer, and was admitted to practice in 1840. In 1868 he was elected judge of the superior court, but resigned the office. Prior to this, however, in 1866, he was appointed United States attorney for the district of North Carolina, and held that office until 1872. He served as a delegate to the secession convention at Raleigh in 1860, and was a delegate to the constitutional convention which met at the same place in 1865. He was a man of magnificent abilities, and rose to marked distinction in his profession.

HON. LEVI M. SCOTT

was born in Rockingham county, N. C., J 8, 1827. In early childhood he accompanied his parents to Guilford county, and his preliminary schooling was obtained in the schools of the latter county. Leaving school at the age of twenty he began his active career as a school teacher, and at about the same time took up the study of law. In 1850 he was appointed postmaster at Greensboro, N. C., and held that office for about three years. In 1852 he was licensed to practice, and a year later received the election as clerk of the superior court, and held that office until 1856. In the latter year Mr. Scott was elected to represent his county in the state legislature, and served a term of two years. In 1858 he was elected solicitor of Guilford county, and for two terms, of four years each, most satisfactorily discharged the duties of that important position. He was appointed as receiver of sequestrated property by the Confederate government in 1862, and was retained in that capacity until the close of the war, his duty having been to collect all debts owing northern creditors from southern debtors, for the benefit of the Confederate States. After the termination of hostilities between north and south, Mr. Scott devoted himself exclusively to the practice of his chosen profession at Greensboro. He served as a member of the board of directors of the state penitentiary from 1885 until 1889, and at the present time is the attorney for the Bank of Guilford. As a lawyer he has won a name of which he may be proud. Dignified and able, his opinions carry weight wherever promulgated, and his reputation as a man of the most rigid integrity but adds to his fame as a distinguished lawyer and citizen.

Mr. Scott has been most happy in his domestic relations, having been united in marriage to Miss Mary E. Weatherly, in 1861. Mrs. Scott is a daughter of Mr. Andrew Weatherly, of Greensboro, N. C. Two children have been born to this blessed union, the surviving one being Mrs. Mary L. Reynolds, now living in Brooklyn, N. Y. Mr. Scott is a prominent member of the I. O. O. F., and in 1866 held the high honor of grand master of the state of North Carolina. John D. Scott, his father, was born in Guilford county, N. C., in 1800. He was given a common school education, and then gave his attention to agriculture, and was engaged in planting all his life. He served as a colonel in the North Carolina militia cavalry, and held his commission until the breaking out of the Civil war. In 1824 he married Miss Jane McLean, a daughter of Marshal McLean, of Guilford county, N. C., and three children were the offspring of the marriage, their names being: Allen H., of Guilford county, N. C.; Levi M., of Greensboro, and William L. Scott, who died in 1872. The father died in 1880, his wife having preceded him to rest in 1845. John D. Scott was the son of Adam Scott, who was a native of Guilford county, N. C., where he was born, in 1782. His demise occurred in 1837. He was a planter all his life. His father was Thomas Scott, a Pennsylvanian, who emigrated to North Carolina in early manhood, and settled in Guilford county. The ancestors of the Hon. Levi M. Scott on the paternal side were from the north of Ireland, and on the maternal side, came from Scotland.

MAJOR JOHN W. GRAHAM

was born in Orange county, N. C., July 22, 1838. He received a thorough preliminary education in the best schools in North Carolina, and for two years in the District of Columbia, his father, Hon. William A. Graham, being at that time secretary of the navy, and residing at Washington city; and he graduated with distinction at the University of North Carolina, in 1857. He remained at that institution as tutor for two or three years, and established a fine reputation for proficiency. Coming to the bar, in 1860, he soon won high esteem for his ability, thoroughness and fine character, an enviable reputation which succeeding years only seemed to enhance. The war breaking out, not withstanding his devotion to the Union and to the principles of the old whig party, of which his father had been such an illustrious leader, on the 22nd day of April, 1861, he entered the service of North Carolina as a lieutenant in the Orange guards, which became a company of the Twenty-seventh North Carolina regiment, and the next year was promoted to be captain of Company D of the Fifty-sixth regiment, afterward assigned to Ransom's brigade; and in September, 1863, was again promoted, being made a major of that regiment. He served with great acceptability and was attentive to every duty, caring for his men with assiduity and sharing in every hardship they were called on to endure in a manner altogether admirable. Brave to a fault and unflinching in the execution of his duties, he won the confidence of all who had intercourse with him, while he displayed a heroism and self-denying spirit that betoken those high qualities that adorn his character. Particularly was he highly complimented for unusual gallantry at the battle of Plymouth. He escaped all the vicisitudes of war, however, until he was seriously wounded in the trenches around Petersburg, and again on the 25th of March, 1865, when in command of the left of the line in the attack on Hare's Hill he was dangerously wounded in both things, and was on the evacuation of Petersburg left in the hands of the Federal forces. It was late in the summer before he reached home. As soon as his strength was somewhat restored he again opened his law office at Hillsborough and, being chosen as solicitor of Orange county, served as such during the years 1866 and 1867 and part of 1868.

In 1867 Major Graham was elected by the democrats of Orange county, to represent them in the constitutional convention of 1868, being one of the few democrats in that body. He then entered upon that career as a public man which has won for him the unqualified respect, esteem and admiration of the thinking people of the state. He opposed the radical changes then proposed in our organic law with a persistence and an address that riveted public attention upon him. He was elected to the state senate of 1868–69, and though there were but a half a dozen democrats in that assembly, he never ceased to oppose improper legislation and to strive for the best interests of the people. He it was who drew the important bill repealing the taxes imposed in the special tax acts and declaring the special tax bonds invalid, and directing them to be returned to the state treasury. Together with Jarvis, Plato Durham, and a few other democratic members, and with the assistance of some of the better element of the republicans, he pushed the repealing legislation to a successful termination, and gained a great triumph for the people in that corrupt legislature. He was again elected to the legislature — that of 1870–72, where he was one of the most efficient members, and he was largely instrumental in shaping the beneficial and remedial measures of that period. In 1872 he was nominated by the democrats for state treasurer, but the ticket failed to be elected by a small adverse vote. He was in the senate of 1876–77, following the adoption of the amendments to the constitution, when he augmented his reputation as one of the most efficient and useful public men in the state. Familiar with every detail of the state government, and a most laborious and industrious member, a thorough lawyer and a practical man of business, he took rank as one of the leaders in that body, and exercised a great influence on the legislation of that session. In 1886 he was chairman of the state board of commissioners, to revise the system of collecting taxes and to equalize the valuation of property, and his report is a valuable state paper. In the fall of that year he was also nominated for congress in the Wake district, but was defeated owing to influences for which he was not responsible.

Major Graham has attained a commanding eminence in his profession, ranking with the foremost lawyers of the state. He was long in partnership with Judge Thomas Ruffin, the younger, and they were employed in many important cases in their circuit. He has been trustee of the North Carolina R. R. and for years administered a trust amounting to many thousands of dollars. As a citizen he has borne a most exemplary character, as a public man his record is without blemish, and as a party leader he has been prudent, conciliatory and patriotic, affable, honest and true, he has the esteem and entire confidence of the people of the state. In 1867 Maj. Graham married Rebecca, daughter of the late Paul C. Cameron, who died in 1883, leaving six children. He was again married in December, 1887, to Miss M. F. Bailey, of Tallahassee, Fla., and one son has blessed their union. Living on the site of the old residence of his father, rebuilding the former home destroyed by fire, he has a small farm on the Eno, adjoining the grounds owned by Mr. P. C. Cameron, and one of the most attractive spots in the central part of the state. Here he delights to spend such time as he can command from the circuit of courts he attends, and to realize that "there is no place like home."

W. H. HAYWOOD.

William Henry Haywood, one of North Carolina's distinguished statesmen, was born in Wake county, N. C., in 1801. He graduated from the University of North Carolina in 1819, studied law and opened a law office at Raleigh for the practice of his profession. In 1831 he was elected a member of the state legislature, first of the house of commons and then of the senate. He was elected to the United States senate in 1843, holding a seat in that body till 1846. He then resigned and returned to his law practice in Raleigh. He was a man of firm and commanding talent, made an able statesman and an eminent law practitioner. Ill health, however, compelled him early to relinquish active business, and for several of the latter years of his life he entirely abstained from the practice of his profession. Mr. Haywood died in Raleigh, October 6, 1852, in the fifty-second year of his age.

HON. MATTHEW LOCKE McCORKLE,

a prominent attorney and ex-judge, at Newton, N. C., was born on Mountain Creek, Catawba county (Lincoln county at that time), November 7, 1817. His father was Francis McCorkle, son of Francis McCorkle, Sr., who fought gallantly at the battles of Ramsoms, at Cowpens, Kings Mountain and other places, during the Revolutionary war for our national independence. His mother was Elizabeth Maria Abernathy, of Lincoln county, N. C. His great-grandfather was Matthew McCorkle, who came to this country about the year 1750, from the north of Ireland, with his wife, Bettie, *nee* Given. His paternal grandmother was Elizabeth Brandon, daughter of Richard Brandon, who married Margaret Locke, of Rowan county, the sister of Judge Frank Locke, and the niece of Matthew Brandon, who represented his district in congress in 1796. His maternal grandmother was Susan Maria Abernathy, and his maternal grandfather was John D. Abernathy, who came from Scotland about 1750. The subject of this sketch is, therefore, of Scotch-Irish descent. He attended the old field schools at intervals, until 1836, and acquired the rudiments of an English education at Lincolnton, under the instruction of Prof. John Dickey. In 1838 he entered Davidson college, and began the study of Latin grammar. Owing to financial embarrassment, he left college in his junior year, and taught one year at Hicksby Grove academy, having a large and flourishing school. He was invited by the philanthropic society, of which he was a member, to deliver to them a lecture, with which he complied. His old class invited him, with the permission of the faculty, to join them in their graduation, which he did, graduating within four years from the time he began his Latin grammar. This was in 1843. He studied law under Chief-Justice Pearson, and obtained license to practice in 1845, settling on the newly laid site of the county seat of Catawba, now the city of Newton, in June of that year.

Mr. McCorkle obtained license to practice in the superior court in 1846, and in the same year was appointed clerk of the superior court of Catawba county, by Hon. John M. Dick, to fill the vacancy caused by the resignation of Isaac Wyckoff, who left the state. He was elected to fill this office in 1846, and held it until 1850. In December of that year, Mr. McCorkle was married to Miss J. M. A. Wilfong, only living daughter of John Wilfong of Hickory, N. C. They were blessed with nine children, five sons and four daughters, seven of whom are now living. The eldest daughter, Elizabeth Lavina, died at the age of three years; the eldest son, Frank Wilfong died in Baltimore while attending medical lectures. The eldest living son, Henry, is in Texas following the business of engineering. The next son, George is a practicing attorney at Newton; the next, John Macon, is a practicing physician, also in Newton; the youngest son, Charles Hilton, is in Catawba college. The eldest daughter, Mary Locke married Eugene Simons; Anna Ellen married Jerome Dowd, of Charlotte, N. C., Lizzie Alberta is still unmarried. Mr. McCorkle volunteered in the late Civil war, raised a company of which he was elected captain. He served one year in the Twenty-third regiment of North Carolina troops. His health giving out, he was compelled to resign. Upon the recovery of his health, Mr. McCorkle was appointed colonel of the North Carolina reserves. In 1864, he was elected to the state senate from the counties of Lincoln, Catawba and Gaston, and continued to represent his district in the senate until the state was thrown into a provisional government. He was elected in 1875 to the constitutional convention.

The law practice of Mr. McCorkle is now in all the courts, and he has met with unprecedented success in his practice before the supreme court of the state. In August, 1890, he was appointed by Gov. Daniel G. Fowle, judge of the superior court of the Eleventh judicial district of North Carolina, to fill the unexpired term of the late Hon. William M. Ship. He rode the ninth judicial circuit, and gave great satisfaction to the bar and to the people. His judgments taken to the supreme court were every one of them affirmed by that tribunal and the public press of his district was the medium of many complimentary notices in praise of the ability, fairness and impartiality of

his judgments and rulings upon the bench.   At the last court he held
in the county of Surry, the attorneys and court officers called a meeting and passed some very complimentary resolutions, laudatory of the
presiding judge.   His health and intellect are in a remarkable state
of preservation, the fruits of a steady and temperate life.

MICHAEL HOKE JUSTICE

was born in Rutherford county, N. C., February 13, 1844.   He is the
son of Rev. T. B. and Harriet (Bailey) Justice, and is the fourth child
in order of birth.   He attended the schools of his native county, and
at the age of ten entered the academy at Rutherfordton, where he
remained for five years.   He then entered the Golden Grove seminary, taught by Prof. Logan.   This school he attended two years when
he left his studies to enter the Confederate army in defense of his
southern home.   He enlisted in the Sixty-second regiment of North
Carolina troops, taking the rank of ordnance officer of that regiment;
was soon promoted to a lieutenancy in his company, then was raised
to the rank of adjutant of his regiment, and was finally elected as ordnance officer of the brigade, serving in that capacity until the war
closed.   His regiment was paroled after the surrender of Lee, he surrendering to Gen. John M. Palmer, at Rutherfordton, who at that time
was stationed there under a flag of truce.   Soon after this Mr. Justice
began studying law with Judge John L. Bailey, at Asheville, N. C.
After two years' study he was licensed to practice in January, 1868.
He immediately opened a law office at Rutherfordton, where he has
ever since practiced.   His business has constantly extended, reaching
out to all the counties contiguous to his own.   In politics he has
closely identified himself with the democratic party.   He has been a
member of the congressional executive committee of his district, and
of the judicial executive committee.   In the legislature of 1876–7 he
represented the district composed of Rutherford and Polk counties
in the state senate, being the first democratic senator who had represented that district since the close of the war.

Mr. Justice was the democratic presidential elector for his district
in 1884.   He is a prominent member of the Masonic order, having
filled the highest official stations in that fraternity.   In religious sentiment he is a Baptist, having been closely identified with that denomination for many years; he is one of the prominent members of the
Rutherfordton Hotel & Improvement company, and one of the chief
directors of the Rutherfordton military institute.   In every progressive interest he takes a deep concern and has given a helping hand
to all the improvements of the town and county of his residence.   In
the Citizens' Building & Loan association he is counsel and one of
the directors.   He drew the charter for the Henrietta Cotton Mills
company.   Mr. Justice drew up the charter that passed the legislature in 1890, incorporating the Asheville & Thermal Belt railroad
company.   On the 21st of March, 1865, he was joined in matrimony
with Miss Maggie L., daughter of James M. and Martha Smith, of

Buncombe county, and they have had six children, four of whom are still living. The eldest son, E. J. Justice, is a graduate of Wake Forest and of G. N. Folk's law school, and a partner in practice with his father. B. A. Justice, the second son, is in Wake Forest college, and Gaston, the third son, is in attendance at the Rutherfordton military institute.

COL. J. A. FORNEY,

an attorney of the city of Rutherfordton, was born in Rutherford county, N. C., in 1849. He is the son of Albert G. and Elizabeth (Logan) Forney, and his grandfather was Jacob Forney, Sr., a Revolutionary soldier. Albert G. Forney died, when his son, the subject of this sketch was an infant, and as the son grew up, he attended the home schools, till his widowed mother required his services in looking after the business left by the father. He finally, however, found opportunity to attend the academy, and in 1874, entered the law school of Chief-Justice Pearson, spending two years under his instruction, at the end of which period he procured license from the supreme court of this state to practice. He at once began the practice of his profession in his native city, where he has ever since remained, and has built up a successful and lucrative law business. Col. Forney is a staunch democrat, and has served as chairman of the democratic executive committee, of Rutherford county, for the past ten years. He has been recognized as a leader in his party, and has taken an active part in all its exciting campaigns, ever since he arrived at his majority. Col. Forney is president of the Rutherfordton Hotel Improvement company, and is classed among the most public spirited citizens, taking a vital interest in every enterprise, that looks to the public improvement of his native city. Col. Forney was united in marriage with Miss Mary Sue Davis, daughter of Col. C. T. N. Davis, who was killed at the battle of Seven Pines, in defense of the Confederate government. The mother of Mrs. J. A. Forney was originally Miss Mira McDowell, who was a granddaughter of Joseph McDowell, who was of Revolutionary fame. Six children have been born to Col. and Mrs. Forney, as follows: Champion Albert, Lewis Berguer, Joseph Francis, McD., Mary Mansfield, Mira Elizabeth, and J. A. Forney, Jr.

GEORGE S. BRADSHAW,

one of the leading citizens of Randolph county, N. C., attorney-at-law and clerk of the superior court, was born in Alamance county, N. C., April 5, 1854. His parents are William S. and Margaret E. (Stockard) Bradshaw, both native North Carolinians. The former is a farmer of the better class, and has been very successful in his occupation. He is numbered among the respectable, worthy, well-known and highly esteemed agriculturists of the county. He was captain in the senior reserves, and took part with his company in the batle of Bentonville, being the last engagement of the war. He has reached the age of seventy-six years, and with his wife is a devout and consistent member of the Methodist Episcopal church. George S. Bradshaw is the third in a family of six children, four of whom are still living. He was educated in Trinity college, graduating therefrom in 1876. He taught with good success a year and a half, then took a course in the law school of Dick & Dillard, and was admitted to the bar in January, 1879. To his law practice Mr. Bradshaw has added the duties of editorship, being principal editor of the Ashboro *Courier* for six years. He was president of the state press association for one year. In 1880 he was elected to the general assembly of the state, serving therein a term of two years as the representative of Randolph county. He was a member of the judiciary and education committees, and was chairman of the printing committee and on the committee on privileges and elections.

Mr. Bradshaw was elected as clerk of the superior court in 1882, and has been re-elected for every succeeding term since by constantly increasing majorities, evincing the high esteem in which he is held as an officer of the court, and showing his popularity among his fellow citizens. He was beaten for a nomination for congress by the narrow majority of one vote and a half, in the nominating convention of the Seventh congressional district, in 1884. He is one of the trustees of the state university, elected thereto by the last legislature, and trustee of Trinity college. He has been a director in the High Point railroad company ever since its organization. In all progressive enterprises and schemes for improvement, he takes a leading part. Mr. Bradshaw was married in 1881, to Miss Lou McCullock, daughter of John and Louise McCullock, of Guilford county. The home of this happy couple has been blessed by the birth of five bright children: Kate, Louise, Samuel, John and Mary. Both parents are members of the Methodist Episcopal church, south. Mr. Bradshaw is a member of the Masonic order, in which association be is held, as he is by all his fellow citizens, in the highest esteem. The personal characteristics of Mr. Bradshaw are great energy, quick preception, positive in his opinions, all re-enforced by an active temperament and a sagacious judgment.

AUGUSTUS W. GRAHAM,

of whom we will now write, was born in Hillsboro, N.C., June 8, 1849. His preparatory schooling was obtained at Mr. Nash's school in Hillsboro, and later at Dr. Alexander Wilson's excellent academy in Alliance county. Entering the University of North Carolina, he was graduated therefrom in 1868. He then commenced the study of law with William Ruffin and Hon. William A. Graham, his distinguished father, and was admitted to the bar in 1872. Until 1888 he was engaged in the practice of his profession at Hillsboro, and then removed to Oxford and became associated with Robert W. Winston, which

W. A. Graham

partnership existed until January 1, 1891. At the latter date Mr. Winston was elected judge of the superior court of the Fifth district. Mr. Graham was elected secretary of the board of arbitration created by the legislatures of Virginia and Maryland in 1873, to settle the boundary dispute between those states, and served in that capacity for three years. In 1885 he was elected a member of the state senate from the counties of Orange, Durham, Person and Caswell, and served one term. For two years, from 1889, he was a member of the Oxford city council. Mr. Graham was happily married in 1876 to Miss Lucy A. Horner, an accomplished lady, daughter of Prof. James H. Horner. Two of the four children born to this union now survive, viz.: Susan W. and Alice R. Mr. Graham is a man of much ability, and is recognized as one of the leading lawyers of North Carolina.

It is eminently proper that this, necessarily short sketch, should be closed with a brief mention of the immediate antecedents of our subject. His grandfather, Joseph Graham, was born in Mecklenberg county, N. C., in 1757. At the age of nineteen he raised a company, of which he was made captain, to fight in the patriot army of the Revolution. At the close of the war he held the rank of major. He participated in the battles of Charlotte, Beatties Ford, was present at Pyle's defeat in Alamance county, N. C., and was in command of the Continental cavalry when Lord Cornwallis was stationed in Hillsboro. At the battle of Charlotte he was grievously wounded, but fought until literally cut down. After the war he became high sheriff of Mecklenberg county, and retained that office for several years, resigning it upon his removal to Lincoln county, where he became the pioneer of the North Carolina iron industry. Upon the organization of the University of North Carolina the distinguished gentleman was made a member of its board of trustees, and took an active and substantial interest in its development. During the war of 1812, we find him once more in the field as a brigadier-general, and he was placed in command of the army sent to suppress the insurrection of the Creek Indians in 1813-14. For his valor in the war of 1812, North Carolina's legislature voted him a handsome sword, appropriately engraved. At this time he retired to his plantation, and conducted it in connection with his iron business until his demise in 1837. Joseph Graham was the son of James Graham, a native of county Down, Ireland, where he was born early in 1700. While a young man he came to America, settling in Chester county, Penn. He was a planter. His father was born in Scotland, and removed to Ireland during his early manhood. The maternal ancestors of Augustus W. Graham were English. His mother was a direct descendant of a brother of George Washington, and her father was a man of refinement and ability.

WILLIAM ALEXANDER GRAHAM,

senator and statesman, was born in Lincoln county, N. C., September 4, 1804. He attended the common schools of the county, and

B—11

afterward received a classical training under Rev. Dr. Muchat, at
Statesville, where it was said of him that he was noted for his thirst
for knowledge and his aptitude for learning. He graduated from the
North Carolina university in 1824, studied law with Judge Ruffin, was
admitted to the bar at Newbern, and opened a law office at Hillsborough. Here he found for associates a large number of able lawyers, who had been or were subsequently called to preside over the
courts—such men as Ruffin, Mangum, Murphy, Badger and Nash, a
brilliant coterie of counselors and jurists. But it was not long before
Mr. Graham stood side by side with them in the ranks of the profession. As an equity lawyer he became highly distinguished; still he
was destined to shine in the political field with equal luster as at the
bar. Between the years 1833 and 1840, he held a seat in the state
legislature, and was several times elected speaker of the house. On
the occurrence of the great political revolution of 1840, he was needed
in the national councils, and was elected United States senator, to fill
the vacancy caused by the resignation of Senator Strange, who
yielded to the instructions of the legislature asking for his resignation.
Mr. Graham's senatorial term extended from December 10, 1840,
to March 3, 1843. He was the colleague of Willie P. Mangum, who
had been elected under similar circumstances with himself. In this
position he became the associate of such distinguished senators as
Clay, Webster, Benton, Buchanan and Wright, and his speeches before the senate did not suffer in comparison with the speeches of these
eminent statesmen. Soon after the completion of his senatorial term
he was elected governor on the whig ticket by an unprecedented
majority. He was re-elected in 1846 by a still greater majority, prov-
ing that his administration had been highly satisfactory to the people
of his state. He was solicited to try a third term, but declined. President Taylor, in 1849, offered Mr. Graham the Spanish mission, and
this he also declined, but, in 1850, accepted from President Fillmore
a place in his cabinet, as secretary of the navy. In the presidential
campaign of 1852, the whig party nominated Gen. Winfield Scott for
president, and William A. Graham for vice-president, but in this campaign the whigs were defeated, and this proved to be the death-blow
of that great party.
While Mr. Graham was secretary of the navy he projected the
Japan expedition which was so successfully accomplished by Commodore Perry, and which has opened not only to this country but to
every commercial nation on the globe, trade relations with that here-
tofore secluded nation which have proved of incalculable advantage
to all. He also projected another expedition to explore the valley of
the Amazon, in South America, the results of which were of great
consequence to this country. In 1854, Mr. Graham was again elected
to the state senate. When North Carolina seceded from the Union,
it found in Mr. Graham an ardent opponent to that measure, but when
the convention met, the ordinance was passed unanimously. He was
elected senator in the second Confederate congress, and held that
office from the 22d of February, 1864, until the close of the war. He

Very truly,
B. H. Brown

was a member of the Union convention which met in Philadelphia, in 1866. He was one of the commissioners appointed to settle the difficult boundary dispute between Maryland and Virginia. He died at Saratoga Springs, August 11, 1875. Mr. Graham married Susan, daughter of John Washington, of Newbern, who bore him two sons, Joseph and John Washington, both of whom were officers in the Confederate army.

HON. BENJAMIN HICKMAN BUNN,

whose name is familiar to every North Carolinian, as the successful lawyer and congressman, first saw the light on the 19th of October, 1844, in Nash county, N. C. He is the son of Redman and Mary Hickman (Bryan) Bunn. His father was for many years a merchant and agriculturist of Nash county, where he reared three of the noblest sons of North Carolina, two of whom fell during the war and the third is the subject of this sketch. Of these brothers William H. Bunn was the eldest. Graduating at the University of North Carolina, he studied law and after being licensed opened his office at Wilson, where he was doing a leading practice when the war broke out. He entered the Confederate army and was killed while commanding a company of cavalry at Burgess' Mills, October 27, 1864. Elias, the second son, left the university and entered the army and was adjutant of Col. Sol Williams' regiment, Twelfth North Carolina troops, when he was killed at Hanover court house, May 27, 1862. The father of Mr. Redman Bunn was also a native of North Carolina, and largely engaged in agriculture. He died at the age of twenty-six, leaving issue only Redman. His widow sometime subsequent married William Dortch, and bore him a large family of children. Several of these children have risen to distinction in the state. Among them may be mentioned the Hon. William T. Dortch, who was a Confederate States senator. Another was Isaac F. Dortch, who became one of the leading physicians of Alabama. Benjamin Bunn, the great-grandfather of our subject, and the one for whom he was named, came with his brother, Redman, from Virginia and settled in North Carolina, soon after the war for American independence. Redman Bunn for many years represented Nash county in the popular branch of the general assembly, and died leaving no descendants. This family is of English extraction, the former of the American branch having come from London, England, early in the history of this country. There is every reason for supposing that it emanated from the same source as the family now bearing that name in England, members of which have risen to fame and distinction in that land. The Hon. William H. Bunn, at present the queen's counsel, is a representative of this branch of the family.

Benjamin Hickman Bunn had but just completed his college preparatory course at the time of the breaking out of the late Rebellion. He gave up further study to enter the ranks of the southern army, and at the age of seventeen enlisted in Company I, Thirtieth North

Carolina infantry, under Capt. Arington. He began his military career as an orderly sergeant, and in September, 1862, was elected junior second lieutenant of Company A, Forty-seventh North Carolina infantry. He was afterward promoted to second lieutenant and then to first lieutenant. Eighteen months prior to the close of the struggle he was placed in command of the Fourth company of sharpshooters of William McRae's North Carolina brigade, in which position he gained the confidence of Gen. McRae, who once remarked to his assistant adjutant-general that he could tell Bunn's company as far as he could see them on the field by their manners without recognizing a single face. It will be seen that he was honored by promotion while still very young, as the date of his enlistment was July 20, 1861. Still, like many another southern lad, he commanded men, while yet a boy, with wisdom and valor. Lieut. Bunn was twice seriously wounded; first in the first day's fight at Gettysburg, and again on the 25th day of March, 1865, before Petersburg. He took a faithful and brave part in the following battles: Gettysburg, Bristol Station, The Wilderness, Spottsylvania Court House, Gaines' Mill, Reams Station, Burgess' Mill, and before Petersburg, where he was wounded when the Federal troops made an attack on the extreme right of the Confederate line. He was conveyed to Winter hospital at Richmond, and remained there until the Sunday morning that Richmond was evacuated and President Davis left the city, which was a few days prior to the surrender of Gen. Lee at Appomatox. Lieut. Bunn had not at this time sufficiently recovered to rise from his bed, but he sent his negro servant to Petersburg, where his baggage had been left, to see if he could not recover it. The boy returned breathless, and with abject terror depicted on his face, exclaiming that the city was being evacuated. This was the first intelligence that Lieut. Bunn had received in regard to the situation, and he immediately arose from his bed and walked to Danville, Va., where he boarded a train for home, arriving home on the day of Lee's surrender. On the first day of December, of that year, Mr. Bunn began the study of law under the tutelage of his uncle, William T. Dortch and Judge George V. Storey, they residing at Goldsboro, N. C., and was licensed to practice in the county courts by the supreme court of that state on the 12th of June, 1866. Twelve months later he was licensed to practice in the superior courts, and since that time has been engaged in the practice of his chosen profession at Rocky Mount, N. C.

As a lawyer, Mr. Bunn excels. He has achieved much honor, and has a widespread reputation as a successful jurist. Keen, progressive and profound, he has brought to the task an indomitable will and a mind thoroughly prepared for his life work. A worthy contemporary in speaking of him says: "I know of but few men who can more deeply probe the essential points of the law. His ability is marked, and his honesty crystal." Mr. Bunn first entered the political arena as a sub-elector in the Seymour-Blair campaign in 1868, and was a member of the constitutional convention in 1875, which framed the present constitution of North Carolina. In November, 1882, he was elected to the state legislature, and while a member of that body was chairman of the joint committee on the code, an honor almost without precedent, where a member of the lower house has been chosen as chairman of a committee formed of members of both the senate and house. This committee which was composed of twenty-two lawyers, formed the present code of the state. In 1884 he was a democratic elector for the Fourth North Carolina district, on the Cleveland ticket, and when the electoral college met in Raleigh, Mr. Bunn was chosen as the messenger to convey the vote of North Carolina to Washington, which he did, polling the vote for Grover Cleveland. Prior to this, however, in 1880, he was a member of the national convention which nominated Hancock. In 1886 he was a candidate for nomination to congress, and led the convention for 212 ballots, but Hon. John M. Graham received the nomination on the 213th ballot, and was defeated at the polls by John Nichols, a republican, who was elected by 1,500 majority. In 1888, however, he was nominated for this distinguished office, by acclamation, and elected by a handsome majority of 2,600 votes. His career in the Fifty-first congress was vindicated by the people in 1890, when he was returned to congress by 6,500 majority.

His speech on the federal elections bill was probably the crowning effort of Mr. Bunn's public career. In it he expressed a true southerner's opinion of the north and their leading ideas discussed, being: "The relative position of the south toward the north and the way to heal dissensions existing between the two sections growing out of the Civil war, and the effect of the negro vote on the presidential elections; showing conclusively that the negroes have for some years held the balance of power." This speech was copied extensively and a part of it was incorporated in the democratic hand-book. He has made over fifty reports from the committee on claims, and is one of its most active members. He was appointed a sub-committee of one to prepare the report on "a bill for the relief of John M. Langston," in which the whole sum expended for expenses in every contested election case since the organization of congress was fully set forth. This is the only document ever published by congress in which this has been done. The report was unanimously adopted by the committee on claims, thus supplanting two reports made by them before on the same subject matter.

On the 7th of November, 1871, the Hon. Mr. Bunn formed a happy marriage alliance with Miss Harriet A. Philips, a lady of much culture and refinement. Mrs. Bunn is the daughter of James J. Philips, who for many years figured as one of the leading physicians of North Carolina. He was the father of a large family of children, among them being the Hon. Fred Philips, judge of the supreme court of that state, and the Hon. James B. Philips, who is now serving his second term in the state legislature. During both terms he has been the chairman of the committee on agriculture, one of the most important and honorable positions in the power of that body to bestow.   Seven children have grown up in the pleasant home of our subject.   Miss Mary is at present a student in St. Mary's college, at Raleigh, N. C.; Hattie A., James P. and Bessie are also in school, and Annie Lee, Redman and Benjamin H., Jr., are still in their early childhood.   The family are communicants of the Protestant Episcopal church.   Mr. Bunn is a man of large and commanding stature, with a keen eye and regular features.   Quick and decisive in his every movement, he at once impresses one as a man of action, one born to command men.   He is thoroughly conversant with the leading questions of the day, and has evidently been a comprehensive and intelligent reader, both of men and books.

HON. DENISON WORTHINGTON.

One of the most prominent lawyers and politicians of North Carolina is the Hon. Denison Worthington.   Mr. Worthington was born in Hertford county, N. C., on the 6th of October, 1843, the son of Dr. Robert H. and Elizabeth (Herbert) Worthington, natives of Albany, N. Y., and Norfolk, Va., respectively.   Robert H. Worthington was a surgeon in the United States army, and while on duty at Norfolk, Va., met and married Miss Herbert.   He afterward settled in Murfreesborough, about the year 1838, and there engaged in the practice of medicine.   During the Civil war he was surgeon of the Seventeeth North Carolina regiment, and subsequently was stationed near Raleigh.   His death occurred at Norfolk, Va., in December, 1871.   Dr. Worthington was grand master of the I. O. O. F. of North Carolina, and was one of the most prominent members of the State Medical society, was a leading democrat and a devout member of the Methodist Episcopal church.   His wife died in 1882.   Of the nine children who blessed this union, four are now living, their names being, Robert Herbert, M. D., the eldest, was a surgeon in the Confederate army, and died at Norfolk, Va., in 1877; George W., lived and died at Norfolk; he was a most gifted poet, and his name now lives in many lines of noted verse; Herbert Livingston, an attorney of Norfolk; Daniel D. R., and Arthur, also of Norfolk; two daughters deceased; and Denison Worthington, the latter the third child.   He was reared at Murfreesborough, and his education was obtained in North Carolina and Maryland.   In 1862 he joined the Eighth North Carolina regiment as a non-commissioned officer, and in 1863 was promoted and assigned to the cammand of scouts on the peninsula, and was taken prisoner in 1864.   He was confined in Fortress Monroe, and subsequently at Point Lookout.   Having obtained his release, he remained with the army until the close.   He then settled at Norfolk, Va., where he read law and was admitted to the bar in 1869.

Subsequently Mr. Worthington removed to North Carolina, locating in Hertford county, where he entered upon the practice of his chosen profession.   In 1880 he was elected judge of the criminal court of Martin county, and in 1881 was elected to the house of representatives of North Carolina, in which body he was chairman of the joint committee for the appointment of magistrates for the state, and in 1883 was again elected from Martin county, and was chosen speaker *pro tem.* of the house, and was also chairman of the committee on rules, and chairman of the joint committee appointed to re-district the state, and was chairman of the committee on military, and also a member of the committee on the judiciary. In May, 1885, he was appointed, by the governor, solicitor of the Third judicial district, and continued in that office until January 1, 1891. Mr. Worthington is a member of the Masonic order, the Knights of Honor, and is a communicant of the Missionary Baptist church. His marriage to Miss Julia Wheeler, daughter of Col. S. J. Wheeler, of Murfreesboro, N.C., was solemnized in November, 1871, and has been blessed by the birth of two children, viz.: Bessie and Samuel Wheeler. Mr. Worthington removed to Rocky Mount, Nash county, in 1891, and is now engaged in the practice of law at that place. He has won an enviable reputation as a jurist, and is recognized as a man of superior mind and great abilities. His public career has never been stained by any dishonorable act, and in his whole life he is regarded as a man of unswerving integrity, and upright, Christian character.

HON. WHARTON J. GREEN

is socially and politically one of North Carolina's most distinguished citizens, as well as a leading industrial factor in the business community. He is the son of Gen. Thomas J. Green, of Mexican fame, was born in Florida, and possesses many of those noble traits of character which were illustrated in the statesmanship and patriotism of his father. Col. Green received a liberal and very thorough education at Georgetown college, the University of Virginia and at West Point. He studied law at Cumberland university, and, on admission to the bar, became the junior partner of the Hon. R. J. Walker, in Washington. When the war broke out he at once joined the Warren guards, of the Twelfth North Carolina regiment, as a private, but was soon promoted to the rank of lieutenant-colonel, commanding the Second North Carolina battalion. He was wounded at Washington, N. C., by a shell; was captured on Roanoke Island, but later was exchanged, and at Gettysburg was again wounded and captured. When peace was declared, Col. Green settled down to a plantation life near Warrenton, N. C., which gave him ample time for reading, a recreation to which he has devoted himself with great assiduity, and he enjoys the enviable reputation of being one of the best informed men of our day. As a statesman, perhaps there is no man in the United States congress that better represents his constituency, and certainly none who is thought more of by the people of his district. He was a delegate to the democratic national conventions in 1868 and 1876, and in the former year was presidential elector. In 1882 Col. Green was elected representative from the Third congressional district of North Carolina, after a close contest, and in 1884 was re-elected by over 4,600 majority. He has shown himself fully worthy the confidence reposed in him by the intelligent people of his district. He has delivered many weighty and well conceived speeches before the house, treating some very important questions in a manner showing he was a thorough master of his subject.

Col. Green is generous in thought, liberal in word and prompt in action. He combines with an easy adaptability to circumstances, a pleasing presence by which he ingratiates himself into the good will of those who have the privilege of an acquaintance with him. He has devoted much attention to the culture of the grape, and upon that subject and its kindred, wine-making, he is an authority. He is the owner of the Tokay vineyard, which was originally planted in 1840. He bought the property in 1879, since which time it has been enlarged and improved. New varieties of grapes have been added, and the owner has spared neither money nor pains in procuring the best known facilities for grape culture and wine manufacture, and to place his products on the market. As a consequence the Tokay wines have taken their place among the standard brands in America, and are sold in every state in the Union except California. In the exhibition of fruits, Col. Green has taken many gold medals as testimonials of the excellence of his products. Tokay is situated three and one-half miles from Fayetteville, and the vineyard is said to be the largest single vineyard this side of the Rocky Mountains, and all visitors have pronounced it one of the most lovely spots on the continent. It is situated on an undulating table land, on Cape Fear river; the eye takes in a semi-circular horizon of twenty odd miles in radius. The vines cover over 100 acres, and the grapes are of some thirty or forty varieties. The vineyard produces annually from 20,000 to 30,000 gallons of wine. The stock on hand is generally 40,000 gallons ready for shipment, and the proprietor owns a storage capacity of 100,000 gallons.

JAMES L. WEBB,

one of the leading attorneys of Shelby, was born November 12, 1853, at Webb's Ford, Rutherford county, N. C. He is the eldest son of Rev. G. M. and Priscilla J. Webb. His grandfather, James Webb, after whom he was named, was one of the pioneer ministers of North Carolina, and during his life time held many positions of honor and trust. Rev. G. M. Webb is still living and has been engaged in preaching the gospel for the past twenty-five years, as it is understood by the Baptist denomination. The subject of this sketch received his primary education in the common schools of the county, and at the age of fourteen years entered Shelby academy. Here he remained three or four years and then entered Wake Forest college. At this institution he remained for two years and a half, when at the urgent solicitation of Hon. Plato Durham, who was at that time publishing *The Shelby Banner*, and was also making the race for congress, he left college and associated himself with Mr. Durham in the management of this paper. He was engaged as editor for some six months and then formed a copartnership with W. C. Durham, and they purchased an entire new outfit and conducted *The Banner* for about two years. Mr. Webb then purchased the interest of his partner and continued the business alone for about eighteen months, at which time he sold out and entered the law office of Hon. Plato Durham, where he remained one year. He then entered the law school of Chief-Justice Pearson, and in June, 1877, was examined before the supreme court at Raleigh, and licensed to practice at the bar. Returning to Shelby, Mr. Webb began the practice of his profession, and in a year's time formed a partnership with Capt. J. W. Gidney. This connection has subsisted ever since, with the exception of a short time during which Mr. Webb was engaged in the government service. This firm acted as the attorneys for Cleveland county for a period of ten years. Their practice extends to the neighboring counties and before the federal courts.

In 1880, Mr. Webb was elected mayor of the city, administering that office for one term with great satisfaction to his constituents, and he has also held the office of alderman for several terms. In 1883 he received the unanimous nomination of the democratic party of the Thirty-eighth senatorial district, composed of the counties of Gaston and Cleveland, to make the race for senator. His opponent was J. H. McBrayer, Esq., but Mr. Webb was elected by an overwhelming majority. He was again nominated by his party in 1887 and elected by a large majority. During this session of the legislature, Mr. Webb frequently acted as president of the senate and ruled with ability and impartiality. Mr. Webb has been actively engaged in politics and in the presidential campaign of 1880, made an extensive canvass of the state. He is chairman of the Cleveland county democratic executive committee, and has held that office for several years. During the Cleveland administration he was appointed postoffice inspector, with headquarters at Lynchburg, Va., but owing to illness in his family, he was obliged to resign his position some months after his appointment. In 1889, Mr. Webb was prominently mentioned as a candidate for lieutenant-governor of the state, but he would not allow his name to go before the convention. He was also offered the solicitorship of his district in 1890. Though not a candidate before the last congressional convention, Mr. Webb received the vote of two counties, and he is named as a candidate in the convention of 1892. He is a Royal Arch Mason and a member of the Baptist church. In all church work he is active and open-handed, ready to contribute liberally of his means and energy for religious culture and improvement, and for the charities of the church. Mr. Webb was married in 1878, to Miss K. L. Andrews, of Shelby, the daughter of Dr. W. P. Andrews. Two daughters and a son have been born into their pleasant home.

JOHN ALSTON ANTHONY,

one of the prominent attorneys and educators of Cleveland county, N. C., was born in York county, S. C., October 23, 1854. He is the second son of Stanhope H. and Margaret Anthony, and moved with his parents to Cleveland county in 1868. He received the rudiments of his education in the public and private schools of his native county, and afterward attended the Kings Mountain high school, in Cleveland county, N. C. He then entered college at Chapel Hill and attended that institution during the sessions of 1881–82. After leaving college he accepted the principalship of the Grover high school, in Cleveland county, and so successful and satisfactory were his services in that position that he was retained for five consecutive years. In 1886 Mr. Anthony was elected superintendent of public schools and is yet filling that responsible and laborious position. During the years 1887 and 1888 he read law with Col. George N. Folk, and in September, 1888, procured license from the supreme court of the state to practice his profession. Since that time he has prosecuted an extensive and successful law practice from his office in Shelby, N. C. Though holding a place in the front rank of his profession, Mr. Anthony has not abandoned his law studies, but keeps himself well posted in the current decisions of the courts, and is a thorough student in elementary law as well as in practice. While he maintains a high standing at the bar, the fine condition of the schools of the county demonstrates the excellence of his admirable superintendence and management. No better test of his efficiency is needed than is shown by the advanced standing, as well in methods as in scholarship, of the schools which come under his superintending care.

Mr. Anthony's paternal grandfather was Jacob Anthony, and his paternal grandmother was Elizabeth Bean, both natives of North Carolina. His maternal grandfather was John Graham, whose father was Maj. Arthur Graham, a major in the Revolutionary war; he came from Ireland to this country about the year 1760. The maternal grandmother of Mr. Anthony was Mary Carruth, and her father was Col. John Carruth, who held the rank of colonel in the Revolutionary war, and he also came from Ireland about the year 1760. October 15, 1889, Mr. Anthony was married to Miss Olive, daughter of Dr. O. P. Gardner, of Shelby, N. C. Mr. Anthony's tastes have not led him into the arena of politics. He prefers pre-eminence in his profession before partisan advancement, and to contribute to the beneficent results to be derived from a superior common school system. In his religious views he is broad and liberal and is a conscientious member of the Methodist Episcopal church.

ALEXANDER MARTIN.

Alexander Martin, senator, was born in New Jersey, about the year 1740. He graduated from Princeton college in 1756, studied law and was admitted to practice. He removed to Virginia, where he remained for a short time, and then, in 1772, took up his residence in Guilford county, N. C., where he was elected a member of the colonial assembly. He was also a member of the first provincial congress, which met at Newbern, in 1774, and was chosen to the same body in 1775. In 1776 he was appointed colonel of the Second North Carolina regiment of volunteers in the Continental service. He joined Gen. Washington's forces and he was engaged, with his regiment, in the battles of Brandywine and Germantown. At the close of the latter battle he was tried by a court-martial for unsoldierly conduct and dismissed from the service. But on his return home, he and others, discharged with him, made themselves very useful in quelling disturbances and punishing the crimes of the tories who had engaged in a course of robberies and murders of the defenseless patriots.

In 1779 to 1782 Col. Martin held a seat in the state senate, and afterward was several times re-elected. During a large part of the time of his senatorship he was the presiding officer. By virtue of that office, he was *ex-officio* governor of the state during the time Gov. Burke was held prisoner by the tories. In 1782 he was elected governor, and was again elected in 1789. He was a member of the convention that framed the Federal constitution. In 1793 he was elected United States senator and served for the full term of six years. In 1793, Princeton college conferred upon him the degree of doctor of laws. As trustee of North Carolina university, he rendered that institution great service, and did much to popularize education throughout the state. In his executive messages, while governor, he recommended a liberal support to the university by state appropriations. He had a taste for literature, imbibed during his collegiate course at Princeton, but was neither a voluminous nor a distinguished writer, and he will be chiefly known to posterity for the high official position he was called by his fellow citizens to occupy. He died at Danbury, in 1807.

DAVID STONE

was born in Hope, Bertie county, N. C., February 17, 1770. In his youth he was schooled by the best teachers to be found in his vicinity, and he well repaid the labor of instruction, by his diligence and aptness for study. When fitted at the academy, he entered Princeton college, from which he graduated with highest honors in 1788. He took up a law course, under the instruction of Gen. William R. Davie, one of the foremost attorneys of his time, and with his quick mind, and naturally studious habits, made rapid proficiency. Mr. Stone came from the teachings of his law preceptor, solidly equipped for a brilliant and successful practice of his profession. This thorough training, under one of the brightest legal lights of his time, added to his superior general education, gave him a prestige which he did not fail to utilize. His character as a private citizen was such as to inspire the confidence of his clients; his abilities as a lawyer were of the first order; he was gentlemanly and urbane in his manners, unselfish and considerate of the rights of all men; it was no wonder that he took a high rank in his profession.

In 1796 when Mr. Stone had only attained his twenty-sixth year, he was called to the bench of the superior courts of law and equity by the voice of the legislature. He had previously held a seat in the house of commons, and had there added largely to his popularity by his solid attainments and his gentlemanly bearing. His conduct upon the bench, where he displayed qualities as a jurist of the highest order raised him still higher in the estimation of his fellow citizens. In 1799 he was elected as a representative in congress, which position he held for two years, and was then elected a United States senator. He had nearly completed his term of six years when, in 1807, he resigned to again take the judgeship of the superior court of his state. The next year he was elected governor, and in that high office exhibited the same exalted qualities which had distinguished him in the other departments of the government. In 1811 Mr. Stone's presence was again required in the state legislature. It was a crisis in the history of that body which called for the best statesmanship, when questions affecting the future political and material interests of the state were to be decided. Gov. Stone's long official experience in all of the departments of the state government, and in the legislative department of the general government, eminently fitted him to take part and lead off in the legislative proceedings in such a juncture.

Though he did not accomplish the results he had undertaken, on account of a strong opposition, yet, that he still retained the confidence and esteem of his fellow members, was demonstrated by the fact that they again elected him to the United States senate, for the full term of six years. This was at the beginning of the war of 1812, against Great Britain, and the voice of North Carolina was almost unanimous for the vigorous prosecution of that war. President Madison needed to have his hands strengthened by wise counsel. It was believed that Gov. Stone was the man for such a purpose. It turned out, however, that Gov. Stone differed from the legislature, and with his colleague in the senate, on some grave questions. He voted against the embargo act, which had passed the house, and was defeated in the senate by two majority. For this the legislature passed a resolution of censure, and Gov. Stone resigned, and this was the close of his brilliant official career. He died in 1818, too prematurely in years, but ripe in conspicuous and useful service to his state.

THEODORUS H. COBB

was born August 20, 1854, at Lincolnton, N. C., and is now residing in Asheville where he practices law with great effectiveness and success. His father was Bartlett Yancey Cobb, and his mother's maiden name was Barbara Milinda Henderson. Both parents were natives of North Carolina, and both were of Scotch-Irish extraction. Bartlett Y. Cobb enlisted in the Confederate army early in the beginning of the war, and gave his life to the cause, dying in the service June 17, 1862. In the fall of the next year the widowed mother removed to Lincolnton, the home of her parents. Theodorus H. Cobb, during the year 1872, engaged in school teaching in the neighboring county

Gaston, having been well trained for such occupation in the schools of Lincoln and Caswell counties. He was acting register of deeds for Lincoln county in 1873-4. He studied law, first under John D. Shaw, of Lincoln county, then, during 1875, at the law school of Hon. R. M. Pearson, at Richmond Hill, Yadkin county. In January, 1876, he was admitted to the bar and immediately began the practice of his profession in company with John D. Shaw, his former preceptor. Their field of practice was Lincoln and adjoining counties, and the partnership continued until 1879, when Mr. Shaw removed to Richmond county. Mr. Cobb then practiced alone until 1881, when he entered into partnership with Judge D. Schenck, the firm continuing for about fifteen months, when Mr. Schenck removed to Greensboro. Mr. Cobb, again left alone, practiced till 1886, when he removed to Asheville where he opened an office and practiced alone until 1887, at which time he went into partnership with J. G. Merrimon, and this connection still exists. The Carolina Central railroad company has retained Mr. Cobb for general counsel for several years, and he still holds that position; he is also city attorney for Asheville, and has been since May, 1889, having been re-elected in May, 1891. His legal attainments are of a high order, and he is a wise counselor and a most effective advocate at the bar. He is a gentleman of refined culture, of courteous manners and a genial temperament, and is a general favorite in society circles. His law practice is continually increasing and there is a propitious future before him. In December, 1879, Mr. Cobb was married to Miss Ellen V., daughter of V. O., and Jane D. Johnson, of Charlotte. Their family circle has been broadened and brightened by the advent of three children: Ellen B., Bartlett J., and Vivian J.

HON. WILLIAM HENRY MALONE,

a prominent lawyer and leading author, of Asheville, N. C., was born in Wythe county, Va., July 24, 1832. He is the son of Theophilus Malone, a Virginian, and a farmer by occupation, who removed to Tennessee prior to the Civil war and died there about 1878. The maiden name of his mother was Martha Holden, a native of Wake county, N. C., who survived her husband only about one year. She was a sister of Benjamin Holden and Richard Holden, wealthy planters, the former of whom died in Wake county in early manhood. The latter removed to a point near Huntsville, Ala., where he accumulated a large estate, having, before the Civil war, 300 slaves and property altogether worth more than a million dollars. His descendants now reside in Huntsville, Ala. Hon. William H. Malone accompanied his parents to Tennessee when a small child, and he was reared to manhood on a farm. He received a thorough early education, and between the ages of eighteen and twenty-two taught school as a temporary pursuit. While thus employed he devoted his leisure time to the study of law, and at the close of his last term of school, entered the law office of Montgomery Thornburg, of New-market, Tenn. He was admitted to the bar in 1854, and at once began the practice of his profession. He devoted himself to his law practice in eastern Tennessee until 1862, being the partner during a portion of the time of Hon. John Baxter, late judge of the United States circuit court. In 1860 he was appointed by Gov. Harris, of Tennessee, attorney-general of the Second judicial district of Tennessee, which he held until the authority passed under Federal control. In 1861 Mr. Malone was elected a delegate to the convention in Tennessee, which was to consider the advisability of seceding from the union. In 1860 he was a Douglas elector in the Knoxville, Tenn., district; he was a democrat but opposed to secession.

In 1862 Mr. Malone entered the service of the Confederate government, and after performing some military work, he was assigned to duty in the manufacture of salt at the Virginia salt works for the state of Tennessee, under the supervision of the governor of that state, and he continued in that capacity until the close of the war. While thus employed his family resided in Knoxville. In 1863, Mr. Malone was arrested by some Federal raiders and was taken to their headquarters at Knoxville. He was required to give a large bond to report to the provost-marshal thirty days later, at the end of which time he and his family were banished by the Federal authority and compelled to remove to a point within Confederate control. In view of the serious trouble growing out of the war in Tennessee, he, in 1865, removed to Caldwell county, N. C., where he soon after resumed the practice of law. In 1868 Mr. Malone was elected to the lower branch of the legislature, from Caldwell county, and served two years. He took a very active part in the discussion of all important matters which came before that legislative body and was a leading member of the judiciary committee. He was one of the few members of that legislature who voted against the adoption of the fifteenth amendment to the constitution of the United States. He opposed it by a strong speech, which made a perceptible impression upon the assembly. It was during this same session that the Ku Klux excitement reached its greatest height and a measure known as the Shoffner bill, which authorized the governor of the state to declare certain counties in a state of insurrection, became a law. Mr. Malone strongly opposed the passage of this bill and in a speech he predicted the disastrous state of affairs which its passage subsequently brought about and denounced it as destructive of the civil liberties of the people. It was the enforcement of this law that led to the subsequent impeachment of the governor, W. W. Holden. While the impeachment trial was in progress, the late Chief-Justice W. N. H. Smith, of North Carolina, then one of his counsel, read the speech of Mr. Malone referred to above as the first exposition of the infamous character of the bill.

Mr. Malone was one of the framers of the first democratic platform of North Carolina, after the close of the war, at a time when the different parties were in a state of chaos. This was in 1868; the state was then under republican rule, the legislature being made up largely of carpet-baggers and negroes. At the close of his legislative term, Mr. Malone retired from politics, declining to be a candidate for re-election. He shortly afterward removed to Asheville, in which place he has since been a leading citizen and a prominent member of the bar. In 1886 he was an independent candidate for congress, making his fight on the following issues: He advocated the free coinage of silver and opposed the contraction of the currency and national banks. He also advocated a protective tariff and opposed the evils of the caucus system in vogue in the national house of representatives. Though he was defeated by the regular democratic nominee, Thomas D. Johnston, he received a very flattering vote, and carried his home county by a handsome majority. Mr. Malone has avoided politics for the most part to devote his attention to his profession, in which he has won a high place, having a wide and well established reputation as a successful and able advocate in both the civil and criminal branches of the law. Throughout a long professional career, he has maintained a most honorable standing, and no blot or act of impropriety can be found upon his record. He is widely known as a lawyer who gives close and careful attention to every case entrusted to his care, and as an attorney who is conscientious in the discharge of his duties.

Mr. Malone has not only reached a high place in the legal circles as a successful practitioner, but he has also made for himself a lasting name as the author of legal works. He published a work entitled, "A Treatise on Real Property Trials" and another called "Criminal Briefs," the former of which was issued in 1883 and the latter in 1886. Both have had extensive circulation, and the supreme court of North Carolina has recently paid the former work a very high tribute, and it is frequently quoted from by that august body and also by the courts of the different states. In politics Mr. Malone is thoroughly independent, and is an ardent protectionist and a warm admirer of James G. Blaine, a very strong resemblance to which distinguished statesman he bears. This latter is so great that it is a very common thing for him to be reminded of it. Mr. Malone is a Master Mason, and is the local attorney for the Richmond & Danville railroad. He is also attorney for the Cranberry Iron & Coal company, the Roan Mountain Steel & Iron company, besides several land corporations. Mr. Malone has been twice married. His first wife was Elizabeth, daughter of Col. Warham Easley, of Grainger county, Tenn., whom he married in 1852. She died in 1864, leaving three sons, two of whom are deceased, and one daughter. In 1866 he married Mrs. Mary E. Murray, of Asheville, a sister of Col. John S. McElroy, of that city.

HON. WILLIAM W. JONES,

a prominent lawyer of Asheville, N. C., was born in Granville county, N. C., July 9, 1841. He is the son of Col. Protheus E. A. Jones, a native also of Granville county born in 1812, and a farmer by occupation who served as a colonel of the state militia. He died in 1871. He was the son of William Jones, a native of Mecklenberg county, Va., and a farmer by pursuit who accompanied his father from Virginia to North Carolina, in the latter part of the eighteenth century. Paternally, the genealogy of the subject of this sketch is of Welsh extraction, his great-grandfather being one of three brothers who came to America from Wales. The mother of Hon. William W. Jones was Mary F. Hawkins, a native of Franklin county, N. C., and the daughter of Hon. John D. Hawkins, also a native of Franklin county, and a prominent citizen who represented his district in both branches of the state legislature. He was a lawyer by profession and one of the influential members of the bar. He was the son of Col. Philemon B. Hawkins, a native of North Carolina and an agriculturist. Mr. Hawkins, Sr., was a captain in the Continental army during the Revolutionary war. He had two brothers in the colonial army, one being Col. Benjamin Hawkins, a commissioned colonel under Washington and the other being William Hawkins who subsequently served as governor of North Carolina. The maternal ancestry dates back to the time of Sir William Hawkins of the British navy. The maternal grandmother of Mr. Jones was a Scotch lady. His mother died in 1872. Hon. William W. Jones was reared to the age of seventeen years in Henderson, Granville county. In 1857 he entered the North Carolina university from which he graduated in 1862. Immediately after completing his collegiate course, he entered the Confederate service in Company G, Third North Carolina regiment commanded by Col. Baker who was succeeded by Col. Moore. Mr. Jones served in Gen. Barringer's brigade of cavalry and was with the command as a private until the close of the war. He served his country patriotically for three years.

Meanwhile, during his collegiate course, Mr. Jones having determined to fit himself for the legal profession, was a member of the law class, and in 1866, resumed the study of law under Judge William H. Battle, one of the supreme judges of North Carolina. He was admitted to the bar in 1867, and in 1868, was admitted to practice in the superior court of the state and the United States supreme court. He at once located at Henderson, N. C., and began the practice of the law. In 1869 he located in Raleigh, and some years later, in 1885, he became a resident of Asheville, the climate there being more congenial to his health. Mr. Jones is one of the ablest and most prominent lawyers in the state. He is a democrat, but has persistently eschewed political preferment throughout his whole career, with the exception of one term in the senate from 1883 till 1885. He has often been solicited to accept other positions of honor and profit. The firm of Jones & Shuford are the attorneys for the National bank at Asheville. The marriage of Mr. Jones occurred in 1871, at which time Miss Bettie E., the daughter of Dr. Charles E. Johnson, a prominent physician of North Carolina, became his wife. They have five children living, one son and four daughters.

Your friend, truly,
Melvin E Carter

CAPT. MELVIN EDMUNDSON CARTER.

Capt. Melvin E. Carter is descended from the Virginia family of the same name; his ancestors came to North Carolina at the close of the Revolutionary war, in which they had taken an honorable part. One of his great-grandfathers served under Washington, and was in twenty-six regular battles. Mr. Carter was born in what is now Madison county, on the 27th day of February, 1843. He was educated at Col. Stephen Lee's classical and mathematical school, near Asheville, and at the university, under Gov. Swain. He studied law under the late Judge Bailey, and was licensed to practice in the county courts in January, 1867, and in the supreme courts in 1869. He has continued actively in the practice of his profession, at Asheville since obtaining his license. Mr. Carter has always been a democrat in politics, but has never aspired to political honors. Under protest, he allowed his friends to elect him to the legislature on four different occasions. He was elected to the house of representatives in 1876, 1878, 1880 and 1888. He held the position of chairman of the committee on elections, chairman of the house branch of the committee on the sale of the western North Carolina railroad, and at his last session, was chairman of the committee on judiciary. It would be impossible in the short space allowed us, to mention in detail, the many important matters of legislation, with which the subject of this sketch was identified during his legislative career. A zealous friend of education, he always urged the most liberal appropriations for the education of both the white and colored children of the state. Mr. Carter always stood by the state's charitable institutions, voting for liberal allowances, to maintain the unfortunates of both races. He feels an especial pride in the part he bore, in the settlement of the state debt. But his friends have probably regarded his efforts in behalf of the completion of the Western North Carolina railroad, as the most important work of his official life.

Mr. Carter served as captain of Company A, of the Sixty-fourth North Carolina regiment in the late war. His regiment was captured at Cumberland Gap, in 1863, and remained in prison until the war closed. He, however, escaped with a few men when his command was captured, and, proceeding to Jonesboro, Tenn., after many days of dodging, stopped for a little rest in the court-house. During the first night, however, an Ohio regiment of infantry ran up on a train from Knoxville, and, reaching Jonesboro, a company was detached to surround and capture the small squad of sleepers in the court-house. Aroused too late to escape, the company of twenty soldiers had time, nevertheless, to fire a volley into the enemy, and in the confusion that followed, Mr. Carter and two of his men escaped. The Ohio regiment proceeded on its way in the direction of southwestern Virginia, and Mr. Carter and his men followed on foot. Reaching a favorable spot they removed a rail, so that the return train would miss the track. Sure enough, when the train was speeding along, the

B—12

next day, on its return trip, the engine was thrown from the track, and, to cut an interesting story short, the regiment was overtaken by the Confederate forces, and captured at Limestone, Tenn., a few miles below Jonesboro. Mr. Carter received the personal thanks of the commanding general for the valuable service he had rendered. Mr. Carter raised another company, and, while in service under Gen. John C. Breckinridge in Tennessee, was captured and sent north by way of Nashville, Louisville and Johnson's Island. While in Jersey City, awaiting a train to carry him, with other prisoners, to Fort Delaware, he again escaped, and, finding his way to Washington, gathered valuable information for his cause, which he succeeded in carrying through Grant's lines to Richmond, receiving the thanks of Gen. Breckinridge, then serving as secretary of war. Mr. Carter was married in 1877, to Susie R. Rawls, of Union, S. C., and an interesting family of six children is the result.

HON. HEZEKIAH A. GUDGER,

a distinguished citizen of Asheville, N. C., and an eminent attorney and statesman, was born May 27, 1849, in Madison county, N. C. He is the son of Jackson J. and Sarah Emeline (Barnard) Gudger, both native North Carolinians. The father was a first class business man, active and energetic, yet careful and prudent. He devoted his attention largely to real estate, and was very successful in his operations. He held the offices of clerk of the superior court and chairman of the county court of Madison county for many years up to 1868. The subject of this sketch began his educational course at the Weaverville high school, which he attended for two years. He then entered upon the study of law at Asheville, under the guidance of Judge J. L. Bailey, and was admitted to the bar in January, 1871. Beginning the practice of his profession the same year, Mr. Gudger opened an office in his native county. His aptitude for public business was soon discovered, and, in 1872, he was elected to the popular branch of the state legislature as the representative of Madison county. The county was strongly republican up to that time, but Mr. Gudger's personal popularity carried him through upon the democratic ticket, and his legislative career justified the choice of the people. He was re-elected at the next trial by an increased majority, and in 1876, was chosen for a third term. He was not there in the interest of a party, but was the capable, efficient and watchful representative of the interests of the district which had entrusted him with those interests. Besides his legislative capacity, Mr. Gudger was well qualified to work in the educational field, and in February, 1877, was elected principal of the state institute for the deaf and dumb, located at Raleigh. His fitness for this position was illustrated by his retention in it for six years.

At the close of the term, in 1884, Mr. Gudger resumed the practice of his profession at Asheville, in partnership with H. B. Carter, Esq. But the state still had need of his services, and at the election in 1884, he was chosen to represent his district in the senate. Already thoroughly experienced in legislation, he made himself efficient in the upper branch not only by his championship of the material concerns of the state, but stood as the fast friend of the free school system, upon which through the education of the masses, the perpetuation of a free government must ever rest. The ideal republic can never be realized but by the education and social elevation of the constituent voter. In a representative government the masses must be intelligent to reach the desired results and these principles were uppermost in Mr. Gudger's political creed. With such sentiments it was fitting that he should be appointed a trustee of the state university, a preferment accorded him by the legislature and which he still holds. At the convention of the instructors for the blind, held in Janesville, Wis., in 1880, Mr. Gudger was a delegate, and so thoroughly identified was he in the general objects of the convention that he was unanimously chosen as its president, though he was the youngest member of that convention. This was the most flattering recognition of his fitness for such a trust and of his ability in the educational field. As an effective public speaker Mr. Gudger has demonstrated his ability in several political campaigns in which he has canvassed the state for the democratic ticket. He is a member of the Masonic fraternity and a Knights Templar, and was chosen deputy grand master of the state. In January, 1891, he was elected grand master of the Grand lodge of North Carolina. He is also a member in good standing of the I. O. O. F. Besides these secret associations, Mr. Gudger is and has for some time been a devoted member of the Methodist Episcopal church, south, and he has on two occasions represented the denomination as a delegate to its annual and general conferences. Mr. Gudger was married in August, 1876, to Miss Jennie H., daughter of B. J. and Sarah E. (Baird) Smith, of Asheville, and they have five children: Francis A., Ada L., Hiram A., Mary and Emma.

GEORGE A. SHUFORD.

Biography has wider and more useful service than in ministering to the vanity of its subject or the pride of its friends; something more noble even than the record of distinction in whatever field of work it has been achieved. Its true mission is to seize upon such points of character and career as may be presented for imitation, emulation or encouragement; and even the humblest of men in conscientious discharge of duty, faithful application of the means opportunity presents to their use, perseverance under opposition, fortitude under adversity, courage under trial, integrity under temptation, may illustrate more usefully and splendidly those characteristics of humanity which ennoble and adorn it, than those more dazzling and striking examples which mankind is more apt and ready to take up as its idols and exemplars. What is worth following, worth imitating, worth worshiping, is not universally found in that higher sphere of action to which ambition chiefly directs its aim. Without question the pages of history are adorned with names so indelibly inscribed with deeds of almost super-human achievement that they can never lose their hold, so long as history and society last and hold together upon human admiration and as spurs to human imitation. But rare are those characters which sustain the scrutiny of analysis, and emerge from it free from the taint of counterbalancing vices and infirmities. It is rather in the more modest walks of life, in that intermediate stage of action, where the actor is playing his part for the present, not like Napoleon, for the "eternity of time" and the admiration of posterity, but with reference to present good and contemporary influence, that the most useful and practical exemplars for the young, and the most encouraging examples for the struggling must be sought. In a few brief, strong words, the Latin poet presents the real ideal of the man who is to make the proper impress upon the present, without concerning himself with the thought of a remote temporal future: "*Justum ac tenacem propositi virum;*" a man just in his dealings with his fellow man, a man fixed in his principles and tenacious in adherence to them, a man so just that he cannot be dishonest, and so brave and sincere that he cannot be corrupt; and when to this lofty heathen ideal is superadded those graces that Christian doctrine so generally imparts, the daily walks of life will provide abundant illustration of useful and admirable character and career without seeking for such in the lofty and resplendent sphere of world renowned public fame and service.

In such daily walk we find the subject of this sketch, George A. Shuford, living illustration of what virtues and characteristics are needed for the perfection of an honorable and useful career, both in its private and public relation. He was born in the county of Buncombe, state of North Carolina, August 1, 1855. His parentage was such as to give assurance of the perpetuation in unbroken line of moral and mental features stamped upon the individuality of a long succession of generations. His father's family was that of German stock, now so firmly rooted in the middle and western portions of North Carolina, into which it was transplanted during the middle of the last century, after having flourished and greatly increased in Pennsylvania. The spirit of emigration seized upon the Pennsylvania colonists when their numbers compelled the occupation of ampler territory; and, governed by characteristic sagacity, the emigrants sought that fertile, beautiful, and then almost unoccupied region, extending parallel with the Blue Ridge through Virginia down into South Carolina, and including the rich valleys watered by the head streams of the many rivers which pursue their devious courses to the distant Atlantic. In this region, with German tenacity, they remained fixed, as if, in the language of the Indian finding the locality that filled all his hopes and wishes, they had said, "here we rest." For though in turn they have sent out their surplus and, with their population, invigorated other lands, the main body still remains where it first planted itself, unchanged in those characteristics of peacefulness, industry, thrift, integrity and fixity of purpose, which have always distinguished that branch of the human family.

The Shuford family were Alsatians, coming early in colonial history to Pennsylvania. From that state, members of it removed before the war of the Revolution, to the county of Lincoln, into that part now known as Catawba, N. C. The great-grandfather of the subject of this sketch was a member of a family of seven brothers, all of them noted for their strength and stature, all of them exceeding six feet in height. All were farmers, prosperous and independent. They were all intelligent, and their names were synonymous with integrity. The early record shows that they filled various places of honor and trust, the legacy of a good and honored name perpetuated to the present day throughout western North Carolina. The great-grandfather of George A. Shuford settled in Buncombe county, in that portion now erected into the county of Transylvania, soon after the close of the Revolutionary war, engaging in stock-raising; to which the character of the country offered peculiar inducements. He lived there useful and honored until his death at ? ripe old age. He had only one son, David Shuford, the grandfather of the subject of this sketch, who, inheriting the characteristics of his ancestors, was noted for his industry, generosity, hospitality and stern integrity. He was endowed with a strong natural intellect, a high sense of honor and justice, and a broad liberality for his fellow men. He was a patriarch and arbiter in the primitive community in which he lived, whose advice was often sought for and whose judgment in matters of controversy among his neighbors was usually final. He raised a large and honorable family of sons and daughters. George Shuford, the eldest son of David Shuford, was the father of the subject of this sketch. In his earlier years he engaged largely in the mechanic arts, in which he became skillful and successful; but his later years were given to the labors and pleasures of the farm, carefully avoiding the cares of public life, passing away in a good old age, leaving behind him the memory of a useful, honest and respected name. He was twice married. His first wife was Louisa M. Beachem, a native of Greenville, S. C. She was of an English family which had for several generations lived in South Carolina. By the first marriage there were five sons and one daughter. On the death of his first wife, Mr. Shuford married again, and the issue of the second marriage was one daughter.

George A. Shuford was the fourth son at the time previously mentioned. His early years, passed like those of most country boys, leave no especial mark for the note of the biographer. His first step in the march of life was into the Sand Hill academy in Buncombe county, near which his father then resided, and afterward he was placed at Davidson's River academy in the present county of Transylvania. His teacher there was Mr. A. D. Farmer, regarded as a well qualified, but somewhat eccentric pedagogue. He entered successively the academies at Brevard, under Dr. McNeil Turner, and the Franklin high school, under Mr. Daniel M. Jones, and attaching himself to that gentleman when he removed to Waynesville. He employed a portion of his time from 1874 to 1876 in teaching; he then entered Emory and Henry college, Virginia, and there completed a special course of study. During the fall of 1877 he taught school, and meanwhile pursued a course of study preparatory to engaging in the study of the law which he had chosen as his profession. Thus, after long years of patient preparation and looking forward, he took the decisive step toward the attainment of those honors, and it may be added, those emoluments which reward the pursuit of the law, of all professions the one most sure to bring into prominence the noblest character of the man, the real qualifications of the student; illustrating the one by illustrating the virtues of integrity and fidelity to responsibilities assumed, and confirming public confidence by the possession of those acquirements of legal learning and enlarged general information without the possession of which the lawyer is imperfectly equipped either for the attainment of honors or for professional reputation.

Mr. Shuford began the study of law in Waynesville, N. C., under the instructions of the Hon. J. C. L. Gudger and Mr. Garland S. Ferguson; the first to become subsequently an honored judge of the Twelfth judicial district; the other for eight years the able solicitor for the same district. He soon afterward entered the law school at Greensboro, N. C., conducted by the Hon. Robert P. Dick, judge of the United States district court, and the Hon. John H. Dillard, then associate-justice of the supreme court of North Carolina. A school under instructors of such eminence assured the solidity of the acquirements of its *eleves;* and, accordingly, after a highly satisfactory and honorable examination before the supreme court of North Carolina, Mr. Shuford was admitted in January, 1879, to practice in all the courts of the state, and at once entered upon the practice of his profession at Waynesville, alone at first, but soon after associating himself with Mr. Alden H. Howell, an experienced practitioner of that town. At the end of two years this partnership was dissolved, Mr. Shuford removing to Asheville, and entering into partnership with the Hon. Thomas D. Johnston, which association was continued until Mr. Johnston was elected to the national congress as a member of the house of representatives. After practicing alone for two years, Mr. Shuford entered into partnership with Mr. W. W. Jones, which connection still exists. A firm unsurpassed in Asheville for its hold upon public confidence, gained through the professional learning of its members, their lofty personal character, their interest in their clients, their inflexible regard to duty. In these gentlemen the profession of the law is illustrated with its traditional lustre and elevated to the dignity through which it should always exact popular reverence.

In 1884 Mr. Shuford was elected presiding justice of the inferior court of Buncombe county, the court was given limited criminal jurisdiction, not embracing capital offenses, yet the cognizance of the lower grades of crime gave ample field for the display of learning, and also for the exercise of firmness, impartiality, and also mercy when wise consideration for the public interest justified it. All these qualifications were so strongly and happily blended in the judicial character of Judge Shuford, that, during the term of the four years during which he served he daily added to the respect and confidence of the people while he inspired a wholesome fear in the minds of of offenders; and then returned to duties of his private pursuits crowned with the reward accorded to the good and faithful officer. With this exception Mr. Shuford has never aspired to office. He is a politician to the extent expected from every good citizen, a man alive to the public interests, feeling sensibly the need of entrusting their conduct to good and able men, jealous of the public liberties, sensitive to the public honor, zealously hostile to whomsoever or whatsoever may attempt to abridge the one or tarnish the other. To this extent he is a politician, and a trusted and watchful member of the democratic party, to which he belongs, and as testimony to his unflinching fidelity to his party principles, and the wisdom and value of his counsels, he has ably served as the chairman of the county democratic executive committe, and of the executive committee of the judicial district in which he resides. But he has steadily suppressed all aspirations for the political honors which, with his consent, would be so readily accorded to him. As a member of the state democratic convention of North Carolina of 1888, he served on the committee on platform and resolutions, and, as one of a sub-committee of two, he, with his associate, drafted the platform which was adopted by the convention, on which the democratic party waged its campaign, and under which a splendid victory was won for democracy. In private life he is of exceptionally amiable disposition, sprightly in conversation, intelligent, and read in the best literature of the day, a sincere and active Christian, a worthy member of the Methodist church. As a citizen he is public-spirited and liberal, and participates and often leads in those intelligent measures having as their object the improvement and advancement of the fine section of which he is a native. In his professional career he has already attained a name and eminence honorable to his character, and his efforts and achievements gained in a comparatively brief professional life. To few men does the pathway of the future open a fairer or more prosperous career.

W. R. DAVIE.

William Richardson Davie was born in Egremont, England, June 20, 1756. In his youth he was brought to this country by his father, Archibald Davie, in 1763, and was adopted by his maternal uncle, Rev. William Richardson. He began school at Charlotte, N. C., entered Princeton college and graduated from that institution in the fall of 1776. Before his graduation he had joined a party of students as volunteers in the northern army. The campaign closing early in the fall, he returned to college, where he graduated with highest honors. He then returned to North Carolina and began the study of law at Salisbury, at the same time aiding to raise a company of cavalry to join the American forces. He was commissioned lieutenant by Gov. Caswell, April 5, 1799. He was afterwards promoted to the command of the company, joined Pulaski's legion and soon took the rank of major. At the battle of Stono he was in command of the right wing of Lincoln's army, and was severely wounded during the fight. He was with Gen. Greene through the southern campaign, fought at the battle of Guilford Court House, Hoblark's Mill and at the evacuation of Camden.

Having served his country gallantly and made a most brilliant military record, Mr. Davie returned to his law studies and was admitted to the bar at Salisbury in September, 1779. His career as a lawyer was equally brilliant and successful with his accomplishments as a soldier, and he immediately placed himself in the foremost rank of his profession. His eloquence and effectiveness at the bar attracted the attention of the public and his services were in demand from every part of the state, his practice extending to all the courts. He was a member of the constitutional convention which met in Philadelphia in May, 1787, but was obliged to leave for his home before the deliberations of that body were completed, and for that reason did not sign the constitution. He was a delegate to the convention at Hillsboro, called to consider the Federal constitution, and was one of the most able advocates in favor of its adoption by the state. Between the years of 1785 and 1798, he was six times elected to the North Carolina house of commons. In the legislature he drew the act for the organization of the North Carolina university, and was foremost in providing for the erection of its buildings, establishing its professorships and arranging its curriculum of studies. Judge Murphey, one of his junior contemporaries, who was an attendant of the house of commons when Gen. Davie was advocating the claims of the university said of him: "I was present in the house of commons when Davie addressed the house for a loan of money for the university, and although thirty years have elapsed, I have a most vivid recollection of the greatness of his manner and the power of his eloquence. In the house of commons he had no rival. His eloquence was irresistible."

In the settlement of the boundary disputes between the Carolinas, Mr. Davie acted at three several times as commissioner on the part of North Carolina. He was appointed brigadier-general of the United States army in 1798, and was the author of a treatise on cavalry tactics. He had previously been appointed major-general of the North Carolina militia. In December, 1799, he was elected governor of the state, but before he had finished his full term, he was appointed by President Adams upon a special embassy to France, in company with Oliver Ellsworth and Chief-Justice William V. Murray. In 1802 he was appointed by President Jefferson an Indian commissioner to treat with the Tuscaroras. In 1803 he was a candidate for congress against Hon. Willis Alston by whom he was defeated. Shortly after this he retired to a farm on the Catawba river, in South Carolina where he spent the remainder of his days. He was offered a commission as major-general of the United States army, in 1813, but declined on account of increasing age, and impaired health. He died in Camden, S. C., November 8, 1820, leaving three sons and three daughters. The mother's maiden name was Sarah Jones, daughter of Allan Jones.

GABRIEL HOLMES

was born in Sampson county, N. C., in 1769. He was educated in the common branches at the public schools and studied the classics under the instruction of Rev. Dr. McCorkle, of Iredell county. He graduated from Harvard university and afterward studied law with Judge Taylor, chief-justice of the supreme court of North Carolina. When he was only twenty-four years of age he was elected to the state legislature where his services were such that he was repeatedly re-elected, holding the office for about twenty years. He then retired for a while to private life, but in 1821 the legislature of the state elected him governor of the state. In 1824 he was elected by his congressional district to a seat in the national house of representatives, and two years afterward was re-elected to the same office. He died September 26, 1829, before his last congressional term had expired, and a tablet in the congressional cemetery perpetuates the date of his decease, and the principal events of his life.   •

Mr. Holmes was not only a finished and profound scholar, but he was the possessor of personal characteristics which gained for him the highest respect and esteem of all with whom he was associated. He was affable in his deportment, kind and sympathetic in his disposition, and by his attainments and culture, was fitted to move in the highest circles of society, where he was ever welcome. His death was an irreparable loss to his family, and not less so to the state which had honored him with the highest office in its gift. He served the state faithfully, honestly and effectively, and shed lustre upon the official trusts which had been reposed in him.

COL. ALLEN TURNER DAVIDSON,

an old and honored citizen and retired lawyer of Asheville, N. C., was born in Haywood county, N. C., on Jonathan Creek, May 9, 1819. He was the son of William Mitchell Davidson, a native of Burke county, N. C., born in 1781, and a farmer by occupation, who died in May, 1846. The latter was a son of William Davidson, a Revolutionary soldier, and the cousin of Gen. William Davidson, who fell at the battle of Cowan's Ford during the struggle for independence. The father of William Davidson was John Davidson, and the father of Gen. William Davidson was George Davidson. John and George Davidson, brothers, came to America from Europe. The mother of the subject of this sketch was Betsy Vance, a native of Burke county, and the daughter of Capt David Vance, of Revolutionary fame. She was also the aunt of United States Senator Vance of this state. Her

birth occurred in 1787, and she died April 15, 1861. Capt. David
Vance was a native of Virginia and a farmer by occupation. The
Vance family are descended from the family of De Vaux, of Nor-
mandy, France. Col. Allen T. Davidson was reared on a farm in
Haywood county, N. C., and received an academic education. At the
age of twenty he found employment in a store owned by his father in
Waynesville. In 1842 he was united in marriage with Miss Elizabeth
A. Howell, an educated Christian lady who greatly assisted him in
his profession and life work. About the time of his marriage, or immediately after, Mr. Davidson took up the study of law, and while a
student in 1843 was appointed clerk and master in equity of Haywood
county. His legal preceptor was Michael Francis. He was admitted
to the bar January 1, 1845, retiring from the above mentioned office
in the spring of 1846. He removed to Murphy, Cherokee county,
where he at once actively entered upon the practive of law. There
he resided until 1863, devoting his whole attention to his professional
labors. He threw his whole soul into his work, and became one of
the leading lawyers of that section. During twelve years of his residence there, Mr. Davidson served as solicitor of Cherokee county.
In April, 1860, the Miners & Planters' bank was organized at Murphy,
and he was chosen president. In 1861 he was a member of the North
Carolina secession convention.

Meantime, in his youth, Col. Davidson had served as a member
of the state militia and was a commissioned colonel before he was
twenty-one years of age. The secession convention, above referred
to, after passing the ordinance of secession, chose him as one of the
North Carolina delegates to the provisional government at Richmond.
He served out the provisional term, and in 1862, was elected a member of the Confederate congress, the permanent government having
meanwhile been established. He served until the spring of 1864, and
in the fall of 1865, located in Macon county, N. C., at Franklin, and
in the spring of 1869 he moved to Asheville. In 1864-5 he served as
a member of the council of Gov. Vance, and in the same year acted as
agent of the commissionary department of the state, it being his duty
to distribute provisions to the widows and families of Confederate
soldiers in western North Carolina. After locating in Asheville, Col.
Davidson devoted his whole attention to his law practice until 1885,
when he retired. His active career covered a period of forty years,
during which he was one of North Carolina's most influential men.
As a lawyer, Col. Davidson stood at the head of his profession in
western North Carolina. Though a very successful lawyer in general, he excelled as a criminal lawyer. He defended fifty-seven cases
for murder and in not a single case was his client executed. He is
president of the Asheville bar association and politically is a democrat. Col. Davidson is a member of the Methodist Episcopal church,
south, and a Royal Arch Mason. He is a stockholder in the First
National bank, of Beaumont, Tex., and also of the North Georgia
railroad. Three sons and three daughters are the living children of
Col. Davidson, one of the former, Hon. T. F. Davidson, being the

present attorney-general of North Carolina. Wilbur S. Davidson is cashier of the National bank, of Beamont, Tex. Robert Vance Davidson is a lawyer in Galveston, Tex.

JOHN W. ELLIS.

John Willis Ellis was a native of Rowan county, N. C.; born November 25, 1820. He was the son of Anderson Ellis. His early education was under private tutors, and he graduated from the North Carolina university in 1841. He studied law in the office of Judge Pearson, afterwards chief-justice of the state, and was admitted to the bar in 1842. He began practice in Salisbury, where he very soon gained a large clientage and carried on a prosperous business. In 1844 he was chosen a member of the house of representatives, to represent Rowan county. His politics were not in accordance with a majority of his constituents, but they elected him, nevertheless, from higher considerations than those of partisanship, and in his course in the legislature, he fully justified the wisdom of their choice, evidenced by several re-elections. He was a true, candid and philanthropic legislator, dealing what he conceived to be justice to all parties. He directed his attention largely, while a member, to the internal improvement of the state, being the friend of the railroad projects and of state educational and charitable institutions.

In 1848 Mr. Ellis was elected one of the judges of the North Carolina superior court, being among the youngest men ever elevated to the bench, yet he proved to be one of the best. His decisions generally met the public approbation, as well as that of the higher courts. He was patient, dignified and impartial in his rulings. He was elected governor of the state in 1858, by an overwhelming majority, over one of the most popular opponents his party could select. He was re-elected by a large majority on the eve of the opening of the Civil war. When that catastrophe happened he was called upon by President Lincoln to furnish troops for the Union cause, which he promptly refused, and on behalf of the state government he took possession of Fort Macon, the public works at Wilmington, and the arsenal at Fayetteville. On the 20th of April, 1861, he ordered the seizure of the United States mint at Charlotte. When the ordinance of secession was under discussion, Gov. Ellis, was one of its most ardent and active supporters. But the cares of state proved too much for his already impaired constitution, and he died in July, 1861, at White Sulphur Springs, whither he had gone in the hope of recuperation. His death at this juncture was a severe loss to the state, and a mournful event to a large circle of personal friends and admirers.

HUTCHINS G. BURTON

was a native of Granville county, N. C. He studied law and settled in Charlotte, Mecklenburg county. In 1810 he was elected to the state legislature and by that body was appointed attorney-general of the state. Afterward he removed to Halifax county, and in 1817 was chosen to represent that county in the state legislature, serving two years. In 1819 he was elected to congress from the Halifax district and was re-elected in 1821. He was elected governor of the state in 1824. In 1826 he was nominated by President John Quincy Adams, as governor of the territory of Arkansas. but the senate failed to confirm the nomination. He married Sally, daughter of Willie and Mary Montford Jones, and granddaughter of Robin Jones. He died in Iredell county, in 1836. Gov. Burton was a man of genial and social disposition, of polite manners and of correct deportment. He was a universal favorite in society, to which he imparted grace and ornament.

HON. CLEMENT DOWD

was born in Moore county, N. C., August 27, 1832. His father was Willis D. Dowd, and the maiden name of his mother, Ann Maria Gaines. They were both natives of South Carolina, the father of Irish and the mother of Scotch descent. Willis D. Dowd was a farmer by occupation, and at the early age of twenty-one was chosen a member of the lower branch of the state legislature. Thereafter he served several times in both branches. He was the son of Cornelius Dowd, also a farmer and a native of Moore county. For twenty-five years he was clerk of the county court in his native county. His father was Couner Dowd, who came from Ireland at an early day and settled in Moore county, where he lived and died, spending his days in the farming industry. Clement Dowd was reared upon the homestead farm, where he learned the lessons of industry and perseverance. Here he worked till seventeen years of age, in the meantime attending the old field schools and obtaining a fair English education. He then began teaching in the public schools of his county. This was the stepping stone to higher and more important stations in life, and by means of the income secured from teaching, Mr. Dowd was enabled to incur the further expense of attending the academies in his neighborhood. By these helps in 1852 he gained admission to the university from which he was graduated in 1856. For two years thereafter he taught the Carthage academy, in which he had formerly been a student. During the two years he studied law, and in January, 1859, was admitted to the bar. The same year he began practice at Carthage. In 1857 Mr. Dowd was married to Miss Lydia Bruce, of Moore county, and they have had three sons and four daughters. In April, 1861, he entered the Confederate army, enlisting in Company H, of the Twenty-sixth North Carolina state troops. This company had been raised by him and others in his county, and he was made first lieutenant. After the battle of Newbern he was promoted to the captaincy of the company, for in this battle the captain had been slain. He was subsequently made first major, but in 1862, by reason of failing health, he was relieved and returned to his home.

In the fall of 1866, Major Dowd came to Charlotte and forming a copartnership in law with Hon. Z. B. Vance, began again the practice of his profession, the partnership continuing for six years. Mr. Dowd was elected mayor of Charlotte and re-elected, holding the office till 1871, when he was elected president of the Merchants & Farmers' National bank, of Charlotte. This position he held until 1874, when he was elected president of the Commercial National bank, of Charlotte, and remained there until 1881. In the fall of 1880 he was elected a member of congress from the Sixth district, by the democratic party, receiving 16,401 votes against 12,366 for W. B. Myers, republican. He was re-elected in 1882 receiving a vote of 15,549. In the Forty-eighth session of congress, Major Dowd was one of the coinage committee, and was chosen to draft a bill for recoining the "trade dollar" and converting it into the standard or "Bland" dollar, providing also for the removal of the government tax on State bank circulation which tax as it then provided granted and now grants a monopoly to National banks which alone can issue bank notes. The bill was not enacted into a law. In 1885 he was appointed by President Cleveland, internal revenue collector for the Sixth district, and held the office until 1887 when it was discontinued. The office came to him unsolicited and he accepted it with reluctance. He was appointed in April, 1888, receiver of the State National bank at Raleigh, which trust he accepted, and efficiently executed. In his calling Major Dowd has achieved a grand success and amassed a handsome fortune, not through speculation but as the legitimate reward of an intelligent and assiduous devotion to his profession added to office salaries unsought by him. But though wealthy, he is not the man to hoard his resources. He is progressive and has invested his means largely in such enterprises as promote the welfare and prosperity of the community at large. Though not a member of any church organization he is a generous patron of religious as well as educational organizations in the promotion of each of which he does not spare his fortune or his personal efforts. He is a trustee of Trinity college of North Carolina, and a member of the Charlotte chamber of commerce. In every aspect of his character, he is broad, liberal, enlightened and closely in touch with the higher and better development of society.

HON. LEE S. OVERMAN,

a leading lawyer and prominent politician residing in Salisbury, N. C., was born in that city January 3, 1854. His father, William Overman, now deceased, was a native of Pasquotank county, N. C. He was a farmer and merchant and came to Salisbury from the eastern part of the state about the year 1838. He resided in Salisbury for half a century, quietly devoted to his life business and died at the mature age of seventy-eight years, enjoying the individual respect of all who knew him. He married Miss Mary E. Slater, a native of Rowan county, and her ancestors were among the distinguished individuals of North Carolina. Her maternal great-grandfather was Maj. James Smith, who was a noted character in the Revolutionary war. He was taken prisoner after the battle of Kings Mountain, and was carried to Charleston, where, with other prisoners, he died with small-pox. William and Mary Overman, the parents of the subject of this sketch, had five sons and one daughter. Lee S. Overman was reared in Salisbury and here received his primary schooling. He was graduated with first honors from North Carolina Trinity college in 1874. Two years later that college conferred upon him the Master's degree. For about two years after his graduation, Mr. Overman taught school, in the meantime directing his attention to the study of law. In 1876 he further pursued the study under the instruction of J. M. McCorkle, Esq., of Salisbury. He finally completed his course under R. H. Battle, of Raleigh, was examined before the supreme court of North Carolina, and duly admitted to the bar in January, 1878. In 1876 he took an active part as a democrat in the political campaign of that year, and when Hon. Z. B. Vance was elected governor in 1877, Mr. Overman was appointed private secretary, remaining as such until that distinguished gentleman was elected United States senator. On the election of Gov. Jarvis, the successor of Gov. Vance, Mr. Overman was continued in the office of private secretary till in December, 1879, when he resigned the position to take up the practice of his profession. In January, 1880, he began practice at Salisbury, where he has from the first secured a large and profitable law business, not second to that of any attorney in the city. He holds a foremost position among his professional associates, not alone in his own city, but in the state at large.

In 1882 Mr. Overman was elected a member of the lower house of the state legislature as a representative from Rowan county. The canvass for his election was a heated one, he being the regular democratic candidate against G. A. Bingham, a prominent candidate of the independent democrats. Mr. Overman was elected and re-elected for the two succeeding terms commencing respectively in 1884 and 1886. In 1888 he declined a nomination for a fourth term. Mr. Overman was the choice of the democrats in 1887 for speaker of the house, being the unanimous choice of the democratic legislative caucus for that office, but he was defeated by a coalition between the republican and independent democratic members. falling only two votes short of an election. Though beaten for the speakership, his distinguished ability gave hin the next highest position in the house, the chairmanship of the judiciary committee. During his legislative career he served as a member of the judiciary committee, the committee on education, on the penitentiary and on the deaf and dumb asylum. In 1885 he was elected by the legislature a member of the board of trustees of the North Carolina state university, and he still continues in that position. In January, 1889, Mr. Overman was appointed by Gov. Fowle, and confirmed by the state senate, a member of the board of directors for the state penitentiary, which membership he still retains. Under the administration of the board during the membership of Mr. Overman, the institution became self-sustaining for the first time in its history. Mr. Overman is a high-minded politician and a citizen whose character is stainless. He is an able lawyer and refined and cultured gentleman. He is a respected member of the order of the K. of P. and of the I. O. O. F. He and his estimable wife are leading members of the Methodist Episcopal church. Mr. Overman married Miss Mary P. Merrimon, of Raleigh, daughter of Chief-Justice A. S. Merrimon, October 31, 1878, and they have had four children, only two of whom, both daughters, survive.

COL. HAMILTON C. JONES

is a native of Rowan county, N. C.; born in Salisbury, November 3, 1837, the son of the late Hamilton C. Jones, of Salisbury. Col. Jones was reared in Salisbury, where, under Prof. Benjamin Summers, he was prepared for the university at Chapel Hill. Entering that institution, he graduated in 1858, just as he came to his majority. While at the university he studied law, under the late Judge Battle. After his graduation he entered the law office of his father, then practicing in Salisbury, where he further pursued his law studies. In 1859 he was admitted to the bar, and began the practice of his chosen profession in his native town. In politics he was a determined whig, having stumped the state for John Bell, for president, in 1860. Mr. Jones was first lieutenant of Rowan's rifle guard, which proceeded under command, to Fort Johnson, on the coast, taking possession of the fort even prior to the passage of the North Carolina ordinance of secession. As a state policy, Col. Jones held, and always has held, that secession was entirely inexpedient, but when it came he accepted the situation, and linked his fate with the Confederate cause. Upon the organization of state troops he was appointed by Gov. Ellis to the captaincy of Company K, of the Fifth regiment of state troops. Soon after the battle of Williamsburg, where he was severely wounded, in May, 1862, he was made lieutenant-colonel of the Fifty-seventh North Carolina regiment, with which he joined the army of northern Virginia, in the fall of the same year. He subsequently participated in the battles of Fredericksburg and Chancellorsville, and in the Gettysburg campaign. At the Rappahannock railroad bridge, November 7, 1863, he was captured, and was thereafter imprisoned in the old Capital prison, at Washington, and subsequently at Johnson's Island, at Lake Erie. In February, 1865, he was sent south in a special exchange. He took command of his regiment, then before Petersburg, its colonel, Archibald C. Goodwin, having been promoted to the rank of brigadier-general. The battle of Hare's Hill followed, in which an assault was made upon Gen. Grant's works. In this assault Col. Jones was again wounded and disabled from further service. Before he had recovered the war ended.

After the war Col. Jones resumed the practice of law at Salisbury, and continued there until August, 1867, when he removed to Charlotte, forming a partnership with Gen. Robert D. Johnston, with whom he practiced for some twenty years. In 1869, Col. Jones was appointed to fill an unexpired term of state senatorship, and the following year he was elected for a full term for the same office. While he was senator the impeachment of Gov. W. W. Holden come on and that official was convicted and deposed. In 1873, Col. Jones was married to Miss Connie, daughter of Col. William R. Meyers, of Charlotte. Col. Jones and family are influential members of St. Peter's Episcopal church, of Charlotte, of which he has been a vestryman for many years. In 1885 he was appointed by President Cleveland United States district-attorney for the western district of North Carolina, which office he held till 1889. As a lawyer Col. Jones holds a distinguished position and has few equals. His knowledge of law is extensive; nature has endowed him with acute legal perceptions; he is accurate and profound in his exposition of the law; clear, pointed and forcible in his statements, and whether before court or jury he is powerful and effective. He combines the best elements of lawyer and jurist, and stands in the front rank of his profession. As a citizen, Col. Jones is of the progressive type and is ever alive to whatever in his judgment promotes the best and the highest interests of the people. As a member of society he is cultured, genial, highminded and is highly respected by all who know hin.

COL. JOHN E. BROWN

is a leading attorney-at-law at Charlotte, and solicitor of the criminal court of Mecklenburgh county. Col. Brown's birthplace was Locust Hill, Caswell county, N. C., where he first saw the light of day in August, 1830, as the son of John E. and Elizabeth C. Brown, both of whom were of good old Carolina stock, the father being for many years the leading physician of his time, and for two terms a member of the state legislature. He was a brother of Senator Bedford Brown. The mother was a lineal descendant of the Carters, of Shirley, Va., one of the first families of the Old Dominion. Our subject received his preparatory education at Yanceysville, N. C., and completed his education in 1853 at Hampden-Sydney college, of Virginia, a Presbyterian institution of high repute. After leaving college he read law at Richmond Hill, under the late Judge Richmond Pearson, at one time Chief-Justice Pearson of North Carolina. He was admitted to the bar in 1856, and in 1857 he came to Charlotte, which has been his home ever since, and with the exception of the four years of the war, he has been in most active practice. He entered the Confederate service in May, 1861. He was commissioned first lieutenant in Company D., of the Seventh North Carolina state troops, which was commanded by Col. Campbell. His first active service was in the battle of Newbern, in March, 1862, soon after which he was commissioned lieutenant-colonel of the Forty-second regiment, which was ordered to Virginia in May, 1862, and brigaded under Gen. Pettigrew. In 1863 he was promoted to the rank of colonel of his regiment, and was engaged around Petersburg and Richmond, till May 20, 1864, when at the battle of Bermuda Hundreds he was wounded in the head by a gunshot. After a brief sickness he returned to the army in front of Richmond, and December 24th, was ordered to Wilmington, and thence to Fort Fisher. Later he joined Gen. Johnson, and his last battle was that of Bentonville, where the regiment surrendered. He held the rank of colonel on his return to Charlotte, and resumed the practice of law, at which he has since continued. In 1872-3 and 1874, Col. Brown served in the lower house of the legislature. In 1879 he married Miss Laura P. Morrison, the daughter of Rev. R. H. Morrison, D. D., one of the leading and most popular divines of North Carolina, of whose life and to whose memory we copy the following tribute from a printed pamphlet prepared and published by his admiring fellow citizens and co-workers.

IN MEMORIAM.

The Rev. Robert Hall Morrison, D. D., born in Rocky River Congregation, Cabarrus county, September 8, 1798; died in Lincoln county, N. C., May 13, 1889, in the ninety-first year of his age. The southern church mingles its sympathies with the presbytery of Mecklenburg, in the death of its oldest minister, this venerated man of God. Society suffers in the removal of one of its strongest supports and truest ornaments. The church, bereft of one of its brightest crowns, mourns over an aching void; a void that can never be filled. An extraordinary character has vacated an extraordinary sphere of usefulness and honor. A bright star whom we have seen shining at Christ's right hand here below is now shining with surpassing splendor with Christ above. Descended from a sterling Scotch-Irish Presbyterian ancestry, he inherited those marked and noble qualities of mind and heart, which, hallowed by grace, made him an honour to the age and a blessing to the world. Early called by the Saviour, in the morning of life, he obeyed the voice of the gracious shepherd, and followed him faithfully to its close. Communion with God, meditation upon the glory of Christ, the study of the Scriptures — which he read through four times each year, with commentaries, dwelling upon their preciousness and power — the perusal of devotional works, were his chief delight. Literary tastes were sanctified, and mind and heart found their highest satisfaction and enjoyment in the green pastures of divine truth and beside the still waters of divine consolation. The grand doctrines of grace, embodied in the Calvinistic system of faith, entered into and moulded his christian experience and made him humble and prayerful, cheerful and strong, decided but liberal, active and zealous, steadfast, immovable, always abounding in the work of the Lord, knowing that his labor was not in vain in the Lord. In his latter years all of his income — after providing for his physical wants — was devoted to the gospel, not restricting himself to his own, but assisting all denominations of Christians. He left a legacy to the American Bible society, having made all his children life-members, and was himself a life-director. His works do follow

B—13

him and will continue to follow him forever! Christians of every
name were received into his confidence and love, but none were left
unaware that the venerable patriarchal and apostolic Presbyterian
church, "the Mother of us all," was the home of his heart and his
chief joy.

Dr. Morrison was graduated at the University of North Carolina,
in 1818; dividing the honor, of his class with President Polk, also of
Presbyterian lineage, and from that Presbyterian section of the state
which gave to the world the first declaration of American independence, May 20, 1775. Dr. Morrison was ordained by Concord Presbytery in 1820, his first charge being Providence church in Mecklenburg
county. He was soon called, thence, to Fayetteville. During his
pastorate there, he was, on the 27th of April, 1824, at Vesuvius Furnace, Lincoln county, N. C., united in marriage with a lady of renowned family, Miss Mary Graham, sister of Gov. William A. Graham, and daughter of Gen. Joseph Graham, of illustrious Revolutionary fame — a devout Christian, and for the last ten or twelve
years of his life, ruling elder in Unity church, Lincoln county.

Dr. Morrison remained in Fayetteville from 1822 to 1827, and
accepted a call to the venerable Sugar Creek church, three miles
from Charlotte; in which historic town, the birthplace of American independence, a Presbyterian church was organized by him,
their membership having been, previously, in the mother church,
Sugar Creek. To these churches he ministered most acceptably. His scholarly attainments, his chaste and elegant diction,
his dignified mien, his impressive delivery, his heart on fire with
the love of Christ and the love of souls, captivated his hearers
and made his ministry a ministry of power. His was no non-com-
mittal, politic, trimming disposition, courting or valuing popular favor,
winking at, if not approving of fashionable folly and iniquity. He
fearlessly denounced worldly conformity in the church. Christ's
name was on his forehead, seen and read by all. He followed the
Lamb whithersoever he went, bearing his cross, following him through
evil as well as good report, regardless of the buzz of dissent, or the
clamor of opposition. His was no half-way offering of himself, but
full and entire, upon the altar of God, and with an ardor that never
cooled, and a zeal that never wavered, he continued a faithful, uncompromising witness to the truth, whether men would hear, or
whether they would forbear, even to the end. David's description of
a citizen of Zion was applicable to him: " In whose eyes a vile person is contemned, but he honoureth them that fear the Lord." " Do
not I hate them, oh Lord, that hate Thee? and am not I grieved with
those that rise up against Thee? I hate them with perfect hatred; I
count them mine enemies."

Deeply impressed by the fact that very few candidates for the
ministry came from the state university and other secular institutions,
and realizing the necessity of a Presbyterian college as a nursery for
the church and its ministers, Dr. Morrison brought before Concord
presbytery, on the 12th of March, 1835, at Prospect church, Rowan

county, a resolution for the establishment within its bounds, of a Presbyterian college, where Presbyterian doctrines should be faithfully taught and expounded. The resolution was adopted and Drs. Morrison and Sparrow were appointed financial agents. They succeeded in raising funds sufficient to start the college on the first of March, 1837. The three presbyteries in charge of it, Concord, Morganton and Bethel, elected Dr. Morrison the first president of Davidson college. The $30,000 thus raised were supplemented in 1855 by a princely donation from Mr. Maxwell Chambers, of Salisbury, N. C. Dr. Morrison appeared before the legislature, and with difficulty, procured a charter, with a limit of $200,000, which was not the whole of Mr. Chambers's donation.

Davidson college, thus brought into being, has risen to eminence among the institutions of America. Its high standard commands the respect of the whole country, north and south, whilst the moral influences which surround and govern it, are equaled by few, surpassed by none. A high-toned faculty and high-toned students are regarded with admiration throughout the land. The Bible forms a part of the college curriculum; and the God of the Bible has set his sacred *imprimatur* upon this consecrated institution. The divine spirit, the fountain of truth, energizes, with signal force "the lively oracles" here dispensed. His vital breath renders fruitful and fragrant this cherished garden of the Lord. During the fifty-two years of its existence, it has given to the church 200 ministers of the gospel! Who is able to compute the sum total of blessing accruing to the world from this one source alone! Who is able to measure its influence for good through all coming time! And who is able to estimate the indebtedness of society, the state, and the church, to its noble founder! Davidson college is his monument! A monument more lasting, and grander far, than stone or brass! A monument perennial, enduring through all ages—all ages of time and the endless ages of eternity! Generations yet unborn will rise up and bless the honored name of Dr. Robert Hall Morrison!

Failing health led Dr. Morrison to resign this most important trust, the presidency of the college, and he retired to his farm in Lincoln county. His delightful home, the home of culture and refinement, of joy and happiness, was proverbial for an overflowing hospitality, which was dispensed from a full heart with a free hand.

His labors in the gospel ministry knew no intermission, but were continued at Unity, Castanea, and Machpelah churches. During the long ministerial term of sixty-five years, it mattered not what the weather was, he was never known to fail to meet an appointment. In recounting his mercies, he stated the remarkable fact, that, though not strong, physically, he was never confined to his bed three consecutive days in his long life, until about ten days before the end came. He was constantly expressing his gratitude for his eyesight being spared, enabling him to read continually, until two weeks before his death. When debarred this privilege by much suffering, he declined being read to, saying: "Fortunately, my mind is stored with very precious promises, and I find many of the hymns very sweet prayers."

When the war broke out, Dr. Morrison, though in principle a strong Union man, cast his lot with his people, and espoused the cause of the Confederacy with all his heart and soul. Three gallant sons, old enough for the service, and five sons-in-law, were officers in the Confederate army. Notably among the latter, was the peerless Gen. (Stonewall) Jackson, the splendor of whose military renown was even surpassed by the lustre of his piety, and the crowning character in the constellation of excellences that illumined his name and invested it with a halo of glory, was that of the fearless, devoted man of God. His piety was the basis of his greatness, the true secret of his military success. He was the Joshua of modern history. An assemblage of similar qualities rendered both illustrious and immortal. Both were raised up by Providence to illustrate the elevating power of religion. In both, the sentiment of DUTY was paramount to every other. Both were characterized by supreme devotion to God. And both, God "set on high," because they "knew" and honored "his name," "on high," on a conspicuous eminence before men, the objects of a world's veneration and love; and, now, again, "on high," among principalities and powers, the noblest chieftains in the kingdom of glory!

The youngest son of Dr. Morrison, Alfred, the Benjamin of the family, a gifted youth, on whom the mantle of his honored father seemed likely to fall and rest, being called of God into the ministry of Jesus Christ, proclaimed the glorious gospel with a fervor, and a power, and a success, that seemed but an earnest of still greater blessings to the church from a long life of devotion to his holy calling. Alas, the vanity of human hopes and expectations! The youthful soldier was soon, how soon! remanded from the field of battle, and called to wear his crown! And he who pens this tribute, in sadness and sorrow, performed the funeral rites and committed his body to the tomb.

We, with our contracted vision, are unable to comprehend, and greatly wonder at the mysterious Providence that cut short a career so full of promise, and are greatly saddened by it. But let us remember that that career is not ended. It was not the meteor's flash, illuminating for a moment its pathway in the heavens, and then expiring in darkness, leaving not a trace of its former light and splendor. No! he set, "as sets the morning star, which goes down beneath the darkened west, nor hides obscured behind the tempests of the sky, but melts away into the light of heaven!" And now he knows, and will forever know, even as he is known. No dim or hazy atmosphere obscures the firmanent of glory. He admires and adores the deep, deep Providence which stumbles us. Like the pillar of cloud and fire, though it be dark on our side, yet on his side it is full of light. There is no night there. He has entered that temple which the glory of God doth lighten, and the Lamb is the light thereof! He has joined the company before the throne. And the blest occupation of earth is still the blest occupation of heaven — preaching the glorious gospel of the son of God! Father and son, now forever associated, together making known "the unsearchable riches of Christ" to the grandest assembly of the universe, to angels and archangels, to cherubim and seraphim, who learn "*from the church* the manifold wisdom of God"—proclaiming to the admiring, adoring principalities of heaven, the fathomless wonders of redeeming love, the unutterably glorious triumphs of amazing grace!

> Worthy the Lamb that died, they cry,
> ' To be exalted thus '!
> 'Worthy the Lamb,' our lips reply,
> ' For He was slain for us ! ' "

The burden of this, and other afflictions — having been previously bereft of a beloved wife and devoted children — pressed heavily upon Dr. Morrison. It pleased his heavenly father to perfect him, even as Christ, the captain of our salvation, was made perfect through much suffering. But throughout the long-protracted discipline of trial, he murmured not, but meekly drank the cup that was given him to drink, in the spirit of Him who said: "Thy will, not mine, be done." And under the culture of sanctified affliction, his Christian character visibly mellowed and ripened fully into fitness for heaven. Though confined to his home by the infirmities of age, he was always working for the Master in distributing Bibles, good books and papers, and writing to many on the importance of preparation for heaven. His conversation was more of heaven than earth. He wrote to each of his absent children almost weekly, and the close of every letter was almost a sermon. His last letter to a beloved daughter ends thus: "I have been deeply impressed by the number of sudden deaths we have had. God seems to remind us often of the frail tenure by which we hold to the things of time and the privileges of the gospel. In such an hour as we think not the messenger comes! The main thing is to have our lamps burning, prepared for the coming of the bridegroom. The more we lay up treasures on high, the less, I presume, we will fear the loss of things below. Among the most solemn impressions is the fact, that all privileges enjoyed here will soon be forever gone, and we have no power to recall them! Let us strive for that kingdom which knows no sorrow, no changes, no death." He delighted in the society of ministers, and loved to encourage his young brethren to persevere in their glorious work for the Master. To a young minister he said, recently, with great animation: "O, my dear young brother, if I had ten thousand lives to live, I would give them all to the gospel!" The graces of the Holy Spirit so abounded in his life as to render his old age very peaceful and beautiful, through much bodily suffering. The habit of secret prayer became so unceasing, his family often feared to enter his room, he was so constantly on his knees. He would admonish all not to faint in prayer, and with great humility would ask all to pray for him. When alone he prayed much aloud, and the burden of his prayer was, that all his descendants might be saved, children and grandchildren and great grandchildren gathered all, an unbroken family, into the heavenly kingdom.

In broken utterances, under great bodily suffering, he gave his dying testimony: "While I can, I wish to bear my dying testimony to the power and the blessedness of the gospel, and to the preciousness of the dear Saviour. In our hours of ease, precious; in hours of trial and distress, a thousand times more precious. I cannot express in words freely, what I mean. O the sweet wonders of the cross!" Marked tokens of the Divine favor were accorded to the dying saint, as cordials to sustain his fainting spirit. And amid the gentle ministries of filial love, and the kind offices of filial devotion, untiring, unfaltering, that ceased not, day nor night — "ministering angels" — relieving the tedium of the sick chamber, soothing the couch of suffering, and mitigating, as far as possible, the pains of dissolution, he sweetly fell asleep.

He has 'eft to his descendants the rich legacy of an honored name, a holy life, an elevated Christian character, and many fervent prayers which have been, and are yet to be, answered in blessings on their heads — a legacy infinitely more precious than all the diadems and treasures of earth. May they all, to the latest generation, secure by faith, the priceless inheritance!

He has gone to see the King in all his beauty, to gaze upon that sacred brow, that for us was crowned with thorns, and to lean his head with adoring confidence and unutterable joy upon his Saviour's loving bosom.

> "Soldier of Christ, well done!
> Praise be thy blest employ,
> And while eternal ages run,
> Rest in thy Saviour's joy!"

> "Who, who would live alway, away from his God,
> Away from yon Heaven, that blissful abode,
> Where the rivers of pleasure flow o'er the bright plains,
> And the noontide of glory eternally reigns!

> Where the saints of all ages in harmony meet,
> Their Saviour and brethren transported to greet;
> While the anthems of rapture unceasingly roll,
> And the smile of the Lord is the feast of the soul!"

JOSEPH HARVEY WILSON.

In September, 1810, in Mecklenburg county, the late Joseph Harvey Wilson was born. For many years he was one of the foremost members of the Charlotte bar. He was the son of the Rev. John McKamie Wilson, of Mecklenburg, N. C. At the early age of fifteen he graduated from Washington college, now Washington & Lee university, of Virginia. He began the study of law at Charlotte, under the supervision of the late Washington Morrison, and in 1831, when only twenty-one years of age, was admitted to the bar. He began the practice of his chosen profession at Charlotte, which was the theatre to him of a long and successful career, ended only by his decease, which occurred in September, 1884. Though comparatively very young at the outset, he at once distinguished himself at the bar,

and his practice soon became extensive, so continuing during a course of practice of more than half a century. His profound knowledge of the law made him an eminent jurist, and his influence at the bar was powerful. Among his legal brethren he was an authority, and his opinions were always eagerly sought. For clearness and perspicuity he was a model. He possessed a strong legal mind, a natural love for the law, and he pursued its study as a searcher for the truth. With such qualifications and characteristics, it might have been expected that a judgeship would have been tendered him, and such was actually the case, but having no desire to enter upon a public career, he declined the proffered honor. He had but little taste either for political preferment, but was induced to serve his county for several terms in the state senate, of which honorable body he was chosen president. Aside from this his life was more or less retired and devoted to the quiet and extensive practice of his profession, in which he was pre-eminently a leader. Notwithstanding his natural reserve and love of quiet, he always manifested much interest in the public welfare and the moral, intellectual and material progress of society. He was a warm and earnest advocate of the church, of liberal education and the general public advancement. For many years Mr. Wilson was an active member of the Presbyterian church, in which he was an elder. As a friend, he was faithful and of a most genial disposition, in his nature he was gentle and domestic. He was twice happily married. His first wife, Miss Patton, died leaving him five children. Subsequently, he married Miss Phifer, of whom two children were born. Mr. Wilson was seventy-five years of age when his death occurred. Such is a brief biography of this able and learned lawyer and jurist, who besides his high intellectual endowments was an honored and esteemed citizen. His life was characterized by honesty, sobriety, piety and usefulness to his fellow men.

RUFUS YANCEY McADEN.

The name of Rufus Yancey McAden represents two of the oldest and most distinguished families in the Carolinas. The name of Yancey, so prominent throughout the south, is found from Mississippi to Virginia, all of them in the foremost and honorable walks of life. The name of Yancey has from time immemorial been associated with the best lawyers of Mississippi, and William Tudor Yancey, Robert Yancey and Charles Yancey are among the prominent members of the justly celebrated bar of Virginia. Rufus Yancey McAden was born in Caswell county, N. C., March 4, 1833. He was a son of Dr. Henry McAden, the most prominent physician of the state. Mr. McAden's paternal great-grandfather was Rev. Hugh McAden, who came as a Presbyterian missionary from Philadelphia to North Carolina in the early days of the state. Dr. John McAden, his son, married Betsy Murphy, a sister of Archibald D. Murphy, the great North Carolina orator. Dr. Henry McAden married Frances Yancey, whose parents were Bartlett and Anne Graves Yancey. The parents of Rufus died while he was yet a boy, and our subject was adopted into the home and family of Mrs. Bartlett Yancey, his grandmother, she being a widow, where he was brought up and received the greater part of his education. He was graduated at Wake Forest college in 1853, aged twenty, and subsequently read law under Judges Nash and Bailey. Being admitted to the bar he first located in his native county. In 1858 he wedded Miss Mary F. Terry, daughter of Dr. B. F. Terry, of Prince Edward county, Va., and in the next year removed to Alamance county, and located at Graham. The next year he entered politics as the whig candidate for the legislature, and was defeated by thirteen votes, reducing the democratic majority some 300. In 1862 he was elected to the legislature and successively re-elected, serving until 1867. In 1866 he acted as speaker of the house of representatives, defeating for this high office Col. R. H. Cowan, a distinguished and honored representative from Wilmington. As speaker of the house Mr. McAden made an excellent presiding officer. During his incumbency of the speaker's desk, Gov. Swain, upon a visit to that city, declared he had not seen such a speaker since the days of Edward Stanly.

In 1867, upon his retirement from both politics and the law, Mr. McAden began a career of business prosperity unparalleled in the history of the state. In that year he was made president of the First National bank, of Charlotte, which position, by reason of his former experience as president of the bank at Graham, he was eminently qualified to fill. In the following year he associated himself with Col. A. S. Buford, a member of the great Kentucky family of that name, for the construction of the air-line railway from Charlotte to Atlanta, Col. Buford being president and he vice-president of the corporation. He also organized and constructed the Spartanburg and Asheville railway, it being through his indefatigable efforts that the road was finished. In 1881 he turned his business energies in the direction of manufacturing, and erected in Gaston county one of the largest cotton mills in the state, giving employment to over 500 men. After a life full of the largest and most beautiful benefactions to his fellow-citizens, Rufus Yancey McAden died January 29, 1889, leaving a wife and five children as the issue of a happy marriage. At the time of his death he was president of the First National bank, of Charlotte, president of the Spartanburg, Union & Columbia railway, the Asheville & Spartanburg railway, the Falls of Neuse Manufacturing company, and the McAden cotton mills. Mr. McAden was a strong man in every phase of his character. From the grandmother who brought him up from poor and youthful orphanage. he learned those characteristics of promptness, honesty, truth and industry, and through his great business career these attributes ran, sanctifying all his transactions and crowning his life work with honor. Mr. McAden, though his life had been devoted to his successful business career, found time to acquire great erudition and personal culture, so much so that he was well posted in the general field of polite and classical literature. He was genial in his nature and true to the southern in-

James H. Osborne

stinct of chivalry and a lavish hospitality. At the bar he was a forceful advocate, and fortified with a high order of forensic eloquence, which quality had attracted the attention of most people of education throughout the south.

JAMES WALKER OSBORNE.

The legal profession of North Carolina has been signalized by a number of distinguished individuals, none of whom has held a higher place than the subject of this sketch, James Walker Osborne. As a lawyer, jurist or private citizen he was pre-eminent. He was born at Salisbury, N. C., December 25, 1811, and died at Charlotte August 10, 1869. He came of an illustrious line, his great progenitor being Alexander Osborne, who came from New Jersey to North Carolina some years previous to 1755, settling in Rowan county. He was a colonel of distinction in the American Revolution, and had one son and several daughters. His son's name was Adlai Osborne, whose mother's maiden name was Agnes McWhorter. She was the sister of Rev. Alexander McWhorter, who at one time was president of Queen's college at Charlotte. Adlai Osborne was educated at Princeton college, graduating in 1768. In January, 1771, he was married to Margaret Lloyd. He studied law and was appointed under the crown, clerk of the courts of Rowan county, holding that office until 1809. His decease occurred in 1815, and he left a large family consisting of both sons and daughters. One son, Edward Jay Osborne, married Harriet Walker, of Wilmington, N. C. He had studied law at Wilmington and was admitted to the bar, but removing to Salisbury established there his permanent home. He attained extraordinary distinction as a learned and able member of the legal profession. He had three daughters and one son, James Walker Osborne, the subject of this sketch. The mother of Mr. Osborne died when he was a child only a year and a half old, and he was adopted into the home of Mr. and Mrs. Robert Davidson, of Mecklenburg county, Mrs. Davidson being an own sister of his father.

The intellectual training of James Walker Osborne began in early life. He was first placed in a private school in charge of Samuel C. Caldwell, D. D., where he was prepared for entering the university at Chapel Hill, from which he graduated, in June, 1830. He entered the law office of Hon. William A. Graham, and taking up the study of law, was admitted to practice at the bar in 1833. In that year he opened up a law office in Charlotte, where he soon became distinguished as an able and effective lawyer, taking rank with the most illustrious members of the profession. Twice he was chosen presidential elector at large for his state. In the Clay campaign of 1844, he was first presidential elector at large, and again he held the same position in the Seymour and Grant campaign. For four years he was superintendent of the United States mints, at Charlotte, being appointed to that important trust by President Millard Fillmore. He was called to the bench of the superior court in 1859, by Gov. Ellis, to fill a vacancy in the judgeship of that court. His appointment was confirmed by the general assembly in November, 1860. He held this position until 1866, when he was displaced by the rule of the republican party, against whose principles he was an active opponent. He represented Mecklenburg county as state senator, which office he held at the time of his decease. April 5, 1842, he was married to Mrs. Mary A. Moore, daughter of John Irwin, deceased, of Charlotte. She was the widow of Thomas J. Moore, son of Gen. Thomas Moore, of South Carolina, who was a member of congress from the Spartanburg district. Thomas J. Moore died at the age of twenty-six years, leaving one son, Dr. Thomas J. Moore, of Richmond, Va. The union of James Walker Osborne and his wife resulted in the birth of four sons, two of whom are deceased. The surviving sons are Francis Irwin Osborne, the present solicitor of the Eleventh judicial district of North Carolina, and James Walker Osborne, the youngest son, also a lawyer by profession in practice in New York city.

Judge Osborne attained great eminence in his profession and attracted the admiration as well as secured the esteem of his associates at the bar. His dignified yet suave manner, as well as his purity of character added grace to the bench, the man conferring dignity upon the office for which he possessed such high qualifications. His name stands eminent in the annals of the jurisprudence of North Carolina. During his brilliant career as a lawyer, he at one time became the law partner of Gen. Rufus Barringer, of Charlotte, who has said of him: "He had a logical and discriminating mind, and his persistent search after truth was marked. He was an extraordinary man, and amid all the cares and vexations of professional life he always found time to devote to the advocacy of the cause of the poor and needy." He was charitable both in his acts and judgments, and was a faithful friend both to white and black. As a legislator he was liberal, high-minded and discreet, and took a broad and intelligent view of all public questions. He was sincere in his convictions, and as a public speaker he was brilliant, forcible, pleasing and eloquent. As a man of letters he was of the highest grade, with a mind abundantly stored with useful knowledge and classic learning. Whenever called upon to make a speech in public, he was always equal to the occasion, and never failed to both please and instruct his audience, always acquitting himself with honor. In politics he was a democrat of the states rights school, perhaps of the new school, for originally he was not a democrat. He was a member of the old whig party with which organization he had long identified himself, and he only left it because he thought it too slow and conservative; because it did not appear to see the dangers that were menacing the south and not prompt in resisting them.

In the secession convention of 1860, Judge Osborne maintained that secession was the best southern policy. He was devoted to the south, its customs, habits and traditions, and fully justified and approved the movement for a separation of the south from the north. As a citizen he was of the progressive stamp, alive to every local interest which looked to a development of the natural resources of the country. He was a pioneer advocate of railroad improvements, prompting the people to lend a helping hand to all feasible railroad projects. He was temperate in his habits and religious in his frame of mind. His character for honesty and probity was unimpeachable, and he was always quick to approve the right and condemn the wrong. His language was always pure and chaste, showing both good breeding and culture. He was a zealous member of the Presbyterian church, for many years holding official positions in that organization, and his christianity was of the active and zealous type. In every undertaking for the advancement and uplifting of society, Judge Osborne was among the foremost leaders, and his learning and ability, his fine taste and discrimination made him an effective power in that direction. He was hardly fifty-eight years of age when death put an end to his useful and praiseworthy career. No nobler, purer spirit ever winged its flight to the blissful regions reserved for the blessed. No more loyal heart, no firmer friend, no more exalted patriot ever found a dwelling place on earth. He has gone to his reward — to the recompense of a pure, unspotted life.

SAMUEL CASPAR WISTAR TATE,

a leading member of the bar at Morganton, N. C., was born June 23, 1825, in the town of his present residence. He was the son of Dr. Samuel Tate, a native of Burke county, N. C., born in 1798. The father died January 27, 1873. He was the son of Hugh Tate, also a native of Burke county, and by occupation a farmer. He served as sheriff of his county several years. The name of Mr. Tate's mother before her marriage to his father was Mrs. Elizabeth Gilliland, widow of Dr. Gilliland, of Bedford, Penn. She died May 10, 1857. The subject of this sketch was reared in Morganton, and received his education in the Morganton academy. In his youth he accompanied his parents to Cherokee, now Clay county, N. C. In a few years the family returned to Morganton where he resumed his studies in the academy then presided over by G. Zelotes Adams. Later on he entered Washington college of East Tennessee, where he remained about two years. He then entered the University of North Carolina where he spent six months, being a member of the senior class. In these different institutions, Mr. Tate obtained a good classical education. On leaving the university he took up the study of law under Hon. B. S. Gaither, of Morganton, and was licensed to practice in the county courts August 7, 1848, and in the superior courts August 6, 1849. Mr. Tate entered upon his professional career at Murphy, Cherokee county, N. C., September 12, 1848, remaining there, however, only during one term of court. He devoted himself to his practice in Burke and adjoining counties, with his home and headquarters at Morganton, until the breaking out of the Civil war. Prior to this event he served as solicitor of Haywood, Burke and Caldwell counties.

In April, 1861, Mr. Tate entered the service of the Confederate army as a volunteer in Company G, First North Carolina state troops, and served with that command for six months as a private. He participated during the time in the battle at Bethel. At the expiration of his term of service, he returned home, and throughout the remainder of the war he served the Confederate government in the way of looking after supplies for the army and upon home guard duty. In October, 1865, he went to Marion, N. C., where, during the winter which followed he taught the Marion academy. Returning to Morganton early in 1866, he resumed the practice of law and has devoted himself to it ever since. He is now one of the ablest lawyers of the Burke county bar. Mr. Tate was born and raised under whig influences, but since the whig party went out of existence he has affiliated with the democratic party. He was a candidate for the state legislature in 1851 and again in 1862, but failed of an election. He has served one term as mayor of Morganton with good acceptance. Mr. Tate is a member of the Episcopal church and of the Masonic fraternity. As a citizen he holds a high rank, and is greatly respected and esteemed by his fellow citizens.

DAVID LOWRY SWAIN,

a distinguished North Carolinian, was born in Asheville, Buncombe county, N. C., January 4, 1801. He was of English descent; his father, George Swain, was a native of Roxboro, Mass. Mr. Swain took a partial course in the North Carolina university, studied law under Hon. John L. Taylor, and was admitted to the bar in 1823, when he opened a law office at Raleigh. In 1824 he was elected to the state legislature, and in 1831 was appointed a judge of the state supreme court. He was elected governor of North Carolina in 1832, being the youngest man ever elected to that office. He held the office of president of the University of North Carolina from 1835 till his death. He was one of the most efficient presidents ever chosen to that position, contributing to the progress and success of that institution through a presidency of more than thirty years. He was a favorite of President Andrew Johnson, and was invited by that functionary to advise and assist in the reconstruction measures of the southern states. In 1841 he received the honorary degree of LL. D., from Princeton college, and in 1842 Yale college conferred upon him the same degree. He was a facile and graphic writer, and was the author of several valuable historical writings, among them, "The British Invasion of North Carolina in 1776," and "The Revolutionary History of North Carolina."

In a lengthy eulogistic notice of Gov. Swain, Gov. Vance said of him: "His knowledge was encyclopedic in its range, especially in English literature. So overwhelming were his stores, that the writer enumerates with grateful pleasure, when, forgetting altogether the subject on hand, he would stand up in front of his class, and in an outgush of eloquence, poetry, history, anecdote and humor, wrap us all as with an enchantment. His most remarkable trait was his powerful memory, and the direction in which that faculty was notably exercised was in biography and genealogy. In this particular he had no superior in America." Gov. Swain rendered his greatest service to the state, by his efficiency as the patron and president of the university. He was its moving spirit before the war, and when Sherman's army spread desolation in its track Gov. Swain was one of the commissioners appointed to meet Gen. Sherman and ask his interposition to save the university from destruction. Gov. Swain was married, January 12, 1824, to Eleanor, daughter of William White. He died at Chapel Hill, September 3, 1868, leaving his widow surviving him.

CHARLES MANLY.

Gov. Charles Manly was born in Chatham county, N. C., May 13, 1795. He was fitted for college by a distinguished educator, Prof. William Bingham, at Pittsboro academy and graduated from the University of North Carolina, in 1814, with first honors. He engaged as a private tutor, in the meantime studying law with Gen. Robert Williams. He was admitted to the bar in 1816, and began practice under most encouraging auspicies. He was appointed reading clerk in the North Carolina house of commons, and as clerk of the commission at Washington, under the treaty of Ghent, to investigate and award claims against Great Britain, for property taken by the British during the war of 1812. In 1830 he was elected chief clerk of the house of commons, which office he held for about eighteen years, with only a single intermission. In 1840 he was one of the presidential electors on the whig ticket, and cast the vote of his state in the electoral college for William H. Harrison and John Tyler. He made an unsuccessful canvass for state senator in 1844, as the representative of Wake county. He filled, respectively, the offices of director of the State bank, commissioner to sell the Cherokee land and collect the proceeds thereof, and of treasurer of the state university.

In 1848 Mr. Manly was the whig candidate for governor, and made a very effective canvass of the entire state. He was elected by a large majority, and administered the office for two years with marked ability and success. He was candidate for another term, but was defeated by one of the strongest democrats in the state, Hon. David S. Reid, the democrats having gained a decided and lasting ascendency in the state. This was the close of Gov. Manly's political career — a career in which he acted a most brilliant and highly creditable part. He was married, in 1817, to Charity, daughter of William H. Haywood, Sr. He died at Raleigh, May 1, 1871, an event doubtless hastened by the anxieties, the ravages and the spoliations of the Civil war. Gov. Manly was a most interesting and brilliant conversationalist; as a public speaker he was eloquent, and as a writer was master of a strong, yet refined rhetoric. He loved society, and his home was the center of the best and most cultured circle of intimates. As a lawyer he was considerate and judicious, and urged the interests of his clients with strength and zeal. In religion he was a devoted and zealous Episcopalian.

HON. JOHN H. SMALL

is one of the leading lawyers of North Carolina. Mr. Small was born in Washington, N. C., on the 9th of August, 1858. He was prepared for college in the schools of his native city, and finished his junior year at Trinity college, after which he took up the study of law in the office of Mr. Charles F. Warren and Judge William B. Rodman, and was admitted to the bar in 1881, since that time having been engaged in practice at Washington. Mr. Small became associated with the Hon. George H. Brown in 1888, and this law firm existed until January 1, 1889. His political career was begun early, as he was appointed reading clerk of the state senate, a few days after his admission to the bar, and he continued in that office during the session of 1881. In 1881, he was elected county superintendent of public instruction, and served as solicitor of the inferior court, from 1882 to 1885, when that court was abolished by law. He entered the journalistic field, as proprietor and editor of the North Carolina *State Press*, in 1883, and soon after changed the name to the *Washington Gazette*, which greatly prospered under his able management, its subscription list being trebled, and the paper greatly enlarged and improved. At the time of his relinquishment of its editorial management, the *Washington Gazette* was the leading organ of the democratic party in the county. Mr. Small has been attorney for the board of county commissioners, since 1888, and was a member of the city council, from May, 1887, to May, 1890; and from 1889 to 1890, he held the office of mayor of Washington. As a member of the committee on graded schools, he did much to place that excellent system on a firm basis, and his assistance and counsels were at all times most valuable. He is the attorney for the Jamesville & Washington railroad, and for the Roanoke Railroad & Lumber company, and also the Wilmington & Weldon railroad company.

In 1888, Mr. Small served as chairman of the democratic executive committee of the First congressional district of North Carolina. As a leading citizen he has done much to stimulate the industrial growth of the city and county, and was largely instrumental in securing the location of the extensive oyster canning establishment of J. S. Farren & Co., at Washington, and in many other ways has contributed to the prosperity of the community. He ranks among the ablest and most successful attorneys of the Beaufort bar, and is held in the highest esteem as a man of superior mind and unbending integrity. He was most happily married June 11, 1890, to Miss Isabella C. Wharton, a daughter of Col. R. W. Wharton, a leading citizen of Beaufort county, N. C., and one child has blessed their union, May Belle Small. Mr. Small is a son of John H. and Sally A. (Sanderson) Small, natives of Chowan and Washington counties, N. C., respectively. His father was a prominent planter of Beaufort county for many years, having settled there about 1835. He is a member of the Methodist Episcopal church, south, and a staunch democrat.

WILLIAM BLOUNT RODMAN

was born at Washington, Beaufort county, N. C., on the 29th of June, 1817. His father's name was William Walton Rodman, from Queens county, New York. The first ancestor of the Rodman family, of whom they know anything, was John Rodman, who was a Quaker, and went from Ireland to Barbadoes, where he died in 1686. He had been imprisoned in Ireland for contempt of court, because he refused to pull off his hat, and was afterward turned out of the Quaker society, because he owned slaves. Quakerism could never have been long lived as a sect. By its very constitution it renounced any army of mercenary priests to defend it. The peculiar garb and speech of the Quakers will soon disappear forever; but the principle of George Fox: that every man is his own priest, and that every man's reason is his divine guide to eternal life, is the logical result of Protestant thought, and must continue to live, until all independence of thought shall have yielded to the infallibility of a pope. His children were Quakers; they emigrated to Rhode Island and New Jersey, and their descendants are now numerous in most or all of the northern states. The parents of Mr. Rodman both died while he was an infant, and he and his two sisters were taken into the family of his maternal grandfather, John Gray Blount, a family well known in the histories of North Carolina and Tennessee. His grandfather sent him to the University of North Carolina, where he graduated with the first honors of his class, in 1836. He read law under Judge Gaston, in Newbern, and was licensed as an attorney in 1838. He resided in the town of his birth, and had an extensive practice in that and the adjoining counties, being also engaged in planting. In September, 1858, he married Camilla, a daughter of Wiley Croom, of Greensboro, Ala., and her death, in 1887, was felt as the greatest misfortune of his life.

Mr. Rodman was educated a democrat, and a believer in the rights of states, as taught by Jefferson and Calhoun. After the breaking out of the late Civil war, he was elected captain of a company of volunteers, and felt bound to accept, under the belief that he was acting in defense of his state, which had a right to his services. With his company he participated in the battle of Newbern, in March, 1862. To show the fratricidal character of that war, two of the descendants of their common ancestor, and bearing the same family name, were engaged in this battle, as officers of a Connecticut regiment. After this battle and resignation of Major Hood, quartermaster of Branch's brigade, Capt. Rodman was promoted to that position. He accompanied the brigade to Virginia, and was present at the battle of Mechanicsville, and at sundry skirmishes. At this time he was appointed by President Davis, to be the presiding judge of a military court, to sit in Richmond, under the command of whatever general might be in command of Richmond. This court had jurisdiction to try all Confederate soldiers and officers, not above the rank of brigadier-general, for all military offenses. His associates were Col. John M. Patton, of Richmond, who had commanded the First regiment of Virginia volunteers, Gen. B. T. Johnson, of Maryland, and later Col. Bateler, of Harper's Ferry, after the resignation of Gen. Johnson. These gentlemen have their places in the history of the Confederacy, and need no encomiums here.

Mr. Rodman continued in Richmond and Petersburg until the evacuation of those places by the Confederates, and accompanied the retreating army of Gen. Lee as far as a place called Pamphitts station on a railroad, where, under the advice of Gen. Matthew Ransom, who said that the Confederate army must certainly surrender in a day or two, he left the army, and proceeded on foot to join that of Gen. Joseph Johnston, which he found near Greensboro, N. C., and which itself surrendered the next day. He received his parole as an officer in Johnson's army. From Greensboro, where his family had sought refuge after the battle of Newbern, he returned to his former residence in Washington. Here he found that he had lost all the property that he had, that could be pillaged or destroyed. Probably no one in the state lost more largely in proportion to his means. His slaves, about 100 in number, had been carried off and scattered, except a few, who came and insisted on living under his care, notwithstanding their emancipation, and these have continued to do so up to this time. His furniture and household goods which he had left in the care of a lady in Washington, had been seized in the name of the United States, as abandoned property; the numerous and comfortable buildings on his plantation nearly opposite the town of Washington had been burned, and even the bricks of the chimneys to their foundations in the ground, with his fruit trees and grape vines, had been dug up and carried off; this was done, however, not by the soldiers of the United States, but by the neighbors who remained at home, and whom the northern soldiers contemptuously called "buffaloes," after a sort of cattle that have no horns. The United States sent soldiers to bring away the negroes from his plantation, and all his horses, machinery and farming utensils, and their proceeds, unless stolen on their way, may still be in the treasury of the great United States. This was to preserve and perpetuate "the Union." This was the way in which the union between England and Ireland was attempted to be perpetuated by William and his successors, with the result that Ireland has been in rebellion ever since, and now after 200 years of conciliation, is ready to ally itself with any nation that England may be at war with. It is to be hoped that the good sense of the southern people will permit no such wound to fester in its heart. Let retribution to the wrong doer come at once and on him, not on his children; and if that is impossible, let the wrong be forgotten.

In 1867, Gen. Canby, commandant of the military department o which North Carolina was a part, called a convention to make such changes in the constitution of the state as would restore it to its place in the Union. Mr. Rodman was popular with the negroes who then voted for the first time, because he had always been a kind master, and with the Confederate soldiers and democrats because he had been one of them, and his interests and theirs were identical, and although he was bitterly opposed by the "buffaloes" he was elected to the convention by a large majority. The convention met in January. 1868. Several of its members were northern men who had come into the state during or after the war. These men were contemptuously called carpet-baggers by the members of the party which then called itself democratic, although a great many of them had never called themselves such, or acted uniformly with that party even during the war. It has been the fashion ever since to describe these men as a set of unprincipled adventurers, intent only on plunder. Some of these deserved to be so classed, as did some who were natives of North Carolina. But the most prominent northern men in the convention, Gen. Abbott, Col. David Heaton, A. W. Tourgee, D. I. Rich and several others, did their duty to the state intelligently and faithfully. Such adventurers are a gain to the state, and it is to be wished that North Carolina had more such. Of course their opinions and prejudices on many subjects were different from ours, and unfortunately as to Judge Tourgee, some of these prejudices have continued in spite of experience and have materially impaired the usefulness of his undoubted literary talents.

Mr. Rodman took an influential part in framing the articles in the constitution on the judiciary, and on revenue and taxation, being greatly assisted in the first by Tourgee and in the last by Heaton. Tourgee is entitled to whatever credit may be due for the first section of the article on the judiciary which abolished the existing practice and procedure in civil actions, and impliedly involved the adoption of the New York on those subjects. Rodman is responsible for the sections in the article on revenue and taxation, fixes the proportion between the tax on property and that on polls, which, so far as we know, had not previously appeared in the constitution of any state; of that which fixes the proportion between the state and county taxes; of that which provides that no income tax shall be levied upon the property from which the income is derived shall be taxed; and of that in the article on corporations which forbids the legislature to charter private corporations by special act; but unfortunately following the constitution of New York, we believe, he added: "Except when in its judgment the objects of the legislature could not be otherwise obtained." The exception to the attempted restraint, a better example for such a restraint may be found in the constitution of Pennsylvania since adopted. The attempted prohibition appealed only to the conscience of legislators, and more than half of every volume of legislative acts since 1868, is filled with acts which are apparently beyond the rightful powers of the general assembly. And so it has been with the section which forbids municipal corporations to contract debts without the sanction of the legislature. This it was

B—14

thought would be difficult to obtain. But alas! it is always granted
without inquiry.

The constitution provided for the appointment of three commissioners to prepare and report to the legislature, a code of the law of
North Carolina; Rodman, Tourgee and Victor Barringer were appointed. As the constitution had abolished the existing law of
practice and procedure, and the administration of justice in civil actions was entirely suspended, prompt action was necessary in supplying another. The commissioners agreed to adopt the code of New
York which had been used for several years in that and numerous
other states, with such alterations as were necessary to adapt it to
the judicial system of North Carolina. These alterations mostly
fell to the lot of Mr. Rodman, and the code as thus hastily, but not
inconsiderately altered, was speedily reported to and adopted by the
legislature which met in 1868. The changes since made in it by
which the pleadings are made up in term time only and not in vacation, as originally provided for, have delayed the trial of actions, and
have not benefited either parties or attorneys. The code originally
provided for the repayment of his necessary expenses in attorneys'
costs to the successful party. But that has been changed rather accidentally than deliberately, and North Carolina is now the only
country in the world in which a litigant party can recover his debt or
property, only at his own expense.

It also fell mainly to the share of Mr. Rodman to draw the acts on
the subjects of criminal procedure. Draining low lands, landlord
and tenant, and marriage, which were enacted by the legislature of
1868, and still remain in the statute book substantially as drawn.
Afterward he prepared with great labor, a more comprehensive code
of penal procedure, which the legislature neglected to consider. At
the election for justices of the supreme court of the state in 1868, Mr.
Rodman was elected as one of them and served in that capacity
until his term expired in 1878. His opinions may be found in volumes from sixty-three to seventy-nine inclusive, in the reports of that
court. It may be said that they are frequently cited with respect by
the succeeding judges of that court. After his retirement from the
bench, he returned to the bar and to the management of a large
plantation which has occupied much of his attention. In politics he
has always been a democrat, except when he voted for Holden for
governor, and for Gen. Grant for president; under the circumstances
which he considered exceptional. He is spending the evening of his
life with a family of sons and daughters, content with having discharged his duties honestly and to the best of his abilities.

JOHN C. DAVIS,

a young, self-made and successful attorney-at-law, practicing and
residing at Wilmington, N. C., where he has lived since 1877, was
born in Carteret county, N. C., and his parents were Samuel E. and
Jane (Roberts) Davis. The father, who was a merchant by occupa-

tion, is now deceased, while the mother resides with her son, in Wilmington. The circumstances of our subject's youth were not at all promising, the war ravaging the wealth of the parents, and at the age of thirteen years, the boy went to sea as a sailor and remained at sea till 1877, when he came to Wilmington, and worked in the Wilmington cotton mills as a weaver. About this time certain friends became interested in him and gave him access to books, for which he soon formed a love, and afterward began the study of law, and under the night instructions by John D. Bellamy, Jr., he became enabled to secure a license to practice at the bar in 1884, since when he has been in the active practice of the profession. He is a consistent member of the Methodist Episcopal church and is a respected citizen. He has taken much interest in church and Sunday-school; was a delegate to the world's Sunday-school convention which met at London, Eng., in 1889. He thus visited Europe and became better schooled in the history of the east, and in 1890 rendered much aid to the rector of the Fifth Street Methodist Episcopal church of Wilmington.

WILLIAM A. WRIGHT.

There were few men in eastern Carolina better known and few in the state more highly esteemed and deservedly so, than William A. Wright. He was the son of the Hon. Joshua G. Wright, and was born in Wilmington in 1807. He was graduated at the University of North Carolina when very young and embraced the profession of the law. He possessed great powers of application, was regarded as a better counselor than advocate, and as a corporation lawyer, as it is termed, had few equals either at home or abroad. He made no pretensions to oratory, and yet his efforts before a jury were often very effective. For many years he was chairman of the county court under the old regime, and upon the death of his brother, Dr. Thomas H. Wright, president of the Bank of Cape Fear, he was elected to that position and proved himself an able financier and man of business. He was the attorney and also a director of the Wilmington & Weldon railroad from the commencement of that great work, and was in continued service the oldest railroad director in the United States. He had a peculiarly happy temperament, was amiable and hospitable to a degree, was fond of a joke and excelled in the telling of one, and delighted in social gatherings where his overflowing humor made him the life of the occasion. He was at the service of his friends at all times and perhaps no member of the profession gave up so much of his time and professional advice also, to others without any hope of compensation; in fact he never seemed happier than when so engaged. The writer recalls numerous occasions when he has seen him so employed, searching up authorities upon intricate points of law and undergoing an amount of mental work that would tax the energies of the most robust. Of modest and retiring disposition, he shrank from the turmoils of politics, but in 1865, while absent from the city, he was elected a member of the convention which met at Raleigh soon after the organization of the provisional government of the state and known as the reconstruction convention. He accepted the position and his well-known habits of industry and application joined to his large experience and recognized ability gave him an influence second to but few in that body, numbering as it did among its members such men as B. F. Moore, Edwin G. Reade, Nathaniel Boyden, Bedford Brown and others who might be mentioned. While he was conservative by nature and opposed to extremes of every kind, he had the courage of his convictions and never hesitated when occasion demanded to express his views upon all questions with a frankness that challenged respect and commanded attention. He was greatly esteemed and respected, in fact was a popular favorite, and it is doubtful if he left behind him an enemy in the world. He died in May, 1878, the Nestor of the Wilmington bar, mourned not only by his legal brethren, but by the community at large, for his public career was without reproach and his personal life blameless. Mr. Wright married Eliza Ann Hill, daughter of William Hill, Esq., and had many children, but they died young, his widow and but one child, a son, surviving him.

JUDGE AVERY.

" It was early in the year 1631 that the ship Arabella landed its passengers at the place where now stand Boston and Charleston, and where Gov. John Winthrop, Sr., had commenced an English settlement the year before. Among the passengers were Christopher Avery and his little son James, then eleven years old." James married Joanna Greenslade and removed to New London in 1651, where he built a stone house which is still standing and is occupied by one of the Averys — the eighth generation from James. At the battle of Groton Heights, when Benedict Arnold, September 5, 1781, captured New London and massacred the garrison, "eleven Averys were killed in the fort and seven wounded." Solomon Avery, writing from Groton to his brother Waightstill, in North Carolina in 1783, said, " Many Averys have been killed in this war. There have been no tories named Avery in these parts." Samuel, the seventh son of James Avery, was born in 1664, and in 1686 married Susan Palms, a daughter of Maj. Palms and granddaughter of Gov. John Winthrop, Jr., of Massachusetts. He had ten children, seven being sons. The sixth child was Humphrey, who was born July 4, 1699, and married Jerusha Morgan, by whom he had twelve children.

Waightstill was born May 10, 1741. He was prepared for college by Samuel Seabury, of Groton, and graduated at Princeton in 1766, where he served as tutor for a year. He subsequently studied law with Lyttleton Dennis, a prominent lawyer of Maryland, and came to North Carolina in 1769. He kept a journal from the day he entered North Carolina, for many years, which has proved of much historic interest. Entering the province in the Albermarle section, he presented his letters of introduction to Iredell and Hewes, and the first

A. C. AVERY, Judge Supreme Court.

men in the colony, and was at once received with friendship and esteem. He located near Charlotte and not far from Salisbury, where the western court was held, boarding with Hezekiah Alexander, and soon found in Mecklenburg his college mates at Princeton, Dr. Ephriam Brevard, Adlai Osborne, and Rev. Hezekiah J. Balch. He was an early friend of liberty and a promoter of all patriotic movements, and soon established himself as one of the most influential leaders in his section of the province. He was a member of the provincial congress of 1775, and also that of 1776, which framed the constitution, and he was one of the committee that brought that instrument forward.

Upon the formation of the state government, in 1777, he was chosen attorney-general, and while attending court at Newbern, he met the young widow, Leah Franks, whom he married in 1778. As she had large landed interests in Jones county, in 1779, he settled in that county, and resigning the office of attorney-general, succeeded Nathan Bryan as colonel of the Jones county militia—the militia being always more or less in active service. In 1777 he had been on a commission to make a treaty with the Cherokees, over the mountains, and was doubtless led, by his journey in the west, to appreciate the salubrious climate of that region. In 1781, eastern Carolina being then invaded, he removed his family to Swan Pond, a tract of land he had acquired in Burke county, where he subsequently resided. He often represented Burke county in the assembly up to 1796. In 1801 he was stricken with paralysis, but continued to practice his profession until a few years before his death in 1821. He was one of the most cultivated men in the state, possessed an extensive library and maintained his knowledge of the Latin language even in his old age. He left three daughters and a son. Elizabeth married William Lenoir, and Louisa, Thomas Lenoir. His only son was Isaac Thomas Avery, who was born at Swan Pond, September 22, 1785, and died December 31, 1864, in his eightieth year. He was several times a member of the legislature, and was an influential gentleman in his section of the state.

In 1815 he married Harriet, the oldest daughter of Col. W. W. Erwin. For more than thirty years he was cashier of the bank at Morganton, and at the same time was largely engaged in agriculture and stock raising. No place in all that region was better known for elegant hospitality than his home at Swan Pond. Here Col. Avery lived with every comfort, surrounded by a devoted family, and beloved and esteemed by all who knew him. His days were prolonged until within the space of one year, he was bereft of his three eldest sons who fell in defense of the south. Col. William Waightstill Avery, the eldest son was born May 25, 1816. Having graduated at the University of North Carolina, he studied law with Judge Gaston and soon entered public life as a states rights democrat. He often represented his county in the legislature, was chairman of the North Carolina delegation in the national delegation of 1856, and again in 1860, and was a member of the provisional congress of the Confederate states, where he rendered efficient public service. No man in the state commanded higher respect for his talents, attainments and worth than Col. Avery. In 1864 an incursion was made by a maurading party from Tennessee into Burke county. They were led by the notorious Col. Kirk. Col. Avery hastily gathered together a body of militia and started in pursuit. In attacking Kirk's force in a strong position in the mountains, he was mortally wounded and died on the 3d of July, 1864, universally lamented throughout the borders of the state.

Col. Clark Moulton Avery was the second of the six sons of Col. Isaac T. Avery. He was born October 3, 1819, and died June 19, 1864, of wounds received at Spottsylvania Court House. He commanded a company at Big Bethel, and rose by merit to be colonel of the Thirty-third regiment North Carolina infantry, and was one of the most gallant and meritorious officers of the service. He married· Elizabeth, a daughter of Thomas Walton, and left four children. Col. Isaac Erwin Avery was born December 20, 1828. He was, when the war broke out, in partnership with Col. C. F. Fisher and S. M. D. Tate, as contractor for building portions of the W. N. C. railroad, and proved himself a most efficient manager of construction work. He raised a company and joined Col. Fisher's regiment; was wounded at Manassas in 1861 and at Gaines' Mills, and became colonel of the Sixth North Carolina troops. On the afternoon of the second day's fight at Gettysburg, Col. Avery was in command of Hoke's brigade, and together with Hay's brigade attacked the Federal works on Cemetery hill, and after an obstinate fight in which the losses were very heavy, entered the works. In the assault Col. Avery was shot through the neck and fell speechless. In his hand was found a bloody scroll upon which he had written, with a pencil, despite his great agony — "Col. Tate, tell my father that I fell with my face to the enemy."

Next to the youngest son of Col. Isaac Avery was Judge Alphonso Calhoun Avery, who was born September 11, 1837. He took first honors at Chapel Hill, and read law with Chief-Justice Pearson. In May, 1861, he was commissioned a lieutenant in Company E, of the Sixth North Carolina troops, and with his brother, Capt. Avery, was complimented for gallantry at Manassas. In 1862 he was promoted to a captaincy, and was later commissioned as major, and assistant adjutant-general of D. H. Hill's division, and in 1863 accompanied Gen. Hill to the western army. He served there on the staff of Breckinridge, Hindman and Hood. Subsequently he was given command of a battalion in North Carolina, but was captured by Stoneman's forces near Salisbury and was kept a prisoner until August, 1865. In 1866 he was elected to the state senate, and served in that the last legislative body elected exclusively by the white people of the state. Two years later he was again returned to the senate, but was not permitted to take his seat. In 1875 he represented Burke in the constitutional convention, and rendered efficient and valuable service in that body. He had always been an active and zealous adherent of the democratic party, and was a member of the state executive committee. In 1876 he was a presidential elector, and in 1878 he was elected judge of the superior court for the Eighth judicial district.

After ten years' service on the superior court bench, in which the people of the state realized the extent of his unusual powers and fine judicial attainments, Judge Avery was elevated to the supreme court bench, where his talents and learning and discriminating judgment have greatly enhanced his reputation as an eminent jurist. Generous, with a kindly disposition, and possessing a fund of humor, he is off the bench a most agreeable companion. Handsome in person, with a splendid physique, full of sympathy and personal magnetism, he is an ornament to society, while his philanthrophy and genuine Christianity and manliness of carriage endear him to a host of admiring friends. On February 27, 1861, Judge Avery was united in marriage with Susan W. Morrison, daughter of the Rev. R. H. Morrison, and a granddaughter of Gen. Joseph Graham, and a sister of the wife of Gen. Stonewall Jackson, and by her had six children, of whom four survive, viz.: Isaac Erwin Avery, of Morganton; Susan W., Alphonso C. and Alfred L. His wife dying in March, 1886, Judge Avery married December 31, 1888, Miss Sallie Love Thomas, a daughter of Col. W. H. Thomas, of Jackson county, by whom he has one son, Lenoir Avery.

DR. KARL VON RUCK,

an able and scholarly physician of Asheville, N. C., gives his sole attention to diseases of the lungs and throat. He was born at Constantinople, Turkey, July 10, 1849, his father, Baron Johann von Ruck, being at the time of his birth the German minister at that place. Dr. von Ruck was reared in Wurtemburg, Germany, and was educated at the Royal gymnasium in Stuttgart, graduating there at the age of seventeen years. He then completed a medical course in the University of Tuebingen; before graduating, however, the Franco-Prussian war had been inaugurated, and he was appointed to a position as assistant under Prof. von Bruns, which he held until the close of the war. Afterward he resumed his studies in the university, and graduating with honors, came to America. Here he entered the medical department of the University of Michigan and completed a course in it, graduating in 1878, thereafter spending about a year in the New York hospitals. Dr. von Ruck now entered upon his professional career at Norwalk, Ohio, where he continued until 1883. At that time Prof. Koch announced the discovery of the germ of tuberculosis, and in order to acquaint himself with the nature of the discovery, Dr. von Ruck went to Berlin and spent about eight months in the Hygienic laboratory under Prof. Koch, and in the Pathological institute of Prof. Virchow. He also, before leaving Germany, visited the private institutions throughout that country for the treatment of consumption. Returning to Ohio in 1884 he now established a private hospital for consumption, and encouraged by the favorable results he obtained, and in order to have the assistance of the best climatic condition as well, he removed to Asheville, N. C., in 1888, where he established the Winyaw Sanitarium for diseases of the lungs and throat. He has conducted that institution since, and it has become one of the famous sanitariums of the kind in the United States, and is modeled and conducted upon the plan of the leading private institutions in Germany. The institution is supported by the leading physicians in all parts of the country who send their patients there for treatment.

Upon the discovery by Prof. Koch, of Berlin, of the remedy for tuberculosis, now called tuberculin, Dr. von Ruck hastened to Berlin and was the first of the army of physicians to secure the remedy for use in a private institution. Since his return, he has administered it to a large number of patients with great success, enjoying now, after the riper reflection of the profession, the distinction of being the first physician to use it in a proper manner. Apart from this remedy which is considered only an aid in suitable cases, the climatic, dietetic, hydropathic and other methods of treatment are carefully carried out, and the records of the institution show now, sixty-nine cured and a great number of permanently arrested and greatly improved cases of consumption. Dr. von Ruck is a member of the American Climatological association, the American Medical association, and a number of other important medical societies, and the author of many important publications relating to his specialty. In the year past there were treated about 100 patients. The institution, besides the offices, laboratory, parlors, billiard rooms, etc., has sixty-five guest rooms, and is unexceptional in all its appointments. Especial attention is given not only to thorough disinfection of all the rooms, but any article with which patients come in contact is subjected to disinfection by steam before it is again used; thus making residence in the establishment not only one of security and prospect for recovery for the invalid, but conferring immunity from infection to the well, and such as seek climate for eradicating the predisposition to the disease, or for convalesence.

DR. JOHN ANDERSON WATSON,

a leading physician of Asheville, N. C., was born at Clay Hill, York county, S. C., December 18, 1849. He is the son of Dr. David M. Watson who also was a physician by profession and who, in his day was one of the prominent practitioners of South Carolina. The latter was also born in York county, the date of his birth being January 24, 1814. He was the son of David Watson, also a native of York county, and a farmer by occupation who was born in 1772. The latter was the son of Col. Samuel Watson, a revolutionary soldier born in 1731. The Watson family descended from an emigrant from the northern part of Ireland, a Scotch-Irishman and Presbyterian, and his faith has been the faith of the many generations which have followed him. Three sons of David Watson, the grandfather of the subject of this sketch, were physicians by profession and another son, Rev. S. L. Watson, was a Presbyterian minister who for forty years was pastor of Bethel church, in York county, and one of the highly respected men of that section. The father of Dr. Watson died August 11, 1855. His mother was Mary J. Anderson, who was a native of York county, the daughter of John Anderson a planter, and the sister of Rev. J. M. Anderson, a Presbyterian divine, who for many years was a member of the faculty of the Davidson college. Maternally as well as paternally, Dr. Watson is of Scotch-Irish descent, the Anderson family in this country having also been founded by an emigrant from the northern part of Ireland.

Dr. Watson spent his early life in York county, S. C., and was educated in the Kings Mountain military academy, of Yorkville, and in the South Carolina university. For a want of means he was obliged to leave the latter institution one year before his graduation would have taken place. Shortly after leaving the university he became possessed of a desire to fit himself for the practice of medicine. Fortunately for him, at this tims, a kinsman, being aware of this desire, offered to provide him with the necessary funds to give him a medical education. He availed himself of this offer, and though the total sum thus advanced him amounted to more than $1,600, it has been paid in full together with interest. In the fall of 1870 Dr. Watson entered the medical department of the University of Maryland, at Baltimore. After taking one course in that school, he became an interne in the university hospital, and graduated in March, 1872. After completing his medical education he became a resident physician in the Bay View hospital, of Baltimore, and held that position about one year, after which he returned to South Carolina, and was shortly afterward appointed demonstrator of anatomy in the South Carolina university. He held that position likewise about one year, at the end of which time he resigned to turn his whole attention to the practice of his profession. Locating at Chester, S. C., he became the partner of Dr. A. P. Wylie, a prominent practitioner of that place. Dr. Wylie died some three or four years later, after which Dr. Watson succeeded to the practice of the firm, which was very large, and to which he devoted himself until 1884. In that year he removed to Asheville, N. C., where he has been in the active and successful practice of his profession ever since, and of which city he is a leading physician.

Dr. Watson was chiefly instrumental in establishing the Mission hospital at Asheville in 1885, being associated in that project with Drs. S. W. Battle and the late Wardlaw McGill. Dr. Watson has been one of the attending physicians of that hospital ever since. While he is a general practitioner, he has paid special attention to the treatment and study of diseases of women, and he is recognized as one of the most competent in that branch of practice in western North Carolina. In view of his fitness for the position, he was upon the establishment of the Mission hospital placed in charge of the women's department, which position he still holds. He is a member of the Buncombe county medical society. In politics he is a conservative democrat, and has served one term as coroner of Buncombe county. He is a member of the Presbyterian church. Dr. Watson was married June 7, 1886, to Miss Arabella, the daughter of James M. Tebbetts, of Great Falls, N. H. Her mother was Hannah E. Brackett, a native of Maine. Dr. Watson has taken three post-graduate courses, two in the polyclinic, and one in the University of New York.

DR. MORAGN LINES NEILSON,

an old and honored physician of Asheville, N. C., was born in Green county, Tenn., March 17, 1822. He was the son of Archibald D. Neilson, a native of North Carolina and a farmer by occupation, who died more than forty years ago. The father served in the war of 1812, and was a recruiting officer under Gen. Jackson, at the battle of New Orleans. The latter was the son of William Neilson, a native of Scotland, who graduated at the University of Glasgow, and came to America shortly after the Revolutionary war, and settled at Lynchburg, Va., where he followed mercantile pursuits. He subsequently removed to Tennessee, and later to North Carolina, locating in the vicinity of what is now known as Hot Springs, which property he owned and improved. The mother of Dr. Neilson was Eliza Lines, a native of South Carolina, and a niece of Gen. Francis Marion. She also died more than forty years ago. The subject of this sketch was reared upon a farm in Greene county, Tenn. He received his education in a country school, and at Greenville college. At the age of twenty-one he entered upon the study of medicine under Drs. Hale and Walker, of Greene county. In the fall of 1842 he entered the Transylvania medical college, of Lexington, and in it he attended one course of lectures. In 1843 he began the practice of medicine in Beech Bottoms, Tenn. He was married in 1844, in Buncombe county, now Madison county, N. C., to Laura Henrietta Vance, sister of United States Senator Z. B. Vance. In 1845 Dr. Neilson located in Asheville, N. C., where he has resided and practiced his profession ever since, with the exception of two years, 1867 and 1868, during which he resided in Spartanburg, S. C., and Tennessee. In the fall of 1851 he entered the Philadelphia college of medicine, graduating in 1852. He served three years of the Civil war as surgeon, resigning the position just before the close of the war, on account of ill health. Dr. Neilson is a general practitioner. He has practiced his profession for nearly a half century, and his career has been a most honorable one. He is a member of the Buncombe county medical society, and belongs to the Methodist Episcopal church, south. In politics he is a democrat. Dr. Neilson and wife have two sons living. Though nearly seventy years of age, Dr. Neilson is still in the active practice of his profession.

DR. JAMES ANTHONY BURROUGHS,

one of the rising and popular young physicians of Asheville, N. C., is a native of Kanawha county, W. Va., and was born December 8, 1858. His parents were James and Sarah (Ruckel) Burroughs, both natives of Bedford county, Va. His father combined farming and merchandising and was highly esteemed in the community. He located in what is now West Virginia, in 1853, and when the Civil war broke out he joined the Confederate army and soon made himself conspicuous for gallant and meritorious conduct in the face of the enemy, for which he was rewarded with a major's commission, holding the same with credit to himself throughout the sanguinary struggle. Dr. J. A. Burroughs began his education in the Virginia schools, afterward entering the Louisville, Ky., medical college, from which he graduated with distinguished honors, in 1882. His close application to his studies was something of a strain upon his physical forces, and he graduated with his health partially impaired. He had mastered his medical course in much less time than is usually consumed for that purpose, and the temporary loss of health was the penalty exacted of him. But his indomitable spirit did not yield, and he started out in the practice of his profession at Paucha Springs, very soon working up an extensive and profitable practice. He soon found, however, that the field at this place was too narrow for the full developments of his powers, and in 1882 he removed to Asheville, which place promised to give his medical genius full scope and ample verge. Here the immediate and continual enlargement of his business shows that he chose a locality where his talents, learning and natural adaptation to the requirements of his profession are duly appreciated, and the extent of his professional engagements is only to be measured by his endurance and strength to answer the calls upon him.

Few practitioners of Mr. Borroughs's age have ever come so rapidly to the front, or exhibited qualities in their profession of a higher grade. Even in the outset of his career, comparatively, he bids fair to soon reach the front rank in his profession, and attain a reputation as wide as the boundaries of the state. Dr. Borroughs is a member of the state medical society of North Carolina, and a member of the Buncombe county medical society. He is city physician of Asheville, and a member of the Asheville board of health. In the midst of his busy practice, and of his official duties, he does not ignore nor neglect the material, social, intellectual and moral improvement of the community in which he has cast his lot, but takes an active concern in this direction. He has a property interest in several large enterprises outside of his professional circles, but is an active agent in every direction for the up-building and improvement of society. In December, 1882, Dr. Burroughs was married to Miss Annie Reynolds, a lady of wide culture and fine accomplishments, the daughter of Dr. John Reynolds, of Asheville.

DR. SAMUEL WESTRAY BATTLE,

a distinguished naval officer and physician was born in Nash county, N. C.. August 4, 1854. His parents were William S. and Elizabeth (Dancy) Battle, both native North Carolinians. The father's occupation was that of a planter and manufacturer and he carried on an extensive business in both, being one of the largest dealers in his section of the country. He brought both energy and intelligence to the task of conducting his varied enterprises and thereby won success. He took a lively interest in politics but never aspired to office holding. Yet his strong common sense and sagacity suggested his fitness for public duties and when the secession movement was inaugurated, he was chosen a member of the state convention which took that subject into consideration. He was also chosen to other offices in his county. Dr. Battle, in his youth, attended Horner's classical and mathematical school at Oxford, N. C., and afterward entered the Bellevue high school in Bedford county, Va. Here he fitted himself for the Virginia state university, and in that institution entered upon a medical and classical course, graduating with honors in 1874. But he was not yet satisfied in his professional researches and entered Bellevue hospital and medical college of New York, from which he graduated in 1875. With this elaborate preparation he entered the United States service as surgeon in the naval department, passing a rigid competitive examination for that position. He fully illustrated his fitness for this important trust by the signal brilliancy of his official career. His field of operation was on the seas and in every naval port, and his services were of the highest order of merit. They were arduous and extended to a term of ten years, from 1875 till 1885. His services were terminated by a collision at sea in which he received a severe wound in his left arm by which he was for a time practically disabled for the performance of surgical operations. He was consequently retired from active naval duty but without the loss of his rank in the service.

In 1879 he was appointed to take charge of the United States hospital in Florida, where he spent about four years. In 1885 he began the practice of his profession as a private practitioner in Asheville, and his business at once became extensive and profitable. Professionally, Dr. Battle is a thorough and progressive student, constantly abreast of the times in medical and surgical sciences. His general intelligence and knowledge of the world, nearly all parts of which he has personally visited, make him a great favorite in social circles, where his suavity of manner and the brilliancy of his conversational powers are duly appreciated. Ever since the establishment of the Asheville city hospital in 1886, Dr. Battle has been in charge and his services therein are a public beneficence. He is very popular as a member of the board of health of the city of Asheville, and is president of the Buncombe county medical society. In business lines he is vice-president of the Asheville Street Railway company, director in the Light & Power company, one of the incorporators, president and a director of the Cosmopolitan club, and vice-president of Asheville Park & Hotel Co. Dr. Battle was married to Miss Alice M., daughter of Admiral George E. Belknap, of New Hampshire, a naval officer of the highest distinction. Dr. and Mrs. Battle have three children, Madelon B., Samuel W. and Belknap Battle. The doctor is a member of the Episcopal church.

DR. WILLIAM D. HILLIARD,

a prominent physician of Asheville, N. C., was born in the city in which he now resides, March 11, 1858. He is the son of Dr. William L. Hilliard, a native of Georgia, and a physician who practiced his profession for more than forty years in Asheville. He died October 11, 1890. The mother of William D. Hilliard was Margaret E., daughter of Col. James R. Love, and she was born at Waynesville, N. C. She is still living. Dr. Hilliard was reared in Asheville, and was educated in Col. Stephen Lee's high school, in which he obtained a knowledge of the classics, in addition to a good English training. At the early age of seventeen he entered upon the study of medicine, under the preceptorship of his father, and in the fall of 1876, entered the Jefferson medical college of Philadelphia, from which he graduated in 1878. He at once began the practice of medicine as the partner of his father, and this partnership continued until 1881. He soon built up a lucrative practice which he resigned in 1882, to accept the position of assistant superintendent of the Western North Carolina insane asylum, at Morganton, N. C. He held that position three years, resigning it in 1884. He then returned to Asheville, where he has since been in the active practice of medicine, and of which city he is now a leading physician and surgeon. Dr. Hilliard is a member of the North Carolina medical society, and of the state board of health. He is the local surgeon of the Richmond & Danville railroad company, and the assistant surgeon general of North Carolina. Dr. Hilliard has served several terms as coroner of Buncombe county. He is a Mason, a Knights Templar and a member of the I. O. O. F. lodge. In politics he is a democrat. Dr. Hilliard was married in 1884 to Miss Mary V. Duffield, of Norfolk, Va., and they have one child, a daughter.

S. T. & P. A. NICHOLSON.

Sir Malile Nicholson left England in 1748 and sought a home in the new world, settling in Halifax county, N. C., on a tract of land granted him by King George II. His son, Thomas Wright Nicholson, was born in Halifax county. He became a very prominent and influential man in the community, and served in the patriot army of 1776 as a colonel. He was a large land owner and slaveholder, and represented his county in the state legislature for several years. As a member of the Methodist Episcopal church he did much toward building up that denomination in his section of the state, and was a man of great force of character and ability. Temperance Winifred Wiggins became his wife and bore him the following named children: James; Joseph, deceased; Timothy, of Mississippi, a prominent lawyer; Blake B., Mary, Laura and Winnie. Blake B. Nicholson was educated at Washington and Lee university, and followed in the footsteps of his father and noble grandsire as a planter. In 1858 he removed to Mississippi, and there became a major in the Mississippi Guards. He returned to Halifax county in 1882, and now resides at Panacea Springs, Halifax county, N. C. He is an active democrat, a prominent Mason, and a steward in the Methodist Episcopal church, south. By his marriage to Miss Lucy C. Thorne, nine children have been born, viz.: Temperance W., wife of E. A. Daniel, of Panacea Springs; Samuel T., M. D.; J. T., of Bath, N. C.; B. B., Jr., assistant treasurer of Trinity college; P. A., of Washington, N. C.; Mary E., wife of Samuel J. Clarke, of Enfield, N. C.; William Edward, manager of the Bath Lumber Co.; Lucilla G., wife of James Clarke, of Enfield, N. C., and Katie, who resides at home. Samuel T. Nicholson, the immediate subject of this biographical mention, was born on the family estate in Halifax county, N. C., December 25, 1855. He was graduated from Fork institute, then under the management of Prof. John Graham, and began to study medicine with Dr. E. T. Taylor, of Washington, and graduated from the College of Physicians and Surgeons at Baltimore, in 1881. In the same year he began the practice of his profession in Beaufort county. He is a member of the state medical society, and for the past eight years has been a United States pension examining surgeon. He is a prominent member of the I. O. O. F., is a school commissioner, and a leading member of the democratic party in the county. Dr. Nicholson has been very active in encouraging and instituting new and important industrial enterprises, and was prominently identified with the organization of the Bath Manufacturing company, in which he is a large stockholder; he was an organizer of the Washington Industrial association, and since its establishment has been treasurer, he is also treasurer of the Young Men's Christian association, of Washington. In 1890 he erected the magnificent hotel at Washington, known as the Hotel Nicholson. On the 4th of July, 1876, his marriage to Miss Annie E. Lucas, daughter of Jesse B. Lucas, of Beaufort county, was solemnized, and has been blessed by the birth of five children: John Lawrence, Lucille Thorne, Elizabeth S., Annie Plummer and Samuel T., Jr. Dr. Nicholson is a steward and treasurer of the Methodist Episcopal church, south, of Washington, and is a leader in every enterprise promising the uplifting of the people. As a physician he has won an enviable reputation for skill and ability, and his name is known throughout that portion of the state.

Plummer A. Nicholson, M. D., was born in Halifax county, N. C., May 25, 1865. He received his scholastic training in the Thorne Branch institute, and later read medicine with Dr. S. T. Nicholson. In 1888 he received his diploma from the College of Physicians and

Surgeons at Baltimore, and at that time formed a partnership with his preceptor. He is a member of the state medical society, a stockholder in the Bath Manufacturing company, and is a prominent democrat. In 1889 he formed a marriage alliance with Miss Estella M. Hunter, daughter of Capt. Samuel B. Hunter, of Halifax county. Dr. Nicholson is a member of the Methodist Episcopal church, south, and also of the Y. M. C. A. He has an extended practice, and is regarded as one of the ablest of the younger physicians of eastern North Carolina.

COL. DAVID N. BOGART.

Among the most prominent business men of Beaufort county, N. C., appears the name of Col. David N. Bogart, the leading druggist of Washington. Col. Bogart was born in Washington, in 1847, and his parents were Gilbert and Christiana (Barden) Bogart. Gilbert Bogart was a very prominent man. He was born in New York in 1804, and came from New Jersey to North Carolina in about 1840, he having graduated from Princeton college. He was principal at different times of the academies at Washington, Edenton and Newbern. He was an elder in the Presbyterian church, and a man of godly life. He died in Washington in 1867. A whig in politics, he served as collector of customs at Washington for two years, and his death occurred while he was the incumbent of that position. As an educator he was able and active. Possessed of superior mind, he had broadened and extended his faculties by years of consistent study and reading. His wife was a native of Beaufort county. She survived her husband until 1879, and then joined him in eternal rest. To these parents three sons and three daughters were born, viz.: Annie, William, cashier of the Greensboro bank; David N., and three others, now deceased. Col. David N. Bogart is the youngest of the living children. In 1864 he joined the Confederate army, as a member of Freeman's North Carolina battalion, regular troops, and was captured by Stoneman's forces, April 12, 1865, and imprisoned at Camp Chase, Ohio. After the close of hostilities he returned home and embarked in the drug business at Washington, in 1868. Two years later he married Miss Mary, daughter of William Z. Morton, of Washington, and their eight children are all living. He served for a time as captain of the Washington light infantry, was then made major of the First North Carolina state troops, and now holds the rank of lieutenant-colonel of the same. Democratic in politics, he is a member of the school committee. He is also a prominent member of the I. O. O. F. and the Knights of Honor, and is a leading communicant of the Presbyterian church, in which he is a deacon. Mrs. Bogart is a member of the Episcopal church.

DR. W. J. T. MILLER

was born April 12, 1805, about four miles south of Rutherfordton, N. C., and died in Shelby, N. C., December 7, 1885. He was the youngest son of John and Susan Miller, and his father and grandfather were leading citizens of western North Carolina. His mother before her marriage was Miss Susan Twitty, whose family was prominent in that part of the state. Dr. Miller graduated with the degree of M. D. at Lexington, Ky., in 1827, and settled on his large plantation south of Shelby, the place taking the name of Poplar Grove. There he engaged in the practice of medicine as well as agriculture and the mercantile trade, remaining there until 1852, when he removed to Shelby. This was his permanent residence for the rest of his life. February 7, 1833, he was married to Miss Elizabeth Fullenwider. daughter of Jacob Fullenwider, of Lincoln county, and ten children were born to them, two of whom were killed in the southern army. Mrs. Miller and four sons, Dr. John F. Miller, of Goldsboro; W. H. Miller, A. C. Miller, and R. B. Miller, of Shelby; and two daughters, Mrs. Moore, of South Carolina, and Mrs. S. G. Brice, of Shelby, survive him. His sons are leading men in their professions and in society, and all are faithful and conscientious members of the church which he in his lifetime loved so well, and served so devotedly. Dr. Miller was possessed of a clear and vigorous intellect and great energy of character, and these attributes made him a most successful practitioner and business man, besides being the mainspring in all other enterprises which he undertook for the promotion of his country. With characteristics which fitted him for a wider sphere, he was not permitted to remain in the private walks of life. His qualities and adaptabilities for public positions were recognized, and in 1836 he was elected to the house of representatives from Rutherford county and served in that body for three successive terms. He was then elected to the senate from the district composed of the counties of Cleveland, Rutherford and Polk. In that body he served a number of terms and at various times, the last being in 1872 and 1874, when he represented the present district composed of Cleveland and Gaston counties.

In 1841, with the aid of his cousin, Michael Hoke, of Lincoln county, and J. G. Bynum, of Rutherford county, Dr. Miller succeeded in passing a bill for the formation of a new county, from parts of Rutherford and Lincoln counties, and at his suggestion the new county was called Cleveland, in honor of the Kings Mountain hero. He was the ruling spirit in the location of the county seat, and he gave it the name of Shelby, of Revolutionary fame. While in the senate Dr. Miller was the leader in the establishment of charitable institutions. He attended the first railroad meeting held in the state, and assisted in procuring a charter for the North Carolina railroad. He aided liberally, both with his valuable influence and with his means, in the construction of the Carolina Central railroad. In 1861 the doctor was a member of the secession convention, and as a whig, he was firmly against anything which threatened the dissolution of the Union. But, like hundreds of others of the greatest men who held the same principles and the same convictions, when the struggle came, he was on the side of his state. In 1874, after eighteen years of public service, Dr. Miller declined further preferment, and from choice, retired to private life, giving himself up to the practice of his profession, and to doing good in the community where he lived. Dr. Miller joined the Methodist Episcopal church in 1836, and was for forty-nine years a member of the church, holding the position of steward for forty years. He was more immediately and constantly identified with the interests of the church than any man in western North Carolina, as a member of the quarterly, district, annual and general conferences, and in all of these gatherings he was the leading genius among the laymen.

DR SAMUEL J. HINSDALE.

One of the most highly respected citizens of Fayetteville, Cumberland county, N. C., is Dr. Samuel J. Hinsdale, a retired business man, having for many years conducted a large pharmacy at that place. Dr. Hinsdale is a native of Middletown, Conn., where he was born in 1817, the son of John and Harriet (Johnston) Hinsdale, who were also natives of Connecticut. The father was an extensive merchant, and also carried on a large shipping business. He was well and favorably known throughout New England, where his death occurred in 1850, at the age of seventy-two; his wife died a few years later. The son, Samuel J., was educated in Connecticut, and graduated from the New York college of pharmacy, in 1837. He then went to Buffalo, N. Y., and there embarked in the drug business, and after about three years, in 1843, removed to Fayetteville, N. C., where he has been an honored citizen since. In 1843, Dr. Hinsdale opened a drug store in his new home, and continued in a large and successful business until 1835, when he retired from active life. In 1841, he was married to Miss Elizabeth, daughter of Ichabod Wetmore, of Fayetteville, and two children were born to them, viz.: Col. John W. Hinsdale, now a prominent attorney of Raleigh, N. C. In 1861, the latter enlisted in the Confederate army as an aide to Gen. Holmes, and before the close of the war, was promoted to the rank of colonel of junior reserves, and with his command, fought in the battle of Bentonville. Although he served during the entire war, he received no wound, nor was taken prisoner. He married a daughter of Maj. John Devereux, of Raleigh, and their children are: Margaret, Samuel, John, Lizzie, Nellie and Annie. The next child is Fannie, wife of Judge J. C. MacRae. The mother of these children died in 1885, aged sixty-six years. She was a life-long communicant of the Episcopal church, and was a woman of excellent attainments. In 1886, Dr. Hinsdale married Mrs. Mary (Waddill) Broadfoot, daughter of Col. Thomas Waddill, late of Cumberland county, N. C. Dr. Hinsdale has been a vestryman for a number of years, and a warden for the past twenty years in the Episcopal church at Fayetteville, and is held in the highest esteem throughout the community.

B—15

CHARLES DUFFY, JR., M. D.,

was born in Onslow county, N. C., July 18, 1838. His father, Dr. Charles Duffy, was born in Ireland, near Dublin. He received his professional training in his native land, and came to the United States in his early manhood, locating in Onslow county. He is a resident of that county at this time, having retired from active practice owing to advanced age. He is a member of the state medical society, an elder in the Presbyterian church and a trustee of the Davidson college. He married Miss Nancy C. Howse, of Onslow county, and twelve children resulted from the union, ten of whom reached maturity: Mrs. A. B. Mosely, Dr. Charles, Jr., Mrs. Elizabeth Merrill (deceased), Lawrence E., Miss Lucy, Francis, M. D., Mrs. Carolina Wooten, Rodolph, Leinster, M. D., and Palmetto (deceased). Our subject was educated in his native county in the Richland academy, and later in an academy in New York city. He began the study of medicine with his father, and was graduated from the medical department of the University of New York, in 1859, and began to practice in Onslow county in the same year. In May, 1861, he joined the Confederate army as a member of Company B, Fourteenth North Carolina volunteer infantry, and in October, 1861, was made assistant surgeon of the regiment, and later was promoted to surgeon of the Fifty-fourth regiment, from which he was transferred to the Forty-ninth, remaining with the latter regiment until the close of the war. He was detached to take charge of a hospital at Blue Sulphur Springs, W. Va., in the early part of the war. Resuming his professional duties in Onslow county, he remained there until 1870, when he removed to Newbern. Dr. Duffy is a member of the state medical society, of which he has been vice-president, and for six years was a member of the state examining board. In 1872 he was vice-president of the state medical society, first president of eastern North Carolina medical society in 1873 and treasurer in 1875-6-7, and in 1878 was president of the state medical society. From 1873 to 1874 he was president of the Craven county medical society, and from 1872 to 1878, was a member of the state board of examiners, and was appointed a member of the committee to organize the state board of health. He is a prominent member of La Fayette lodge, No. 83, of which he was worshipful master, and Newbern chapter of the Royal Arch Masons, and is also a member of the I. O. O. F. A loyal democrat, he is now a member of the state board of charities, having been appointed by Gov. Fowle, and is now president of this board. In 1881 Dr. Duffy was married to Miss S. B. Moore, daughter of William P. Moore, of Newbern, and three children have been born to them, of whom only one survives, named Richard M., Jr.

Dr. Francis Duffy, M. D., was born in Richland township, Onslow county, N. C., June 24, 1847. His literary education was obtained in different private schools and by private tutors. He read medicine with his father, Dr. Charles Duffy, and graduated from the University of Virginia in 1868, and from the college of Physicians and Surgeons in New York in 1875, and from Bellevue hospital in 1873. In 1869 he located in Jacksonville, N. C., and opened an office, but in 1879 removed to Newbern, and has since been associated with his brother, Dr. Charles Duffy, Jr. He is a member of the American medical association; North Carolina state medical society, and was a member of the State examining board from 1884 to 1890. He is a director in the Winston Salem Land & Investment company, and also in the Building & Loan association and of the Virginia Life Insurance company. As a physician he excels. His medical training was of the best and was made use of to the best advantage. The result has been honorable.

RICHARD DILLARD, M. D.,

was born in Sussex county, Va., December 1, 1822. His father was James Dillard. He was graduated from the University of Virginia, and received his medical diploma from the University of Pennsylvania. When a young man he took up his residence in Chowan county, N. C., and married Miss Mary Louisa Bevely Cross. He was a sound democrat of the old school, and soon became a leader of the party in his new home. He was twice elected to represent Chowan and Gates counties in the state senate, and served as a member of the secession convention from Chowan county. By reason of his loyalty to his adopted state during the war, he was despoiled of his property. After the war he located at Edenton, and by strict application to his profession was enabled to repair his losses, and at the time of his death was regarded as one of the substantial men of the county. He was an honorary member of the state medical society. During the war he was appointed aide-de-camp to Gov. Clarke, with the rank of colonel, and ordered to inspect fortifications at Roanoke Island, and later was acting brigade-surgeon for Gen. Roger A. Pryor. His death occurred in 1887, and his wife's in 1880. The two children now living of the four born to them, are Richard and Sally, the latter being the wife of M. H. Dixon, of Edenton.

Richard Dillard, Jr., read medicine with his father; he entered the Jefferson medical college of Philadelphia, and in 1879, completed the course there, and subsequently attended the New York Polyclinic. Dr. Dillard at once opened an office in Edenton, and has rapidly risen to the front ranks of his profession in the state. He is a prominent member of the state medical society, and in 1890, was one of its vice-presidents. He is also a member of the Phi Kappa Sigma fraternity, and holds the office of contract surgeon in the United States marine hospital service at Edenton. Dr. Dillard interested in agriculture in the county, and has real estate interests in Virginia. As a democrat he is active and efficient. Major James Dillard, his grandfather, was a native of Sussex county, Virginia, and served in the legislature of the Old Dominion state. He was a major during the Mexican war, and rendered distinguished services. Mrs. Mary L. B. Dillard, the mother of our subject, was a direct descendant of the Brownrigg family, of Winfield, N. C., which is one of the oldest and most honored connections of the state.

DR. HIRAM TARLTON CHAPIN,

one of the rising physicians and surgeons of Chatham county, was born in Wayne county, N. C., July 30, 1858. His parents are Dr. Ansel B. and Argent E. (Thompson) Chapin, the father a native of Granby, Conn., and the mother of Wayne county. The former was a graduate from Jefferson medical college, Philadelphia. He had a position on the Atlantic & North Carolina railroad about the year 1855, in charge of a force of hands in building that road. Later he took charge of a newspaper in Goldsboro and subsequently at Beaufort, N. C. In 1859 he moved to Ore Hill, Chatham county, and there began the practice of his profession, which he continued a few months, when he was ordered to report at Pittsboro in the service of the Confederate States. Before the day of departure arrived he went to Gov. Vance and obtained leave of absence for the purchase of land in the eastern part of the state, and while there went to Washington and applied for a position as surgeon in the United States army. He passed the examination and was accepted as an army surgeon, and served during the war in the northern army and for two years longer. In 1867 he resigned his commission and moved to Greensboro, N. C., and engaged in the drug business. At the same time he was editor of the *Union Register*, which position he filled for two years. Attacked by rheumatism, he sold out in Greensboro in 1870, and moved to his old farm at Ore Hill. Dr. Chapin was assistant assessor in the internal revenue service from 1870 to 1872. He had the farm carried on during this time, and then exchanged it for one at Hadley's Mills in the same county, where he moved and engaged in farming and milling. In 1883 he exchanged that property for property in Beaufort county, and there he removed and engaged in the drug business, and is postmaster at that place.

Dr. Chapin was married in June, 1857, to Miss A. E. Thompson, of Goldsboro, N. C., and they have had three children: Hiram T., Jo   W., a farmer at Aurora, N. C., and Lillius B., an attorney at Lillington, N. C. During the war, the mother and her three children remained in the Confederacy. For fourteen months she never heard from her husband. He came home in 1865, but did not resign his commission until 1867. His wife died in 1885, at the age of forty-nine years. She was a devoted member of the Methodist Episcopal church. Dr. Hiram T. Chapin, the immediate subject of this sketch, was educated at Sylvan academy. He taught school for one year and began to read medicine in 1881, opening a drug store in Pittsboro on the 7th of November, that year. He attended medical lectures at the college of Physicians and Surgeons at Baltimore during the winters of 1883 and 1884. In 1886, Dr. Chapin graduated from the Louisville medical college and began practice at once, after having obtained license from the state medical board. He has been practicing here ever since with very satisfactory results. Dr. Chapin is superintendent of health for Chatham county, and is a member of the North Carolina state medical society. December 20, 1882, he was married to Miss Annie M., daughter of William F. Foushee, who was clerk of the superior court of Chatham county for sixteen years. They have one child, William B. Chapin. Dr. Chapin is a member of the Society of Friends. The drug business has been carried on successfully, first under the name of H. T. Chapin, and in 1890 a partner, Dr. William E. Headen, was taken in, and the firm name was changed to Chapin & Headen. July 3, 1891, Drs. Chapin & Headen disposed of their drug business to L. H. Merritt, so as to devote their whole time to their profession.

JOSIAH B. DAVIS, M. D.,

of Beaufort, N. C., was born in Carteret county, N. C., on the 7th of August, 1831, and is a son of Allen and Mary Jane (Simpson) Davis. Allen Davis is a native of the same county as his son, and for many years has been engaged in agriculture near Beaufort. He has attained the advanced age of eighty-four years, and his wife is still living at the age of seventy-nine years. These parents reared a family of seven children, five of whom are now living. They are Josiah B., Rufus W., a planter of Carteret county; Bryant E., also of Beaufort, and a carpenter by trade; Clarkey, wife of William T. Davis, of Beaufort; and Ruth Jane, wife of James Longest, of Carteret county. Dr. Davis obtained but a limited education in the public schools of his native city. He was determined, however, to thoroughly equip himself by diligent study and reading, and most of his education was obtained solely by his own efforts. At the age of twenty-one he engaged as a laborer in a Beaufort ship-yard, and later taught school for three years. He took up the study of medicine, and in 1862 began its practice, having attended his first course of lectures in 1859-60. In 1865 he took a second course of lectures, and was graduated from the University of New York city in the following year. From 1862 to 1864 he was engaged in the mercantile business at Beaufort, and for many years past has conducted a large drug business, being a leading druggist of the city. He is a prominent republican, and has held the office of town commissioner, and in 1884 was appointed United States pension examining surgeon, a position he still retains. In 1865 he married Miss Mary A. Sewell, daughter of Thomas B. Sewell, of Baltimore, Md., and their children are: Mary Jane, wife of Robert R. Robinson, of Beaufort; George, Annie and Rose, all residing at Beaufort. Dr. Davis is an active and consistent communicant of the Baptist church, and he is a trustee of the church at Beaufort. Active and progressive, he has made much of opportunity, and has come to be one of the leading citizens of his native county.

NATHANIEL ALEXANDER,

a prominent physician, was born in Mecklenburg county, in 1756. His early education was at a school near his father's residence, kept in a log cabin. He graduated from Princeton college in 1776, after which he took up the study of medicine and carried on a successful practice. His practice, however, was interrupted by the necessity of the country for soldiers to defend its liberties from the encroachments of the British government. Through the latter years of the Revolution, Dr. Alexander rendered effective service in the southern army. When the war was over he returned to his practice. He was elected a member of the house of commons in 1797, and of the state senate in 1802. In 1803 he was elected a member of congress from the Mecklenburg district and served for the full term of two years. He was elected governor of the state in 1805 in which office he served until his death which occurred at Salisbury, March 8, 1808. He married a daughter of Col. Thomas Polk.

E. BURKE HAYWOOD, A. M., M. D., LL. D.

Dr. Edmund Burke Haywood, born in Raleigh, N. C., January 15, 1825, is the most eminent physician who resides at the state capital. When Raleigh was laid off in 1792, and the city lots sold by the state, John Haywood, the father of Dr. Burke Haywood, as the subject of this sketch is always called, purchased a handsome square on Newbern avenue and built thereon a commodious residence. In that house Dr. Burke Haywood was born, and there he still resides. His father, John Haywood, was treasurer of the state from 1787 to 1827, and was much esteemed for his high integrity of character and estimable qualities. He was a planter, and had considerable landed interests. He was the first vestryman elected for Christ church, Raleigh. In his honor the legislature in 1808 established the county of Haywood, and the town of Haywood is also called after him. The father of Treasurer Haywood was Col. William Haywood, a distinguished personage in Carolina in the Colonial days. He filled various offices, civil and military, and was a patriotic and useful citizen. In 1765 he was colonel of the county of Edgecombe, and in 1775, when the provincial congress appointed committees of safety, he was appointed chairman of the committee for Edgecombe county. He was a member of the state congress held at Halifax in the spring of 1776, as well as that held in November of that year, which adopted the constitution, and he was a member of the committee that framed that instrument. He was chosen, in December, 1776, one of the counselors of state, provided for in the new constitution. He died in 1779.

John Haywood, the father of Col. William Haywood, and the founder of the family in North Carolina, was in the employment of Earl Granville, being his agent, with Edward Moseley, in laying off and selling Granville's lands in North Carolina. He was treasurer of

the northern counties in colonial times. The family came originally from Worcestershire, England. Many distinguished men have sprung from this Haywood stock, and in each generation they have played an important part in North Carolina. A first cousin of Treasurer Haywood was John Haywood, who was esteemed in his day the strongest legal luminary of the state. He was elected attorney-general in 1791, and three years later was transferred to the supreme court bench of the state. This post he held until he resigned it in 1804. Some years later Judge Haywood was induced to move to Tennessee, to locate certain land grants, and recover a large territory for some clients, and he became so greatly interested in these lands that he permanently settled there, where he became judge of the supreme court. He was the author of a " Manual of Laws of North Carolina," " Haywood's Justice," " Haywood's Reports;" of a very valuable history of Tennessee, and various other works. It was of him that Chief-Justice Henderson remarked in one of his decisions, "that he disparaged neither the living nor the dead when he said that an abler man than John Haywood never appeared at the bar or sat on the bench of North Carolina."

The mother of Dr. Burke Haywood was Eliza Eagles Williams, a daughter of John Pugh Williams, who in April, 1776, was made captain of the North Carolina troops in the Edenton district, and in November, 1776, commissioned colonel of the Ninth regiment of the Continental line. He served with distinction during the war and was greatly esteemed for his sterling worth. His brother, Hon. Benjamin Williams, who resided in Moore county, was a member of congress from 1793, to 1795; was elected governor in 1799, and twice thereafter consecutively, and again in 1807. Among the brothers of Dr. Burke Haywood were Dr. Fabius J. Haywood, the elder, who for many years was a leading practitioner at Raleigh, one of whose daughters intermarried with the lamented Gov. Daniel G. Fowle; and another brother was George W. Haywood, an eminent attorney and counselor-at-law, at Raleigh, who after the war removed to Alabama, where he died in 1891. A sister, Miss Eliza Eagles Haywood, whose social accomplishments and intellectual capacity alike distinguished her, was one of the most charming of her sex. Dr Haywood's early education was under the Rev Dr. McPheeters, Silas Bigelow and J. M. Lovejoy, who were successively the preceptors at the Raleigh academy. He entered the University of North Carolina in 1843, and took first distinction, but was compelled by ill health to leave that institution before graduating. Among his classmates were Gen. Johnston Pettigrew, Senator John Pool and Senator Matthew W. Ransom, and they have ever maintained the college friendship that existed between them.

Dr. Haywood studied medicine at the University of Pennsylvania where he received his degree of M. D. in 1849, and the following year he became a member of the medical society of North Carolina, and entered on a lucrative practice at the capital of the state. In May, 1861, he patriotically abandoned his practice and joined the Raleigh light infantry, and was elected surgeon of that command. In May, 1861, he organized, at Raleigh, N. C., the first military hospital established in North Carolina during the late war between the states; but the state authorities had other duties for him to perform. Gov. Ellis, appreciating his fine abilities, sent him in May, 1861, on a tour of inspection and observation of the military hospitals on Morris Island, S. C. On the 16th of May, 1861, he was appointed surgeon of the North Carolina state troops, and placed in charge of the Fair Grounds hospital. At the same time he was appointed, by the governor, surgeon of the military post at Raleigh, N. C., with the assimilated rank of major. On the 20th of May, 1861, he was assigned by the governor to the camp of instruction, near Raleigh, N. C., as chief surgeon, with the assimilated rank of major, the commission to date from May 16, 1861. On the 20th of May, 1861, he was authorized by Adjutant-General Hoke, to appoint a druggist, two assistant surgeons and two nurses for the hospital at the camp of instruction near Raleigh, N. C. On the 4th of June, 1861, he was appointed surgeon of post, at Raleigh, of the state troops of North Carolina. On the 15th of July, 1861, he was appointed president of a board of surgeons to examine applicants for the position of surgeon to the North Carolina troops.

Dr. Haywood remained in the military service of North Carolina as surgeon until December 4, 1862, when he was appointed by James A. Sedden, secretary of war, surgeon in the Provisional army in the service of the Confederate States, to rank as such from August 1, 1862. In the fights around Richmond he was on duty at Seabrook's hospital. In 1862 he was appointed president of the medical board for granting furloughs and discharges from the Confederate States army, for Raleigh, N. C., and in the same year was appointed acting medical director in the Confederate States army for the department of North Carolina. When the war ended he remained in charge of the wounded Confederate soldiers in Pettigrew's hospital at Raleigh, N. C., faithfully and patriotically rendering them his best service, and it was not until July 4, 1865, that he resumed his civil practice, the last wounded soldier under his charge being then discharged from the hospital cured and able to return to his home.

In June, 1866, Dr. Haywood was elected vice-president of the medical society of the state of North Carolina, and also to the chair of surgery of the board of medical examiners of North Carolina for a term of six years. Two years later he was chosen president of the medical society and the University of North Carolina conferred upon him the honorary degree of A. M. The following year upon retiring from the presidency of the medical society he delivered an address on the subject of " The Physician, His Relations to the Community and the Law." This address, which was published by the request of the society increased his reputation and brought him into still greater repute among the members of the medical fraternity. In it he portrayed the moral heroism and self-sacrifice of the physician who conscientiously performs his duties to society and to the medical profession. With great force and acumen he urged the necessity for habits of close observation and he enlarged upon the importance of a more extended knowledge of medical jurisprudence. An address so replete with sound views and couched in such chaste and elegant language could not fail to add largely to the fame of Dr. Haywood. In 1870 he was one of the organizers of the Raleigh Academy of Medicine, and the succeeding year he served as a member on the committee of publication of the transactions of the medical society, which position he also held in 1872 and 1873. In 1872 he was elected secretary of the Raleigh Academy of Medicine and was also appointed by the medical society a member of the board to examine druggists. In the same year he brought suit in Wake superior court to establish the right of physicians and surgeons to extra compensation when summoned to testify as experts, and the supreme court of the state on appeal sustained his contention. In 1873 he served as a member of the board of censors established by the medical society and in March of that year was elected corresponding member of the Gynecological society, of Boston, Mass.

In January, 1874, Dr. Haywood became president of the Raleigh academy of medicine, and in October, 1875, he attended as a delegate to the annual session of the association of medical officers of the Confederate army and navy which convened in Richmond. Notwithstanding he was politically opposed to the party in power at the time, he was, on March 16, 1866, appointed a member of the board of directors of the North Carolina insane asylum, in which capacity he served that institution until 1875, when he was elected president of its board of directors. He held continuously that office until August 10, 1889, when he resigned and was appointed chairman of the board of public charities by Gov. Fowle. He was delegate from the medical society of the state to the American medical association in the years 1869, 1870, 1875 and 1876, and he was also a delegate to the international medical congress held in Philadelphia in September, 1876, and also to the ninth international medical congress held in Washington city, September, 1887. In February, 1889, he was appointed by Gov. Fowle as a delegate on behalf the state to attend the national quarantine conference held at Montgomery, Ala., and in June of that year the University of North Carolina conferred upon him the degree of LL. D., he being the first physician in North Carolina upon whom the university ever conferred this degree. In April, 1890, he was appointed by Gov. Fowle a delegate to the seventeenth national conference of charities and corrections held in Baltimore in May of that year. On April 18, 1891, he was appointed by Gov. Holt a delegate to the eighteenth national conference of charities and corrections to be held at Indianapolis, May 13-20, 1891.

It will be seen that Dr. Haywood in addition to his practice has performed much work in the line of his profession. He has always been indefatigable in seeking to promote the comfort and welfare of the insane and he has been influential in accomplishing much for this unhappy class of unfortunates. When in 1875 the general assembly proposed to utilize the Marine hospital building at Wilmington as a branch asylum for the colored insane he urged the impossibility of rendering that building suitable for that purpose, and that the general assembly should take the proper steps to build an asylum for that class. At his instance a commission was appointed and a site selected near Goldsboro, and he had the satisfaction of seeing that commodious institution erected near that town. In like manner he urged the establishment of the Western insane asylum at Morganton, where the state now has the finest and best appointed institution in the south. Dr. Haywood's long connection with the noble charity in the state, and his devoted attention for so many years to the unfortunate insane has eminently qualified him for the position of president of the board of charities having general supervision and charge over all such institutions in North Carolina, and it is to be regretted that in 1891 he declined a re-election to this responsible position continuing, however, to serve as a member of the board.

In the course of his extensive practice, in which he has long been regarded as the most eminent surgeon and practitioner, Dr. Haywood has performed successfully, many of the more important surgical operations. In August, 1874, he performed the cæsarean section, with success. In the same year he operated on four cases of strangulated inguinal hernia, of which two were cured. In 1875, he operated sucessfully in two cases of lacerated perineum. Indeed, it may be said of him, that he has performed more such operations than any other surgeon in North Carolina. In 1869, he successfully performed ligation of the right external iliac artery for traumatic aneurism of femoral artery, the first operation of the kind ever performed in North Carolina, and the case was considered so important, that it was published in pamphlet form, by order of the Raleigh Academy of Medicine and the North Carolina medical society. He has also removed cancerous tumors of the mammæ, and he was the first to use anæsthetics in obstetrics and puerperal convulsions in the state. In April, 1869, he assisted Dr. Washington Atlee, of Philadelphia, in performing at Raleigh, an operation for ovariotomy. The patient being left entirely in Dr. Haywood's charge, recovered, and has since become the mother of three children. He has operated twice successfully for the removal of submucus fibroid of the uterus. He has performed several other notable surgical operations among the most important of which may be mentioned: Aspiration of the pericardium for hydropsy, pericardii, external esophagotomy for impacted foreign body low down in esophagus, amputation of thigh in its upper third for gangrene of leg and thigh caused by traumatic femoral aneurism, tracheotomy for foreign body in bronchus.

Dr. Haywood's time has been so fully occupied by the demands of his extensive practice, that he has but little opportunity for authorship; but among his contributions to medical literature may be mentioned: " Report of an operation for traumatic aneurism of femoral artery, cured by ligature;" "Report of a case of compound comminuted fracture of middle and lower thirds of both bones of right leg;"

"Comminuted fracture of right femur;" "Compound fracture of left femur, just above the condyles;" "Report of a successful operation for traumatic aneurism of the superficial palmar arch;" "A case of craniotomy;" "An operation for vesico vaginal fistula;" "Report of a successful operation for compound comminuted fracture of cranium, with extensive depression and several large fragments driven into the brain;" "Report of a case of total necrosis of diaphysis of the tibia, periosteum not necessary for osteo-genesis;" "Report of a case of membraneous croup, tracheotemy successfully performed, and the child entirely recovered;" "Report of a case of amputation of the right thigh at the upper third, for gelatinous arthritis;" "Report of an operation for fistula in and with the elastic ligature."

But with all his professional duties, which he has so conscientiously performed, Dr. Haywood has ever found time to discharge other duties as well. He is a member of Christ church, Raleigh, and for twenty years was an active member of the vestry; he was president of the board of health for Wake county, and is a member of the board of directors and physician to the Peace institute, at Raleigh, N. C. He was surgeon to the Confederate survivors association. In June, 1889, he was elected one of the physicians to the institution for the deaf, dumb and blind, in which capacity he still serves that institution. He was medical director for the North Carolina Life Insurance company at Raleigh. He is now medical examiner for Raleigh of the Mutual, the Equitable, the New York, the Manhattan and the United States Life Insurance companies, all of New York, and also of the Life Insurance company of Virgina, and the Maryland Life Insurance company. He is also medical referee of the Mutual Benefit Life Insurance company of Newark, N. J. His high rank in his profession, in which he is justly distinguished, is equalled by his high social standing. His spotless character, his patriotic life work at the insane asylum, his self-sacrificing service during the war are all so many claims upon the reverence and esteem of the public, and his g eat learning and fine ability only enhance the regard in which he is held.

But while properly appreciating the genuine admiration which his friends entertain for him, Dr. Haywood is modest and unobtrusive to a remarkable degree, and he quietly and unostentatiously performs his daily task in his laborious profession. He is mild in his carriage, gentle in his manner, and considerate of the feelings of others. It is only to those who know him well that the full nobility of his character is evident. He is a man of great decision and quickness of apprehension, and whether in his professional work or when engaged on other subjects, he intuitively seizes on the strong point of the matter and goes to the bottom of it. As eminent as he is and wearing so worthily the distinction of being the first physician of the state, he passes through life without the least assumption.

In November, 1850, Dr. Haywood married Miss Lucy A. Williams, daughter of Mr. Alfred Williams, whose firm name of "Alfred Williams & Co.," book-sellers, has for more than fifty years been well

known all over North Carolina. He has one daughter, the wife of
Mr. Preston L. Bridgers, of Wilmington; and six sons, Edmund
Burke Haywood, a planter; Alfred Williams Haywood and Ernest
Haywood, who are practicing law together and are well known attorneys throughout the state; and Dr. Hubert Haywood, who is now
a partner with his father in the practice of medicine, and Edgar Haywood, who is associated with the book house of Alfred Williams & Co.,,
which was founded by his grandfather; and John Haywood, who
is a cotton dealer in Alabama. Alfred W. Haywood married Miss
Louise M. Holt, daughter of Gov. Thomas M. Holt, May 23, 1883.
Dr. Hubert Haywood married Miss Emily R. Benbury, December 14,
1881.

JOHN H. CRAWFORD

was born in Wayne county, N. C., January 17, 1832. He received his
early education in the common schools in that county, which he regularly attended until 1845. When in his thirteenth year he suffered the
loss of his father. To assist his mother he left school at an early age
and went to Smithfield, N. C., to superintend the business of Dr.
Alexander Telfair. During the year 1851, when but nineteen years
old he was employed to superintend the store and distillery belonging
to Col. John F. Sanders, of Johnston county, N. C. In January, 1852,
he married Patience A. Stevens, daughter of Jacob A. Stevens,
of Johnston county, N. C., and to them were born seven children, of
whom four now survive: John W. Crawford, of Raleigh, N. C.; Mattie A., wife of L. Brown, of Asheville, N. C.; Lulu, wife of Rufus
Horton, of Raleigh, N. C.; Alonzo J. Crawford, of Raleigh, N. C. In
1853,the subject of this sketch entered the jewelry business, at Goldsboro, N. C., and for five years continued it with success, and then he
studied dentistry under Dr. S. A. McDowell for two years, at the
end of which time he commenced to practice that profession at Goldsboro and in its vicinity. In 1862, during the war, he went with the
Goldsboro militia to Newbern, and was in the battle of Newbern.
After that battle, being appointed hospital steward, by the secretary
of war of the Confederate States, he served in that capacity until the
close of the war. When peace came Dr. Crawford removed to
Raleigh, where he entered upon a lucrative practice of his profession,
and where he has since resided, being one of the finest and best
known dentists in the state, and a most worthy and honorable citizen,
respected by the entire community. Dr. Crawford belongs to
Hiram lodge, No. 40, F. & A. M., and is also a member of Seaton
Gales lodge, No. 64, I. O O. F., and Litchford Encampment. No. 26,
I. O. O. F. He is a valuable member of the Presbyterian church, and
by his Christian motives and gentlemanly address, has won the esteem of his brethren, friends and all who come into contact with him.
   John Bemis Crawford, Dr. Crawford's father, was born in New
York in 1800, and coming to North Carolina at the age of twenty-
eight, settled in Raleigh. He afterward moved to Wayne county,

where he died in 1845. He was a man of superior education, and by profession was a teacher. He was appointed a magistrate of Wayne county, and served in that capacity for a number of years. In 1828 he married Louisa Talbert Harris, and to them were born five children, as follows: James D. Crawford, of Robinson county, N. C.; Sarah (deceased), wife of Nathan Stanley (deceased), of Goldsboro, N. C.; John H. Crawford, of Raleigh, N. C.; William W. Crawford, of Goldsboro, N. C.; Mary A., wife of Allen S. Ballinger, of Greene county, N. C. Dr. Crawford's grandfather, James Daniel Crawford, was born near Saratoga, N. Y., and lived there all his life. Archibald C. Crawford, Dr. Crawford's great-grandfather, was born in Scotland, but came to America and settled at Saratoga Springs, N. Y., where he died June 8, 1806. Dr. Crawford's ancestors on his mother's side were from Ireland.

MR. JOHN R. WILLIAMS,

whose name has been for more than half a century connected with the drug business in Raleigh, was born in Franklin county, N. C., March 4, 1820. He received his education in the academic schools of Franklin and Wake counties. When just sixteen years of age he entered the drug store of Williams & Haywood, owned by his elder brother, Alfred Williams, and Fabius Haywood (now deceased), and after eight years' service as clerk, he was admitted a partner under the firm name of Williams. Haywood & Co., and the firm so continued until 1855, when Mr. Alfred Williams retired, and the business has since been continued under the style of Williams & Haywood. Although Dr. Haywood died in 1880, the business has been carried on by Mr. Williams, under the old name, as surviving partner. During this long period Mr. Williams has steadily maintained the highest reputation for intelligence and thoroughness in the drug business, and no house is better known or has enjoyed a wider reputation throughout central North Carolina than that of Williams & Haywood. In 1845 Mr. Williams was fortunately united in marriage with Miss Ariadne E. Smith, daughter of Benjamin B. Smith, Esq., a prominent merchant of Raleigh, to whom were born five children, of whom three now survive, Robert J. Williams, George H. Williams and Mary A. Williams. Mr. Williams has ever been esteemed as one of the most exemplary and excellent citizens of Raleigh. He and Mrs. Williams are consistent members of the Methodist Episcopal church, and their influence has been promotive of good works in the community. Mr. Williams has never actively participated in public affairs, but has always steadily maintained the principles of the democratic party. He has, however, on several occasions served the city as alderman, and for a number of years he was a director of the institute for the the deaf, dumb and blind, freely giving his service to ameliorate the condition of those unfortunate wards of the state.

NATHANIEL ALEXANDER,

a prominent physician, was born in Mecklenburg county, in 1756. His early education was at a school near his father's residence, kept in a log cabin. He graduated from Princeton college in 1776, after which he took up the study of medicine and carried on a successful practice. His practice, however, was interrupted by the necessity of the country for soldiers to defend its liberties from the encroachments of the British government. Through the latter years of the Revolution, Dr. Alexander rendered effective service in the southern army. When the war was over he returned to his practice. He was elected a member of the house of commons in 1797, and of the state senate in 1802. In 1803 he was elected a member of congress from the Mecklenburg district and served for the full term of two years. He was elected governor of the state in 1805 in which office he served until his death which occurred at Salisbury, March 8, 1808. He married a daughter of Col. Thomas Polk.

E. BURKE HAYWOOD, A. M., M. D., LL. D.

Dr. Edmund Burke Haywood, born in Raleigh, N. C., January 15, 1825, is the most eminent physician who resides at the state capital. When Raleigh was laid off in 1792, and the city lots sold by the state, John Haywood, the father of Dr. Burke Haywood, as the subject of this sketch is always called, purchased a handsome square on Newbern avenue and built thereon a commodious residence. In that house Dr. Burke Haywood was born, and there he still resides. His father, John Haywood, was treasurer of the state from 1787 to 1827, and was much esteemed for his high integrity of character and estimable qualities. He was a planter, and had considerable landed interests. He was the first vestryman elected for Christ church, Raleigh. In his honor the legislature in 1808 established the county of Haywood, and the town of Haywood is also called after him. The father of Treasurer Haywood was Col. William Haywood, a distinguished personage in Carolina in the Colonial days. He filled various offices, civil and military, and was a patriotic and useful citizen. In 1765 he was colonel of the county of Edgecombe, and in 1775, when the provincial congress appointed committees of safety, he was appointed chairman of the committee for Edgecombe county. He was a member of the state congress held at Halifax in the spring of 1776, as well as that held in November of that year, which adopted the constitution, and he was a member of the committee that framed that instrument. He was chosen, in December, 1776, one of the counselors of state, provided for in the new constitution. He died in 1779.

John Haywood, the father of Col. William Haywood, and the founder of the family in North Carolina, was in the employment of Earl Granville, being his agent, with Edward Moseley, in laying off and selling Granville's lands in North Carolina. He was treasurer of

ginia C., wife of Rev. J. H. Howell, of Yanceyville, N. C.; Indiana G., wife of John B. Collins, of Raleigh, N. C.; Dr. Wisconsin I. Royster and V. C. Royster, of Raleigh, and O. M. Royster, of Columbia, S. C. Mr. James Royster died at Raleigh, February 5, 1890, at the age of ninety-three years, and his wife followed him to the grave on April 6, 1890.

DR. WILLIAM HENRY McKEE

was born at Raleigh, N. C., on the 7th day of September, 1814. His father, James McKee, was a native of Orange county, a kind hearted, generous friend, and an industrious, useful and respected citizen. He moved to Wake county in early life, and was married, in 1810, to Miss Priscilla Macon, of Franklin county, a niece of Hon. Nathaniel Macon. She was rarely endowed with estimable qualities of mind and heart, which shone with beautiful lustre among the trying responsibilities of her life. Their wedded life had continued through only nine years when, in April 1819, the husband and father was removed by death. Their union had been blessed with four children, three daughters, Narcissa, Mary and Priscilla, and one son, the subject of this sketch. Left thus in early widowhood, without fortune and with four little children to rear, her position was one of peculiar trial and responsibility, but with a true mother's heart and an unfaltering trust in the God of the widow and the Father of the fatherless, she bore up bravely under her sorrows, and faithfully discharged her duty to Him and to them. This noble Christian mother died in 1832, leaving the impress of her pious example and the savor of her righteous counsels to adorn the character and the lives of her children. William Henry began the battle of life at an early age, without other resources than a courageous spirit, virtuous principles and meagre rudiments of education received at home. When about fifteen years of age he obtained employment as a clerk in the apothecary store of Mr. C. D. Lehman. Here he was assiduous, faithful and courteous in the discharge of his duties, winning and retaining the confidence and esteem of his employer. Eager in the pursuit of knowledge he soon became a skillful pharmacist. When Mr. Lehman retired from business, Messrs. Williams & Haywood, druggists of this city, secured the services of the young apothecary, who soon rose to partnership in the firm. While occupying this position he prosecuted the study of medicine. In 1837 he went to Philadelphia, matriculated at the University of Philadelphia, and became while there a resident physician of the alms-house. He graduated in 1839, but continued to reside in Philadelphia until the close of the year. Returning to Raleigh, he commenced the practice of his profession here in the year 1840, and soon acquired an enviable reputation as a physician, not only among the people in general but signally also among the members of his profession.

In 1849 Dr. McKee was chosen secretary of the state medical convention, and was one of the leading projectors of the state medical society. He was elected as the first secretary of the society, serving efficiently and zealously in that capacity for three consecutive years. At the session of the society held at Edenton, in 1857, he was elected president and was re-elected in 1858. He repeatedly filled the honorable mission of representative of the state medical society in the national medical association, and was also chosen by the society as a member of the first board of medical examiners, under the act of legislature of 1859. Deservedly popular, he was eminently trusted as a true and valued citizen, in positions unconnected with his professional walk. He was, year after year, an efficient member of the board of commissioners of this city and served for years as the president of the board of directors of the state institution for the deaf and dumb and the blind, being also its physician. He was an honored member of the noble, beneficent fraternity, the I. O. O. F., and was elected grand master of their grand lodge of North Carolina. Dr. McKee was twice married. His first wife was Miss Susan E. Battle, to whom he was married in March, 1842. His last wife was Miss Eliza O. Nixon, whom he married in November, 1854. By the former marriage there were four children, only one of whom survives, Dr. James McKee. By the last marriage he left one daughter, Eliza, who resides in Raleigh. He was a devoted son, administered consolation and cheer to the burdened heart of his afflicted mother. His affection for her to the end of his days was indeed beautiful and noble. A loving brother, he reciprocated the offices of pure sisterly affection with grateful tenderness and care. He was a fond and faithful husband and an affectionate and thoughtful father. As a friend he was generous, honorable and true. As a man he was imbued with the pure, warm spirit of benevolence, dispensing with a liberal but modest hand, to the distresses and necessities of his fellow men. While ever ready to respond to the appeals that were made for charity at his own door, he was magnanimously generous in ministering, in his professional labors, to the indigent and helpless, from whom he could expect no reward beyond the expression of gratitude. Truly we may say of him that as an humble disciple of the Great Physician, " he went about doing good," and his memory will long be cherished in many a lowly household to which he bore in hours of sickness and distress the aid of his skill and the balm of his sympathy.

Supplying the want of early advantages by patient study and conscientious devotion to the duties of his profession, he became the peer of its leader in the state. His constitution became enfeebled, but he continued to pursue his arduous practice with occasional intermissions, his health the meanwhile gradually but surely declining, until the spring of 1874. Though suffering much he continued his wonted labors to within a few weeks of his death, which occurred at his home on the 24th of April in the midst of his weeping family and sympathizing friends. Dr. S. S. Satchwell, a contemporary, said of him: "His virtues were those which most adorn human nature and mostly ennoble our always noble profession. True to friendship, to

Truly yours

James McKee M.D.

the demands and wants of his profession, to the instincts and needs of patriotism, and to the calls of poverty and the cries of suffering humanity, his services and sacrifices in these important relations have embalmed him in the lasting admiration, love and esteem of his professional brethren and in the enduring plaudits, gratitude and affection of the public, not alone of his native city and county, but of the entire state. The instincts of his benevolent nature to relieve pain and distress, his proverbial readiness at all times to go, as he ever went, to the calls of the poor and down-trodden, as well as to the calls of the affluent and prosperous, placed the laurel leaves of honor and victory upon his brow. Thus it is that this distinguished member of the profession and prominent citizen of the state stands enshrined in the gratitude and affections of our people, and that his name and fame will be a hallowed household word around the altars and firesides of tens of thousands of the poor and distressed, as well as the wealthy families of North Carolina."

JAMES McKEE, M. D.,

one of the leading physicians of North Carolina, was born in the city of Raleigh, January 5, 1844. His preliminary schooling was obtained in the old Lovejoy school which was ably presided over by J. M. Lovejoy. Later he entered the University of North Carolina, but left there in 1861 to give his services to the Confederate army. He enlisted in Company D, First regiment North Carolina volunteers, and was mustered out in October, 1861, when he enlisted as lieutenant in 1862. Until December, 1862, he acted as drill master in the Raleigh and Morganton camps of instruction, after which he went into active service. After the battle of Kinston, N. C., in which he participated, he was assigned to the Seventh North Carolina regiment, then stationed around Petersburg. In the latter part of January, 1865, that regiment was ordered to North Carolina to intercept deserters, and Lieut. McKee accompanied it on this duty. About the 1st of April the regiment was re-called to the army. In the meantime Richmond had fallen and the Seventh was detained at Danville, Va., by order of President Davis, and was the last regiment to leave Danville, following the train that carried Davis from Danville to Greensboro. Lieut. McKee took an active part in these battles: Kinston, Jones Farm, below Petersburg, and was on picket duty around Petersburg during the three days' fight. Returning home from the army he acted as special messenger for the National Express and Transportation company for about a year, and then entered the office of his father, Dr. W. H. McKee, under whose direction he began the study of medicine. In October, 1867, he entered Bellevue hospital college in New York city, and was graduated from that institution March 1, 1869. He then returned to Raleigh and began the practice of the profession that he had chosen as his life work.

Dr. McKee has won wide distinction in the medical world. He is a member of the North Carolina state medical society of which he

B—16

has been secretary; has served as president of the Raleigh medical academy, of which he is a member, and has been a delegate to the American medical association. As an alderman of Raleigh and member of the board of health of that city, Dr. McKee has shown an aptitude for public work. He has filled these offices since 1881, and is also a member of the Wake county board of health. He has been a professor of the Leonard medical college of Shaw university from its inception to the present time, being at present the incumbent of the chair of obstetrics, diseases of women and children, and is also visiting physician to the Leonard medical school hospital, and to St. John's guild hospital, and local surgeon of the North Carolina division of the Richmond & Danville railroad. Dr. McKee was the first physician to instruct the negro in medical science, and is now surrounded in the Leonard medical college by a corps of assistants and professors that are not excelled. Dr. McKee was happily united in marriage to Miss Mildred Sasser, daughter of John W. Sasser, of Wayne county, September 30, 1873. Six children have been born into this cultured home, named as follows: William H., John S., James B., Edwin B., Lewis M. and Philip S. Dr. McKee is the son of William H. McKee, M. D., one of the most eminent physicians that North Carolina has ever produced, and a sketch of whose life precedes this one. The subject of this sketch was the first, and is the present, superintendent of the board of health of Wake county, and is the present president of the local board of health of Raleigh, and is the author of the present well devised ordinances, by which the good health of Raleigh is maintained. To him is due the credit of the present system of collecting and registering the vital statistics of Raleigh which cannot be excelled. The sanitary bureau of Raleigh was organized by him and the organization is so thorough and complete that the number and kind of contagious and infectious diseases can be shown at any time — a rare thing.

FRANCIS TAYLOR FULLER, M. D.

In every vocation of life there arise men who tower above their fellows in force of character and intellectual competency; who draw to them that esteem and deference which mankind yields to superior endowment; they are those who have lived to good purpose and who will not soon fade away from human consideration. These are such as live devoted to their life work, and their influence for good will long continue to act; their characteristics are fixed and ineffaceable; and in affectionate rememberance, such men will long live as men of purity, devotion, superiority and worth. To this class of men belongs Francis Taylor Fuller, M. D., whose respected name introduces this biographical mention. And before giving an outline of this distinguished gentleman's career, mention of his ancestry may fittingly be made.

During the trouble between the Stuarts and the House of Hanover, Esquire John Taylor and his wife, the Lady Anne Cradock,

C. T. Hullen. M.D.

moved from England and settled in Virginia, at Bowling Green. About the same time two of the brothers of John Taylor also came to Virginia, and one of these was the ancestor of President Taylor and of Gen. Richard Taylor, and the other was an ancestor of John Taylor, of Caroline county, Va., the author of a noted work on agriculture, and also an ancestor of President Madison on his mother's side. John Taylor, of Bowling Green, had four sons; one was captain of a merchant ship and suffered a long and painful imprisonment by Algerine pirates; the two youngest fell in battle in the cause of liberty, one at the battle of Cowpens, the other at Brandywine. The remaining son, Major Francis Taylor, passed through many perils, but fortunately survived them. He was a bold and enterprising officer, and possessed a daring and adventurous spirit. He was several times wounded and once so seriously about the hip that he walked lame the rest of his life. He was twice captured; on the first occasion he was carried prisoner to Charleston, but managed to escape, tradition says, by bribing one of the guard with his mother's gold watch which he had concealed in his boot; he hastened to report to Gen. Greene, then in North Carolina, on whose staff he served as aide. Subsequently being sent by Gen. Greene with dispatches to Gen. Washington, he was captured and taken to the house of a tory, near Ramseur's Mills. N. C. Again managing to escape, he sprang upon the horse of a British colonel, in the stable, and began a flight in which he was hotly pursued. His horse being a fine one he distanced all but two of the pursuers. As these approached him, he drew from the holsters the colonel's pistols and killed one of men first, and finally killed the horse the other rode. Making good his escape, he proceeded to the north and safely delivered his dispatches to Gen. Washington.

Major Taylor married Mrs. Pattie Thorpe and settled at Locust Hill, Franklin county, N. C., where he died in April, 1816, at the age of seventy-six years, honored and beloved by all who knew him. His wife, widow Thorpe, was a sister of Gen. Tom Person. The Persons coming from England, settled in Gloucester county, Va. The name was said to have been Personne, and Gen. Person pronounced it Personne, which was the origin of the common way of calling it Passon or Passons. Mrs. Taylor survived the major and lived to the great age of ninety-eight years. She was buried by the side of her husband at old Locust Hill, Franklin county. Among the children of Maj. Taylor was Thomas Person Taylor, who was born in Franklin county in 1793, and died in 1871, and whose daughter, Martha A. Taylor, married James N. Fuller, of Granville county, and became the mother of the subject of this sketch. She was born April 11, 1815. The father of James N. Fuller was William Fuller, Esq., of Granville county, and was of Scotch and English lineage. He was a man of strong force of character and of influence among his countrymen, and died in 1840, in a respected old age. His son, James N. Fuller, was born November 18, 1802, in Granville county, and on August 29, 1833, married Martha A. Taylor, then just eighteen years

of age. He was a farmer and a man of sterling principles and integrity. He was high-minded in all his actions, and generous, hospitable
and kind. He was a good neighbor and faithful in the discharge of
all his duties, religious as well as civil and social. During the course
of his life he held different county offices which he filled with credit
to himself and acceptably to the people. He died at the advanced age
of seventy-nine years, his death occurring May 27, 1881, leaving seven
children surviving him: Francis T. Fuller, subject of this sketch;
Celestia W., John A., Mrs. Anna Gill, Erastus, Emma, and Lucy, the
wife of James Thompson, Esq.

Francis Taylor Fuller, M. D., was born in Granville, N. C.,
June 14, 1835. His early education was obtained at the South Lowell
academy in Orange county, N. C. In 1851 he left the academy and
returned to Granville county where he taught school for a time, and
subsequently took up the study of medicine under the direction of
Dr. William R. Hicks, of Oxford, and in 1854 became a student at
the medical department of the University of Pennsylvania. In the
summer of 1855 he placed himself under the tutelage of Dr. Charles
E. Johnson, late of Raleigh, and remained with him until his return
to Philadelphia to re-enter the university, from which he was graduated in 1856. Dr. Robert Hicks was a classmate of Dr. Fuller, as
was also Dr. Kelly, late of Granville county, N. C., and Dr. Jacobs,
late of Person county. After his graduation the young physician
was requested by Dr. Charles E. Johnson, then acting superintendent
of the North Carolina insane asylum, which had been opened in
February, 1856, to assist him in his duties, and soon after, at a meeting of the board of directors, Dr. Fuller was elected first assistant
physician, which position he has held ever since. For twelve years
he served under Dr. Edward C. Fisher, who was succeeded in 1868
by Dr. Eugene Grissom, who held the superintendency of the asylum
until September, 1889. During his long career Dr. Fuller has
evinced wonderful ability in the care of the insane. He brought to
his work a mind thoroughly prepared by study and inclination for
the profession he had chosen. The reputation of his skill has spread
throughout the length and breadth of the state, and the people of
North Carolina repose esteem and confidence in him to a marked
degree. Indeed, Dr. Fuller is favorably known among the eminent
specialists of the United States and Canada. It is seldom that a man
remains so long in a position requiring so much exertion and tact,
and it is still more unusual for a physican holding such a place to be
regarded with such uniform respect and admiration by officers and
employers alike.

Dr. Fisher, the admirable superintendent of the institution, in his
report for 1858, in referring to his obligations to those who have rendered official services, thus spoke of Dr. Fuller: "In an especial
manner are those obligations due to the assistant physician, Dr. F. T.
Fuller, for his untiring devotion to duty at all times. Most faithfully
did he conduct the affairs of the institution in my absence the past
and previous summers, and while assuring you of his entire capability

and efficiency for the duties of his office, I present you with but an imperfect idea of my appreciation of his worth as an officer." In his report, November 1, 1868, Dr. Grissom, the accomplished superintendent, said, "To the officers and others with whom I have been connected, I tender my thanks for their efficient discharge of duty, and to Dr. Francis T. Fuller, assistant physician, I am under peculiar obligations, for the skill and fidelity with which he executes his laborious trust." And again, in 1870, Dr. Grissom said in his report: "The assistant physician, Dr. F. T. Fuller, by his experience, industry and constant devotion to the welfare of the patients, has placed the institution and the state under a debt of gratitude." Dr. J. G. Ramsay, president of the board in 1876, thus refers to Dr. Fuller: "F. T. Fuller, M. D., who has held the position and faithfully performed the duty of assistant physician continuously for the last twenty years, was in like manner re-elected for the ensuing four years."

In the report of 1878, Superintendent Grissom said: "It can be considered no invidious distinction to mention the obligations of the institution and the people of the state to Dr. F. T. Fuller for his long and efficient services to the unfortunate under our charge." And again in his report of 1888, he said: "Dr. F. T. Fuller, our first assistant physician, whose faithful services in the institution extend through a period of over thirty years and who has entitled himself to the gratitude of the people of the state, by his fidelity and usefulness, has been granted a leave of absence by order of the executive committee to enable him to recruit his health. I hope that time and rest will restore him to the position he has filled so long, so faithfully and so efficiently." Later, Dr. E. Burke Haywood, as president of the board, reported: "It affords us great pleasure to inform you that Dr. F. T. Fuller, our faithful and efficient first assistant physician, who has been suffering from a painful and serious illness of eleven months duration, has so far recovered as to be able to resume his duties." Indeed in nearly every report from 1856 to 1889, favorable reference to Dr. Fuller's services as assistant physician of the institution is made. The Statesville *Landmark*, edited by the prudent and careful Joseph Caldwell, said of him: "The Raleigh *Christian Advocate* very truly says: 'There is not a more faithful public officer in this or any other state than Dr. Fuller. The state owes him more than it will ever pay him for his faithful services for so many years. In a quiet way, he has done a vast deal for unfortunate humanity.'"

The foregoing are but a few of the many tributes paid his worth. Indeed, it is well known that the North Carolina insane asylum owes the greater part of its successful management to the skill and unremitting care of Dr. Fuller. He has remained at his post when others failed; his words of cheer and hope have supplemented his medical skill in calming and restoring reason to many who otherwise might have continued hopelessly insane. The patients know him, and his presence exercises a salutary influence upon them. The hundreds who have been returned to society from the institution have cause to feel the utmost gratitude for his kind ministration and his merit and goodness and sympathetic disposition and unselfish devotion to his charge are recognized throughout the state. Quietly he has pursued his course, not seeking promotion and fame, but the latter has come to him unasked, and promotion he has had the privilege to decline. In 1882, he was appointed a director of the Western North Carolina insane asylum, and besides his other arduous duties he filled that position until 1889. One of the most important labors of his life was in connection with that institution. He was greatly interested in securing its establishment, and he was influential in its organization. Had he not virtually refused the advancement, he would doubtless have been elected as the superintendent of the new institution, but he preferred to retain his position in the North Carolina insane asylum, to which he was attached by reason of his long association with it, and with his friends in the city of Raleigh. At times he has administered its affairs, and always with credit to himself.

Dr. Fuller has taken pride in his profession, and is a member of the Raleigh academy of medicine, of the state medical society, and of the association of medical superintendents of American institutions for the insane, and of the Medico-Legal society of New York. He is a member of the Protestant Episcopal church, and is a vestryman of Christ church, Raleigh. As a citizen he is of the progressive order and among men he is esteemed and respected for his moral and intellectual culture, and socially he is pleasant, affable and courteous. He is unostentatious and unassuming in character, and is respected for his meekness and mildness of temperament. Not only is he a man of kind and unselfish heart, but especially is he charitable in disposition, and many have been his gifts to charity, but given in a quiet and unpretending way.

DR. JOHN D. BELLAMY.

This prominent and very worthy gentleman was born in All Saints Parish, S. C., September 18, 1817. His parents were John and Elizabeth Bellamy and his ancestors were planters, independent gentlemen who held no important offices, and did not desire any. Our subject was educated in South Carolina, first at Marion academy and finished at the celebrated Rice Creek institution which more than rivaled the Columbia college which had declined considerably. In 1835 he removed to Wilmington, and applied himself to the study of medicine under the supervision and instruction of the late Dr. William J. Harris. He entered the University of Pennsylvania in 1837, and graduated from that institution in 1839. He practiced his profession with great success in Wilmington, for fifteen years when he was compelled to retire from active business on account of ill health, and his large planting interest in the county required his time and attention. He has served as a director in banks and in railroads, and was regarded as a very conservative and efficient officer. He married in 1839, Eliza M. Harris, daughter of the late Dr. William J. Harris and had several sons and daughters and grandchildren. Dr. Bellamy has never held any political office and though urged time and again to do so has always refused to accept as he considered a private station more desirable and equally as honorable for a gentleman of integrity. The same rule of action in regard to public office was conspicuous in his ancestors, none of them would accept and though they were not highly distinguished in life, none of them was ever dishonored. Dr. Bellamy is now advanced in years and lives in retirement. He is a gentleman of education and culture, with a naturally strong mind and which has been improved by study and observation. He is greatly respected in his community in which so many years of his life have been passed and justly so, for during his long life he has been upright in his actions and has wronged no man.

DR. WILLIAM J. LOVE.

This skillful physician and most estimable gentleman was born at the village of South Washington in New Hanover county, on April 21, 1834, and received his early education in Wilmington. He then entered the University of North Carolina at Chapel Hill, and in 1857 he received the degree of A. B., and in 1859 that of A. M. from that institution. He chose the science of medicine for a profession, and pursued his studies under the supervision of the late Dr. James H. Dickson, of Wilmington, a man of varied learning and one of the most accomplished physicians in the state. In 1858 he entered the University of New York, but remained but one session when he removed to the South Carolina medical college at Charleston, where he graduated in 1861. Returning to Wilmington, he at at once commenced the practice of his profession. His abilities were readily recognized, and he soon commanded a large and lucrative practice, which has continued to increase as his faculties expanded under the experience of maturer years. He has always been a student devoted to his profession, and has kept fully up with the progress made in that science. His great forte is self-reliance. Conscious of his own capacities he seldom hesitates in any crisis, but acts promptly and with decision, and his success is the best evidence of the soundness of his judgment and his skill as a fearless operator. He ranks deservedly very high in his profession; is a member of the North Carolina state medical society, and of the New Hanover medical society also, in which latter he has served as president for three terms. He has devoted himself entirely to his profession, escaping politics, and not only not seeking but not even desiring public office, and possessing in an enviable degree the entire confidence of all classes of our people.

DR. WILLIAM J. H. BELLAMY

is the son of Dr. John D. and Eliza M. Bellamy, and was born in Wilmington, September 16, 1844. His first preceptor was that thorough teacher of youth, Prof. George W. Jewett, who died but a few years ago. Under his tutelage young Bellamy soon became proficient in his studies, and gave promise of ripe scholarship in the future, a promise which his after life has amply fulfilled. In 1860 he entered the University of North Carolina, and remained there until 1861, when he enlisted in the Confederate army, and served one year, when he again entered the university, remaining, however, one session, and in 1863 he again entered the service as captain of a company in the state home guards. which surrendered with Gen. Johnston's army, in 1865. After the close of the war he began the study of medicine, and, upon careful preparation, entered the University of New York, where he graduated in March, 1868, and at once commenced the practice of his profession in Wilmington. He has been very successful, and ranks high as a skillful physician. He served as a member of the board of medical examiners of 1884 to 1890. He is also a member of the state and county medical associations, and has been since he began to practice medicine, and in the latter he has served as secretary and president. He is a member of the Knights of Honor, and also state examiner for that order, and is a member of the I. O. O. F., being the oldest presiding officer. He married, on November 10, 1869, Miss Mary W. Russell, of Wilmington, who has borne him three sons and three daughters. Dr. Bellamy is a rising man in his profession, is exceedingly attentive to his duties, and possesses the entire confidence of all who know him. He has a son, Russell Bellamy, who is his oldest son, and he recently received, from the board of examiners, a license to practice medicine, and on examination he received the highest record of the seventy-five students examined. He is hardly twenty-one years old. He will now graduate at the New York city university, and then will take up his practice.

DR. WILLIAM WALTER LANE, A. M., M. D.,

surgeon in charge of the City hospital, was born in New Hanover county, near the city of Wilmington, in 1831. He is the son of Levin and Margaret M. Lane, both natives of this county and state. Levin Lane, the father of the subject of this sketch, was the son of Ezekiel Lane, who was one of the most successful planters in this section of the state. He, like his father before him, cultivated the soil and amassed a large estate, and had sons and daughters born unto him, Dr. W. W. Lane. whom we are now noticing, being the third son. His early education was acquired in the schools of Wilmington, and later at St. Timothy's Hall, Catonsville, Md. He entered the University of North Carolina, at Chapel Hill, in 1849, and graduated in 1852, with the degree of A. B. Soon after his graduation, and following the bent of his inclinations he began the study of medicine in the office and under the supervision of Dr. James F. McRee, of Wilmington, one of the most prominent physicians in the state, with whom he remained for some time. In the fall of 1853 he entered the University of New York, in the city of New York, and graduated from that institution in 1855. In order to complete his medical education, and to improve himself as much as possible in the profession, he spent the following year, 1856, in Europe, visiting the hospitals at Paris, London, Berlin and other European cities. He returned to the United States in the winter of 1857, spent a short time at his home in Wilmington, and then removed to the state of Mississippi, where for some years he engaged in the cultivation of cotton in addition to the practice of his profession. He remained in Mississippi, until the year 1863, when he returned to his native state, and enlisted himself with the Confederate army as assistant surgeon, in which capacity he served until the surrender of Gen. Johnston, in April, 1865.

At the close of the war Dr. Lane resumed the active practice of medicine until the year 1875, when he was appointed surgeon of the United States marine hospital, at Wilmington, and served in that capacity for four years. In 1881 he was very active in urging upon the authorities the necessity for a city hospital, and when principally by his exertions it was established and organized, he was appointed physician and surgeon in charge, which position he still holds, and discharges the duties, sometimes very onerous ones, to the entire satisfaction of the authorities and the public generally. He has always been especially fond of surgery, and during his extended practice has performed many difficult and delicate operations, which have been very favorably noticed by many leading members of the profession. He is a member of the state medical society and of the medical society of the city of Wilmington. He has never taken any active part in politics, but has devoted himself entirely to his professional duties, in which he takes great delight, and is a skillful, conscientious, and in every respect reliable practitioner.

DR. ARMAND JOHN DeROSSET.

This gentleman, one of Wilmington's oldest and most honored citizens, was born in that city October 6, 1807, and in the house in which he now resides. His parents were Dr. Armand J. and Catherine DeRosset (*nee* Fullerton). His father, like himself, was a native of Wilmington, while his mother was born in Charleston, S. C. His grandfather was Dr. Moses John DeRosset, a native of London, England, born in 1726, and who graduated with distinction in one of the leading colleges of that city. In 1760, in company with his brother, Louis H. DeRosset, who had been appointed a member of the colonial council, he emigrated to America and settled on the Cape Fear river, near Wilmington, where he began the practice of his profession and was eminently successful. During his life he held many important public positions, and was mayor of Wilmington during the troublous times of the Revolution, in which latter capacity he exhibited great courage, firmness and devotion to the cause of the colonies. He was father of two children, a son and a daughter. The son, Dr. Armand J. DeRosset, Sr., followed in the footsteps of his father and embraced the medical profession. He graduated at Princeton college and then entered the University of Pennsylvania, and was one of the first three graduates of that institution.   He followed his profession in Wilmington during his whole lifetime, which was a long and honorable one, and died in the city where he was born in 1859, at the ripe age of four score and twelve years, leaving behind him an unsullied reputation and not one enemy in the world.   His son, the subject of this notice, acquired his early education in the schools of Wilmington, and principally at the hands of Prof. James W. Mitchell, an experienced teacher and of more than ordinary attainments.   As a student he was exceptionally bright, for when he was but fourteen years old he was able to enter the sophomore class of the University of North Carolina, at Chapel Hill, and graduated with distinction in 1824 when but seventeen years of age.   In choosing a profession, his early inclination was for that of arms, but when he was about to enter a military school he, for some reason unknown to the writer of this, abandoned this and applied himself to the study of medicine, spending one year at South Carolina medical college at Charleston, and completing his medical education at the University of Pennsylvania, graduating in 1828, when he had scarcely reached his majority. He entered upon the practice of his profession in connection with his father, and their practice was large and lucrative, but the profession was distasteful to him and he soon tired from it, preferring a mercantile life.

In 1837 he formed a co-partnership with an estimable gentleman, the late P. K. Dickinson, for the purpose of carrying on the lumber business, which he continued until 1839, when he withdrew and founded the house of DeRosset & Brown, general commission merchants, of Wilmington, and Brown & DeRossett, of New York.   This business was immense, and was conducted very successfully until 1861, when the opening of hostilities between the north and south compelled the suspension of all active operations.   Upon the close of the war he resumed his business with his sons under the firm name of DeRosset & Company, and continued until 1882, when he finally withdrew, and since that time has been engaged in the general insurance business.   He was first married in 1829 to Miss Eliza Jane, daughter of the late William C. Lord, who bore him eleven children, seven sons and four daughters.   One of these sons became a prominent physician in the city of New York.   The second wife was Miss Catherine Kennedy, who is still living.   Dr. DeRosset has never taken an active part in political life nor sought public office, but has held many positions of responsibility which have been conferred upon him.   He has been for years, almost since its organization, an active director in the Wilmington & Weldon R. R., and was sent by that company, in 1849, to England to negotiate its bonds and purchase rails for the use of that road, which he successfully accomplished.   The effects of the war were ruinous to the road, and his financial ability was again put in requisition to restore its credit.   At the earnest solicitation of the board of directors he again visited Europe in 1865 and 1866, for the purpose of obtaining an extension of time on the original bonds, which were running rapidly to maturity, and placing

JOSEPH GRAHAM, M. D.

additional securities on the market, in which he was again successful and which is a monument to his financial skill. He has been for the greater part of his life a consistent member of the Protestant Episcopal church, senior warden of St. James parish and treasurer of the diocese of east Carolina, has been an active, energetic, public-spirited citizen, and has done as much perhaps as any one man to advance the interests and increase the prosperity of his native city. No man is more respected and esteemed than he, and justly so, for during his long and active business life his integrity has never been questioned, and his name is the synonym for all that is honorable and true.

JAMES H. DURHAM, M. D., D. D. S.

One of the most promising physicians and dentists of the state of North Carolina is Dr. James H. Durham, of Wilmington. He has accomplished within a score of years what it has taken many men of talent a lifetime to accomplish, and other men of talent have never accomplished at all. He was born in Wayne county, August 27, 1850. His parents were Dawson O. and Julia (Smith) Durham. They came from good old "North State" stock, and both are natives of North Carolina. Dawson Durham, the father, was an old-time southern planter, which he followed all his life. living in the ease and comfort peculiar to that class. He died, lamented by a large circle of admiring friends, in 1880. Our subject received his preparatory education in Trinity college, and completed it at the University of Virginia, where he took the full collegiate and medical course, which he completed in 1872. He then attended two years for the sake of the experiences to be gained thereby, at Bellevue hospital, New York city, and immediately when completing his course there he went to Philadelphia, and attended the Philadelphia dental college, from which institution he graduated in 1875, with the degree of D. D. S. In 1873 the young physician and dental surgeon, commenced to practice his profession in Wilmington, where he has continued his work with great success ever since. Dr. Durham was married, in 1882, to Nellie Alston, of Durham county. Two children have blessed this happy union, one son and one daughter. Dr. Durham is a member of the Royal Arch Masons and Knights of Pythias, and has built up a large and lucrative practice, of which many older men might well be proud. He is president of the state dental society, and a member of the state medical examining board, in which last capacity he is serving his third term.

JOSEPH GRAHAM, M. D.,

was born in Newbern, N. C., April 15, 1837. He was reared, not in the city of his birth, but at Hillsborough, N. C., the birthplace of his parents. His early days were spent at the Caldwell institute at Hillsborough. When he had arrived at the age of thirteen, his parents removed to Washington, D. C., his father holding an official position in that city, under the Federal government. Young Graham was then placed, for the two years during which his father remained in office, in the classical and mathematical academy at Georgetown, under the instruction of the distinguished Prof. Abbott. In 1853 he entered the North Carolina university at Chapel Hill, from which he graduated in June, 1857. For three months thereafter he studied medicine under the instruction of Dr. Edmund Strudwick, at Hillsborough. In the fall of 1857 he entered Jefferson medical college, of Philadelphia, where, after completing a thorough course, he graduated in the spring of 1859. The following summer and fall were spent in the hospitals of Philadelphia. Returning to Hillsborough in October, Dr. Graham was united in marriage, on the 26th day of that month, with Miss Elizabeth, the eldest daughter of the late Thomas Blount Hill. They have had five children, three sons and two daughters, the latter and only one son now surviving. The surviving son is Dr. William A. Graham, who is a partner with his father in the practice of medicine. In January, 1860, Dr. Joseph Graham moved to Charlotte, N. C., and there locating, began the practice of his profession, pursuing that practice until his state passed the ordinance of secession in May, 1861. He then aided in raising a company of light artillery, known as Brem's battery, but subsequently as Graham's North Carolina battery. With this company he entered the Confederate service with the rank of first-lieutenant, and upon the resignation of Capt. Brem, early in the war, Dr. Graham was promoted to the captaincy of the company. This rank he held until in January, 1864, when desiring to return to the practice of his profession, he was commissioned as surgeon of a North Carolina regiment, remaining as such until the close of the war.

Returning home from the field of battle, Dr. Graham found himself at the foot of the ladder in a financial sense, the result of war's ravages, and he was thus compelled with thousands of his fellow citizens, to begin in his business life anew. He decided to return to the practice of his profession in Gaston county, where he removed his family, and where he continued to reside and practice up to the spring of 1869. He then returned to Charlotte, where a year later, he formed a partnership with the late Dr. Johnston B. Jones, with whom he continued until the death of Dr. Jones, in March, 1889. Since that date a son of Dr. Jones and his own son, Dr. William A. Graham, have been his partners. Dr. Graham is in the foremost rank of medical practitioners in North Carolina, and his practice has been signalized by a large degree of success. He is a member of the Southern Surgical and Gynecological society, of the Charlotte academy of medicine, and ex-member of the North Carolina board of examiners. He is an ex-president of the North Carolina state medical society, besides holding so conspicuous a rank in his profession. Dr. Graham is a representative citizen, and enjoys a high social standing. He is a member of the Charlotte chamber of commerce, and has served as a member of the city council. Dr. Graham is a gentleman of the highest respectability, is honored by his fellow citizens throughout the state, and comes of an excellent ancestry, as is noted elsewhere in this volume.

GEORGE W. GRAHAM, M. D.,

born in Hillsborough, Orange county, N. C., August 19, 1847, is the sixth son of the late Hon. William A. Graham, whose biography appears in these pages. At an early age he developed those qualities of cool judgment, kindness of heart and strength of mind, together with most strict habits, so essential to the success of a good physician, and having completed his academical preparation in the common schools of his state, entered and was graduated from the state university in 1868. In 1869 he spent a year in the celebrated medical department of the University of Virginia, and afterward graduated in medicine with high honors from the University of New York city. He located immediately after his graduation in Atlanta, Ga., where in the face of some of the most eminent specialists in contagious and infectious diseases, he remained for two years, enjoying in the meanwhile a large and most lucrative practice. Subequently he completed in the Manhattan hospital of New York city, a special course in ophthalmology and otology, and then returned to Raleigh, N. C., where he remained for seven years in the active practice as an eye and ear specialist. In 1873, Dr. Graham was married to Miss Sally S. Shaver, of Atlanta, Ga., who survived fourteen years of her married life, she having died in 1887, leaving three children. In 1880 he returned to Charlotte, where he permanently settled and where he has since become widely known as a skillful operator in his specialty. Dr. Graham was married the second time in Charlotte, to Miss Alice L. Alexandra, of that city, with whom he has lived most happily ever since. In his profession he ranks among the foremost men of his state. He holds a membership in the state medical association and the Charlotte academy of medicine, is president of the Scotch-Irish society of North Carolina, and also president of the Charlotte literary and library association. Dr. Graham is a devout lover of literature, in which he is thoroughly versed, and is considered an authority upon literary questions.

J. WELLINGTON BYERS, M. D.,

of Charlotte, N. C., is a physician by profession, and a writer upon medical and allied sciences, of considerable reputation. He was born on the 8th day of May, 1859, at Parkersburg, then Virginia, now West Virginia. His parents were Wellington Byers and Mary E. Byers, *nee* Peers, and both were natives of Virginia, and of Scotch-Irish ancestry. They had established a home at Parkersburg, for only a few years when the Civil war broke out; and being of strong southern proclivities and sympathy, were forced for refuge from Parkersburg, and settling at Charlottesville, Va., the birthplace and former home of young Byers' father, his parents continued to reside here till 1870, in which year the family moved to Atlanta, Ga. In 1876 young Byers left Atlanta and entered the freshman class of the North Georgia college, a branch of the state university, at Dahlonega. Here, for several terms, he pursued a scientific, classical and literary course, achieving distinction in metaphysics and bellesletters; he was esteemed to be one of the most profound and proficient students in mental philosophy and rhetoric the institution had ever sent forth; and in his subsequent pursuits and achievements have been manifest this character of mind and learning. It was during his college days at Dahlonega that he first gave promise of prominence in literature, and first began to exercise his tendencies as a writer, his first work being editorial writing for the college paper, so often the first avenue presented for the future distinction of literary workers. The publisher of the local newspaper at Dahlonega, being favorably impressed with his ability as a writer, invited him to become a contributor to his journal, known as the *Dahloncga Signal*, and accepting the invitation, his work upon this journal soon brought it into notice as the best and most communicative paper the town had ever had.

However, young Byers soon left college, and also severed his connection with this newspaper, but continued to write for various newspapers and periodicals, producing a number of miscellaneous articles upon politics and literature, and as early as 1879, at the age of twenty he wrote an able review of the early English drama, which was published in the *New York Clipper*. In 1880 he returned to Charlottesville, Va., his purpose being to enter the University of Virginia. He spent several months under the tutelage of Rev. E. Woods, of the Pantops school, reviewing mathematics and classics, that he might be fresh in these studies upon entering the university for which he was well prepared, but financial contingencies necessitated a change of his plans, and he was forced to relinquish his purpose of entering the university, and returning to his home at Atlanta, he began preparations for the study of medicine. In the fall of 1880, he entered the Atlanta medical college, from which institution he graduated with distinction in February, 1882, as fifth in a class of fifty-three. At once he began the practice of his chosen profession at Atlanta, under most promising prospects. Being solicited to locate in Charlotte, N. C., Dr. Byers removed in 1883, to that city, where he has since continued to reside. Three years later, 1886, he chose a wife, wedding Miss Catherine L. Leary, an accomplished lady, and a daughter of the late William A. Leary, a noted book publisher of Philadelphia, Penn.

Dr. Byers has taken post-graduate courses in northern schools, and has established an excellent reputation for skill, ability, learning and culture as a physician and surgeon. As a writer, especially upon medical and allied sciences, he has attained to a prominence second to that of no other young man in the south; and although a young man, and of hardly a decade of years experience in the medical profession, his career has been brilliant and successful, and he gives great promise of eminence in his chosen profession. He is author of several standard articles in medical and correlative sciences, some of which have appeared in standard medical works, such as, " Woods' Reference Handbook" and "Keating's Cyclopedia." In both of these he is author of the chapters upon "Influence of Race and Nationality upon Disease;" also, those upon the "General Principles of the Prevention of Disease," " Diseases and Injuries of the Shoulder Blade." In the department of ethnological medicine, Dr. Byers is regarded as a foremost authority in this country, and his opinions and conclusions are accepted as most complete and thorough among those of investigators of these questions. For several years he has been a regular contributor to various medical and scientific journals; and he is a member of the editorial staff of the *Southern Medical Record*, published at Atlanta, Ga., and is also an associate editor of the *Climatologist*, a journal of high character, devoted to hygiene and climate, published at Philadelphia, Penn. In his writings, Dr. Byers, style is scholarly, graceful and philosophical. His language is chaste and classical, and his productions bear evidence of a student, and of a man of experience and scientific research. In habit he is seclusive rather than demonstrative. In scientific research he is thorough, methodical, systematical and original; rather inventive, and possessed of a striking capacity for original discovery in scientific medicine. He has, in the *New York Medical Record*, February 14, 1891, set claim to the discovery of the germicidal action of the blood, in connection with the germ theory of disease, an important and highly interesting question to all physiological and pathological investigators. Dr. Byers is a member of the North Carolina state medical society, and an honorary member of several literary and other medical societies.

JOHNSTON BLAKELEY JONES, M. D.,

an eminent physician and a man of remarkable intellectual and social culture, was born in Chatham county, N. C., September 12, 1814, at " Rock Rest," the residence of his father. He died in Charlotte, N. C., March 1, 1889. His father, Edward Jones, was a native of Ireland, and a lineal descendant of Jeremy Taylor, as may be seen in a note appended by Bishop Heber to his life of Jeremy Taylor. Mr. Jones came to North Carolina when quite a young man, and soon attained great eminence at the bar, being for over thirty years solicitor-general of the state. He married Mary E., daughter of Peter Mollet, of Fayetteville, by whom he was the father of a numerous family. The subject of this sketch, the youngest child of the above marriage, was prepared for college at the old Episcopal school in Raleigh, under that eminent scholar, bibliographer and educator, Mr. Joseph G. Cogswell, a notable name in the literary history of America. Mr. Cogswell was a man specially qualified to exert a stimulating and refining influence upon the inquisitive and discriminating mind of his pupil, and Dr. Jones probably owed to him much of that literary taste and general intellectual culture for which he was remarkable. From the school in Raleigh he proceeded to the University of North

Carolina, at Chapel Hill, where he remained several years, but did not take a degree. We next find him beginning the study of medicine in the medical college at Charleston, S. C., but his health being delicate, he was advised to try a residence in Europe. He therefore went to Paris, and continued his professional studies under the instruction of the eminent professors who then taught the science and practice of medicine in that city. After two years thus spent in Paris, and a visit of six months to friends and kinsfolk in Scotland and Ireland, he returned to America and took his degree in medicine in the Charleston college where he had begun his course. He entered upon the practice of his profession at Chapel Hill, N. C., in 1841, and there remained in the successful pursuit of its honorable rewards until the breaking up of the University of North Carolina, in 1868, in consequence of the political troubles of that period. He then removed to Charlotte, and in this new field continued the active and beneficent exercise of his profession until disabled by the infirmity of age, in June, 1886. A little less than three years of retirement and rest brought him peacefully to the end. In 1871 he had formed a co-partnership in practice with his friend Dr. Joseph Graham, and in 1883, a third partner was added in the person of his son, Dr. Simmons B. Jones.

From the beginning of his professional life, Dr. Jones took a high stand in the estimate of the public, and of his brethren. To that faithfulness, unselfishness and unwearied diligence in the service of humanity, which is the common honor of the profession, he added a special intelligence, patience and sympathy, which made his services as grateful to the feelings of his patients as his skill made them useful to their necessities. His scientific attainments are believed to have been surpassed by none of his contemporaries in this state. Among them it seemed to be recognized and acknowledged that as a general practitioner he stood at the head of his profession. His reputation was probably more widely extended over the state than that of any physician of his time. He carried into the performance of his daily duties the spirit of a student and a humanitarian; he had nothing of the *commercial* instinct, and could not make the most extensive practice the source of a large income. With him the fee was still the *honorarium* by which gratitude expressed its recognition of benevolence and skill. Not only were his services ready at the call of the poorest, but he did not exact from affluence the due reward of his time and labor spent in its behalf. After nearly fifty years of full practice, he died a poor man, so far as worldly goods go, but rich in the respect and gratitude of those who had known his kindness, and who had experienced his beneficence. He was one of the prime movers in the organization of the North Carolina medical society, and always took a deep interest in its welfare.

Dr. Jones was not more respected for his attainments in science and for his skill as a physician than he was esteemed for his magnanimity, sincerity, and sweetness of disposition. Outside of his professional learning his information was extensive and accurate, and his mind was acute, vigorous and original. He possessed powers of analysis and generalization in a remarkable degree. But a subtle and inquisitive intellect was balanced by a heart singularly retentive of youthful affection and loyal to early convictions. Few men have been so generally beloved, because few men have been so uniformly kind, interesting, agreeable and true, in social intercourse. After a partial paralysis had rendered him almost helpless, he was none the less an eagerly welcomed guest, whom it was a pleasure and an honor to entertain and to serve.

It is a small matter, perhaps, but necessary to the perfect picture of the man, to add that from his youth he was remarkable for physical beauty which seemed but the expression in outward form of the luminous mind within. He is said to have been known in Paris during his student days, as "the handsome American." Dr. Jones married, October 21, 1841, Mary Ann Stuart, daughter of Gabriel Stuart, of Halifax county, and granddaughter of Dr. Simmons J. Baker. Their eldest son, Edward S. Jones, lost his life in the war between the states, their eldest daughter also died before them; two sons and two daughters survived their father: Johnston B. Jones, Jr., Dr. Simmons B. Jones, Mrs. Lucien H. Walker and Miss Carolina D. Jones.

DR. JOHN H. McADEN,

president of the Merchants & Farmers' bank of Charlotte, N. C., and also one of the leading and public-spirited citizens, was born in Caswell county, March 13, 1835. He received a liberal English education at Wake Forest college and the university at Chapel Hill. He studied medicine under Dr. A. G. Yancey, at Yanceyville, Caswell county, and in 1857 graduated from Jefferson medical college of Philadelphia. He practiced medicine in Caswell county from the year of his graduation until the outbreak of the Civil war, at which time he was appointed surgeon of the Thirteenth North Carolina regiment, and subsequently made senior surgeon of Gen. A. M. Scales' brigade. In this capacity he served until the close of the war, surrendering with Lee's army at Appomatox. Soon after the war Dr. McAden located in Charlotte and embarked in the drug business, which is still continued in his interest. In 1875 he was elected president of the Merchants & Farmers' National bank, of Charlotte, and has since continued a successful administrator of the affairs of that institution. Dr. McAden has for some time been interested in several industrial enterprises, and at present is the president of two cotton works, namely, the McAden Cotton mills, of Gaston county, and the Falls of Neuse Cotton mills, of Alamance county; he is ex-president of the Charlotte chamber of commerce, of which he is a charter member. As a business man Dr. McAden ranks far above the ordinary class. He is careful, judicious, far-seeing and intelligent, and has been continuously identified with the business world since the close of the war, not confining his whole attention to the medical profession.

In 1871 he was united in marriage with Miss Sallie, daughter of

B—17

Mr. Joel H. Jenkins, a merchant of Salisbury, N. C. They have seven children. Dr. McAden is a Knight Templar of high order in the Masonic fraternity, having been eminent commander of the Knights Templar, of Charlotte. He is a man of fine intellect, a clear thinker, and is endowed with an extraordinary memory. He is a lover of literature, and is well versed in the biographical and historic lore of North Carolina, in which he takes great interest. Dr. McAden comes of conspicuous parentage. His father, Dr. Henry McAden, was the son of Dr. John McAden, both of whom were among the most eminent physicians in the state. Dr. John McAden, the grandfather, was a son of Rev. Hugh McAden (sometimes spelled " McCadden ") who was the first missionary to settle in the state. Dr. McAden, the immediate subject of this sketch, is a great-grandson of this venerable man. His mother was Frances Yancey, daughter of Bartlett and Annie (Graves) Yancey, of Caswell county. When a small boy Dr. McAden was left an orphan and was placed in the care of his maternal grandmother, Mrs. Bartlett Yancey, then a widow, who received and educated him, and to her sterling qualities and her moral and religious training does he largely owe the excellence and integrity of his character.

R. J. BREVARD, M. D.,

is at the present writing, mayor of the city of Charlotte, N. C. His birthplace was Tallahasse, Fla., and the date of his birth was December 5, 1848. He is the son of Theodore W. and Caroline (Mays) Brevard, the former of whom was a native of North Carolina and the latter of South Carolina. The father was a lawyer of eminence; he was the son of Alexander Brevard, son of the Hon. Ephraim Brevard, a citizen of Mecklenburg county, N. C. Dr. Brevard was educated at Davidson college, North Carolina, at which institution he received a liberal English education. He began the study of medicine in 1866 at Lincolnton, N. C., under the instruction of his brother, Ephraim Brevard, M. D., during the war surgeon of the Fifth Virginia regiment of Stonewall Jackson's brigade, and who was killed in 1871, by a fall from his horse. He was a promising physician, possessing ability of a high order. In February, 1872, Dr. Brevard graduated from the medical department of the University of New York city, with high honors, having been appointed the valedictorian of a class of 120 graduates. His was the only instance in the history of the university in which a southern student had received that high distinction. Immediately after his graduating he located at Lincolnton, and began the practice of his profession. In January, 1882, he located in Charlotte where he has ever since continued to practice. He is a member of the state medical association, and is one of the leading progressive members of the medical fraternity. His politics are democratic and he is a Master Mason.

During his residence in Lincolnton Dr. Brevard served as mayor of that town with much credit to himself and to the satisfaction of the citizens. Since removing to Charlotte he has served several times as a member of the city council, and was elected mayor in May, 1891. In December, 1881, Dr. Brevard was married to Miss Mary Stoney, an accomplished lady of a distinguished South Carolina family. Dr. Brevard has taken an active interest in the material progress of Charlotte and is a leading member of the chamber of commerce of that city. He has wielded a powerful influence in his political party and during 1886 and 1888 was president of the Charlotte democratic club. Socially he is a great favorite and suave and affable in his manner. He is a man of forceful will-power, a characteristic subordinated by a wise and generous discretion.

D. O'DONOUGHUE, M. D.,

whose name introduces the following biography, is a native of Ireland, being born in that country December 8, 1841. He received a thorough education in the national schools of Ireland, in which schools he was a most successful teacher during a period of ten years, afterward entering Trinity college, Dublin, and in this college and its normal training school he completed a thorough classical and scientific education, becoming proficient in natural philosophy, chemistry, higher mathematics and other sciences, thus gaining a rare and thorough knowledge of the sciences. Thinking the United States would afford a better opportunity for the application of such a scientific education, accordingly, in 1871, he emigrated to this country, landing in New York city in April of this year, and the third of the following May arrived in Washington, D. C. He was now penniless, but having, in Washington city, a sister and an uncle, he for a time, made his home with these relatives, and soon he was to gain a position. May 26, 1871, he secured in the Saint Elizabeth government insane asylum, at Washington, a position as an attendant, and in this position earned his first money in this country. In the following September, 1871, he and six others were examined for positions in the signal service department of the United States government, which department had been established only the year before. Of the seven applicants who were examined, only he and two others were successful, he standing first. September 13th, he gave up his position in the asylum and was made sergeant in the signal service. Five weeks later he had received full instructions, and in November was sent to Mobile, Ala., to take charge of the signal station there; of this station he remained in charge till in September, 1876. Being aided by an assistant, he had more or less leisure time, and becoming acquainted with leading physicians of Mobile, who foresaw that in the medical profession he would be pre-eminently successful, he was, at their instance, induced to take up the study of medicine. Accordingly, he began to utilize his leisure time from his office by attending the Alabama medical college at Mobile, which college he entered in 1872, and from which he graduated in 1874, with honors, in a class of thirty-three graduates receiving the degree of M. D. Then, with Dr. J. T. Gilmore, the renowned surgeon of Alabama, Dr. O'Donoughue continued to practice till in September, 1876, and in the meantime continued to discharge his official work in charge of the signal station.

In September, 1876, he was called to Washington, where he was made clerk in the signal service department, remaining as such till in October of 1878. During the time he took a post-graduate course in the Columbian university and attending the hospitals of Washington. October 3, 1878, he was ordered by signal service to Charlotte, N. C., to establish a signal station, in charge of which he remained till February, 1886, at which date he was called to Washington, for promotion in the signal service. While at Charlotte he had, after 1879, continued a general practice in medicine, in connection with continuing to discharge his work in charge of the signal station. Having here established a large and lucrative practice, and having accumulated property here, and desiring besides to settle in life at Charlotte, where he might devote his entire attention to the practice of medicine, he resigned from the signal service April, 1886, and located permanently at Charlotte, where he has since been actively engaged in the practice of his profession. He ranks among the foremost physicians of Charlotte, and is a member of the North Carolina state medical association, and is secretary of the Charlotte academy of medicine. Although he does a general practice, he gives special attention to gynecology and private diseases. The doctor has twice been happily married. In June 1873, while at Mobile, he married Miss Margaret Bookle, of that city. She died at Washington, in August, 1878. In October of 1883, he married for a second wife, Mrs. Agnes Sullivan, of Washington, D. C. She died at Charlotte, in April of 1889. Dr. D. O'Donoughue is a character of more than ordinary interest, and has led an eventful life. Educated in his native land, Ireland, he taught in its national schools, attaining distinction as an educator, and then emigrating to the United States without money and position he began the struggle of life under adverse circumstances. His determined will, noble ambition and character, together with a superior intellect and education fittingly applied in all his undertakings, his efforts have been crowned with success, and now he ranks among the most respected citizens and representative physicians.

HENRY TULL, M. D.

The paternal grandfather of our subject was Henry Tull, who was a native of New England. In early manhood Henry Tull settled in Lenoir county, N. C., and there amassed a large fortune. He was the largest land-owner and slaveholder in the county, having about 400 slaves. He was prominent in public affairs and a leader in political circles, and was a man of splendid education. His son, John, was born in Lenoir county September 19, 1832. He was given an excellent academic training, and has followed in his father's footsteps as an agriculturist, and before the Civil war, had become even more prosperous than his father before him, who was so successful. Before the war he was a leading member of the whig party, but after the disruption of that political party, became a staunch democrat. For several years he has held the office of justice of the peace of the county, and is a prominent member of the farmers' alliance of Lenoir county, and is a Knight of Honor. His marriage to Cynthia A. Dunn resulted in the birth of two children. The mother died in 1860. Mr. Tull was again married, Miss Winnie R. Jackson becoming his wife. Rowena, Hettie S., John L., Edward S., Frank R., Isaac M., Katie and Reed, are the children of this second union, and Henry Tull, M. D., and Cynthia, of the first. Henry Tull, M. D., the principal of this biographical mention, and one of the leading physicians of the state, was born on his father's estate in Lenoir county, on the 4th of January, 1855. Having completed a thorough academic course in the Kinston schools, and later at Bingham military institute, from which he was graduated with the rank of first lieutenant. In 1881 there was erected at Kinston a monument to the memory of Gov. Caswell, first governor of North Carolina, and this occasion was under military honors. Dr. Tull was then captain of Kinston Rifles, Company K, First regiment, N. C. S. G., which company, with others, participated. Dr. Tull so won the admiration of the guards on this occasion, by his participation in the ceremonies. and by rendering skillful professional aid to certain members of the Raleigh light infantry who, under the oppressive heat of the day, were stricken; that this infantry passed resolutions of respect and thanks to Dr. Tull, presenting him with a token in a handsome gold-headed ebony cane. He entered Harvard medical school, and in 1876 was graduated from the medical department of the University of Pennsylvania, and since that time has been engaged in active and successful practice at Kinston.

Dr. Tull is an honored member of the state medical society, and is a Knight of Honor. In 1881-2 he was chairman of the democratic executive committee of Lenoir county, and for several years was county physician. He has been earnestly interested in the industrial growth of Kinston and the vicinity, and was a prime mover in the organization of the Orion Knitting Mill company, and in 1886 erected a fine hotel building in Kinston, known as the " Hotel Tull." His marriage to Miss Myrtie Wooten, daughter of W. T. and Elizabeth J. Wooten, was solemnized in 1882, and two children, Bettie and Lottie, have blessed the union. W. T. Wooten was a captain in the Confederate service, and was killed while fighting for the cause he loved. He fills an honored soldier's grave. Henry Tull, M. D., is a man of great ability and learning in his profession. He has rapidly risen to the front ranks of his profession in the state; the same force of character which made him the careful, painstaking student, has won for him an honored reputation. Such men are not kept waiting for weary years before success comes. As a citizen he is public-spirited and progressive, and is esteemed as a man of unbending integrity.

DR. JAMES M. HODGES

was born near La Grange, Lenoir county, N. C., February 14, 1862. He is the son of Simon E. and Persis S. (Harper) Hodges, both of whom were natives of Lenoir county. The name of Dr. Hodges' grandfather was James E. Hodges, who was a native of Greene county, N. C., and of English lineage. He was a planter of much prominence and respectability. His son, the father of the subject of this sketch, followed the occupation of his father in Lenoir county, of which he was a leading and prominent citizen. Simon Hodges' political views were democratic, and in his religious faith he adhered to the Church of the Disciples. He was twice married, first to Miss Nancy Turnage, of Pitt county, and they had three children, whose respective names were Edward M., of Kinston, N. C.; George L., a farmer of Lenoir county, was register of deeds for six years, and Addie G., wife of Edward Mosely, of Lenoir county. His second marriage resulted in the birth of James M., F. R., Paul A., Robert G., and Lillie P. Hodges.

Dr. Hodges was educated at Chapel Hill university, and afterward studied medicine under the able instruction of Dr. J. D. Spicer, of Goldsboro. He attended Bellevue hospital, from which he graduated in March, 1883. After his graduation Dr. Hodges began his professional career at La Grange, where he has established an extensive and successful practice. His reputation as a physician is not confined to the field of his immediate practice, but he is favorably known throughout the state. He is a member of the state medical society, and also a member of the Masonic fraternity. In political faith he adheres to the democratic party, and in religion he subscribes to the creed of the Methodist Episcopal church, south. In 1884 Dr. Hodges was married to Miss Emma E., daughter of James H. Fields, of La Grange, and this union has been blessed with two children, Cyrus W. and Harry M. Hodges.

JOHN A. POLLOCK, M. D.,

was born in Onslow county, N. C., November 1, 1844, the son of W. A. J. Pollock, who is also a native of Onslow county. The father was educated in Wilmington, N. C., under Dr. Freeman, and later in New York city under the tutelage of Dr. Beach. For over fifty years he was engaged in the practice of medicine in Onslow and Lenoir counties, and is now retired and living in Kinston, having won a reputation as a most skillful and intelligent physician. He married Miss Olivia B. Humphrey, daughter of Lott Humphrey, of Onslow county, who was an extensive planter and a noted public man, having served in the legislature for many years. In 1850 Mrs. Pollock died, leaving three children, Andrew, an eminent physician of Florida. He served as president of the yellow fever commission during the course of that terrible epidemic recently in Florida. As captain of Company H, Fifty-fifth North Carolina regiment, he fought for the cause of the southland during the greater portion of the Civil war. Dr. Pollock is an ex-member of the Florida legislature. John A., and Virginia, wife of James G. Cox, of Kinston, being the other children. The father was again married, Miss Annie Loftin becoming his wife. By this marriage two children were born, viz.: William D. and Sarah. The Pollock connection is of Scotch descent, William Pollock, the great-grandfather of our subject, having come from Scotland to America in early times. He settled in Onslow county, N. C., and fought in the patriot army of the Revolution. He became a leading man in the county, and served as a justice of the peace for several years, and also as county surveyor for sometime. John Pollock, his son, was also born in Onslow county, and became an extensive planter. His brother, Elijah, served through the war of 1812. John Pollock was a justice of the peace and surveyor of the county, and was a staunch democrat. Of his four children, all are dead with the exception of W. A. J. Pollock, M. D. One son settled in New York, one in Georgia, and another, John, was a leading politician, and for several years was a member of the state senate from Onslow county. During the Mexican war he volunteered in the United States army, and was made colonel of militia in after years.

We will now write more particularly of John A. Pollock, M. D. Mr. Pollock lived in his native county until 1850, when he removed to Lenoir county. His education was received at the Kinston academy, and in January, 1862, he enlisted in Company H, Fifty-fifth North Carolina regiment, but soon after was transferred to the Third North Carolina cavalry, and served in that regiment with distinction until the close of the war, when he returned home and studied medicine under the direction of his father and Dr. William H. Moore. Entering the University of New York, he was graduated therefrom with the class of 1886, with the degree of M. D., and has since practiced at Kinston. From 1865 until 1874 he was interested in the drug business at Kinston. Dr. Pollock is a member of the state medical society, and he is also prominently identified with the Lenoir county medical society, the Masonic fraternity and the I. O. O. F., and is past noble grand and regent of the Royal Arcanum. As medical examiner of Lenoir county he rendered the highest degree of satisfaction. Always a staunch democrat, he was offered the nomination for state senator, but declined and nominated Col. Whitfield. Dr. Pollock was chairman of the Kinston graded school board and president of the Kinston collegiate institute. In 1867 he married Miss Agnes P. Jones, a daughter of William C. Jones, of this county, and three children have blessed the union, viz.: Mozelle, Raymond and Emily. The family are communicants of the Baptist church, of which he is a trustee.

HENRY OTIS HYATT, M. D.,

who is one of the best known and skilled physicians in the state of North Carolina, resides at Kinston, where he has led a most active life, busy in the practice of his profession for a number of years. He was born May 5, 1848, at Tarboro, Edgecombe county, N. C. His parents were Jesse B. and Margaret A. (Shirley) Hyatt, of English lineage and of families which for three generations lived in Edgecombe county where they became well and favorably known. The progenitors of these families were for the greater part planters, the maternal grandfather of Dr. Hyatt being one of the most prominent and wealthy slave-holders in his county. He was a man of more than ordinary intellectual powers and a mathematician of some note, his descendants inheriting much of his ability in this science. Jesse B. Hyatt was a farmer by vocation, though he did some merchandising. He was twice married, Dr. H. O. Hyatt being the only child by his first wife, while the second marriage gave issue to several children. The father died but a few years ago, the mother of Dr. Hyatt departing this life when he was an infant. She was a woman of vigorous intellect of stout, yet symmetrical figure, and in these particulars it may be said that her son bears strong resemblance. She was noted as being a beautiful and most excellent woman, and though she could not live to foster her son, nature gave to him her individuality. He was reared in the town of Tarboro, where he received a thorough education in a male academy, advancing beyond the common branches into the higher sciences and into the study of Greek and Latin. When ready for college he began to answer a call, drafting seventeen-year old youths into the Confederate service, but before enlisting the great civil conflict was closed, and though he had inherited wealth from his mother's estate, consisting of many slaves, the result of the war reduced him to a condition little better than poverty.

Further education was no longer attempted, and realizing the importance of having a trade, Mr. Hyatt set about to prepare for a livelihood. Being of a mechanical turn of mind he resolved to apply for an apprenticeship as a blacksmith. Upon going to a certain blacksmith (an Englishman) of Tarboro, the smith, thinking the youth once of wealth, was making light, indignantly refused his offer and so passing further along the street, he entered the office of Dr. N. J. Pittman and asked to be accepted as a student in medicine. Dr. Pittman, after a thorough examination, became the preceptor of Mr. Hyatt and two years later he graduated from the University of Pennsylvania in March, 1868. Returning to Tarboro, Dr. Hyatt received on the 5th of May following, an appointment as acting assistant surgeon in the United States army, and was stationed at Fort Hatteras on quarantine duty. A few months later, being able to purchase a horse and drugs, he located at Falkland, Pitt county, N. C., and began the practice of his profession. Two years later he removed to Greenville where he remained for two years and on the 1st of January, 1872, he located at Kinston, N. C., where he has ever since resided and continued an active and extensive practitioner. He has ever been a hard student in his profession, and has made much scientific investigation. While his practice has been general, in surgery and chronic diseases he has become the peer of any physician in the state, and his work has been attended with marked skill and success. In 1872, at Kinston he performed successfully, asperating the stomach through the abdominal wall in a case of laudanum poisoning. This was the first operation of the kind ever performed and it was reported in the *London Medical Times and Gazette*, and was translated and published in all the medical journals of the day. He has performed a number of successful ovariaotomy operations and devised a method for replacing the lacerations produced by childbirth. To gynecology, or diseases of women, he has given special study and attention, and in this kind of work stands at the head of his profession in the state. In 1883 Dr. Hyatt operated for stone in the bladder, improving the method of cutting through the lower part of the abdomen, which method is now used by the more advanced surgeons of the day. He has reported many cases of importance and has written several highly prized articles on medical subjects.

Among Dr. Hyatt's contributions to medical literature may be mentioned: Incised wounds of knee joint; physiology of spinal cord; a ready method of arresting hemorrhage after child-birth; hot water in urine therapeutics; milk diet in albuminuria of pregnancy; electricity in treatment of fibroid tumors of the womb; a new operation for lacertious of pirineum; the anatomy of valvo vaginal orifice; plaster of Paris as a surgical dressing; high operation for stone in the bladder; the physiology of conception; treatment of gin saw wounds and many others. These articles have appeared in the *North Carolina Medical Journal*, the *Virginia Medical Monthly*, the *American Journal of Obstetrics, Philadelphia Medical World*, and *The Obstetrical Journal*, of Great Britain and Ireland. For some time past Dr. Hyatt has given special attention to the diseases of the eye and in 1891 spent several months in Will's eye hospital, of Philadelphia, and has performed various operations upon the eye, He is the founder and editor of the *Herald of Health*, published at Kinston and at this place he also conducts a sanitarium known as the "Waverly." Dr. Hyatt is a leading citizen as well as physician and is a man of most happy domestic relations. In 1876 Miss Sybil Miller became his wife and their home has been blessed with the birth of two daughters and a son. Dr. Hyatt is not connected with any religious denomination and takes very little interest in any matters that are not connected directly with his profession. As he grows older, the more devoted he has become to his chosen calling and instead of getting careless in his work, the greater amount of pains he takes with cases. Like all men with scientific minds, he has developed a passion for accuracy.

DR. JACOB M. HADLEY,

a noted physician of La Grange, was born in Chatham county, N. C.,
November 30. 1835. His father was William Penn Hadley, and his
mother's maiden name was Hannah McPherson, the former a native
of Chatham county, and the latter of Alamance county, N. C. Dr.
Hadley's great-grandfather, Joshua Hadley, was the first of the
family to settle in Chatham county. He was a quaker of English descent, and moved to Chatham county, from South Hadley, Mass.
His children were Simon, who married Miss Thompson, and moved
from Chatham county, to Hendricks county, Ind.; John and William
moved to Todd's Fork, Clinton county, Ohio, in 1800; Thomas
moved to Morgan county, Ind.; Jonathan was a surveyor, and married a Miss Long, of Alamance county. He died in that county and
his family moved to Parke county, Ind. Jerry moved to Plainfield,
Ind.; Jacob lived and died at Hadley's Mills, on Terrill's creek; he
first married a Miss Chambers, of Orange county; afterward a Miss
Pickett, of Chatham county, by whom he had two sons and five
daughters; Joshua married Rebecca Hinshaw, and moved to Hendricks county, about 1838; Joseph married Miss Hinshaw, of Chatham county, and moved to the state of Iowa about 1844. The
eldest daughter married Hugh Woody, of Chatham county. The
second daughter married Jerry Pickett, of Alamance county;
the third daughter married Jesse Dixon, of Alamance county.
Jacob Hadley, the grandfather of Dr. Hadley, was a prominent farmer and a mill owner. He established the present Hadley's Mills, and the postoffice was named for him. William P.
Hadley, Dr. Hadley's father, was born May 29, 1810. He was educated in the schools of that period, and has always been engaged in
farming and milling, in Chatham county, where he now resides in his
eighty-second year. He was a justice of the peace many years, and in
1864 was a member of the lower house of the legislature. He was
formerly a whig in politics, but after the war joined the democratic
party. He is a stockholder in the Fayetteville bank and is a prominent and influential member of the Methodist Protestant church. He
is a large land owner, and owns one of the finest flouring mills in
Chatham county, his ownership dating back more than thirty years.
He has reared ten children whose names are as follows: Jacob M.,
the subject of this sketch; William C., who died November 11, 1880,
and was a member of the Second North Carolina cavalry, with the
rank of second lieutenant. He served through the war, and was
severely wounded at Brandy Station; Sarah A., wife of Van R. May,
of Wayne county; Oliver Newton, a member of Company C, Twenty-
sixth North Carolina infantry, died of typhoid pneumonia, at Morehead City, in 1861; Phœba A., of Chatham county; Annie C., wife of
Romulus Eubanks, of Chatham county; John W., a member of the
Second North Carolina cavalry, killed in battle at Stephensburg, Va.;
James A., of Beston, Wayne county, a merchant and farmer; Frank-

lin M., of Siler City, Chatham county, farmer and merchant, and Martha, deceased.

Dr. Jacob M. Hadley began his education at the New Garden school and finished at Trinity college, after which he engaged in teaching and studying medicine under Dr. Alfred Lindley, of Chatham county. He graduated from the University of Pennsylvania in March, 1860, and practiced in Craven county till the breaking out of the war. In 1861 he volunteered in Col. Clark's regiment, of New-bern, after the fall of which he was appointed assistant surgeon and had charge of the hospital at Raleigh, with Surgeons James P. Bryan and E. Burke Haywood. In the fall of 1862 he was appointed surgeon of the Fourth North Carolina state infantry in Lee's army of northern Virginia, and served in that capacity until the close of the war and was paroled from Appomatox, on April 9, 1865. He was taken prisoner at Martinsburg, Va. After three months duty in the lines, was complimented and paroled by Gen. Andrew T. McReynolds, commander of the post. After the close of the war, Dr. Hadley resumed the practice of his profession at Oakes, Orange county, but in February, 1867, removed to La Grange, where he has ever since been in active practice. Dr. Hadley stands high in his profession and has the reputation of a skilled and successful practitioner. He is a member of the state medical society, was a representative to the Virginia medical convention and was appointed a delegate to the American medical association at its meeting at Washington, D. C., in May, 1891. He was one of the organizers of Lenoir medical association and has served as president of that society. He is secretary of the county board of health. He is a member of the Masonic fraternity, of the Independent Order of Odd Fellows, of the Knights of Honor and of the Patrons of Husbandry. Dr. Hadley is the owner of 2,000 acres of farm land and is an extensive real estate owner in La Grange. September 4, 1860, he married Miss Lizzie E. Kirkpatrick, of Orange county, N. C., and they have had three children whose names were William Newton, now deceased; Lillie H., deceased, also, and George B. W. Hadley, A. B., principal of La Grange collegiate institute. Dr. Hadley is a trustee of and a prominent member in the Methodist Protestant church of La Grange, and has been a representative to several annual conferences and to every session of general conference since 1877.

HUGH M. McDONALD,

druggist, of La Grange, was born in Moore county, N. C., May 7, 1840. His parents, Daniel and Mary McDonald, were natives of Scotland, and came to America while children, with their respective parents, and settled upon Cape Fear river. Here after reaching their maturity they were married, and afterward moved to Moore county. Daniel McDonald was a tailor by occupation, which trade he followed until his death, which took place in 1868. His wife died in 1865. They were both members of the Presbyterian church, Mr. McDonald holding the office of elder. They reared a family of seven children, four of whom still survive. Their respective names were: Alexander D., a practicing physician of Wilmington, N. C.; Angus P., who died in 1861; Christina J., deceased; Sarah A., now Mrs. Jones, of Moore county; Hugh M.; Catherine J., wife of Duncan Thompson, of Richmond, N. C., and Mary Alice, deceased. Hugh M. McDonald was reared in Moore county. He attended the common schools, afterward graduating in pharmacy at Bluff Falls, Md. In 1861 he joined the Confederate army, enlisting in Company C, of the Thirty-fifth North Carolina infantry. He was promoted to the rank of orderly sergeant, and served until June 17, 1864. He was then taken prisoner at Five Forks, Va., and confined in prison at Elmira, N. Y. He participated in the battles of Richmond, Fredericksburg, Malvern Hill, the Wilderness, Spottsylvania, and several less important engagements. After the war was over he located in Wilmington, N. C., where he read medicine with his brother, devoting his attention largely to pharmacy. In 1870 he engaged in the drug house at Wilmington as a clerk for one year. He came to La Grange in 1873, and established his present business as a druggist, where he has ever since conducted the only drug store in the town. Mr. McDonald is a member of the Masonic fraternity, of the Knights of Pythias, and of the Knights of Honor. In political faith he is a democrat. In 1880 Mr. McDonald was married to Miss Hattie N. Hall, the daughter of Albert C. Hall, of Pindar county, N. C., and they have one child, Alexander Milton McDonald. Mr. McDonald is an active member of the Presbyterian church, in which he is an elder, and when the present church edifice was built, he rendered efficient aid both in material means and in encouragement by his wise counsel.

JAMES GRAHAM RAMSAY, M. D.,

a prominent physician of Rowan county, N. C., was born in Iredell county, March 1, 1823, the son of Col. David Ramsay, who was also a native of Iredell county. Col. Ramsay was of Scotch-Irish descent, and the progenitors of the family in North Carolina came direct from Pennsylvania, but originally from Scotland. They settled in Iredell county, and their descendants are to be found throughout the country; many of them, like the subject of this sketch, have become highly distinguished. His father was for many years a prominent and substantial farmer, and an honored citizen of Iredell county, in which he lived and died. Col. Ramsay was twice married, his first wife being Miss Graham, by whom he had two sons and five daughters, all dead except the subject of this sketch. His second wife was the mother of three children, of whom only one, a daughter, now survives. Dr. James G. Ramsay, was reared and passed his earlier days upon his father's farm, availing himself of what educational privileges were within his reach. He graduated from Davidson college in 1841, and subsequently taught school for a short time. In 1848, he graduated from the Jefferson medical college of Philadelphia. When he first

entered upon the practice of his profession, he located in Rowan county, about sixteen miles west of Salisbury. Here he has continued a long, active and successful practice of medicine, rising to the foremost rank of his profession. He has been an active member of both the North Carolina and Rowan county medical associations, and is regarded among his professional associates, as one of the most learned and skillful of their number. Throughout his entire career, he has been a close and constant student, and his researches have extended far outside the domain of medical science. In politics he was an adherent of the whig principles, as held by Henry Clay, Daniel Webster and other great lights of that once powerful party.

In 1846 Dr. Ramsay was elected to the state senate from Rowan and Davie counties, and so ably and faithfully did he represent that district that he was re-elected for several terms. When the great civil struggle cast its ominous shadow before, he was an ardent "peace man" and stubbornly opposed all measures looking toward a dissolution of the union by force of arms. When the actual conflict came, however, he cast his lot with the people of his own section, and was an earnest participant in the great struggle against the Federal government. He was elected to represent his district in the Confederate congress and took part in the deliberations of its second session. Since the close of the war Dr. Ramsay has been identified politically with the republican party. He was chosen a presidential elector upon the Grant ticket in 1872, was again a candidate for elector on the ticket in 1880, but was defeated as was the whole republican ticket of that year in his section. In every political campaign since the war he has taken an active part as a republican, and is one of the ablest and most effective public speakers and campaigners in his party. In 1846 Dr. Ramsay was united in marriage with Miss Sarah Foster, a native of Davie county, and a worthy and highly respected lady. The marriage has resulted in the birth of two daughters and six sons, named as follows: Margaret F., Florence May, who died in infancy; David A., deceased; James H., Edgar B., William G., who died a few years ago while superintending a gold mine in Africa; Robert L. and Claudius C. Dr. Ramsay and his wife have long been members of the Presbyterian church of which he has been a ruling elder many years. In the Masonic fraternity he is a member of the Royal Arch degree. Dr. Ramsay's life has not only been a useful but an eventful one. Not alone in his profession has he proved himself of great use to his fellow men; his upright, intelligent, conservative and consistent course as a citizen, both in public and in private life, has made him a worthy example for the emulation of all who have been cognizant of his spotless career, and the intelligence and integrity which have been his distinguishing characteristics.

JOSEPH JOHN SUMMERELL, M. D.,

was born in Halifax county, N. C., November 1, 1819. His father, John Summerell, was a Virginian by birth, and was married to Mary

Perry, a native of Halifax county, N. C. He was a successful farmer, and accumulated a considerable estate, and was able to afford his children the advantages of a liberal education. Of his marriage with Miss Perry there were born four children, only two of whom lived to maturity. The eldest, Mary A. E. Summerell, married Capt. E. N. Peterson, and now lives in Weldon, N. C. Joseph John, three years younger than his sister, was graduated from the University of North Carolina in 1842, and studying medicine, was graduated as a physician from the University of Pennsylvania in 1844. Soon after receiving his degree of doctor of medicine, he settled in Salisbury, N. C., where he has continued ever since in the successful practice of his profession. He has confined himself strictly to his calling, and never sought public office. His fellow-citizens, however, for many years, secured his services as a justice of the peace of Rowan county, and for two years he was chairman of the county court. For over thirty years he has also been superintendent of public health for Rowan county, and physician for the county home for the aged and infirm. In this office he has been able to do much for the health of the county and town, for the relief of prisoners, and for the comfort of the unfortunate and destitute. In 1855 Dr. Summerell became a member of the state medical society, and in 1862 was elected president of that learned body. He still continues a member, and is interested in all their labors for the relief of the suffering.

In 1844 Dr. Summerell was married to Miss Ellen H., daughter of Elisha Mitchell, D. D., professor in the University of North Carolina. Seven children, four sons and three daughters, blessed this marriage. Of these, two sons and two daughters still survive. The eldest son, the Rev. J. N. H. Summerell, is a Presbyterian minister, and the beloved pastor of the Presbyterian church in Tarboro, N. C. The other son, Elisha Mitchell Summerell, M. D., is a practicing physician in Rowan county, N. C. The eldest daughter, Mrs. Anna Maria Coit, resides with her father in Salisbury; and the youngest daughter, Mrs. Gertrude Hope Chamberlain, is the wife of Prof. J. R. Chamberlain, of the Agricultural and Mechanical college, at Raleigh, N. C. Dr. Summerell became a member of the Salisbury Presbyterian church in 1847, was ordained a deacon in 1852, and a ruling elder in 1866, and has continued to serve his church in the latter office to the present. He has represented his church in presbytery, in synod and in the general assembly, with fidelity. His life has been characterized by the faithful performance of all known duties, and his intercourse with the people has been marked by remarkable candor and courage. In every relation of life he had the confidence of his fellow citizens. He has had a long and laborious life of nearly fifty years in his profession in the same community, and during all that time has enjoyed the respect of his profession and the affection of patients and cherished friends. Now in his seventy-third year he is still able to do a reasonable amount of professional work, and is seen almost daily on the streets of Salisbury, going his accustomed rounds, and finds his chief earthly pleasure in relieving the sick and suffering.

DR. JULIUS ANDREW CALDWELL,

of Salisbury, N. C., is a son of Judge D. F. Caldwell, a sketch of whom will be found elsewhere in this volume. Dr. Caldwell was born at Salisbury, February 9, 1830. He graduated from the North Carolina university in June, 1850, and soon after began the study of medicine in his native city, under the instruction of the late Dr. M. Whitehead, who acted as his preceptor. He likewise attended the medical college at Charleston for one term, and then entered the University of Pennsylvania at Philadelphia, and graduated from the medical department of that institution in 1854. In the same year he located at Lincolnton, N. C., and began the practice of his profession. He remained there four years and then, in 1858, removed to Salisbury, where he has ever since remained. Dr. Caldwell is a kind, unobtrusive gentleman, modest and retiring, but a most excellent and painstaking practitioner. He gives most of his time to his profession, and takes a lively interest in public affairs, though he has never sought office. As a physician his efforts have been crowned with success. He enjoys the profound respect, not only of his professional brethren, but of the community which is the field of his practice. In the professional ranks he is among the foremost, and as a citizen he is universally honored and esteemed. In August, 1868, Dr. Caldwell and Miss Fannie M. Miller were united in marriage, and the fruit of this happy union has been the birth of three sons and three daughters, but they have been called to mourn the death of one son and one daughter. Dr. Caldwell and his family are members of the Episcopal church, and in the society circles and among the leading families of Salisbury they enjoy a high social standing.

JOHN HEARTWELL TUCKER.

John H. Tucker, M. D., is a native of Virginia. He was born in Brunswick county, October 27, 1842. A sound foundation for his education was laid in Hanover academy, and at William and Mary college and the Virginia military institute. He left the last named institution in June, 1861, to enlist in Company I, Third Virginia cavalry, as a private. After a faithful service of twelve months he received his honorable discharge on account of physical disability, and then resumed the study of medicine, having carried on a course in that science in addition to the regular collegiate course prior to his enlistment. In the spring of 1864 he was graduated from the Virginia medical college, and immediately re-entered the Confederate service as assistant surgeon, being assigned to the Chimborazo hospital at Richmond. In September, 1864, he was commissioned assistant surgeon of the Confederate navy, and was assigned for duty to the gunboat " Pee Dee," then stationed near Georgetown, S. C. He served until the fall of Charleston, and was then sent to the Marine hospital at Drury's Bluff, where he was captured in the spring of

1865, and was subsequently paroled at Richmond, Va. Beside many skirmishes and engagements of minor importance Dr. Tucker participated in the battles of Williamsburg, West Point and Seven Pines. After the close of hostilities he removed to Okolona, Miss., and was there engaged in the active practice of his profession and also in planting for seven years, five years of which time he was associated with Dr. John S. Cain, now of Nashville, Tenn. In 1874 Dr. Tucker changed his residence to Henderson, N. C., and has since made that his home. Since coming to Henderson he has won distinction as a skilled physician, and as a business man of much ability and foresight. He has risen to the front ranks of his profession in the state, and is a prominent member of the state medical society, also of the American medical association and of the state board of health, and at the present time is the president of the Vance county health board. He has been active in furthering the best interests of North Carolina, and is a director and vice-president of the proposed Atlantic, Henderson & Virginia railroad company. He is a Mason and Knights Templar, and a consistent communicant of the Episcopal church.

In 1872, Dr. Tucker was very happily married to Miss Willie Ruffin Hill, a daughter of the late Dr. John Hill, of Wilmington, N. C., and eight children have been born into their home, named: Eliza C., John H. Jr., Edward B., Willie Julia, Fannie J., Maria and two others now deceased. Edward B. Tucker, the father of the principal of this mention, was also a Virginian, having been born in Brunswick county in 1812. He was an extensive planter and owned large landed interests in Mississippi and Virginia. He was a magistrate and a member of the county court of his native county for many years. His marriage to Miss Eliza Cummin, daughter of James Cummin, of Armagh, Ireland, was solemnized in 1836 and resulted in the birth of eleven children, only four of whom reached maturity; they are: John H., William C., and Thomas Goode, of Brunswick county, Va.; and Maria Tucker. The latter (now deceased) was the wife of the late Dr. John A. Field, of Brunswick county, Va. The father of these children died in 1885, his wife having preceded him to rest in 1876. Edward B. Tucker was the son of Col. John Tucker. He was born in Virginia in 1774, and was a man of wide influence. An extensive planter, he was a politician of ability, having served several terms as a member of the state senate, and for many years was high sheriff of Brunswick county. His demise occurred in 1842. The American branch of this family descended from Capt. Joseph Tucker, of the British army. He settled in Bermuda, but later came to Virginia. He was descended from the Tudor branch of the Tucker family, who were originally from England. The maternal ancestors of our subject were from Armagh, Ireland. They were of noble blood and had wealth and influence. The maternal grand-ancestors of Dr. Tucker were the Virginia Goodes. The Goode family has an honorable history. It originally settled in Chesterfield county, Va., and many of its members were prominent in public affairs in the proud old state. William O. Goode was for eighteen years a member of congress from Virginia, prior to the Civil war, and the Hon. John Goode and Col. Thomas F. Goode are distinguished living representatives of the Virginia family.

DR. FLETCHER R. HARRIS,

one of the most eminent and successful physicians of Henderson, N. C., is a native of Granville county, N. C., where he was born on the 28th of September, 1859. In 1881 he was graduated from the University of Virginia, and in the fall of that year entered the college of physicians and surgeons of New York city, and subsequently attended the Post Graduate school in that city. In 1883 he returned to Henderson, and commenced the practice of his profession. Dr. Harris is a member of the American medical association, the North Carolina state medical society, and also of the Vance county board of health. In 1884 he was happily married to Miss Cary, daughter of Jesse H. Page, of Slatesville, N. C., and two children are the offspring of their union, namely: Agnes Reese Harris and Jessie Harris. Dr. Harris is the son of Benjamin F. Harris, a native of Granville county, having first seen the light there in 1806. He was a prominent planter and merchant during his active career, having removed from Granville county, to Oxford, N. C., in his later life. In 1848, he was united in marriage to Miss Ann E. Rogers, daughter of Samuel Rogers, of Granville county, and five children were born to them George B. Harris, a resident of Henderson, N. C.; Samuel R. Harris, also of Henderson; Benjamin F. Harris, died in 1876 at the age of twenty years; Fletcher R. Harris, and A. J. Harris, of Henderson. The family is one of the oldest and most highly esteemed in the state.

D. MALLOY PRINCE, M. D.,

one of the leading physicians and surgeons of North Carolina, was born in Marlborough county, S. C., in 1848. His parents were L. B. and Mary (McEachin) Prince, the former a native of South Carolina, and the latter of North Carolina. L. B. Prince was a planter in early manhood, and later in life devoted himself to teaching. He was a son of Lawrence and Charlotte Benton Prince. The mother was a daughter of Col. Benton, who figured so prominently as a patriot soldier in the Revolutionary war, and later as a congressman from South Carolina. Charles Prince, the great-grandfather of D. Malloy Prince, was a captain in the British army prior to the war for American independence. Lawrence died at the age of sixty-five years, and his wife at the age of eighty-two. Of their eleven children but four now survive. Our immediate subject, D. Malloy Prince, M. D., was engaged in obtaining an education in the schools of Cheraw and Sumter until his fifteenth year, when he enlisted in a regiment of boys under Col. Harington in 1863, thereby offering his services to the Confederate government. This regiment served with valor in

B—18

numerous skirmishes and small engagements, but took part in.no
large battle. After the close of the war Dr. Prince resumed his
studies, and subsequently took up the medical science under the
tutelage of Dr. Cornelius Kollock, of Cheraw, and later attended the
Charleston medical college, from which institution he was graduated,
the first honors of the class being equally divided between himself
and two classmates. After graduation he began practice in Cheraw,
and about a year later removed to Laurel Hill, N. C., where he became associated with Dr. Patterson. After several years' residence
in that place, Dr. Prince took up his abode at Laurenburg, and there
formed a partnership with Dr. Dixon, and this firm still exists. Dr.
Prince has completed a course of study in the medical department of
Johns Hopkins university, and is an ardent student of medicine, perhaps having no superior as a surgeon in this portion of the state. He
is an honorary member of the South Carolina medical association.

PETER W. STANSILL, M. D.

Probably one of the most eminent physicians Richmond county,
N. C., ever produced was Peter W. Stansill, M. D. Born on the 29th
of August, 1812, his useful career was prolonged until April 16, 1890,
when he passed from this world, firmly trusting in his Redeemer's
power to save. Dr. Stansill was one of nine children born to Peter
and Sallie (Jones) Stansill. The father removed to Rockingham from
Northampton. N· C., in 1790, and settled on the spot now occupied by
the Richmond hotel. These parents were intelligent and respected
people, but did not possess means sufficient to give their children educational advantages. Their son Peter was ambitious, however, and
in early boyhood determined to acquire a thorough education. He
was apprenticed to a blacksmith, and while working at his trade devoted himself to persistent study. Having decided to fit himself for
the medical profession, at the age of twenty-five he began reading
under Dr. C. C. Covington, although still obliged to remain at the
anvil to earn his living. Under the most discouraging surroundings
he pursued most faithfully his scientific research, and after several
years succeeded in borrowing sufficient money from his friend, Mr.
James P. Leak, to defray his expenses while attending a course of
lectures at the Charleston medical college. After completing the
course he returned to Rockingham, where he practiced for a year or
two, after which Anson county became his home; but after a residence
there of two years, he, in 1846, returned to Charleston and took a
more advanced medical course. Subsequently Dr. Stansill settled
once more in Rockingham, and it was in the latter place that the
greater part of his life was spent. In 1847 he married Miss Eliza
Ellerbe McQueen, of Chesterfield, S. C. She was a descendant of
the Ellerbes, of South Carolina, who came from England in 1766, and
furnished several patriot soldiers in the Revolution. Six children
blessed this marriage, viz.: John, Cecilia, Anna, Cora, Ida and Willie.

- When Dr. Stansill entered upon his professional career, the treatment of typhoid fever was such that but few contracting the disease recovered. The ardent young physician saw that something was wrong and determined to remedy the defect of science. Devoting his clear, disciplined mind to the subject, he was successful in discovering an entirely new treatment which proved so beneficial that his name was soon given widespread prominence throughout the state. Rapidly the man rose to the front ranks of his profession, and his personality was such that not only the people at large respected his decisions, but also his brethren in medicine. It was but natural that a man possessed of such a mind and heart as he should early own his allegiance to God, and assume his share of the burden of elevating the world to the standard set by the Saviour. At the age of eighteen he joined the Methodist Episcopal church, and his after life was noted for its piety and uprightness. His death was a public calamity, and he was mourned in the rich man's house as well as in the habitation of the poor. None may know until the final day how pure was his life, how many destitute and fallen he raised, and what comfort his ministrations brought to the bed of the dying. He felt that his calling was not only to restore physical health, but also to bind up the bleeding heart, and direct the famished soul to its God and Maker. His memory lives in the hearts of those who loved him and the influence of his life cast on the side of right can never be lost. In politics he was a democrat, and during the struggle between north and south, he upheld the cause of his people, because he thought it right. Too old to bear the brunt of battle, he assisted as well as he could by his counsels and support. His son and successor is John McQueen Stansill, M. D., who was born in Rockingham, Richmond county, N. C., June 30, 1849. His preparatory education was obtained in the Rockingham academy, and later in the University of Maryland, where he was graduated in 1872. He then took special courses of study in Baltimore and New York medical colleges, after which he returned to Rockingham and began the practice of his profession. He is a member of the Rockingham medical association, and also of the state association, and for several years has been superintendent of health board of the county. February 23, 1882, Miss Willie B. Baldwin, daughter of T. R. and Minnie (LeGrand) Baldwin, of Richmond county, became his wife, and three children, named Minnie L., Eliza, and Cora C., have been born to them. Both Dr. and Mrs. Stansill are communicants of the Methodist Episcopal church, in which he is a trustee and steward. As a physician he is able and progressive, and has met with marked success.

A. W. HAMER, M. D.,

a leading physician of Richmond county, N. C., was born in Marlborough county, S. C., December 29, 1834. Alfred and Martha (Wallace) Hamer, his parents, were natives of South and North Carolina, respectively. The father was a prominent planter, and was a man of

influence and ability; a consistent member of the Methodist Episcopal church. He died in 1855, aged forty-nine years. His widow still
survives him with powers of mind and body remarkably well preserved, having attained the age of eighty years. Of the fourteen
children born to these parents, eleven reached maturity, and five are
still living. The son, A. W. Hamer, the principal of this mention,
was educated in private schools in Marlborough county, S. C., and began the study of medicine under the tutelage of Dr. W. D. Wallace,
of Bennettsville, and subsequently attending the course of lectures
at the Charleston medical college, he was graduated from that
famous institution with the class of 1858. Locating in Rockingham,
he at once entered upon the active practice of his chosen profession,
and continued at Rockingham with marked success until the secession of the state, when he enlisted in Company D, Twenty-third regiment volunteer infantry., and served as a private until the following
September, when he was honorably discharged on account of physical disability, and returned home. In 1862 he went to Richmond,
Va., where he received the appointment of acting assistant-surgeon
in Hospital 20, at Richmond, and retained that office until 1863, when
the hospital was closed. Returning to South Carolina, he resumed
his practice, and remained in Marlborough until January, 1881, when
he removed to Laurinburg, N. C. Dr. Hamer is a prominent member of the state medical association, and also of the Masonic fraternity, being a past master of his lodge, and is a member of the K. of P.,
having held the office of first district deputy grand chancellor of
Laurinburg; the K. of H., and the K. & L. of H. In 1864 Dr.
Hamer married Miss Elizabeth Douglass, of Marlborough county,
S. C., the daughter of Duncan Douglass, her mother being Sarah
(McLaurin) Douglass, a sister of Duncan McLaurin, for whom the
city of Laurinburg was named. Dr. and Mrs. Hamer are the parents
of these children: Sallie D., wife of Peter McIntosh; Mattie, Kate and
Douglas, who is a member of the junior class in the state university,
and Wallace, deceased at the age of ten years, in 1888. Mrs. Hamer
is a communicant of the Presbyterian church, while her husband and
children are members of the Methodist Episcopal church, south.

DR. EDWARD P. SNIPES,

one of the leading physicians and surgeons of Moore county, also a
druggist and pharmacist, was born in Chatham county, N. C., July 26,
1853. He is the son of B. F. and T. B. Snipes, the maiden name of
his mother being Norwood. Both parents are natives of North Carolina, the former being a farmer and merchant of Snipesville. He
served as county commissioner some years since for one term, but
takes little interest in politics, giving his undivided attention to business. He is quite an extensive farmer for that part of the country
and is a prominent and official member of the Methodist Episcopal
church, and though quiet and reserved in his disposition is widely
and favorably known throughout the county. He is respected as a

high-minded and an honorable business man, and a good citizen in the best sense of the term. He was born in 1810, and saw much of pioneer life in the south. His wife, who is still living, was born in 1818, and she too is a life-long and devoted member of the Methodist Episcopal church. Her parents were natives of Virginia, coming to North Carolina in an early day. The subject of this sketch is the fifth born in a family of six children, whose names are G. B., a farmer residing in Chatham county; James, who enlisted in 1863 and took part in several of the most sanguinary battles of the Civil war. He was a lieutenant in his company, and was mortally wounded in the last Manassas battle, receiving a gun shot wound of the hip. He was left at a spring in charge of J. J. Norwood, a cousin. The army was on the retreat. Neither of these individuals have ever since been heard from, though the father of young Snipes went to the battle-ground and searched in the neighborhood of the spring for three weeks. His age was seventeen years. Sarah, wife of A. W. Norwood, residing on a farm in Chatham county; Josephine, wife of J. J. Hackney; Dr. Edward P., and Nora, wife of James Norwood, a farmer of Chatham county.

Dr. Snipes was educated at Hugh's academy, and read medicine under Dr. William P. Mallet of Chapel Hill. He attended medical lectures at Vanderbilt university, graduating therefrom in 1890. He is also a graduate of the same university in the class of 1891. Dr. Snipes began the practice of medicine in 1879, at Snipesville. As a practitioner he has met with great success, and bids fair to take a foremost position among his professional associates in the county. He has kept a drug store in connection with his practice for the past eight years at Jonesboro. He went to that place in 1880, and has resided there since. Dr. Snipes is a member of the North Carolina state medical society, and the medical examiner for several insurance companies. He is a stockholder in the Jonesboro cotton mills and is business manager of the *Jonesboro Leader*. He has been town commissioner for several terms and is chairman of the board of health for the town of Jonesboro. In all the enterprises which promise the prosperity and advancement for his town Dr. Snipes takes a foremost rank. He is a member of the Methodist church, and is past grand in the Independent Order of Odd Fellows, of which organization he is delegate to the grand lodge of the state. In the community where he resides, he enjoys universal respect and esteem.

HON. THOMAS P. BRASWELL,

of Battleboro, Nash county, N. C.. was born in Edgecombe county, N. C., in the year 1833, and is now fifty-seven years old. He did not enjoy the advantages of a collegiate education, having acquired what he possesses by teaching himself while working upon the farm, which he did until twenty-one years of age; then he was elected district constable, and served his people in this capacity as well as that of deputy sheriff a few years. During the late war he was a regimental militia officer, railroad contractor and supply agent. Mr. Braswell moved to Nash county in 1866, and has since been extensively engaged in farming, and is one of the most successful and prosperous farmers in his state. He is a large land-owner and operates several large farms, is extensively engaged in the cultivation of tobacco and the first in erecting a warehouse for the sale of leaf tobacco in east North Carolina. Mr. Braswell has always been liberal and enterprising, substantially contributing to the building of all the schools and churches in his section. He was among the first to engage in cultivating grasses and raising improved stock, and has now at his home farm near Battlesboro the largest and finest-bred herd of Jersey cattle in the state. Mr. Braswell has filled creditably many useful public positions in his county and state; was first appointed by the governor a justice of the peace, afterward elected by the people; a part of the time chairman of the county board of magistrates. For many years he was county commissioner, serving as chairman of the board and once chairman of the county democratic executive committee. He was nominated by the democratic party and elected a member of the state legislature and served in the sessions of 1876-7, declining a renomination in 1878. He is a prominent member of the A. F. & A. M. lodge, I. O. O. F.. Knights of Honor, and in politics a democrat.

While Mr. Braswell's greatest interest is in farming he has contributed largely to the building up of his county towns; having built and now owning business houses in Nashville, Rocky Mount and Battleboro, he is a stockholder and promoter of the Rocky Mount West End Land and Improvement company, and is president of the Eastern Carolina Agricultural and Mechanical Fair association. Mr. Braswell married Miss Emily Stallings, a native of Edgecombe county, N. C., in his early manhood, and their four children are: M. C. Braswell, Esq., of Battleboro, N. C., a large merchant and broker, conducting the largest business in his county. He was prepared for college at Homes Henderson, attended college at University of North Carolina, and Poughkeepsie, N. Y.; J. C. Braswell, B. S., University of North Carolina, a tobacconist at Rocky Mount, N. C.; T. C. Braswell, Jr., aged fifteen years, at school. M. R. Braswell, M. D., born in Edgecombe county, N. C., December 12, 1865, prepared for college at his home and Bingham school, and attended college at Wake Forest and the University of North Carolina, and March 17, 1886, was graduated from the University of Maryland, with the degree of M. D., at the age of twenty years. He obtained license to practice his profession from the state board of medical examiners in May of the same year, and commenced the practice of medicine at Rocky Mount, of the same year, and has since then continued to build up an extensive practice, being notably successful in the treatment of all diseases to which he is called to see. He is a member of the North Carolina state medical society, and an active member of the Corinthian lodge No. 230, A. F. & A. M. He is medical examiner for four-fifths of the life insurance companies doing business in his town. He is public spirited and lends a helping influence to all worthy enterprises. Besides his extensive practice, he operates successfully a tobacco farm. Was a promoter and is a stock owner of the Rocky Mount West End Land and Improvement company, and is considered a progressive and able business man as well as a skillful and intelligent physician, as few have gained such distinction at his age. His political faith is of the principles of the democratic party.

DR. JOHN F. BELLAMY

was born in Edgecombe county, N.C., in 1827. He is the son of John F. and Ann Nicholson Bellamy, who were both natives of North Carolina. John F. was the son of John Bellamy, also a native of the same state, and he in turn was the son of William, a North Carolinian. He was the father of two sons, John and William, and both were residents of the state. William was a minister, and held the commission of lieutenant during the Revolutionary war, in a company of home guards. He died in October, 1846. John Bellamy, the grandfather of the subject of this sketch, died when but a young man. John F. Bellamy was born about 1790; studied medicine and practiced for a number of years in the state; enlisted in the United States army in 1812, as a private, and afterward served as surgeon. At the close of the war he settled near Battleborough, where he followed the practice of his profession until 1836. He then retired from business, and died in 1846. He was married about 1817, to the mother of the subject of this sketch. She bore him one son and one daughter, and then died. He was married again in 1836, to Mrs. Coffield, who bore him one son. He took no part in politics, and he was an earnest and consistent member of the Methodist church.

John F. Bellamy, the subject of this sketch, received his early education in the schools of the county, and completed his course in the University of Virginia, graduating from that institution in 1847. He began the study of medicine under Dr. William Hunter, and graduated from Jefferson college, Philadelphia, in 1849. He began practice near Enfield, and continued it until 1870, since which time he has been engaged in farming and cotton spinning. He was married in 1858, to Miss Sarah Coffield, his step-sister. The issue of this union has been one son and one daughter. Mr. Bellamy has taken some interest in politics, and has been offered several offices by his fellow-citizens. He is a member of the Odd Fellows and Masonic organizations, and of the Methodist Protestant church. He is one of the prominent men of Enfield, and enjoys the respect and esteem of its citizens.

DR. WILLIAM D. McMILLEN,

a leading physician of Magnolia, was born in New Hanover county, N. C., in a part now in Pindar county, in the year 1844. He received his early education in the Wilmington schools and in the Bula military academy. On the secession of the state, in 1861, he enlisted in the Papsail Rifles for one year and did service in coast defense. That company was disbanded in 1862, and he then enlisted in the first battalion of artillery and served with that through the Virginia campaign. But in 1863, he was transferred to the Fifty-first North Carolina infantry and served with that regiment until the surrender in 1865, with Johnston's army. He was in the battles around Petersburg, at Cold Harbor, and among others was wounded at Fort Harrison by a shot through the left shoulder. After the close of the war he began the study of medicine under Dr. W. G. Thomas, with whom he remained one year. He entered the Maryland university in the latter part of 1867 and graduated from there in 1869. In 1870, he began practice in New Hanover county and remained there six years; he then moved to New River where he remained five years, and then removed to Magnolia where he now resides. He is a member of the county medical society, of which he is president, and was for some time a member of the state society. He has never taken any active part in politics, but served as chairman of Onslow county democratic committee. He enjoys an extensive and lucrative practice, and is highly esteemed by all who know him.

JOHN B. BECKWITH, M. D.,

was born in Pasquotank county, N. C., on the 8th of November, 1816, the son of Watrous and Susan E. (Bailey) Beckwith. The father was a native of Poughkeepsie, N. Y., and came to North Carolina with his brother, Dr. John Beckwith, settling in Newbern in 1808. John engaged in the practice of medicine in his new home, where he married Miss Stanly, a sister of John Stanly. Subsequently, he removed to Raleigh, and in 1840 went to Petersburg, Va., going thence to New York sometime later, he died in the latter state in 1870. He was the father of Bishop John W. Beckwith, of Georgia, and of Dr. Thomas Stanly Beckwith, of Petersburg, Va. Watrous Beckwith was an eminent lawyer and legislator. He read law under the direction of a Mr. Martin, and in 1812 located in Smithfield, Johnston county, N. C. In 1815 he removed to Elizabeth City, where he married. In 1829 Plymouth, Washington county, became his residence, and his demise occurred at this place on the 10th of April, 1850. He was a prominent member of the whig party, and represented his county in the house of representatives of North Carolina in 1831. His father was John Beckwith, who was born in Lyme, Conn., and later in life he removed to Poughkeepsie, N. Y. He was born April 17, 1752, and died September 12, 1834. His wife, Chloe Bosworth Beckwith, was born at Washington, Conn., December 5, 1759, and died October 9, 1834, the same year as her husband. These parents had three sons: Dr. John Beckwith; Nathaniel, who died in 1840, and Watrous, the father of our subject. The maiden name of

Susan E. Beckwith was Bailey, and she was a daughter of Mr. John Bailey, of Pasquotank county, N. C. She was a devout member of the Methodist Episcopal church, and was a woman of lovely Christian character. She went to her eternal rest October 23, 1862. The six children born to her were: John B; Nathaniel, a prominent lawyer of Hyde county, N. C., he died October 30, 1886. In September, 1849, he married Miss Mary Elizabeth Wynne, of Franklin county, and their children are: Watrous, Sidney, Stewart, Norma, who married Terry Welborn; Dr. James L. S. Beckwith, who died in Craven county, March 30, 1866; he married Evelyn C. Clifton, of Johnston county, who bore him these children: Dr. Roe B.; Bosworth C., a lawyer; Annie, wife of John Thaxton, and Miss Susan W. Thomas Beckwith died in Smithfield in 1863; he was a lawyer by profession, and during the Civil war served in Company I, Twenty-fourth North Carolina infantry; Henrietta J. Phelps, of Washington county, became his wife in 1856, and their children are: John Percy; Dr. Thomas L., born January 14, 1860, and died in December, 1883; Chloe Ann, who died in 1847, aged nineteen years; Georgette, also deceased in early childhood.

The immediate subject of this biographical mention is John B. Beckwith, M. D. Until his fourteenth year Dr. Beckwith remained in his native county. He was educated at Vine Hill academy, in Halifax county, and subsequently began the study of medicine under the tutelage of Prof. Eli Geldings, in 1834. Entering the University of Maryland he was graduated from that institution in the class of 1837, and in that year began the active practice of his chosen profession in Wake county, N. C., but in 1841 he removed to Smithfield, and has since been prominently identified with the interests of that place, having won for himself a position in the front ranks of the medical profession of the state. He is a member of the state medical society, and also of the Johnston county medical association, he having been very active in the organization of the latter mentioned society, and its first president. Dr. Beckwith has given much attention to agriculture, and is recognized as one of the most successful and progressive planters in the county. During the great struggle between the north and south, he remained true to the principles so dearly beloved by the "Southland," and was a commissioned surgeon in the Confederate service, and he was also appointed to look after the families of soldiers, to provide them with the necessities of life. He was first married in 1849, to Miss Annie G. Thompson, daughter of Rev. David Thompson, of Smithfield. One year later this estimable lady died. In 1856, Miss Julia M. Sanders, a daughter of Major Ashley Sanders, of Johnston county, became his wife. In 1859 death again entered this home, and terminated his happy domestic life, his wife having died in that year, leaving no issue. Dr. Beckwith is a valued member of the Methodist Episcopal church, south, and has been a steward, and the superintendent of its Sabbath school, at Smithfield since 1855.

N. J. PITTMAN, M. D.

Among North Carolina's most prominent physicians appears the name of N. J. Pittman, M. D., who was born in Halifax county, N. C., August 9, 1818. His great-grandfather was an Englishman by birth, and settled in Virginia in 1650. John, Ambrose and Arthur Pittman removed to Halifax about 1776. Ambrose was the grandfather of our subject. His father fled to America from England, on account of the persecution of Oliver Cromwell, and became a planter and prominent man in the colonies. John Pittman, his son, and the father of N. J. Pittman, was born in Halifax county, N. C. He became a large planter and slaveowner. By his marriage to Miss Catherine Jones, of Halifax county, he had nine children. By a second marriage two children were born. The only surviving member of this family is Dr. Pittman. The latter received a thorough literary education, and for a time read law. Later his attention was turned to medicine, and in 1839 he received his diploma from the University of Pennsylvania. Until 1850 he was engaged in practice at the Falls of Tar river, when he decided to take a more extended course in the medical schools of Europe. For two years he remained in Paris, then the city of sciences, and later pursued his studies at Berlin, and also gained an intimate knowledge in the schools of London. During his residence abroad Dr. Pittman became personally known to many of the great scientific men of the day. In 1853 he returned to his native country and resumed his practice at Tarboro, where he has since resided. In 1857 Dr. Pittman was elected president of the Edgecombe county medical society, and one year later was made president of the state medical association, he having been most active in the organization of both these societies, and also as an organizer of the state medical board, of which he was the second president. He is a member of the Society of Science, Letters and Art, of London, Eng., and has a very fine badge which was presented him by the society.

During the recent Civil strife, he cast his influence and service with the south, and served as a surgeon in Branch's brigade, having been captured with the Confederate forces that surrendered at Newbern. From 1866 to 1872, Dr. Pittman was a member of the state board of medical examiners; and in 1877, he presided as first vice-president of the National medical association, which met at Chicago, and in 1881, was a delegate to the International medical congress in London from the American medical and North Carolina medical societies; and in the same year was a delegate to the British medical association, which met at Ryde, Isle of Wight. This eminent gentleman has contributed many valuable medical papers, the most important ones being on gynecology, of which he has made an especial study. At one time he was a corresponding member of the Tennessee medical society. In addition to his professional work, he is also very extensively interested in agriculture and stock raising, and owns some 3000 acres of land in Edgecombe county; his large herds of

Very truly yours

N. G. Pittman M.D.

Shropshire sheep, and Devon and Jersey cattle, are among the finest in the south, and have made their owner famous as a stock-raiser. Dr. Pittman is a stockholder in the Atlantic Coast Line railroad, and is a director in the Tarboro cotton mill, he having been very prominent in the organization of that company. Miss M. A. Pittman, a distant relative, became his wife in his early manhood, and bore him two children, one, Minerva, now surviving. By his marriage to Miss Mary Eliza, daughter of the late James S. Battle, of Edgecombe county two more children have been born, Eliza and Cornelia B., now deceased. He is a Master Mason and a senior warden in the Episcopal church.

JOHN E. LOGAN, M. D.,

was born in Greensboro, N. C., July 14, 1835. His education was received in the University of North Carolina, where he was graduated in 1857. He then entered Jefferson medical college at Philadelphia, and finished the course there in 1859. After a year spent in the hospitals of Philadelphia, Dr. Logan returned to Greensboro and entered upon his professional career. At the outbreak of the recent Rebellion he became the company surgeon of the Guilford Grays, an independent company organized in Guilford county, N. C., and in the fall of 1861 he was assigned to the Fourteenth North Carolina regiment of state troops as assistant surgeon, and during the latter part of the war acted as surgeon of the regiment. After the close of hostilities between north and south, Dr. Logan returned to Greensboro and resumed the practice of medicine, in which he has since met with success. In the year 1868 he was most fortunate in forming a marriage alliance with Miss Frances Mebane Sloan, daughter of Robert M. Sloan, of Greensboro. Dr. Logan is a member of the Masonic fraternity, and occupies a high place in the esteem of the community in which he lives. His father was John M. Logan, who was born near Londonderry, in the county Londonderry, Ireland, in 1797, and came to the United States when twenty-one years old, settling in Guilford county, N. C. For many years he was a leading merchant of Greensboro, and for a long period held the office of clerk of the county court, and was the incumbent of that position at the time of his demise in 1853. He was quite prominent in military circles, and held the commission of major-general in the North Carolina militia. In 1829, Miss Elizabeth Ambler Strange, daughter of Robert Strange, of Bedford county, Va., became his wife, and to them were born four children, all of whom died in infancy, with the exception of John E. The mother of these children died in 1845. John M. Logan was the son of Alexander Logan, who was born in Ireland. He was an officer in the British army. His father's name was also Alexander, and he was a native of Scotland. The maternal great-great-grandfather of Dr. J. E. Logan was Gen. Leftwitch, of Revolutionary fame. He was a Virginian. Bishop Early, the eminent Virginia clergyman, was a great-uncle of our subject, whose ancestors on both sides have been men of ability and note.

JAMES ELLIS MALONE, M. D.,

was born in De Soto county, Miss., November 19, 1851. While he was still in his infancy his parents removed to Louisburg, N. C., and it was in the latter place that the boy was educated, having been a student in the excellent school taught by Mr. M. S. Davis. At the age of seventeen he went to Baltimore, Md., and remained for about a year. Returning to his home he took up the study of medicine under the tutelage of his father, Dr. Ellis Malone, and in 1872 entered Bellevue hospital medical college in New York city, from which institution he was graduated in 1875. From 1875 to 1878, Dr. Malone was associated with his father in the practice of his profession. In 1890 he was appointed medical examiner for the Fourth congressional district to examine candidates for West Point. In 1889 Gov. Fowle appointed him a delegate to the national sanitary convention held at Montgomery, Ala. Dr. Malone is a prominent member of the Franklin county medical society, and also of the farmers' alliance. His marriage to Miss Anna Richmond, daughter of Jones Fuller, of Louisburg, N. C., was solemnized in 1878, and five children are the offspring of the union, namely: Jones Fuller, Carrie Hill, Edward Hutchison, Mary Ellis and Anna Richmond Malone. Ellis Malone, M. D., father of the above mentioned, was born in Caswell county, N. C., November 5, 1805, and came to Franklin county in 1853, having resided in Mississippi for seven years prior to that date. He was graduated from the Jefferson medical college at Philadelphia, and arose to great eminence in his profession. At one time he was deputy grand master of the grand lodge of F. & A. M. of North Carolina. In addition to a large practice he owned extensive agricultural interests, both in Mississippi and North Carolina. He was twice married, his second wife having been Miss Martha Caroline Hill, to whom he was married in 1845. Their children were: Mary E. (deceased), wife of Edwin W. Fuller (deceased), a noted poet of Louisburg, N. C., who died April 22, 1877, and James Ellis Malone. The grandfather of these children was James Glencoe Malone, who was born in Pennsylvania and emigrated to Caswell county, N. C., in early life. He was a tobacco planter. Dr. James E. Malone has been prominently identified with the advancement of the interests of Franklin county since entering upon the active duties of his professional career. In 1884 he had the entire charge of the magnificent exhibit of Franklin county at the exposition held in Raleigh, and by his skillful management made his department a great success.

DR. WILLIAM M. B. BROWN

was a Virginian by birth. In early manhood he settled in Pitt county, N. C., with a Virginia colony, and died prior to the war of 1812, leaving a large family of children. One of his sons was Wiley Brown, who was born in Pitt county. He was quite extensively interested in agriculture. He married Nancy Moye, also a native of Pitt county. Wiley Brown died in 1867, his wife having preceded him to rest in 1843. These parents reared five children to maturity, their names being, Wyatt Moye Brown, who was a physician, and from 1854 until 1859, was an assistant surgeon in the United States navy. Resigning he engaged in practice of medicine in Greenville, N. C. At the outbreak of the Civil war he offered his services to the navy of North Carolina, and was an active medical officer until the war ended. After the war he became a member of the commission house of Marmaduke & Brown, and died in Macon, Miss., where he had married in 1863. The second child is Susan, wife of William M. Merritt, of Ridge Spring, S. C. Annie, wife of J. J. Thomas, of North Carolina, is the next, and Martha, who married S. B. Wilson, of Greenville, N. C., is the fourth. The eldest child is William M. B. Brown, M. D., who was born in Greenville, Pitt county, N. C., on the 9th of October, 1823. He received his education in the schools of his native state, and then began the study of medicine with Dr. E. H. Goelett, of Greenville. In 1846 he was graduated from the medical department of the University of New York, and in the same year began the practice of his profession in Pitt county.

In 1854 Dr. Brown removed to Greenville, and has since been a resident and practitioner of that town. As a democrat he is active and loyal. During the Civil war Dr. Brown rendered valuable assistance to the Confederate service by caring for the families of Confederate soldiers, and in other ways earnestly forwarded the cause. In connection with his professional duties he now operates a plantation. He married Miss Jane M. Greene, a daughter of Charles Greene, Esq., of Greenville, N. C., in 1854. This union has resulted in the birth of five sons and one daughter. Wyatt L. Brown is an insurance agent at Greenville; William is a member of the firm of Brown & Hooker, merchants of Greenville; Jennie, wife of L. V. Morrill, of Pitt county, N. C.; Zeno Brown, M. D., educated at the University of North Carolina, and entering Bellevue hospital college, completed the medical course there in 1885, since which time he has practiced at Greenville; James and Wiley Brown are associated together in the mercantile business under the firm name of Brown Brothers. The family are active members of the Episcopal and Methodist churches.

CHARLES JAMES O'HAGEN, M. D.

Among the most eminent of North Carolina's many noted physicians we find the name of Charles James O'Hagen, M. D., of Greenville, N. C. Dr. O'Hagen is an Irishman by birth, having been born in county Londonderry, Ireland, September 16, 1821, the son of John P. and Martha (O'Kane) O'Hagen. The parents came to the United States in 1840, and settled in New York. The father was a gentleman of rare refinement and ability. He was a literateur of considerable note, and for several years edited a paper in Ireland, and after his removal to this country was in editorial charge of a leading Brooklyn (N. Y.) journal. Dr. O'Hagen was educated in Londonderry, later at Belfast, and his scholastic training was completed at Trinity college, Dublin. In 1842 he joined his parents in America. It was his ambition to become a physician, but before proceeding further with his studies it was necessary for him to obtain money sufficient to pay the expenses of a medical course. For some time he taught school in Lenoir, Greene and Pitt counties, N. C., and by that means managed to save enough to keep him while a student in the New York medical college. While engaged in teaching, Dr. O'Hagen had given every spare moment to the study of medicine, and consequently entered college under favorable circumstances. He was graduated from the New York medical college in 1855, and in the same year located at Greenville, N. C.

In 1861 he cast his fortunes with the cause of the Confederacy and offered his services to the army. He was made surgeon of the First North Carolina cavalry, subsequently being transferred to the Thirty-fifth infantry, Gen. Ransom's brigade, and served with that command until the final surrender at Appomatox. Surgeon O'Hagen fought in the battles of Malvern Hill, Fredericksburg, Richmond, Antietam, Drury's Bluff and Sharpsburg. The war closing, he resumed his practice at Greenville. He has been president of the state medical society, a member of the board of censors, is a member of the American medical association, and for two years served as president of the board of medical examiners of the state. Dr. O'Hagen has been twice married. In January, 1846, his marriage to Miss Eliza Forest, of Greene county, N. C., was solemnized. She died in 1871, leaving two children, viz.: Eliza, wife of J. J. Loughinghouse, of Pitt county, N. C.; and Martha. Miss Elmira Clarke, also of Pitt county, became his wife in 1877, and their union was blessed by the birth of one child, Charles James, Jr. Mrs. O'Hagen's demise occurred on the 15th of November, 1889. As a democrat Dr. O'Hagen has been active and loyal at all times. He has been mayor of Greenville, and is a most enthusiastic supporter of the public school system.

DR. J. D. GROOM

was born in New Hanover county, N. C., December 22, 1844, the son of John B. and Mary (McDuffie) Croom, both North Carolinians. The father is an extensive planter, and has held the office of magistrate for over thirty years. He served in the senior reserves of the Confederate army during the Civil war. His wife died in 1874, aged fifty-two. She was a life-long member of the Presbyterian church, and the influence of her life will be felt in the community in which she lived for good. These parents had ten children, nine of whom survive. J. D. Croom was educated in the private schools of his native county, and in the spring of 1862 enlisted in the heavy artillery service of the Confederate army, being at the time of his enlistment but seventeen years of age. Most of his service was in North Carolina, but near the close of the conflict he was transferred with his regiment to the department of Virginia. After a service of three years he surrendered with Johnston, having fought at Fort Anderson, Kinston, Bentonville, where he was wounded, and several other engagements of minor importance. After the final surrender he resumed his studies for a time, and then began the study of medicine. At this time, however, he was married to Miss Mortimer Blake, daughter of Isham Blake, of Fayetteville, N. C., the ceremony having been solemnized September 1, 1868. After completing his medical course in the college of Physicians and Surgeons, at Baltimore, which institution he left in 1873, he embarked in the drug business at Maxton, N. C. In 1875-6 Dr. Croom attended the lectures at the South Carolina medical college, and was graduated in the latter year. He is a prominent member of the state medical society, and has held the office of president of the North Carolina pharmaceutical association, and has also served as a member of the board of aldermen of Maxton for several terms, and at the present time is a director in the Building & Loan association of Maxton. Jimmie M., Mary F., Robert D., James D., and Arthur D., are the children that have been born to Mr. and Mrs. Croom. His wife is a communicant of the Methodist Episcopal church, while he is a deacon in the Presbyterian denomination, and he is also a Mason, is past chancellor of the K. of P., and is secretary of the lodge of Chosen Friends.

H. W. McNATT, M. D.,

was born in Robeson county, N. C., October 24, 1859, the son of Daniel and Carolina (Gillis) McNatt, who were both natives of the same state as their son. Daniel McNatt was an extensive turpentine operator, having been the largest in the south in 1872. He served three years in the Confederate army, and surrendered with Gen. Lee at Appomatox, having been a member of a cavalry company with whom he participated in most of the great battles of the Civil war. His death occurred December 25, 1885, in his sixty-first year. He was a devout member of the Presbyterian church, as is also his wife, who survives him. Three sons and two daughters were born to these parents, four of whom are living. H. W. McNatt obtained his preliminary schooling in the Jonesboro high school, then under the charge of Prof. J. D. Arnold. Entering the University of North Carolina, he took a partial course there, and in 1878 began the study of medicine with Dr. T. W. Harris. He attended lectures in Bellevue hospital college, in New York during the winter of 1879-80, and graduated from the medical department of the University of Maryland in 1881. In April, 1881, Dr. McNatt began the practice of his profession at Maxton, N. C. He has rapidly risen in his profession, and is now acknowledged to be among the leading physicians in that portion of the state. He has been a medical examiner for the New York Life, Manhattan Life, and also the Connecticut Mutual Life Insurance companies, and since coming to Maxton has been a member of the town board of health. Miss Jessie McRea, a daughter of

John McRae, of Robeson county, became his wife October 31, 1888. Dr. McNatt is a prominent member of several secret organizations, among them the K. of P., the K. of H., and the Masonic fraternity. Progressive and liberal, he is honored in the community not only for his professional skill, but also for his intelligent view of what constitutes good citizenship.

W. B. HOUSTON, D. D. S.,

was born in Union county, N. C., on the 5th of March, 1862. He is a son of Mr. W. H Houston, who is likewise a native of Union county, and a leading stockdealer of Darlington, S. C.   His marriage to Miss A. J. Stevens has been blessed by the birth of three children, whose names we give below: Annie, who is the wife of J. O. Muldrow, a resident of Darlington; D. Frank, a resident of Spartanburg, S. C., where he is superintendent of the city schools.   Prof. Houston is a graduate of the University of South Carolina, and for one year was a member of the faculty of his *alma mater;* he is an educator of exceptional promise; and W. B. Houston.   The latter was educated in the common schools, and was graduated from the dental department of Vanderbilt university in 1885, and at once began his professional duties at Monroe, where he has since succeeded in building up an extended practice and a reputation second to none in that portion of the state.   As a citizen he is progressive and liberal, and is interested in every movement promising the uplifting of the community, and the enlargement of its industrial resources.   Dr. Houston was most happily married in 1888, to Miss M. H. Fitzgerald, an accomplished daughter of Mr. I. A. Fitzgerald, of Davidson county, N. C. Two children have been born to this union: Henry Addison and Annie Fitzgerald; the first named died February 12, 1891, aged but nineteen months.   Both Dr. and Mrs. Houston are active and consistent members of the Methodist Episcopal church, south.

I. H. BLAIR, M. D.,

is one of ten children born to Joseph and Thirza (Hilton) Blair, natives of North and South Carolina, respectively.   The father was a mill-wright by trade, but subsequently became a planter.   He was a man of affairs, and was held in the highest esteem wherever known. Both himself and wife were devout members of the Presbyterian church.   I. H. Blair was born in Lancaster county, S. C., July 5, 1833. He received a thorough academic education at the Franklin academy, Lancaster, S. C., and in March, 1855, was graduated from the South Carolina medical college at Charleston, at once beginning the practice of his chosen profession in Mecklenburg county, N. C., but after a short time he returned to Lancaster county, S. C., and for five years practiced there in partnership with Drs. Wylie and Strait.   He then went to Jefferson, Chesterfield county, S. C., and in 1871 settled at Monroe, N. C., where he now resides.   During the Civil war Dr. Blair served on the examining board of conscripts for the First congressional district of South Carolina, and later enlisted as a private in the state troops, being appointed regimental surgeon of Goodwin's regiment, and at the time of the final surrender he held that office, part of the time having served as brigade-surgeon. In 1855 Miss Laura McCullough became his wife, and bore him one child, Richard W. He graduated from the South Carolina medical college at Charleston, and was practicing at Walkerville, Union county, N. C., when death ended his career. He died August 16, 1878, aged twenty-three years; he was possessed of a brilliant mind, and gave great promise of a bright future. The mother died March 19, 1859.

July 22, 1860, Miss L. M. Miller, of Chesterfield, S. C., was joined in marriage to Dr. Blair, and six children are the offspring of the union, their names being: Joseph R., a successful lawyer of Troy, Montgomery county, N. C.; John M., who graduated from the Louisville medical college, in 1887, and is now associated with his father; Stephen O., a graduate of the Baltimore college of pharmacy, and now engaged in the drug business at Monroe. He married Miss Lottie Fitzgerald, daughter of Col. Fitzgerald, of Monroe, and Isaac H. is their child; Rochelle K., the fourth son of Dr. I. H. and L. M. Blair, who is a student in the Baltimore college of pharmacy; Mary M. and Jennie L., the two last mentioned being still of the home circle. Dr. and Mrs. Blair are members of the Methodist Episcopal church, south, as are also the two daughters. Dr. Blair is very prominent in several of the secret fraternities, being a member of the Masonic order, the I. O. O. F., the K. of H., and the American Legion of Honor. He stands among the leaders of his profession in the state, and is a man of wide intelligence, and of the strictest integrity. Samuel Hilton, his great-grandfather on the maternal side, was a patriot soldier in the Revolutionary war, and during the Mexican war forty-seven of his immediate kinsmen fought in the United States army, all either bearing the name of Hilton, or being immediate descendants of that proud old connection.

JOHN F. SHAFFNER, M. D.

Among the most eminent of North Carolina's many distinguished physicians appears the name of John F. Shaffner, M. D., who is a native of Salem, Forsyth county, N. C., where he first saw the light on the 14th of July, 1838. He was given the best of educational facilities in the excellent public schools of his native town and with different private tutors. At the age of eighteen he began the study of medicine, and in 1860 was graduated from Jefferson medical college. Returing to his home he had completed the first year of active practice when the Civil war broke out, and in 1861 he enlisted in Company F, Twenty-first regiment, North Carolina volunteer infantry, as a private. After one month's service he was transferred to the Seventh North Carolina regiment as assistant surgeon, and after three months was detailed on special duty at Manassas, where he remained for about two months. He was then transferred to the Thirty-third regiment of North Carolina volunteers as assistant surgeon, and in March, 1862, was commissioned surgeon, and detailed as inspector for North Carolina and Virginia. At this time the battle of Newbern was fought, and the surgeon of the Thirty-third regiment being captured, Surgeon Shaffner was appointed to fill his place, and he remained with that regiment until April, 1863, acting as brigade surgeon. In the latter year and month he was transferred to the Fourth North Carolina, and remained with the Fourth regiment until the final surrender at Appomatox, and his whole term of service was marked by complete devotion to his duty.

After the cessation of hostilities, Dr. Shaffner returned to Salem and resumed his practice, and in 1867 established a drug business, which he still operates in connection with his practice. In 1865, in the month of February, his marriage to Miss Carrie L. Fries, daughter of the late Francis Fries, was solemnized, and has resulted in the birth of five children, the four living ones being: Henry F., William, Carrie Lizette and John F. Shaffner, Jr. For seven years Dr. Shaffner satisfactorily filled the office of mayor of Salem, and for some time he was a member of the Forsyth county democratic executive committee. He is a prominent member of the state medical society, and for six years was a member of the state board of medical examiners. He is also a member of the American medical society, and in 1872 was a delegate to the National convention for the North Carolina state society. In 1879 and 1880 he was president of the North Carolina state medical association, and for several years was director in the Northwestern North Carolina Railroad company. Henry Shaffner, the father of Dr. J. F. Shaffner, was born in Canton Basle, Switzerland, in the year 1798. He came to America in 1834, and located at Salem, N. C., where he assumed the management of the Salem Pottery company, and was at the head of that concern at the time of his death in 1877. He was twice married, his first wife having been Miss Lavinta Hauser, to whom he was married in 1835, and who bore him two children, the surviving one being John F. The wife and mother died in 1840. She was a daughter of Peter Hauser, who was a native of North Carolina.

CHARLES J. WATKINS, D. D. S.,

one of the leading dentists of Forsyth county, N. C., was born in the latter county August 4, 1836. Until his twenty-first year he was a student in the schools of his native county, and subsequently at Smith Grove academy in Davie county, N. C. He commenced his active career as a school teacher, and he was engaged in that calling in Forsyth, Davie and Davidson counties until the breaking out of the Civil war. In 1862 he enlisted in the Sixteenth North Carolina battalion of cavalry, as a private, and was promoted to first-sergeant, and later to brigade forage sergeant, and he held the latter rank at the time of Lee's surrender at Appomatox. He served in the battles of

Black and White's station, around Petersburg, and many other engagements, in all of which he bore himself as a true soldier and patriot. After the final surrender he turned his attention to the study of dental surgery, and in the fall of 1866 entered the old Pennsylvania dental college at Philadelphia, and graduated therefrom in 1868. He located at Kernersville, N. C., and was engaged in practice there until 1873, when he removed to Winston, N. C., where he has since been most successfully engaged in his profession, residing in Salem. In 1873 Dr. Watkins married Miss Flora O. Conrad, daughter of J. J. Conrad, of Yadkin county, N. C., and their children are: Joseph C., William H. and Bessie. Dr. Watkins is one of the oldest deacons of the First Baptist church of Winston. In church work he has been very prominent, and was instrumental in building that church, it being conceded by all that he did more in that direction than any other one man. He has also been very active in Sunday-school work, and for eighteen years has been connected with the same, having during that time, served as superintendent and teacher. In temperance work the doctor has always been prominent and active, he being a strong advocate of prohibition in any shape or form. He is a member of the Masonic order. His father, Abel C. Watkins, was born in Guilford county, N. C., in 1800, and spent his life as a planter. He was married in 1823, to Hannah Teague, daughter of Isaac Teague, of Davidson county, N. C., and eleven children were born to them: Susan, wife of William Hasten; Rebecca, wife of Anselm Reid; Mary, wife of William Crews; Charles J., and Sarah, wife of Bennett Sprinkle, being the surviving members. The father died in 1872, and the mother in 1866. Abel was the son of Josiah Watkins, who was born in Virginia, and came to North Carolina in early life. He was a successful farmer, and died in 1810. Dr. Watkins was elected to the honorable position of first vice-president of the North Carolina dental association, which he held for two years.

ROBAH F. GRAY, M. D.

Among the leading physicians of Forsyth county, N. C., may be found the name of Robah F. Gray, M. D., of Winston. Dr. Gray was born December 24, 1852, in the city where he now resides. His education was begun in the schools of his native city, and continued in the Emory and Henry college of Virginia. After completing his junior year in the latter institution, he returned to Winston in 1872 and began the study of medicine with Dr. Keehlan, with whom he remained for two years, after which he accepted a position on the editorial staff of the *Western Sentinel*, and for two years was engaged in editing that journal. At this time Dr. Gray entered the Louisville medical college, and was graduated therefrom in 1877. He then went to New York city, and in 1878 completed the course in the Bellevue medical college there. Once more returning to Winston, he opened an office and entered upon his professional career. During the small-pox epidemic of 1882, he held the office of city health officer, and to his efficient service the community owes much.   He has had marked success in his calling, and is ranked among the ablest physicians of the county.   Dr. Gray was very fortunate in his marriage to Miss Lelia R. Wilson, an accomplished daughter of James H. Wilson, of Charlotte county, Va.   Their union was solemnized in 1878, and has been blessed by the birth of six children, named as follows: May Belle, Eugene P., Robah F., Samuel W., Alice S. and George P. Robert Gray, the father of the above mentioned subject, was born in Randolph county, N. C., in 1814.   He was given a good common schooling, and then engaged in the mercantile business in Gladesboro county, N. C., but in 1850 removed to Winston, N. C., where he established a mercantile house of large proportions.   He was married in 1842 to Miss Mary Millis Wiley, daughter of Mr. Wiley, of Guilford county, N. C., and their children are: Samuel W., was killed at Gettysburg while commanding Company D, Fifty-seventh regiment, North Carolina volunteer infantry — held the rank of captain; Martha E., wife of A. P. Gibson; James A., Robert T., Mary I., wife of Thomas Barber; Robah F., Eugene C., Emory S. and Willie T., colonel of the Third regiment North Carolina state militia.   The father died in 1881, but his wife still survives him.

DR. JAMES L. RUCKER

was born in 1832, in Rutherford county, N. C.   He was the third child of William and Lavinia Rucker. and his preliminary education was acquired at the schools of his native county.   He read medicine with Dr. Calaway, at Rutherfordton, and then attended the medical school at Augusta, Ga., for a time, finally graduating with honors at the Medical college at Louisville, Ky.   After completing his medical education he began the practice of his profession at Morganton, Ga., where he soon worked up an extensive business.   But not tarrying long there, he removed to Texas, where he practiced until the breaking out of the Civil war.   At this time he returned to his native home and entered the Confederate army in defense of his country.   He served as surgeon throughout the war and made himself very useful to the soldiers under his medical charge, gaining their love and respect for his invaluable services to them.   At the close of the war, at the earnest solicitation of his many friends, Dr. Rucker located himself at Rutherfordton, and began there the practice of his profession.   He was not long in acquiring an extensive and lucrative practice which he successfully prosecuted until his death, which occurred March 13, 1884.   His loss to the community in which he moved, both professionally and socially, was a sad blow and left a void which could not be readily filled.   Politically, Dr. Rucker was an ardent and thorough going democrat, but he took no prominent action in partisan strifes, being strictly devoted to his profession.

Soon after the close of the war Dr. Rucker was united in marriage with Miss Fanning, daughter of Rev. F. M. Fanning, of Asheville, N. C.   The fruit of this marriage was the birth of two children, William Fanning and Myra Lavinia, both of whom survive. Dr. Rucker was one of the most prominent members of the Masonic fraternity in western North Carolina, having filled all the chairs in that organization. He lived up to the high principles and maxims of the order, standing upon the broad platform of its charitable and religious teachings. He was not a Mason simply in name, wearing its insignia for display and knowing its mysteries for selfish ends, but he was a Mason in its grander and more unselfish spirit, and he was universally respected by all members of the order who enjoyed the privilege of his acquaintance.

JOHN MILLER CRATON, M. D.,

was born at Rutherfordton, N. C. March 9, 1823. He is the eldest son of Isaac and Elizabeth Craton, both deceased. The home schools furnished young Craton his preliminary education, and at the age of sixteen he went to Gainesville, Ga., where for two years he was engaged in a dry goods store. He read medicine one year with Dr. Banks, at that time one of the best physicians in Georgia. From Gainesville Mr. Craton went to Charleston, S. C., where in 1843 he entered the medical college. Here he attended two full courses of lectures, graduating in 1845. Dr. Craton then came to Cleveland county, N. C., and began the practice of medicine in company with his uncle, Dr. W. J. T. Miller. Here he remained one year and then removed to his native town and formed a co-partnership with Dr. Calloway, the firm continuing from 1846 to 1851, in the medical prac tice. At this time Dr. Craton was seized with a desire to locate in some other state, and to this end made an extended tour through Georgia and Alabama in search of a desirable location. But his search was unavailing, and he returned to Rutherfordton and, in 1851, settled permanently in the practice of his profession, where he has doubtles secured the most extensive practice of any physician in western North Carolina. Notwithstanding his devotion to his profession, Dr. Craton has not neglected the material interests of his city and county; he is public spirited and has liberally contributed of his means and efforts for the public improvement. In politics he has never taken an active part, though repeatedly solicited to represent his county in the state legislature. He is a thorough democrat and has always been identified with that party. In his religious views he is a devout Methodist, having been associated with that church for more than thirty years.

April 8, 1847, Dr. Craton was united in marriage at Syracuse, N. Y., with Miss Margaret Williams, daughter of Dr. Williams, of that city, and granddaughter of Judge Forman, formerly of New York, but later of Rutherfordton. Judge Forman was the founder of Syracuse and was a prime mover in the construction of the Erie canal. Nine children have been born to Dr. and Mrs. Craton, whose names are respectively as follows: Mrs. Carrie Guthrie, Mrs. Alice Simpson, John Williams, Marshall, at present practicing medicine at Carrolton,

Mo.; Mrs. Maggie Sevier, of Spartanburg; Mrs. Florence Dixon, of Florence, S. C.; S. Boyce, physician at Syracuse, N. Y.; Mrs. Hattie Chapman, of Spartanburg; Mary Willie Craton. Doctor and Mrs. Craton are a most amiable couple and one only has to visit their home to find the very ideal of generous hospitality and true but unostentatious politeness. Dr. Craton has exercised great care and liberality in the education of his family.

DR. JOHN McENTIRE

was born in Burke county, N. C., in 1791. He was the youngest son of James McEntire who came from Ireland to the United States at an early day. John McEntire spent his early days in Morgantown, N. C. He chose the medical profession for his life work and attended two terms of medical lectures at Charleston, S. C,, after which he completed his studies at Philadelphia. His medical training being perfected, he located at Rutherfordton, and began the practice of his profession. In those early days his territory was extensive, reaching south as far as the South Carolina line. The result of his wide practice was the accumulation of a large fortune, but in 1830 failing health compelled him to retire from his laborious practice. About this date he was elected to the legislature in which he served his state with great dignity and efficiency, and with great credit to himself. During his legislative career he made the acquaintance of Miss Mary Jane Lancaster, of Franklin county, daughter of Rev. William Lancaster, a prominent Baptist divine. The acquaintance ripened into an engagement, and Dr. McEntire and Miss Lancaster were married in 1832. The young wife of that period still survives her husband at the ripe age of ninety-two years, with a mind fresh and unimpaired by the lapse of this unusual extension of her physical and intellectual faculties. She is still remarkable sprightly for a lady of her years and the charm and vivacity of her mind are in keeping with this physical healthfulness and strength. She is the honored mother of two sons. William T., and John J., both of whom were gallant soldiers in the Confederate army, and both of whom bore marks of their valor in the shape of honorable wounds. The eldest son died of his wounds a sacrifice to his patriotism and chivalry. Mrs. McEntire was also the mother of Mrs. Martha Ann Morris, who is still living in Rutherfordton; of Mrs. Jane Eliza Shotwell, whose heroic husband fell in the engagement around Richmond; and of Mrs. Laura Eugenia Hicks, wife of Dr. Hicks of Rutherfordton. William Thomas McEntire left two daughters, who since his death have married. Dr. McEntire died in December, 1856. He was greatly beloved by all who knew him, and his days were spent in rendering himself useful to the community in which he lived. In all his acts he was charitable, and humane and the memory of his noble characteristics and of his exemplary life is a perpetual solace to his well preserved and lovable surviving widow.

THE WARD FAMILY

has furnished the prominent physicians of Washington county, N. C., for four generations. The first of the name to settle in North Carolina was Francis Ward, an Englishman, who was the first register of deeds and of colonists under the Earl of Granville, in Tyrell county, and Ward's Bridge, his home, was named for him. Francis Ward, Sr., was the first of the family to practice medicine in Plymouth. His son was named for him, and followed in his father's footsteps as a physician. He was born at Ward's Bridge and received a collegiate education. For many years he was the leading practitioner of Plymouth. For one term he served in the state senate, and in 1832 was a presidential elector, having cast his vote for Andrew Jackson. W. W. Ward, M. D., was his son and successor in the medical profession. He was born in Martin county, at Ward's Bridge, in 1817, and was educated in the schools of that county. He attended lectures at the University of Pennsylvania, and was graduated from the University of Maryland in 1847. In the same year he began his practice at Plymouth. During the late war Dr. Ward served as surgeon in the Confederate States army until discharged for deafness. His reputation as a physician was well known in the eastern part of the state, and his name was known throughout the state. He was a prominent Mason, and a communicant of the Episcopal church, and his political faith was founded on the principles of the republican party. His death occurred in 1879. His wife, Alexina Boyle Ward, is a native of Petersburgh, Va., and still survives him. But two of their seven children are living, viz.: Johnson G., of Philadelphia, Penn., and William H. Ward, M. D. The latter was born in Plymouth, N. C., on the 3rd of January, 1857. His education was obtained in the schools of his native city and at Buckhorn academy. He read medicine under the tutelage of his distinguished father, and was graduated from the University of Maryland in 1881. Dr. Ward is a member of the state medical society, of the I. O. O. F. lodge No. 528, and also of the Knights of Honor and Masons. As a democrat he is active and loyal, and is now county physician, and for several years held the office of United States pension surgeon. He was married in 1883 to Miss Jessie M., daughter of Maj. A. F. Garrett, of Washington county, N. C. Dr. Ward is a member of the Episcopal church.

CHARLES E. MOORE, M. D.,

of Wilson county, N. C., is a native of Edgecombe county, N. C., where he was born on the 10th of June, 1854. His parents were Moses and Esther (Peel) Moore. Moses Moore was a prominent and influential planter of Edgecombe county, which he left in 1855 to take up his residence in Nash county. He continued in agriculture there up to the time of his death in 1890. As a democrat he was active and efficient, and served as a member of the board of county commissioners for several terms. During the Civil war he served in the Confederate army for some time, subsequently furnishing a substitute. His widow still survives him, being a resident of Nash county. Both became identified with the Primitive Baptist church in early life. Of the five children born to them, three are living, viz.: W. H. Moore, of Nash county, N. C.; Charles E. and R. M. Moore. The latter is a leading planter of Nash county. Charles E. Moore obtained his scholastic training in the public schools of Edgecombe and Wilson counties, and also under the instruction of private tutors. His medical education was begun under the direction of Dr. N. J. Pittman, of Tarboro, N. C., and was completed in the Bellevue medical college, of New York, from which institution he was graduated with the class of 1875. Dr. Moore practiced in Nash county until March, 1886, when he removed to Wilson, where he has since resided and practiced. As a physician he has won an enviable reputation, and is a prominent member of the state and Wilson county medical societies. He is a progressive and valued citizen, and is deeply interested in public affairs as a democrat. For the past few years he has been quite extensively interested in agriculture, and now operates a large plantation. Dr. Moore was very happily married in 1878, to Miss Minnie R. Taylor, a daughter of K. C. Taylor, Esq., of Nash county, N. C., and five children have blessed their union, their names being: Charles E., Jr., Thomas H., Karl C., Clyde and Elsie Moore.

DR. JOHN K. RUFFIN.

Hon. Thomas Ruffin was descended from one of the oldest families of the south. The connection has furnished many eminent professional men, among whom may be found several judges of unusual distinction. Thomas Ruffin was born in King and Queen county, Va. He was prepared for college at Warrenton, N. C., and subsequently graduated from Princeton college. Having chosen the law as his life work, he settled in Orange county, N. C., and rapidly rose to the front ranks of the bar in the state. For several terms he was a member of the house of representatives of the state, and was a judge of the superior court. Although able and dignified at all times, the crowning work of his life was accomplished as chief-justice of the supreme court of North Carolina. After filling that honored position for many years, he retired at last with ermine unspotted, and a name of wide-spread prominence as a wise and able judge. His many decisions are remarkable for their clearness and soundness. This distinguished gentleman was born November 17th, 1787, and died in 1870. He was a prominent democrat, and was particularly interested in agriculture, having been at one time president of the State Agricultural Fair association. By his marriage to Miss Anne M. Kirkland fourteen children were born, six of whom survive. The mother died in 1875. Thomas Ruffin was the son of Sterling Ruffin, a Virginian by birth. Late in life he settled in Caswell county, N. C.,

where he labored as a local preacher in the Methodist Episcopal church. He married Miss Alice Roane. Anne, wife of Paul Cameron, of Hillsboro, Orange county, N. C.; Sterling, of the same county; Peter B., also a resident of Orange county, where he is secretary and treasurer of the N. C. R. R.; Jane M. Ruffin, of Norfolk, Va.; Martha P. Ruffin, of New York city; and John K. Ruffin, M. D., are the surviving children born to Thomas and Anne Ruffin.

The immediate subject of this sketch is John K. Ruffin, M. D., who was born in Orange county, N. C., March 6, 1834. His scholastic training was obtained at Bingham's school and the University of North Carolina, where he was graduated in 1854. Dr. James E. Williamson, of Caswell county, became his preceptor in the study of medicine, and in 1857 he completed the medical course of the University of Pennsylvania. At this time Dr. Ruffin entered upon his professional career at Graham, Alamance county, N. C., moving from there to Washington in Beaufort county, later on. As surgeon of the Forty-ninth North Carolina regiment he served through the entire Civil war with fidelity and efficiency. After the declaration of peace between north and south he resumed his practice at Graham, and in 1876 came to Wilson, where he has since practiced, being now the oldest practitioner of the town. Dr. Ruffin is a prominent member of the state medical society, and also of the Wilson county medical association, and is a member of the Royal Arch chapter of the Masonic fraternity. He has taken interest in public affairs as a staunch democrat, and is the present coroner of Wilson county. His marriage to Miss Sally E. Tayloe, a daughter of Col. Joshua Tayloe, of Washington, N. C., in 1858, resulted in the birth of the following named children: Kate R., who married Abram Sydnor, of Halifax county, Va.; Sally T., Anne C., wife of William Sims, of Halifax county, Va.; David T., a resident of Fort Townsend, Wash., where he conducts a successful drug business; Sterling, a clerk in the United States treasury department at Washington city, and M. D. by profession, practicing in Washington, D. C., at present; Mary, Thomas and George M. The mother died in 1883. Dr. Ruffin was married a second time, March 3, 1886, Miss Nina W. Ruffin, of Franklin county, N. C., becoming his wife. She died May 12, 1891. Dr. Ruffin is recognized as one of the ablest physicians of the state. Thomas Ruffin, a brother of the above mentioned subject, was a brilliant lawyer. His death occurred at his residence in Orange county, N. C. For several years he was solicitor of the Fifth district. During the Civil war he served as captain of the Alamance Grays, and left the service with the rank of lieutenant-colonel. As an associate-justice of the state supreme bench he ably represented the honored family name.

WILLIAM J. JONES, M. D.,

was born in Greene county, N. C., February 15, 1838. His parents were Wiley and Winifred (Edmundson) Jones, who were born in the same county as their son. Wiley Jones was an extensive planter, owning many slaves. William J. Jones was given every educational advantage. His early training was received in Franklin institute, and in 1855 he became a student in the office of L. Jeffries, M. D., of Franklin county. Subsequently he entered the medical department of the University of Virginia, and in March 1858, was graduated from the University of New York. By competitive examination he obtained a position in Bellevue hospital, New York, and served there for fourteen months as resident physician. He then returned to North Carolina and entered upon the active practice of his profession at Snow Hill, in his native county, where for twenty-four years he resided and practiced with great success. In 1884, he removed to Goldsboro, and has since built up one of the most extensive practices in the county. Since 1859 he has been a member of the state medical society, and has served as vice-president of the same. He is also a member of the American medical association, and also of the Masonic fraternity. Dr. Jones has not confined his active life exclusively to the medical profession, but for some years has carried on extensive agricultural interests in Jones and Greene counties. In 1864 he married Miss Clara E. Ernull, of Craven county, and three children have been born to them. Their names being as follows: William J., Jr., now a student at the University of New York; Wiley Street, attending the University of North Carolina, at Chapel Hill; and Henry Spicer Jones, who resides at home with his parents.

GEORGE L. KIRBY, M. D.,

a leading physician and surgeon of Wayne county, N. C., was born in Sampson county, N. C., near Clinton, on July 11, 1834, the son of William and Elizabeth (Cromartie) Kirby. The mother was a descendant of the Cromartie who settled in Bladen county, on the South river. William Kirby, grandfather of our subject, moved from Southampton county, Va., of which county he was a native, in 1800, and settled near Clinton, N. C., where he owned a large estate. His entire property, including many slaves, was lost during the recent war. The father of our present subject settled near Clinton, where he engaged in farming, and both himself and wife remained on the farm until their death. Dr. George L. Kirby was given a thorough preliminary education in the Clinton academy, then presided over by John G. Elliott. He entered the medical department of the University of New York, and where he completed a course in 1860, and was graduated from the Long Island hospital college. He then studied for one year in Paris, having returned at the breaking out of the war. He was the second man to volunteer his services from his native county, and joined Capt. Marsh's company, known as the Sampson Rangers. The company was sent to Smithfield for duty, and he was appointed assistant surgeon and assigned to the Second North Carolina regiment, then stationed at Garysburg under Surgeon J. B. Hughes. Dr. Hughes subsequently resigned and Dr. Kirby was then made surgeon of the regiment, and held that office until December,

1864, when he was relieved from field duty and assigned to hospital work, and was ordered to establish a hospital at Wytheville, Va.

Dr. Kirby was with his regiment in the battles of Mechanicsville, Cold Harbor, Malvern Hill; and the regiment then being transferred to "Stonewall" Jackson's division, he participated in the battles of Fredericksburg, Chancellorsville, Spottsylvania C. H., second Cold Harbor, Cedar Creek, Winchester, South Mountain, Antietam and Kelly's Ford, where he was captured and sent to Fort McHenry and confined there for several months. In June, 1865, Dr. Kirby was discharged from further hospital duty at Wytheville, and in August of that year came to Goldsboro and entered upon the practice which has since proven so honorable to him. On the 7th of June, 1866, he was happily married to Miss Mary C. Green, daughter of John A. Green, one of the oldest citizens of Goldsboro. For six years Dr. Kirby was a member of the North Carolina state examining board, and for twelve years was coroner of Wayne county, and he is now a member of the state medical society. A prominent member of the Masonic order, he has always been a loyal democrat, and is recognized as one of the most skillful physicians in the county. He brought to his life work a mind well prepared for serious action. His exceptional educational advantages were made the most of, and with native ability to grasp them his professional career has proven a success.

ALEXANDER W. ROWLAND.

A leading business man of Wilson county, N. C., is Alexander W. Rowland, whose birth occurred in Granville county, N. C., March 17, 1841. He is the eldest son of Horace H. and Martha W. Rowland, natives of Granville county. His mother was a daughter of the late Isham Cheatham, who was one of the most influential citizens of the county. Henry Rowland, the father of Horace H., was born in Granville county, where he was an extensive planter for many years. Mr. H. H. Rowland's death occurred in May, 1886, his wife surviving him until January, 1889. Both were devout and beloved members of the Methodist Episcopal church, south, and died in the sweet confidence of their Saviour. Their children are, Alexander, William B., who died in 1860; Benjamin W., of Tyler, Tex., who is a prominent druggist and president of the Tyler water works; Edwin S., of the same city; Isham C., of Henderson, N. C.; Horace H., president of the Tyler (Texas) First National bank; and Parry W., of Tyler. Alexander Rowland was educated in the schools of his native county, and at the Henderson military institute, while his brothers were all educated at Wake Forest college. The Granville Grays was the first company to offer its services to the cause of the south from Granville county, and we find Mr. Rowland a member of that company from the first. After serving eighteen months in this company he was transferred to the Fifth North Carolina cavalry. He proved a loyal and valiant soldier and was in the engagements at Hanover C. H., Mechanicsville, Cold Harbor, Fair Oaks and Malvern Hill, while in infantry. In the latter engagement all the commissioned officers having been wounded, he led his company, and in that engagement was twice wounded. He was in nearly all the important engagements in Virginia and Maryland, and at the battle of South Mountain was taken prisoner and confined for two months in Fort Delaware. After the close of the war he engaged in the drug business at Henderson, N. C., as a member of the firm of Cheatham, Andrews & Co. In 1870 his business was burned out, and in the fall of that year he removed to Wilson, where he has from that time conducted the most extensive drug business of the town. In all his business ventures he has been eminently successful. Democratic in politics, he takes a deep interest in public affairs, and was a member of the democratic executive committee of his county. Mr. Rowland was happily married in 1869, to Miss Elizabeth A. Speed, daughter of Rufus K. Speed, of Gates county, N. C., who for a number of years was a member of the state senate. Mrs. Rowland died in 1884. She, as is her husband, was a devoted communicant of the Episcopal church, of which he is a vestryman. Mr. Rowland is also a member of the state pharmaceutical association, having been one of its founders, and at one time president of the organization. He is also a member of the North Carolina board of pharmacy.

DR. WILLIAM GEORGE THOMAS

was born in Louisburg, N. C., March 23, 1818, and died in Wilmington on the 18th of February, 1890. He received a common school education at Louisburg, and entered upon the study of medicine in the office of Dr. Wiley Perry, Louisburg. He graduated in 1840 at the University of Pennsylvania, at the time when that splended old school had for its faculty George B. Wood as professor of materia medica and therapeutics, Nathan Chapman as professor of practice, William Gibson as professor of surgery, Robert Rogers professor of chemistry, and Hodge as professor of obstetrics. Impressed with the dignity of his career, inspired by the zeal of his teachers, with a native fund of energy, a strong brain, and an overwhelming sense of honor, he entered upon his profession in his native state at Tarboro. There were two things specially which seemed to predominate among the early objects of his study — the deep impression that he must pursue the investigation of climatic diseases, and so supply the lack of knowledge dwelt on by his professor of materia medica and therapeutics, and the neglected study of obstetrics and diseases of women. He did not neglect other branches of his profession, but in these he was assiduous, and in these he excelled. When the writer first obtained personal knowledge of Dr. Thomas (1852) he learned that he was considered an innovator, and his innovation largely consisted in the boldness with which he used quinine, venturing upon five-grain doses two or three hours apart in the period of intermission and remission, and his boldness in the use of obstetrical forceps. These may seem now to be slight things, but climatic fevers were then treated with such small doses of quinine as are now known to be trivial, and the obstetric forceps, when constituting the outfit of the physician, was a reserve power, so sacredly held, and so exceptionally employed, that it was an obsolete instrument.

Dr. Thomas came to Wilmington from Tarboro in 1850. He was then thirty-two years of age, with a handsome face, a kindly expression, marked physical vigor, attractive as a horseback rider (in which way he then principally visited his patients), and he at once took a place in the community. At the bedside his manner was re-assuring, pleasant, painstaking, sympathetic. The good of the sufferer was the object of his visit, and the friends of the patient were won by his persistent attention to the smaller details in his behalf.

When the call was made for a medical convention for the purpose of forming a state medical society, Dr. Thomas responded and be-came one of the original members. His attachment to the society was for work, and this distinguished his membership. He was made secretary in 1856, and continued in this office until 1867, during which time he was the moving spirit in the society. Once he was chosen its president, but with his accustomed magnanimity he declined in favor of a friend, and he continued to plod on for years for the future welfare of the society. It was only after the lapse of our Civil war, during which time there had been a suspension of the active life of the society, that he consented to be its president. He presided in Tarboro, where he had spent his early years, and where he was married in 1843. Doubtless it was a proud day for him, for he received an ovation at the hands of his old friends. The society was then small, but not feeble, although not much given to literary con-tributions. Dr. Thomas' address was well worthy of the occasion, indicating his freshness and vigor of professional practice, and his knowledge of the scientific current, but his misgivings about his literary ability induced him to withhold his address, and no amount of persuasion could induce him to allow it to be printed.

Dr. Thomas was always a worker. He was willing that his friends, especially his worthy juniors, should have society promotions; his sole ambition was to see the great undertakings of the profession, especially the board of examiners, established upon a sure founda-tion. His contributions to the literature of medicine are very few, his only lengthy paper being an account of the yellow fever epidemic as it occurred in Wilmington in 1862, in reply to a paper on the same subject by Dr. E. A. Anderson. When the yellow fever epidemic occurred in Wilmington in 1862 Dr. Thomas had already been in practice here twelve years. It was an ordeal through which none of the resident physicians had ever passed. In the very earliest of it Dr. James H. Dickson had died, Dr. Thomas was taken sick and went to his old home in Louisburg, to recruit, where he had a relapse. From this attack he seemed to have passed from the middle to old age by one bound, so feeble was his health for years after, and then he reached a new stage of his life marked by ripened vigor of body and brain.

Among the pioneers in gynecology Dr. Thomas must be rightly numbered. Before Marion Sims had enunciated the methods which formed the foundation of this branch of surgery, he had been working in the same direction, and had actually applied the wire suture for the closure of a vesico-vaginal fistula, bringing the local blacksmith into requisition to devise for him a duck-bill speculum; but at the earliest day after Sims had fully demonstrated his processes, Dr. Thomas became a dili-, gent gynecologist, laboring assiduously with patience and zeal among the patients who had already been attracted by his skill. He was a most earnest patriot. When the alarm of war was sounded and the clash was inevitable, he put all his energies in the preparation of the men for the field, and had it not been for the overwhelming weight of his duty to the sick at home he would have gone to the field. As it was, though, he spent all he had in the fortunes of the Confederacy, beginning the world anew in 1865, with very little more than his profession, but he bravely conquered all difficulties, having always a full practice. Indeed, so large was his practice that he had little time for any reading but the current medical journals, but in the line of periodical literature he always had the best and in abundance, and for this reason he may be said never to have been an old doctor. The newest and the best he always mastered, and you could always find at the bedside of his patients the most recent of the reputable remedies. His juniors found that in consultation he had no obstinate bias for the obsolete therapeutic legacies of the good old times, nor was he under the dominion of the last book he read, but he preserved that intellectual aplomb which made him equal to the task before him. His marked characteristics were truth and moral courage. His steadfastness for God's revealed Word and for the right made it always sure on which side of every important question he could be found. Exceeding the time allotted to man, maintaining his vigor of body and of mind to the last, in him was fulfilled the Scripture, " Thou shalt come to thy grave in a full age like as a shock of corn cometh in in his season."

SAMUEL SWANN.

The most commanding figure in Colonial days in North Carolina was Speaker Sam Swann. He was the son of Major Sam Swann, by his wife Elizabeth, daughter of Gov. Lillington. William Swann, the grandfather of Major Swann, settled Swann's Point, opposite Jamestown, Va., of which city he had been alderman, and died there in 1638. Major Swann's first wife was Sarah, a daughter of Gov. Drummond, first governor of Carolina. After her death he married, 1694, Elizabeth Lillington, and had two daughters, Sarah, who married Col. Thomas Jones; Elizabeth, who married John Baptista Ashe; and two sons, John and Sam. Major Swann died in 1707, and his widow married Col. Maurice Moore, in 1713. The subject of this sketch was born October 31, 1704, and came to manhood under the training of Col. Moore and Edward Moseley. He became a practical surveyor, and ran the dividing line between North Carolina and Virginia in 1729, being the first white man to cross Dismal Swamp. He was elected to represent Perquimans county in the assembly of 1725, and continued a member of that body for forty years. In 1731 he removed to Swann's Point, below Rocky Point, where his uncle, Edward Moseley, who thirty-five years had been the leader of the popular party, abdicated the speaker's chair, Sam. Swann, in 1742, succeeded to the position. He occupied the chair until 1762, when he retired, and his nephew, John Ashe, succeeded him. In 1746 he was appointed, with Moseley, to revise the laws, and the first book published in the colony was Swann's Revisal "Yellow Jacket." He was a lawyer of learning, and as speaker and the head of the party opposed to the prerogatives claimed by the governors as representatives of the crown, he gave direction to the affairs of the province. He exalted the speaker's office, and wielded an influence superior to that of the royal governors. The struggle he successfully maintained against attempted encroachments upon the liberties of the people entitle him to the admiration of posterity. Gov. Johnston constantly referred to him as the head of the republican junto, bent on engrossing the executive power of the crown. Retiring from the assembly in 1762, he continued to practice law until his death in 1772. He married Miss Mildred Lyon, and left several daughters and one son, Major Sam Swann, an officer of the Revolution, who some years after the war was killed in a duel with Mr. Bradley, at Wilmington, N. C.

GEN. SAM ASHE,

the youngest son of John Baptista Ashe, was born in 1725; was educated at the north, studied law with his uncle, Sam Swann, was an active participant in all measures in opposition to the crown, and was a leader in the extreme democratic wing of our public men. He was conspicuous in every movement for independence. He was a member of the congress of 1775, and of the provincial council of thirteen (of which he was chosen president), to whom was committed the administration when congress was not in session, was a member of the committee that framed the constitution, and was speaker of the first senate held under the constitution, and by that assembly was elected presiding judge of the supreme court, which position he held for eighteen years. This court was the first in America to refuse to obey a legislative act, on the ground of unconstitutionality. In after years Judge Haywood saidg "For this Judge Ashe deserves the gratitude of his country and posterity." He resigned his judicial office in 1795, to accept that of governor, to which he was thrice elected. He warmly advocated democratic principles, opposed the ratification of the Federal constitution until it was amended, and was a leader of the opposition to the federal party. He died at Rocky Point, in 1813, at the age of eighty-eight years. He married first Mary Porter, a granddaughter of Col. Maurice Moore, and had by her two sons,

John Baptista, and Sam; and after her death married Mrs. Elizabeth Merrick and had one son, Thomas.

His son, John Baptista Ashe, was born at Rocky Point in 1748; was at the battle of Alamance in 1771, and at the battle of Morris' creek in February, 1776; was appointed a captain in the Sixth Continentals in April, 1776; major, January, 1777, and lieutenant-colonel in November, 1778. He served with credit throughout the war, and particularly distinguished himself at the bloody battle of Eutaw Springs, in 1781. He sat in the house of commons for Halifax from 1784-86, being speaker of that body; was a member of the last congress of the Confederation; was a member of the state senate of 1789, and a member of the constitutional convention of 1789, that ratified the Federal constitution. As chairman of the committee of the whole, he presided over all the deliberations of that body during the discussion of the instrument. He had opposed the adoption of the constitution without amendments, and like his father and brother-in-law, Willie Jones, was strongly imbued with the spirit of democracy. At the first election for members of congress, he was chosen to that body, and was re-elected in 1791. He again represented Halifax in the assembly of 1795, but then retired from public life. Three years after his father retired from the office of governor, he himself was elected, but after signifying his acceptance, he died in November, 1802, before entering upon the office. He married Miss Montfort, of Halifax, and resided there. He left one son, Samuel Porter Ashe, whose descendants live in Tennessee.

Samuel Ashe, the second son of Gov. Ashe, was born in 1763, entered the Continental service at the age of sixteen, served two campaigns at the north, was taken prisoner at Charleston, and when exchanged served with La Fayette in Virginia and then with Gen. Greene in South Carolina until the end of the war. He was greatly revered for his lofty character and noble virtues. He married Elizabeth Shepperd, of Hillsboro, and raised a large family. To give his daughters the highest educational advantages, he maintained a residence for them at Bordentown, N. J. His sons were: Samuel, John Baptista, a member of congress from Tennessee, and then a resident of Texas, William Shepperd, Thomas Henry and Dr. Richard Porter Ashe. The latter served in the Mexican war and settled in San Francisco, Cal., where his family still resides.

William S. Ashe was educated at Trinity college, Connecticut; studied law; was a planter; was often in the state legislature from New Hanover county; was a member of congress from 1849 to 1855; was president of the Wilmington & Weldon railroad from 1854 to 1862, when he was killed by an accident on that road. He was a strong democrat—a man of great capacity and high character. At the beginning of the war in 1861 he was appointed major and quartermaster, and was placed in control of all the transportation over railroad lines from New Orleans to Richmond. In 1862 he was commissioned colonel with authority to raise a legion of artillery, cavalry and infantry, but soon afterward, September, 1862, was killed. He

S. A. Ashe

married Sarah Green, and left several daughters and two sons, John Grange Ashe, who attained the rank of major during the war of 1860–5; and left two sons in Texas, and Samuel A. Ashe, of Raleigh, N. C., who was educated at the naval school; studied history and law until the war began; entered the service in April, 1861; became a private in Company I, Eighteenth North Carolina regiment; was appointed in regular army of the Confederate States; served at Charleston in the spring of 1862; was captain and adjutant-general of Pender's brigade in the summer of 1862; was captured after the second battle of Manassas; when exchanged was assigned to duty with Clingman's brigade at the south; was assigned to duty at battery Wagner as ordnance officer during its siege, and then ordered to Fayetteville, where he remained as assistant to the commanding officer of the arsenal of construction until the end of the war; studied law after the war; located at Wilmington; represented New Hanover county in the assembly of 1870, the sole democratic representation from the county for twenty years. He married Miss Hannah Willard, of Raleigh, in 1871, and located in Raleigh, where he formed a law partnership with Hon. A. S. Merrimon, now chief-justice of the state, and Col. T. C. Fuller, now judge of the United States land court of claims, which continued for seven years, when he, in 1879, purchased the *Observer* newspaper and entered journalism. The next year the *News* was consolidated with the *Observer*, he remaining the editor. Mr. Ashe has always been interested in politics, and was for many years a member of the state executive committee, of which at one time he was chairman. He was appointed postmaster of Raleigh by President Cleveland. He has found time to indulge a fondness for books, and has for twenty years been an original investigator in North Carolina history.

THOMAS S. ASHE,

A prominent and worthy descendant of Gov. Sam Ashe, through his son Thomas, whose descendants are scattered throughout the south, was Thomas Samuel Ashe, who was born in Orange county, June, 1812. He graduated at the University of North Carolina in 1832, sharing the first honors with Senator Thomas L. Clingman and Hon. James C. Dobbin, secretary of the navy. He studied law under Chief-Justice Ruffin, and located at Wadesboro. In 1842 he was elected to the house of commons as a whig; and in 1854 to the state senate. He was long a solicitor for his judicial district. During the war he was a representative from his district in the Confederate congress, and was, without his knowledge, elected to the senate of the Confederate states. In 1868 he was nominated by the democrats for governor of North Carolina, but was beaten by Gov. Holden. He was elected to the United States congress in 1872, and again in 1874. "No member of either party stood higher in the house, for integrity, intelligence and fidelity to the constitution." He was a member of the judiciary committee, and was one of the committee of three ex-

B—20

amining Hon. James G. Blaine about the Credit Mobilier and Mul-
ligan letters when Mr. Blaine's illness stopped the proceedings. In
1878 he was elected to the supreme court of North Carolina, and
again in 1886. He was one of the eminent men of his generation and
was universally esteemed in North Carolina. He died February 4,
1887. He married early in life Caroline Burgwin, and left several
daughters and one son, Samuel S. Ashe.

JOHN BAPTISTA ASHE.

A gentleman, many years ago, referring to "notices of the Ashe
family printed in 1710," wrote "that in the mother country for several generations they were the strenuous opponents of arbitrary power,
and were not only actors, but sufferers in the paternal and also in the
maternal line." "A gentleman of this family compelled to sell his
estate in Wiltshire, England, by the pecuniary embarrassments, in
which an excess of zeal had involved him, migrated to South Carolina at an early period in the history of that province. Thence one
of his sons removed to North Carolina, whose character and abilities
made him a prominent member of that colony, and from that time to
the year 1814 the name of Ashe was always conspicuous either in the
forum, the senate or the field, and in the highest offices of the state."
In the long parliament that maintained the liberties of England
against the arbitrary power of Charles the First, were two brothers,
John and Sam Ashe, of Wiltshire. In the next generation a scion of
that family, John Ashe, settled in South Carolina, where he became
an influential member of the assembly. When the bigoted Lord
Granville sought to oppress the dissenters of Carolina, Ashe was
selected by the principal inhabitants of South Carolina to represent
their grievances to the crown. While at Charleston to take shipping,
his opponents raised a riot against him that lasted five days, and he
was under the necessity of making his way through the wilderness to
Albemarle. He was resolute, bold and high-spirited. The mild
Quaker, Archdale, said that he did not seem well qualified for the
work — "not that he wanted wit — but temper." His lofty spirit could
not tolerate with patience attempted oppression. Arriving at London,
he drew up "The Representation," but died in 1703 before it was all
printed, "not without suspicion of foul play." Defoe, the novelist,
then took the work up and published his pamphlet, "Oppression in
Carolina," and the train was laid that finally led to the downfall of
proprietary rule.

A son of this John Ashe, John Baptista Ashe, was in the Albemarle settlement in 1719, and in that year married Elizabeth Swann,
daughter of Col. Sam Swann, and granddaughter of Maj. Alexander
Lillington, and by this marriage became closely connected with Moseley, Moore, Porter and the other leaders of the popular party in
North Carolina. When Gov. Burrington first came to the colony, he
tells us that having known several members of Mr. Ashe's family in

England, he made him his friend. Burrington, at that time co-operated with the popular party, and Ashe was speaker of the assembly in 1725, which remonstrated against Burrington's removal. When Burrington returned as the first royal governor in 1731, he brought a commission for Ashe as one of his council, hoping for his aid; but Ashe opposed all measures to extend the prerogative of the crown, and organized the council against the governor and defeated his measures even in that body, despite the fact that his kinsman, Edward Ashe, was one of the lords of the board of trade, having the affairs of the colony in charge. Great animosity sprang up between them, and the defeated governor had Ashe illegally thrown into prison; but the representations of Ashe and Rice, the attorney-general, papers of marked ability, resulted in the speedy removal of the governor. Ashe died in 1734, and was buried on his plantation, Grovely, near old Brunswick, whither he had removed in 1727. He left two sons, John and Sam, and a daughter Mary. The latter married George Moore, of the Cape Fear.

GEN. JOHN ASHE,

the oldest son of John Baptista Ashe, was born on the Albemarle, in 1720. His parents dying while he was still a boy, he was reared to manhood by his guardian, Sam Swann. He inherited a large estate, received a liberal and thorough education, possessed a fine library; was an orator, a soldier and a statesman. "He struck the chords of passion with a master hand. His words roused the soul like the roll of a drum or the roar of artilery at the commencement of an action." "Mr. Sam Strudwith, who had mingled in the fashionable and political circles of London, declared that there were not four men in London superior in intellect to John Ashe," and that at a time when Pitt, Burke and their brilliant associates adorned British annals. He early entered the assembly and soon became the most influential member of the body on the floor. He was one of the committee on correspondence, was denounced as early as 1758 for his republicanism by Gov. Johnston, who habitually wrote of Ashe, Swann and their associates, as the republican junta. He succeeded his uncle, Sam Swann, in the chair in 1762, and as speaker, warned Gov. Tryon, in 1765, that the people would resist the stamp act "unto blood." He was a director chosen by the people, in the military movement, in February, 1766, forcing the British war vessels in port and the crown officers to disregard the stamp act and release the vessels they had seized for violating that law. On the repeal of that law, a wave of loyalty swept over the country, and the new assembly was on better terms with the governor. John Harvey succeeded Ashe in the chair, but later he was elected treasurer of the southern district notwithstanding Tryon's opposition. In the regulation troubles, he actively sustained the government of the province against the anarchy threatened by the regulators, and was a major-general in Tryon's army.

In 1773 he was one of the committee of correspondence in regard to British oppression, and was ever among the foremost patriots in the colony. Acting on the idea suggested by Speaker Harvey, in 1774, he caused the notices to be sent out by the Wilmington committee for the election of delegates to a provincial congress, the first revolutionary legislative body elected by any colony. In July, 1775, at the head of 500 men, he took possession of Fort Johnson, and in the presence of the British vessels, burned it to the ground. He had been an aide to Col. Innis in the Indian war, and solicited the command of the first Continental regiment, but this being bestowed, by a majority of one vote, on his brother-in-law, Gen. James Moore, he raised troops at his private expense, and participated gallantly in the campaign against the tories in February, 1776. In April, 1776, he was appointed brigadier-general of the Wilmington district, and was in command of the 7,000 troops assembled on the Cape Fear to meet the forces under Gen. Clinton should they attempt to penetrate the interior. He continued to serve as a member of the congress, and was an advocate of ultra democratic principles. He was a member of the committee that framed the state constitution in December, 1776. In 1778 he was major-general and marched that winter to the aid of Gen. Lincoln on the Savannah river. He drove the enemy from Augusta, and followed them down the river, on the west side, until he reached the confluence of Briar creek, which protected his front. Called to consult with Lincoln and Rutherford, whose forces lay further down on the east side of the river, he returned to camp to find the enemy was active; and he sent out parties to obtain intelligence, and made dispositions to resist an attack. At three o'clock the next evening, March 2, 1779, the enemy approached from the north. Ashe advanced a quarter of a mile to meet them, his force being about 600. His militia did not stand the fire of the British regulars, and soon fled to the swamp, the British capturing 162 privates and 24 officers. The terms for which these men were enlisted expired a month later, and they returned to North Carolina. Gen. Ashe was afterward treasurer of the southern district. Maj. Craig occupied Wilmington, in January, 1781, and sent out scouting parties to subdue the country. He held as prisoners, under sentence of death, two of Gen. Ashe's sons, Maj. Samuel Ashe, of the Continental light horse, and William, a mere boy. Later he contrived to capture the general himself. During his confinement Gen. Ashe contracted the small-pox, and was eventually paroled only to die. He expired during the month of October, 1781, at Col. Sampson's in Sampson county. Early in life Gen. Ashe was married to Miss Mary Moore, a daughter of Col. Maurice Moore, and a sister of Gen. James Moore, by whom he had Samuel Ashe, a major of light horse in the Continental army, who served with Washington at the north; John Ashe, who was captain in the Fourth Continentals, A'Court and William. His sons left no issue. Among the descendants of his daughters the following have attained distinction: Gov. Joseph Alston, of South Carolina, who married Theodoria Burr; William H. Wright, of the

Thos. M. Holt

engineers; Griffith J. McRee, and Samuel Hall, judge of the supreme court of Georgia.

GOV. HOLT.

While North Carolina may well be proud of her statesmen and her soldiers, and freely acknowledge her indebtedness to them, yet she is equally indebted to those captains of industry who have put in operation the spindle and the shuttle within her borders. And among these none deserve more the thanks of the state than the family of the Holts. They have done much more to develop the manufacturing of cotton, with its attendant industries and incidental business, than any other family in North Carolina. They were pioneers and leaders in this enterprise, and the force of their successful example has been of inestimable advantage to the people of their native state.

Edwin M. Holt, the father of Gov. Thomas M. Holt, established the first cotton factory in central North Carolina, and some time before the war he operated another factory on Haw river. Here Gov. Holt entered actively into the milling business, and from that nucleus has been developed by his skill and superb management, one of the largest manufacturing interests of the south. While nineteen mills have been built in Alamance county, in a large number of which the Holts and their connections are interested, Gov. Holt himself, in his celebrated Plaid mills, operates nearly 9,000 spindles and about 450 looms, and gives employment to 500 hands. His father, Mr. Edwin M. Holt, was one of the most estimable citizens of the state. By prudent management of his farms and milling interests he amassed a large fortune which was carefully invested. His home was famed for its hospitality, and he enjoyed the respect and confidence of all the business men of North Carolina. He married Emily Farrish, a daughter of Thomas and Fannie Banks Farrish, by whom he had a large family of children.

Thomas M. Holt, a son of this union, was born July 15, 1831, in that part of Old Orange county, which has since been set off into Alamance county. He was prepared for college at Caldwell institute, Hillsboro, and when eighteen years of age, entered the University of North Carolina. But without finishing his course at the college, he left and spent a year in the mercantile business in Philadelphia, learning there the practical part of the business of manufacturing. So thoroughly did he master these details that when twenty years of age his father took him for an assistant, and soon began to lean on his judgment and confide in his skill and management. When only twenty-one years of age he was honored by an appointment by the legislature as a magistrate, and served as chairman of the board of finance of Alamance county. In 1872 he was elected chairman of the board of county commissioners and served for four years. His kindly disposition, his unswerving integrity, his courteous demeanor and neighborly interest in the people of his county, nearly every one of whom he has long known personally, have made him very popular, and he has never been brought forward for office without receiving not only the full strength of his party, but many votes from others. In 1876 he was elected state senator, receiving 650 more votes than any candidate for that office had ever obtained. In the senate, his services were highly useful to the state. He had been a director in the N. C. R. R., in which the state had an interest of $3,000,000, since 1869, and was elected president of the company in 1875. He was also largely interested in agriculture and was president of the North Carolina agricultural society for twelve years. His varied experience and ripe judgment and sterling character made him one of the most influential senators. He labored successfully for the establishment of the agricultural department, and was, by virtue of his position as president of the agricultural society, made a member of the board controlling it.

In 1883 he was returned to the house of representatives; and again in 1885. when the house, in recognition of his eminent fitness and patriotic services, chose him for speaker. He was a member of the house again in 1887, and at the succeeding election was called by the people to the office of lieutenant-governor, and as such, he presided over the deliberations of the senate. As a member on the floor of the assembly, he had been able, efficient and practical; and as a presiding officer he was fair and impartial, courteous towards all and a wise administrator of the rules. During the period of his legislative service he won the confidence of the whole state, and when on the 8th day of April, 1891, he was called to the executive chair, on the sudden death of Gov. Fowle, the people were entirely satisfied that the affairs of state were in good hands, and that the duties of that high office would be discharged with ability, intelligence and a lofty patriotism. For sixteen years he had administered the affairs of the North Carolina railroad, as its president, with zeal and good judgment, and he laid down that office on becoming governor, with the consciousness that all of his acts had met public approval.

As we have said, for thirteen years he was president of the North Carolina state agricultural society, and he contributed not only his time, but also his money, to make that institution worthy of the state. A practical farmer, well versed in agriculture, and successful in the business, he used every exertion to utilize our state fairs for developing our agricultural resources and stimulating the people to advanced methods of culture. With liberal views, always seeking improvement, he kept abreast with the progress in farming, just as he has done in his milling operations, and he has presented an example that the intelligent farmers of the state can follow with advantage. But notwithstanding all of the varied duties that have claimed his attention, his chief interest has ever centered in his cotton factories. At Haw river he has so enlarged his fine mill, that he has had to erect about 150 buildings, for his employes, and for the purposes connected with his business. In addition he has there a five-story flour mill, a large mercantile establishment, and he has erected an attractive church edifice for the benefit of the community. On the opposite side of the river, spreading themselves over a gradually ascending eminence lie his princely premises — one of the finest country residences in the state, where nature and art are combined to illustrate the taste and elegance of a cultured family. But it is at Linwood, his splendid plantation on the North Carolina road, that Gov. Holt finds his greatest pleasure. There his fine stock, and his beautiful fields yield their increase and delight the eye of the practiced farmer.

In October, 1855, Gov. Holt was happily married to Louisa, the accomplished daughter of Samuel and Mary A. Bethel Moore. To them have been born five children: Charles T. Holt, Cora M., who married Dr. E. Chambers Laird, of Virginia; Dazie M., who married Alfred W. Haywood, one of the most skillful lawyers of Raleigh; Ella N., who married Charles Bruce Wright, of Wilmington, but now a resident of Raleigh; and Thomas M. Holt, Jr. Although his residence has been the seat of elegant hospitality, and Gov. Holt's large business interests have occupied him very closely, yet he has always found time to attend to other duties. He has participated actively on the stump in nearly every campaign, and not content with liberal giving, has devoted his time and talents to the promotion of party weal. He is also a Royal Arch Mason; and he has faithfully discharged his religious duties. For thirty years he has been a consistent member of the Presbyterian church, and for many years he has been an elder in that denomination. Indeed, in all the relations of life he has been foremost. His honesty is proverbial; his dealings are always fair and just; and in his friendships he is constant and unwavering. He never deviates from lofty principles, and North Carolina has no more patriotic son than this eminent citizen.

DONALD W. BAIN.

The Bain family of which the present treasurer of North Carolina is a descendant, is of Scotch origin, and traces its lineage to the early part of the eighteenth century. Among the relatives have been some of the most distinguished men of the United States, of which the single name of Adams is enough to pronounce. Donald Bain was born near the city of Glasgow, Scotland, whence he came to America about the close of the war for independence. He settled near Wilmington, in North Carolina, and there in 1785, he was married to Frances Eliza Hall. Providence favored them with five children, of whom William T., was one, born in Bladen county, N. C., November, 1793. William T. Bain was educated principally at the famous Bingham school, the founder of that institution being his teacher, and for a while after reaching manhood, was engaged in teaching school. He was for a long series of years, one of the most distinguished Masons of the state. From 1836 to his death in 1867, he occupied the position of secretary of the Masonic Grand Lodge of North Carolina, excepting a short interval of four years. His wife was Martha A., daughter of Green Hill, who bore him a family of six children, five of whom are now living, viz.: Elizabeth F., wife of the late Andrew J. Partin, of Petersburg, Va.; Mary A., wife of B. L. Bitting, of Forsyth county, N. C.; Donald W. Bain, of Raleigh, N. C.; Julia G., of Raleigh; Thomas H., of Germanton, Stokes county, N. C. Donald W. Bain was born in Raleigh, N. C., April 2, 1841. His educational training was secured in the schools of his native place, and in the high schools at South Lowell and Pittsboro. Upon leaving school in 1857, he entered the office of the comptroller of state and remained there until April, 1865. In July of the same year he was appointed chief clerk of the state treasury department by Jonathan Worth, provisional treasurer. Mr. Bain continued in that capacity until January, 1885, at which time he assumed the duties of state treasurer, to which he had been elected in November preceding. In the fall of 1888 he was elected to the second term of four years, which will expire in January, 1893. His administration of the state's finances has been satisfactory to the public and gratifying to his friends. After having spent a great part of his lifetime in the office over which he now presides, it was but a fitting tribute to his probity and uprightness, his fidelity and energy, when his fellow citizens called him by their suffrage to discharge the responsible duties of this high office. In 1879 he was chosen as one of the commisioners to adjust and renew the bonds issued by the state, on account of the North Carolina railroad.

Like his father, Mr. Bain is an ardent member of the Masonic fraternity, and has devoted much of his time and talents to that eminent order, whose foundation goes back to the dawn of authentic history. In February, 1867, he was appointed to succeed his father in the office of grand secretary of the Grand Lodge of North Carolina, and from that time to this he has discharged the duties of that honorable place. He is also secretary of the Grand Royal Arch chapter and recorder of the Grand Council. For the two terms of 1885 to 1887 he was grand commander of the Knights Templar for the state of North Carolina. As a member of the Scottish Rite he has been the recipient of thirty-two degrees, thus testifying that he is held in high esteem by all branches of this ancient and respected order. Mr. Bain is also a conspicuous figure in the circles of Odd Fellowship. January 26, 1865, he was married to Adelaide V. Hill, a daughter of the late Dr. William G. Hill, of Raleigh. To this union have been born four children, of whom these three are now living: William H., Ernest B. and Adelaide V. Mr. Bain's paternal ancestry was of French extraction, and belonged to that sect known as Huguenots, the persecution of which in France has handed them down to history as the most cruelly treated people which the annals of intolerance bear. When in 1598, Henry the IV. of France issued his famous edict of Nantes, it secured to this unhappy class a release from persecution for nearly a century. But when, in 1685, Louis the XIV. revoked this edict the work of hate again commenced. France was on that account speedily abandoned by many thousands of her best and most industrious citizens. A large number of these found their way to America where, with their knowledge of the arts and their habits of sobriety and industry, they soon became an important factor of the population. It was from this class that Franees E. Hall, Mr. Bain's paternal grandmother, descended. Mr. Bain has been for many years a leading member of the Methodist Episcopal church, south.

GOV. EDWARD B. DUDLEY.

This gentleman, so distinguished in the annals North Carolina, was born in Onslow county, N. C. His first appearance in public life was as a member of the state legislature from his native county, in 1811–13. Removing to Wilmington shortly after the expiration of his term of service he made that town his home, and in 1816–'17, and again in 1834, he was the representative of that ancient borough in the general assembly of the state. In 1829 he was elected to the congress of the United States, from the Cape Fear district, but served one term only, positively refusing a re-election, and giving as a reason for his refusal, that he did not think congress a fit place for any man who wanted to be honest. What a striking contrast between his action and the devious and tortuous paths now so generally pursued in this progressive age, by those ambitious of political preferment, it is refreshing to note it, and to note also how much more highly he prized his integrity and self-respect than all the allurements of official station. He identified himself with the cause of internal improvements in North Carolina, giving to it his time, his talents and his wealth. He was the active and ardent friend of that great work, the Wilmington & Weldon railroad, and was the largest individual subscriber to its stock. He was the first president of the company, and did more, perhaps, than any one man to secure its completion. In all of its difficulties and embarrassments, he was its staunch friend, and while others desponded and almost despaired, he never lost faith in its ultimate triumph, and he lived to witness in its successful operation the gratifying results of his practical sagacity.

When the constitution of North Carolina was amended by the convention held in 1835, among other changes made, the election of governor, which prior to that time had been made by the legislature, was given to the people. The democratic party was in the ascendent in the state, and the gubernatorial chair was filled by Richard Dobbs Spaight, a democrat who had served one term and who had been nominated by his party for re-election. The opposition with remarkable unanimity centered upon Edward B. Dudley as their leader in the contest for that elevated position, and without any action on his part to secure it, he was nominated and elected, being the first governor of North Carolina ever chosen to that office by the direct vote of the people. His administration of the duties of his high office was so satisfactory that at the expiration of his first term there was no organized opposition to his re-election, a compliment, creditable alike to a faithful public servant and to the people who thus showed their appreciation of his character and public services. When his second term expired he returned to his home in Wilmington, where he continued to reside until his death, in October, 1855.

Gov. Dudley was no ordinary man, for despite the defects of his early education he rose to distinction by his natural abilities and force of character. Nature had been kind to him, had given him a commanding presence, a vigorous intellect, and that faculty which grasps as it were by intuition, the salient points of a subject when presented for consideration, and a judgment that seldom erred in its conclusions. He was a man of liberal and enlarged views, of a genial disposition and generous impulses, and of spotless integrity. He could not tolerate prevarication or deceit, for he was one of the most sincere of men, and never hesitated to express what he thought, not offensively but with firmness, and with a dignity of manner that commanded respect. He was frank and manly in his intercourse with the world, could not have practiced deceit if his life had depended on it, and abhorred it in others. His ample fortune enabled him to dispense a profuse hospitality and in which he greatly delighted, for in administering to the pleasures or happiness of others he was but obeying the promptings of his heart and giving expression to the kindly feelings of his nature. His purse was always open at the call of charity, and merit, it mattered not how humble or obscure it might be, was promptly recognized and generously assisted. He sleeps his last sleep in the beautiful cemetery near Wilmington, one of the most beautiful in the south, and tender affection has erected a massive monument over his remains in commemoration of his virtues and noble qualities. North Carolina has had few more worthy sons than Edward B. Dudley.

HON. JOHN POOL.

This distinguished man was born in Pasquotank county, N. C., June 16, 1826, and died in the city of Washington, August 16, 1884. He was fifty-eight years and two months old. He was born on a plantation near Elizabeth City, and reared there until he entered the University of North Carolina, where he graduated second in the distinguished class of 1847. The same year he was admitted to the bar, and commenced the practice in his native county, in Elizabeth City. He soon went to the front, at a bar renowned for its learning and eloquence. Such men as Ruffin, Badgers, Pearson, and Stanly, eminent in the state and nation, had to be encountered. It is no small honor that he won his reputation at such a period. But the forum was not the field on which he was to achieve his chief success. He entered early the domain of politics and statesmanship. His high mental endowments forbade his occupying a secondary place. It was impossible for him to breathe the air of mediocrity, he was by nature destined to tread the ice-clad ranges of jurisprudence. Indeed the practice of his profession, the conflict of procuring testimony, and the struggle to select juries influenced by particular interests, were distasteful. The subjects involved in political life were more congenial. He naturally drifted into that channel. He entered the field at the most intense period in the conquest over slavery, and after his own state had passed entirely over to the ranks of the slave interest. Largely interested in that institution, he never regarded it as divine or entitled to the reverence of the American people. This became the controlling political question in the south. It appeared upon the hustings, in the press, in the pulpit, and in all the avenues of social life. The intense feeling had grown with the deepening interests in the extension of the institution over new territory. The growth of the free states demanded for free labor the new teritory, and the disadvantages 'and crime of slavery had made a deep impression in the north. Gradually these two forces were dividing upon geographical lines, until the year 1820 introduced the Missouri struggle. The settlement of this question was but a drawn battle. The conflict in no respect abated. The admission of Texas introduced the war with Mexico, and it gave a more violent form to the impending issue, but the country passed peacefully this crisis, as it had that of the annexation of Texas. The repeal of the Missouri Compromise and the opening up of the new territories consecrated to freedom by that measure brought the conflict to the scene of violence.

It was at this eventful crisis that Mr. Pool entered political life. He was raised and educated in the whig faith, and had he not been, his fine powers of head and heart would have carried him to that party. It was then in the days of its decline, indeed. in its expiring agonies. Its splendid orators and statesmen had vainly sought to save the country from a civil war, and to preserve the union of the states. The spirit of freedom in the free labor states had demanded the unsettled territory for free men. The south were demanding with still more intense feelings their rights under the constitution, to carry there their slaves. Rapidly those two forces were absorbing all the political elements in each section till the national party standing between them had in a great measure disappeared. In his boyhood he had followed the banner of Mr. Clay, borne by the dauntless Kenneth Rayner, to whom he ever remained devoted. In the course of time the pupil became the leader, and was supported by his former mentor with all his heroic enthusiasm. Though the great political forces had concentrated in geographical lines Mr. Pool abated in no respect his firm national sentiment. The whig party retained its vitality in the border slave states long after it had disappeared from the extreme north and south. The border state whig, of necessity, was in conflict with both the great antagonistic forces at that time. He sought to avert the nation from the bloody banquet spread before it. His influence was in a great measure dissipated by the conflict of interest, association and sympathy with his patriotism and judgment.

In the years 1856 and 1858 Mr. Pool was returned to the state senate from his district. It is needless to say that he distinguished himself in that body. So marked was the impression, that in the year 1860 the whigs chose him as their candidate for governor. He made a gallant and impressive canvass, and after this was ranked among the ablest statesmen and political advocates in the state. He was defeated, but he had greatly reduced the majority of the opposition. He pleaded for the union of the states, and the exercise of reason and forbearance. It was against the tide of opinion and the wild shout for southern rights. This effort to save the people from the threatened calamity was so earnest and rational, that the better sentiment was convinced, and ranked him among their ablest men. The hour of trial had come, and no power could avert the catastrophe. He foresaw the fatal sacrifice of the young men of the south, and deplored the dreadful consequences of that rash counsel that was leading them to their doom. He had done all that he could to avert the calamity, and nothing was left for him but to retire to his home and await the issue. He remained at home during the eventful years of war, until 1864 brought a gleam of peace. He was elected to the state senate as a peace man, and entered that body with the hope of inducing such a rational spirit as could compel the Confederate government to listen to honorable terms of peace. He introduced his celebrated peace resolutions, but the hour for reason had not yet returned, and these well-made endeavors proved abortive. These resolutions contemplated separate state action, in the event that the Confederate government should refuse to make peace. They, in that event, proposed to withdraw North Carolina from the Confederacy and restore her to the Union. This was done while the war was still flagrant, and at great peril. No bolder, braver, wiser movement was ever made. The war continued until the Confederate army was so overthrown at every point that their arms were wrested from their hands. It was a conquest thorough and absolute. The south was placed at the mercy of the victors.

The war closed virtually with the surrender of Gen. Lee. The assassination of Mr. Lincoln soon followed, and Mr. Johnson came into the presidential chair April, 1865. May 25th, the president issued his proclamation for the re-organization of civil government in North Carolina. The Hon. W. W. Holden was appointed provisional governor and authorized to call a convention of the people of the state for that purpose. Mr. Pool was a member of that body and served with distinction in it. He and Hon. W. A. Graham were elected to the United States senate; congress did not deem it safe to admit the states as re-organized by President Johnson and remanded them to military rule, consequently the members returned from the insurrectionary states were not admitted to their seats. When the state was reconstructed under the act of congress, Mr. Pool was again elected to the United States senate, and took his seat in 1868, which he held till 1873, when the state passed into the hands of the opposition. Since that period he has been practicing his profession in the city of Washington. During his services in the senate he was regarded as one of the ablest men of that body. He served on some of the leading committees with usefulness to the country and honor to himself. It was during his senatorial term that North Carolina, with other southern states, was infested by organized bands of out-laws, defying law and order and rendering the life, property and peace of the citizens who differed in their political sentiments not only insecure but a perpetual dread. Its history is without parallel in the annals of the Anglo-Saxon race. Mr. Pool believed that the proper enforcement of the law was the only and certain remedy. He undertook the work of enacting such a law as would secure pro-tection to the citizen in the enjoyment of his political and other rights. Then the due and reasonable enforcement of these laws re-ceived his wise counsel and aid. The remedy was successful and delivered the state from the most terrible and fearful scourge that has ever darkened the pages of history. For this noble stand he was cruelly abused by the opposition. The day is coming when full just-ness will be done him in this matter. In this movement he counseled none but strictly legal measures. He believed that law could be executed in due form with more lasting effect than by any other means. To Mr. Pool and Judge Bond is due the credit of the over-throw of the Ku-klux scourge in the United States. The result vindicated his judgment and patriotism.

Mr. Pool was at no time the friend of war, he believed it adverse to all generous and noble sentiments, brutal and irrational in its methods, destructive of the public good, and useless as an agent in the adjustment of national disputes. He was an earnest friend and an active member of the " National Arbitration League." He longed to see the peace of the world assured, not by devouring armies trained for the butchery of their race, but by the devout methods and profound worship of humanity. His love of humanity was not bounded by the limits of his country, it extended wherever the race was struggling for a higher good. It is the duty of the more ad-vanced to lift the degraded to a higher plane, not to despoil and de-stroy them. He regarded war as the crime of all crimes, the scourge of all nations, the organized foe of the race. Its machinery was a cruel and never-ending curse, the instrument of tyranny, and the consumer of the people's labor. He thought it the duty of all good men to unite their efforts to put an end to an unreasonable and cruel crime against all the virtues. Some two years since his fine health gave way and since that time he had apprehended serious conse-quences until more recently he appeared to have recovered his usual elasticity. The day preceding his fatal illness he seemed in the full enjoyment of health and cheerful vigor. But Friday night the 15th, after having as usual enjoyed the society of his family, where he was always the center of devoted attachment, in the full glow of joyous amusement he retired with his little granddaughter to rest. She arose in the morning on the 16th at the usual time, leaving her grand-father to enjoy his morning sleep. He did not appear at breakfast, and some of the family sought his room to call him to his meal, and found that noiselessly he had passed into that " dreamless sleep " that knows no waking. His peaceful exit was in supreme harmony with the calm and dignified life of the man.

No state in this Union has contributed to its country's history more conspicuous individual and personal worth than North Carolina. From the first page of her history up to this good hour, she has furnished her full share of distinguished merit, and her story is replete with illustrious memories. In all the grand achievements of the nation, her sons have filled and more, the measure of expectation. High among these illustrious names, the muse of history will write the name of our silent friend. He was the representative child of his native state. In an eminent degree, he possessed her virtues and none of her vices. His portraiture would be more truly the representative North Carolinian than any other man. His education was the best that the university could afford, and her efforts were not wasted. The seed fell in fertile soil and yielded an abundant harvest. Highly esteemed by the faculty, he was the favorite of his fellow students. His rich capacity and freedom from ambition relieved him from antagonism in this, the dawn of his promising intelligence. His mind was one of order, and all his information was carefully classified and arranged. He was a scientific lawyer and had all his principles so classified that he could at once refer any subject to its proper place. The same was true in regard to all his information on every subject. As a legal and political advocate, he addressed himself to the understanding and reason. He made thorough preparation, "scorning to utter an unconsidered word" to a court or the people. He indulged in no appeals to passion, he believed this unworthy the advocate. Nor did he often, if ever, appeal to the more tender sentiments of our nature, though he was by no means destitute of these feelings, on the contrary, he was readily moved by an appeal to tender sensibilities. His emotional nature was not only active, but easily aroused by injustice, oppression or tyranny. The strong side of his character was the esthetic. He loved the beautiful in form, color and sound, and was more readily moved by the moral than by natural beauty. As an advocate, his voice was clear, benevolent in tone, soft and gentle. His articulation was so distinct, that he was readily heard without an effort in the open air, or in large rooms. His manner, gesture, voice and the whole man were always under the dominion of reason. His powers of analysis were of the highest. In some respects he resembled President Johnson in this particular mental faculty. He was a more highly endowed man, had greater powers of invention and a richer imagination. They differed on many points and especially in their ambition; this was the supreme motor in Mr. Johnson, Mr. Pool was entirely free from it. He believed that the people should select their agents unsolicited, whilst Mr. Johnson pressed his claims. No man was ever more thoroughly self-poised, he carried this into every relation of life, in the domestic circle, in the drawing room, in the senate, in the tumultuous assemblies where the populace were torn by passion, he was always the same unruffled, calm, gentle, unpretending gentleman, and a man more thoroughly master of himself was never known. He was above passion and incapable of blind resentment. His simple, elegant taste characterized all his actions and his intellectual operations. His mind was one of great comprehension and his judgment exact. His knowledge of mechanical forces and his capacity to use them would have made him one of the first inventors of the age had he directed his attention exclusively to that subject.

To the firmness of the martyr he joined the meekness of a child. He loved all children and was beloved by them in turn. He knew their natures and trusted them implicitly, and was seldom deceived. Sincere and faithful to his friendships, he secured the confidence of all with whom he came in contact. His gentle loving nature never permitted him to neglect a child. He treated them as persons of distinction entitled to attention and respect. His friendship was warm and did not depend upon place, rank or wealth. He was the true friend of humanity, his heart bled freely for all who felt the heavy hand of affliction. He never cast off a faithful friend stricken by misfortune. Conscious of his own worth and proud of his noble qualities, he could with the Cid have shared his bed with the leper, and with Sydney, have passed the cup of water to the humble soldier whose wants were still greater than his. There was no human sufferer so humble that he would not reach forth his hand to secure from distress. I have seen him under all the conditions that could elevate or depress the human heart, yet I never heard from him an angry word, an intemperate expression, or one unchaste or profane, no matter who his auditors. He rose above all dogmas, or vulgar superstitions, and bowed with reverence before the worship of all sincere persons. Truthful to his convictions, he laid no claim to superior sanctity, and put on no vulgar assumption of importance. He intended to merit the good will of his kind, and gave little attention to public opinion; he knew that it was unreliable; to-day it was a blessing, to-morrow cursing, but in the end, trusted in public justness if it was deserved. He was by no means indifferent to the culture of his religious sentiments. If " religion is the emotion of reverence which the presence of the universal mind excites in the individual," then was Mr. Pool one of the most religious of men. All nature was instinct with the Divine from the lowest forms of insensate matter up through all the forms of vegetable and animal life. His heart was responsive to its presence in every form of life. His comprehensive intelligence, his warm affections embraced all, protected all, reverenced all. His was the religion of cheerfulness and duty. No gloomy fears shrouded humanity in habiliments of woe. Every object around, from the ephemera sporting in the sunlight to the distant stars that shine in glory through all the countless ages, were ministering angels inspiring love and reverence. The suppression of passion, the exercise of reason, and the cultivation of a living love for all men, all life, were the supreme duties of man. The strongest element of his nature was the love of liberty, of soul and body. Subordination of the spirit to the will of another was the worst form of slavery. He detested every form of dominion over the hearts and bodies of men. As he loved liberty for its own sake, he rejoiced to see all other men enjoy it. Out of this element grew his political principles and conduct. A whig before the war, he readily became a republican, which party has, since it was established in North Carolina, received his warmest support until the contest of 1880. In this contest, he supported Gen. Hancock, not only for his superior military services, but for fine intelligence and manly virtues, but he believed that the southern republicans had been unjustly treated, and defeat would lead the party to act with better faith toward their real allies. He confided in the progressive character of the republicans but believed that a long lease of power had rendered them neglectful to their duties and recreant to good faith.

The life of Mr. Pool was an eventful one. Born under a declining civilization, he grew up during the discussion of its merits and participated in its extinction in every part of the republic. He saw the old passing away, and on his vision broke the dawn of a grander day. From Nebo's loftiest peaks he looked into the promised land and passed over and dwelt beneath the shadow of the tree of liberty, and saw "a new heaven and a new earth," that had risen out of the old. He did not live long enough to realize in full the glorious promise of his labors, but long enough to felicitate himself upon the sacrifices he had made for the consummation of the coming age. He largely participated in working out for his native state and the nation one of the grandest moral revolutions in time. He aided to dispose of a civilization that consigned a large part of its population to the condition of chattels, tore from the mother's breast the sentiments of maternal affection and annihilated the father of the child. Under his and his colleague's labors, life has been endowed with a new value far above the shambles. The graces and virtues of home have been sanctified, justice has received a new meaning, her domain has been enlarged, and her worship purified by a living and universal faith. Labor has been emancipated from the lash, and its author has been lifted from a beast of burden to the condition of Amercan manhood. The education of the whole people has been made the life of the commonwealth. The reign of fear has given place to the reign of love and duty. This beneficent change has worked inconvenience to a few, but is full of promise to a regenerated people. Every year will attest his prescience by the increased knowledge, the growth of virtue, the accumulation of wealth, and the adoption of creative interests. Though calumniated by those who did not realize the demands of the age and the wants of a growing community, in time a new commonwealth will attest his wisdom and honor his memory. A renewed life will dissolve all the resentments and partisan prejudices. The good will survive the shock of resentment that annoyed his tranquillity. The benefactors of mankind hope not to receive a grateful return for their services, they seldom escape the scourge, the cross of calumny. They have always been consecrated to the public good through sighs, and groans and tears. For their sufferings the tears of sorrow must forever flow. The champions of a new era cannot escape the malignant arrows of an expiring one. But the hour has passed, "no steel, nor poison, malice domestic, foreign levy, nothing can touch him farther."

This tender, strong man, so dignified in life, without a struggle or a sigh, has retired to his endless rest. No kinder friend, no more loving and devoted husband, father or brother, has crossed the "sunless river's flow." In all the relations of life he has modestly and faithfully performed his duty. To him we may justly apply the words of the greatest of Roman poets:

> " Justum et tenacem proposite virem
> Non civium ardor prava juventium,
> Non vultus instantis tyranni
> Mente quatit solida neque Auster
> Dux inquieti turbidus Adrae
> Nec fulminantes magna Jovis manus:
> Si fractus illabatur orbis,
> Impavidum ferient ruinde."

Mr. Pool was twice married; first, to Miss Narcissa D. Sawyer, of Elizabeth City, N. C., of whom one child, Mrs. Dr. Sessford, of Washington, D. C., survives; second, to Miss Mollie Mebane, of Bertie county, N. C., of whom two children, Miss Mamie and Mr. John Pool, of Washington, D. C., survive. He was a classmate at the university of the very highly gifted and distinguished Gen. J. Johnston Pettigrew, who early fell in the Civil war, and of the Hon. M. W. Ransom, at present United States senator from North Carolina.

GEN. LAWRENCE O'BRIAN BRANCH.

The subject of this sketch was of distinguished lineage, his ancestors having been prominent for many generations in the affairs of North Carolina. He was born in Halifax county, N. C., November 28, 1820. On Christmas day, 1825, his mother died; and in 1827 his father, who had removed to Tennessee, also died. Gov. John Branch, who was his guardian, brought him back to North Carolina, and being appointed secretary of the navy in 1829, carried him to Washington city. He studied under various preceptors, among others Salmon P. Chase, afterward chief-justice of the United States. He entered Chapel Hill in 1835, but the same year, left and entered Princeton, where he graduated in 1838, taking the first honor. He removed to Florida to practice law, and in the early part of 1841, he served in the Seminole war. After a residence of eight years in Florida, he removed to Raleigh, N. C., having in 1844, married Miss Blount, the accomplished daughter of Gen. William A. Blount of Washington, N. C. In 1852 he was an elector on the Pierce and King ticket, and in the same year he was elected president of the Raleigh & Gaston railroad company, which position he held until he was elected to congress in 1855. He continued in congress until the war began, winning the esteem and confidence of all his party associates.

In December, 1860, on the resignation of Hon. Howell Cobb, Gen Branch was tendered, by President Buchanan, the position of secre

tary of the treasury, but declined it. He was appointed quartermas-
ter-general of North Carolina on the day the state seceded from the
Union, and in September, 1861, was commissioned colonel of the
Thirty-third regiment North Carolina troops. On the 17th of January, 1862, he was promoted to be brigadier-general. His brigade
consisted of the Seventh, Eighteenth, Twenty-eighth, Thirty-third
and Thirty-seventh North Carolina regiments. His first service was
at Newbern, where he disputed Burnside's approach, March 14, 1862.
His brigade was attached to A. P. Hill's light division, and it was the
first to open the fights around Richmond at Hanover Court House.
It was also the first to cross the Chickahominy and to encounter the
Federal forces. With about 3,000 men, it lost 1,250 in killed and
wounded, and of five colonels, two were killed, two were wounded
and one was taken prisoner. In those battles the brigade, no less
than Gen. Branch himself, won imperishable fame. Gen. Branch
bore himself with distinguished courage and was idolized by his men.
He participated in the battles of Cedar Run, Second Manassas, Fairfax Court House and Harper's Ferry. Hurrying from that great
achievement at Harper's Ferry to Sharpsburg, he reached that fatal
field to be of essential service to Gen. Lee's hard pushed army. He
had, with his command, just swept the enemy from his front, when
Gens. Gregg and Archer pointed out a column approaching. Stepping up to these generals, a group was formed that attracted the attention of a sharpshooter, and a bullet came crashing through his
brain and he fell dying into the arms of his staff officer, Maj. Engelhard. As a lawyer, a statesman and a soldier, Gen. Branch took
high rank, and he was one of the foremost men of North Carolina of
his age. He left one son, Hon. W. A. Branch, the representative of
the First North Carolina district in congress, and two daughters.

GEN. JAMES JOHNSTON PETTIGREW.

Among the brilliant men who have adorned the annals of Carolina none takes precedence of James Johnston Pettigrew, who was
born July 4, 1828, at his father's residence, "Bonarva" on the shore
of the beautiful lake Scuppemong, in Tyrrell county, N. C. One of
his ancestors was James Pettigrew, a distinguished officer in King
William's army at the battle of the Boyne, whose youngest son,
James, emigrated to America in 1740, and finally settled at Abbeville,
S. C. His son Charles Pettigrew, settled in North Carolina, and was
ordained a minister in 1775, and after the Revolution was chosen the
first bishop of North Carolina, but was never consecrated. The only
son of Bishop Pettigrew was Hon. Ebenezer Pettigrew, who was a
member of congress from eastern North Carolina. He married
Ann B. Shepard, a daughter of one of the most distinguished families of Newbern, and from that union sprang the subject of this
sketch. After a thorough preparatory education at Bingham's and
elsewhere, Johnston Pettigrew, as he was called, entered Chapel Hill,

where he won greater distinction than any other student there has ever done.

He was a marvelous scholar, and upon graduating, in 1847, so great was his capacity, especially in mathematics, that President Polk, at the suggestion of Commodore Maury, tendered him one of the assistant professorships at the observatory in Washington, he being then only nineteen years of age. The law, however, attracted the brilliant student and after a year's work with Maury, he studied law, first with James M. Campbell, of Baltimore, and then with his cousin, the great James L. Pettigrew, at Charleston, S. C. In 1850 he began an extended tour of Europe, and spent two years in travel and study on the continent. On his return to Charleston he took rank with the first men of South Carolina, and being in the legislature of 1856, when the slavery question was much discussed, he became an honored and conspicuous figure in that body. The Italian war breaking out in 1859, his sympathies were strongly enlisted for the Sardinians and he sailed for Europe, determined to offer his assistance. He was tendered an appointment in that service, but the war ended before he could reach the scene. Shortly after his return he published a very interesting and instructive volume, "Spain and the Spaniards," that is worthy of his high ambition.

When the war broke out, he was colonel of the First regiment of Charleston rifles, and rendered efficient service at that point, but the Confederate government declining' to receive the officers of that organization, he was chosen colonel of the Twelfth North Carolina regiment which afterward was known as the Twenty-second North Carolina troops. His fine bearing, his unusual accomplishments, his proficiency in military studies, and the great personal esteem in which he was held singled him out as a proper object for promotion, but he declined the offer of a commission to be brigadier-general, until he had greater experience. Later he accepted the offer and was assigned to a brigade. At the battle of Seven Pines, June 1, 1862, his brigade was heavily engaged, and as he was gallantly leading one of his regiments in a charge upon a strong position, he was wounded and fell insensible on the field; when he regained consciousness he was a prisoner. After two months confinement he was exchanged, but for some time being an invalid, was employed as commander of the post of Petersburg. Here a new brigade was formed for him — composed of the Eleventh, Twenty-sixth, Forty-fourth, Thirty-second and Fifty-second, North Carolina troops. During the fall of 1862, he was ordered to North Carolina with his brigade, and he repelled the Federal raid into Martin county, and Gen. Foster's expedition in December, against Goldsboro, and he rendered conspicious service in the demonstration against the town of Washington, N. C., in the spring; at Blount's creek, he illustrated his fine abilities as a commander.

When Stoneman made his raid north of Richmond, Pettigrew was in command of the defenses of that city. Later his brigade was assigned to Heth's division, and marched with Lee to Gettysburg. He led his brigade in the assault on the first day of that great battle

and if his fame and that of his brigade were to rest on that engagement of July 1st, alone, they would be imperishable; but as heroic as
were their achievements then, they were surpassed on July 3d, in the
famous Confederate charge.   Maj.-Gen. Heth being wounded, Gen.
Pettigrew succeeded to the command of the division, and on the
morning of the 3d reported to Gen. Longstreet.   The division advanced on a line with Pickett's fresh Virginians on the right, across
the plain to the crest of Cemetery Ridge, and took possession of the
stone wall which had served the Federal forces as a breastwork.
Nothing in history has surpassed that grand charge, and Pettigrew's
name has become immortal.   Of the 3,000 men and officers composing the brigade, 1,100 were killed and wounded at Gettysburg.   The
Twenty-sixth regiment, commanded by Col. Henry Burgroyn, out of
800 men, lost 549, the greatest loss ever sustained in modern warfare
by any regiment.   Officers and men were alike mowed down, and
Gen. Pettigrew himself was painfully wounded.   On the return of the
army to Virginia on the morning of the 14th of Jul , near Falling
Waters, on the Potomac, Gen. Pettigrew was ordered to remain with
his command as a rear guard.   A small body of cavalry, some forty
in number, made a sudden dash upon a bevy of officers, of whom
Gen. Pettigrew was one, and being mistaken for Confederates were
not fired on by the troops.   In the melee Gen. Pettigrew was mortally wounded, and on the 17th day of July he expired near Martinsburg, Va.   Thus perished one of the most gifted and brilliant men
known to American annals, whose name is inseparably connected
with the most heroic feat of arms in modern times.

GOVERNOR JOHN OWEN.

The memory of but few North Carolinians deserves to be held in
higher esteem than that of Gov. John Owen.   He was the son of
Col. Thomas Owen, a gallant officer during the Revolution, who
married Eleanor Porterfield, a daughter of Maj. James Porterfield,
an Irishman by birth, who had settled at Fayetteville, and was a leading whig, and whose son, Capt. Dennis Porterfield, was a conspicuous
officer in the continental line, and at last fell fighting gloriously at the
battle of Eutaw Springs.   By her Col. Owen had two sons, Gen. James
Owen, who was a member of congress in 1817-18, and later president
of the Wilmington and Raleigh railroad — a gentleman of the highest character and reputation, who died about 1860; and John Owen,
the subject of this sketch, who was born in 1787.   He was a gentleman of singular purity of life, sweetness of temper and refined
culture.   He served the people of Bladen in the assembly from 1812 for
sixteen years, being elected governor of the state in 1828.   After
three years in the executive chair he was brought forward for United
States senator, and came within one vote of an election.   He was
president of the whig national convention which, in 1840, nominated
Gen. Harrison for president, and he was tendered the nomination for
vice-president, but he could not bring himself to accept the honor

since he presided over the body. He declined it for that reason. He died a year later at Pittsboro, N. C., much lamented in North Carolina and by his friends throughout the Union. He married a daughter of Gen. Thomas Brown, of Bladen county, a Revolutionary patriot and officer who was the hero of the battle of Elizabethtown, leaving an only daughter, who married Hon. Haywood Guion — a distinguished lawyer and the author of "The Comet" — a book of rare merit.

GEN. JAMES B. GORDON.

John George Gordon came to this country, from Scotland, about the year 1724. He was the great-grandfather of the subject of this sketch, whose ancestors, for four generations, lie buried in the family burying ground, at Wilkesborough, Wilkes county, N. C. James B. Gordon was born at the old homestead, November 2, 1822, and at the age of ten years was placed at school, with Peter S. Ney, in Iredell county. At the age of eighteen he entered Emory and Henry college, Virginia, and then became a merchant at Wilkesborough. He represented his county in the legislature, in 1850, and was always active in political affairs. At the first call to arms, he volunteered in the Wilkes county guards, and was chosen a lieutenant. The company was assigned as Company B, to the First regiment of state troops, and Gordon was appointed captain of it. Soon afterward he was appointed major of the First cavalry, and went to the front in Virginia, where the regiment (Col. Robert Ransom) was placed under the command of Brig.-Gen. J. E. B. Stuart. Maj. Gordon led the first charge on the Federal forces, at Vienna, Halifax county, Va. In the spring of 1862 he was promoted to be lieutenant-colonel, and in the spring of 1863 he was commissioned colonel and given command of the Second North Carolina cavalry. He won his promotion by his gallantry on many a hard fought field. In September, 1863, he was commissioned brigadier-general, and the First, Second, Third and Fifth regiments of North Carolina cavalry were assigned to him, as his brigade. He addressed himself to the task of promoting the efficiency of his command, and soon established thorough confidence and reliance upon each other among his regiments. At Auburn, October 13, 1863, he was wounded, but he successfully passed through hundreds of dangerous encounters.

In the memorable campaign of 1864, Gordon's outposts were the first to meet the Federal forces as they crossed the Rapidan near the Wilderness, and for days the most terrible struggle raged throughout that section. On the evening of the 10th of May, Stuart and Fitz Lee were hastening with the brigades of Lomax, Gordon and Wickham, to intercept the Federal cavalry in its march on Richmond. It was a critical moment. Between Stuart and Gordon there existed the warmest friendship; together they had performed feats of prodigious valor and had made the fame of the Confederate cavalry immortal. They had fought together as brothers: they were to die together as heroes. Gordon drove the opposing force at Ground Squirrel Church on the 11th, and attacked Sheridan near Brook Church, almost in the suburbs of Richmond on the morning of the 12th. On the evening before Stuart had fallen at Yellow Tavern, and at Brook Church, with Richmond almost in sight, Sheridan fought with great obstinacy. With his inferior force, Gordon held the road, and reckless of self, exposed his life with unusual daring to encourage his men to the utmost resistance. He was severely wounded, but held his position until Confederate infantry came up and Richmond was saved. For six days he lingered, and then died at the hospital at Richmond, May 18, 1864. His death was lamented throughout the army, and "filled his entire command with grief and consternation."

GEN. STEPHEN D. RAMSEUR.

But few North Carolinians have displayed greater military capacity than the subject of this sketch. He was a worthy descendant of John Wilfong, a Revolutionary hero, who fought valiantly at Kings Mountain and Eutaw Springs. Stephen D. Ramseur, the second child of Jacob A. and Lucy M. Ramseur, was born May 31, 1837, at Lincolnton, Lincoln county, N. C., where his ancestors had settled several generations before. His early education was received at the preparatory schools in Lincolnton and Milton, and at Davidson college, North Carolina. In 1855 he entered the military academy at West Point, and graduated there with distinction in 1860. He was appointed a lieutenant in the light artillery, but in April, 1861, resigned his commission and took service with the Confederate States government, then at Montgomery. He was soon afterward offered the command of the Ellis light artillery, a Raleigh company, and in the summer was ordered with his company to Smithfield, Va. The next spring his company was at Yorktown, in front of Gen. McClellan, and Ramseur was put in charge of all the Confederate artillery, and later was commissioned major. Subsequently he was elected colonel of the Forty-ninth regiment North Carolina troops, and was assigned to the brigade of Gen. Robert Ransom. In the seven days fights he won distinction, and at Malvern Hill was severely wounded. While still disabled he was appointed brigadier-general, and in October was sufficiently recovered to take the field. His brigade was composed of the Second, Fourth, Fourteenth and Thirtieth North Carolina regiments, and was attached to Rhodes' division of Jackson's corps.

At the battle of Chancellorsville Gen. Ramseur particularly distinguished himself. Gen. Lee writing of his brigade to Gov. Vance, June 4, 1863, said: "I consider its brigade and regimental commanders as among the best of their respective grades in the army, and in the battle of Chancellorsville, where the brigade was much distinguished and suffered severely, Gen. Ramseur was among those whose conduct was especially commended to my notice, by Lieut.-Gen. Jackson, in a message sent to me after he was wounded." Again

Truly Yours
William Hawkins

in the first day's fight at Gettysburg, Ramseur's brigade secured the ridge known as Oak Hill, the key to the field. At Spottsylvania Court House, May 12, 1864, he again won unstinted praise for gallantry and heroism unsurpassed during the war. After the battle, Generals Lee and Ewell thanked Ramseur in person, for his conduct and that of his brigade at the "Angle of death." His heroism won him a commission as major-general, and he was assigned to the command of Early's division. After the battle of Coal Harbor, Early's corps was ordered to the valley of Virginia, and there Gen. Ramseur displayed the highest military acumen. But after passing through many dangers unscathed, on the afternoon of the 19th of October, 1864, in the battle of Cedar Creek, he was mortally wounded, and fell into the hands of the Federal forces. On the 22nd of October, 1863, he had married Miss Ellen E. Richmond, of Milton, N. C.; on the day preceding this battle he had received intelligence of the birth of a daughter. He died the next day. His dying words were: "Bear this message to my precious wife: — I die a Christian and hope to meet her in Heaven."

THE HAWKINS FAMILY.

The first of this distinguished family to settle in America was Philemon Hawkins, who was a descendant of the celebrated admiral, Sir John Hawkins, whose deeds redounded to England's glory, through his son Sir Richard Hawkins. Philemon was born in England in 1690, and his wife, Ann Howard, was born in 1695. He came to this country in 1715, and made his home in Gloucester county, Va., where he died in 1725. Mrs. Hawkins survived him seventeen years, and died at the residence of her son, Philemon, in Bute, now Warren county, N. C. Philemon, the second, was born near Todd's Bridge, Gloucester county, Va., in 1717. Removing to Bute county, N. C., he soon became a man of prominence in that region, and his home became a seat of elegant hospitality. He served as an aid to Gov. Tryon at the battle of Alamance, and was an officer under the colonial government, but later was a warm advocate of the movement for independence. His long life was one of usefulness. He died in 1801, in his eighty-third year. By his marriage with Delia Martin, of Brunswick county, Va., in 1743, he had four sons and several daughters. The sons were: Philemon, Benjamin, Joseph and John.

Benjamin, the second son, was born 1754. He was educated at Princeton college, and was proficient, not only in Latin and Greek, but in French. He was at Princeton with his younger brother Joseph, when that institution was closed during the Revolutionary war; he then joined the army and served at Washington's headquarters for nearly a year; his proficiency in modern languages, especially French, caused Washington to appoint him interpreter between the American and French officers of his staff. In 1780 he was appointed by the state of North Carolina a commercial agent to secure supplies from abroad. From 1781 to 1784 he was a member of the Continental congress, and witnessed at Annapolis the resignation by Gen. Washington, of the command of the army. In 1785 he was appointed a commissioner to treat with the Cherokee Indians, and also on a commission to treat with the Creeks. The next year found him again in congress, and upon North Carolina's adopting the Federal constitution and entering the Union, he and the distinguished Sam Johnston, were selected as the first senators to represent the state in the United States senate. At the end of his six years' term in the senate, he was appointed by President Washington, agent for superintending all the Indians south of the Ohio. He remained in this responsible position through all administrations, rendering most valuable service to his country until his death, in 1816, at Fort Hawkins, Ga. He was a man of mark in his day and generation; was a fine scholar, and an author. He left works on topography, and on the Indian language, and a sketch of the Creek country. One son, Madison Hawkins, and three daughters survive him.

Col. Joseph Hawkins, the third son of Philemon and Delia, left Princeton college during the Revolutionary war, and joined the army. He served in Canada, and rendered efficient service in the cause of his country. He died unmarried. The fourth brother was Col. John Hawkins, who married a sister of Hon. Nathaniel Macon, and left a large family. Among his sons were Gen. John H. Hawkins, Joseph, and Gen. Micajah Thomas, who were all prominent public men. The eldest of these brothers was Philemon the third. He was born in 1752 and died in 1833, in his eighty-first year. He married Lucy Davis, and had seven sons and five daughters. The sons were: John D., William, Dr. Joseph, Benjamin, Philemon, George and Dr. Frank. The last four died unmarried. Dr. Joseph W. Hawkins, having graduated at the University of North Carolina, received the degree of M. D. at the University of Pennsylvania, in 1808. He was an eminent physician, and enjoyed a large practice. He was greatly esteemed and beloved, and his death was lamented by the entire community where he resided. He married Mary Boyd, by whom he had eight children.

Governor William Hawkins, the second son of Philemon and Lucy, was for many years esteemed the most popular public man of Warren county. He often served in the assembly, and was governor of the state for three years, from 1811 to 1814, covering the period of the second war with Great Britain, and was called "the war governor." He administered his responsible office during the war with great acceptability to the people and received many evidences of popular appreciation. He married Ann Boyd, to whom were born eight children. He died at Sparta, Ga., in May of 1819. The daughters of Philemon and Lucy were Eleanor, who married Sherwood Haywood, and had many children; one, Delia, became the second wife of Hon. George E. Badger; Ann, who married William P. Little; Delia, who married Stephen Haywood; Lucy, who married Louis D. Henry, and Sarah, who married Col. William Polk. One of her sons was Bishop Polk —

Yours Truly
W. J. Hawkins

the bishop-general, who was killed during the Confederate war. One of her daughters, Mary, was the first wife of Hon. George E. Badger; and another, Susan, married Hon. Kenneth Raynor.

The eldest son of Philemon and Lucy was Col. John D. Hawkins, who was born at the old homestead, "Pleasant Hill," in Warren county, in 1781, and died in 1858, in his seventy-eighth year. His wife, Jane A. Hawkins, was born in 1784 and died in 1875. Col. Hawkins was a graduate of the University of North Carolina, and for fifty years was a trustee of that institution. He was a lawyer and a political leader. He served many terms in the assembly and was prominent in all internal improvement movements in his county and state. He spent much time on his plantation and was greatly interested in agriculture. He had six sons and five daughters, viz.: James B. Hawkins, who married Ariella Alston, and resides in Matagorda county, Tex., where since the war he has converted his large sugar plantation into a stock farm. Frank Hawkins, who was born in 1815, and is living at Winona, Montgomery county, Miss., where he is engaged in planting. John D. Hawkins, born February 5, 1821, a resident of New Orleans, a cotton factor and a large and successful planter in Mississippi. Philemon B. Hawkins, born May 11, 1823, and died in Franklin county, N. C., January 2, 1891. Dr. Alexander B. Hawkins, born January 25, 1825; he practiced his profession some years in Warren and Franklin counties, and then moved to Florida, where he became largely engaged in agricultural pursuits and was eminently successful as a planter and in business affairs. The daughters were: Ann, who married Col. W. W. Young, of Virginia; Lucy, who became the wife of T. Kean, of Newbern, who after her death moved to LaGrange, Tenn.; Mary, who married P. E. A. Jones, of Granville county, N. C.; Virginia, who married William J. Andrews of Edgecombe, one of whose sons being Col. Alexander B. Andrews, vice-president of the R. & D. R. R. system; and Jane A. Hawkins, who did not marry.

The third son of Col. John D. Hawkins and Jane was William J. Hawkins, who was born in Franklin county, May 27, 1819. He entered the University of North Carolina in 1837, but in 1839 he left that institution, and entered William and Mary college, in Virginia, where he graduated in 1840. Thence he went to the University of Pennsylvania, where he graduated in the medical department in 1842. Settling at Ridgeway, N. C., in the vicinity of his home, he practiced his profession for several years, displaying rare skill and unusual talent. In 1855 he was elected president of the Raleigh & Gaston railroad company, and in this position, his executive ability and capacity for the management of business at once attracted attention. He continued in the presidency of that company (except for the space of a year and a half), until October, 1875, when he retired on account of the condition of his health. His management of the affairs of the company, with the limited facilities and unlimited difficulties of the memorable days of the war, called forth the highest encomiums, and his acknowledged abilities and decided southern attachment caused the Confed-

erate authorities frequently to ask his aid. He strained every nerve
to render service to the Confederate cause, and his railroad line,
which was an important link in transportation, was maintained in the
highest state of efficiency that the circumstances permitted. In 1870
he founded the Citizens' bank of Raleigh, N. C., and under his management it has ever been one of the most successful banking institutions of the south. He selected Col. William E. Anderson for its
president, but on Col. Anderson's death in 1890, he himself took the
position. For many years he has been a trustee of the university,
and he has warmly promoted all plans for the advancement of that
institution.

Always cool and self-poised, cautious and clear-headed, deliberate
in council but firm when a conclusion had been reached, gifted with
quick perceptions and possessing a remarkably sound judgment, Dr.
Hawkins combines those elements that have entered into the character of the distinguished members of the family in past generations,
and which would have assured him conspicuous success in any department of activity that he might have chosen. His achievements
as a railroad manager, especially in the difficult time of the war, and
his success in the administration of the Citizens' bank, and the high
esteem in which his judgment is held by business men, are evidences
of mental scope and intellectual power equal to any undertaking in
ordinary life. His tastes did not lead him to take part in the scramble
for office, and though always interested in political contests, he has
held no official station in government. But he has always exerted an
influence in public affairs which has ever proven beneficial to his state
and been of advantage to the people.

On January 4, 1844, Dr. Hawkins married Mary Alethea Clark
(daughter of David Clark, Esq., of Halifax county, N. C.), who died
on the 19th of September, 1850, leaving two sons, Colin M. Hawkins,
born December 26, 1846, now a citizen of Raleigh; president of the
Raleigh Gas & Electric company, of the North Carolina Phosphate company, the Citizens' Trust company, and a director in
the Citizens' National bank, and Marmaduke J. Hawkins, born September 9, 1850, a resident of Ridgeway, N. C., and a lawyer by profession. On December 27, 1855, Dr. Hawkins married a second time,
Lucy N. Clark, who died October 9, 1867, leaving two daughters,
Louisa, who married William McGee, Esq., a merchant of Raleigh,
and Alethea, who married Mr. J. M. Lamar, a merchant of Monti-
cello, Fla. On the the 12th day of May, 1869, Dr. Hawkins married
a third time, Mary A. White, the daughter of Andrew B. White, of
Pottsville, Penn. They have one daughter, Lucy C. Hawkins.

DOLPHIN ALSTON DAVIS.

Few men in western North Carolina have lived a more useful and
exemplary life than did Dolphin Alston Davis. He, in his lifetime,
set an example well worthy of imitation, one which may be regarded
as a beneficence to his fellow citizens. Mr. Davis was born in Fay-

etteville, N. C., in July, 1802. His father was a native of Halifax county, Va., and was a soldier in the Revolutionary war, taking part in the famous batttle of Kings Mountain. Soon after the close of the Revolution his father settled in Fayetteville and married Ann Stevenson, a daughter of one of the Scotch emigrants who came to Cape Fear shortly after the battle of Culloden. The fruits of that marriage were five sons and three daughters. Dolphin A. Davis was the youngest son and next to the youngest child. Both of his parents were devout and religious people, and his father was long a ruling elder in the Presbyterian church. Mr. Davis lost his parents when he was but a youth, as he was sixteen years old when his father died and one year later the death of his mother occurred. The estate left him was but small and the inheritance of a Christian father's blessing, his exemplary life and his blameless character was a legacy more precious and valuable than gold — which contributed more to the development of his manly characteristics than material wealth could do. His education was limited, probably owing to the early death of his parents. He enjoyed, however, the advantage of the best schools and academies of those days by which he attained a good English education. At the death of his father, the son was appointed clerk in the Fayetteville branch of the Bank of the United States. In May, 1825, he purchased a farm near Fayetteville, and spent twelve years in pursuit of agriculture. In 1837 he was elected cashier of the branch bank of Cape Fear at Salisbury, and in the same year removed to this city with his wife and two children.

For several years before his removal from Fayetteville, Mr. Davis had been a magistrate and the financial agent of Cumberland county. He was soon chosen to the same position in Rowan county. His accuracy, his integrity and ability soon won for him the confidence of his fellow citizens, and there was scarcely an enterprise originated in which his services were not demanded. He became a stockholder in the Salisbury cotton mills, a director of the Salisbury and Taylorsville plank road company, a director of the North Carolina railroad company, chairman of the special court, warden of the poor and county commissioner, holding the last office to his death. To his prudence and sagacity was due for many years the safe condition of the finances of Rowan county. He was ever a friend and promoter of schools and a higher education, and to his wisdom and foresight was due the advantageous management of the Rowan school fund prior to the war. He was for many years a trustee of Davidson college, and a member of the executive and finance committee of the college. His counsel and management helped to tide over the college through many shoals and quicksands. He was able to provide for his family liberally, and gave them all a finished education. To the Davidson college, to which he so generously and prudently lent his aid and influence, he sent his four sons, and they were all graduated from that college. Mr. Davis, in his lifetime, showed his adaptation to all the business situations he assumed, yet his efficiency and success as a financier marked him specially as an adept. For over fifty years he was in the banking business, and when in 1864 or 1865, the branch bank of Cape Fear, at Salisbury, of which he had remained cashier from the first, was discontinued, Mr. Davis established the private bank of D. A. Davis, which he continued until his death. His moral and religious character was upon an exalted basis. In a private letter to a friend he wrote: " If I am a Christian, I owe it under God, to the precepts and examples of a pious father who was a ruling elder in the Presbyterian church for many years, as well as the prayers of a mother, whose constant practice it was to spend a season of private prayer for her children and family every night. If I could have in me any love of country, I have justly inherited it from my father, whose life was jeoparded in the Revolution to free his country from a foreign yoke. And as I am a Presbyterian, I am justly entitled to my predilections, as I am descended directly on the materternal side from the Scottish Covenanters."

At the age of twenty years, Mr. Davis became a member of the Presbyterian church at Fayetteville, and in a short time was ordained to the eldership in this church. On removing his family to Salisbury in 1837, he and his wife were two weeks later received into the communion of the Salisbury Presbyterian church. In December, 1839, he was elected an elder in this church and served in that capacity till his death. Mr. Davis often represented his church in the presbytery, the synod and the general assembly. Many years ago he was made clerk and treasurer of the session. As treasurer, he had the management of the funds of the church and the supervision of the property connected with it. These duties he performed faithfully to the last. He lived to see his eight children members of the church of their fathers, and all of them but one survived him. Two sons and one grandson are faithful ministers of the Presbyterian church, and one son a ruling elder in the church. Rev. John W. Davis, one of his sons is a faithful missionary in Soo Chou, China, and the children then surviving were all but him permitted to stand around the death-bed of their father and receive his blessing. Mr. Davis died December 14, 1881. In 1849 Mr. Davis became a Master Mason and in 1850 he was exalted to the degree of Royal Arch. Mr. Davis had strong and marked characteristics, his leading traits being decision, order and system in business. In his attachments he was constant and affectionate, traits which shone out in his relations of husband, father and friend. It is worthy of mention, that his son, Mr. O. D. Davis has ably and successfully followed in many of the positions vacated by the death of his father and has continued the established banking business of his father. He was born in Rowan county, N. C., February 27, 1851, and graduated with honors from Davidson college in 1873. He taught for one year and then went to the business college, at Poughkeepsie, N. Y., where he graduated in November, 1874. Returning home he was made cashier of the private bank of his father, at Salisbury, remaining as such till his father's death. Immediately after this, he and Mr. Samuel H. Wiley established a private bank, doing business as Davis & Wiley, bankers, till

July 1, 1889, when they associated some of the prominent business men of Salisbury with them and established Davis & Wiley bank, Mr. Samuel H. Wiley being president, and Mr. Davis the cashier, the institution being a state bank, and it is still doing a successful business. Mr. Davis has for years been a member of the Presbyterian church in which he has been an elder for eleven years. He has for about the same time been treasurer of the invested funds of the church. He was town treasurer of Salisbury for three years, and is one of the substantial citizens highly respected in the community in which he resides. Mr. Davis was united in marriage, May 5, 1880, with Miss May, the daughter of J. M. McCorkle, deceased, who in his lifetime was a prominent lawyer in Salisbury. Mr. and Mrs. Davis have three children.

SAMUEL H. WILEY.

Samuel H. Wiley, Esq., of Salisbury, is one of the best known and most prominent of bank presidents and business men in the eastern part of North Carolina. His parents were Shannon and Nancy (Millis) Wiley, and the father was a nephew of Alexander Hamilton. He was a farmer by occupation and of Scottish ancestry. The mother was of French descent, her parents being of a family of exiled Huguenots. The father reached the age of seventy-seven, and the mother lived till she was eighty-five. Both parents were universally respected wherever known. Samuel H. Wiley received a thorough literary education at the classical school of E. W. Caruthers and at the Caldwell institute, then among the foremost educational institutions in the state. Among his schoolmates were Col. Julius A. Gray, Gov. A. M. Scales and other characters who have risen to eminence. Moved by a laudable ambition Mr. Wiley was destined for success in life. By teaching school he obtained the means of completing his education. As a teacher he was faithful, instructive, and on completing a classical course the degree of master of arts was conferred upon him by the University of North Carolina. After studying civil engineering under Gen. J. F. Gilmer, Mr. Wiley served for some time as a surveyor of public lands in the west. Without solicitation on his part he was appointed collector of internal revenue of North Carolina in 1865, and with great credit to himself and satisfaction to the public, held the position till 1872, when he resigned that he might give a more undivided attention to his own private business.

Although Mr. Wiley has never been a politician, nor a candidate for office, he has filled several positions of trust with signal ability. He has for a number of years been largely interested in various financial and industrial enterprises and has always given freely of his time and resources to the material upbuilding of his town and section. He is the president of the Davis & Wiley bank of Salisbury, and is vice-president and the largest stockholder in the Salisbury cotton mills. He is treasurer of the North Carolina steel and iron company at

Greensboro, N. C.; a director of the Western North Carolina railroad company; a director of the Salisbury water works company; a director of the Salisbury gas company as well as of the Connelly Springs company, the Yadkin railroad company, the North Carolina Bessemer company; trustee and treasurer of Davidson college; member of the finance committee of the North Carolina railroad company, of which he has been chairman for fourteen years. All these as well as other similar positions are evidences of the esteem and confidence his fellow citizens repose in his wisdom and integrity. Mr. Wiley has been instrumental in the development of the new celebrated Cranberry and Ore Hill iron properties. In 1861, Mr. Wiley was married to Miss Miriam C. Murdock, who with five children, the fruit of this union, still lives to bless his home. Mr. Wiley has been an extensive traveler both in this country and in Europe. He is thoroughly well informed on all subjects of general interest, and throughout his useful and active career, has ever been a warm friend and supporter of educational and religious institutions. He has been a lifelong member of the Presbyterian church of Salisbury, in which he has been a ruling elder for many years. Perhaps the most important achievements of Mr. Wiley's life were the success of his efforts in conjunction with those of Col. A. B. Anderson, of Raleigh, in the construction and completion of the Western North Carolina and Yadkin railroads.

COL. JAMES G. BURR

is a native of Wilmington and has resided in that city the whole of his life. He married Miss Mary Anna Berry of the same city, a descendant of Chief-Justice Charles Berry, who held office under the Colonial government; she was also a niece of Admiral John Ancrum Winslow, of Alabama fame, and who was also a native of Wilmington. He had issue three sons and four daughters, but only four children are now living. Col. Burr has held many positions of trust and honor under the government. In 1848, he was appointed by President Taylor, postmaster of Wilmington, was removed by President Pierce for political reasons solely, being a whig, and retired from office with the reputation of having made one of the most efficient officers the city has ever had. In 1853 he was appointed teller in the bank of Cape Fear, an institution having a capital of one million and a half dollars, with seven branches in different parts of the state, and in 1861, on the death of the cashier, was elected to fill that vacancy which he had held until 1866, when the bank went into bankruptcy, having been ruined by the war. He was a director and acting president of the Wilmington & Manchester railroad from 1860 to 1873. In 1866 was elected one of the aldermen of the city, and by a standing resolution of the board, acting mayor during the absence of that officer; was a state director of the insane asylum at Raleigh, and for nearly twenty-five years a vestryman of St. James church in this city. Early in the war he was commissioned by Gov. Vance, colonel of the Seventh regiment state guards, and though not liable to military

duty, he accepted the position, and with his regiment, was appointed to the defense of the city of Wilmington. At the bombardment of Fort Fisher, he was ordered to its defense, but had no chance to participate in the affairs as Gen. Bragg did not think it prudent to attack the enemy's intrenchments. On the evacuation of Wilmington, he marched with his regiment to Raleigh, N. C., and served on the staff of Gov. Vance, who sent him, with ex-Govs. Swain and Graham, to meet Gen. Sherman and surrender the city, which they satisfactorily accomplished. At the close of the war he returned to Wilmington, where he has since resided. Col. Burr possesses a vigorous mind and an intellect of a high order. As a writer and lecturer he is surpassed by few. In him is combined that rare faculty of uniting pathos with wit, one moment holding his audience in tears, the next convulsed with laughter. Generous to a fault, his heart as trusting as a child's, is ever ready to respond to the cry of distress, like his purse which is always open to those who need. A gentleman of the Cape Fear, brave, chivalrous and courtly. North Carolina may well be proud of her sons.

GEORGE W. WILLIAMS.

Among the men of North Carolina, who have achieved success in business circles, appears the subject of this mention. Mr. George W. Williams, a native of this state, was born in Chatham county, February 2, 1831. He spent his early life in his native county, and received his education in the schools of the state and at the hands of private tutors, but was denied the advantages of a collegiate education. He first entered business near Fayetteville, N. C., in a small way, in January, 1852, conducting a general merchandise store which he carried on successfully until 1853 when he was offered the advantage of a partnership with his elder brother, Mr. John D. Williams, now president of the bank of Fayetteville which he accepted, the firm being known as G. W. Williams & Co. Mr. Williams assumed the management of the business and conducted it until the early part of 1866, when he connected himself with Capt. David Murchison and became the senior member of the firm of Williams & Murchison of Wilmington. His connection with Capt. Murchison in all his successful transactions is well known and further mention of them can be found in the sketch of Capt. Murchison which appears elsewhere in this work. On the death of Capt. Murchison in 1882, Mr. Williams was appointed administrator of the immense estate and by his judicious management saved the heirs many thousands of dollars. He has continued the business built up by the firm, having after the death of Capt. Murchison formed a partnership with his brother, Col. K. M. Murchison, continuing the business under the old name. Mr. Williams is also senior member of a firm which conducts one of the largest wholesale grocery houses in the state, and he took an active part in the organization of the bank of New Hanover of Wilmington, of which he is vice-president and director. Mr. Williams was happily wedded to Miss Kate A., daughter of D. Murchison, and the sister of Capt. D. R. Murchison, on April 12, 1854. This union has been blessed by five sons and three daughters now living. Mr. Williams is a member of the Masonic fraternity and has been a lifelong communicant of the Presbyterian church. He has never taken any active part in politics or sought public honors, preferring to give his whole attention to his business interests. He has shown himself to be a man possessed of more than ordinary ability, and during his long residence in Wilmington, has by his honesty and uprightness gained m w m personal friends and the respect and esteem of all that know him.

EUGENE A. EBERT.

One of the leading and most enterprising business men of Forsyth county, N. C., is Eugene A. Ebert. Mr. Ebert is a native of Salem, N. C., having first seen the light there, May 27, 1850. He left school at the age of sixteen, and at that time entered upon his mercantile career as a clerk in a Salem store. He remained with one firm for ten years, and at the expiration of that period embarked in business for himself, and for eight years successfully conducted a large business. During the last two years of this time he was cashier in the internal revenue office. Selling out his store, he engaged in the tobacco business, and still is interested in that leading industry. In 1888, at the organization of the Forsyth Savings bank, Mr. Ebert was elected its president, and still holds that office. He is secretary of the Winston Development company, and is a stockholder in the Roanoke & Southern railroad company. In 1877 he was happily united in marriage to Miss Dora Starbuck, daughter of D. H. Starbuck, of Winston, N. C., and to their union three children have been born, one of whom survives, namely, Ellen. Christian Ebert, the father of the above, was born in Forsyth county, N. C., in 1812. He was a hatter by trade. He married Miss Lucinda Rothass in 1838, and became the father of four children, two of whom now survive him: Leonora A., wife of John I. Nissen, of Salem, and E. A. Ebert. The father of these children was a son of Solomon Ebert, who was born in Pennsylvania, in 1775, and came to North Carolina with his parents when a youth. He died in 1838.

HON. DAVID F. CALDWELL.

One of North Carolina's most prominent citizens is the Hon. David F. Caldwell. David Franklin Caldwell, son of Thomas and Elizabeth Caldwell, was born one mile west of the city of Greensboro, N. C., Guilford county, on the 5th of November, 1814. His parents removed to Greensboro when he was but one year old, and his scholastic training was obtained in the schools of that city. For a time he worked on his father's farm, and in 1841 left the farm to enter the mercantile business in Greensboro, and continued in that enterprise until 1849. In 1848 he was elected to the house of representatives of the state, and was re-elected for five successive terms, only retiring in 1861. In 1860 he began the study of law, and one year later was admitted to the bar. He practiced at Greensboro until the new code was adopted, when he abandoned his profession in disgust. In 1864 he was elected county attorney and served until his retirement from the law. He was a delegate to the constitutional convention of 1865, and in the same year was nominated for congress, but was counted out by Gen. Canby, at Charleston, S. C. In 1872 he was a delegate to the convention that nominated Greeley and Brown for the presidency and vice-presidency, respectively, of the United States, and in 1879 was sent to the state senate, where he remained one term, and in the same year was appointed a member of the committee chosen to compromise the state debt. Mr. Caldwell's course as a member of the legislature was dignified and able. In 1848 he framed, and had passed a tax bill, revolutionizing the tax system of the state, and despite the bitterest opposition, finally brought his measure into so great favor with the people that he was practically their unanimous choice for the legislature until his voluntary retirement from public life. He was more than prominent in the organization and building of the North Carolina railroad, and was a prime mover in the establishment of the Greensboro & Cheraw and Cape Fear & Yadkin Valley railroads.

At the outbreak of the Civil war, Mr. Caldwell was engaged in a lucrative law practice with the late James A. Long. He was opposed to secession, and like many another southerner who proved loyal to his people when the test came, yet foresaw too far into the future to think that good could come of the disruption of the Union. When his state seceded David Caldwell went with the majority, and in 1861 enlisted in the Confederate army, he being at that time captain of Senior reserves, but owing to the refusal of the governor to issue his commission, he served as a private. He was refused a captain's commission because of his previous opposition to secession, and because the governor of the state had doubts of his loyalty. Mr. Caldwell proved his love for his people, and his name was vindicated by them when he was elected to the legislature by an overwhelming majority. As a financier, Mr. Caldwell is able and safe. He has large landed interests, is a stockholder in various railroad enterprises of the state, and is extensively interested in different cotton factories. In 1889 he organized the bank of Guilford, and was made its president, an office he still holds. Thomas Caldwell, the father of our subject, was the first clerk of the superior court of Guilford county, having been first appointed to that office by Judge Duncan Cameron, at Martinsville, in 1806. For more than fifty years he discharged the duties of that important office. When the county seat was changed in 1808 from its former location to Greensboro, Thomas Caldwell bought some property in the now thriving city, and erected the first brick dwelling of the present city. His family moved into this abode in 1815, and the son, David, has continued to reside in that house ever since.

As a boy, David Caldwell was not vigorous in body. His parents were obliged to take him from school in order to allow him to recuperate, and he was placed in a coach-shop to gain strength by manual labor. This had the desired effect. His first appearance in political life was in the campaign of 1840, when he cast his first vote for "Tippecanoe and Tyler too." He is a man of magnificent abilities, and his life has not been lived "apart unto himself," but his talents and energies have been directed toward the upbuilding of his state, and the uplifting of her people.

THOMAS A. GREEN,

a member of the banking house of Green, Foy & Co., was born in Newbern, N. C., June 25, 1846, and is a son of Thomas and Annie M. (Curtis) Green, both of Craven county, N. C. The father was a sea captain, being joint owner in the vessel he commanded, which was in the West India trade. He was lost at sea in 1852. Our subject was raised in Newbern, and received his scholastic training in the public schools of that town. At the age of twelve years Mr. Green was "bound out" to Mr. Fred Lane, by his guardian, A. T. Jerkins, Esq., to learn the carpenter's trade. On the 14th day of March, 1862, the city of Newbern was captured by Gen. Burnside, and on that day he was left a barefooted and bare-headed boy, without a penny to call his own. During the war he obtained employment at such odd jobs as he could pick up, and in 1868, having saved his earnings, he engaged in the mercantile business with Capt. Gates, the firm name being Gates & Green. In 1872 Mr. Green purchased the entire business, which he successfully conducted until 1885. In the latter year he became associated in the banking business with the present firm of Green, Foy & Co., he controlling a one-half interest. Early in life he was thrown on his own resources, and the reputation he has won as an able business man is vastly more to his credit than if he had not started life as a drayman in the streets of the city where he is now recognized as its leading banker, and where for years he has conducted the largest mercantile establishment in the vicinity. Mr. Green was one of the prime movers in the establishment of the Cotton Exchange at Newbern, and has been treasurer of that institution since its organization in 1879. He has also served as president of the Newbern board of trade. He is now the president of the Neuse & Trent River Steamboat company, and at one time was president of the Newbern Cotton Mill company. Mr. Green is a member of St. John lodge, A. F. & A. M., of which he is past master and present treasurer. He is a director in the Oxford orphan asylum, at Oxford, N. C., and has served as an alderman of his city. He is the oldest living fireman in the city, and has been chief of the department. A trustee of the Newbern academy, he was one of its principal supporters, and has ever taken an active interest in the welfare of the people. He is one of the largest tax payers in the city. In 1868 he was married to Miss Harriet H. Meadows, daughter of J. A. Meadows. The marriage has been blessed by the birth of six children, of whom two survive, namely: Maud Louisa and Clara Maria. The family are communicants of the Methodist Episcopal church, south, and he has been chairman of the board of stewards of that church for several years.

CLAUDIUS E. FOY,

a member of the banking firm of Green, Foy & Co., of Newbern, N. C., is a descendant of an old French Huguenot family of North Carolina. He was born in Jones county, N. C., on the 10th day of May, 1850, his father, Charles H. Foy, being also a native of that county, born September 20, 1816. He was a prominent planter of that section, a colonel in the state militia and a leading member of the whig party, taking an active interest in all questions of public improvements. He was a consistent member of the Methodist Episcopal church, south, and lived within a half a mile of Lee's Chapel church, where he held his membership. Mr. Foy was very fond of society, and he entertained his friends with the old-time southern hospitality. His first marriage was to Miss Elizabeth A., daughter of Col. John S. Smith, of Newbern, and occurred October 13, 1840. She died July 30, 1843, without children. Mr. Foy was married to Miss Elizabeth P., daughter of John Oliver, of Jones county, on the 20th of June, 1849, and this union was blessed with the following children: James O., born April 4, 1852, now editor of the Winston *Twin City Daily Sentinel;* Laura E., born February 7, 1854, married James C. Holland, of Onslow county; Charles H., born November 2, 1856, a prosperous farmer of Jones county, and Claudius E. Foy. The father died August 20, 1856, having contracted a fatal illness while canvassing Jones county as a candidate for the state legislature. His wife, who was a member of the Piney Grove Baptist church of Jones county, and a most devout woman, died February 23, 1863.

The paternal grandparents of Claudius E. Foy were Enoch Foy who was the son of James Foy and Elizabeth Ward, his wife, who was born in Onslow county on May 17, 1777. Enoch Foy moved to Jones county and settled on the south side of Trent river, about fifteen miles above Newbern. He became an extensive planter and large slaveowner. Wheeler's History of North Carolina says that he was nine times a member of the state legislature from Jones county between the years 1803 and 1838; five times a member of the house of commons and four times a member of the senate. He belonged to the whig party. His wife, the mother of Charles H. Foy, was Phœbe Sanderson, daughter of Joseph Sanderson. He was a member of the Methodist Episcopal church, south, at Lee's chapel, in Jones county, and died October 6, 1846. James Foy, the father of Enoch Foy and the paternal great-grandfather of C. E. Foy, was the son of John Foy, a French Huguenot, who with a number of others came to this country from France in the early part of the seventeenth century, fleeing to escape the terrible persecution which they were

subjected to in their native land.   He first settled on the south side
of Trent river, in the neighborhood of the Pembroke Ferry, near
Newbern, and afterwards moved to Onslow county, on Hick's run.
The wife of James Foy was Elizabeth Ward, who was a member of
the church of England.   James Foy fought in the Revolutionary war
for American independence and was in the battles of Cowpens, Kings
Mountain, Guilford Court House and Moore's Creek Bridge, at which
place he was wounded in the wrist.   He died at the age of eighty-
five years.   American history says of the French Protestants or
Huguenots: " No better class of emigrants could have been desired.
They represented not only the best bone and sinew, but the best intellect and conscience of France.   They brought with them that
power and influence which springs not from rank or money, but from
character."

John Oliver, the maternal grandfather of our subject, was the son
of James Oliver and Macey Brady, his wife, and was born January 19,
1799, and died July 26, 1863.   He was a large slave owner and extensive planter of the Piney Grove section of Jones county.   He married a Mrs. Penelope Simmons, *nee* Loftin, and the widow of F. G.
Simmons, Sr., of Jones county, who had one son, F. G. Simmons, for
many years a prominent planter of Jones county, and now a resident
of Newbern.   He is the father of ex-Congressman F. M. Simmons,
of Winston, N. C.   Penelope B. Loftin, wife of John Oliver, was the
daughter of Joseph Loftin and Mary Becton, his wife.   She was born
February 24, 1805, and died October 24, 1872.   Their four children,
whose names were Harriet C., born March 14, 1835, and married
Thomas S. Gillett, died July 30, 1862; Penelope B., born February 10,
1840, died April 7, 1863; Elizabeth P., who was the wife of Charles H.
Foy, was born October 27, 1831, and died February 23, 1863; Joseph
John, their only son, was born May 13, 1842, and entered the Confederate army, July 1, 1862, as a member of Company K, Sixty-first regiment, North Carolina state troops.   He was wounded mortally at
the battle near Petersburg, Va., and died in the hospital at Petersburg, October 29, 1864, from the effects of his wounds; the above
mentioned are all deceased.   Olivers, a postoffice in Jones county,
was named in honor of John Oliver and is situated near his old homestead.   He and his wife were consistent members of the Piney Grove
Baptist church, and he was a whig in politics.

The principal of this biographical mention, Claudius E. Foy, is a
native of Jones county, and early embarked in an active business
life.   The Civil war had destroyed everything belonging to the Foy
family with the exception of their lands in Jones county, and there
was nothing left to work with.   His first effort was as a clerk in a
country store for Dr. W. H. Barker, of Carolina city, Carteret county,
beginning there July 1, 1865, at the age of fifteen years.   Subsequently Dr. Barker removed to Swansboro, in Onslow county, in the
early part of 1866 where he formed a partnership with Robert S. Mc-
Lean under the firm name of Barker & McLean.   Mr. Foy was
retained in their employment until the fall of 1866, when on account

of ill health he had to give up his position. In the early part of 1867 he came to Newbern and secured a clerkship with J. A. Bell, general merchant, and remained with him until July 1, 1869, when at the age of nineteen, with the assistance of his uncle he embarked in the general mercantile business for himself. His first visit to New York was made in September, 1869, for the purpose of purchasing goods for the fall trade. He then entered upon the career which has since been so prosperous and honorable. In 1871, Mr. Foy removed his business to Polloksville in Jones county and remained there until February, 1873, when he returned to Newbern, and formed a copartnership with Capt. Thomas Gates for the prosecution of the general mercantile and cotton commission business under the firm name of Gates, Foy & Co. This concern existed until February 13, 1880, it having met with marked success. At this time, Mr. Gates retired from the firm, and Mr. Foy conducted it alone under the firm name of C. E. Foy & Co. until January, 1885. During the year 1884 he took an extensive trip throughout the west, going to Denver, Col., with a possible view of locating and investing in business. But he decided to return to Newbern, and on the 29th of January, 1885 the banking house of Green, Foy & Co. was organized by Thomas A. Green and Claudius E. Foy, F. M. Simmons and Clement Manly. Messrs Green and Foy soon afterward purchased the entire interest of the concern, and have since conducted it under the name of Green, Foy & Company.

Mr. Foy has ever taken a deep interest in the development of Jones county. He was the promoter of the first government appropriation in 1879, of $7,000 for the improving of Trent river, and was appointed by the people of that county to go to Washington, D. C., and look after the interests of their section. Up to this time, more than $40,000 have been expended under the direction of Gen. Robert Ransom, in opening up the river to navigation from its mouth to Trenton, the county seat of Jones. Mr. Foy organized the Trent River Transportation company, and was president of the same for several years. They ran a regular line of freight and passenger steamers on the Trent river. Mr. Foy has been a member and director of the Newbern cotton and grain exchange since its organization, and is one of the charter members of the Newbern board of trade, and for several years was a director of the Atlantic & North Carolina railroad. He was the promoter of the East Carolina Land & Railway company, which had for its object the building of a railroad from Jacksonville, Onslow county, to Newbern. The charter was sold to a New York syndicate who are now exgaged in constructing the road. Mr. Foy is a director in this company. He is prominently identified with the democratic party, and is one of its active workers. He is a member of the Royal Arcanum, Knights of Honor, American Legion of Honor and Chosen Friends. On the 6th day of July, 1871, he was so fortunate as to form a marriage alliance with Miss Agnes C. Paton, a native of Edinburgh, Scotland. Her father was David Paton, the son of John and Eleanor (Roper)

Paton, the latter a sister of Sir Timothy Roper, of England. The father of John Paton was also named David. He is the great-grandfather of Mrs. Foy, and his wife was Eleanor Campbell, the sister of Lord Campbell of Monzie Castle, and one of the oldest families in Scotland. The mother of Eleanor Campbell descended from the Earl of Breadalbine of Taymouth Castle. David Paton, the father of Mrs. Foy, was twice married. His first wife was Miss Nicol, the daughter of Andrew Nicol, Esq., of Scotland, and they became the parents of one daughter, Eleanor, who married John Wyld, now deceased. She now lives at Mount Ellen, near Glasgow, Scotland. Mrs. Paton died in Scotland, and Mr. Paton subsequently came to America, making a prospecting tour through the United States and Canada.

David Paton was an architect by profession, and while in New York, just on the eve of returning to Scotland, he was engaged by a committee from North Carolina to come to Raleigh and draw the plans for the new state capitol. Wheeler's History of North Carolina says of this structure: "That for correctness of architecture and perfect adaptation to its intended purposes, it has no superior in these United States." While living in Raleigh during the course of the construction of this capitol, Mr. Paton met Miss Annie B. Farrow, a daughter of Hezekiah and Theresa (Jones) Farrow, of Washington, N. C., and made her his wife. Soon after this they went to Scotland, and after living there nine years, they returned to this country and took up their residence in Brooklyn, N. Y. He was a professor in the American architectutal institute at Brooklyn and professor on the mechanical institute of New York for more than thirty years. His death occurred in 1883 and that of his wife in 1875. To his second marriage were born these children: Theresa J., now Mrs. E. Snedeker, of Brooklyn, N. Y.; Hettie S., wife of Horace F. Hopkins and John Paton, of the same city; Sarah D.; Mrs. N. D. Bush, of Nyack, N. Y.; Matilda S.; Mrs. W. Van Gorden, of Newburg; Mary A.; Mrs. John O. Silvey, of Denver, Col., and Agnes C., wife of C. E. Foy, of Newbern, N. C. Mr. Paton's father was largely interested in building the Dean bridge across the Leith near Edinburgh. Four children have been born to Mr. and Mrs. Foy. They are: Claudius B., eighteen years of age, now at Major Bingham's military school; David F., aged fifteen years; Agnes G., aged thirteen years, and Annie E., aged nine years. The last three are attending the Newbern collegiate institute. Mr. and Mrs. Foy are active and valued communicants of the Newbern Presbyterian church in which he is an elder.

COL. JOHN W. ALSPAUGH

was born in Forsyth county, in July, 1831, and received his education mainly through his own efforts at Trinity college, N. C., graduating at that institution with distinction in 1855. Leaving the farm on which he had been reared, he came to Winston, from which point he went to Greensboro, and began the study of law under Hon. Robert P. Dick, and was admitted to the bar in 1856. As is often the case with young men who have been admitted to the practice of law, and who have little or no means, he sought employment which he might pursue to aid him in accumulating means with which to start in life, and being of a literary turn of mind, he connected himself with the *Western Sentinel*, and soon became the sole editor, publisher and proprietor of that so well and favorably known weekly newspaper in North Carolina. As editor of this democratic paper, he soon brought himself into notice throughout the state; and any one who has examined the old files of the *Sentinel*, published previous to, and during the war, will testify to the ability with which he maintained the cause of the south, and of the Confederacy during this trying period. He remained in charge of the editorial chair of this paper until 1866, during which time he was offered the editorial control of the *North Carolina Standard*, published at Raleigh, and of the *Charlotte Democrat*, published at Charlotte, N. C. After retiring from the active management of the *Sentinal*, in 1866, Col Alspaugh returned to the practice of the law. Establishing an office in Winston, he offered his services as a lawyer, confining his practice to civil causes. In the practice of law he set out, as in everything else he has undertaken, with the intention to succeed, and soon by close application to business and faithfulness to his clients, he found himself supplied with the very best class of clients which the country afforded and a large number of them. His business continued to increase year after year, and no lawyer had a better class of paying business than he. He then conceived that the necessities of the community in this section of North Carolina demanded more capital, and he determined to withdraw from the practice of law and establish a National bank in Winston.

During his experience at the bar Col. Alspaugh had so gained the confidence of parties who had money to invest that he managed the funds of many capitalists in this section of the state, and consequently when he retired from the law to take up banking he brought to bear in his position as cashier of the First National bank of Winston, which was established in 1876, with a capital stock of $100,000, and now increased to $200,000, with a deposit account of over $300,000, a ripe experience and a fine knowledge of business; he has been the cashier of this bank since its foundation in 1876, and as such has been largely instrumental in aiding in the establishment of many of the large manufacturing institutions which adorn and enrich the flourishing city of Winston. Col. Alspaugh has never allowed the use of his name in connection with any public office, with the exception of filling for five years the position of chief clerk of the North Carolina senate, and being mayor and commissioner of Winston for a number of times. There are many large and rich manufacturing establishments in the city of Winston in which Col. Alspaugh has been instrumental in having brought to Winston, and in aiding, by loaning money and lending the proprietors the use of his name in procuring money to successfully operate. There is not a railroad running into

Winston which has not had the benefit of his time, experience and money in being located and built to this place. Ready at all times, day or night, to lend the use of his influence and his money to do whatever his fellows citizens agree upon as the best thing to be done for the city and community, it might justly be said of him that his native county seat has every reason to be proud of his services and to wish for his continued prosperity and success. No one man has done as much for the city as he, and though advancing in years, his zeal for the welfare of Winston has not in the least abated, and his fondest wish is to live long enough to see Winston the largest town in North Carolina, as she is already the most progressive and flourishing.

Another quality which Col. Alspaugh possesses has made his name familiar to the people of this section; he is one of the most liberal and public-spirited citizens in the state. There is not a schoolhouse nor a church in the community built by subscription, to which he has not been a large contributor. And the North Carolina conference of the Methodist Episcopal church well know the fact, that but for his fidelity to the cause of education, his energy and skill in the management of difficult affairs, Trinity college now the pride of the church and the coming glory of the state would have been numbered among the things that were. Rallying to its support in the hour of despair when almost all others had abandoned it to a thraldom of debt that seemed impossible to be removed, he has lived to see the last dollar of its indebtedness canceled and a large nucleus of endowment created, the college thoroughly reconstructed, re-organized and rapidly growing into one of the broadest and most comprehensive universities of the south, and it can be truly said of him that he has never "turned his face from any poor man," but he is ready at all times to aid any deserving person or object. In addition to other enterprises which might be mentioned in connection with his services is the origin of the Winston graded school, the city water works, and electric lights. Another trait of his character which has so endeared him to the citizens of this city is the interest which he has always manifested in young men. He can count by the score, the number of young men whom he has given a start in life, either by giving them employment, lending them money or endorsing for them to enable them to procure money with which to open a business for themselves; and it is a very remarkable fact, that notwithstanding the large number of persons he has habitually aided in this way, he has very rarely ever lost a dollar by this course, though at times the parties he assisted have been comparatively strangers.

Col. Alspaugh is a member of the Masonic fraternity (Royal Arcanum) and encampment. He has been married twice, the first time in 1861, to Olivia G. Stedman, who died in 1869. There were no children by this marriage. He married again in 1872, to Celeste Tucker, daughter of Thomas Tucker, of Iredell county, and to them have been born three children: Emma Celeste, John W., Jr., and Violet G., all very interesting and bright children. Col. Alspaugh's father, the Rev. John Alspaugh, was born in 1804, and is still living.

Paul. C. Cameron

His father was admitted to the ministry of the Methodist Episcopal church in 1824, and continued in active service of the church as a local preacher up to 1880, when advancing years compelled him to give up his regular charge. He was an aggressive and popular preacher, and has done much in his day to strengthen the Methodist church in Forsyth county, and to entitle it to the love and confidence of the people. Rev. John Alspaugh was married in 1825, to Elizabeth Lashmit, and to them were born nine children. Two of his sons, James and Albert, gave their lives to the Confederate cause, James dying in a hospital in Charlottesville, Va., from disease contracted in the service, and Albert was killed in a charge at the head of his company, at the battle of Gettysburg. The Alspaughs came originally from Germany, Henry Alspaugh, the grandfather of Col. J. W. Alspaugh, came to this country from Germany, about the time of the Revolutionary war, settling in the Wachovia settlement, now known as Salem. He was a soldier in the war of 1812. His maternal grandfather, Elias Lashmit, was a soldier in the Continental army and was severely wounded at the battle of Guilford Court House during the Revolution.

PAUL CARRINGTON CAMERON

was born on the 25th day of September, 1808, at Stagville, in the then county of Orange, now Durham county, N. C. His father was Judge Duncan Cameron, of whom a sketch appears elsewhere in this volume. His early boyhood was passed at Fairntosh, the residence of his father, and at school in the vicinity. His first preceptor was an old, country school-master, who taught at the farm known as Ellerslie, two miles from Fairntosh. He was then placed under the charge of Willie P. Mangum, a resident of the family of Judge Cameron, as a law student, as was also at the same time, William H. Haywood, the only law students, with the exception of his son, that Judge Cameron ever had, the two names afterward prominent in public life and both honoring seats in the senate of the United States. Subsequently he was placed under Mr. John Rogers, at Hillsboro, and when of sufficient age, was sent to Dr. McPheeters, at Raleigh, a gentleman celebrated in hisd ay as a teacher, and living yet in affectionate remembrance as a good man and able divine. From Raleigh he was sent to the celebrated military school at Middletown, Conn., famous as "Capt. Partridge's School," the principal having been a Revolutionary officer and a good tactician, his school in its best days, presuming a rivalry with West Point. Here Mr. Cameron early developed his character as a leader, for he was soon ranking captain of the four companies of cadets. Leaving this school with an honored and brilliant record, he entered the University of North Carolina in the fall of 1825. His appearance must have been a very striking one, being clad in a full suit of red homespun; his head was fiery red, and his complexion beamed with a ruddy glow. The boys promptly dubbed him the

"Red Bird," which title he as promptly resented with a continued fusilade of red brick-bats with such effect as to bring about his expulsion on the day of his admission to the university. He was, however, taken back. His pugnacity was a bar to his graduation. One morning in the chapel, while President Caldwell was conducting prayers, Mr. Cameron engaged in a fight with one of the seniors, much to the scandal of the place and the occasion. The faculty thought that in the interest of discipline, the expulsion of both was necessary. Mr. Cameron justified his own conduct and so did his father and friends. The sentence of expulsion was not executed; but after spending two years at the university, he left and entered Washington (now Trinity) college, Hartford, Conn., where he graduated in 1829. Half a century later, he delivered the commencement address.

His predilections led him to study law, a calling suited to his tastes, the character of his mind, and the ardor of his temperament, an avocation, in his young days especially, to give active employment to the accumulated stores of a liberal education and a becoming equipment for the future attainment of those high political honors to which his position might justly entitle him to aspire. He, therefore, read law with his father, and was admitted to the bar, but he never engaged in the practice of the profession, because of the burden which fell upon him in aiding his father in the management of his vast and varied interests. This duty unavoidably devolved upon him, and he cheerfully sacrificed the ambitions to be gratified in a professional or political career, to the more obscure, more exacting, more responsible, but not less useful, life of the intelligent planter. He saw in the planter something more noble than the mere tiller of the soil; in agriculture, some aim higher than the extraction from the earth, by the rude process of unskilled labor, those products in all ages recognized as indispensable to human sustenance and comfort. He saw in the great mainspring of commerce, of prosperity, of social happiness, the foundation upon which was laid the great superstructure of human advancement and enlightenment. With such views, he saw that agriculture was an avocation that must be advanced by intelligently applied skill, and elevated by all the appliances that might be exacted from science. He also saw, in his case, that, in the control of such wide territory, such an army of laborers, and such magnitude and variety of productions, demanded successful direction and harmonious reconciliation of various conditions, there were required executive and administrative qualifications scarcely inferior to those called out in the government of a state or the command of an army. He, therefore, devoted himself to the study of agriculture, both practical and theoretical, with earnestness equal to that which had marked his acquisition of what are regarded as the liberal branches of education. He became the model of a farmer; he infused his own ideas into others; he became president of the first agricultural society organized in North Carolina; an address delivered by him before the society at Hillsboro in 1830 was so replete with practical wisdom, and so adorned with literary excellence that it was called for,

for publication, and long remained as a model of its kind, a guide to those who chose to follow in his enterprising footsteps.

Mr. Cameron exhibited in the conduct of his responsibilities, for more than a half century, an administrative and financial ability, an energy and integrity which would have secured him high honors in any field of action. His career was characterized by the simple, straightforward devotion to what he conceived to be duty in every relation of life. As a son, as the head of a family, as a citizen, and as a guardian of 1,900 slaves, his course may challenge inquiry, and would doubtless repay it. The very mistakes of such men are instructive. That he never erred, no one will affirm; that he has ever been able to please everyone in the conduct of his multifarious interests, is equally doubtful; but his strict sense of honor, of justice, and his unflinching adherence to what appeared to him at the time right, has never been called into question. An independent thinker, with expanded observation, he acted out his own line of thought with fearless confidence, only controlled by that governing principle of right and duty that shaped the conduct of his life. With a mind so active as his was, with information so extensive, with the prominence and responsibility of his station, he could not be indifferent to the strong influences that were agitating the public mind, either in their relation to material or mental welfare, or to the political questions in which the peace of the country or the safety of the domestic institutions of the south were involved. He was active and zealous, and no man entered into the new measures undertaken for the development of state interests and advancement of internal improvements, with more enthusiasm than did Mr. Cameron. He was an active promoter of the building of the North Carolina railroad, designed as the great central artery of the state in its ultimate perfected railroad system. When the work on it was begun he was among the first to undertake a large contract, and he was the first contractor to turn over his finished work. He was, for a number of years, a director in the company, and when Col. Charles F. Fisher, its president, resigned that position in July, 1861, to take command of the Sixth North Carolina regiment, on the point of marching to the seat of war in Virginia, he was succeeded by Mr. Cameron, who for one year managed the affairs of the corporation with energy and ability, and with much self-sacrifice in his private affairs, which in such time of general confusion suffered from enforced neglect. He was also for many years a director of the Raleigh & Gaston and of the Raleigh & Augusta Air Line railroad companies. He was also from their beginning, a stockholder in the two leading banks of Raleigh, the Citizens' and the Raleigh National. He became also largely interested in the cotton manufacture, and was a large stockholder and director in two of the largest factories at Rockingham, Richmond county, a large stockholder in the cotton mills at Rocky Mount, and also in two of the largest mills in Augusta, Ga.

As a politician Mr. Cameron had strong, clear and decisive views. He has grown up as a whig of the old school, and had clung tenaciously to his party principles and measures, until, as the portentious question which began to overcast the political sky, his party, in its northern wing, gave unmistakable token that it had become sectional-ized, and that the peace of the whole country was imperiled and the institutions of the south menaced with ruin through the favor ex-tended to the unconstitutional purposes of the abolitionists, then, with many other prominent gentlemen of the state, he promptly and unre-servedly surrendered his old convictions and ranged himself in line with the democratic party; and to that party, proved by the test of experience to be pure, honest and patriotic, he undeviatingly adhered to the day of his death. He did not want political preferment. Once only did he yield to the call of his countrymen; in 1856 he represented Orange county in the state senate. He was made chairman of sev-eral important committees of the senate, and as such the public felt secure that the business in hand would be done, and well done. It was in such duty rather than a frequent speaker on the floor of the senate, that he gained distinction as one of the most laborious, useful and able members of that body to which he belonged. The occasions were rare which enforced his participation with public political life. Once, again, indeed, he took prominent place as chairman of the North Carolina delegation to the democratic convention which met at St. Louis in 1876, and in which Mr. Tilden was nominated for the presidency.

But it was his interest in the education of youth that brought him into the most intimate relations with the intelligence of his state. He had the appreciation of the educational needs of the people, and was the earnest advocate of every liberal measure devised to supply them. He performed his part of the noble work by giving his care to the maintenance of such leading institutions as might shed abroad their light for good in the most extended beneficence. In the decay of the old Episcopal school for boys, established in Raleigh in 1833, upon the sale of the property, Judge Duncan Cameron became the purchaser, and by his wish, and under his directions, St. Mary's school for girls became the successor of the Episcopal school for boys. Upon his death, Mr. Cameron succeeded to the property; and, carry-ing out with filial piety the wishes of his father, the institution under his solicitous care and liberal provision, has thriven without hinder-ance, and now after the lapse of nearly a half century, prosperous in unchecked vigor. The same interest, but with less happy issue, attached to the Military academy established near Hillsboro in 1859, by Col. C. C. Tew, and prospering as such through the war; then, with the fate that darkened all southern fortunes, falling into decay. The death of Col. Tew, who fell in the war, made necessary as soon as it was practicable to effect it, a settlement of his estate. A sale of the institute property was made, and Mr. Cameron became the pur-chaser. His purpose was to establish a school for boys of the highest grade in relation to classical, literary and business education, with a military feature recognized, but subordinate. With this view he secured for its conduct two gentlemen of the highest qualifications to be found in North Carolina — Mr. Ralph H. Graves and Mr. James H. Horner — both natives of the state, both graduates of its university, and both educators of long experience and repute. The school was opened under the brightest auspices, it prospered to the most sanguine expectations. Mr. Graves died very suddenly; the health of Mr. Horner completely failed him, and he was forced to abandon his work. Competent successors for two men so remarkably fitted for their duties could not readily be found, and after much and unsatisfactory efforts to that end, the doors of the school were closed and so remain to this day.

It was, however, in the welfare of the state university that the interest of Mr. Cameron was most actively enlisted. To this object he was thoroughly drawn by his own conception of duty. His grandfather — Mr. Richard Bennehan — was one of its founders and earliest benefactors. His father and his uncle were faithful trustees. He was a student under President Caldwell's administration, and, as the faculty of the university, recently further said, in tribute of his memory, a "friend and counselor under Swain, a father and guide under Battle." But it was in the dark days which overshadowed the university after the war that his interest was developed in its fullest intensity. Ruin, material and financial, menaced its existence. Its decay seemed inevitable, and for long duration the dismal catastrophe seemed certain. Happily, it was averted; and the university once again lifts its head as the great central light for the intellectual illumination of the commonwealth. No one lent his aid with more readiness, more earnestness, more efficiency than Mr. Cameron. He took upon himself, as the cherished mission of his latter days, the work of encouragement, of counsel, of supervision. His judicious and liberal pecuniary advancement to the work of repair resulted in the renovation or completion of dilapidated or unfinished buildings, and secured to the university the present possession of structures ample for existing needs, and worthy of the spirit and purpose that called them into existence. With none of those structures is the name of Mr. Cameron so closely identified as with the Memorial hall, that grand, capacious and unique monument to its long-time president of the university, David L. Swain — to all its great and good men — trustees, professors, alumni, who had reflected honor upon their *alma mater;* and most touchingly and appropriately to those of the latter who had gone forth at the call of patriotic duty, and laid down their lives for a cause sacred to them. Upon no one does the honor fall with more distinguished lustre than upon Mr. Cameron.

Mr. Cameron grew to regard the university with the solicitude with which a fond father watches the destiny of a loved and hopeful child. His visits to it were frequent, often on business more often from an affectionate wish to watch its gain in strength and growth in usefulness. It need not be suggested that he was never absent from any meeting of the board of trustees, or ever failed to respond to any invitation to attend any meeting of the faculty, to which he was frequently called in the capacity of adviser. At every commencement for years he was present, the most conspicuous figure amid thousands, his majestic person, his ruddy countenance aglow with health and resolution. His strong features, his noble brow and piercing eyes, crowned with a wealth of snow-white locks, formed a picture which was delightful to behold and which could not be easily forgotten. At the annual festivals, he was often called upon to speak, and he performed his duty with readiness, with dignity and with power; for he had fine gifts as a public speaker, which were always called into play whenever he spoke on commencement or other occasions. In fact he was a capital public speaker, always going to the point, commanding attention; always effective. In 1885 he delivered the oration at commencement on the dedication of Memorial hall; this was in his seventy-seventh year, yet his address was characterized by vigorous thought, deep feeling, scholarly diction. The year before he had generously supplied the funds necessary to complete the hall.

An evidence of the public estimate of the value of Mr. Cameron's services to the university is seen in the fact that he was unanimously elected chairman of the Alumni association, and continued for a succession of years against his earnest protest, as not being a graduate. In his habits he was plain and unostentatious, and in manners somewhat unconventional. This was the result of his characteristic honesty and directness. With him there was no pretense; no evasion; no subterfuge. A manly courage and an honest heart impelled him to speak out openly what he thought; to act out fearlessly what his judgment counseled as right and proper. What was apparent to all men was his unflinching honesty of purpose; his undeviating sense of justice; his exercised inflexibility, fairness and frankness. He stood among people an unobtrusive, yet undeniably a great man — adequate to meet any demands upon any one or all of his dominating qualities. He was possessed of a rare perpetuation of mental faculties in reference to the current public and local affairs, to the day of his final illness in the extremes of his old age. He watched the course of public events with intelligent solicitude; he scanned the public prints with sharpness of criticism; he received public policy, or the measures and conduct of public men, with just and keen discrimination; he observed with intelligent eye the questions in which the good of the state was involved, and in social life he was no less the same careful, accomplished and distinguished man.

Death came to him later than to most men. Mr. Cameron died at his residence in Hillsboro, January 6, 1891. He was interred in the cemetery of St. Matthews church adjacent to his own beautiful grounds, and under the evergreens he had planted and nurtured. The funeral was of that imposing kind appropriate to the character and disposition of the deceased; and was attended by the governor of the state and other officials and prominent gentlemen, of Raleigh, of Durham; by almost the entire population of Hillsboro, his home, and by the president, some of the faculty and a deputation of students of the university. Relatives from abroad, as well as the members of his household, swelled the solemn and imposing cortege. A striking feature of the solemnities of the funeral was the presence of a large body of the former slaves of the deceased; some of them grown when they became freemen; others, children at the time of liberation; and many of them continuing in his service until his death. With affectionate remembrance, they gathered around the remains to render their last tribute to their old master and life-long friend. Surely there is some vivifying spirit in slavery which could thus so perpetuate in all their freshness and strength, loving and gentle emotions, in the hearts of the slaves, sometimes ignorantly and unjustly assumed to be unnatural and impossible.

Mr. Cameron, on the 20th of December, 1832, married Anne, daughter of Thomas Ruffin, who was a distinguished jurist and chief-justice of North Carolina. He passed a happy wedded life of a little more than fifty-nine years; his domestic relations were most happy. A large family blessed a happy union. Two children, the first-born, died in infancy; a daughter, Mary, died at the age of twelve or fourteen. all the others reached maturity. His eldest son, Duncan, married Mary, daughter of Col. H. B. Short, and died in 1886, at the age of thirty-seven, leaving three children. His son, Bennehan, his daughter Annie, wife of Maj. George Collins; Margaret, wife of Capt. Robert B. Peebles; Pauline, wife of Mr. William B. Shepherd, and Mildred, unmarried, are the surviving children. Rebecca, wife of Maj. John W. Graham, died some years ago, leaving six children. Such is the outline of the life of one whose impression upon his times will not soon be effaced, whose strong personality is stamped on features not to be forgotten, and whose influence for good will long act upon those who fell within his sphere. The lines of the poet Armstrong furnishes of him an illustration so nearly apt, that in conclusion we quote them:

"Though old, he still retained
His manly sense, and energy of mind;
Virtuous and wise he was, but not severe;
He still remembered that he once was young;
His easy presence checked no decent joy,
Him even the dissolute admired; for he
A graceful looseness when he pleased put on,
And laughing, could instruct."

HON. JAMES M. WINSTEAD,

of Greensboro, N. C., belongs to one of the oldest and most influential families of that state, whose members have at different times held high positions in the state and national governments, always with unquestioned character and ability. His father, Samuel Winstead, was born in Person county, N. C., where he died in 1829, having been engaged in agriculture all his life. In 1804 he married Miss Elizabeth Sergeant, and by her had thirteen children, of whom five are now living, viz.: Alexander, born June 11, 1809, now of Person county;

William G., born in 1814; Henry J., born in 1818; Charles S., born in 1822, and James M., the subject of this sketch. His mother died June 28, 1863, being seventy-nine years of age. James M. Winstead was born in Person county, N. C., May 10, 1824, and received his education in the schools of his native county. At the age of thirteen he was employed in a store at Sergeantsville, where he remained for two years. He then went to Danville, Va., and after two years spent in a store at that place, came to Madison, N. C., where he clerked for four years. After this he returned to Person county, and embarked with his brother in the mercantile business. In the course of four years he sold out his interest in this business, and turned his attention to speculating. At the beginning of the war he was engaged in planting, and also took government contracts. In 1862 he was appointed one of the assistant state treasurers and government depositaries under the Confederate States.

After the close of the war, Mr. Winstead embarked in the tobacco trade, which he successfully carried on until 1870. In the latter year he went to Greensboro to accept the position of chief deputy collector under his brother, Charles S. Winstead, who was United States collector of internal revenue. This position he held for seven years, being practically in charge of the office. In 1878 he visited the city of Atlanta, Ga., and there established and successfully managed a wholesale drug business for four years. He subsequently returned to Greensboro, and in 1887, on the organization of the People's Five Cents Savings bank, was elected its president, and in 1889 became cashier and director of the Piedmont bank. These positions he still holds; and is also a member of the firm of E. D. Winstead & Co., of Milton, N. C., manufacturers of tobacco, and president of the Henry P. Scales Tobacco company, of Atlanta, Ga. In 1875, he married Mrs. Maria A. Scales, daughter of Pleasant Black, a successful merchant of Madison, N. C. Mr. Winstead was independent in politics until prohibition became a political issue in North Carolina. Then, actuated by what he believed a controlling principle of individual conduct, he joined the prohibition party, and became its candidate for congress in 1886. The large and complimentary vote he received from the best element of both the old political parties, showed the high esteem in which he is held. It is almost needless to say that so long and active a life, joined with such high qualities of head and heart, have brought wealth and position; and that he is universally regarded as one of the ablest and safest business men of his state, exercising a widespread influence even beyond its borders.

F. W. KERCHNER.

The gentleman who forms the subject of this sketch has been closely identified with the business interests of Wilmington for twenty-six years, and is noted for his thorough business qualifications, sterling integrity and liberality, and during a business career of many years, he has fully sustained his reputation. Col. F. W. Kerchner occupies a prominent position here as promoting most materially the mercantile importance of this city and port. The importance of the cotton trade of Wilmington, and its great influence upon the prosperity of the community has been a frequent subject of comment, but not until each separate venture in this line of trade is examined, is the true magnitude of the industry understood and appreciated, and in this connection we must chronicle the establishment of Col. Kerchner's business, which he established in 1865 just after the close of the war; afterward associating with him in business Messrs. Calder Bros., which firm transacted a large wholesale grocery and commission business, and also dealing in cotton and fertilizers, until November, 1886, when the firm dissolved, and Col. Kerchner continued the cotton and commission business, in which enterprising industry he commands the confidence and trade of influential merchants throughout North and South Carolina.

Col. F. W. Kerchner is the efficient and enthusiastic president of the chamber of commerce, which position he holds with honor and credit to himself, and the satisfaction of the community. He was formerly a citizen of Baltimore, but since his adoption of this city as his home, in 1865, he has always been alive to her interests and contributed materially to her progress and advancement, assisting with brains and means to elevate all worthy industries, animating others by his example and efforts. He is a worthy citizen and holds a high position in the public estimation. He is a director in several of the enterprises he has established, and still takes an active part in all of them. Through his intimate business knowledge he has given material assistance to all of them and they have proven successful. He was an ardent supporter of the cause of the south during our Civil war, and he gave liberally of his time and his means to insure its success, and frequently at great personal risks to himself. He is now at the head of a wholesale hardware house, of Gleaves Hardware company, one of the most reliable houses in North Carolina, and doing a large and lucrative business. There are few men better known in the state than F. W. Kerchner, his genial manner and generous impulses have made him troops of friends and he has a faculty, a very happy one it is too, of retaining friendships when once formed. He is now in the vigor of life and with every prospect for a long and useful career.

CHARLES W. RANEY.

Among the many intelligent and enterprising business men of Vance county, N. C., may be found the name of Charles W. Raney. Mr. Raney has been a resident of North Carolina since his fourth year, having been brought to Granville county from Virginia by his parents about the year 1843. He was born in Mecklenburg county, Va., on the 5th of December, 1839. In 1861 he left the South Lowell academy, in Orange county, to enlist in the Confederate army, having joined Company B, Twelfth North Carolina infantry, in April of that

B—23

year. Until 1862 he remained with that company, when he was transferred to the Fifth North Carolina cavalry, and served until the surrender at Appomatox. The battles of Hanover Court House, Reams'
Station and numerous other engagements found him at his post. In
1864 Mr. Raney was detailed as a clerk in the office of Assistant
Inspector-General Dabney, and he remained in that capacity until
the end came. After the war he went to Kittrell, N. C., and until
1870 was engaged in agriculture. In the latter year he became one
of the proprietors of the Kittrell Springs hotel, at Kittrell, and after
one year spent in the hotel business, embarked in the mercantile
trade at the same place. In 1875 he turned his attention to the cotton
industry, and has since been engaged in that business with marked
success. He owns large farming interests in Vance county, carries
on an extensive guano enterprise and gins some 1,200 bales of cotton
per year. Mr. Raney was united in marriage in 1866, to Miss Sallie C.,
daughter of George Kittrell, who was one of the wealthiest and most
prominent farmers in that portion of the state. Mr. Raney is a
Mason. It is to such men that Vance county owes its increasing prosperity and importance as a great farming community and coming
commercial center.

JONATHAN McGEE HECK.

The Heck family, noted from its earliest history for its devotion to
religious and political liberty, came to the new world seeking both in
1727. Johann Jacob Heck, son of Johann Jost and Eva Maria Heck, with
400 other members, as their ancestors had been before them since
1560, of the German Reform church, left his home in the German
platinate and found shelter in the hospitable province of Pennsylvania. Moving westward the little colony reached the county of Bercks
(Berks) and here built their new homes, around their little church, fit
emblem of that religion for which they had sacrificed so much. Here
Johann Jacob Heck married his wife Judith, and here was born to
them in 1754 their son, Johann Jost Heck. The baptismal certificate
of his birth, still in the possession of the family, is a curious old document, illustrative of the state of the art of drawing and illuminated
penmanship in the colony. Johann Jost Heck was in the prime of
his young manhood, when the first drum calls of the war of the Revolution echoed through the land, and found him ready to answer its
dread summons. Joining the army, he fought under Gen. Washington at the battle of Long Island, and followed his varying fortunes
until the glorious victory at the surrender of Yorktown. After the
declaration of peace he and his young wife, Rachel, moved westward,
living a few years in Maryland, but finally settling in that part of
Virginia (since the war West Virginia), which afterward became
Monongalia county. Among the first to reach this then far west there
was many a hard battle to be fought with wild nature and with
wilder savages. Nevertheless, indomitable energy prevailed and the
land which became valuable under his management is still the prop-

erty of the Heck family. Here his ten children were born. The eldest, Jacob Jost, born in 1792, had not reached his majority when again the alarm of war made the young republic shudder. Young as he was, he was one of the first volunteers of the war of 1812. But a more deadly enemy than British bullets was to cut short the young soldier's career. He died, one of the fever's many victims, in Norfolk, Va. The eldest born fallen, his next brother, Adam, a mere lad, was ready to take his place and was marching to the front when the glad news of peace flew over the land. George Heck, seventh son of Johann Jost Heck, and father of the subject of this sketch, was born in 1803 and was married to Susan McGee in 1827. A quiet man, of great power of purpose, breadth of thought, religious conviction and personal strength, the unwritten life of George Heck is one of those which goes to make our country what it is to-day — the greatest of nations.

His second son, Jonathan McGee Heck, was born May 5, 1831. Educated in the best schools which the neighborhood afforded, he sought higher education in Rector college, then one of the best schools of all that region. Leaving college, he determined to enter the profession of the law, and for this purpose studied law with Hon. Edgar C. Wilson, of Virginia, in Morgantown, the county seat of Monongalia county. Admitted to the bar, he had soon a large and growing practice, and at the beginning of the war was commonwealth's attorney. On March 10, 1859, he was married to Mattie A. Callendine, daughter of Martin B. and Anna Callendine, and a descendant of the Scudder family of New Jersey. Elected colonel of the militia, it was one of his chief pleasures to perfect his regiment in military exercises, especially that company called for him the " Heck Riflemen." But sterner deeds of war were near, though they litttle thought how near, and already this border land between north and south was torn with internecine dissension. From the first, Col. Heck was a firm believer in the sovereignty of the states, and believed he owed his first allegiance to the state of Virginia. With growing anxiety he watched the course of events, every personal interest of home and property being with the north, but every conviction of duty to his country being with the south. The final crash came, and leaving his young wife and child and the handsome home which he had provided for them, renouncing all his former ambitions and accumulated wealth, he came to Richmond, and once and forever cast his lot with that of the southern states. Before the Virginia troops were transferred to the Confederacy he received his commission of colonel from Gov. Letcher, of Virginia. He was then sent by Gen. R. E. Lee to the valley of Virginia to raise and equip a regiment. This he succeeded in doing winning much praise from his superiors in rank for his promptness and determination. Perhaps a finer body of men was never collected than this Thirty-first regiment, but it may be well to add, as a matter of history, that Virginia was obliged to arm them with old flintlock muskets. With this regiment he marched to meet the large army under

Gen. McClellan, which was then marching into Virginia from Ohio. After the battle of Rich Mountain he was, with others, paroled by Gen. McClellan, and for some unaccountable reason, was held under parole long after those with him were allowed to return to active service. During this period he was sent by the soldiers from his section, to the Virginia convention, where, with many of her bravest and best, he was a signer of the celebrated declaration of secession. As soon after as his parole would allow, he again gave his best efforts to actively pushing forward the cause he had espoused, his organizing and mechanical ability making him very successful in the collection and manufacture of the munitions of war for the Confederate government. Having been allowed through the personal kindness of Gen. McClellan, to bring his family through the enemy's lines, he located with them in Raleigh, N. C., where with the exception of two years, he has ever since resided. Having purchased the large and then far-famed health resort, Jones's Springs, in Warren county, he with generous-hearted liberality threw it open to the many homeless refugees, who were then seeking refuge in North Carolina.

Crushed, but not broken by the issue of the war and the fearful period of "reconstruction," he set to work from the wreck of old things to create for himself a new fortune, and, as far as in him lay, for his country a new south. With Hon. K. P. Battle, Dr. W. J. Hawkins and Capt. P. B. Williamson, like liberal-minded men, he formed a company whose purpose was the peopling of the deserted fields of the south with northern emigrants. Thus while raising the fallen fortunes of their loved south, they hoped to hasten the healing of the yawning chasm war had torn between the two sections. For this purpose they began the edition of a paper, opened a land office in New York, and would have been eminently successful but for the rife rumor of confiscating all southern lands. Finding that for the present they could expect no help but in the south's own ability to regain her lost position, this attempt was abandoned and Col. Heck and his partners returned to North Carolina. Here he became interested in southern farming and mineral land, and in the latter his chief wealth now consists, owning large and valuable iron property in North Carolina, copper in Virginia, and coal in Tennessee. As his fortunes rose he was a liberal contributor to many causes for his town and state; he with one other gentleman giving the money to build the handsome library and society halls at the Wake Forest college, helping to establish a female college in Raleigh, assisting in the re-organization of the state agricultural association, offering a handsome house and property for a North Carolina Confederate soldiers' home, etc. A Baptist and member of the First Baptist church of Raleigh, he has been honored by his denomination by being made president of the Baptist state convention, state Sunday-school convention, etc. Blessed with a large family, his sons are: George C. Heck, John M. Heck, William Harry Heck and Charles M. Heck, and his daughters are: Mary Lou Heck (Mrs. W. H. Pace), Minnie Callendine Heck (Mrs. B. G. Cowper), Mattie A. Heck (Mrs. J. D. Boushall), Fannie E. Scudder Heck,

Susie McGee Heck and Pearl Chadwick Heck. While in the state of his adoption Col. Heck has never sought or held any political office; it is but just to say that few men have had her interests more at heart, few made her welfare more their first thought, and few who will leave a deeper impress for noble manhood and unfaltering integrity upon her annals.

FRANCIS HAWKS CAMERON

was born in Hillsboro, Orange county, N. C., June 1, 1839, and received his early education at Caldwell institute, at that place. He then attended the academy at Newbern for two years, and in 1855 entered the United States service. At the breaking out of the war he was stationed north on coast survey duty, but upon the bombardment of Fort Sumter he promptly resigned his position in the Federal service and returning home in April, 1861, at once tendered his services to the Confederate authorities, receiving the commission of lieutenant in the regular service. His first duty under the Confederacy was at Pensacola, Fla., under Gen. Bragg, who was then organizing what was afterward known as the Army of the West. It was while stationed at Pensacola that Lieut. Cameron volunteered for duty and served on the expedition commanded by Col. Stevens, of the engineer corps, who performed the dangerous work of placing obstructions in the harbor and blocking the channel immediately under the guns of forts Pickens and Barrancos. In the fall of 1861 he was assigned to duty on the coast of South Carolina and Georgia, and participated in the battles of Port Royal and many other minor engagements.

Early in 1862, Lieut. Cameron's command (First battalion of Marines) was ordered to Virginia, and was in the engagement at Drury's Bluff, when the monitors were successfully repulsed. Then in the seven days' fight around Richmond, and in numerous engagements on James river, at Harrison's Landing, Bermuda Hundreds, and at the second battle of Drury's Bluff, when Gen. Benjamin F. Butler was repulsed, and his attempts to capture Richmond defeated. In this last named battle, Cameron commanded the left wing of the Confederate skirmish line, and though unsupported and greatly outnumbered by the enemy in his front, who several times nearly succeeded in turning his flanks, he stubbornly held his ground, and succeeded in repulsing every attempt made to force his line. After this campaign, Lieut. Cameron was in command of "Camp Beall," at Drury's Bluff, for some months. He was then at the opening of the last campaign, and with his command and other forces, covered the retreat of Lee's army at High Bridge, when the rear guard suffered so severely. His command formed part of the rear guard during the entire retreat to Appomatox, and suffered heavily, losing over eighty per cent. in killed wounded and prisoners. On the morning of the 10th of April, they were at the front and took part in the last forward movement made by the Confederate army, a few hours before its surrender.

With the return of peace Mr. Cameron settled in Wilmington, engaging in the insurance business. In 1873 having married Miss Haywood of Raleigh, he moved to the state capital, where he has since resided, continuing in the insurance business, in which but few men in the state are better known, or have a larger acquaintance. In 1878, he was elected captain of the Raleigh light infantry, and the next year, 1879, he was appointed inspector-general of North Carolina by Gov. Jarvis, which office he held until the spring of 1891, when he tendered his resignation. During this time he manifested a deep interest in the state guard, which indeed may be said to owe its efficiency and perpetuation to his zeal in its behalf. As the inspector-general, he visited every company frequently, and his inspections were rigid, requiring a strict compliance with the regulations. He has not hesitated to cause some of the favorite companies to be dropped from the roll, and his enforcement of proper discipline while highly creditable to himself has been most salutary in promoting the efficiency of the corps. At the time of his resignation, he was oldest in commission of the inspector-generals of the states in the Union, and was confessedly one of most zealous and efficient of them. His resignation called from the members of the state guard many expressions of regret.

In 1878 Col. Cameron was a delegate to the national convention of the board of trade that convened in New Orleans, where he represented North Carolina with intelligence and credit. Col. Cameron is a gentleman of the nicest sense of honor, and of the highest social standing. Associated from his boyhood with military officers of the regular service he has cherished those refinements of conduct and carriage for which many of these gentlemen were noted. In 1871 Col. Cameron married Margaret N. Haywood, a daughter of the late United States Senator Haywood, of Raleigh, N. C., and to them were born two sons. His first wife dying in 1879, he was married again in 1881 to Miss Eugenie L. Weaver, of Selma, Ala., and by whom he has had several children. Col. Cameron, while much occupied by his attention to his insurance business which keeps him much away from home inspecting agencies, settling claims, etc., has not been neglectful of other duties. He is a member of the Masonic order, being a thirty-second degree Mason, and for years was vestryman in Christ church parish, at Raleigh, N. C. He was also for some years a director and member of the executive committee of the North Carolina insane asylum, at Raleigh, and for three successive terms was elected president of the southern chamber of life insurance and of the local board of underwriters at Raleigh.

As his name indicates, Col. Cameron is of Scotch descent. His father, Mr. John Cameron, was born near Petersburg, Va., about the year 1812, and came to North Carolina when quite a child with his parents who were the owners of considerable landed property in Orange county when they settled. He was educated at the University of North Carolina and was a gentleman of fine attainments and elegant scholarship. He married in 1837, Frances, daughter of Francis Hawks, Esq., of Newbern, a lady of rare social and intellectual attainments, and had by her, two children: Francis Hawks Cameron and John M. Cameron. He died at his residence "Lochiel," near Hillsboro, N. C., in August, 1883. Mrs. Cameron died in 1857. The grandfather of Col. Cameron was William Cameron, who was born in Virginia, and came to North Carolina about 1825, locating in Orange county, where he was an extensive planter. He married Annie, only daughter of Hon. Daniel Call, of Richmond, Va., one of the most eminent jurists of his day, and for many years a partner in the practice of the law with his distinguished brother-in-law, the late Chief-Justice Marshall, of Virginia. Mr. William Cameron's father was the Rev. Dr. John Cameron, who belonged to the clan Cameron, and who emigrated from Scotland to America about 1745, after the battle of Culloden, settling near Petersburg, Va. There Blandforch church was soon after built, the material being brought from England, and he was appointed rector of it. He was a minister of the established church, a man of great learning and unusual piety and was a preacher of renown in his time. He married Miss Ann Owen Nash, a niece of Gen. Francis Nash, of Revolutionary fame, killed at the battle of Germantown.

The mother of Col. Cameron, nee Frances S. Hawks, was a sister of Bishop Cicero Hawks, bishop of the diocese of Missouri, and of Rev. Dr. Francis L. Hawks, rector of Calvary church, New York, one of the most eloquent and distinguished ministers of the Episcopal church; and also of Rev. Dr. William N. Hawks, for many years rector of the Episcopal church at Newbern, and afterward at Columbus, Ga., where he died. We should mention that the brothers of William Cameron, the grandfather of Col. Cameron, were Judge Duncan Cameron, for many years a judge of the superior court of North Carolina, and then president of the State bank of North Carolina; and Judge J. A. Cameron, who was a member of the supreme court of Florida for many years; and who was lost at sea many years ago, on the ill-fated steamer, Pulaski; and Dr. Thomas N. Cameron, of Fayetteville, N. C. With an ancestry and relations so distinguished, as might be expected, Col. Cameron has maintained through life a highly honorable character and is known among the gentlemen of the state as no less upright in his business dealings than chivalrous and polished in his social intercourse.

JAMES R. YOUNG,

one of the most successful and efficient insurance men of Vance county, N. C., is a native of North Carolina, having been born at Oxford, on the 17th of February, 1853. In 1870 he was graduated from the Hampden-Sidney college in Virginia, and after graduating returned to Oxford and secured a clerkship in the drug store of T. D. Crawford & Co., with whom he remained for about eighteen months. At the expiration of that time Mr. Young removed to Henderson — about 1873 — and opened a drug store in partnership with D. Y.

Cooper and H. Lassiter, the firm existing until 1882. In 1881 Mr. Young was elected clerk of the Vance county superior court, and served in that honorable position until December, 1890. In 1877 he became interested in the real estate and insurance business in a small way, but has since succeeded in building up a large and constantly increasing business. Mr. Young is active, not only in state but religious work. He is a stirring Sunday-school worker, and is also one of the most prominent workers in the state in the Young Mens' Christian association, being president of the state convention in 1890. Mr. Young is a member of the I. O. O. F., and also of the Masonic order. His father, Dr. Peter Wesley Young, was born in Granville county, N. C., in 1832. He was graduated from the medical department of the University of Pennsylvania. During the late war he served in the army of northern Virginia from its commencement until the surrender at Appomatox, having been surgeon of the brigade commanded by Ex-Gov. Scales, of North Carolina. In 1852 he married Miss Jane Cooper, daughter of J. C. Cooper, of Granville county, N. C. The father died in 1886. His father was David Young, of Granville county, N. C. He was a merchant during his active life, and died in Granville county about 1850.

JOHN W. THOMPSON,

one of the most popular citizens of Wake county, is now clerk of the superior court for that county. He was born in Wake, August 27, 1850, and after attending the local schools was duly entered at Wake Forest college. Leaving that institution in 1868 he engaged in mercantile business at Wake Forest, and was afterward in the lumber business. Mr. Thompson, springing from an influential family and being an ardent democrat, soon attained local prominence in party councils and in 1880 he served with fidelity and efficiency as the chairman of the county executive committee. In the following year he was appointed to the responsible position of steward and purchasing agent of the North Carolina insane asylum, which position he held until 1889, when he preferred charges against the superintendent, Dr. Grissom, for improper conduct, and a trial resulted that excited more interest throughout the state than any other trial that has ever occurred within her borders. Mr. Thompson's conduct throughout the affair was highly commended as honorable and manly and patriotic. On his retirement from the asylum, Mr. Thompson acted as general manager of the Manhattan Life insurance company, for North Carolina; but the people desired his services in a public capacity, and in the very exciting political year of 1890, when the farmers' alliance was in full control of the county and party spirit ran high, Mr. Thompson was selected over the president of the county alliance for the nomination of clerk, and in November, he was triumphantly elected over a republican nominee who had held the position for twelve years, whom many supposed it was quite impossible to beat. This important office he now fills to the satisfaction of the public, being well equipped to discharge its responsible functions, having served for several years in the capacity of a justice of the peace. In February, 1874, Mr. Thompson was united in marriage to Sallie J. Ellington, daughter of J. McC. Ellington, of Chatham county, and to them have been born five children: Lillian, Daisy, Herbert C., John S, and Francis V. Thompson. Mr. Thompson is a gentleman of kindly disposition and pleasing address. He is full of the milk of human kindness and seeks to do good to his fellowmen. He is an active member of the Masonic fraternity, Raleigh commandery No. 4, K. T., Enoch council, Raleigh chapter Royal Arch Masons, and is past master of William G. Hill lodge, No. 218, A. F. & A. M. He is also an Odd Fellow, being a member of Seaton Gales lodge, 64, I. O. O. F., of Raleigh. In 1888 Mr Thompson was a delegate to the convention of the young men's national democratic club, which met at Baltimore, Md., in July of that year, and took a prominent part in the proceedings of that body. He was honored by being selected as vice-president of the convention for the state of North Carolina.

The father of Mr. Thompson, was Michael Thompson, who was born in Wake county, N. C., in 1816. He was a farmer and stood high in his county, for many years being a magistrate. He married Martha J. Crenshaw, daughter of William Crenshaw, Esq., and to them were born ten children, of whom five survive: Isabella C. Thompson, Glovenia M., wife of James S. West, Esq., of Raleigh; John W. Thompson, and Dr. S. W. Thompson, of Wake county, and James C. Thompson, of Raleigh. Mr. Michael Thompson died in 1877, and his widow survived him but a year.

WILLIAM J. HICKS

is one of those self-made men, who by application and native ability, have risen to prominence in their calling. He was born in Spottsylvania county, Va., February 18, 1827. During his youth he enjoyed no educational advantages, but after attaining manhood he went to school during the winter season, when his work was interrupted. In 1849 he engaged in the quarrying and stonecutting business in Louisa City, Va., and so continued for two years, gaining valuable experience that was to stand him in good stead in after life. He was led, however, to learn the millwright and carpenter's trades, and worked in that line some three years, when he was engaged by a New York firm to put up its machinery in their gold mine, near Greensboro, in Guilford county, N. C. This led to his residence in that part of the state for a couple of years, when he was employed in putting machinery in the Neuse papermill, on Neuse river, Wake county. When that had been satisfactorily accomplished, he located permanently in Raleigh, where he has since resided. He at first followed the busi-

ness of contractor to build houses, and while so engaged, was early in
1862, selected to erect a powdermill near Raleigh, and he remained as
superintendent of the mill, making powder; which was the best small-
arm powder by far, that the Confederate States had, until the close
of the war. He then engaged in the resin business for a year or so,
when he again undertook the work of a contractor, and was so engaged until August, 1869. At that time he was appointed by the
directors of the penitentiary, to be superintendent and assistant architect of that work. The location near Raleigh was determined on, and
ground was soon broken for the buildings. Col. Hicks's judgment
and experience were relied on to a large degree in deciding on the
details of construction, and without injustice to others it may be said
that the North Carolina penitentiary was more his creation than that
of any other person. In 1872 he was elected warden and architect of
the penitentiary, which position he has ever since held, establishing
himself year by year more firmly in the confidence of the authorities
and of the state legislature.

Col. Hicks' sound judgment has led to his being consulted on various occasions and matters not connected with this work; and he
has for years been a member of the state agricultural society. He has
ever been an active worker in the advancement of Raleigh's prosperity, and he is a stockholder in the Raleigh Wagon company and in the
Raleigh Savings bank, of which indeed he was a director until he
resigned that position. He is also a member of the Masonic order,
being a thirty-second degree Mason and nine degrees in the York
rite, and he has filled all the chairs in the council and the chapter.

Col. Hicks is a member of the Baptist church and stands high
among the people of Raleigh for a consistent walk in life. It goes
without saying that one who has been in continuous office under the
state government for twenty years is associated, politically, with the
dominant party, and Col. Hicks is a democrat in his political faith.
Col. Hicks was married in 1858 to Julia L. Harrison, daughter of Col.
John R. Harrison, of Raleigh, and to them have been born eight children, of whom five survive, viz.: John M. W. Hicks, of New York;
William B. Hicks, of Moore county, N. C.; Julia F., wife of Dr. A. J.
Buffalo, of Raleigh; Elizabeth W. and Bertha M. Hicks. The father
of our subject was Martin Hicks, a native of Spottsylvania county, Va.,
born in 1797. He was a farmer. He married about 1813, Nancy, a
daughter of Robert Pendleton of the same county, by whom he had
eight children, of whom but two now survive — Francis R. Hicks and
Col. Hicks. He died in 1849, his wife having died about 1825. Col.
Hicks' grandfather was Peter Hicks, who was a native of Virginia,
where he was born about 1750. He was of English descent, his father
being born in England in 1720 and coming to Virginia in early manhood. He, too, was a farmer; he was also high sheriff of Spottsylvania
county for a number of years, and he served in the Revolutionary
war. He attained a great age and passed away in 1844, much
esteemed and venerated in his community.

R. D. SPAIGHT.

Richard Dobbs Spaight, governor, was born in Newbern, N. C., March 25, 1758. His father, Richard Spaight, in provincial times, was secretary and clerk of the crown. His mother was the sister of Arthur Dobbs, for more than ten years governor of the province. He was left an orphan at a tender age, and was sent abroad to be educated when only nine years old. He pursued his academic studies in Ireland, entered the University of Glasgow, from which he graduated in 1778. He returned to his native land to find it in the midst of a war for its separation from the mother country. Though not of age, he immediately volunteered in the service of his country, and was appointed aide on the staff of Gen. Richard Caswell. He was present with that general at the battle of Camden, August 16, 1780. He was a brave and gallant soldier, but he had talents which so aptly fitted him for a legislator that he was elected as a member of the general assembly to represent the Newbern district. He was re-elected in 1782 and 1783. He was then chosen a member of congress and appointed upon a committee to devise a temporary form of government for the western territory. He was a member of the convention to frame the Federal constitution, and was one of the most active and useful members of that body; he was also a member of the North Carolina state convention which met at Hillsboro, July 21, 1788, to consider the constitution he had aided in framing, and was an ardent advocate of its adoption by the state, although he had identified himself with the Jeffersonian democracy and believed in the sovereignty of the states. But he could not prevail upon the convention to adopt the constitution. All this time he was in correspondence with Gen. Washington upon the subject, and it was through a visit to North Carolina of Gen. Washington, on the invitation of Mr. Spaight, that by their combined counsels, the state reconsidered its action, and on the 21st of November, 1789, adopted the constitution. This was one of the triumphs of cool, dispassionate and conciliatory measures to effect an object which was not practicable by the exercise of less judgment and good sense.

In 1792 Mr. Spaight was again elected to the general assembly, by which body he was immediately chosen governor—the first native citizen that had ever before held that office. While holding the office of chief magistrate he was chosen a presidential elector, and again in 1797 he held that office. He was elected a member of congress in 1797, holding the office for two terms, when he was again returned to the state senate. This proved to be his last election. In those days politics ran high, legislative discussions were earnest and often acrimonious. In a dispute of this nature Gov. Spaight and John Stanly, political opponents, became involved in an excited controversy; Stanly sent a taunting and offensive challenge to his adversary, which was accepted. The duel occurred September 5, 1802, and Spaight was mortally wounded, surviving but a single day after the rencontre. This tragic and truly lamentable occurrence deprived the state and the nation of one of their wisest and most brilliant statesmen and counselors, and threw a beloved family into the deepest mourning. At his funeral his eulogist, Rev. T. P. Irving, said of him:

"Uniform in his conduct, respectful to authority, and influential in his example, hospitality was conspicuous trait of his character. The stranger was welcome, treated with cordiality and entertained with kindness. His charity was universal. For the tale of sorrow he ever had a tear of relief. He was an effectionate husband, an indulgent father, and a compassionate master, consistent in his hours of study and recreation, no irregularities disturbed his course, or improper indulgence his repose." Gov. Spaight married Miss Polly Leach who bore him three sons and one daughter; the latter, Margaret became the wife of Hon. John R. Donnel, one of the state judges. Two sons died, one in infancy and one unmarried, Richard Dobbs, the second son, was a leading statesman, member of the legislature, of congress and governor of the state. He too died unmarried.

CHARLES B. ROOT,

one of the leading citizens of North Carolina, was born at Montague, Mass., October 31, 1818. He was given good educational advantages and was a student in the academy at Greenfield, Mass., until his seventeenth year, when he went to New York city, but almost immediately after removed to Raleigh, N. C. Arriving in Raleigh in 1837, he engaged in trade. For five years he had charge of the business owned by Bernard Dupuy, whom he subsequently bought out. In 1860 Mr. Root sold the concern, and never again engaged in business. Immediately after the war, he was elected president of the Raleigh gas company, and for eighteen years served in that capacity. In 1884 he was elected city tax collector of Raleigh and still holds that office. He has served as a county commissioner, having been chairman of the board, for many years he has been a magistrate and for fifteen years was a city alderman. For two years he was mayor of Raleigh, having been elected to that office by the democratic party, of which he has ever been a firm adherent. Mr. Root was married in 1848, to Miss Anna Freeman Gales, daughter of Weston R. Gales, of Raleigh, and a niece of Joseph Gales, editor of the old *National Intelligencer*. Three children are the fruit of this happy union: Love Gales, wife of Dr. V. E. Turner, of Raleigh, N. C., and Charles, also of Raleigh, and another child now deceased. Mr. Root is regarded as one of the leading business men of the state. His whole career has been marked by great ability and sterling integrity. He is descended from one of the oldest and most distinguished of the New England families.

His father was Elihu Root, who was born in Montague, Mass., in 1767. He was a speculator, and engaged in various pursuits, although principally interested in agriculture. He filled nearly all the munici pal offices of Montague, and was generally esteemed throughout the community. In 1804 he was married to Miss Sophia Gunn, daughter of Samuel Gunn, who was a Revolutionary soldier. Their children were five, but one of whom now survives. The father died in 1859, and the mother in 1821. Elihu was the son of Moses, a native of Montague, Mass., where he was born in 1742. He was a farmer and large landed proprietor. His death occurred December 17, 1817. His father was Capt. Joseph Root, also a native of Montague, where he first saw the light in 1713. He died April 24, 1781. He was the son of Joseph, born July 3, 1686, in Northampton; died February 16, 1710. He was the son of Joseph Root, whose birth occurred at Northampton on the 15th of January, 1664, where he died October 23, 1690. His father was also named Joseph. The latter was a native of the state of Connecticut, having come into the world in Hartford, that state, in 1637. His demise occurred January 28, 1691. All these honored sires were farmers, and were active in the development of the New England states. As tillers of the soil they helped form the backbone of the community, and as large land owners had a voice in the formation of the country. Thomas Root was born in England January 16, 1605, and sought a new home in America in 1637. He was one of the first settlers of Hartford, Conn., where he became a leading spirit. He died on his farm in 1694.

JOHN M. HORAH,

one of the oldest and best known citizens of Salisbury, N. C., was born in that city March 18, 1824. His father was William H. Horah, also a native of Salisbury, and he was the son of Hugh Horah, who was likewise born in the same city. He was the son of Henry Horah, a native of Ireland who came to this country in an early day, not later than 1750, settling in Salisbury, where he lived many years, devoted, it is believed, to farming. Henry Horah had two sons and one daughter, Hugh, Henry and Esther, who married William Brandon. Hugh Horah was a silver-smith by occupation, and lived and died in Salisbury, leaving one son, William H. Horah, who was the father of the subject of this sketch. His early occupation was that of a silver-smith, but for many years afterward he was cashier of the state bank at Salisbury, which was wound up in 1833 or 1834. He then engaged as a clerk in the Cape Fear bank, a branch being established at Salisbury. He was the father of twelve children, and died in 1863. In 1814 or 1815 Mr. William H. Horah was married to Louisa Furr. John M. Horah was reared in Salisbury, here acquiring an academic education, and beginning his business life at the age of eighteen as a clerk in a store. In 1846 he went into the branch bank of Cape Fear at Salisbury, as clerk. This bank was wound up in 1864 or 1865, and he then engaged as clerk with S. H. Wiley, internal revenue collector for seven years, during which he established a first class reputation as a business man. In 1874 he was elected clerk of the superior court

for Rowan county, and retained that office for sixteen years, discharging his duties with credit to himself and to the satisfaction of
the public. He is now a deputy clerk in the same office. Mr. Horah
is a man of sterling qualities and is highly respected by his fellow
citizens. In 1847 Mr. Horah was united in marriage with Miss
Margaret S. Ballard, and by her has had three children, a daughter
and two sons. His family are all members of the Presbyterian church.
He would have joined the Confederate army in defense of his state
during the Civil war, but was examined and rejected because of physical disability.

JAMES H. RAMSAY,

the subject of this brief sketch, was born in Rowan county, N. C.,
February 9, 1855. He is the son of Dr. James G. Ramsay, a sketch of
whom will be found elsewhere in this volume. His early life was
spent upon the farm of his father in Rowan county, where he gained
a thorough academic education. He spent one year as a teacher in
his native county, and in 1875, accepted a position as bookkeeper
and general manager of the mercantile business of Ford & Fowler,
and bookkeeper for the tobacco manufacturing business of Ford &
Company of South River, N. C. In 1880 he engaged as bookkeeper
for Merroney Bros., general merchants at Salisbury. In 1881 he took a
clerkship in the office of the internal revenue collector for the western
district of North Carolina, at Statesville. Eighteen months later he
was appointed by President Arthur as postmaster at Salisbury, which
position he held till in July, 1885, when he was superceded by the ap-
pointee of the Cleveland administration. Mr. Ramsay returned to
the occupation of bookkeeper for Merroney Bros., of Salisbury, with
whom he remained till the spring of 1886, when he became interested
in the tobacco manufacturing business in which he continued until
1889. He was then re-appointed postmaster at Salisbury under the
Harrison administration, and is now the efficient and acceptable incumbent of that office. His many and excellent business qualifications make him a fit officer for that position and his upright character
as a private citizen makes him popular with all. Though never an
active partisan, his politics are republican, with which party he has
always been identified. He is a member of the Masonic fraternity;
having attained the degree of Master Mason. Mr. Ramsay enjoys in
a high degree the esteem and respect of his fellow citizens.

COLONEL JOHN D. TAYLOR.

This gentleman, one of the most worthy of the many estimable
citizens of Wilmington, was born in that city March 24, 1831. He is
the son of the late John A. Taylor and Catherine M. Taylor, his wife.
His father was a native of the city of New York, but removed to
Wilmington in 1820, where he married and lived many years, and
died at a ripe old age, carrying with him to the grave the respect of

the entire community. He was an active and successful business man, and for many years acted as agent for a line of mail steamers plying between Wilmington and Charleston. His only son, the subject of this notice, received a classical education and was graduated at the university of the state in 1853. Shortly afterward he visited Europe and spent four months in travel, principally on the continent. Upon his return home he engaged in rice planting in the adjoining counties of Brunswick and Bladen, and served until the early part of 1862, when he enlisted as a private in Company K, Thirty-sixth North Carolina state troops, artillery service. His merits were soon discovered, and he was rapidly promoted, soon reaching the rank of lieutenant-colonel, in which position he did the state much service. When the evacuation of Wilmington took place in 1865 he joined Gen. Joe Johnston's army, and was badly wounded at the battle of Bentonville, losing an arm in that engagement. After the close of hostilities he resumed the planting of rice, which he continued until 1878, when he was appointed to the office of clerk of the superior court of New Hanover county to fill an unexpired term. In 1884 he was elected city clerk and treasurer, and served in that capacity for three years, giving very general satisfaction. In 1890 he was elected superior court clerk, which office he now holds.

Col. Taylor was happily married in 1859 to Miss Elizabeth Walker, and has been blessed with three sons and five daughters, who are all living. His eldest son is a member of the firm of I. C. Stevenson & Taylor, wholesale grocers, who carry on a large and profitable business; his second son, Walter, is a member of the firm of Hodges & Taylor, general insurance agents, representing companies of first class standing. There are few men more popular and more deservedly so than Col. Taylor. Of genial manners and pleasant address he endears himself to all. He is one of those men to whom one in trouble would go and not hesitate to unbosom himself freely, for he would feel assured of warm sympathy, kindly advice and generous assistance. It is doubtful if he has an enemy in the world, and he enjoys the fullest confidence of all classes, irrespective of color or "previous condition of servitude." He is a man of the strictest integrity, of great amiability of character, and above all a Christian gentleman, the highest type of a true manhood.

JOHN PORTER.

In 1663, John Porter, a member of the Virginia house of burgesses from lower Norfolk county, was arraigned before the house for being "loving to the Quakers" and being at their meetings. He was also charged with being "against the baptism of children." As Bancroft tells us, he was expelled — the house resolving that he was well affected towards the Quakers. Afterward John Porter with his wife Mary, and children, among them being Edmund and John Porter, Jr., removed to Chowan precinct where he established himself as a merchant, trading to Boston, at least, and accumulated wealth. In the Albemarle region he became a man of first consequence, not, however, ordinarily taking part in political matters. His daughter Sarah married John Lillington, and his son John married Sarah Lillington and by these marriages his family became connected with the Swanns, Moseleys, Moores and Lillingtons.

In 1704, when Lord Granville undertook to enforce the act of the British parliament, requiring all officers to take certain oaths and excluding Quakers from holding places under government and undertook to set up a state church in Carolina, John Porter sent his son Edmund to England to co-operate with John Ashe, who was sent from South Carolina, to secure a redress of grievances. Col. Daniel, the deputy governor for North Carolina, was as a result of that mission dismissed; and Sir Nathaniel Johnson, governor, residing at Charleston, then sent Col. Carey as deputy governor. Col. Carey, however, followed in Daniel's footsteps, and in 1706, John Porter himself went to England, to have the matter settled. He obtained a commission suspending the power of Sir Nathaniel Johnson to appoint a deputy governor for North Carolina, and removing Col. Carey, and also new deputations, appointing Porter and his friends deputies of the lords proprietors, to act as members of the council, and with power for the council to choose a president among themselves. In fact, the entire management of public affairs of the colony was committed to Mr. Porter. Thus equipped with full power, Porter reached home in October, 1707. At first he had Glover, one of the councilors, chosen president of the council; but Glover soon began to ignore these instructions; and calling together the councilors, Porter set aside Glover's election, and Carey agreeing to obey them, he caused Carey to be proclaimed president and governor. Glover would not submit; and so the two contending presidents agreed to submit the matter to an assembly, to be elected on a day agreed on.

At that election the Carey or Porter party was entirely successful. The election of Edward Moseley, one of the Porter party was, however, contested; but the assembly seated Moseley and chose him speaker. Porter himself was elected a member and took the oaths, but some Quakers were chosen who merely affirmed as had always been the practice under the constitution of the colony. Glover then declared that the assembly was not a lawful body and that he would not submit to its judgment as he had agreed to do. He and Col. Pollock fled to Virginia. Col. Carey continued to administer the affairs of the colony until the arrival of Edward Hyde, who was sent out to be governor of North Carolina, but whose commission had not reached him. Carey and Porter and all others in the fall of the year 1710, joined in asking Hyde, who was cousin to the queen, to become president of the council and to take the administration, which he did. But he at once fell under the influence of Col. Pollock and the Glover party, and would not allow Quakers to hold office unless they took the oaths, excluding them from the assembly, which thus was dominated by the Glover faction. Carey and Porter and Moseley were arrested, but the former managed to escape and Carey fortified himself in a strong position. Hyde marched against him without success. Carey then raised a force and sailed from the Pamlico section toward Edenton, but his expedition came to naught, and in July, Carey and Porter abandoned opposition and went to Virginia to take shipping for England. There they were arrested by the governor of Virginia and sent to England. Porter remained in England, and a few months afterward died at Bridgewater, where his will was proved in the summer of 1712. His wife remained in Carolina, dying there in 1717. He left Edmund, John, Matthew, Joshua and Sarah and Eliza.

Edmund Porter was a strong supporter of Careys, and left the colony at the same time. It is said that he went to Scotland and engaged in rebellion there, perhaps in 1715. Later he returned to the colony and was an active manager of public affairs, was judge of the court of admiralty, and was a member as the royal council, which post he held at the time of his death in 1739.

John Porter, the second, was born in Virginia, in the year 1664, and was admitted as a lawyer to practice in the courts of North Carolina, soon after becoming of age. He married Sarah, daughter of Gov. Alexander Lillington, and in the year 1711, was residing near the present town of Beaufort, he being a vestryman of St. Thomas Parish, which included Bath. In the same vicinity lived John Lillington, who had married his sister Sarah, the mother of Gen. Alexander Lillington. In the Indian massacre of September, 1711, the Indians burnt both their residences, and Col. Porter's family barely escaped. A negro had their infant son, John, near the house when the Indians came up. One of the band seized the child and was in the act of dashing its brains out against a tree, when Mrs. Porter rushed out and rescued him. Capt. Patrick Manle was in the house, and together with Col. Porter made defense from the front, while the family prepared to leave by the rear. They succeeded in reaching a boat at the landing and found safety on a vessel anchored in the harbor. Captain Manle, who married Eliza Porter, afterward fought bravely in the Indian war.

Col. Porter was a member of the assembly of 1715, and afterward moved to New Hanover, where he died in 1734, leaving John Porter (the third), born in 1709, and Mary Porter, born in 1712. This Mary Porter became the second wife of Col. Maurice Moore and was the mother of Judge Maurice Moore, Gen. James Moore and Rebecca, the wife of Gen. John Ashe.

John Porter (the third) resided at Porter's Neck, New Hanover county and was a wealthy merchant. He was one of the original incorporators of the town of Wilmington, and an active man of business. He married Mary, daughter of Col. Maurice Moore. He died in 1744, leaving John Swann Porter and several daughters, who all died unmarried except Mary, who married Gov. Sam Ashe, and was the mother of Col. John Baptista Ashe and Col. Sam Ashe.

B—24

JOHN M. SMITH,

one of the leading citizens of Rockingham, sheriff, tax collector and treasurer of Richmond county, N. C., was born in that county, December, 1856. His parents were Calvin and Lucy Smith, both natives of South Carolina. Calvin Smith was a farmer and mechanic, and was well and favorably known in Marlborough county, S. C. His death occurred in 1867, when he had arrived at the age of fifty-eight years. His wife survived him many years, dying November 3, 1890, aged seventy-eight years. John M. Smith is the only child of these parents. The mother's first husband was Nelson Stevens, by whom she became the mother of seven children, four of whom are now living. At the age of eleven years, the subject of this sketch began the turpentine business and assisted very materially in the support of his mother and her daughters. He learned the cooper's trade and continued in that business until 1876. He then worked on the railroad as a section hand for a year, when he was promoted to station agent at Sand Hill. Here he remained until he was elected sheriff in 1882, when he resigned his position on the railroad. At the election in 1884 he was defeated for the office. He then was employed by the same railroad company as book-keeper at Hamlet. In 1886 he was again elected sheriff and was re-elected in 1888 and in 1890. His present term of office will not expire till 1892. That he has administered the office to the satisfaction of his constituents and all concerned is amply demonstrated by his continuous re-elections to the same office. As a private citizen, Mr. Smith is numbered among the most responsible, worthy and enterprising of the community in which he lives. He was married in 1881 to Miss Catura L. Newton, daughter of Cornelius D. Newton, of Marlborough county, S. C. The home of this couple has been brightened by the birth of four children whose names are Holland, Nellie V., Carl and Ruby L. Mr. Smith is a republican in politics and was appointed alternate delegate from his district to the national conventions held in Chicago in 1884 and 1888, the former, which nominated James G. Blaine, and the latter Benjamin Harrison, for president.

J. W. SCOTT, JR.,

mayor of the village of Sanford and a dealer in furniture, was born in Chatham county, March 8, 1863. He is the son of J. W. Scott, Sr., and Kate L. Scott, both natives of North Carolina and still living. The father is a speculator and one of the wealthy and prominent business men of Moore county. He is widely known and highly respected; is one of the substantial citizens of his community, and gives much attention to politics. He is not, however, an office seeker. Mr. Scott operates principally in buying and selling lands, but deals in other commodities whenever opportunity offers. He is a member and an elder in the Presbyterian church to which his wife also belongs. They have five children living: Mary W., wife of T. M. Cross; J. W. Jr.; Katie; Charles L., who is baggage master on the C. F. & Y. V. railroad, and Samuel V. The last named and Katie are still inmates of the parental home. J. W. Scott., Jr., was educated at the academy at Haywood, there completing an English course. He was prepared to enter the sophomore class in college, but his health failing, the prosecution of a further educational course was abandoned. He began business for himself at the age of twenty years as editor of the Moore *Gazette*, published at Carthage. He continued in this position for four years, selling out the concern in February, 1887. He then resumed the printing business at Sanford, in which he remained one year, and then embarked in the furniture traffic, in which he is at the present time engaged. The business is done under the firm name of the Sanford Furniture company, and a fair degree of success has attended the operation. Mr. Scott has the only house in the county which handles furniture exclusively. He is also agent for the Manhattan Life Insurance company, beside representing several fire insurance companies. In this line he is working up a good trade.

Mr. Scott is not of the standstill class of men, but possesses energy and push, and is numbered among the most enterprising men of the county. He was chosen one of the policemen of the town of Sanford in 1889, holding the position for one year. In 1890 he was elected mayor of Sanford by a handsome majority, and he makes an excellent and highly popular executive official. Mr. Scott was united in marriage in 1885, with Miss Kate J., daughter of Dr. E. M. Howerton, of Clarksville, Va. Their home has been blessed by the birth of two children: Edward W. and Jessie. Mrs. Scott is a member of the Presbyterian church. Mr. Scott enjoys the confidence, respect and esteem of his fellow citizens. He is secretary and treasurer of the Sanford Loan Improvement company, and was the originator of the enterprise. He thus stands to the front in all the leading affairs which promote the prosperity and advancement of his town. His public spirit, and broad ideas of business methods are a beneficence in the community in which he lives.

GOV. WILLIAM HAWKINS.

One of the most popular men of his time in North Carolina was William Hawkins, of Granville county, who at the early age of thirty-four years, was called to the gubernatorial chair during the troubles with Great Britain, and was twice re-elected, serving from 1811 to 1814. He was known as the war governor of North Carolina. He was a member of the influential family bearing his name, whose history has been intimately connected with public affairs in North Carolina for nearly a century and a half. He was the son of Philemon Hawkins and Lucy, and was born at the old homestead in Granville county, October 20, 1777. Having received a finished collegiate education, he read law with Judge Williams, of Williamsboro, Granville county, who was the father-in-law of Judge Henderson. But before entering on the practice, his uncle, Benjamin Hawkins, who had been a member of the Continental congress, and later one of the first senators elected by North Carolina to the Federal congress, and who was then general agent for all Indians south, urgently desired him to come to the agency at Fort Hawkins, near Macon, Ga., as his assistant. In conformity with this request, young William, in December, 1797, repaired to the agency and spent two years assisting his uncle, who became very much attached to him, and being unmarried, purposed making him his heir.

At the end of two years Col. Hawkins discovered that William was restless in the wilderness and seeing few others than Indians and he provided him with means and induced him to go to Philadelphia, Penn., and spend two years studying law and reviewing some of his former studies, especially French, so as to perfect himself in that language both by study and in the society of the numerous prominent Frenchmen then residing in that city. After two years profitably passed at Philadelphia, then the seat of the United States government, William, in the winter of 1801, returned to North Carolina and was appointed by Gov. Turner, in 1802, to settle some disputes with the Tuscarora Indians. In 1804, becoming enamoured of Miss Ann Boyd, of Mecklenburg county, Va., he was married to her and relinquished all idea of returning to Georgia, settled on a fine plantation on Nutbush creek, near Williamsboro, Granville county, and near the old homestead where his father resided. Here, in 1804, he built his residence, which became a seat of refined hospitality and social culture. In 1809, 1810 and 1811, he represented Granville county in the house of commons, and so highly esteemed was he for personal worth and so warmly was he appreciated by the public men of that period, that he was elected governor by the legislature of 1811, at the early age of thirty-four, being the youngest governor ever elected in North Carolina. His term was continued by re-election as long as the constitution permitted, and covered the very interesting period of the second war with Great Britain. He was active, able and patriotic in the discharge of the duties of the executive office during the war, and his administration reflected credit alike on himself and on the people of the state. With zeal he applied himself to measures of defense and he rendered the Federal government all the aid possible. During his administration the new governor's mansion at the foot of Fayetteville street, Raleigh, was prepared for occupancy, and he was the first governor to reside in it.

About the end of his term as governor, his uncle Benjamin, who was then advancing in years, felt the growing need of an assistant in his affairs at Fort Hawkins, Ga., and asked Gov. Hawkins to prevail on his younger brother, Capt. Philemon Hawkins, who had graduated at the University of North Carolina in 1809, and who was then a captain of artillery in the United States army, to resign his commission and come to his aid. This he did, and Capt. Hawkins on reaching Fort Hawkins, in 1815, found his uncle in feeble health, and in the succeeding year, 1816, Col. Benjamin Hawkins died. As remarked before, Col. Hawkins had as far back as 1797, intended to make his nephew, Gov. Hawkins, his heir, but later he married and children were born to him. Gov. Hawkins knowing the extreme punctiliousness of his uncle, thereupon wrote to him that he recalled with grateful recollection all of his past favors and his expressed intention to make him his heir, but that circumstances had changed and his children were the natural objects of his bounty, and he protested his own unwillingness to share in his estate, and released him from all moral obligation. Col. Hawkins had not seen him in many years, but in his will he provided that his estate, which was considered a large one (over $200,000) for that time, should be divided among his wife, his six children and his nephew William, share and share alike, and made his nephew William sole executor.

Gov. Hawkins accepted the trust, qualified as executer, and settled up the estate; but would retain nothing either of the bequest, or commissions, or in compensation for his own expenses in the matter. A year or two later, in May, 1819, Gov. Hawkins himself died, at Sparta, Ga., at the age of forty-two. He left eight children. One of the sisters of Gov. Hawkins, Sarah, married Col. Polk, of Raleigh, and her son Leonidas, was the bishop-general of the Confederate army; a son of his, Dr. Polk, obtained eminence in his profession in New York city, and died near Asheville, N. C., in the summer of 1891. Two other sisters married Haywoods, of Raleigh, and one married Mr. Little, of Halifax. The four sisters were left widows with large estates, and with large families, and they were each made sole executrix, and settled up their trusts with great credit to themselves. The first wife of Hon. Louis D. Henry was another sister of Gov. Hawkins.

JAMES McNIGHT MORROW

was born in Lancaster county, S. C., April 12, 1831. His father, Allen Morrow, was also a native of Lancaster county, and he was the son of James Morrow, a Virginian by birth, but who early emigrated from Virginia, and settled in Lancaster district, S. C. He was of Irish descent and had five sons and four daughters. His wife was Miss Watson who came from Virginia of which state she was a native. Allen Morrow, the father of James was twice married. His first wife was Agnes Potts, of Union, N. C., formerly a part of Mecklenburg county. She was of Irish lineage. James was her only child, and she died while he was an infant. For a second wife Allen Morrow married Clarissa A. Spears of Mecklenburg county, and they had two sons and three daughters. He was a farmer by occupation in which he achieved both prominence and success. He had no political aspirations, preferring the honor, respect and independence which ever crown a faithful devotion to that calling. He died in Lancaster district. James McNight Morrow was reared amid the scenes o plantation life, acquiring a liberal English education at the hig school in the neighborhood of his father's homestead. He remained with his father until twenty-one years of age, and then left his home to grapple with the realities of life on his own account. He first secured the position of clerk in which occupation he was engaged three years. In 1855 he was united in marriage with Margarete Potts, of Lancaster county, where he settled on a farm. He followed farming till 1869 in which year he sold his farm, and removed to Charlotte, N. C.

Mr. Morrow abandoned farming in consequence of the free labor system, which resulted from the Civil war. A lameness in his left foot and ankle unfitted him for the active work of the farm, and when deprived of slave labor he was practically compelled to give up farming. He secured a clerkship in the grocery store of E. M. Holt & Co., a wholesale and retail establishment in Charlotte. In this capacity he continued for two years, when he engaged as bookkeeper for R. M. Miller & Sons, wholesale and retail grocers, where he remained for four years. Then he engaged in the same capacity for Joseph McLaughlin during a term of nine years. He then took a like position with T. R. Magill, in the same business, and this engagement lasted about four years. In 1886 Mr. Morrow was elected clerk of the superior court of Mecklenburg county, and in 1890 was reelected for a second term. In November, 1886, his wife died, leaving him three children; February 13, 1890, he married as his second wife, Miss Bettie H. Williams, of Charlotte. Mr. Morrow is a member of the First Presbyterian church at Charlotte, of which he is an influential communicant. He enjoys the highest respect as a private citizen, and as a court official is regarded as one of the best and most efficient clerks ever entrusted with the duties of that office.

CORNELIUS HARNETT,

a Revolutionary patriot, was born in 1723, probably in the Albemarle section of North Carolina, as his father, Cornelius Harnett, was settled there about that time. In 1726 his father was residing on the lower Cape Fear, being one of the first settlers on that river. Cornelius Harnett, the elder, was a friend of Gov. Burrington during his first term as governor in 1724, and on his return as the representative of the crown, Burrington brought with him a commission for Harnett to be of the council. Harnett, however, joined Ashe in his opposition to Burrington, and aided in defeating the adoption of all prerogative measures. Of the early life of the son, but little is known. He received a good education; was a gentleman of elegant manners and refined appearance. He was a genius in music, and a writer of force and elegance. In the stamp act troubles of February, 1766, he was a leader in the movement to secure the release of the captured vessels. And from that time onward he bore a conspicuous part as a whig patriot. So beloved was he by the people of Wilmington that the legislature enacted that his residence at Hilton, some distance from the town, should be attached to the town, so that he might represent the town in the assembly.

When, in 1773, Josiah Quincy visited the Cape Fear to ascertain the temper of the people, he spoke of Mr. Harnett as the Samuel Adams, of North Carolina. He boldly espoused the cause of his country, and took rank with the foremost men of the colony. He was a member of the committee of safety; was a leading member of the provincial congresses; was chosen president of the committee of thirteen, in whom the administration was lodged before the adoption of the constitution, and drew up the resolution declaring for independence and separation in April, 1776. When Clinton arrived in the Cape Fear in the spring of 1776, Harnett with Howe was honored by being excepted from the general offer of pardon. He was a member of the committee that framed the constitution of the state, and doubtless many of those fine state papers of that period which are so creditable to North Carolina were his productions. He served as a delegate to the Continental congress in 1777, 1778, 1779 and the early months of 1780. He signed the articles of confederation. In that body he had but few superiors. In 1781 Maj. Craig occupied Wilmington, and as soon as the fleet entered the river Mr. Harnett, who was then at Hilton, sought safety in Onslow county. A detachment of dragoons was sent to capture him, and being seized with an attack of the gout, he was unable to escape. Carried to Wilmington after rough treatment he was paroled — but his malady was fatal, and he died April 20, 1781. He was not a believer in Christianity; and his tombstone bears an epitaph written by his own hand when near his end:

> "Slave to no sect, he took no private road,
> But looked through Nature, up to Nature's God."

J. W. COBB,

the subject of this sketch, was born in York county, S. C., September 30, 1855. His father, Dr. B. M. Cobb, was a native of Lincoln county, N. C., born in 1822 and of English lineage. He was the son of John Cobb, who was born and reared in Catawba county, N. C., and was by occupation a farmer. He had five sons and three daughters. Dr. B. M. Cobb was reared in his native county, receiving there a liberal English education. He studied medicine under Dr. Caldwell, in Lincolnton, and afterward attended the Medical university at New York city and Jefferson medical college, of Philadelphia, from which two institutions he graduated. He began practice in Lincoln county and for several years pursued his practice in that county, Gaston and Catawba counties. In 1848 he removed to Fort Mills, York county, S. C., where he remained till 1868. He married Catherine Lonergau, born in Ireland in 1825, and who came to this country with her parents in 1830. She was the daughter of Edward Lonergau, and died in 1888, leaving six sons and two daughters. J. W.

Cobb was the fifth in succession of births. He was reared in York county, N. C., and received a fair English education at Fort Mills. In June, 1870, at the age of fifteen, he came to Charlotte and accepted a position as clerk in a store, where he remained about six years. In 1876 he was employed in the county register's office as clerk, where he remained till 1884. He was then elected register of deeds, and for every term of two years since, he has been re-elected to the same office. His superior qualifications as a clerk, his long experience and his sterling characteristics as a citizen have amply equipped him for the position he has so long and so satisfactorily filled. He began life in straightened circumstances, financially, but by excellent business habits, unimpeachable integrity, unerring judgment and an indomitable perseverance, he has fairly won success. October 15, 1885, he was married to Miss Mary L. Groove, of Charlotte, and their union has been blessed by the birth of three children. They are both members of the Catholic church.

THOMAS A. WATTS,

ex-sheriff of Iredell county, was born on the farm where he now resides, in the township of Shiloh, Iredell county, N. C., May 5, 1837. His family was of the purest Scotch-Irish descent, and his ancestors moved from Pennsylvania to North Carolina at an early day. His father was Fielding Watts, his paternal grandfather William Watts, and his mother was Sarah, daughter of William Steele and Bettie Watts. His ancestors were prominent members of the Presbyterian church in Iredell county, his father being an elder in the Concord church, and two of his uncles were clergymen in that denomination in the fellowship of the North Carolina synod. Before the war he and his connections were whigs and union men. Thomas A. Watts was the fourth son of his father. When the war began he was major of the North Carolina militia, and, by order of Gov. Vance, was ordered to remain at home on protective duty. During the war he was captain of one of the two companies of Iredell county home guards, but did not go into active service. Immediately after the war he was appointed by provisional Gov. Holden, a justice of the peace, and took an active part in re-establishing the county government. He was subsequently elected by the people and served until August, 1874, when he was elected sheriff of Iredell county, defeating his cousin, J. A. F. Watts, who had the support of the old sheriff and most, if not all, of the other county officers. He was elected by a vote of more than three to one. At the next election in 1876, Mr. Watts was elected without opposition, and was again elected in the same way in 1878. In 1880 S. C. Hager was the republican candidate, and Mr. Watts was elected by more than 1,500 majority, while the democratic majority on the presidential and gubernatorial tickets was only 743. Prohibition was the leading issue in 1881, and Sheriff Watts took an active part in the campaign on that side. The ticket was defeated by more than two to one.

In 1882 a great effort was made by the republicans and certain anti-prohibition democrats to defeat Mr. Watts for sheriff. His opponent was W. F. Sharpe, a man of spotless character, but Mr. Watts was elected by a majority of 822, while the democratic majority on the state ticket was only 543. He declined a nomination in 1884, and retired from the political field. During his incumbency of the office of sheriff, county scrip was worth 100 cents to the dollar, and throughout his official career he retained the confidence and respect of the people. In 1888 Mr. Watts was elected chairman of the democratic county executive committee, a preferment which was again accorded him in 1890. He has been a leader in the democratic party in his county ever since the war, and his qualities as an organizer have earned for him the name of "the Samuel J. Tilden of Iredell county." January 11, 1865, Mr. Watts was united in marriage with Miss Margaret E. Morrison, and they have been blessed by the birth of nine children, four sons and five daughters, one of whom is deceased. Mr. Watts now divides his occupation between farming and milling.

DR. MOSES JOHN DeROSSET.

The subject of this sketch was one of the patriots of the Cape Fear section in the days of the stamp act troubles. He was the brother of Lewis Henry DeRosset, who represented the borough of Wilmington in the assembly in 1752, and was in the winter of that year made a member of the upper house, which position he continued to hold until the Revolution, and who is described as a gentleman of elegant culture and refinement. Dr. Moses John DeRosset, who received his degree of M. D. doubtless at some English university, was an officer in the troops raised in 1754, to go to the aid of Virginia against the threatened invasion of the French and Indians. He was the mayor of Wilmington, in 1765, and was in thorough sympathy with the people in their movements against the stamp act. When it was known that an effort would be made to enforce the odious law the people of that town rose equal to the emergency. On the 19th of October, 1765, they had a public demonstration, burnt "a certain honorable gentleman" in effigy, drank toasts to liberty, property and no stamp duty, and confusion to Lord Bute and all his adherents. On the 31st of that month they again assembled and paraded with an effigy of liberty, which they put in a coffin and marched in a solemn procession to the churchyard, a drum in mourning beating before them and the town bell muffled, ringing a doleful knell. But before committing the body to the ground, they thought it advisable to feel its pulse, when finding some remains of life they returned to the bonfire and placed the effigy before it in a large, two-armed chair, and concluded the evening with great rejoicings on finding that liberty had still an existence in the colonies. On the 16th of November, William Houston, the stamp master, came to town from Duplin county, and the people took him to the court house and made him resign his commission, and they had further proceedings of the same character as on previous occasions. Houston's resignation and declaration not to execute the law were left with Mayor DeRosset.

Gov. Tryon, who was a man of great policy and address, sought to have the law executed at least in part but without avail. Shortly afterward two vessels came into the harbor without having stamps on their clearing papers, and were seized by the British war ships in port. These war ships were supplied with provisions from the town but the town authorities determined they should have no more supplies until the seized vessels were released. The people embodied and marched to Brunswick to secure a redress of grievances. The war ships were being starved for the want of provisions. A boat sent to Wilmington to obtain supplies was captured; the crew was put in jail, and the people marched in procession through the streets, hauling the captured boat in triumph. Without supplies, and with a large force of armed people occupying the town of Brunswick, where the governor and provincial officers resided, the British captains saw no other course open than to yield to the demands of the people, and being starved out, they surrendered the vessels they had seized, much to the disgust of Gov. Tryon. Without doubt this proceeding on the part of the people was open, flagrant war, and during the whole course of the matter Dr. DeRosset, as mayor of the corporation, bore his part with firmness and credit. His correspondence with Gov. Tryon was firm, manly, highly honorable and worthy of the patriots whose action shed such glorious lustre upon the annals of Wilmington and of the Cape Fear country. There was no evasion or palliation suggested for any act.

In reply to the communication of the governor, desiring to know why bread was not allowed to be supplied to the ships, he says: "An agreement was entered into not to supply his majesty's ships with any more provisions, unless the particular restrictions on this port were taken off," etc. "As to the boatmen being put in gaol, it was done by the people, who had collected themselves together to procure a redress of their grievances, and to prevent their going down; and not only they, but every other person going to Brunswick were stopped." That is, no communication was to be allowed with the enemy at Brunswick — the governor, the provincial officers and his majesty's ships of war! After the stamp act was repealed a wave of popular rejoicing passed over the country, and the borough of Wilmington made an address of appreciation to Gov. Tryon. To this he replied, making reference to some personal disrespect shown him, which called out an answer, signed among others, by the mayor. The following extract shows the spirit of it: "If oppressed by the late act some commotions of the country seemed to threaten a departure from moderation, your excellency, we hope, will not impute these transactions to any other motive than a conviction that moderation ceases to be a virtue when the liberty of British subjects is in danger." Of all the manly spirits of his time, none excelled in character, attainments and patriotic ardor, the young soldier of 1754, who now had become the head of the chief town corporation of the province.

Unhappily for his country, Mayor DeRosset died before the Revolutionary struggle came on. He left one son, Armand John DeRosset; and his widow married Adam Boyd, who before the Revolution, printed *The Mercury* newspaper at Wilmington, and who afterward was a chaplain in the North Carolina line, and in 1787 was ordained an Episcopal minister, and served in Augusta, Ga., from 1790 to 1799. Dr. Armand John DeRosset was born November 17, 1767. He matriculated at Princeton, 1784. Four years later he became a pupil of the celebrated Dr. Rush, of Philadelphia, and received his diploma in 1790. In 1822 he was elected a director of the bank of Cape Fear, which position he retained until the day of his death. No man was more esteemed in the community. He resided his whole life in the brick building at the intersection of Market and Third streets within the shadow of the Episcopal church (St. James), of which he was one of the supporting pillars. He died April 1, 1859, at the age of ninety-two years. His mantle descended on his son, Dr. Armand John De Rosset, Jr., who was born in 1807, graduated at the University of North Carolina in 1824, A. B., and during a life of more than four score years, has ever been an ornament to his native town, as his ancestors were before him.

DAVID A. JENKINS.

There have been few characters in North Carolina, more favorably known than the subject of this sketch, David A. Jenkins. He was a native of Gaston county, and was born April 5, 1822, the eldest child of Aaron and Mary Jenkins. Aaron Jenkins who died August 13, 1891, was a native of Rowan county and his wife was a daughter of Joseph Jenkins, a native North Carolinian and a granddaughter of Col. Hamright who commanded the American forces at the famous battle of Kings Mountain. David A. Jenkins was reared in his native county and attended the old field schools where he gained a fair English education, and at the early age of fourteen years he began teaching school. Subsequently he chopped wood, which he sold to the proprietors of the Fullenwider furnace and received in return, goods manufactured at this furnace, selling the same. In his early life he did farm work and split rails for little compensation, and by means of hard toil and economy, became prosperous and highly respected. Mr. Jenkins was united in marriage early in life with Miss Lodema, daughter of Jesse Holland. To this union were born ten children, all living with the exception of two. Mr. Jenkins was elected to the office of constable and subsequently to that of magistrate, in the latter position serving many years. Although he was devoted to the southern people, their customs and habits, he foresaw the inexpediency of secession, which meant war, and was bitterly opposed to it. But when war came, he being a magistrate, was exempted from active field duty. Mr. Jenkins accepted the reconstruction act and was from the close of the war identified with the republican party. In 1866, both republicans and democrats solicited and supported him for the legislature, to which body he was elected and served faithfully for two years.

In 1868 Mr. Jenkins became the republican candidate for treasurer of the state, and was elected to that position. He was re-elected in 1872, serving two terms of four years each. He was a wise and cautious official, and being a man of keen financial judgment and ability, his administration of the office of state treasurer met with the universal approbation and support of the entire state. During his last term in this position, Mr. Jenkins removed his family to Charlotte for a time, later returning to his native county and locating at Gastonia, where he built a handsome residence and retired to private life. In 1880 Mr. Jenkins was urged by his admiring friends to become the republican candidate for governor of the state, but owing to the then recent death of his wife, he declined to enter the canvass. Upon his refusal to make the race for the governorship, his son, A. D. Jenkins, was by the republican convention unanimously nominated for treasurer of the state, and though not elected, carried his own county which was largely democratic, and reduced the democratic majority of the state. In 1881 Mr. Jenkins supported the prohibition party. In all his political career he was highly esteemed, and the confidence of the people was his. He was given the name of " Honest Dave Jenkins," which sobriquet was ever afterward applied to him. Faithful to the interests of the people, a financier of repute, and a man of sterling qualities and strong force of character, he was ever an honest servant of his constituents in the halls of legislation, and other official positions. His death occurred at Gastonia, September 10, 1886. Mr. Jenkins was an active member of the Baptist church, and in his death there ended a long, active and exemplary life.

REV. JAMES H. CORDON, D. D.,

was born at Washington, N. C., July 9, 1851, and was educated at Bingham's school in Orange county, N. C., where he completed his studies in 1871, including a post-graduate course of a year at that institution. Being elected register of deeds, in Beaufort county, N. C., in 1872, he served two years, in that capacity, during which time he studied law under Hon. Edwin G. Reade, who was then a justice of the supreme court of North Carolina. Mr. Cordon was admitted to the bar in 1874, and opened a law office in Washington, N. C., where he practiced for about three years. During that period Mr. Cordon became greatly interested in the subject of religion, and uniting with a highly moral character a conscientious purpose to discharge all duties, his convictions led him to long for a closer walk with the Saviour. With warm religious fervor he undertook the work in life whereinto he was called, and abandoning the law, he in 1877 joined the North Carolina conference of the M. E. church, south. He was first sent to the Mattamuskeet circuit where he continued three years. During that time he was ordained a deacon, at Winston in 1879, and

Yours Very Sincerely,

G. W. Sanderlin.

two years later he was ordained elder. After leaving the Matta-muskeet circuit, he was stationed four years on the South Edgecombe circuit, when he was transfered to the Statesville station. Two years of delightful ministry at Statesville were followed by an equal term at Wilson, when he was stationed at Raleigh, as the pastor of the leading congregation in the conference — the Edenton street church. The congregation now numbers 730, and Dr. Cordon most faith-fully, and acceptably serves this large congregation who accord to him unbounded affection and esteem.

Mr. Cordon is a member of Seaton Gales lodge. No. 64, I. O. O. F., and has held all the chairs in the subordinate lodge, and belongs to Litchford encampment, I. O. O. F. Dr. Cordon was grand master of the I. O. O. F., of the state of North Carolina during the year from May, 1888, to May, 1889, and was elected grand representative to the sovereign grand lodge in 1890, and still holds that office. He also belongs to William G. Hill lodge, F. & A. M., and to Raleigh chapter, Royal Arch Masons. The degree of D. D. was conferred on Dr. Cordon in 1890 by the University of North Carolina in recog-nition of his eminence in his profession and his purity of life. Dr. Cordon was married November 19, 1872, to Mattie Telfair, daughter of Thomas Telfair, of Washington, N. C., and niece of Gov. D. G. Fowle, and to them were born ten children, of whom five now sur-vive, as follows: Mary Stewart Cordon, Laura Cordon, Etta Cordon, Nanny Cordon and James H. Cordon, Jr.

Dr. Cordon's father, William S. Cordon, was born in 1812, in Beaufort county, N. C., where the family for several generations had resided. He was a farmer during his early life, and for the last twenty-one years of his life he was clerk of the court and register of deeds, and during that time he never had but two opponents, and of these it is said that one received six votes in the county, and the other twelve. He was a decided whig all his life. He was a Presbyterian and in 1842 was married to Nancy Satchwell, daughter of James and Elizabeth Satchwell, of Beaufort county, N. C., and to them were born three children, of whom two now survive, as follows: Laura S., wife of H. F. Price, of Wilson, N. C.; Rev. James H. Cordon, of Raleigh, N. C. Dr. Cordon's father died in 1866, and his mother in 1882.

HON. GEORGE W. SANDERLIN, LL. D.,

was born in Camden county, N. C., on the 22d day of February, 1843. His father was by name Maxcy Sanderlin, Esq., who was a native of Camden county, N. C., being born in that county in the year 1798. He was a successful planter by occupation, and was respected as a gentleman of honor, integrity and industry. He was of Scotch line-age, his ancestors being among the Scotch settlers of the state, many of whose noble and excellent families trace their origin to that noble race of the Scotchman, ever characteristic for his high sense of honor, for his integrity, patriotism and for his unswerving nature and superior intelligence. For many years Maxcy Sanderlin lived in Camden, his native county, but in 1848 removed to Pasquotank county, and died in that county in 1874, at the advanced age of seventy-six years. In the year 1818 he was united in marriage with Martha Sanderson, daughter of Caleb Sanderson, who was a respected citizen of Currituck county, N. C. Unto the above union were born thirteen children and on the 12th day of December, 1862, the beloved mother was called away in death at the age of sixty years. Like her husband she was of Scottish ancestry, and her life was one of devotion and piety. These parents, Maxcy Sanderlin and wife, in their thirteen children gave blessing to their humble though useful and exemplary lives, and of these thirteen children we are most interested in the life of George W., whose honored name introduces this sketch.

Hon. George W. Sanderlin, LL. D., was prepared for college in the schools of Elizabeth City, N. C., and then entered Wake Forest college, which college he left in August, 1861, to enter the Confederate army. However, after returning from army service he was given a diploma as a graduate from this college, being recognized as a member of the graduating class of 1862. Dr. Sanderlin enlisted as a private in Company E, Thirty-third regiment North Carolina volunteers, commanded by Col. C. M. Avery. He soon received well-merited promotions, first to sergeant and successively was promoted to the rank of a captain, and on more than one occasion was in command of his regiment. On the battlefield of Newbern Mr. Sanderlin, in consequence of his gallantry on the field was promoted from first sergeant to third lieutenant, by Col. C. M. Avery. On this battlefield, March 14, 1862, Mr. Sanderlin, in performing the duty assigned by his colonel, bravely surmounted the Confederate breastworks, and heroically underwent heavy firing from the advancing column under Gen. Reno, of the Federal army. On the third day of the battle of Gettysburg, Lieut. Sanderlin led his company, together with two others, in a charge against the Federal breastworks near Cemetery Hill, and captured and held them for some ten minutes, but not being reinforced, was compelled to fall back. It was a brilliant charge, and Col. Avery at once made Mr. Sanderlin a captain. Capt. Sanderlin took an active part in many hard fought fields, participating, among others, in the following important battles of the war: Newbern, Hanover Court House, seven days' fight around Richmond (including the battles of Mechanicsville, Gaines' Mills, Cold Harbor and Malvern Hill), and other important battles were Cedar Run, Warrenton Springs, second Bull Run, second Manassass, Chantilly, Va., Harper's Ferry, Sharpsburg, Antietam, first Fredericksburg, second Fredericksburg, Wilderness, Chancellorsville, Gettysburg, Hagerstown, Falling Waters, Snicker's Gap, Mine Run, Spottsylvania Court House, second battle of the Wilderness, Petersburg, Fussel's Mill (in front of Richmond), Burgess's Mill, Jones' Farm, Belfield and Hare's Hill.

Mr. Sanderlin commanded 300 sharpshooters on the skirmish line at Petersburg on the morning the break was made, April 2, 1865, repelling with his small force entrenched in rifle pits, three attacks of 3,000 Federal troops, at Jones' farm. An hour afterward the Federals broke the Confederate lines at Burgess' Mill, two miles to the right of Jones' farm, where the Federals had unsuccessfully made the attack on that portion of the Confederate line commanded by Capt. Sanderlin. At Appomatox Court House Capt. Sanderlin was with his regiment fighting in the front ranks, when Gen. Custer rode into his regiment and announced the surrender of Gen. Lee; and thus it is observed that Mr. Sanderlin continued in gallant and active service in the defense of the Confederacy till the disaster at Appomatox Court House ended the greatest of civil conflicts. It is true that Mr. Sanderlin saw the hardest-fought of battles and when Gen. Maxcy Gregg, of South Carolina, fell at the first battle of Fredericksburg, Mr. Sanderlin was near by in line of battle; and he was also near Gen. L. O'Brian Branch, of Raleigh, N. C., when that brave and gallant soldier and able general fell, at Antietam, and at Chancellorsville, when "Stonewall" Jackson was killed, Mr. Sanderlin was stationed within a few paces of him in command of the skirmishing line. Mr. Sanderlin was three times wounded, receiving a slight wound at each of the battles of Newbern, Richmond and Petersburg. He served four years and participated in as many as forty battles; was one time in a hospital; was never taken prisoner, and was given but one furlough, this being for a brief time in January, 1865, but during his absence no fighting was done by his regiment; in fact he missed scarcely a skirmish, fight or march in which the army of northern Virginia participated, and when the dreadful war was ended Mr. Sanderlin had made a brilliant and most excellent record as a soldier; and as gallant as were the spirits of that fine command of which he was, there were none who displayed more devotion, a more unflinching courage than Capt. George W. Sanderlin. Maj.-Gen. R. F. Hoke, at one time lieutenant-colonel commanding the Thirty-third North Carolina regiment; and who was afterwards known as the "Hero of Plymouth" has said of Capt. Sanderlin, who was at one time a member of the above regiment: "I know his war record thoroughly. I know that he was always present for duty and always true to duty."

On the close of the war Capt. Sanderlin returned to Elizabeth city, N. C., and at once began to arrange for completing his education. He had intended studying the law, but feeling called to the ministry he entered the Southern Baptist Theological seminary at Greenville, S. C., where with honor he graduated in 1867, two years later. He graduated in ten of the eleven schools of this seminary, completing the course in Hebrew in the brief period of ten months. During his academical and collegiate courses, Mr. Sanderlin graduated in seven different languages; and as both a classical and scientific scholar he has a wide and well earned reputation. After leaving the seminary Dr. Sanderlin returned to North Carolina, and for one year continued general Sabbath school work. In the spring of 1868 he was ordained to preach, being ordained in the chapel of Wake Forest college, his *alma mater*, President Wingate, Reverend Doctors Royall,

Prichard and others participating in the services. Subsequently Dr. Sanderlin assumed pastoral charge of the church at Goldsboro, N. C., and for three years continued the able and beloved pastor of this church, resigning in consequence of a purpose of making a tour of Egypt and Palestine, in company with the distinguished Dr. John A. Broadus (once his preceptor) who awaited him at Rome. But, missing the only steamer by which he could meet Dr. Broadus, Dr. Sanderlin was compelled to abandon the trip. About this time, while in Baltimore he preached with such effect in the Franklin Square Baptist church of that city, the pulpit of which had but recently been vacated by Rev. Dr. J. B. Hawthorne, now of Atlanta, that subsequent to his return to North Carolina he received a unanimous call to that church. Entering upon duties of pastor in March, 1871, he remained there until in 1876, when the arduous work having undermined his health, he was compelled to retire from the pastoral charge of this church and from the active ministry as well.

Dr. Sanderlin now settled near Goldsboro, N. C., and turned his attention to agriculture, remaining for some time on his plantation. He soon became well known to the agricultural world, becoming a voluminous writer for the farming journals of the country. Taking an advanced interest in agriculture and agricultural journalism, he finally became the agricultural editor of the *Kinston Free Press*, and also an able contributor to other papers. His articles on "Upland Rice Culture" attracted widespread attention, and gave origin in the state to an agricultural crop that has since become an important product, now yielding more than $1,000,000, annually. Dr. Sanderlin became widely and favorably known throughout the state, and in 1888 he was pressed by his many friends throughout the state to accept the nomination for state auditor, and finally consented to become a candidate. He soon won reputation as an able speaker and campaigner. He spoke from the Seaboard to the Tennessee line with great and pleasing effect; and so generous was his campaign and so great his personal popularity that he was deservingly and fittingly elected; and in January, 1889, he was inaugurated state auditor. It is needless to make mention of his wise administration of the affairs of this office, more than to say that in every report submitted on the condition of state government by different committees this department has been especially commended.

He is a man of high sense of honor; a man of wisdom and excellent executive ability, and many are his friends throughout the state anxious to promote and elevate him to the highest and most honored position; and his name is very prominently mentioned as a candidate for governor in the approaching campaign of 1892, and there seems to be a general sentiment throughout the state, that he be made the gubernatorial candidate. Dr. Sanderlin has continued his interest in church work and in education. While not in the active ministerial work, he still preaches on occasions, and is one of the most eloquent, learned and profound divines of the state. He is vice-president of the North Carolina Baptist state convention, and a prominent member of the mission and Sunday-school board of the North Carolina convention. Dr. Sanderlin has ever taken a manifest interest in education, and he has been for some time a trustee of Wake Forest college. Recently he received, on the same day, the degree of LL. D. from Wake Forest and Judson colleges. He is a prominent Mason, Odd Fellow and Knight of Pythias. On the 23d of February, 1869, Dr. Sanderlin and Miss Eliza W. Wooten, daughter of Council Wooten, of Lenoir county, N. C., were united in marriage, and their union has been blessed by the birth of six children, of whom four are living. Dr. Sanderlin resides with his family in Raleigh, his duties as state auditor requiring his residence there. The living children are, Beulah, Georgia, Pattie, and Rosalie.

REV. DR. DAVID CALDWELL.

The subject of this sketch was one of the great educators of North Carolina. He was born in Lancaster county, Penn., on the 22d of March, 1725, of highly respectable parents. He graduated at Princeton in 1761, and the next year offered to be taken on trial as a candidate for gospel ministry. He served after getting his license, August 18, 1763, at various points in New Jersey, and on May 16, 1765, he was appointed to labor one year in North Carolina, and was then ordained. In 1766, he married in North Carolina, Rachel, a daughter of Rev. Alexander Craighead, of Mecklenburg county, and in 1767 opened a school in what is now Guilford county, which was one of the earliest in the western part of the state as it became the most famous. He was instrumental in bringing more men into the learned professions than any other educator of his day in the southern states. Many of them became eminent as statesmen, lawyers, judges, physicians and ministers. Five of his pupils became governors of different states and many more members of congress; others adorned the bench, the bar and the pulpit. No man had a greater reputation as a teacher or was more beloved by his pupils. The number of his scholars ran from fifty to sixty, drawn from great distances. Later in life he studied medicine and added the practice of that science to his duties. From the organization of Orange presbytery he acted as stated clerk till 1776. When the synod of North Carolina held its first meeting in 1788, he was its leading member. He continued to be a beloved and esteemed minister until his death, August 25, 1824, being then in his ninetieth year. The University of North Carolina, in recognition of his learning, conferred upon him the degree of D. D., and he was greatly esteemed throughout the state for the excellence of his character, his purity, piety and patriotism.

Soon after his arrival in North Carolina, the regulation troubles broke out in his immediate section, and many persons connected with the congregations he served were involved. He sympathized greatly with the people in their troubles, but counseled against violence, and in 1771 sought to be a peace-maker, addressing the people and urging them against intemperate measures. He was a member

B—25

of the state convention of 1776 that framed the state constitution, and was also a member of the convention of 1788 that declined to accept or ratify the constitution of the United States, he acting with the majority of the convention.

REV. FRANK L. REID, D. D.

Dr. Reid was born in Rockingham county, N. C., June 16, 1851. He is the second son of Rev. Numa F. Reid, D. D., and Mrs. Ann E. Reid, and the grandson of Rev. James Reid. The grandfather and father were members of the North Carolina annual conference of the Methodist Episcopal church, south, at the time of their decease. Dr. Reid being the son of an itinerant Methodist preacher, was reared as it were "on the wing," his father having occupied many of the most prominent stations in the conference, and having been in charge of several districts as presiding elder. Dr. Reid at the age of fifteen years entered the freshman class, half advanced at Trinity college, North Carolina. In May, 1870, he was licensed to preach at a quarterly conference over which his father presided as presiding elder, and of which the late Rev. Braxton Craven, D. D., LL. D., was secretary. He graduated and received the degree of A. B. at Trinity college, June 16, 1870, the day he was nineteen years of age. He was soon thereafter elected principal of Kernersville high school at Kernersville, N. C., where he taught until the close of the year. He joined the North Carolina conference of the Methodist Episcopal church, south, at Greensboro, N. C., in December, 1870, and was appointed to Madison circuit in his native county by special petition of the board of stewards of that pastoral charge. He served this charge three years. Dr. Reid's grandfathers were James Reid and James Wright. His grandmothers were Martha Edwards (paternal) and Ella Wall (maternal), all of Rockingham county. There is an unusual line of succession connected with the social life of the Reid family; a grandfather of Dr. Reid, his father, two brothers and he married in Rockingham county; a sister also married a native of that county. Dr. Reid's grandfather served the circuit in Rockingham county, and went to Louisburg; about twenty years after his father served the same charges in succession, as did Dr. Reid himself about twenty years after his father.

Dr. Reid was married June 3, 1873, to Miss Minnie E. Cardwell, daughter of James L. and Sarah F. Cardwell, of Rockingham county. From this marriage four children have been born, namely: W. Fuller, Minnie LeGrande, Lola McGee and Annie Field, all of whom are living. In January, 1874, he took charge of the Louisburg station by appointment of Bishop Keener, and served the charge four years, the whole of the legal limit. While there his health failed and he contracted a throat disease, which affected his pulpit ministrations and forced his retirement from active pastoral duties. He was, in 1877, elected president of the Louisburg female college, which position he resigned in June, 1878, as a necessity for absolute rest and restoration of health. His season of rest was short, however. In October, 1878, he, with Rev. W. S. Black, D. D., purchased the *Raleigh Christian Advocate*, the organ of the North Carolina conference, of the Methodist Episcopal church, south. On the 19th of December, 1884, he purchased Dr. Black's interest and became the sole owner and editor of the *Advocate*, and so continues. He was appointed pastor of Edenton street Methodist Episcopal church, south, in the city of Raleigh, N. C., in October, 1881, on the death of Rev. A. A. Boshamer, the pastor, and presiding elder of the Raleigh district on the death of Rev. N. H. D. Wilson, D. D., in May, 1888. He received the honorary degree of master of arts, from Trinity college, in 1873, at the age of twenty-two, and of doctor of divinity from the University of North Carolina, in the year 1890, at the age of thirty-nine. He was a delegate to the general conference of the Methodist Episcopal church, south, held at St. Louis, Mo., in May, 1890, and was appointed a delegate to the Ecumenical Methodist conference to be held in Washington, D. C., in October, 1891.

Dr. Reid became a Mason at the age of twenty-one, and has twice been grand chaplain of the grand lodge of North Carolina, which office was filled by his grandfather, James Reid, and by his father. He has attained to the degree of Royal Arch, and is a true exponent of the principles of Masonry, both in precept and example. He has filled important civil positions, principally as a director of the state penitentiary, and during his term as such he was secretary of the board, and chairman of the committee of finance. He was a member of the school committee of Raleigh, and after serving one term was re-elected, but soon resigned on account of feeble health. While Dr. Reid is prominently known and esteemed in his state as an able minister of the gospel and as possessing, in an eminent degree, the culture and qualities necessary in the work of a successful educator, yet, in the broad field of editorial work, in the publication of the *Raleigh Christian Advocate*, are his distinguished abilities more generally recognized throughout the southern Methodist church.

REV. C. T. BAILEY,

editor and proprietor of the *Biblical Recorder*, at Raleigh, N. C., was born in James City county, near Williamsburg, Va., October 24, 1835. His father, the late William Moody Bailey, a quiet and successful farmer, was the son of Anselm J. Bailey, a Scotchman, who settled first on the eastern shore of Virginia, in Accomac county, and in middle life removed to New Kent county, where he died in 1840. Mr. William M. Bailey married when quite a young man and raised a family of ten children, five boys and five girls. Their names were Robert Wesley, William M., Jr., James Morris, Christopher Thomas, John Goodall, Mary J., Ann E., Sarah Alice, Amanda and Louisa. A son named Lemuel Park died in infancy. In 1850, Mr. Bailey, the father of the subject of this sketch, removed to Williamsburg in order to educate his younger children. The city at that time had in it schools, surpassing all others in the state, excepting the state university at Charlottesville. William and Mary collegegone of the oldest and best colleges in America, was in the height of its prosperity, under the presidency of Bishop Johns. Christopher John Dickinson Prior, a teacher of national reputation, had a large and prosperous school for boys and young men and drew patronage from many of the states of the south, while Profs. Morrisett and Peyton had charge of the Williamsburg academy. There was also a good college or seminary for girls under the management of the Episcopalians, and a special school for young ladies under the management of the Misses Clopton, daughters of Judge Clopton. Before his removal to Williamsburg, Mr. Bailey had sent his children to such schools as he and his neighbors secured in the country.

The subject of this sketch, after finishing the course in the academy under Profs. Morrisett and Peyton, studied law under Prof. Minor, of William and Mary college,and at that time fully expected to follow that profession, but he had made a profession of religion in his seventeenth year, and being often called upon by his father to attend the meetings at the colored Baptist church, in order to make the meeting lawful, and so prevent interruptions by the town constable, and as the pastor of the church could not readyit fell to him as a duty to read the scriptures for the preacher. From this he was gradually led into preaching to the people, and after a while found himself a preacher without intent or design. His father died in 1855, and his mother, a devout Christian, earnestly exhorted him to give up the law and go to Richmond college in Richmond, Va., then under the presidency of Rev. Dr. Robert Ryland, now living in Lexington, Ky. Dr. Ryland had in his early ministry baptized Mrs. Bailey. In the fall of 1856, young Mr. Bailey entered Richmond college as a student for the ministry. He spent three years there and failed to graduate, as he refused to stand the final examinations in Latin, having had a personal difficulty with Dr. Dabney, who was the teacher in that department. He and Dr. Ryland were warmly attached to each other, and continue so to this day. Dr. Ryland has been for some years a regular correspondent of his paper, and made its pages bright by his wisdom and piety. On leaving college in June, 1859, on the advice of the late Dr. J. B. Jeter, Mr. Bailey accepted a call to a very poor church in Surrey county, Va.. at that time one of the most destitute counties in the state. His salary was $75 a year. On the call of this church he was ordained in the Baptist church at Williamsburg, Rev. Dr. William M. Young, then pastor, Rev. Dr. William Martin and Rev. William A. Crandall, taking part in the services. On returning to Surrey county to enter his life's work, he made it a point to visit all the members of his charge. They were widely scattered and many of them very poor, but he spent a day or a night with every family that could afford to have him do so. By reason of this his $75 salary was amply sufficient to meet his wants. Here the war found him; his heart was with the south, and he accepted the issue. Much of the time between 1861 and 1865 he was with the Sixteenth infantry and the Thirteenth Virginia cavalry, many of the members of these regiments being from Surrey and Sussex counties, Va., and some of them were members of the Moore's Swamp church, in Surrey county, and the Antioch church in Sussex county, where he preached.

Mr. Bailey got badly whipped by the war, and upon its close in April, 1865, he took the oath of allegiance to the states, and accepted the situation, returning to the work of the pastorate. Three of his brothers, Robert, James and William fill soldiers' graves far away from the resting place of their parents. In May, 1865, the churches of all that section of Virginia being dismantled and scattered, he in company with his schoolmate, Dr. A. E. Owen of Portsmouth, Va., set out on a voluntary mission to encourage the churches of that association, and held meetings in the counties of Brunswick, Greensville, Southampton, Surrey, Sussex and Isle of Wight, and greatly aided in re-establishing the cause. They were young men, each owning a horse, and nothing else of worldly goods; their books had been captured by the Federal raiders, but all they asked was something to eat, and a place to lodge at night. On the 21st of November, 1865, Mr. Bailey married Miss Annie S., eldest daughter of the late Rev. Josiah C. Bailey of Greenville county, Va., Rev. Dr. A. E. Owen officiating. He and his wife were not related to each other, he being of Scotch descent, and she of English. During this year Mr. Bailey removed to North Carolina, and became principal of the Reynoldson academy in Gates county, and pastor of two churches, one in Virginia, and the other in North Carolina. From Reynoldson he was called to the pastorate of the Baptist church in Edenton, where he spent four happy years. In 1871 he was called to Warrenton, N. C., and spent five years at busy, happy work as pastor. These churches paid him, as pastor, four hundred and five hundred dollars respectively, and so much did they improve and develop under his ministry that each of them was enabled to give his successor $1,000 and house rent.

In 1875 Mr. Bailey was advised by his brethren to buy the *Biblical Recorder*, the organ of the Baptists of North Carolina. This paper had been regularly published since 1835, and had had as editors such men as Rev. Thomas Meredith, Rev. J. J. James, Mr. J. H. Mills and Rev. Dr. J. D. Hufham, four of the ablest men in the state, but at that time had only about 2,000 subscribers. He bought the paper and entered upon his work as editor July 1, 1875, Rev. Dr. J. D. Hufham as associate. The *Recorder* under his management has now become the best established paper in North Carolina, with 6,000 regular subscribers. As editor he came to the paper at a most auspicious time, and has been privileged to see not only his subscription list trebled, but the Baptists of the state more than trebled in numbers. The college at Wake Forest increased its endowment from $35,000 to over $200,000, and the contributions of the churches for missions, home, foreign and state, raised from $5,000 to more than $80,000. Mr. Bailey as editor cannot be said to possess anything like genius other than great capacity for work. He is cheerful, full of fun and humor likes to tell or hear a good joke about as well as Senator Vance or the Rev. Dr. Lafferty, of Virginia, does, and is generally in a good humor. He loves his brethren and his work and has no favorites. He has been for years pastor of poor county and village churches, and knows how to sympathize with all such. He is fair to all men and makes it a special point to not only be fair but generous to all who differ from him. While a Baptist and honestly believing that he is right, he can and does treat other denominations with respect. The first article in his creed is " *This is a free country.*" His disposition to joke has greatly annoyed some of his friends, and even damaged him with many of the solemn and straight-faced brethren of his own and other denominations. He is generous in his views, and makes it a point to subscribe to the building of all Baptist churches and every worthy cause. He gives to every one who asks him for help without reference to class or creeds. He is strictly honest, fair and open in all of his dealings, pays his debts promptly and expects others to do the same. He has no use for what he calls "side shows" in religion, and hates proud hypocrisy and double dealing; has no use for cranks and fanatics in or out of the church, believes with all his soul in liberty of conscience for himself and for all mankind, and bears no malice. He can readily forgive an injury and will laugh at a joke on himself as heartily as on another fellow, and has great pity for the man who cannot do this. Rev. Bailey has four children: a daughter, Mrs. W. N. Jones, and three sons; C. T., Jr., graduated from Wake Forest college in June, 1889, in his eighteenth year, and is now business manager of the *Recorder;* Josiah William, now a student in Wake Forest college, and Edmunds Lamar, a student in the Agricultural and Mechanical college at Raleigh. The youngest son, Bayard Yates, died when only eighteen months old. Wake Forest college conferred the degree of doctor of divivity upon Mr. Bailey some years ago, but he neither accepted nor declined it, and has never used it.

REV. MATTHIAS MURRAY MARSHALL, D. D.,

an eloquent preacher and one of the most eminent divines in North Carolina, was born in Pittsboro, Chatham county, N. C., August 13, 1841, and after attending the academic department of the schools in his native town and at Graham, N. C., entered Trinity college, Hartford, Conn., in December, 1858, and studied there until May, 1861, when the war called him home. He at once enlisted as a private in the Confederate army and was commissioned a lieutenant, but his health becoming impaired he soon retired from the army and entered the University of North Carolina, graduating with honors in June, 1863. Two years afterward he received the degrees of A. M. and A. B. from the University of North Carolina, and in 1874 the degree of D. D. was conferred upon him by William and Mary college, Williamsburg, Va. In December, 1863, Dr. Marshall entered the ministry of the Protestant Episcopal church, being ordained deacon at Emanuel church, Warrenton, N. C., by the Rt. Rev. Thomas Atkinson, bishop of the diocese, and immediately afterward he was sent as chaplain to the Seventh regiment North Carolina troops in the army of northern Virginia. His health, however, became precarious, and after a short service in the field, he returned to North Carolina and was sent to Kittrell Springs as minister in charge of the Episcopal church there and as chaplain of the Confederate hospital at that place. He remained in the acceptable discharge of these duties until 1865, when he accepted a call to Christ church, Elizabeth City, N. C., where during the next two years he faithfully ministered to his charge and endeared himself to his parish.

On September 3, 1865, he was ordained priest by Bishop Atkinson, and in July, 1867, he accepted a call to Emanuel church, Warrenton. Here he spent seven years, increasing in reputation, beloved by his congregation and highly esteemed by all the citizens of the community, irrespective of their religious affiliations. In 1874, on the death of the learned and beloved Dr. Mason, for many years the rector of Christ church, Raleigh, the vestry of that congregation unanimously called Dr. Marshall to take charge of that parish. There for seven teen years, he has served his congregation with fidelity and great acceptability. On one occasion, when his health was impaired, his throat giving him serious trouble, he felt impelled to tender his resignation; but his congregation appreciated his excellence so thoroughly and were so attached to him, that they gave him a year's leave of absence, with a liberal provision for his family while he should be away, in hopes of a restoration of his health. The rest proved beneficial, and his trouble has been removed. Dr. Marshall has had the satisfaction of seeing much substantial work done in Christ church parish since his connection with it. The large church debt has been paid, and many improvements have been made under his advice. He has always urged that the pew system should be abandoned, and he has had the gratification of seeing this so fully accomplished that Christ church is now virtually a free church. He also was a warm advocate for the division of the diocese, and this has likewise been accomplished.

Although Dr. Marshall's sermons are models of elegant diction and sound church doctrine and elevated sentiments, yet he enjoys a still higher reputation for the beauty of his reading, there being but few divines more gifted in this respect. Uniting with these accomplishments a fervor and zeal and unusual learning, Dr. Marshall is justly esteemed as one of the foremost men in the diocese. He is president of the standing commitee which is the governing authority of the diocese in the absence of the bishop, and has co-ordinate authority with him in many matters, and he has for years been president of the diocesan convention, and one of the examining chaplains of the diocese, and he is the clerical deputy of longest service from the diocese to the general convention. On July 12, 1866, Dr. Marshall married Miss Margaret Susan Wingfield, only daughter of Rev. John H. Wingfield, D. D., who was for fifty years rector of Trinity church, Portsmouth, Va., and the sister of the Rt. Rev. J. H. D.

Wingfield, D. D., LL. D., bishop of northern California. This union has been blessed with eight children, of whom six survive, viz.: John Wingfield Marshall, Eliza Simpson, the wife of T. L. Eberhardt, Esq.; Maud Murray Marshall, Joel King Marshall, Margaret Susan and Theodora Marshall.

Dr. Marshall's father, Abel Marshall, was born in Virginia in 1813, but removed in early manhood to Pittsboro, N. C., where in 1840 he married Miss Delana Gunter, daughter of Abner Gunter, who for more than forty years was the register of deeds of Chatham county, N. C., and to them were born six children, of whom but two now survive, Henrietta Marshall and the subject of this sketch. Mr. Abel Marshall was a cabinet maker, and was famed for his mechanical skill and genius. He was a magistrate of Chatham county, and for a number of years one of the town commissioners of Pittsboro. He possessed the entire confidence and esteem of the community in which he lived, and died much lamented in 1857.

Dr. Marshall has written much that has elicited high praise and given him an established reputation; but we will only refer to the sermon preached by him before the diocesan convention in St. Luke's church, Salisbury, N. C., in May, 1872, which attracted a great deal of attention, and an article on "the Episcopal church of North Carolina, its present condition and prospects," which was received with great approbation.

JOSEPH CALDWELL, D. D.,

the distinguished gentleman who was the first president of the University of North Carolina, was born in 1773, and died in 1835. He was professor of mathematics in the university from 1796 to 1817; and from 1817 till his death in 1835, he was president of the university. The first astronomical observatory in the United States was erected by him in Chapel Hill, the seat of the university. He was a leading spirit in the cause of public education and internal improvement in North Carolina. Dr. Caldwell was introduced to the board of trustees of the university and the people of North Carolina by Mr. Charles Harris, of Cabarrus county, N. C., to whom the state owes a lasting debt of gratitude for such presentation. Dr. Caldwell, in agreeing to come to Chapel Hill, acted on the advice of his best informed relatives and friends, and even after he had taken leave of his duties and friends at Princeton, where he was a tutor, he rejected favorable inducements held out to him to remain in Philadelphia, in charge of a congregation there, as their pastor, and continuing his journey to his destination at Chapel Hill, he remained here to the end of his days, in labors most unremitting, living a life of self-denial, and the good man was as cool and deliberate as he was fearless, and his trials were many, but he bore them with patience, and his character made him the well qualified professor and president of the university that he was. In the obscure village of Chapel Hill, in such insubordination, he lived, a president, a preacher, a teacher and a bachelor. Was it not a martyrdom to duty? Marrying first Miss Susan Rowan, of whom, as well as of an infant daughter, he was deprived three years afterward by death, subsequently associating himself in marriage with the honored name of Hooper, he became a land-owner and a slaveholder, thus making his citizenship in North Carolina complete. His second wife died early. A man small of stature, quick in motion, light in his step, he was every inch a man, born to control, ever equal to his office and duty. From this he never asked relief. Did the state fail to provide funds, did the south building stand uncovered for two years at the second story? He volunteered to collect money for its completion. Not in term time, but in the six weeks' vacation in the summer of 1811, in his stick-sulky he canvassed the state. Having headed the list by a substantial subscription, he brought home and paid over to the treasurer of the board, $12,000, with which it was completed. Continuing his labors and well directed efforts till in January, 1835, in his little brick office in his yard, his sufferings and his life ended, and a great benefactor was no more. Not many men have died in this state more honored whilst living, or reverenced when dead.

EDMUND FANNING.

Col. Edmund Fanning, who was so obnoxious to the regulators of Orange county during the troubles that culminated in the battle of Alamance, was a native of Long Island. He graduated at Yale college in 1757, and in 1764 received the degree of A. M. from Harvard as well as from his *alma mater*. He studied law, and in 1760 came to North Carolina, being in that year sworn in as an attorney at Hillsboro, where he settled. Three years later he was appointed register for Orange county, which office he continued to hold until he left the province in 1771. In 1766 he was appointed an assistant judge in the place of Maurice Moore, whom Gov. Tryon suspended because of his ardent conduct in the stamp act troubles. He was elected in that year also a member of the assembly from Orange county and became the fast friend of Gov. Tryon, whom he accompanied as chief executive officer of the escort on the expedition to run the boundary line. When the regulation troubles began in 1766, objection was early made to the illegal fees taken by the register as well as the clerk. Fanning had submitted to the justices of the inferior court in Orange the question of what fees he was entitled to and charged according to their decision. However, he was indicted in 1768 and submitted his case to the judges, denying any criminal intent, because he was acting under the direction of the inferior court. The judges took the case under advisement and referred the point to learned counsel in England, and it was never decided. The disturbances of that year led Gov. Tryon to appoint him colonel of the militia of Orange county, and he violently opposed the regulators who fired into his house and otherwise showed their ill-will toward him. The governor, in 1769, proposed to appoint him associate judge, but he declined.

In 1770 a new assembly was called, and the regulators elected Herman Husband instead of Fanning to represent them. Gov. Tryon thereupon erected Hillsboro into "a borough-town" with the right of a member, and Fanning was elected to the assembly from Hillsboro. The regulators, subsequently in September of that year, broke up the court, dragged Fanning by the heels from the courthouse, whipped him severely and tore down his house and destroyed his furniture. If any one man was the irritating cause of their violence, it was undoubtedly Fanning. After the battle of Alamance, he returned to New York, where indeed he had for some time been "surveyor general of the province." It seems that he came to North Carolina a poor young man, and when he left he was much better off in worldly goods.

In 1772, Columbia college in New York conferred the degree of A. M. upon him, and in 1774, he received the degree of doctor of civil law from Oxford, England, and 1803, the degree of doctor of laws from both Yale and Dartmouth college. When the Revolution came on he enlisted a corps of loyalists called the King's American Regiment of Foot, which was disbanded in 1783. In September, 1783, he was appointed lieutenant governor of Nova Scotia, and for nineteen years he was lieutenant governor of Prince Edwards Island, In 1793 he was made major-general in the British army, and in 1799 lieutenant-general, and in 1808 a full general. He died at his house in London, on February 28, 1818, leaving a widow and three daughters. Evidently he was a man of fine education and brilliant parts, and he won for himself more degrees at an early age than have ever been conferred upon any other resident of North Carolina. He was esteemed by the gentlemen of the province as a man of integrity and worthy of their confidence and association, and he expressed himself as being greatly mortified and wounded that the people of Orange county became averse to him.

REV. FRANCIS J. MURDOCH, S. T. D.,

is a native of Buncombe county, N. C., born March 17, 1846. His parents William and Margaret (Nixon) Murdoch were natives of Ireland, and after emigrating to the United States resided for two years in Pennsylvania. In 1845 they removed to North Carolina and settled near Asheville. William Murdoch was a farmer by occupation and dealt in fine stock. He is said to have been the first to export fine breeds of cattle to this county and was regarded as a model farmer and an excellent citizen. His death occurred in 1865. Rev. Dr. F. J. Murdoch was reared amid rural scenes in which he learned the lessons of industry, economy, integrity and perseverance, characteristics illustrated in all his after life. In youth he attended Col. Stephen Lee's school, an excellent educational institute in Asheville. Subsequently, after removing to South Carolina he entered the military academy of that state, first at Columbia and then at Charleston. In 1868, Dr. Murdoch was inducted into the sacred office of the gospel ministry, accepting the pastorate of St. John's Episcopal church of Gaston county, N. C., where he remained for two years. For the next two years he devoted himself to missionary work at Asheville. He was called to Salisbury in 1872, and became the rector of St. Luke's Episcopal church, where he has ever since been an active and zealous worker in the vineyard of his Divine Master. He has built four churches in Rowan county. He is much beloved as a pastor and is regarded as one of the most able and learned clergymen in the state. In 1890 the degree of Doctor of Sacred Theology was conferred upon him by the Episcopal University of the South at Sewanee, Tenn. The high estimate set upon Dr. Murdoch's character and abilities by his brethren, is evidenced by the varied and responsible positions to which they have called him. In 1889 he was selected as a deputy to the general convention of the Episcopal church, convened in New York, and he is president of the church conference of Rowan and adjoining counties, and was the originator of the church school for boys at Salisbury.

Besides his clerical qualities he is a highly valued citizen of the progressive order. He has become interested in the cotton manufacturing industry at Salisbury, where he was efficient in organizing the Salisbury cotton mills and the Rowan knitting company, of both of which he is now secretary and treasurer. He is also president of the Vance cotton mills, and secretary and treasurer of the Salisbury Building & Loan association. He is also the president of the Yadkin Falls manufacturing company, whose cotton mill is in Montgomery county, and is a director and practically the manager of more than one land company. He has manifested much interest in education, and is ex-secretary and examiner of the Salisbury graded schools. He has developed not only remarkable abilities as a practical business man, but as a successful financier, and he enjoys the unlimited confidence and esteem of all who know him. Rev. Dr. Murdoch was married to Miss Lila Marsh, of Salisbury, in 1884. They have been blessed with two children, a son and a daughter.

JETHRO RUMPLE, D. D.,

is a native of Cabarrus county, N. C., born March 10, 1827. He was reared on a farm and received his primary education in the country schools. At the age of eighteen he made a profession of religion and soon after undertook to secure a classical education, relying upon his own personal efforts to meet the expense. By alternately teaching and attending the neighboring academies Mr. Rumple was enabled to enter Davidson college, from which he graduated with distinction in 1850. Subsequently he taught school for several years, accumulating sufficient means to defray the expenses of his literary and theological education. In 1854, under the patronage of the Concord presbytery, he entered the theological seminary at Columbia, S. C., in which J. H. Thornwell, D. D., was then professor of theology. He here remained two years, and July 31, 1856, he was licensed by the Concord presbytery to preach, and on January 9, 1857, he was ordained by the same authority to the ministry, and was installed as pastor of the Providence and Sharon churches in Mecklenburg county, N. C. After holding this pastorate for four years he was called to the Presbyterian church at Salisbury, and was installed as its pastor November 24, 1860. There he has continued the faithful and beloved pastor up to the present time. His labors have been abundantly blessed; the church has trebled its membership under his charge and is now one of the largest and most prosperous churches in the state. During his pastorate six young men of his church have entered the ministry. As an evidence of the high esteem in which he is held by his brethren Dr. Rumple has been called to occupy various and responsible positions. For thirty years he has been a trustee of Davidson college and a director of the Union Theological seminary of Virginia. He has been a commissioner to several general assemblies, and in synod and presbytery has served the church in well nigh all the most honorable and important positions.

In 1874 he was moderator of the North Carolina Presbyterian synod, and in 1884 was a member of the general council of the Presbyterian alliance which met in Belfast, Ireland. On this occasion, Dr. Rumple availed himself of an opportunity to visit Glasgow, Edinburgh, the highlands, the western lakes of England, London and Paris. Dr. Rumple is highly distinguished as a minister, and as a pastor he is prudent, laborious and of the sympathetic temperament which gains the unreserved love and respect of his parishioners. His style as a preacher is forcible, earnest and eloquent. He is a lover of literature and history as well as of theology. He has spent much labor in writing up the "History of Presbyterianism in North Carolina," which he has contemplated publishing in book form, and such a work would prove a valuable addition to the church literature of the state. In 1881, was published a valuable history of Rowan county, N. C., of which Dr. Rumple is the author. In 1887 he edited the "First Semi-Centenary Celebration of Davidson College," giving the addresses, historical and commemorative of that occasion, and in which publication he is the author of an excellent and well written historical sketch of Davidson college. October 16, 1857, Dr. Rumple was married to Miss Jane E. Wharton, of Greensboro, N. C. This marriage has been blessed by the birth of three children, the eldest of whom, Watson Wharton Rumple, died at the age of eighteen, while a member of the senior class of Davidson college. The surviving children are, James W. and Linda Lee. James W. Rumple is a lawyer by profession, and the daughter is a talented and accomplished musician, the wife of Rev C. G. Vardell, pastor of the Presbyterian church of Newbern, N. C.

RT. REV. THOMAS ATKINSON, D. D., LL. D.

There have been more brilliant men in public service — men of more marked characteristics who have stamped their individuality upon the age in which they lived, and men of more extraordinary genius, but it is seldom that a character is found so complete, so harmonious, and so evenly balanced, so thoroughly rounded in all of its proportions, so symmetrical and beautiful in the essentials of a godlike man as that of the late bishop of North Carolina, Thomas Atkinson, of blessed memory. The influence for good of such a character and of such a life as his cannot be over-estimated. As the refreshing dew falls alike upon the delicate plant and the coarse fibre of the weed, causing each to bloom and blossom, so does such a life shed its sweet influences around. We cannot contemplate too frequently such a character, and we should be thankful that there is virtue enough still left among men to enable them to recognize and appreciate such an embodiment of goodness in human nature. The grandfather of Bishop Atkinson was the son of a clergyman of the church of England. He came to this country in early youth, and after his marriage to Miss Pleasants of Curls Neck, on the James river, Va., settled near Petersburg in Dinwiddie county, on a farm known as Mansfield, named after the great English jurist, Lord Mansfield. The bishop's parents were Robert and Mary (Tabb) Atkinson, who inherited the family seat Mansfield, and to them eleven children were born; Thomas, the subject of this sketch being the sixth in order, was born August 6, 1807. Upon reaching the age of sixteen he was sent to Yale college, but remained there not quite a year, owing to a difficulty in which he became involved with the faculty. In 1825 he entered Hampden-Sidney college, Virginia, and graduated at nineteen years of age with distinction in a class that numbered among its members the eloquent John S. Preston, and William Ballard Preston, the latter secretary of the navy during the administration of Gen. Taylor.

He married in 1828, and about that time he was licensed to the bar, and practiced his profession with great success, and would doubtless have risen to distinction as a jurist had it not pleased God to call him to a different sphere of action, the life of a laborious and self-sacrificing minister of the cross. While rector of Grace church, Baltimore, in 1853, the diocese of North Carolina called upon him to be its bishop. He accepted the call and was consecrated the same year in St. John's chapel, New York, and at once entered upon his duties. Bishop Atkinson assumed charge of the diocese of North Carolina at a very trying time in its history. Bishop Ives, the successor of the great Ravenscroft, had abandoned his charge and had joined the Roman Catholic communion. There was anxiety throughout the diocese as to the effect upon the church in North Carolina of the defection of its chief pastor, and it was feared that he who should be called to that high office would meet with more than ordinary difficulty in calming the troubled waters and bringing order out of chaos. Dr. Atkinson, upon whom the choice fell, was personally known to but few in the diocese, but the hand of God was evident in the selection, for under his wise administration dissensions ceased, confidence was restored, and the diocese remained true to the teachings of the uncompromising Ravenscroft and "to the faith once delivered to the saints."

In his personal endowments he was greatly favored; he was dignified yet courteous and affable in manner, with a deference for the opinions of others, yet with a steady reliance upon himself. He would attract attention in any assembly, and would be at once recognized as a leader of men. He was intensely intellectual, yet keenly alive to all the kindly impulses and more gentle virtues of our nature, a truly great man and remarkable in this that in whatever circle he moved, whether in the church, in society, or in the ordinary vocations of life, he exercised a mighty influence for good, for his example was the reflex of the precepts he inculcated. In the house of bishops his influence was very great, and whenever he rose to speak he commanded the attention of the members. As a pulpit orator he was distinguished for keen analysis, sound logic and effective reasoning. His style was chaste, and more conversational than declamatory, but his great power lay in the faculty he possessed of impressing all who heard him with the conviction of his sincerity, and this had an overpowering influence upon all with whom he came in contact. He was strong in debate, a close reasoner, and if the premises he laid down were admitted, there could be no escaping his conclusions.

Bishop Atkinson was a man of large brain, a just man, true to his convictions, to his friends and kinsfolks, and above all, to his God. He was a lover of books and a thinker, and notwithstanding the cares and responsibilities of his office, found time to keep up with the best literature of the day and frequently in the lecture room delighted large audiences from the rich stores of his varied learning. But it was as an expounder of divine truth and as a ruler in the church that he was most distinguished. He was conservative by nature, not timid and yet not aggressive. His prudence and his wisdom were manifest to all, and when these are combined as they were in him with a sincere and unselfish piety they are irresistible, for it is such men as he was, men of prayer and men of truth who constitute the strength and power of a state. Few men were more honored and beloved than he, and not by his own flock only, but by all classes and conditions in life " for this Duncan had borne his faculties so meek, had been so clear in his great office " that all peoples did do him reverence, and so when he fell asleep on January 4, 1881, bishops and priests, the high and the low, the rich and the poor, gathered around his bier with bowed heads and stifled sobs as he was borne onward to the grave — for he was a good man.

RT. REV. ALFRED A. WATSON, D. D.

This able and faithful minister of God is the greatly respected and beloved bishop of the diocese of east Carolina. He was born in New York city, August 21, 1818, his parents being Jesse and Hannah Maria Watson. He graduated at the University of New York, in 1837, and applying himself to the study of law, was admitted to the bar of the supreme court in 1841. He did not, however, continue long in the legal profession, but moved by strong convictions early abandoned it for the laborious and self-sacrificing life of a minister of the cross, and was made deacon in St. Ann's church, Brooklyn, N. Y., November 3, 1844, and ordained priest in St. John's church, Fayetteville, N. C., in 1845. He was rector of Grace church parish, at Plymouth, N. C., from 1845 to 1858, and of Christ church parish, Newbern, from 1858 to 1865. In 1863 he took charge of St. James parish, Wilmington, N. C., as assistant to the Rt. Rev. Thomas Atkinson, D. D., and was elected rector of that parish in 1864, where he remained until his elevation to the episcopate April 17, 1884. Previous to the division of the diocese of North Carolina, he was clerical deputy to the general convention from that diocese from 1850 to 1883, with the exception of the period of the war, and during a portion of the time was chairman of the committee on canons of that body. When the new diocese of east Carolina was formed, he was, with remarkable unanimity elected its bishop and was consecrated in the St. James' church, Wilmington, in which he had served as rector for more than twenty years, April 17, 1884.

To a mind singularly acute and discriminating, Bishop Watson possesses great powers of application and tenacity of purpose that enable him to master any subject requiring rigid investigation, to which his faculties may be applied. He has been a student all his life, and possesses the happy faculty of giving expression to his ideas in language terse, chaste and to the point, and so lucidly as to be easily understood even by the unlettered. He seldom indulges in rhetorical display, but preaches the gospel in its utmost purity, and his appeals to the heart and understanding are fervid and convincing. As a parish priest, he was faithful, diligent and zealous, and carried the lamp of truth in his hand; as a bishop he has proved himself to be a true leader of the hosts of God, whose trumpet never gives forth an uncertain sound. By precept and example, by the elevated tone of his morality and the purity of his life, he exerts a most wholesome influence over all who come within the sphere of its action, and greatly advances the cause of true religion. He is greatly beloved in his diocese and esteemed and respected by all classes and denominations of professing Christians, for he is a true man, who would suffer martyrdom rather than sacrifice principle.

REV. M. L. WOOD, D. D.,

one of the leading divines of the North Carolina conference of the Methodist Episcopal church, south, now pastor in charge of the Rockingham church, was born in Randolph county, N. C., October 23, 1829, the son of Jones K. and Ruth (Loftin) Wood, both North Carolinians by birth, and both descendants of Virginia families. The father was a planter, and an influential man in the community in which he lived. He was an earnest and consistent member of the Methodist Episcopal church, and for eighty years was absent but a few times from his place of worship. His death occurred September 5, 1880, he having attained the ripe age of ninety years: his wife died in 1868, aged seventy-five years. She was a most godly woman, and had been a member of the Methodist Episcopal church since 1824, having joined at the same time as her husband. Fourteen children were born to these parents, all of whom lived through childhood, and eight of them now survive, the Rev. Dr. Wood being the tenth child. He was graduated from Trinity college, in July, 1855, having entered college with but five dollars with which to defray his expenses. His early boyhood was spent on his father's plantation, and he worked as a planter until his twenty-first year. He became connected with the Methodist Episcopal church in his fourteenth year, and joined the North Carolina conference, in 1855, and was engaged as a circuit preacher until November, 1859, when he was sent by the missionary board of his church as a missionary to Shanghai, China. Here he labored until December, 1866, when he returned to his native land, arriving in New York March 20, 1867. In the same year he returned to North Carolina, and lectured in several places in the state until the fall of 1867, when he again entered the itinerancy, being appointed to Mount Airy, where he remained three years, after which, during the years 1871-2-3-4, he was presiding elder of the Salisbury district.

In 1875-6 he preached on the Iredell circuit, and from 1877 to 1879 was presiding elder on the Greensboro district, and from 1880 to June, 1883, he was on the Charlotte district. At the latter date Dr. Wood was elected president of Trinity college, a position he resigned December 24, 1884. At this time he was appointed to the Shelby district as presiding elder, and in 1888 Rockingham became the scene of his labors. September 19, 1859, his marriage to Miss Ellen E. Morphis was solemnized. Two children were born to this happy union, viz.: Edwin H., who died at the age of twenty-three years. He was born in Shanghai, China. At the time of his sad demise he was superintendent of weaving in the Naomi Falls factory, in Randolph county. He died from heart disease, April 6, 1884; and Charles V., bookkeeper in the tobacco factory of W. A. Whittaker at Winston, N. C. The mother died in Shanghai, China, March 16, 1864, aged twenty-nine years. Ellen Morphis was born January 7, 1835. She educated herself at Greensborough female college, graduating therefrom in 1856. For a little over two years she was engaged in teaching school at Thomasville, and later she became a member of the faculty of her *alma mater*. Dr. Wood was married a second time, Miss Carrie Pickett becoming his wife March 2, 1869. She bore him three children: Fanny L., Thomas Pickett and Maggie G. Mrs. Wood died in 1873, at the age of thirty years. Mrs. Amanda (Alford) Robins was made his wife November 29, 1875. March 9, 1890, at the age of fifty-seven years, she, too, went to rest. Dr. Wood is a member of the Royal Arch Masons, and has been W. M. of two lodges. His appointment to many of the best charges in the conference, and the success that has universally attended his work, fully attest his ability. Possessed of a mind of rare strength, disciplined and made symmetrical by the judicious, intelligent study of years, he is well fitted to fill theyleading pulpits of his church.

REV. SOLOMON POOL, D. D.,

a native of North Carolina, was born at Elizabeth City, Pasquotank county, April 21, 1832. His father was Solomon Pool, Sr., and the maiden name of his mother was Martha Gaskins. They were both natives of North Carolina, his father being of English descent and his mother of French. They had seven children, of whom the following named reached maturity: George D. Pool, who spent his life as a farmer. He had two sons of prominence, one now deceased, Hon. Walter F. Pool, who was a member of congress; the other, Hon. C. C. Pool, now residing in Elizabeth City, is a lawyer by profession and has been a circuit judge of his state. Another brother of the subject of this sketch was the late Hon. John Pool, a United States senator from North Carolina. Another brother was William G. Pool, M. D., now deceased, who was graduated at the North Carolina university and was a physician by profession. Solomon Pool, Jr., is the youngest of this family. He was reared amid the scenes of plantation life, and in 1849, at the age of seventeen, entered the state university, where he graduated in 1853. In December of the latter year he was elected tutor of mathematics in his *alma mater*, and in 1860 was raised to the adjunct professorship of mathematics, a position which he held for six years. He then accepted a government position in the revenue service, resigning the same in 1869 to accept the presidency of the university tendered him in that year. This position he held until 1875, when he severed his connection with the university and became principal of a school in Cary, N. C., of which he remained in charge for three years.

As an educator Dr. Pool was recognized as a success, possessing an extraordinary adaptability for that high profession. Since 1875 and especially since 1878 he has devoted his time and attention to the ministry, since the latter date his time being exclusively spent in preaching the gospel as held by the Methodist Episcopal church, south. He has successively hadycharge of the churches at Greensboro, Raleigh, Winston and Smithfield. Since 1888 he has had a congregation at Charlotte, where he has preached to general acceptance. Dr. Pool is a ripe scholar, a sound theologian, and is a most eloquent expounder of gospel truths. He is a thorough student, keeping himself well u in the theological literature of the times. His piety is unaffected,psimple and sincere; his manner in the pulpit is earnest, and his ideas clearly expressed. He is eminently happy in his pastoral relations, and is sincerely beloved by his people. A master of rhetoric and oratory in the pulpit, Dr. Pool is easy, graceful and instructive in conversation, and in the home circle he is peculiarly happy. In 1856 he was united in marriage with Miss Cornelia Kirk-

B—26

land, of Chapel Hill, N. C., and their union has been blessed with the birth of eight living children.

REV. ALEXANDER GILMER McMANAWAY, D. D.,

is a native of Bedford county, Va., and was born August 19, 1852. His father, Charles H. McManaway, was a farmer, and his mother's maiden name was Ann Wright. Both parents were of Scotch-Irish descent. The subject of this sketch is the eldest of eight children, four sons and four daughters. He was reared upon the homestead farm, and in his youth attended the country schools. At the age of nineteen he began teaching in the public schools of his native county, and continued to teach in that county and Botetourt for three years. He then gave up teaching and spent three years at the Richmond, Va., college, and received a liberal education, both scientific and classical, graduating in several scientific branches of the course, but not completing the full curriculum of the college, which institution he left in the fall of 1877. He then entered the Southern Baptist theological seminary, at Louisville, Ky., where he remained only a few months, leaving in consequence of failing health. After leaving the seminary he supplied, for four months of 1878, a vacancy in the College Hill Baptist church, of Lynchburg, Va. In May, of that year he was married to Miss Maria J. Robertson, of Petersburg, by whom he has five living children. Taking up regular pastoral work he located at Blacksburg, Va., in June, 1878, where he preached to a congregation till February, 1881, when he took a charge at Louisburg, N. C. Here and at Franklinton, he preached until October, 1885, when he was called to Charlotte, to take charge of the congregation at the Tryon Street Baptist church, where he still remains. His work as a minister has been effectual in building up several congregations and in increasing the membership of the churches under his charge. He came to Charlotte when his church numbered only 175 members. Since then more than 300 new members have been added to the church, and at his instance a new church building was erected in 1888, on Trade street, Charlotte. Some fifty members of the Tryon street congregation transferred their membership to the new church and others joined to give strength to the new organization. It has grown rapidly in membership and strength, and now has a pastor of its own.

Dr. McManaway has done effective work in assisting the pastors of other churches of his denomination in revival meetings, and has visited many congregations which he has aided materially in building up. His visits have extended to Greenville, Bennettsville and Darlington, S. C., Savannah, Ga., Durham, Weldon, Wadesborough, Wake Forest, Wilson and Lumberton, N. C., and Portsmouth, Va. He is vice-president of the home mission board of the southern Baptist convention for North Carolina, and in this capacity has canvassed the several associations of the state. He is a trustee of the Baptist female university at Raleigh, and of the Baptist orphanage at Thomasville. He is also an active member of the Charlotte

Y. M. C. A., and has taken much interest in literary work, having been a valued contributor to several periodicals, both religious and general. In 1889, in company with his brother, Rev. J. M. McManaway, he began the work of publishing a selection of sermons delivered by the renowned Rev. Charles H. Spurgeon, a Baptist divine of London. He visited London and held an interview with Mr. Spurgeon to arrange for the publication of twenty-three selected sermons from some two thousand which had been delivered by this celebrated divine. While on this tour Dr. McManaway visited, beside England, Scotland, Ireland and France. Returning, he and his brother in 1890 completed the compilation and published in book form the sermons mentioned above. This publication is one of great merit, and is highly appreciated by the devotees of sacred literature. Dr. McManaway is a lover of the study of theology, and has an extensive and well-selected library, in which his well-used volumes demonstate the extent of his devotion to study and the profundity of his learning. He is an easy and fluent speaker of rare eloquence, and his diction is a model of purity and strength. With such characteristics and endowments it can readily be seen that his effectiveness in pulpit oratory must be very great. In June, 1891, he was made a doctor of divinity by Keachie college, Louisiana. In August of the same year he became one of the editors of the *North Carolina Baptist*, a new and popular paper published at Fayetteville, N. C., and in connection with his pastorate is devoting his best energies to building up the influence and circulation of that journal.

ROBERT ZENAS JOHNSTON

was born in Rowan county, N. C., December 14, 1834. He is the son of Rufus D. and Aly (Graham) Johnston, the former a substantial and well-to-do farmer. The Johnstons and Grahams were devout members of the Presbyterian church and worshiped at the Third Creek church. They were constant and liberal supporters and officers in that church, and their children were brought up within the precincts and under its conservative influence. The best schools were selected for their training. Robert Z. Johnston was the second of six children, and is the only survivor of the six. He worked on his father's farm, on the South Yadkin river, until he was fifteen years old, when his father sent him to Bethany academy, in Iredell county. He was there fitted for and from there entered Davidson college, finishing the regular course and graduating in July, 1858, at which time he delivered the Latin salutatory on commencement day. He often represented his class on public occasions during the course, and at the semi-centennial, in 1887, he delivered the address on Dr. Lacy's administration as president of the college. In October, 1858, he entered Columbia (S. C.) theological seminary and graduated in regular course in May, 1861. On the 15th of May of the same year, he married Miss Katharine Caldwell, of Chester, S. C., and November 17, 1861, was ordained to the ministry of the gospel by Concord presbytery at Providence church, and was installed pastor of the Providence and Sharon churches, in Mecklenburg county. This relation continued until 1872. During the Civil war the churches were reduced to impoverishment, both pastor and flock. Rev. Mr. Johnston reluctantly accepted a call to Lincolnton, and in 1872 removed his family to that place, where he has faithfully discharged the duties of pastor and evangelist ever since. He has preached seven years at Shelby, N. C., until that church was enabled to call a pastor. He also officiated at Dallas, Goshen, Mount Holly, Iron Station and at the Lincolnton paper mills.

Under Mr. Johnston's effective ministrations new churches were organized, houses of worship were built and memberships increased. In 1868 he was elected stated clerk of the Concord presbytery and in 1869, when Mecklenburg presbytery was organized, he was transferred to that presbytery and made its stated clerk, which office he has continued to fill. He was instrumental in improving the public school laws of North Carolina and was elected superintendent of public instruction for Lincoln county. He conducted the county institutes, visited and addressed public schools for years and is now chairman of the board of education of Lincoln county. His interest in the schools never falters and he often delivers addresses in public upon educational topics and the improvement of the young. Mrs. Johnston, having been early schooled in the church, is a willing and efficient helper in the educational work of her husband. Though laboring in a field in which other church organizations are established there is no clashing of interests, but their interrelations are pleasant and their pronounced Presbyterian views are always respected. Large congregations have usually attended the religious services conducted by Rev. Johnston. He generally preaches without manuscript and his sermons are listened to with rare interest. To the leading religious journals he is a frequent and welcome correspondent. He performs missionary service in his county so far as his strength will permit, after delivering three sermons on Sundays. Mr. and Mrs. Johnston have raised six daughters and three sons and trained them in the Lincolnton schools. In 1886 great grief was brought to the family by the accidental death of the eldest son, Robert. He met his untimely end in a furious storm near Wilkesbarre, Penn., an event which long cast its shadow upon the before happy and undivided household.

REV. HILARY THOMAS HUDSON, D. D.,

is a native of Davie county, N. C., born November 15, 1823. He is the son of John Hudson who was born and raised in the same county. His mother was Diana Hughes, and both parents are now dead, the former dying when his son, the subject of this sketch, was but five years old. He is the eldest of three children, his brother J. W. Hudson and his sister, Susan Parnell, deceased. He worked on a farm until he was nineteen years of age, when he was apprenticed to a carriage builder. During the time he was employed at his trade he improved his spare hours in studying grammar and other useful branches. His studious habits and desire to learn caused his friends to open the way to send him to the Mocksville academy, then conducted by the Rev. Baxter Clegg. In this school he made rapid advancement, so that when he had finished his academic course his friends again provided for his entering Randolph-Macon college in Virginia, but not having the means to complete the course at that institution, he returned home and taught school at Snow Creek in Iredell county. While teaching here he was licensed to preach in the Methodist Episcopal church, south. In 1851 he joined the North Carolina conference at Salisbury, and was sent as the pastor of the Methodist church at Washington, N. C. Since that time he has been the pastor at Chapel Hill, Wilson, Greensboro, Fayettville, Rockingham and Raleigh. He has also been chosen presiding elder in the Salisbury and Shelby districts. While at Raleigh, Dr. Hudson became the editor and proprietor of *The Raleigh Christian Advocate*, of which he is still associate editor. He has been elected and served as a delegate to the general conference of the Methodist Episcopal church twice. He wields a facile and trenchant pen, and has probably contributed more articles in the way of religious literature than any of his clerical brethren in the state. He is the author of The Methodist Armor, a book which is now having a wide circulation all through the Methodist church, south. The opinions of the press have been very profuse and generous in their praises of his book. Besides The Armor, Dr. Hudson is the author of several smaller publications, as The Shield of The Young Methodist, The Red Dragon, The Sun-Clad Woman, The Prohibition Trumpet and Children's Lamp. All his books have had quick and ready sales.

At present Dr. Hudson is located at Shelby, N. C., where he acts as pastor and associate editor of the *Raleigh Christian Advocate*, the organ of the North Carolina conference, and one of the ablest and most influential religious papers in the state. His family consists of himself, his most excellent wife and a son — H. T. Hudson, Jr., about twenty-three years old, a talented young lawyer with a bright future in immediate prospect. Dr. Hudson has been twice married. His first wife was Miss Hattie, daughter of the late Dr. Cole, of Greensboro, a most estimable woman in every sense of the word. She died in Raleigh in 1868, leaving H. T. Hudson, Jr., her only child. In 1872 Dr. Hudson married Miss Mary T. Lee, daughter of the late David M. Lee, of Mecklenburg county. She is an educated and cultured woman, a bright ornament in the Christian society in which she moves.

WILLIAM HOOPER,

one of the signers of the Declaration of Independence, was born June 17, 1742, in Boston, Mass., where his father, Rev. William, pastor of Trinity church, enjoyed the affection and reverence of a cultured congregation, and was admired for his elegance of mannersan d impressive eloquence. The subject of this sketch was given the best education that could be obtained in America, graduating with distinction at Harvard, taking A. B. in 1760 and A. M. in 1763. He studied law under James Otis, who is recognized as one of the earliest and boldest advocates of American rights, and doubtless took his coloring from Otis' avowed principles. In 1764 he came to North Carolina and settled at Wilmington, and three years later married, in Boston, Miss Ann Clark, of Wilmington, daughter of Thomas Clark, deceased, and sister of Col. Thomas Clark, of the North Carolina Continental line, and afterward a general in the army of the United States. In his profession Mr. Hooper speedily attained eminence. His superior education and training were united to natural gifts of the highest order. He was an orator of the Ciceronian school, polished, rhetorical, stately and diffusive, and his accomplishments and admirable characteristics won him friends on all sides in his new home. Indeed at that time there clustered at Wilmington a bevy of elegant gentlemen who had no superiors in America, the Cape Fear region being justly famed for the politeness and elegance and culture of its inhabitants. And in such company Mr. Hooper took rank as a star of the first magnitude, and added lustre to the radiance of the Cape Fear.

In the regulation troubles in 1771 he was an active supporter of the government. At the next election, 1773, he was chosen to represent Wilmington in the assembly, and again in 1774 he was in the assembly, and in the provincial congress. Indeed the provincial congress was called only after conference with him. He was one of the first patriots of that early day. He was in 1775 elected a delegate to the Continental congress, and again in 1776 by the body that first instructed its delegates in congress to concur in declaring independence. In the Continental congress Mr. Hooper deservedly took rank with the foremost members of the body. There were few, if any, superior to him in ability, in scholastic attainments, in polished oratory, and in patriotic ardor. His first speech in congress commanded profound silence, and was listened to with the most earnest attention. Some of the most notable state papers were the product of his pen alone. He signed the Declaration of Independence, and took a conspicuous part in the proceedings of congress. In 1777, however, the courts were again opened in North Carolina, after a suspension of several years, and the expense of living in Philadelphia being great, Mr. Hooper returned to the practice, but continued to serve in the state assembly, maintaining his position as one of the foremost men in North Carolina. He resided at Masonboro Sound, eight miles from Wilmington, and when that section was invaded, in 1781, he removed his family to Wilmington, where they would be free from the insults of marauding parties, and himself retired to Edenton, where he was very ill. Writing in the darkest hours of the Revolution he said he had never doubted that America would achieve her independence. He was a warm personal friend of Judge Iredell, who wrote to Mrs. Iredell — " I wish to be like him." Indeed the admiration of Judge Iredell for him was unbounded.

Mr. Hooper continued in the assembly until 1784. He was not an admirer or follower of Jefferson, and warmly expoused the proposed Federal constitution, but was defeated for the convention. At that time he lived in Hillsboro and the western part of the state was opposed to the constitution. Mr. Hooper was of a delicate organization and constitution, and his health was at times poor. He had frequent spells of violent illness. In the fall of 1790 he suffered greatly. It appears that his mind became unsettled and he passed away October 19, of that year, at the age of forty-eight. Of Mr. Hooper it may be truly said that as brilliant as were Howe, Harnett, Iredell, Ashe and Moore, and all of those renowned names that adorned North Carolina's annals during his time, taking a view of the entire galaxy, none surpassed him in shining talents and fine accomplishments, and none deserves more grateful appreciation by North Carolinians.

REV. THOMAS HENDERSON PRITCHARD, D. D.,

who has been for many years the most distinguished Baptist minister, perhaps, of North Carolina, was born in Charlotte, N. C., February 8, 1832. His father, the Rev. Joseph Price Pritchard, was the son of Benjamin Pritchard, a merchant of Charleston, S. C., and his aunt, Madam Juliana DuPre, for half a century presided over a famous school for young ladies in that city. Dr. Pritchard's paternal grandmother was Esther Sass, who belonged to an English family distinguished for attainments in art, her brother, Richard Sass, being a noted painter and president of an academy of design, in London. His mother was Eliza Hunter Henderson, a daughter of Dr. Samuel Henderson, and a descendant of the Martin and Henderson families, who played a conspicuous part in the earlier history of the state. Her grandmother was Jane Martin, the wife of Col. Thomas Henderson, and the sister of Alexander Martin, who was three times governor of North Carolina, the only man who ever enjoyed such an honor, except Gov. Zebulon B. Vance. Judge James Martin, of Mobile, Ala., and H. C. Jones, the author of "Cousin Sallie Dillard," also belonged to this family. Of the Hendersons, there were many eminent men. Richard Henderson, an ante-Revolutionary judge, who figured in the "War of the Regulators," and who sent Daniel Boone, of historical fame, to Kentucky and purchased that state from the Indians, was the brother of her grandfather, Col. Thomas Henderson; another brother, William, commanded with distinguished gallantry Sumter's brigade at the battle of Eutaw Springs; and still another brother, Major Pleasant Henderson, of Chapel Hill, was for forty years clerk of the house of commons of North Carolina without ever asking a man for his vote. Judge Richard Henderson was the father of Leonard Henderson, who died in 1833, chief-justice of North Carolina, and of Archibald Henderson, of Salisbury, who represented his district in congress, and was offered a position on the supreme court bench by the side of his brother Leonard. His grandson, John S. Henderson, is now congressman from the same district. Another gifted member of this family was Dr. Pleasant Henderson, son of the Major Pleasant Henderson named above, who was pronounced by Daniel Webster to be the "most accomplished man he ever knew."

Dr. T. H. Pritchard was prepared for college at a popular academy taught in Mocksville, N. C., by the Rev. Baxter Clegg, a Methodist preacher, and among his school-mates were Judge Victor C. Barringer, who has attained high honors in Egypt; Col. R. I. Dodge, U. S. A.; Rev. S. M. Frost, D. D., and Rev. H. T. Hudson, D. D. His father being a poor man with a large family, he worked his way through college, and was graduated from Wake Forest college in 1854, delivering the valedictory. Mr. J. H. Mills, who has founded two orphanages, and Judge W. T. Faircloth, who was at one time a justice of the supreme court of the state, divided the honors of the class with him. After traveling for a year as agent of Wake Forest college he was ordained as pastor of the Baptist church of Hertford, November, 1855, Rev. William Hooper, D. D., LL. D., preaching the sermon of the occasion. After preaching and teaching in Hertford for a few years, and paying his college debts, he went to Charlottesville, Va., to read theology with Dr. John A. Broadus, and attend the famous University of Virginia. Dr. Pritchard has held many responsible positions and been greatly honored of his brethren, and has probably dedicated more churches and preached at the ordination of more ministers than any other man now living in North Carolina. His pastorates have been Hertford, N. C.; Fredericksburg, Va.; Franklin Square, Baltimore, Md.; Petersburg, Va.; Broadway church, Louisville, Ky.; First church, Raleigh; and First church, Wilmington. His longest terms of service were in Raleigh, where he was twice pastor, and for nearly fourteen years, and his present charge, Wilmington, where he has been nearly eight years.

In September, 1879, Dr. Pritchard became president of Wake Forest college, and during his administration of three years traveled over 15,000 miles and addressed 60,000 people on the subject of education, and brought up the patronage of the college from 118 to 183 students. Many of his friends think these three years the most useful of his life, but his heart yearned for his chosen life work and he soon returned to the pastorate. Dr. Pritchard was for seven years chairman of the board of missions of his church, a good part of the time discharging the duties of the corresponding secretary as well. He is fond of writing for the press and has been twice associate editor of the *Biblical Recorder*, the Baptist organ in North Carolina, and is now one of the editors of *Charity and Children*, the organ of the Baptist orphanage. He has been a trustee of the Southern Baptist theological seminary for twenty-two years; a trustee of Wake Forest college about as long; is also a trustee of the state university, of a female university, of the white Baptist orphanage and also of a colored orphanage. In 1872 he was chosen one of a committee with Senator Joseph E. Brown, of Georgia, Dr. J. L. Burrus, of Virginia, Dr.

Boyce, of South Carolina, and three others to locate the Southern Baptist theological seminary, and on the recommendation of this committee it was moved from Greenville, S. C., to Louisville, Ky. In 1874, Dr. Pritchard preached the opening sermon of the Southern Baptist convention in Charleston, S. C.; in 1888 he represented his church in the World's missionary conference in London, and in 1891 he was appointed, with Drs. T. T. Eaton, F. M. Ellis, H. H. Harris and I. T. Tiechnor, a committee to arrange for the centennial of modern missions in 1892.

In stature Dr. Pritchard is of medium height and is stoutly built; his manners are genial; his disposition is cheerful; his spirit boyish, and he is very fond of young people. He takes great pleasure in field sports, especially quail shooting, and has the reputation of being a good wing-shot, and is an indefatigable hunter. He received the doctorate of divinity from the State University of North Carolina in 1868, at the age of thirty-six years.

Dr. Pritchard married Miss Fannie G. Brinson, of Newbern, N. C., in 1858, who still survives to brighten his life and help him in his work. She is a famous Sunday-school teacher, having a Bible class of eighty-four young men. Mr. and Mrs. Pritchard have five children, three sons and two daughters. The eldest son, W. B. Pritchard, M. D., though under thirty, is a lecturer in the New York Polyclinic, and as a writer is already an authority on nervous diseases. In his eldest daughter, Mrs. A. D. Jenkins, also a resident of New York, the genius for music, which distinguished her ancestors on both sides, the Hendersons and Sasses, has found its crowning development, as she is a singer of surpassing sweetness and power. We subjoin a sketch of the character of Dr. Pritchard, as drawn by his friend, Rev. H. W. Battle:

An elegant writer has said, "The heart is the standard of the man." Measured by this standard, Thomas Henderson Pritchard is surely one of the manliest of men. His sensibilities are exquisitely refined, and all his impulses pay court to honor. A close observer may discover in each individual some secret clue to the character, more reliable than popular estimate or public act. If the individual be accustomed to expressing his deepest convictions, for the purpose of influencing public sentiment, his words—such is the subtle union between words and principles—may be accepted as the magic keys to reveal the very sacristy of his nature. The writer observed, soon after meeting Dr. Pritchard, that there was one word he often used, always with unconscious accentuation, and that word subsequently blended its tender strength with each line in the mind's picture of the man: that word was, "Gentle-man."

Nature, as well as early associations, did much for Dr. Pritchard. All good stars shone at his natal hour. A splendid physique, a noble heart, brimming with kindly sympathies and joyous life, and a brilliant intellect, filled the measure of heaven's royal largess. But Dr. Pritchard was not born to be a student; the elements were not so mixed in him. His love for letters brings him into easy sympathies with the good and beautiful in the literature of the ages, but his love for the society of friends and for "the free air" renders impossible that rigid discipline of the mind which adds to the elegant accomplishments of the gentleman, the erudition of the profound scholar. As a preacher, his ideas are synthetic and come naturally out of the text, his sentences are exceedingly chaste and often very beautiful, his gestures graceful, and his voice singularly sweet and flexible. If we look deeper than "the high art of sermonizing," we shall find a fidelity to evangelical truth — as the fathers held it — which never falters, and a personal devotion to God and man that throbs like a heart-beat in every sentence.

As a platform speaker upon religious themes, Dr. Pritchard is often at his best. His mind is not an alembic that tests at once, with unerring precision, the quality of each question presented; he often finds it difficult, when good men may differ, to decide, and at times this hesitancy might be attributed, by those who did not know him, to a too lax grasp of moral conviction — such a conclusion would be far from correct. In devotion to right he would not swerve a hair-breadth to escape the martyr's crown. His moral courage is equal to any emergency, and if he errs in his estimate of men and measures, his mistake "leans to virtue's side." As might be inferred from what has been said, Dr. Pritchard is admirably fitted for the pastoral relation — a charming conversationalist, a warm-hearted friend and a wise counselor, his words are instinct with cordiality and his very presence is a benediction. When the summons "come up higher," shall call the faithful minister, unselfish friend and Christian gentleman from the scenes of earth, then may it be said of Thomas Henderson Pritchard, as Lord Brooke said of Sir Philip Sidney: "His wit and understanding beat upon his heart, to make himself and others, not in word or opinion, but in life and action, good and great."

REV. PROF. F. W. E. PESCHAU, D. D.

The Peschau family has had its home in the city of Clansthal-Zellerfeld, on the Hartz mountains, in the kingdom of Hanover, Germany, for about one hundred and fifty years. Two branches of the family migrated from the old family seat, and their descendants are chiefly residing in the United States.

Hon. Edward Peschau, German imperial consul in the port of Wilmington, is the son of Rev. George Ludwig Peschau, who spent his whole life in Germany, and was the first minister in the family's history. He was a graduate of the far-famed University of Goettingen, and after being ordained to the holy ministry, took charge of the Lutheran church at Altenbroch, near the city of Bremen. Here he lived and labored for forty-five years, and here he died and is buried. One of his sons is a physician in Germany, and a nephew of his, Dr. Hermann Peschau, resides in Nebraska.

Rev. Prof. F. W. E. Peschau, D, D., of Wilmington, N. C., the subject of our sketch, was born in the city of Clansthal-Zellerfeld,

Hanover, February 17, 1849. He is the eldest child and only son of Henry and Wilhelmine (Muehlhahn) Peschau and had but one sister. The family came to the United States in 1853, on the ship North Carolina, and landed in Baltimore, where they resided a short time, and then removed to Wheeling, W. Va., to take up a permanent residence. In Wheeling the aged father, Henry Peschau, and his only daughter, Mrs. C. Fuhr, still reside, the mother having died, March 9, 1877. She was buried in Mount Zion Evangelical Lutheran cemetery. Having spent his boyhood days in Wheeling, where he attended both a German parochial school and the public school, and having been confirmed, he was sent in 1867 to study for the holy ministry, in the celebrated Lutheran college and theological seminary at Gettysburg, Penn. Here he spent six years. At his graduation he had the honor of delivering the German oration of his class, which was the largest class the institution had graduated up to that time.

It is customary in Germany, that when young Lutheran theologues have finished their course, that they teach either in private families or in a school, to use what they have learned and to get practical experience and to learn to understand life and the world, that their public teaching may be practical, wise and useful. This wish was cherished by the father, and so Prof. Peschau accepted the honorable position tendered him, and became superintendent of German in the public schools, and professor of German in the high school in the city of Evansville, Ind. This position he held three years when he resigned that he might give himself exclusively to the ministry. He was asked by the board to re-consider and re-call his resignation after its presentation, as he had given entire satisfaction. Called as Lutheran pastor to Nebraska City, Neb., he was soon after his removal there unanimously chosen superintendent of the public schools and served in this capacity two years. He also became professor of German in Nebraska college, an Episcopal institution located there, and for two years taught in it, under the lamented Bishop Clarkson. All this was done in addition to his pastoral labors. Shortly after his removal to Nashville, Tenn., he became professor of German in Dr. Ward's large female seminary, at that time the largest in the south, and also in Vanderbilt university, so that he taught continually for about ten years. Recognizing his talents, proficiency, experience and success both as a professor and superintendent, the board of trustees of North Carolina college, in 1883, unanimously elected him president of North Carolina college, but he declined the high and distinguished honor of a college presidency. As superintendent and professor he has had under his care about 100 teachers and 3,800 children and students.

He has been a prolific writer. For five years he was editor of the "German Gleanings," in *The Lutheran Observer*, of Philadelphia, the largest and most widely circulated English Lutheran church paper in the world. When *The Southern Illustrated Monthly Magazine* was begun in Nashville, Tenn., which was one of the finest efforts in this line ever made in the south, but for lack of means failed, he was

chosen editor. For about ten years he has been associate editor of
The Lutheran Visitor, the leading southern Lutheran church paper.
Besides all this he has been special correspondent of several papers
in both English and German.

He has not only lectured to his students in German university
style, but has also delivered many addresses and lectures on educational and other topics before teachers' institutes, county, district and
state conventions, schools, seminaries, colleges and universities. He
has lectured in the following twenty states: Alabama, Florida,
Georgia, Iowa, Indiana, Illinois, Kansas, Kentucky, Maryland, Missouri, Nebraska, New Jersey, New York, North Carolina, Ohio, Pennsylvania, Tennessee, South Carolina, Virginia and West Virginia.
His lectures on " The Cemetery of the Sea," " Foreigners," " Luther,"
"The Lutheran Church," and "Moral Training in Public Schools,"
have been delivered before thousands of people and received great
encomiums from the press, from faculties of institutions, from private
letters, etc. We append just a few. The Charleston *News and
Courier* says: " The learned and gifted speaker selected as his subject ' Foreigners,' and answered who and what they are and what they
have done for this country. The effort was grand and the audience
was delighted." *Die Deutsche Zeitung*, of Wheeling, W. Va.: " Pastor
Peschau is an extraordinarily fine speaker." Charlotte, N. C., *Observer:* " Mr. Peschau is a lecturer of fine ability and his lecture is one
of the finest literary productions we have known to emanate from the
· pen of our home talent." Nashville *Daily American:* " In regard to
the lecture I can only repeat what all others have said who have
heard it, that it was grand, beautiful, sublime."

The sole aim and object of his public life has been to prove himself a faithful pastor, and gospel preacher in the Evangelical
Lutheran church; whilst he has talents in other directions and delights
to use them to do good, the ministry is his chief delight, as it is his
chief calling. Even as a student he organized two Sunday-schools,
and whilst engaged in the busy duties of superintendent and professor
at Evansville, Ind., he began, and maintained and built up a mission
in the court house, that had a Sunday-school of almost 400 scholars.
His first regular pastorate was in Nebraska City, Neb., where he
succeeded the distinguished Rev. Dr. Eli Huber, who had been called
to Philadelphia, as pastor of the large Messiah church. One Easter-tide
while pastor here he confirmed forty-eight catechumens. The work
prospered in every direction, but the climate was too severe for the
young pastor, and so on the united and urgent advice of several physicians he came south, accepting a call to the first church in the city
of Nashville, Tenn. The parting of the pastor and people in Nebraska City was a touching one. The most pleasant relations possible,
had existed, the work was prosperous, and pastor and people were
mutually pleased and satisfied, so that it was painful to each side to
speak the parting word. In Nashville, Tenn., the pastoral relations
were always pleasant, and both the congregation and Sunday-school,
grew steadily for years. The church being German, English services

were introduced that were much appreciated and well attended, and proved to be of incalcuable advantage to the church and its work. About four years were spent in the famous capital of Tennessee, and Rev. Mr. Peschau often speaks of them with delight, and of the kindness shown him, while there, from the the governor down to the humblest citizen. Having been unanimously called as pastor of St. Paul's Evangelical Lutheran church of Wilmington, N. C., in December, 1881, he accepted the call and removed to Wilmington, early in 1882. He will soon complete ten years of pastoral work in Wilmington. He has ever enjoyed the esteem of his congregations. The first two pastorates he served have endeavored several times to have him return as pastor, when they were vacant, and St. Paul's, in Wilmington, paid him the unusual honor and kindness of adopting a resolution unanimously and heartily in 1884, expressing the desire that he might remain its pastor during the days of his natural life.

During his labors in Wilmington the parsonage interior has been completed and much improved and the exterior painted. The interior of the church has also undergone entire renovation. The interior has been finely frescoed, new chandeliers, new carpets, etc., and a grand new pipe organ secured and improvements made in many directions. Luther memorial building, an elegant edifice, was erected in 1884. In 1890 a lot was purchased and a fine chapel erected thereon in Brooklyn, known as St. Matthew's Mission. The congregation and Sunday-school have both enjoyed a steady growth and are both in a flourishing condition. Up to the present time Rev. Mr. Peschau has had charge of and under his own supervision about 1,500 Sunday-school scholars. He has added to the various churches he has served about 300 by certificate, 300 by confirmation, and 400 by baptism, or about 1,000. Being an active church worker, he has held many positions of trust, and has received many church honors. Fully two-thirds of the time of his being in the ministry he has been a synodical officer. He has occupied almost every possible office of ecclesiastical secretaryship, from the lowest to the highest. For four years consecutively he was president of the North Carolina synod, an honor no other man ever enjoyed in the history of this old body. He was the last president of the general synod, south, at Roanoke, Va., and as the first president of the united synod, south, opened its convention in Savannah, Ga., in 1887, so that he was twice the chief officer in the entire southern Lutheran church. The general southern Lutheran body chose him as its representative to the northern general synod, in 1887. He has frequently represented district synods, both as delegate to the general body and also to other district synods. June 10, 1891, he was complimented with the honorary degree of D. D., which was unanimously and heartily bestowed upon him, by the board of trustees of North Carolina college and the excellent faculty of said institution. Dr. Bemheim, his predecessor, writes: "Your congregation is certainly advancing under your administration and I say this sincerely and not as a mere compliment; the work speaks for itself." *The Lutheran Home*, in a notice of him, says: "We are

glad to have such a worker in so important a field of labor. Those
who bear the banner of the cross successfully are worthy of all honor.
We sometimes overlook the esteem due them — due not to pamper
pride, but to 'give honor to whom honor is due.' We offer, therefore, no apology for this extended biography of one to whom God
has given superior talents and the energy to use them."

On June 3, 1873, he married Miss Clara J. Myers, eldest daughter
of Hon. A. K. Myers, Sr., of York Springs, Penn. They have five
children living, namely, four daughters and one son. Dr. Peschau
has published a number of songs of his own composition, as: "Ode
to Gen. Andrew Jackson." This ode was sung by the Phil-har-
monic society, and played by the Columbia (Tenn.) band, at the unveiling of the Jackson equestrian statute in Nashville, in 1880. "Ode
to Mrs. Ex-President James K. Polk," "God Bless Our Noble Fire-
men," "There is no Home but Heaven," "The Orphan's Plea," and
Father Ryon's celebrated "Conquered Banner," which later he
translated to German and set to music of his own. He has published
tracts, quite a number of sermons, a small book of poems, sketch of
Mrs. James K. Polk, etc. He has been elected honorary member
by a number of literary societies, connected with literary institutions,
as Vanderbilt university, North Carolina college, etc. Various
historical societies of national reputation and influence have elected
him honorary member, as the Tennessee historical society, the
finest in all the soutland, and the German historical society of
Maryland, which is the finest in its line in the United States,
Trinity historical society, of Dallas, Tex., etc. He is corresponding secretary of the Wilmington historical society. He has been a
director in the Wilmington library association for some eight years,
was acting chaplain of the Porter Rifles, the best infantry company
of Nashville, Tenn., and often officiated as chaplain in both the house
and senate of the Tennessee legislative bodies. He has been delegate to county, state and inter-national Sunday-school conventions a
number of times, and was chosen a vice-president of the North Carolina Sunday-school convention in Charlotte.

The doctor has received a number of calls from different churches,
and besides these has been offered other calls during his stay in Wilmington, but he declined them all. Prominent among them was a
flattering and pressing call extended him in February, 1891, by "The
Church of the Holy Ascension," of Savannah, Ga., the largest Lutheran church and congregation in the southern states, the church
having cost about $75,000. All these facts prove a recognition and
appreciation of his talents and services on the part of the church. As
to his scholarship we need but say that he not only studied Hebrew,
Greek and Latin and the full college course, but that he speaks, reads,
writes and uses English and German with equal fluency, ease and
accuracy, and has so far mastered the Norwegian language as to be
able to hold services for Scandinavian seamen, which are most highly
appreciated. His ability as a writer is demonstrated by the fact of
his having been editor for so many years. The many church offices

he has held prove that he is a parliamentarian of recognized merit. The positions occupied in educational institutions demonstrate that he is a successful educator. The many things written and accomplished by him establish his reputation as a many-sided and indefatigable worker. His success as pastor and preacher is attested by the work done and the calls he has been honored with. His theological attainments have been recognized and endorsed by the honorary degree of D. D. His oratorical powers have often been complimented, and at the eighty-eighth convention of the North Carolina synod he was publicly introduced as "The silver-tongued orator of the North Carolina synod," and *The Lutheran Visitor's* reporter from South Carolina, who was present, published in his account, the following: "He was introduced as the silver-tongued orator of the North Carolina synod, and fully sustained that reputation. The address was a learned, able and eloquent presentation of the subject, and is highly complimented by all." Whilst he has talents, he has that which is better, namely, industry; and whilst he has an enviable popularity, he has that which is better, namely, humility. He ascribes all he has and all he has been able to do, to the blessing and help of God, whose child and servant he is—and his one ambition is to spend and be spent, to fullest extent, in the Master's service.

In concluding this sketch, which is a labor of love, the writer wishes yet to add to what has been said above, that he has known Rev. Mr. Peschau for the last ten years intimately, though he is not a member of his church. No minister in the city of Wilmington, of any denomination, has the confidence and general esteem of the entire community to a greater degree than he. He is the only minister in our knowledge, experience and observation of fifty years, in all the south, that has the extraordinary ability to conduct the services of the church in three different languages, a thing he has done and is doing from Sabbath to Sabbath in the German, Norwegian and English languages. Our talented friend, just a little over forty years old, is still in the prime of life, and we feel sure still higher honors await him in the golden future. In whatever way and from whatever source they may come, they can not be bestowed upon one more worthy in every way, for he would grace any station in life, and give dignity and worth to the highest official position.

GEN. ROBERT HOWE

was born in Brunswick county in 1732 and died in the same place in 1785. He was descended from an English family, and his parents having died while he was yet an infant, his early education was scant and unfinished. He married while yet a youth, taking his wife to England where they remained for two years; after his return in 1766, he was appointed commandant of Fort Johnson by Gov. Tryon and baron of the exchequer. He was a member of the assembly in 1772-3, and a delegate to the colonial congress that met at Newbern in 1774. On the 21st of August of the same year he was appointed colonel of the Second North Carolina regiment, and was ordered to duty in Virginia, and for gallant service against Lord Dunmore, he was promoted to the rank of a brigader-general. In October of the next year he was commissioned a major-general, and in the next year made his expedition against Florida, where his troops were attacked by contagious diseases and he was compelled to retreat to Savannah, Ga. For some stigma cast upon his political career by Christopher Gadsden, Gen. Howe challenged that gentleman and the duel took place at Cannonsburg; Howe's ball pierced Gadsden's ear, and the latter fired his pistol into the air. The affair became the subject of a humorous poem of some merit, by Maj. Andre. Later, he was sent to Philadelphia to quell some riotous regiments, and for his bravery and discretion upon that occasion, received the thanks of Gen. Washington. Upon returning from this expedition he was sent to treat with western Indians. At the beginning of the last year of his life he was elected to the general assembly, but died before taking his seat.

WILLIAM A. GRAHAM, JR.,

was born in Hillsboro, Lincoln county, N. C., December 26, 1839. His education was obtained at the University of North Carolina and at Princeton college, from which he graduated in 1860. He entered the Confederate army as first lieutenant of Company K, Second regiment of North Carolina cavalry, in May, 1862, and was soon promoted to the rank of captain. At the battle of Gettysburg, July 3, 1863, he commanded his company and was wounded. He was then made adjutant-general, which rank he held until the close of the war. In 1874 Gen. Graham was elected to the state senate as the representative of Lincoln and Catawba counties. Such was his popularity that he had no opposition, and he received every vote cast in the district for senator. He was re-elected at the next election in 1876. His name was prominently mentioned as a candidate for congress as the successor of Hon. Walter L. Steele. In 1864 Gen. Graham was united in marriage with Miss Julia, daughter of John W. Lane, of Amelia county, N. C., and they have a bright, intelligent and interesting family.

ELISHA MITCHELL, D. D.,

who was professor of mathematics in the University of North Carolina, 1817-1825, and professor of chemistry and mineralogy in the same institution from 1825 to 1857, was one of the most distinguished educators and scientists known in the history of education in North Carolina. He was born in Washington, Litchfield county, Conn., on the 19th of August, 1793, and perished on Saturday, the 27th of June, 1857, in the sixty-fourth year of his age. He perished in an attempt to descend alone Mt. Mitchell, the highest peak of the Black mountains, which are in Yancy county, N. C. It was his fifth visit paid to the Black mountains, the others being in 1835, 1838 and 1856, respectively. His object was partly personal and partly scientific. He wished to correct the mistakes into which some had been led concerning his earlier visits, and to so compare the indications of the spirit level and the barometer, that future explorers of mountain heights might have increased confidence in the results afforded them by these instruments. His untimely end left both parts of this work to be completed by the pious hands of others. Dr. Mitchell was buried at Asheville, N. C., but at the earnest solicitation of many friends, and especially of the mountain men of Yancy, his family allowed his body to be removed and deposited on the top of Mt. Mitchell, given his name in honor to him. This was done June 16, 1858. There he rests in a mausoleum such as no other man has ever had. Before him lies the North Carolina he loved so well and served so faithfully. Dr. Mitchell graduated at Yale college in 1813. On quitting college, he taught in a school for boys, under the care of Dr. Eigenbrodt, at Jamaica, in Long Island. Afterward, in the spring of 1815, he took charge of a school for girls in New London, Conn. Here he formed an acquaintance with Miss Maria S. North, who was the daughter of an eminent physician of that place, and became his wife in 1819, and who, with fidelity and grace presided over his household for nearly forty years.

In 1816 Dr. Mitchell became a tutor in Yale college, and while so engaged he was recommended to the favorable notice of the trustees of the University of North Carolina, and in 1817 he was appointed to the chair of mathematics in the University of North Carolina, and after spending a short time at the theological seminary at Andover, Mass., and receiving a license to preach the gospel from an orthodox Congregational association in Connecticut, Dr. Mitchell reached Chapel Hill on the last day of January, 1818, and immediately began a labor from which he ceased only by reason of death. In 1825 he was transferred to the chair of chemistry and mineralogy, which he held at the time of his death. As a professor he displayed the greatest energy and accomplished greatest results. The pursuit of natural science was always a delightful employment with Dr. Mitchell, and no one of his day was better acquainted with the mountains, valleys and plains of North Carolina than he, or knew more about its birds, beasts, bugs, fishes and shells, its trees, flowers, vines and mosses, its rocks, stones, sands, clays and marls. As a divine he was learned and devout; and being a man of high intellectual, moral and religious culture, of abundant generosity, and of affable disposition, he was esteemed, respected and beloved, and will long live in affectionate remembrance as the good divine, distinguished and accomplished professor. Dr. Mitchell was the eldest son of Abner Mitchell, a respectable farmer by vocation, whose wife, Phœbe Eliot, was a descendant in the fifth generation of John Eliot, the celebrated "Apostle to the Indians." Dr. Mitchell was thus a member of a family now very widely spread over the United States, and reckoning many who have exercised much influence in commerce, politics, science and religion.

B—27

DANIEL HARVEY HILL,

soldier, author, educator, was born at Hill's Iron Works, York district, S. C., on the 12th of July, 1821. On both his father's and his mother's side he was descended from American soldiers, and his earliest longings were for a soldier's life. In furtherance of this desire, he, at sixteen, secured an appointment to West Point, and in 1842 was graduated from that institution in a class that afterward gave eight generals to the Confederate service and twelve to the Federal army. Upon graduation, he was assigned to the Fourth artillery and served in garrisons in Maine, and at Savannah, Charleston and Fortress Monroe, until the opening of the Mexican war. He took part in all the most important battles of this war, and was one of the few officers, in the whole army, who were twice breveted — having been made brevet-captain for "gallant and meritorious conduct" in the battles of Contreras and of Churubusco, and brevet-major for being a volunteer in the desperate storming party at Chapultepec. In the bloody assault on the entrenched heights of Chapultepec, he and Lieut. Stewart had a foot-race as they were trying to see who could be the first to force his way into one of the stoutly defended Mexican forts. Stewart proved the swifter of foot but was killed just as he entered the fort, and so Capt. Hill gained the coveted honor. The state of South Carolina presented him with a gold sword in token of its appreciation of his heroic actions and services rendered in this war.

Shortly after the treaty of peace was ratified, Maj. Hill resigned his commission, and accepted the chair of mathematics in what is now Washington and Lee university, but what was then known as Washington college. After five years of successful work in this college, he accepted the same chair in Davidson college, N. C. Of his work in this college, Dr. McKimmon, in a speech in Georgia, said: "Ever since Gen. Hill went there, Davidson has maintained a high and thorough standard of instruction." In 1859 he was called to the presidency of the North Carolina military institute, at Charlotte, N. C., an institution from which was culled many of the noblest young officers that perished in the Confederacy. In the spring of 1861, Gov. Ellis, of North Carolina, invited Maj. Hill to Raleigh, and there he organized the first camp of instruction. Shortly afterward, as colonel of the First North Carolina regiment, he fought at Bethel, the first battle of the war. Promoted to be a brigadier-general, July 10, 1861, he took part in the Yorktown defenses, and then, being appointed a major-general in April, 1862, he commanded a division in the battles around Richmond. At Seven Pines, his division, composed almost entirely of North Carolinians, accomplished a feat rare in military annals — they drove a whole division (Casey's) from its entrenchments. Afterward, with one of Longstreet's brigades (R. H. Anderson's), they repulsed the whole of Keyes' corps, and on Sunday morning gathered up seven thousand muskets, thrown down by the retreating Federals. His division took an active part in all the series of battles that culminated with Malvern Hill.

Gen. Hill took part in the Maryland campaign, and during Gen. Lee's retreat, fought single-handed the battle of Boonsboro, or South Mountain, a battle that has often been called the Thermopylae of the war, for, with 5,000 men, Gen. Hill held these mountain passes, against McClellan's 80,000, from sunrise till 3 p. m., and by his bold stand enabled J   to re-unite with Lee, and this saved the Confederate army from being crushed. At Sharpsburg and Fredericksburg his men were actively engaged. During Gen. Lee's invasion of Pennsylvania, Gen. Hill was entrusted with the defenses around Richmond. In the summer of 1863, President Davis asked Gen. Hill to take command of a corps in the western army, and appointed him a lieutenant-general, July 10, 1863. In speaking of his joining this army, a recent writer says: "The western army had lately gained as successor to Hardee in command of his old corps, a stern and dauntless soldier from the army of northern Virginia, in D. H. Hill, whose vigor, coolness and unconquerable pertinacity in fight had already stamped him of heroic temper. Of the religious school of Stonewall Jackson, his earnest convictions never chilled his ardor for battle, and in another age he would have been found worthy to charge with Cromwell at Dunbar." At Chickamauga his corps did its full share in defeating Rosecrans. For some years after the war, Gen. Hill published a monthly magazine, *The Land We Love*, at Charlotte, N. C. In 1877 he was asked to accept the presidency of the University of Arkansas, and he, accepting the offer, built up one of the most successful of the western colleges. In 1884, his health becoming feeble, he resigned and rested a year in Macon, Ga. In 1885 he assumed the presidency of the Military and Agricultural college at Milledgeville, Ga., and remained there until within a few weeks of his death. He died in Charlotte, N. C., September 24, 1889.

Gen. Hill was a constant contributor to current literature, and is the author of three books: "A Consideration of the Sermon on the Mount," "The Crucifixion of Christ," and "The Elements of Algebra." One who knew Gen. Hill well wrote the following graphic sketch of his *personnel:* "Fancy a man in whom the grim determination of a veteran warrior is united to a gentle tenderness of manner which would not be inappropriate in the most womanly of women . . . . affix a pair of eyes that possess the most indisputably honest and kindly expression; animate him with a mind clear, deep and comprehensive, and imbued with a humor as rich as it is effective; infuse man and mind with a soul which, in its lofty views, compels subordination of the material to the spiritual, and holds a supreme trust in the wisdom and goodness of the Almighty; is zealous in the discharge of duty, and looks with scorn on all that is mean and sinful. Add to all these a courage which is indomitable, and a love of truth and honor which is sublime, and you have the earthly embodiment of D. H. Hill."

HUGH MORSON,

the learned principal of the Raleigh male academy, was born in Stafford county, Va., July 19, 1850, and having received his preparatory education in a school taught by Judge Richard Coleman, brother of the celebrated teacher, Frederick Coleman, of Caroline county, Va., entered the University of Virginia, where he graduated with distinction in 1871. Well trained and with a scholarly disposition, Mr. Morson was drawn by circumstances to adopt the profession of a teacher. He taught two years in Virginia, and in 1874 he accepted the chair of languages in the military academy of Horner & Graves, at Hillsboro, N. C. He occupied this position with credit to himself and satisfaction to the institution until 1877, when he came to Raleigh, and associated with Mr. C. H. Scott, in a private school, known as the Raleigh high school. This partnership continued for a year, when Mr. Scott retired and Capt. J. J. Fray, of Virginia, a graduate of the University of Virginia, joined Mr. Morson, and together they established the Raleigh male academy,.the fitting counterpart of those admirable female seminaries, St. Mary's and Peace, which have made Raleigh a widely known educational center. After six years of ardent labor, Capt. Fray fell into ill health and died, greatly lamented; and Capt. C. B. Denson, long known as one of the most accomplished educators of the state, took the vacant place, and is now associated with Mr. Morson in the academy. Of Mr. Morson it may be said that no teacher has been more esteemed in Raleigh, and that he is regarded as a fit successor to those venerated gentlemen, Dr. McPheeters and Mr. Lovejoy, who for fifty years maintained at Raleigh academies of the highest excellence. In particular is Mr. Morson regarded as a master in mathematics, and as with few equals in the teaching of Latin. Mr. Morson is a gentleman of kindly disposition and pleasing manners, and seeks to discharge all his duties in life. He is a devout Christian, being an active member of the Episcopal church, and vestryman of the church of the Good Shepherd, and he is also a member of Seaton Gales lodge, No. 64, I. O. O. F.

On April 15, 1879, Mr. Morson was married to Miss Sallie F. Field, a daughter of Stephen W. Field, of Gloucester county, Va., and to them have been born four children: Harriet L., Hugh A., William F. and John L. Morson. His father was Hugh Morson, who was a native of Stafford county, Va., born in 1805, and after having graduated as doctor of medicine at the University of Pennsylvania, was appointed as surgeon in the United States navy. This position he held until 1846, seeing much service and gaining much experience, but in that year he resigned, and, settling in Stafford county, retired from professional labor. In 1847 he was married to Rosalie Virginia Lightfoot, daughter of Philip L. Lightfoot, of Port Royal, Caroline county, Va., and to them were born five children, of whom three survived: Hugh Morson, of Raleigh; Sallie L. Morson, of Raleigh; and Philip L. Morson, of Newport News, Va. Dr. Morson died in 1876,

S. M. FINGER, Supt. Public Instruction.

and his widow in 1889, at the residence of her son, in Raleigh. The grandfather of the subject of this sketch was Alexander Morson, a native of Virginia. He was a farmer and was a large land-owner in Stafford county, Va., and died there in 1830. He was named for his father, Alexander Morson, a native of Scotland, who came to this country in colonial times, and was collector of customs for King George, at Tappahannock, Va. From his day, to the present generation, the family of Morsons have ever been held in high esteem and regard by their neighbors and a wide circle of friends.

SIDNEY M. FINGER,

the efficient and distinguished superintendent of public instruction of the state of North Carolina, was born in Lincoln county, N. C., May 24, 1837. He received his early education in the public schools in his native county, entering at the age of five years. His studies were faithfully pursued at home and at the age of eighteen he was well prepared for college. He remained nearly four years at Catawba college, Catawba county, a portion of the time acting as tutor. During his connection with this institution, he during vacation taught public schools, and at the age of twenty-two he entered Bowdoin college, in Maine, where he graduated with distinction in 1861. Returning home in May of that year, he succeeded in reaching Alexandria, Va., on May 20, the very day North Carolina seceded from the Union. For a time he taught school in Bishopville, S. C., but in March, 1862, he enlisted as a private in Company I, Eleventh regiment, North Carolina troops. He was put on duty as quartermaster-sergeant, and served as such until the battle of Gettysburg. After that battle he was promoted to be captain and ordered to Charlotte, N. C., as assistant quartermaster charged with the duty of collecting the "tax in kind" provisions for the army in that district. So efficient was he in this business, that subsequently he was promoted to be major and given charge of collecting that tax throughout the state. At the close of the war he returned home and in June, 1865, opened a school in Catawba county. After a few months he formed a partnership with Rev. J. C. Clapp and organized the Catawba high school in Newton, in the buildings of the Catawba college, which continued until 1874, when, his health failing, he ceased to teach and engaged in merchandising and cotton manufacturing in the same place. In the fall of that year the people of his county chose him to represent them in the house of representatives, and he served so acceptably that at the next election he was chosen to the senate from the district embracing Catawba and Lincoln. In 1881 he was again elected to the senate. He made a reputation as an intelligent and faithful legislator, devoting himself specially to educational and financial matters. In 1882 Gov. Jarvis appointed him on the board of directors of the Morganton insane asylum; that being the first board and the one that opened that magnificent institution for the reception of patients. Maj. Finger had now become known to the public men of the state, and his fine address, agreeable manners, high intelligence and sound judgment have won for him general esteem. Always interested in public education he was now thought of for the responsible position of state superintendent, and at the ensuing democratic convention he was nominated, and in 1884 he was elected to that office, which he filled with such great acceptability that he was re-elected in 1888 without any considerable opposition. During the seven years he has administered the affairs of that office, he has accomplished a great deal for the cause of public education in North Carolina. He has incessantly advocated larger appropriations, more schools and a higher grade of teachers, and that the school terms should be up at least to the constitutional limit.

It has been Maj. Finger's privilege to see many of his measures carried into effect; normal schools created, the agricultural college and the normal schools for girls established, and while the university and colleges have flourished, he has had the privilege of seeing the common school fund largely increased and public education advance more rapidly than during any other period of the state's history. Although devoted to his educational work, Maj. Finger has continued his interests in manufacturing and is concerned in factories in Salisbury as well as at Newton. He is also interested in a flouring mill and in general merchandizing in Newton. Maj. Finger was married in December, 1866, to Miss Sarah Hoyle Rhyne, daughter of Daniel Rhyne, Esq., a prominent planter of Gaston county, N. C. His father was Daniel Finger, a native of Lincoln county, who was born in 1806. He was a farmer and conducted a tannery. He was widely known for his hospitality and for his charitable deeds. He was likewise a great friend of public education. He was married twice, first in 1832, to Sarah Finger, daughter of Peter Finger, of Wilkes county, by whom he has several children: Elizabeth; Monroe, who died in 1863, from wounds received at the battle of Chancellorsville; Sidney M. Finger, the subject of the sketch; Mary, widow of Joseph Fry; Robert, lost in the battle of Gettysburg, aged about twenty years; Franklin, who died in the Confederate service in January, 1865, at the age of seventeen, and Caroline F., wife of J. Dallas Rowe, of Catawba county, N. C. Our subject's mother dying in 1856, his father was married the second time in 1868, to Harriet E. Little, by whom he had one child, Lilly. His father died in 1887. Maj. Finger's grandfather was Daniel Finger, a native of Lincoln county, where he was a farmer all his life. The father of Daniel Finger was born in Germany about 1730. He came with his parents to this country when a child, first stopping in Pennsylvania, and then, about 1760, along with many other Germans, settling in Lincoln county. During the Revolutionary war he was a whig, and he served on the patriot side in that struggle.

THOMAS JEFFERSON GREEN

was a soldier from boyhood. All his early hopes and aspirations were centered on a military career, so there is but little wonder that he should have begun a military training so early and ultimately have attained such eminence as a soldier. He was born in Warren county, N. C., in 1801. He came from a line of distinguished soldiers, and was accordingly educated with that profession in view. Before his education he removed to Texas and joined with that state in her struggle ·for independence. So conspicuously daring was the character of his services rendered there that he rose by successive gradations of promotion to the rank of brigadier-general, and in Texas to this day the name of no man stands higher and no man's memory is more revered. In 1843, acting with a number of his fellow-officers, he refused to obey the orders of Gen. Summerville. Gen. Green claims that Summerville was not loyal. After having dissolved his allegiance to Gen. Summerville, he left the main body of the Texan army, and collecting a small force, made a vigorous dash against the town of Mier. This battle was disastrous to the Texans, 193 officers and men being taken prisoners. They made an attempt to escape, but were recaptured and taken to the City of Mexico, where every tenth man was ordered to be shot by Santa Anna. Green was kept a prisoner till September 16, 1844, when, with 103 officers, he was released. He afterward removed to California, where he served with distinction as a member of the state senate and brigadier-general of the state militia. He returned to North Carolina in 1863 and took part in some of the early campaigns of the Civil war, during which time he published a book on the "Mier campaign," which is said to be an able military production. He died in Warren county, December 13, 1863.

JAMES DINWIDDIE

is a Virginian, having been born in Campbell county, that state, June 29, 1837. He was educated in Samuel Davie's institute in Halifax county, Va., and later at Hampton-Sidney college in Prince Edward county, Va., graduating from the latter institution in 1855. He then taught school in Albemarle county, and in 1858 entered the University of Virginia, taking the degree of A. M. in June, 1861. After completing his course at the university he at once entered the Confederate service as a member of the "University volunteers," which was assigned to the Fifty-ninth regiment of Virginia volunteers. Mr. Dinwiddie was promoted to lieutenant soon after his enlistment, and subsequently was made assistant-adjutant-general of the brigade assigned to the Wise legion. In December, 1861, the University volunteers were disbanded, and he then became a member of the Wise legion, with whom he went to Roanoke Island. When that island was surrendered he escaped and made his way to Norfolk, Va., and thence back to Charlottesville, where he joined the artillery company of which he was made first lieutenant. His company joined "Stonewall" Jackson's army corps in the valley of Virginia, remaining with that command until after the battle of Fredericksburg, in December, 1863, when Lieut. Dinwiddie was promoted to a captaincy in the artillery, and assigned to ordnance duty at Richmond, Va., where he was in charge of contracts and supplies for the army of northern Virginia. At this time he was made major of infantry and placed in command of the arsenal battalion of the reserve corps, serving there until the close of the war. He surrendered with Gen. Robert E. Lee's army. Major Dinwiddie took an active valorous part in the following named engagements: Cross Keys, Port Republic, seven days' fight around Richmond, second Manassas, first battle of Fredericksburg, Roanoke Island, Bermuda Hundreds, Fort Harrison, and many minor engagements.

After the war Major Dinwiddie remained on a farm until 1869, when he was elected principal of Sayre female institute of Lexington, Ky., where he remained but a year. He was then elected professor of mathematics in the southwestern Presbyterian university at Clarksville, Tenn. From 1870 until 1880 he held the latter position with great credit to himself, and much benefit to the institution. In the latter year Prof. Dinwiddie was offered the chair of mathematics in the state university at Knoxville, Tenn., and accepted that call, filling the chair until 1885, when he went to Gordonsville, Va., and purchased the Central female institute, which he still owns. He remained in that place as principal of the institution until 1890. At this time he was tendered the presidency of Peace institute, at Raleigh, N. C., and has since been occupied in discharging the arduous and delicate duties connected with that honored position. This is one of the oldest educational institutions in the south, and ranks high among its sister schools. Professor Dinwiddie is an elder in the Presbyterian church, and is much interested in church work. He is recognized as one of the foremost educators in the state, and is a man of rare attainments, having a mind of great force and erudition. The Dinwiddie family is of Scotch origin, the name having been originally "Dun, of Wody." William Dinwiddie, the father of the above, was born in Lynchburg, Va., January 4, 1804. He was educated in the common schools of Campbell county, and then turned his attention to farming. He died in 1884 in Albemarle county. In 1826 he married Nancy Bryan, whose mother was Catherine Evans, who afterward married Reese Bryan. To the union of William and Nancy were born eleven children, seven of whom survive the parents: Frances, wife of Judge Reese Bryan, of Montgomery City, Mo.; Rev. William Dinwiddie, D. D., of Albemarle county, Va.; Dr. Joseph, of Fayetteville, Tenn.; Rev. John Dinwiddie, of Leesburg, Va.; James, of Raleigh; Marshall, of Swopes, Va.; Walter, of Charlottesville, Va.; Edgar Evans Dinwiddie, of Charlottesville, and those deceased are: Mary, Reese, and Harmon, who was a member of the "university volunteers," and died at Lewisburg, Va., in 1861, from exposure while in the Confederate service. The mother of these children died in 1881. Joseph Dinwiddie, the paternal grandfather, was born in Virginia, in 1773, and died in 1863. His father was William, who came from England and settled in Virginia. He was in the Revolutionary war and fought at Kings Mountain and Cowpens.

JOHN C. SCARBOROUGH,

the commissioner of labor statistics for North Carolina, is a native of Wake county, N. C., where he was born September 22, 1841. Having received a good preparatory education, he was about to enter college when the war broke out, and with that high spirit which he has ever displayed, he enlisted as a private in the Raleigh rifles, on April 16, 1861. His company was assigned to the Fourth regiment, North Carolina volunteers, afterward known as the Fourteenth regiment, North Carolina troops. For two years the subject of this sketch remained in that command, being appointed sergeant of his company, and on January 1, 1863, at his request he was transferred to Company I, First regiment North Carolina troops, Col. Montford S. Stokes commanding, and he continued with this company until the end of the war, surrendering at Appomatox. He participated in the following battles: Williamsburg, Seven Pines, Mechanicsville, Cold Harbor, White Oak Swamp, Malvern Hill, the second battle of Manassas, the battles around Winchester, South Mountain, and at Sharpsburg (Antietam), where he was captured with most of his regiment. Fortunately at that time the cartel of exchange was in force, and after a confinement of only twenty-two days at Fort Delaware, he was exchanged and returned home. Before a month had expired he was again with his regiment and participated in the fight at Jordon's Mills (first battle of Fredericksburg), and later in the battles of Chancellorsville, Gettysburg, Mine Run, second battle of Fredericksburg, the Wilderness, Lynchburg, Harper's Ferry and Monocacy. He was in Early's command in the raid on Washington City, and was engaged in the battles of Snicker's Gap, Winchester, Bear River, Fisher's Hill and Cedar Creek, where he was badly wounded and sent home on a furlough in consequence. On regaining his strength he returned to his command then at Petersburg, and was engaged around Petersburg and at Farmville, and fought at Appomatox. No man was steadier in his devotion to the Confederate cause or more truly admirable in conduct or more courageous in the discharge of every duty, whether on the field of battle, or on the march, than Sergeant Scarborough was during the entire continuance of the war. Returning home when the Confederate flag was furled, he at once went at work on his father's farm to aid in making a crop for the support of the family.

In January, 1866, he determined to complete his education and entered Wake Forest college, where he graduated in June, 1869. The following fall he accepted a position as tutor in the college, and re mained there in that capacity for two years. In August, 1871, he established an academy at Selma, Johnston county, N. C., and successfully conducted it until the summer of 1876, when he was nominated by the state democratic convention for the position of state superintendent of public instruction, and was triumphantly elected. In that campaign Mr. Scarborough made many speeches which won for him great reputation as a public speaker. He administered his responsible office with satisfaction to the people, and particularly to the friends of public education, and was re-elected without opposition in 1880, continuing to discharge its duties with great service to the state until 1885. During his term Mr. Scarborough made numerous addresses on the subject of education, and won the esteem and confidence of the people throughout the state.

After the expiration of his second term, Mr. Scarborough resided on his farm in Johnston county until February, 1888, when he accepted a position as teacher in the Thomasville female college, teaching there until March 4, 1889, when Gov. Fowle appointed him commissioner of the bureau of labor statistics for North Carolina, which position he has since held with credit to himself and satisfaction to the public. When the campaign of 1890 came on, Mr. Scarborough, who was a member of the alliance, was brought forward as a candidate for the democratic nomination for congress, and he received a warm support, but withdrew his name from the contest, and earnestly supported Mr. Bunn, the nominee.

On January 12, 1876, Mr. Scarborough was married to Julia Vass Moore, the daughter of Walter R. Moore, of Johnston county, N. C., and to them were born six children, of whom three survive, as follows: Hartwell V., Anna R. and Julia M. Scarborough. Mr. Scarborough's parents were both natives of Wake county. His father, Daniel Scarborough, was born in Wake county in 1797, and was a farmer. He was also a magistrate and a member of the county court, and possessed the confidence of his neighbors to an unusual degree. He settled many estates, and for about thirty years was warden of the poor. In 1820 he married Cynthia Horton, daughter of Hartwell Horton, a native of Wake county, and had by her ten children, of whom five survive: Rebecca, wife of P. P. Pace; Mrs. Emily Eddins; John C. Scarborough; Helen, wife of Henry V. Bunch, and Charles W. Scarborough, a Baptist minister. Daniel Scarborough died in June, 1878, and his wife on June 4, 1856, aged fifty-six years. The grandfather of the subject of this sketch was John Scarborough, who was born in Wake county, in 1760, and was a farmer. He died in 1854. The father of John Scarborough was Samuel Scarborough, who was a native of Dinwiddie county, Va., and was of English descent. He moved to Wake county in early manhood, and served in the Revolutionary army. Our subject's maternal great-grandfather was Moses Horton, who was of Scotch descent. He also was a soldier in the Revolutionary war.

WILLIAM J. YOUNG,

the principal of the North Carolina institute for the deaf, dumb and blind, was born in Franklin county, N. C., August 10, 1832, and received his education at Wake Forest college; but being compelled by illness to leave before graduating at that institution, he attended Randolph-Macon college, in Virginia, for some time, leaving there in 1857. Returning home he was employed to teach in the male academy at Louisburg, and then he opened a private school at Raleigh; but soon afterward was led to join his brother in the mercantile business, and was so engaged until December, 1860, when he was elected a teacher in the blind department of the institution for the deaf, dumb and blind in Raleigh. He had now found his vocation in life. Gentle, patient and kind, he was peculiarly fitted for this work, and for twenty-three years he continued as an instructor of the blind, carrying light where before was darkness. His sympathetic spirit and fine intelligence admirably equipped him for this congenial work, and year by year his efficiency was more thoroughly appreciated by the authorities, and was made more evident by the practical results that attended his instruction. In 1883 the directors, recognizing his value as an officer of fine judgment, sterling worth and thorough knowledge of the institution in all its departments, elected him principal, and he still remains at the head of the institution, generally esteemed in every part of the state as the right man in the right place. In 1866 Mr. Young received from Trinity college the degree of master of arts, and his long career as a teacher has given him a literary turn. He was at its session in 1888 elected first vice-president of the American association of instructors of the blind. To his natural gentle character there is united a high degree of Christian excellence. He has for many years been a prominent and devout member of Edenton Street Methodist church, and was long a leader of its choir. He is now an official member, chairman of the official board, superintendent of the Sabbath-school, and a trustee of that large and influential church. His good works have not been without their influence in the community where he has long lived, and but few citizens of Raleigh enjoy more esteem than the subject of this sketch. The public generally highly appreciate his worth and excellence, while the teachers, pupils, patients and directors of the institution thoroughly love him. He is quiet and unobtrusive in his deportment, a model gentleman, but is true to his duties, his church, his country and his God.

On November 12, 1860, Mr. Young was married to Sarah Ellen Cook, daughter of Samuel T. Cook, Esq., of Barry, Vt., and to them were born three children: Ellen Grace Young; Emma Hunter, wife of James E. Brown, and Daisy Winston Young. The father of Mr. Young was John Young, who was born in Franklin county in 1794, and who married Grace Hight, by whom he had nine children, two only now surviving, Martha E. Young and the subject of this sketch. Mr. John Young died January, 1875, and his wife in 1868. Mr. Young's grandfather was Samuel Young, a native of Franklin county. He was a farmer and was the son of Rev. John Young, a native of the state of North Carolina, who was a Methodist Episcopal preacher, a man of ability and character, and who for fifty years preached the Word in Franklin county.

GEN. JAMES MOORE.

When, in 1713, Col. James Moore, hastening through the wilderness, brought aid from Charleston to the North Carolina settlers, then in danger of extermination by the hostile Tuscaroras, his younger brother, Maurice, accompanied him, and afterward found sufficient attractions in Albemarle to cast his fortunes there. They were the sons of Gov. James Moore, of South Carolina, a descendant of Roger Moore, who led the Irish rebellion of 1641, and who was sprung from the ancient kings of Ireland; and their mother was Elizabeth, a daughter of Sir John Yeamans, the first governor of Carolina, who, in 1665, made the settlement at Old Town, on the Cape Fear river. About a year after his arrival in North Carolina, the Indians being then subdued, Col. Maurice Moore married Elizabeth, a daughter of Major Alexander Lillington, and the widow of Col. Sam Swann. The Yamasee Indians having risen against the southern colony in 1715, Col. Moore was sent with a force from Albemarle to assist in their subjugation, and so well did he perform his duty that the South Carolina assembly invited him into their hall, and through their speaker formally thanked him in person for his services.

In 1718, when the pirate Blackbeard lay in Albemarle and Pamlico sounds, and was plying his nefarious trade with the connivance of Tobias Knight, the secretary and friend of Gov. Eden, Moore and his brother-in-law, Edward Moseley, with the determination of securing evidence of their illicit dealings, took possession of the secretary's office and forcibly held possession until they had examined the records on file. By this he incurred the enmity of Eden and was tried and punished. But he continued to interest himself in all affairs that affected the welfare of the colony, and was a leader of the popular party. When Gov. Burrington arrived, Moore and his friends induced him to adopt their measures, one of which was the opening up of the Cape Fear river for settlement, and about 1724, Moore laid off a town at Brunswick, and soon afterward he and many friends and connections moved to the Cape Fear. Burrington was quickly superceded, and on Gov. Everard's arrival the legislature met, choosing Moore as speaker. Everard not liking the outlook, prorogued the assembly, but Speaker Moore denied his right to do that, and a conflict at once arose between the assembly and the new governor.

On the Cape Fear, Moore's neighbors were Moseley and John Porter and Sam and John Swann, his step-sons, and he long continued the adviser and counselor of the popular leaders. By his second wife, Mary Porter, he had two sons, Maurice and James. Maurice studied law and was appointed a judge in 1765, but his patriotic ardor at the time of the stamp act disturbances displeased Gov. Tryon, and his commission was taken from him. Later, when those differences were healed, he was again appointed to the bench and was of the court at the time of the Regulation troubles. He afterward addressed a letter to Gov. Tryon, signed Atticus, that shows that he deserves to rank with the foremost men in America for literary ability. He married Miss Anne Grange, and left two children: Alfred Moore, who afterward was a justice of the supreme court of the United States, and Mary, who became the wife of Gen. Francis Nash.

Col. Maurice Moore's second son, James, was an officer in the Indian wars, and thus gained experience that stood him in good stead when the Revolution broke out. He, like his brother Maurice, participated in public affairs, and was frequently a member of the assembly. He was an officer in the Tryon expedition against the regulators in 1771. He was a warm patriot, and ardently co-operated with the other gentlemen of the Cape Fear in their zeal for American freedom. When the congress met in 1775, and steps were taken to organize a military force for defense, James Moore was chosen colonel of the First regiment, and he was in command of the forces on the Cape Fear when the tories embodied on the upper waters of that stream, under Gen. McDonald, and prepared to march upon Wilmington. Col. Moore hastened to oppose them, and in a campaign skillfully planned and admirably conducted as to merit the highest encomium by a series of brilliant movements, he succeeded in preventing their juncture with the British forces and secured a victory of lasting benefit to the cause. Immediately afterward, on March 1, 1776, he was promoted by the Continental congress to be brigadier-general, and with his North Carolina brigade hurried to Charleston, then the object of British attack. Here he served with Gen. Lee until the latter went south to invade Florida, when Moore was left in command of Charleston. In September, 1776, Lee returned to the north and the department of the south was entrusted to the care of Gen. Moore.

In January, 1777, Gen. Moore's health gave away, and he returned to his home and died. He was a man of delicate organization, and a frail constitution in strange contrast with his heroic soul and fine intellectual capacity. It is related that he and his brother Judge Maurice expired in the same house on the same day. Of Gen. Moore it may be said that he was perhaps the most masterful military man furnished by North Carolina to the war of independence, and that probably he had no superior in military genius on the continent. Gen. Moore married Miss Anna Ivey and left two sons, Duncan and James, and two daughters who became Mrs. Swann, and Mrs. Waters.

REV. HENRY MARTIN TUPPER, D. D.,

president of the Shaw university, was born at Monson, Mass., April, 1831. His father was Earl Tupper, who was also a native of Monson, Mass., where he first saw the light August 11, 1798. He was a farmer by occupation. In September, 1830, he married Permelia Norris, of Stafford, Conn., by whom he had nine children, of whom our subject was the eldest. The father died October 31, 1864, his wife surviving him until May 13, 1881. The Tupper family is of ancient origin, and it is eminently proper that an outline of its descent, so far as it relates to the immediate branch of the distinguished subject, should be here given. The following brief mention is taken from the advanced sheets of a genealogy of the family. The Tuppers are of ancient Saxon origin. In the early part of the thirteenth century there was a Thuringian chief, by the name of Conrad Von Treffurth, who in 1260 became chief lord, and afterward bore the appellation of Von Toppherr. He was at the head of several families, and the names of the clan or septs were very similar, as Topfer, Tophern, Tapfer and Toepfern. They owned large real estates, and had castles at Kleintoopfer and at Grostoepfer, nearly midway between Weimar and Hesse Cassel. In later Saxon records the name was spelt, Toppfer, Topfer, Topfor, Topper and Toffer. In the reign of Charles V. the family suffered great persecution from the Catholics as "obstinate Lutherans" and "lost all." The phrase "lost all" gave origin to the name of Toutperd and Toutpert, by which the family was known in France. Tout, all, and perd from the verb perre, to lose, and by a slight modification pronounced Toupard in the Netherlands.

After having been driven from their Thuringian estates they fled to Hesse Cassel, Upper Saxony, about 1520. Two brothers left the country; one settled in Holland, and in 1813, a descendant, Daniel Tupper was burgomaster of Rotterdam. The other brother fled to Switzerland and was the ancestor of Rodolph Topffer, the celebrated author. The other members of the Tupper family fled from Hesse Cassel in 1522, to the "low countries," and thence took refuge in England in the reign of Henry VIII. Robert and Henry first settled in Chichester, Sussex, and William in London. Robert afterward moved to Sandwich, and Henry in 1548 went to Guernsey. Martin Farquhar Tupper is a descendant of Henry. John, his eldest son, married "Mary, sole child and heiress of Peter LePelly." and the family has always ranked high and been considered among the principal gentry of the island; and their arms and crest granted and registered in England, bear evidence of well earned augmentation. Many of their descendants have been greatly distinguished for their valor. Thomas Tupper, who emigrated to America, was probably the grandson of Robert of Sandwich, born 1576, and landed at Saugus, Mass., about 1630. There was another Thomas Tupper, "clergyman

of the Barbadoes," who in 1635, in the Admiralty records, is registered among the emigrants taking passage at St. Christopher, W. I.,
but he was the grandson of Henry of Guernsey. Thomas Tupper became one of the incorporators of Sandwich, Mass. He had a son
Thomas, born January, 1638, who married Martha Mayhew, the
daughter of Gov. Mayhew of Martha's Vineyard. They had eleven
children, seven sons and four daughters. Six of the sons became the
heads of families, to wit: Thomas, Israel, Ichabod, Eldad, Medad and
Eliakim. From these sons have descended all the Tuppers in this
country and Canada.

Henry Martin Tupper's grandfather was Ezra Tupper, who was
born in Middleborough, Mass., March 31, 1763. He was a farmer
and a fife-major in the Revolutionary army, and died September 30,
1849. His wife was Hulda Spencer, of Campton, N. H. He was the
son of William Tupper, who was born in Middleborough, Mass., September 14, 1735. He was a farmer and a colonel in the Revolutionary
war, and his son Ezra served in his regiment. He was married January 22, 1761, to Susanna Clapp, and died November 25, 1824. His
father was Thomas Tupper, who was born in Sandwich, Mass., December 20, 1714. He was also a farmer and was engaged in the
French wars. He married Rebecca Bumpus, of Middleborough,
Mass., June 19, 1734. His death occurred December, 1810. Ichabod,
his father, was born August 11, 1673, at Sandwich, Mass. He was a
sea captain, and was twice married, his first wife having been Mary
Tinkham, and his second wife Hannah Tinkham, of Middleborough,
Mass. Thomas Tupper, Jr., his father, was born in Sandwich, Mass.,
January 16, 1638, one year after the town was founded. For many
years he held different military positions and was a member of the
council of war, was town clerk and selectman for forty years. In
1682 he was representative to general court. He was a large land
holder. October 22, 1661, he married Martha, daughter of Gov.
Mayhew, of Martha's Vineyard, and died in May, 1706. His father's
name was Thomas, Sr. He was a native of England, having been
born at Sandwich, that country, June 28, 1578. About 1630, he came
to America, and became one of the founders of Sandwich, Mass. He
was a selectman, deputy, magistrate and missionary to the Indians.
Thomas Tupper, Sr., died March 28, 1676. He was a descendant of
Robert Tupper, of Sandwich. England, probably the grandson, who,
in 1522, fled with his two brothers, Henry and William, from Hesse
Cassel, Upper Saxony, to escape persecution by Charles V.

The Rev. Henry Martin Tupper, D. D., a brief mention of whose
career will now follow, grew to the years of manhood on his father's
farm in the town of Monson. He was given but few early educational advantages, his attendance at the district school being but short.
Possessing a thirst for knowledge he read every book and paper that
fell in his way, and while a mere lad formed decided opinions on the
questions of the day, especially in regard to slavery. In his eighteenth
year he became a student at Monson academy, and while in that institution was converted. Being obliged meanwhile to support him-

self by his own exertions, he kept on in his search for a higher edu·
cation and finally matriculated in Amherst college, from which he
was graduated in 1859. He then entered the Newton theological institution, from which he was graduated June 26, 1862, that being the
date of the battle of Fair Oaks. On the 14th of July he answered
Gov. Andrew's, of Mass., call for privates by enlisting as a common
soldier. A few days afterward he was ordained as a minister of the
Baptist church and joined the army of the Potomac, about the time
of the battles of South Mountain and Antietam. He was in the battle of Fredericksburg, and followed the Ninth Army corps into Kentucky, was in the campaign against Vicksburg, and in the raid upon
Jackson, Miss., under Gen. Sherman. In one engagement a shell
burst so near his face that it scorched his flesh, but though others at
the right and left fell by the flying pieces, this man was spared for
the great after-battle. While in the army he was constantly engaged
in Christian work. He held meetings among his comrades, wrote
letters for the sick and wounded, often performed the duties of
chaplain and cheered all around him who were blighted by the
stroke of battle. During these years he embraced the opportutity for
becoming acquainted with the colored people who flocked to the camps.
While a student Dr. Tupper had been very desirous of becoming a
missionary to Africa, and had had a large Sunday-school class of
colored youth.

January 25, 1864, he was married to Sarah Baker Leonard, of Stafford,
Conn., the daughter of Gen. Jacob Leonard — a family of distinction
and great benevolence. A few weeks after the close of the Civil war
and previous to his discharge from the army, he received a commission from the American Baptist home mission society to go south
as a missionary to the freedmen. This came to him without his previous knowledge and seemed the divine command. It was left to his
own discretion to select a proper field for his labors, and accordingly,
after due deliberation, he decided upon Raleigh, N. C., as a point
advantageous for his operations. He was discharged from the army
July 14, 1865, and on the first of the following October, started with
his wife for Raleigh. They reached that city October 10th, after
days of hard travel, the communication having been disrupted by the
hostilities that had been in progress there for so long. They came
by the first train that passed over the Seaboard road since the close
of the war, having purchased tickets numbers one and two.

Without entering into further details in regard to the founding of
the university by Dr. Tupper, only to mention the date of its real
establishment, which was December 1, 1865, we will bring this sketch
to a close by generalizing a little on the plan and scope of the institution. Shaw university was one of the pioneer colleges established
in the interest of the black man of the south. Its humble beginning
promised but little. To-day it is a complete, thorough university,
with many beautiful and substantial buildings, and a large corps of
able and enthusiastic teachers. It fits its graduates for the higher
walks of life, and aims to inculcate a manly, self-reliant feeling in the

breast of the colored man—to eliminate that feeling of false independence, which inevitably came to him the day he was made free, and in its stead to give true independence by personal worth and higher education. The university has done a grand work. It has from five to six hundred students, and its alumni have already honored themselves in the world. Teachers, merchants, lawyers, doctors and members of congress have been sent from its walls. It met with opposition; the first building was erected by its president, and the first work was supported by the earnings of himself and his faithful wife, they having kept a night school for the purpose. To-day it rears its proud dome aloft among the educational institutions of the land, a magnificent monument to the grand man who founded it with his prayers and persistent labors. Man can leave no grander mausoleum than this; can leave no grander heritage than the sacrifices and benefactions for a downtrodden, uncultured people, many of whom he has raised to the true freedom of thought and Christianity. Long after soldiers and statesmen are forgotten the name of Henry Martin Tupper will live in the grateful hearts of the colored people of America.

RICHARD CASWELL

was a soldier by preference and profession and was born in the state of Maryland on the 3rd of August, 1725. He removed to North Carolina in 1746, and held various offices and positions of trust and honor and for some years practiced law with great success. He was a member of the colonial assembly for many years and was the speaker of that body from 1770 to 1771. At the breaking out of the Revolution he became the colonel of a regiment of patriots and did good fighting in the patriot cause. He was a member of congress in 1774, and was made treasurer of the state in 1775. For three years he was president of the provincial congress which framed the state constitution, and was governor of the state during 1777-9. One of the most brilliant events of his life was his conduct at the battle of Moore's Creek, where he commanded the patriot army and defeated a large body of loyalists, commanded by no less a soldier than Gen. McDonald. In this engagement he took the loyalist commander prisoner, for which he received the thanks of congress and promotion to the rank of major-general. In 1780 he led the state troops in the disastrous battle of Camden. After his retirement from the military service he was chosen speaker of the senate, and comptroller-general in 1772; he was again governor from 1784 to 1786, and was a delegate to the convention which framed the Federal constitution in 1787. He was again elected to the senate in 1789, and while presiding over that body was struck with paralysis, from which death ensued in a few days.

GEN. JAMES HOGUN.

It is to be regretted that so little has been preserved concerning Gen. James Hogun. His first appearance in public life was as a

B—28

member of the provincial congress, which met at Halifax, in April,
1776. He was then a resident of Halifax county. That congress re-
organized the military forces of the state, and James Hogun, who
had previously been a major of the minute men in Halifax, was appointed paymaster of the Third regiment of continentals and of the
three companies of light horse. In the following November, three
other continental regiments were raised, and Hogun was made
colonel of one of the new regiments, and in 1777 marched to the aid
of Gen. Washington. Howe had been detached from his brigade
and made a major-general. Gen. Moore had after a brilliant record
sunk into a patriot's grave. Gen. Nash had fallen upon the field, and
Germantown and our six regiments of continentals, without a North
Carolina brigadier, were commanded by Gen. Alexander McDougal,
of New York. In May, 1778, so great had their ranks been depleted,
these regiments were consolidated into three, and in January, 1779,
Col. Hogun was promoted to be brigadier, and assigned to the command of the brigade. This was ordered by congress, despite the
fact that the legislature of the state had petitioned that Col. Clarke,
a gentleman of undoubted patriotism and an officer of fine abilities,
should be promoted to the position. But Col. Hogun had been greatly
distinguished in battle and in fact won his promotion by his intrepidity at Germantown. He had endured the sufferings at Valley
Forge, and had proved himself every inch a soldier, whether in camp
or in battle.

In November, 1779, under orders from Gen. Washington, Gen.
Hogun marched his brigade from the north to the relief of South
Carolina, whither Gen. Sumner's brigade had preceded him. In the
spring of 1780, having joined Gen. Lincoln, he and the entire North
Carolina continental line were beleagured in Charleston, along
with about a thousand North Carolina militia, and many other
troops from other states. The city was thoroughly invested by the
royal forces, and after a protracted siege, during which the North
Carolina troops suffered heavily, and were subjected to many hardships and trying vicissitudes, Gen. Lincoln surrendered his army as
prisoners of war. Gen. Sumner fortunately was not present at the
time and thus escaped capture. There were surrendered 743 North
Carolina continentals and over 500 North Carolina militia. These
were confined on board the prison ships, the Sandwich and the Concord, and they were subjected to the most intolerable usage. Several hundred of them were carried to Jamaica and were enrolled in
Lord Charles Montague's regiment. The officers as well as the men
were treated with great severity, and many died from scurvy, fever
and other diseases generated from the crowded condition of the
hulks and from harsh treatment. At length, after a year's suffering,
those who survived were, under a cartel of exchange secured by
Gen. Greene, May 3, 1781, delivered to the American agent of exchange at Jamestown, Va., on June 15, 1781. The cruelties and hardships of their long confinement had, however, proved fatal to many,
and among those who had died in captivity was the brave Gen.

Hogun. There is no record of his burial place. Gen. Hogun left a family resident in Halifax, but his name does not appear to be perpetuated in North Carolina.

GEORGE W. GREENE.

Biographical history can find no subject more worthy than the educator. As popular education increases so must the importance of the teacher's profession increase. The instructor of youth is moulding the destiny of our nation; if his work be not well done it is a calamity; if he is consistent and faithful, to him be the honor. In the following lines may be found a brief outline of the career of George W. Greene, a man of much ability and integrity. Mr. Greene was born in Watauga county, N. C., June 29, 1852, and was educated at Wake Forest college, and at the Southern Baptist theological seminary of Greenville, S. C., having graduated from the former institution with the class of 1870, and from the latter five years subsequent. Having been ordained a minister, he devoted about five months succeeding that event to Sabbath-school work in different parts of North Carolina, after which he went to Hickory, N. C., as pastor of the church there. In 1877 he removed to Moravian Falls, N. C., and for thirteen years thereafter was president of the Moravian Falls academy, and also filled the pastorate there. In 1890 he was elected professor of Latin at Wake Forest college. Still a young man, should life and health be spared him much may be hoped from the industrious labors of years to come. He is a scholar of profound thought, has thoroughly informed himself on all live topics, and as a linguist excels. As a teacher he is patient and persistent, having that happy faculty of imparting to others that which he knows himself, a quality unfortunately lacking in many scholars of repute. He has found time to write a a valuable work on elementary English grammar, which has received much favorable comment.

On the 26th day of December, 1876, Prof. Greene was joined in marriage to an accomplished lady of Greenville, S. C., Miss Dora Mauldin, daughter of Joab Mauldin. Mrs. Greene died October 26, 1890, leaving three children, named: Anna, Pansy and Felix. Her loss was irreparable to husband, children and friends. David Greene, father of the above mentioned, was born in Watauga county, N. C., in 1823. He was given a good common school training, and then turned his attention to agriculture. At the outbreak of the war between north and south he enlisted in 1861, in the Confederate army, as a member of the Thirty-seventh regiment North Carolina volunteer infantry, commanded by Col. Z. B. Vance. He was promoted to the lieutenancy of Company B. After a year he was transferred, or rather re-enlisted in the Fifty-eighth regiment North Carolina infantry as a private. He was taken ill soon after his re-enlistment and died in December, 1863, two days after his return home. In 1846 he married Miss Kate Smith, daughter of George Smith, of Caldwell county,

N. C., and to them were born eight children, named as follows: Smith F., who died in the Confederate service in 1863; Elizabeth, wife of M. E. Thompson, of Caldwell county, N. C.; Mary, wife of Henry Steele, of Caldwell county, N. C.; George W., of Wake Forest, N. C.; Joseph W., died in 1888; Rebecca, wife of Smith Coffey, of Caldwell county, N. C.; Amanda Greene, of Caldwell county, and David L. Greene, who died in infancy. The mother of these children died in 1864. Joseph Greene, the paternal grandfather of our subject, was born in Watauga county, N. C., in 1790. He was a planter of considerable prominence, and died in 1861. His father, Richard Greene, was a native of New Jersey, having been born about the year 1740. He came to North Carolina in 1785, and died early in 1800. The family is of English origin, and comes from the same line as Gen. Greene of Revolutionary fame.

WILLIAM L. POTEAT, A. M.,

professor of natural history at Wake Forest college, is a native of North Carolina, having been born in Caswell county, October 20, 1856. Having obtained an academic preliminary schooling, he entered Wake Forest college and was graduated with the class of 1877. For the following year he was engaged in reading law, but in 1878 was made a tutor at Wake Forest college and served in that capacity until June, 1880, when he was elected assistant professor of natural science, and after three years in that position he was called to the chair of natural history. In 1881 Prof. Poteat was married to Miss Emma Purefoy, daughter of A. F. Purefoy, and granddaughter of the eminent Rev. James S. Purefoy, late of Wake Forest. Two children have blessed this union, named Hubert McNeill and Louie Poteat. Prof. Poteat has contributed valuable articles to the scientific press, of which may be mentioned "A tube-building spider," and an article on " North Carolina Desmids." They were both published in the *Elisha Mitchell Scientific Society's Journal*, issued from the University of North Carolina, and attracted widespread attention. James Poteat, the father of our subject, was born in Caswell county, N. C., in 1807. He was a planter and a large slaveholder, owning about 3,000 acres of tillable land. For many years prior to the war, and during the war, he was engaged in the commission business at Richmond, Va. He was twice married, his second wife, Julia A. (McNeill) Poteat, daughter of Hosea McNeill, of Caswell county, being the mother of Prof. William L. Poteat. They were united in marriage in 1855, and of the four children born to them three survive: William L., Ida B. and Edwin M. Poteat, pastor of Calvary Baptist church in New Haven, Conn. The father of these children died in January, 1889. He was the son of Miles Poteat, also a planter and native of Caswell county, N. C. In 1888 Prof. Poteat and a brother, Edwin, studied in Europe, the former in the zoological department of the famous University of Berlin.

CHARLES E. BREWER

was born in Wake Forest, N. C., and after having received a thorough preparation entered Wake Forest college, from which he was graduated in June, 1886. He then took a post-graduate course in chemistry, under the tutelage of Dr. J. R. Duggan, of Wake Forest. After eighteen months spent in this additional course he entered Johns Hopkins university, and remained there for a year and a half, having made chemistry a specialty. Returning to Wake Forest in 1889, he was called to the chair of chemistry in his *alma mater* and has since held that position. Wake Forest college conferred upon him the degree of A. M., in 1886. John M. Brewer, his father, was born in Virginia, his native county being Nansemond, and the date of his birth the year 1820. He went to Wake Forest as a student in 1838, and has since remained there, having turned his attention to agriculture. In 1844 he married Miss Ann Eliza Wait, daughter of Rev. Samuel Wait, a native of New York, who came to North Carolina in 1827. From 1834 to 1844 he was president of Wake Forest college. To the latter marriage were born ten children, of whom all are living except one; those remaining are: John B., president of the Murfreesboro female college; Mary, wife of W. P. Perry, of Wake county, N. C.; Samuel Wait, of Raleigh; William Cary, of Wake Forest; Sallie M., wife of L. W. Bagley, a resident of Littleton, N. C.; Richard L., of Wake Forest; Hattie B., wife of Dr. J. B. Powers, a physician of Wake Forest; Lydia, wife of N. B. Josey, of Scotland Neck, N. C., and Charles E. Brewer. The grandfather of these children was John Brewer, a Virginian, having been born in 1793. His demise occurred in 1833. He was an extensive planter of good repute. The family is of Scotch origin, and many of its members have risen to honor and distinction in the United States.

WILLIAM B. ROYALL.

For many generations the Royall family has furnished intelligent and patriotic American citizens. Many years prior to the Revolution its American founder left England to seek a home and country across the sea. From that time to this the old Palmetto state has been the home of his descendants. Going back five generations, we find that William Royall was born near Charleston, S. C., in 1754. He was a planter, and at one time was engaged in mercantile pursuits at Charleston. He fought in the patriot army during the war for American independence, and died in 1833. His son William was born on James Island, S. C., in 1797, and followed in his father's footsteps as a planter, and later as a merchant of Charleston, and died in 1863. The Rev. William Royall, D. D., LL. D., an eminent educator of North Carolina, is the son of the last mentioned. Dr. Royall first saw the light in Edgefield county, S. C., in the year 1823. While he was still in early youth his parents removed to Charleston, and the son was reared in that city. Having been given the best educational advantages at hand, he was graduated from the University of South Carolina in the class of 1841. Three years later he was ordained a minister in the Baptist church, but the great effort of his life has been in the education of the young. For a time he held a position as instructor in Charleston, S. C., and later taught in Furman University for several years. In 1860 he accepted the chair of Latin at Wake Forest college, but in 1874 went to Texas, and accepted the presidency of the Baylor female college at Independence, Tex., prior to that having presided over the Raleigh female seminary, and subsequently over the Louisburg female college. In 1880 Dr. Royall returned to Wake Forest college, as professor of modern languages, and at the present time fills the chair of English in that noted institution. Dr. Royall was united in marriage in 1843, to Miss Elizabeth, daughter of Dr. Robert S. Bailey, of Charleston, S. C., and to them seven children have been born, of whom five are now living, viz.: William Bailey; Mary A., wife of Prof. F. P. Hobgood, of Oxford, N. C.; Petrona, wife of W. C. Powell, of Savannah, Ga.; Robert E., of Wake Forest, N. C.; and Minta, wife of Thomas E. Holding, also of Wake Forest. Dr. Royall entered the Confederate service in 1862, as chaplain of the Fifty-fifth North Carolina volunteer infantry, and served for fourteen months. Furman university conferred upon him the degree of doctor of divinity, and the University of North Carolina honored him with LL. D.

William Bailey Royall was born at Mount Pleasant, Berkeley county, S. C., September 2, 1844. He entered Furman university and was about to complete his course there when his father became a professor at Wake Forest college, and the son accordingly became a student in the latter institution, from which he was graduated in the class of 1861. In the fall of the same year he enlisted in the Confederate army, and for nearly a year served as corporal in the Santee artillery of Manigault's South Carolina battalion. In 1862 he was transferred to the Fifty-fifth North Carolina infantry, of which his father was chaplain, was at that time commissioned commissary sergeant, and for the remainder of the war held that office. He was on duty at the battles of Gettysburg, Bristow Station, Wilderness, Spottsylvania, Cold Harbor (second battle), was at the siege of Petersburg and with Lee at Appomatox Court House. After the close of the war Mr. Royall turned his attention to teaching, and accepted a position at Forestville, N. C., 1865. One year later he was appointed as tutor at Wake Forest college, and in 1868 was made assistant professor of languages. In 1871 he was elected to fill the chair of Greek at the same place, and is now recognized as one of the ablest linguists in the state. Wake Forest college gave him the degree A. M., and Judson college conferred the title of doctor of divinity upon him, he having been ordained a minister in the Baptist church in 1869.

Miss Sarah J. Hall, an accomplished daughter of John W. Hall, of Columbus county, N. C., became his wife in 1871, and six children have been born to them, viz.: William, John Hall, Robert Henry, James Bruce Royall, and two others deceased.

BENJAMIN FRANCIS SLEDD,

a prominent and successful educator, now professor of modern languages in Wake Forest college, is a Virginian by birth, having been born in Bedford county, on the 27th of August, 1864. In June, 1886, he was graduated from Washington and Lee university, at Lexington, Va., with the degree of A. M., and then entered Johns Hopkins university, where he took a post-graduate course. At this time he accepted a position at Charlotte Hall military academy, Charlotte Hall, Md., and remained there for one year, when he was elected, in September, 1888, to fill the chair of modern languages in Wake Forest college. In June, 1889, Prof. Sledd was married to Miss Neda Purefoy, daughter of F. M. Purefoy, of Wake Forest, N. C., and a granddaughter of James S. Purefoy, who was one of the founders of the college. Prof. Sledd is the son of William E. Sledd, who was born in Bedford county, Va., in 1827. He was a planter on an extensive scale, and for many years held the office of magistrate of Bedford county. For two years he served in the army of northern Virginia under Robert E. Lee. In 1846 he married Arabella Hobson, daughter of Richard Hobson, of Virginia, by whom he had nine children, eight of whom survive: Mrs. Ann H. Campbell, James R., Eliza, wife of William R. Cornelius; Dr. Samuel D., Mrs. Ida Garnett, Mrs. Louisa Wilson, William E. and Benjamin F. Sledd. The father of these children died in 1888, and the mother in March, 1889. The grandfather of the children last mentioned was James Sledd, who was born in Bedford county, Va., in 1800. He owned large tracts of land. His death occurred in 1846. His father was Rev. John Sledd, a Baptist divine, who was a native of Virginia. He was born in Albemarle county, but went to Bedford county among its first settlers. In his later life he obtained large tracts of land near Paducah, Ky. His demise occurred between 1820 and 1830. Thomas Sledd, the father of the last mentioned, was born in England, and came to America some time prior to the Revolution, in which war he took an active part as a captain in the patriot army.

CHARLES E. TAYLOR.

For many years Wake Forest college has been in the front ranks of the educational institutions of the south. Its alumni number thousands, and many have risen to distinction in the different walks of life. Its standard has always been kept high, and the men who have formed its faculty from time to time have been men of ability and known worth. In the following lines we shall attempt to give a brief but comprehensive sketch of the life and professional career of the present president of Wake Forest college, the Rev. Charles Elisha Taylor, B. L., B. S., A. M., LL. D. He was born in Richmond, Va., on the 28th of October, 1842. He was given ample educational advantages, having graduated from Richmond college and subsequently from the University of Virginia, in July, 1870. The succeeding four or five months were spent in travel on the continent of Europe, and late in the winter of 1870 he came to Wake Forest to accept the chair of Latin in Wake Forest college. In November, 1884, he was elected president of the institution, and has since been its honored head. Dr. Taylor was so fortunate as to form a marriage alliance September 13, 1873, with Miss Mary H. Pritchard, of Wilmington, N. C., a lady of great taste and rare refinement. To this happy union seven children have been born, named as follows: Charles, Fannie, Miriam, Ethel, Jane, Agnes and Edith Taylor. Mrs. Taylor is the daughter of the late John L. Pritchard. In 1870 Dr. Taylor was ordained a minister of the Baptist church.

So much for his personal and professional career; we now turn to his military record and find that he enlisted in the Confederate service on the 17th of April, 1861, the day Virginia seceded, and was assigned to Company F, of Richmond, Va. This organization became a part of the Twenty-first Virginia volunteer infantry. He was wounded at Kernstown, and transferred to the Tenth Virginia cavalry. During the last year of the war he was acting adjutant of the Confederate secret service bureau. Serving in the army of northern Virginia under Lee, he took part in the battles of Romney, Kernstown, Brandy Station, Gettysburg, Sharpsburg (Antietam), and several other engagements of less moment. Dr. Taylor is the son of James B. Taylor, a native of Barton, England, where he was born in 1804. His parents brought him to America in his early boyhood. First locating in New York, they removed to Mecklenburg county, Va., after some ten years, and in 1825 came to Oxford, N. C., where the son was educated. In 1826 he was ordained a clergyman in the Baptist denomination.

PROF. JOSEPH REDDINGTON CHAMBERLAIN

was born in Bath, N. Y., September 22, 1861, and received his education in the district school in Bath, Hareveling free academy at Bath, and Cornell university, Ithaca, N. Y., where he graduated in 1888. He came to Raleigh, N. C., two weeks after he graduated and was appointed agriculturist of the experimental station of the North Carolina agricultural college, holding that position until October, 1890. Prof. Chamberlain's high qualities and engaging address soon won him warm friends in his new home, and so thoroughly and satisfactorily did he perform his duties that in June, 1889, he was appointed professor of agriculture, live stock and dairying of the North Carolina state agricultural college, which position he now holds, with the increasing approbation of all who are officially concerned in that institution. Prof. Chamberlain has besides attended many institutes and meetings in the state, delivering addresses on agriculture that have been most favorably received. Prof. Chamberlain's father, Jesse M. Chamberlain, was born in Bath, N. Y., in 1825, and was educated in the Bath schools, and Prattsburg academy, Steuben county, N. Y. He is a farmer. In 1859, he married Ervilla Ingham, daughter of Isaac Ingham, of Cooperstown, N. Y., and to them were born three children: Joseph R. Chamberlain, William H. Chamberlain, assistant secretary of the Southern Inter-State immigration bureau, at Raleigh, N. C., and Lucy C. Chamberlain of Bath, N. Y. Prof. Chamberlain's grandfather was Joseph Chamberlain, who was born in Vermont, where his parents had long lived, in 1790, and removed to New York when a young man, settling in Steuben county. He was a farmer and died in 1844.

PROF. W. T. GANNAWAY,

professor of Latin in Trinity college, N. C., was born in Wythe county, Va., June 10, 1825. His parents were John and Ann (Trigg) Gannaway, both natives of the Old Dominion. From boyhood the father was a farmer, and both parents were conscientious members of the Methodist Episcopal church. Mrs. Gannaway was a devoted mother, a loving wife, and a sterling example of the devout and exemplary Christian, a helpmeet indeed for a Christian husband. Both went to the reward of the pure in heart — the father in 1865, at the age of seventy-two, and the mother in 1873, aged seventy-six years. They left surviving them five children, of whom the subject of this sketch was the eldest. He was educated at Emory and Henry college, Virginia, and graduated from that institution June 2, 1845. He then took charge of an academy in Jacksonville, Floyd county, Va., remaining there nine years. Mr. Gannaway began with but few pupils, but the numbers rapidly increased; the school assumed the name of Floyd institute, and took a rank among the first educational institutions in the country. Pupils were drawn from all parts of Virginia and the Carolinas. His next work was at Germanton, N. C., where he was called in 1854 to take charge of the Masonic institute. He remained there three years with a very liberal patronage from Virginia, North and South Carolina. His excellent reputation as an educator had gone before him and given him a prestige which contributed largely to his success. In September, 1857, he was elected professor in Latin and Greek at Trinity college, a position which he held for about three years. Prof. Gannaway was then made professor of Latin and history, holding the latter position for about ten years. In 1886 he was chosen professor of Latin and French, holding that position three years, when he was elected to the chair of Latin exclusively, which position he has ever since filled. He was appointed president of Trinity college in 1863, and held the position until after the close of the war. It is a significant fact that, during his presidency, his was the only institution of its kind in the seceded states that did not suspend operations during the continuance of hostilities. Gen. Hardee's army, in April, 1865, had its headquarters pitched upon the college campus. Upon the arrival of Gen. Hardee's corps, the schools under charge of Pres. Gannaway were temporarily suspended until the following fall, when they were again re-organized. During the war there was a full faculty and a very liberal patronage, considering the disturbed condition of the country.

Prof. Gannaway holds an enviable position among the educators of the state. He has met his classes in the same room for thirty-four years, a circumstance which, it is believed, has no parallel in the southern states. To the vantage ground of this long experience he adds every real improvement in the modes of instruction of the present time and keeps up with the new revelations of the arts and sciences. During the long period in which Prof. Gannaway has held a chair in the college, his health has been so exceptionally good that for thirty-four years he has not lost two months' time from sickness, disability, or any other cause. October 15, 1855, Prof. Gannaway was united in marriage with Miss Mary W. Bethel, daughter of Rev. Joshua Bethel, of the North Carolina conference. Four children have been born to brighten the home of Mr. and Mrs. Gannaway, all of them having now come to mature age. They are Ida, wife of Rev. N. E. Coltrane, of the North Carolina conference; Florence, wife of John E. Field, a merchant of Leaksville, N. C.; W. Edgar, who has charge of his father's farm, and Mamie, wife of Capt. Jefferson Davis, professor in the Davis military school at Winston, N. C. Parents and children are all members of the Methodist Episcopal church, south. Prof. Gannaway is a member of the Masonic order, Blue lodge and Chapter. At his graduation he received the first honors of his class, being assigned to deliver the classical oration, and he was chosen by the literary society of which he was a member to deliver the valedictory address in behalf of its graduates. He was also chosen president of the alumni association for the year following his graduation, thus taking the highest honors of his class and of the society to which he belonged.

W. T. R. BELL,

of Rutherfordton, N. C., was born in Accomac county, Va., September 1, 1843. He is the youngest of the family of George H. and Margaret R. Bell. His early education was acquired at Bradford's Neck academy in his home county, and at the age of nine years he entered a boarding school at Locustsville in his native county. Soon after his entry into this school his mother died, and two years later he had the misfortune also to lose his father, but he still remained at school until about the age of thirteen, when he entered Hampton military academy, at Hampton, Va., the principal of which was Prof. John B. Cary, the present superintendent of the Richmond, Va., city schools. At the time of young Bell's attendance at Hampton the academy was one of the finest educational institutions in the United States. He continued at this academy until 1861, when he left the senior class to give his service to the Confederate army. He enlisted in the Richmond light infantry blues, commanded by O. Jennings Wise. The company was attached to the Wise legion, which carried on a campaign in West Virginia. The first year of the war Private Bell was detached as drill master, and during this period the Wise legion was taken prisoners. In April, 1862, they were paroled and exchanged. Mr. Bell was commissioned lieutenant in the regular army of the Confederate States in 1862. After special service at Camp Lee he was breveted captain and assigned to the command of Company F, Ninth Virginia regiment, Armistead's brigade, and was with the command in most of its engagements. He was wounded at Gettysburg, and early in 1865 was sent on special service and met Gen. Sheridan's advance with detachments of cavalry. He followed that general in his efforts to reach Lynchburg, in which he failed. Capt. Bell was with the army at the surrender at Appomatox Court House.

After he returned from the field of battle, Capt. Bell entered the University of Virginia in October, 1865, where for two years he pursued a special course. In 1867 he went to North Carolina and engaged in teaching as a private tutor in Carteret county, his tutorship lasting four years. He was then elected to the state senate to represent in that body the counties of Jones, Carteret and Onslow, serving through the sessions of 1874-5. In 1877 Capt. Bell removed to the western part of North Carolina, settling at Kings Mountain, where he established the Kings Mountain high school. He was superintendent of that school for a continuous term of ten years, the attendance being over 1,500 students, representing every southern state. In 1887 Capt. Bell associated himself with S. E. Gedwy in the joint management of the Shelby military institute, which was soon merged into the Shelby graded school. After successfully establishing these schools, Capt. Bell returned to his accustomed work and is now principal of the Rutherford military institute with most flattering promises of complete success, having at the first session 108 students, representing four states and one territory, the majority of them being boarding students. Capt. Bell is a member of Franklin lodge, F. & A. M.; he is a consistent and devoted member of the Methodist church. In 1868 he was united in marriage with Miss Mamie B., daughter of H. B. Hill, of Carteret county. They have had three sons and one daughter, all now living. The eldest son is a leading correspondent of a number of the principal periodicals of North and South Carolina. His *nom de plume* is " Launcelot."

ALEXANDER GRAHAM,

prominent among the educators of North Carolina, was born near Fayetteville, Cumberland county, N. C., on the 12th of September, 1844. He was prepared for college in the schools of his county town, Fayetteville. During 1860 and 1861 he taught public country schools, and in 1862 was elected principal of Richmond academy, N. C. In July, 1866, he joined the class of 1869 at the University of North

Carolina, entering the sophomore class. In November, 1868, while a member of the senior class, he was elected principal of an academy in Bladen county, N. C., and held this position until October, 1871, when he was elected a teacher in the Anthon grammar school of New York city. He filled this position and entered the Columbia college law school, from which school he was graduated in May, 1873, and in the same month he was licensed to practice in New York city and state. In January, 1875, he returned to North Carolina and was admitted, by the supreme court, to practice law in this state. He continued the practice of law until 1878, when he was elected superintendent of the city schools of Fayetteville, his county town By re-elections he continued in charge of these schools for ten years, during which time the degree of A. M. was conferred upon him by the state university. In February, 1888, he was elected superintendent of the city schools of Charlotte, N. C., which position he now holds.

GEN. FRANCIS NASH

was born in Prince Edward county, Va., May 10, 1720. He was a brother of Gen. Abner Nash, belonging to the celebrated Virginia family of that name. Many are still to be found in the Old Dominion. Of the very early life and educational and social training of Mr. Nash we find very little information in any of the biographical histories of North Carolina or Virginia. He seems at a very early age to have been appointed clerk of the superior court of Orange county, from which we take it that at that time he was a lawyer of some promise, as the administration of that office in all the colonial states which had adopted the English form of judicial procedure, then, as it does even now to a qualified extent, required the training and technical knowledge of a lawyer. A few years later he accepted a captain's commission under the crown, and in that capacity served against the regulars in the battle of Alamance in 1771. He was a member of the the provincial congress of 1775, and by that body was appointed a colonel of one of the two regiments that were at that time forming for the continental service. He was commissioned a brigadier-general by the continental congress in 1777. In the battle of Germantown he was complimented by Washington on the field. After his death congress appropriated $5,000 for a monument to his memory on the battle field at Germantown, but the scheme was never carried out.

PROF. JOSEPH KINSEY,

originator, owner and principal of Kinsey female seminary at La Grange, N. C., was born in Jones county, June 17, 1843. He is the son of Joseph B. and Nancy (Brown) Kinsey, both natives of Jones county. He was early prepared for and entered Trinity college, but before his graduation, the Civil war being in progress and his home threatened with invasion by the Federal forces, he enlisted in Company E, of the Sixty-first North Carolina infantry, and was soon promoted to the second lieutenancy of the company. He was taken prisoner at Charleston, S. C., and confined at Johnson Island, O., where he remained more than twenty months. He bore himself gallantly in the army, and after the surrender of Gen. Johnston's forces returned to Jones county and engaged in teaching a private school as a means of support in the impoverished condition to which the ravages of war had reduced him. In 1869 he came to Lenoir county, where he continued the occupation of school teaching up to 1874, when he settled in La Grange. He kept a mixed school until 1881, when he engaged in the cotton business for five years, except that during that time he taught school one year in Kinston. In 1886 he established his present female seminary, beginning only with a very small number, which steadily and constantly increased until he now has one of the most successful female schools in North Carolina. No school of its class in the south offers greater facilities for the acquisition of the useful and polite branches of female education. Music, drawing, painting, type-writing, shorthand and a full course of literary and mathematical instruction are taught. A large corps of assistants is employed in the various classes called from various states in the Union. Prof. Kinsey has built up his school, involving a heavy outlay for buildings and fixtures, from his own resources and by indomitable perseverance his success is a triumph of individual enterprise and strict devotion to his chosen calling.

Professor Kinsey is a member of the Masonic fraternity and of the Knights of Honor. In political sentiment he is a democrat, though taking but little interest in partisan contests. In 1868 he was joined in marriage with Miss Fannie Kinsey, daughter of J. H. Kinsey, of Jones county, and they have had five children named: Eva, Ina, Bingham, Robert and James. Mr. and Mrs. Kinsey are members of the Disciples church, in which he holds the office of elder and clerk. His father was a prominent farmer in Jones county, and the family were Scotch and German descent, coming to America and settling in Newbern. One of his ancestors participated in the Revolutionary war. Joseph Kinsey, the grandfather of Prof. Kinsey, was a prominent planter and slaveholder in Jones county. His family were all members of the church of the Disciples. Prof. Kinsey's father died in Jones county, and his widow was later married to J. J. Armstrong, and moved to Iowa, where she died. Prof. Kinsey is an eminent example of the higher type of teachers who from individual effort and rare natural talent have achieved a great success in their profession.

A. H. MERRITT.

Abram Haywood Merritt, one of the foremost men of Chatham co nty, N. C., was born in that county on the 18th day of July, 1832. He came of excellent parentage. His father, William Merritt, was a successful farmer, and for many years was a prominent justice of the peace; he was considered one of the very best men in the county; a man of sound judgment, his advice was eagerly sought on business matters; a man of generous feelings, he scattered his kind deeds all around him; his name was a synonym for honesty and virtue. He married Sally Rencher, a sister of the late Gov. Rencher, who represented North Carolina in the Federal congress for many years; later he was minister to Portugal, and then governor of New Mexico. Mrs. Merritt was a remarkable woman. There never was a better mother nor a more devoted Christian; cheerful and bright, she shed around her the aroma of a beautiful character. Five children were born to these parents: William G. Merritt became a leading farmer in DeSoto county, Miss., and died soon after the war from disease contracted in camp. The two sisters married brothers, belonging to one of the prominent families of the state—Mrs. Elizabeth Jones, widow of the late A. S. Jones, lives in Mississippi, Mrs. Sarah Jones lives in Wake county and is the wife of Rufus H. Jones. Leonidas J. Merritt graduated at the University of North Carolina with high honor, studied law under Judge Pearson, located in Pittsborough, and was fast rising to prominence in his profession when the war came on; he was a member of the secession convention and took a high stand in that body as one of the most promising young men of the state; he entered the army as a private, was promoted, and was instantly killed at Malvern Hill. Never did a bullet strike a purer or a nobler man.

A. H. Merritt was the youngest member of this family. He graduated at the University of North Carolina, with honor, in 1856, editing the *University Magazine* during his senior year. He taught school very successfully for several years, and at the opening of the war he was the principal of Olin high school in Iredell county. Returning to his native county, Mr. Merritt discharged the duties of clerk and master of the court of equity for Chatham county, from the beginning of the war, till the court was abolished by law after the war was ended. The delicate and responsible duties of this office during those troublous times he managed with great prudence and with high commendation from the presiding judges. After the war he again went to the teacher's desk, and as principal of the Cary high school and later of a classical school in Pittsborough, he maintained and extended his enviable reputation as a teacher. In 1879, Mr. Merritt was elected state senator for his district by a most flattering vote. He declined the position of one of the presiding justices of the inferior court, to which he had been elected, and took his seat in the senate. He served in the legislature four years, and has since declined every solicitation to be returned to that body. As a legislator Mr. Merritt took a prominent position from the start. At every term of his service he was chairman of the committee of education, and was largely instrumental in formulating the present admirable school law. He served on other important committees, and took a leading part in all the important measures before that body. His

Truly &c.
John W. Starnes

speeches on the geological survey of the state and on the Cape Fear and Yadkin Valley railroad were particularly complimented. Mr. Merritt has never been an office seeker, but his friends strongly urged his name for the position of state superintendent of public instruction, and he received a flattering vote in convention. From 1884 to 1889 Mr. Merritt owned and edited *The Home*, a democratic, family newspaper. Under him the paper grew in patonage and influence, and the press and people gave its editor the credit for being an excellent writer, of discriminating tact, fairness and ability. For many years Mr. Merritt has held the position of trustee of the University of North Carolina, in which institution he takes great interest, and is one of the most active and trusted members of the board. He was married, in 1861, to Miss S. E. Purvis, daughter of Rev. J. Purvis, of blessed memory. She is a woman of great intellect and purity of character, and is the mother of seven bright children, all of whom give great promise of useful lives. Mr. Merritt is now living on his farm near Pittsborough. He has held the office of superintendent of public instruction for the county for ten years, and has done much to elevate and make efficient our system of public schools. He takes an active and intelligent interest in all public matters, and is a frequent contributor to the press. He is considered a good speaker, and many of his more elaborate speeches on literary subjects, Sunday-schools and temperance have been greatly complimented. Col. Cameron, the Nestor of the press in North Carolina, says: " He is a gentleman of great modesty, he is a finished scholar, he is industrious, he is energetic, he is intelligent, and he is pure." In this estimate of his character his hosts of personal friends and acquaintances all over the state heartily agree.

JOHN WESLEY STARNES.

John W. Starnes, one of the representative men of Asheville, N. C., was born in the western part of Buncombe county, N. C., May 13, 1849. He is the son of Thomas A. and Elizabeth Starnes, and on the paternal side is of German descent. His great-grandfather, John Starnes, Sr., was a native of Germany and came to America when a boy about the year 1770. He volunteered as a private in the Revolutionary war and was several times promoted and finally placed in command of a battalion with the rank of colonel, which position he held until the independence of the colonies was acknowledged. Col. Starnes was especially expert and valuable during the war in thwarting the plans of the tories and Indians, and on account of his success in that direction, he was kept continually at that work during the last two years of the war. The tories and Indians were consequently embittered against him, and these two enemies to American rights thirsted for the gallant young colonel's blood. When the heroes of his command were disbanded, he started home to enjoy the liberty he had fought for, but the savages lay in ambush for him, and as he

was nearing his home, they sprang upon him and killed him with
their tomahawks. He left a widow and two little sons, John and
Frederick. When John Starnes grew to manhood, he married Mary
Etta Hice and settled in what is now Starnes' Cove in the western
part of Buncombe county, where he and his wife reared a family of
ten children, and accumulated a large estate of land and negroes,
most of which sank with the southern Confederacy. The maiden
name of the mother of our subject was Morgan, a name which has
illumined nearly every battle field in the history of America, and has
been conspicuous under every administration of the government.
Her father was Jesse Morgan, Sr., who was of English descent, and
he married a Miss Grant.

John W. Starnes was reared on his father's farm among the hills
of Buncombe county. His education was obtained principally in the
common schools of the county, and that too after he had almost attained his majority, his opportunities having been limited and inter-
fered with by the Civil war. He did not, however, depend altogether
upon the school room, but applied himself diligently at home and
was a hard student between the ages of nineteen and twenty-five
years. At the latter age, having fully equipped himself for teaching
school, he began that calling and for six years taught school most of
the time in his home district. In 1877 he was appointed a teacher in
the Western academy and removed to Asheville at that time. After
a year spent in that position, he resigned the same, and for four
years following was engaged in the dry goods business. But the
principal work of our subject's life, and the one wherein he gained
his prominence as an educator and school worker, was accomplished
as superintendent of schools of Buncombe county. He was first
elected to that position in 1883, to fill an unexpired term, and was
successively re-elected in 1884-86-88, each time with but little opposition and the last time by acclamation. When he assumed the duties
of the office of county superintendent in 1883, the schools of the
country were being taught in old church buildings and tenement
houses, there being but two comfortable school buildings, in the county
owned by the school committees. During his seven years' incumbency many new districts were formed and more than three score new
buildings erected. When he entered the office the standard of the
public schools was very low and the office of school superintendent
itself had been resigned by those elected to it. But during Mr.
Starnes' administration a radical change and improvements were
made, and there is no doubt but that to his efforts and untiring labor
the impetus was due in a great degree which has resulted in the
present excellent condition of the county. Also, to his efforts are
due, in a measure, the establishment of the graded schools of Asheville.

Each year of his superintendency Prof. Starnes held two county
institutes, one for the white, and one for the colored teachers, and
which were uniformly successful. His colored institutes were among
the first ever held in the state, and he was highly complimented upon

the proficiency attained by the colored teachers who attended the same. He always advised his teachers to "do right because it is right to do right," which motto he has himself ever followed. Prof. Starnes was a charter member of the North Carolina teachers' assembly, organized in 1884, and was a member of the first committee on organization, being elected first vice-president. By promotion he became president of the second meeting of the assembly, but served only long enough to organize the meeting, and then resigned, requesting that his successor be elected at once and he be relieved, as he preferred the active work on the floor where his services were needed. He was one among the first to deliver addresses before the assembly, the addresses always being upon topics pertaining to educational work. He has also delivered numerous other addresses at different times and places in the state, which attracted considerable attention and were given wide publicity. The principal ones were those on the topics of "Shall Women Vote," "Music," "Signs of the Times," and "Latter Day Politics." Since leaving the office of superintendent, which he resigned in 1890, Mr. Starnes has continued to hold his interest in the public schools and educational work. He has for years been quite prominent in local political affairs, but not as a seeker for office. By industry and the exercise of his naturally excellent business talents, he has succeeded in obtaining a competent estate. He is a democrat and a member of the Masonic fraternity. On February 20, 1878, Mr. Starnes was married to Miss Mary Brand, who was born in Asheville, N. C., and to their union four children have been born, two sons and two daughters, as follows: Brand, Elizabeth (Bethie), Mary (Maidie) and John W., Jr.

The following short impromptu was written by Mr. Starnes in church on the morning of May the 4th, 1890, after hearing his Sunday-school class recite, while the choir was singing, between 10 and 11 A. M., describing the day: "Sunday morning opens out the mildest of days. Love hangs out his curtains across the firmament shutting away the fervid sun and we walk beneath the shadows. A glorious umbrella spreads, anon, over our heads and we breath the pure air of heaven 'neath the smiles of His own tender providence. Last night it was stormy. The rain fell in torrents. We slept, but dreamed of bursting volcanoes, rolling cyclones and hurricanes. This morning we almost feared to look abroad. But ah! the distant horizon stands skirted with friendly clouds and nature smiles in sweetest halcyon. The storm, last night, was only the bursting up of war in the elements. The delicate fingers of spring, now and then, protrude a soft ray through the veil, opening out the petals, till in a few hours the husbandman has spread a carpet of vernal beauty clear across the face of the earth. The sickening heat is gone from the air, and purity from Pisgah steals down upon the city. Precious day! There is an air of holiness and pure incense of love floating in the morning. God is in motion. Not nature's God, but the God of nature. This is not a God belonging to nature but a nature belonging to God."

B—29

JOHN S. LONG, A. M., LL. D.,

was born in Plymouth, Washington county, N. C., on the 3rd of October, 1830 — his parents, John and Mary E. (Armstrong) Long, also being natives of that county. The father was a merchant, and afterward a farmer, owning a number of slaves. He was baptized in the Episcopal church, but subsequently gave his allegiance to the Methodist Episcopal church. He was a man of sterling integrity and worth, and was held in the highest esteem in the community. From a beginning without means he came to be successful in business. His death occurred in 1860, his wife following him to rest two years later. The family are direct descendants of an English bishop, one or more of whose sons came from England with Lord Baltimore. Of their descendants, three brothers settled in North Carolina, one in Randolph, one in Halifax and the other in Bertie county. John Long had four children, all of whom are deceased with the exception of John S., of whom we write. The latter passed his boyhood in Washington, Beaufort county, and was prepared for college by Gilbert Bogart, a graduate of Princeton college. Mr. Long entered the sophomore class in Randolph-Macon college in 1848, and was graduated therefrom in 1851, with high honors in oratory and English composition. In 1851 he entered the law department of the University of North Carolina, and in 1852 obtained his license to practice in the county courts, and in 1853 in the superior courts. Almost immediately thereafter he was elected solicitor of Beaufort county, and practiced law there until 1857, when he entered the ministry of the Methodist Episcopal church, and was stationed at Goldsboro, Wilmington, Raleigh and other prominent points. In 1868 he retired to his farm in Beaufort county, remaining there until 1872, when he removed to Newbern and turned his attention to educational and literary work. For twelve years he has been superintendent of the Craven county schools, and in 1878 was mayor of Newbern.

For several successive terms Mr. Long was president of the board of trustees of the Newbern academy. In 1867 he went on the lecture platform with these topics, "Ethics of History" and "Bishop Bascom." First delivered in the larger chapel of the University of New York, they were repeated in Baltimore and almost all the principal towns of North Carolina. His lecture on the "College Graduate in Pursuit of a Living," was delivered before the University of North Carolina, and also at Wake Forest college, and was received in the most flattering manner. In 1885 he delivered the memorial address at Wilmington, N. C., and the industrial address at Goldsboro, and the thousands of people who heard them were greatly impressed with the ability of the lecturer. In 1889 he delivered the annual address at the "Boys' Home" in Baltimore. His efforts as a literateur have been attended with like success. In 1890 the degree of LL. D. was conferred upon him by the University of North Carolina. Mr. Long was one of the founders of the Delta Kappa Epsilon fraternity's chapter at the University of North Carolina. During the war the chapter was disorganized and the records destroyed. It was then rechartered as the Beta Alpha chapter. Columbia college, of New York, having established a chapter which took the former's old name, refused to relinquish it. The matter was left to arbitration, and Dr. Long was chosen as the representative of the University of North Carolina, but the plan failed. The fraternity convention, which finally settled the difference, met at Cincinnati in 1888. North Carolina's university won the day, and Dr. Long achieved high credit by the result. In 1852 Dr. Long married Miss Mary A. Marsh, daughter of James B. Marsh, by whom he has had two children: Nellie, the wife of W. F. Yost, of the National Union bank, of Baltimore, and Minnie, the wife of S. S. Willett, formerly of the United States navy. Mr. Long is a member of the Chosen Friends, and also of the Legion of Honor, and of the Episcopal church.

GEORGE WASHINGTON NEAL

was born in Warren county, N. C., on the 10th of September, 1823. His parents were Cuthbert and Lucy Neal, the former being a successful farmer. When the parents removed to Virginia the son was still in early boyhood. His scholastic training was begun in the "old field school" in Mecklenburg county, Va. Subsequently he became a student in a private school of high standing and made remarkable progress. In 1844 he removed to Hertford county, N. C., and attended Buckhorn academy for some time. Being thoroughly equipped for his collegiate career, Mr. Neal entered the University of North Carolina, and was graduated with due honor, after which he turned his attention to educational work. His first experience as a teacher had been gained while he was still a student, his progress having been so substantial as to warrant his instructors in appointing him an assistant to teach a few classes each day. After leaving college he returned to Buckhorn academy as a professor, and after three years of success there accepted an offer to establish a male and female academy at Williamston, N. C. Here he remained until 1856, when he was elected professor of higher mathematics and ancient languages in the Wesleyan female college at Murfreesboro. For three years he conducted a flourishing school at Franklin, N. C., and at the expiration of that time was offered a large salary to found a college at Marianna, Fla. $24,000 was raised by the trustees of the town to erect a suitable building, and Prof. Neal entered upon his duties as president in November, 1860. Upon the breaking out of the war he decided to return to North Carolina, and did so, assuming charge of a school at Franklinton, N. C., where he remained for seven or eight years. In 1870 he accepted the office of principal of the Newbern academy, and discharged the duties of that position with universal satisfaction for seven years. He then became the head of the Rockingham academy, at Rockingham, N. C., and in the year 1881 returned to Newbern and opened a high school. Since that time he has conducted different schools in the city with uniform success.

During the last two years Prof. Neal has filled the chair of higher mathematics and civil engineering in the Newbern collegiate institute. Early in his professional career his *alma mater* conferred upon him the degree of A. M. For twenty-seven years he has been a local preacher in the Methodist Episcopal church, and is now a local elder; and he has also served as a trustee and steward of the same denomination, and for two years was president of the Evangelical alliance at Newbern. On the 5th of September, 1854, Prof. Neal formed a marriage alliance with Miss Fanny Pauline Hart, a native of Southampton county, Va. Her parents names were John and Elizabeth A. Hart. The children of this union are: Fanny, wife of John Hughes Bell, an employe in the pension bureau at Washington, D. C.; Walter Hart, attorney-at-law in Laurinburg, N. C.—at present the attorney for the Carolina Central railroad, chairman of the democratic executive committee of the Sixth congressional district, and a member of the state democratic executive committee; Lizzie Clark, a successful teacher; Benjamin Baxter, junior member of the firm of L. H. Cutler & Co., and John Hughes Neal, who is at present acquiring a knowledge of the machinists trade. Prof. Neal is a man of unusual ability. His predominating characteristic is perseverance. A lifelong student he has brought to his noble calling a mind well stored with knowledge, and especially does he excel as a mathematician and scientist. Few men entering the ranks of educators succeed in more thoroughly grasping the details of their work than has this man. It has been his study to get from each student that which was in him. He has elevated his position, which is but true genius itself, by consistent, persistent effort.

ALEXANDER MEBANE.

This eminent statesman was born in Philadelphia, November 26, 1754. In December, 1776, he was a member of the provincial congress that formed the state constitution. He was also a member of the convention at Hillsboro, which rejected the constitution of the United States. After this he was almost unanimously elected to represent his district in the general assembly, which office he held from 1783 to 1792. At the end of his legislative career at home, during which he had rendered such splendid services, he was elected to a seat in the congress of the United States, but died before taking his seat. Mr. Mebane was a man distinguished for his stern integrity and indomitable firmness. He was married first to Mary Armstrong, of Orange county, and his second wife was Mary Claypole, of Philadelphia. Several of his children survived him, James, William and Dr. John A. Mebane, of Greensboro. The distinguished family to which Mr. Mebane belonged is one of the largest in the south, and the family will be found scattered broadcast throughout Tennessee, Mississippi, Indiana, Kentucky, Arkansas, Texas and Virginia.

REV. BENJAMIN FRANKLIN DIXON,

late superintendent of the Oxford orphan asylum, was born in Cleveland county, N. C., March 26, 1846. His parents, Thomas and Mary W. Dixon, were of foreign extraction, the one of English and the other of Irish parentage. Mr. Dixon's earlier education was acquired at a high school, which he left when only a boy of fifteen to enter the Confederate service as a private soldier. He joined Company D, of the Fourth North Carolina infantry, afterward known as the Fourteenth regiment. He was promoted to a lieutenancy in 1863, and for gallant conduct before the enemy was afterward raised to the captaincy of his company, being still a minor. His military career was distinguished for daring bravery and coolness in battle. He was several times wounded, receiving a shot in his right arm at Drury's Bluff, in the left arm at Malvern Hill, and one in the side at Petersburg.

At the close of the war Mr. Dixon began teaching in his native county, which he followed for two years. At the end of this time he went before an examining board in theology, was approved and joined the conference of the South Carolina Methodist Episcopal church, south, thereafter entering the ministry of that church. His first charge was at Sumter, S. C., where his services were instrumental in bringing about much good. He was afterward stationed at Monroe. Subsequently he was transferred to the North Carolina conference, was stationed at Monroe, as above noted, and then was appointed upon the Shelby circuit. His health being somewhat impaired he remained stationary in this circuit. While engaged in teaching he had pursued a course of medical studies. At this point of time he completed his course at Charleston and began practice at Kings Mountain. His practice proved to be a success and he pursued it for ten years, at the end of which he was elected superintendent of the Oxford orphan asylum, the duties of which he administered with signal success for six years.

In September, 1890, he was elected by a unanimous vote of the trustees as president of the Greensboro female college. Here he not only received the highest approbation of the trustees, but gained the respect and esteem of the pupils in attendance upon the institution. He stands in the very front rank as an educator. He is a distinguished member of the Masonic fraternity, and is a bright exemplar of a Christian gentleman. In July, 1877, he was married to Miss Nora C. Tracy, daughter of Dr. J. W. Tracy, of Kings Mountain. They have three children: Pearl, Benjamin F., and Wright T. When Dr. Dixon left the Oxford institution, the *Public Ledger* closed a notice of the event with the following appreciative words of Mrs. Dixon: A host of friends in Oxford regret the departure of Mrs. Dr. B. F. Dixon and her interesting family for their future home in Greensboro. During her long stay in Oxford she has won the love of all classes of people, and is looked upon by all as being one of the most admirable women in North Carolina.

Rev. Mr. Dixon served in the following battles during the Civil war: Yorktown, Seven Pines, seven days' fight around Richmond, Fredericksburg, Wilderness, Chancellorsville, Gettysburg, Drury's Bluff, siege of Petersburg, and during the engagement at Five Forks, April 1, 1865, he was captured by the Federal troops, and for three months was held a prisoner of war. Mr. Dixon is the son of Thomas Dixon, who was born in Lincoln, now Cleveland county, N. C., in 1803. He was a planter, and a man of considerable prominence in the community. In 1828 he married Miss Mary A. Winter, daughter of John Winter, a native of Ireland. Her mother was Mary Dilworth, also of Irish birth. Seven children were born to them, the two surviving being Martha, wife of Polk Collins, of Bluntsville, Ala., and Benjamin Franklin Dixon, of Greensboro, N. C. The mother died in 1886, and the father in 1856. The latter was a son of Robert Dixon, who was born in North Carolina in 1771. Like his son, he followed agriculture all his life, dying in 1857. His father was a native of England. He came to America in 1760, and settled in North Carolina, where he was engaged in planting at the time of the breaking out of the war for American independence. He fought as a patriot soldier. The Winter family is also an old connection in this county, and is of Scotch origin. Mary Winter Dixon was a relative of Hon. Clement Clay, of Alabama, who served as a United States senator for many years. His son, Clement C. Clay, Jr., was also a man of great prominence, and was a senator in the Confederate congress, being imprisoned with President Davis. Major-Gen. Jones Winter, of Mobile, Ala., served with distinction in the Confederate army, and John Winter, of Huntsville, Ala., was assistant adjutant-general of the Confederate States, and was a cousin of our subject's mother.

LEONIDAS L. POLK.

This distinguished journalist and politician, to whom so much attention has been recently called by reason of his conspicuity as the leader of the farmers' alliance in the south, is a well-known figure in southern politics and journalism. His recent friendship to the farmer is nothing new in the history of Col. Polk, but a favorable political opportunity, for all his life has been devoted to advancing the condition of that class of men, as a glance at his life will show. He was born April 24, 1837, in Anson county. He is of honorable Irish extraction, one of his ancestors, Thomas Polk, having been a signer of the Mecklenburg Declaration of Independence, and a colonel in the Revolutionary war. He is the son of Andrew Polk, a farmer of Mecklenburg county, and was himself educated for the same calling. After attending the common schools he took a course at the Davidson Presbyterian college, and studied especially scientific agriculture. At the age of fourteen he was left an orphan. A few years later he married Sarah P. Gaddy, the daughter of a prosperous farmer, Joel W. Gaddy, and purchasing his father's estate settled down to the business of his

life. He was elected by the whigs to the legislature of 1860, which passed the ordinance of secession.

Mr. Polk's military career was a bright one. He enlisted as a private in Col. Vance's regiment, the Twentieth North Carolina, of which he became sergeant-major, and later on was made first lieutenant of his company. His regiment did some of the best fighting in the war, having participated in the following campaigns: Newbern, Washington, Plymouth, Gettysburg, where he was seriously wounded in the foot; Richmond, Hanover Junction, Bethesda Church, Berryville, Kernstown, Fisher's Hill, Cedar Creek and Winchester. He was called from active duty, in 1864, to fill a term in the legislature. After the war he devoted himself assiduously to the duties of his farm, and for two years served as a magistrate, and ran a weekly newspaper called the *Ansonian*, besides conducting an extensive mercantile business.

In 1873 the Carolina Central railroad approaching his farm, Mr. Polk built upon a tract near the line a village called Polkton in his honor. He was chairman of the committee of the state grange of North Carolina, and assisted in drawing the bill for the establishment of the department of agriculture, the passage of which, by the legislature, he was deputed to promote and succeeded in effecting. The bill as passed provides for a commissioner of agriculture, to be elected by the state board of agriculture, to consist of the governor of the state, the president of the state agricultural society, the president of the state university, the state geologist, the master of the state grange, and two practical agriculturists. By this board, duly organized under the law, he was chosen commissioner, April 6, 1877, and at once entered upon the discharge of the responsible duties of the office. The system of the department, as defined in the law, is more comprehensive than that of any other like department in the United States, and the system finds in him a zealous and efficient administrator—himself a thoroughly practical agriculturist, familiar by actual experience with every branch of the art, and taking delight in all of them.

JOSEPH EDWARD ROBINSON,

proprietor and editor of the Goldsboro *Daily and Weekly Argus*, was born in Lenoir county, N. C., September 23, 1858, his parents being John and Margaret (Dillon) Robinson, both of Irish nationality Mr. Robinson's parents removed to Goldsboro while he was an infant, consequently his career is closely identified with that place. He was educated in the St. Charles college, of Maryland (Society of St. Sulpice), graduating therefrom in the class of 1879, after which he took up the study of law. Having read under the direction of Mr. A. K. Smedes, of Goldsboro, he was admitted to the bar in 1881, and for four years practiced in the Wayne county courts. He then accepted a position on the editorial staff of the Goldsboro *Messenger*, and in April, 1885, he established the *Daily and Weekly Argus*, which now ranks with the leading papers of the eastern portion of the state.

It is the only daily in the county, and wields a strong influence under the able management of its editor. Democratic in politics, it is recognized as one of the leading party organs of the state. Mr. Robinson was as great a success as a lawyer as he is in the editorial room. He was attorney for the M. N. C. railroad from its inception until it passed into the hands of a receiver. During two administrations he ably filled the office of city attorney of Goldsboro and retired from that position to found the *Argus*. He has held frequent commissions from the governor for special service, and is at present state proxy of the A. & N. C. railroad, and also a member of the democratic executive committee of Wayne county. Few men of his age attain such an influence in a community as has Joseph E. Robinson. He has ever been an enthusiastic supporter of public education, was a constant advocate of its claims through the *Messenger*, when on the staff of that paper, and has delivered a number of telling speeches throughout the county in favor of the free school system. If life and health be spared him a brilliant career doubtless awaits him.

THOMAS R. JERNIGAN

was born in Hertford county, N. C., February 24, 1847. His father, Lemuel R. Jernigan, was a prosperous planter and influential citizen, and many years a presiding justice in the court of common pleas and quarter sessions; he was related to Spencer Jarnigan, at one time a United States senator from Tennessee. His mother was Mary Harrell, and a near relative of the late W. N. H. Smith, chief-justice of the supreme court of North Carolina. Mr. Jernigan received his primary education at the academy of his native village, Harrellsville, and soon after the close of the war entered the University of Virginia, where he took a classical course of two years, and then studied law for one year at the same institution. He obtained a license to practice law the year he attained his majority, and practiced his profession in the county in which he was born. In 1870 he was nominated for the legislature by the democratic party of his county, and although the usual republican majority was over two hundred, he was declared legally elected and given the certificate of election. While the election was to every appearance fairly conducted, and the certificate awarded in strict conformity to law, a canvass of the popular vote showed that Mr. Jernigan was defeated by sixteen majority. When convinced that there was no mistake in the count of the popular vote he promptly resigned his certificate of election, declining to serve. Many of Mr. Jernigan's political friends expressed dissatisfaction with his course, but all admired his manly firmness, and sense of equity and justice. In 1874 Mr. Jernigan was nominated by his political friends for the state senate. The senatorial district embraced seven counties, casting about 12,000 votes. Mr. Jernigan began his canvass in the face of a republican majority of 750, but was elected by 355 majority. He served as state senator for two years, was always prepared for the

W. R. Jernigan

work before him, and aided in laying the foundation for the settlement of the public debt of his state.

During the presidential candidacy of Gen. Hancock, Mr. Jernigan
was one of the presidential electors of his state, and his canvass was
very highly complimented by the press. As a speaker he is logical
and chaste in his language, aggressive and of easy manner and pleasant delivery. In 1885 Mr. Jernigan was appointed by President
Cleveland as United States consul at Osako and Hiogo, Japan where
he remained nearly four years, and performed his duty to the
marked satisfaction of his own government and of the government
to which he was accredited. Returning home he settled at Raleigh,
the capital of the state, where he established the *North Carolina Intelligencer*, edited and conducted by him for one year, when it was
consolidated with the *News and Observer*, the organ of the democratic
party of North Carolina, of which he is now one of the chief editors
and a stockholder. Mr. Jernigan was married in 1885 to Miss Fannie Sharp, a daughter of the late Col. Starkey Sharp, who was a
wealthy and highly influential citizen of Hertford county. Mr. and
Mrs. Jernigan have three children, two boys and one girl, all born at
the United States consulate, Hiogo, Japan. A very good likeness of
the subject of this sketch appears in connection herewith. Mr. Jerni-
gen is of slender build, weighing about 130 pounds. He has always
been very active in the public affairs of his state. He is fearless in
the advocacy of whatever he believes to be right, and his political
friends and enemies always know where to find him, and in consequence of his firmness and ability he is admired by both.

SPEAKER JOHN HARVEY.

The Harveys were among the early settlers in Virginia, where
they occupied high station. Shortly after the first settlement was
made on the shores of the Albemarle, they came southward and
located on Harvey's Neck at the mouth of Perquimans river. In 1679
John Harvey as president of the council administered the affairs of
colony, and in 1797, his son Thomas Harvey was as deputy governor
likewise at the head of the colony. Possessing wealth and education
as well as vigorous mental powers, the family occupied a prominent
position in the province for more than a century. The subject of this
sketch, Speaker John Harvey, was endowed with a vigorous mind, and
having enjoyed the most liberal opportunities for its cultivation he
added the ornaments of an education to the hereditary qualities of a
polished gentleman. His first appearance in public life was a member from his native county of Perquimans in the assembly of 1746,
when Gov. Johnston sought to deprive the northern counties of their
accustomed representation. During the eight years following, under
advice of himself and associates, Perquimans, like the other northern
counties, was not represented in the assembly. It was a bold course
to pursue, but it was successful. In 1754 the obnoxious act was repealed by the crown, and the upper counties were again represented,

and from that date to his death John Harvey was a prominent actor in North Carolina affairs. He was an able coadjutor of Swann, Starkey and Ashe in the conflict with Gov. Dobbs. With Gov. Tryon's administration the stamp act troubles began, and no assembly was convened by him during their continuance.

When the stamp act was repealed in 1766, a wave of intense loyalty and fervid gratitude swept over the continent, and when the new assembly met in the fall of that year, it testified its good will and gratitude by complying with the desires of Gov. Tryon. It fixed the seat of government at Newbern, and gave him £10,000 to build him a palace there. It was in this era of good will that John Harvey was elected speaker of the house, and Gov. Tryon, who was a most accomplished and astute manager, kept the assembly on good terms with him. The chief troubles of those years were the regulation disturbances, and as to them the assembly sustained the governor, who kept it in existence until 1770, during the whole of the period Harvey being the speaker. In that year, 1770, Tryon expected to leave the colony, and the regulators having pressed for a new assembly, he issued writs for a new election. When the new body convened, Caswell was elected speaker. The assembly, Harvey being a ·member, however, strongly sustained the governor in the regulation troubles, and a majority of the members went with him on the expedition ending in the battle of Alamance.

Governor Tryon, when about to set out, wrote to Harvey, thanking him for his kind present last winter, and wishing him a perfect re-establishment of his health, and "if you think you can procure me, with the assistance of Col. Taylor, a company of fifty men, I should be glad to take them. I wish your son could command the company." His personal relations with the governor seems to have been friendly, and his failure to be re-elected speaker was perhaps due to his ill-health. In a few months Tryon had left the colony and Josiah Martin succeeded him. A difference sprung up between this assembly and Gov. Martin about taxes, and he dissolved it. In the fall of 1772 a new election was held, and when the assembly met Harvey was chosen speaker. From that time onward the controversies with Gov. Martin as the representative of the crown became stronger and stronger, and Harvey, in the commanding position of speaker, was the leader of the popular party.

On the 21st of December, 1773, Gov. Martin suddenly prorogued the assembly. As soon as the house understood his purpose it appointed a committee, of which John Harvey was the head, to prepare an address to the king, beseeching him to withdraw his royal instructions to the governor; and it was unanimously resolved to address Gov. Tryon, who was then in England, and implore that he would present the address to the king and that he would accept this important trust as a testimony of the great affection this colony bore him. The house met again March 1st, but after a sharp conflict with Gov. Martin, was dissolved. The private secretary of the governor mentioned to Speaker Harvey that the governor did not intend to

convene another assembly until he saw a chance of getting a better one. Harvey replied that then the people would convene one themselves. Harvey mentioned this to Willie Jones, and then to Col. Buncombe and Sam Johnston, who wrote to William Hooper about it the next day, April 5, 1774, and begged him to speak of it to Mr. Harnett and Col. Ashe. The result was that some weeks later hand bills were issued by the Wilmington committee inviting the people to elect delegates to a convention to be held in Newbern, August 25th. Thus Col. Harvey's suggestion was the germ of the first provincial congress, the earliest revolutionary body elected by the people in any colony. When it met the body elected him moderator.

And now the era of the Revolution was reached and instead of struggling for the rights of the colony against the instructions of the king, Harvey and his associates struck out boldly for the rights of America. They resolved that after January 1, 1775, they would neither import nor purchase any goods of British manufacture, and they took advanced whig ground in all their actions. They also resolved not to import or purchase any slave brought into this province from any part of the world after the 1st day of November, 1774. Having completed its work this congress resolved that Col. Harvey should call it together at his pleasure, and it "thanked him for the faithful exercise of the office of moderator and the service he has thereby rendered this province and the freedom of America in general." His health even then appears to have been precarious, for provision was made in case of his death for Sam Johnston to take his place. On the 11th of February, 1775, Harvey, as moderator, issued notices requesting the people to elect deputies to represent them in a provincial congress, to meet on April 3d, the day appointed for the meeting of the colonial assembly. This was at once denounced by Gov. Martin, in a flaming proclamation, but without avail. The two bodies were composed of nearly the same men. The assembly chose Harvey speaker, and the congress elected him moderator. Four days later, however, the governor dissolved the assembly, and that was the last assembly that met in North Carolina until 1777. Within a fortnight after the provincial congress adjourned Gov. Martin fled from Newbern; and two months later, June 5, 1777, the patriot, Harvey himself, had passed away. He was a bold and strenuous advocate of the liberties of the colonies, and his death was greatly deplored.

COL. R. B. CREECY.

The only surviving member of the family of Joshua S. and Mary (Benbury) Creecy is the Hon. Richard B. Creecy, one of the ablest journalists of eastern North Carolina. Col. Creecy was born in Chowan county, N. C., on the 19th of December, 1813. The family lived in Chowan county for several generations, and was influential and prominent. Lemuel Creecy, the grandfather of our subject, was an extensive planter. His son, Joshua, was a colonel of militia, and rendered distinguished service to the government during the war of 1812. He too was a planter. His wife was a daughter of Thomas Benbury, who served as the first collector of the port of Edenton, having been appointed to that position by President Washington. He served in the patriot army all during the Revolution, and was promoted to the rank of general for valiant field work. Thomas Benbury was speaker of the house of commons of North Carolina. Joshua Creecy died in 1817, and his wife in 1822. Their son Richard was given exceptional educational advantages, and in 1835 was graduated from the University of North Carolina. In 1842 he was admitted to the bar, and in the following year located at Elizabeth City, where he was engaged in successful practice until 1851, at which time he retired and turned his attention to agriculture. In 1872 Col. Creecy resumed active work in his profession, and at that time became the owner and editor of the *Economist*. He has made this the leading journal of the county, and one of the most important and ablest democratic organs in the state. Possessed of a superior mind, he has greatly enlarged and broadened it by years of careful study and reading; keen and ready, with unusual versatility, he has won a widespread reputation as a safe and brilliant writer. In early life Col. Creecy was a candidate for the state senate, but was defeated. President Cleveland appointed him collector of the port of Elizabeth City, and he served during that administration. In 1844 he was most happily married to Miss Mary B. Perkins, daughter of Edmund Perkins, of this county. In 1868 Mrs. Creecy died, leaving nine children, viz.: Mrs. Elizabeth Winston, of Windsor, N. C.; Edward P., of St. Louis, Mo.; Mrs. Mary Lawton, of Philadelphia; Mrs. Ella G. Lamb, of Elizabeth City; Richard B., Jr., of Elizabeth City; Henrietta, Joshua C., Nannie B. and Paul are at home, with the exception of Joshua C., who resides in St. Louis, Mo.

JAMES INNES.

The subject of this sketch was born in Scotland, of a distinguished family. We first knew of him as a resident of New Havover, where, in 1734, he was made a justice of the peace. In the same year Gov. Johnston recommended him as a member of the council. The next year he was appointed assistant baron of the exchequer court. It appears that he had seen service in the British army, and in 1740, when Gov. Johnston raised a North Carolina battalion to send to Florida, he appointed Innes to the command. The same troops went under him in the expedition against Carthagena, in South America. There he appears to have won an enviable reputation. Later he was colonel of militia in New Hanover county and one of Granville's agents for the sale of land. In 1750 he was appointed a member of the council in the place of Eleazer Allen, who had died. When the French and Indian war broke out, in 1754, North Carolina promptly responded to the appeal of Virginia for aid and took steps to raise a regiment, Col. Innes being appointed its colonel. Gov. Dinwiddie who seems to have known him well, addressing him as "dear James" and conveying in his letters messages from "his wife and daughters," tendered him the position of commander-in-chief of the expedition. This Col. Innes hesitated to accept because of his age, and sent John Ashe, as his aide-de-camp, to Virginia, to see the governor, who insisted, saying that his merit required him to take the command. And Col. Washington declared that he would be glad to serve under such an experienced officer and man of sense.

Thus pressed, Col. Innes accepted the chief command, and hastened on the Virginia frontier. Five months later, however, in November, 1754, the king designated Gov. Sharpe, of Maryland, as commander-in-chief, and Col. Innes proposed to retire. But Gov. Dinwiddie prevailed on him to remain in the service, and appointed him camp-master-general, and he remained at Fort Cumberland on the confines of Virginia, making treaties with the Indians, constructing forts and virtually in command. On June 24, 1755, Gen. Braddock reached Fort Cumberland on his ill-fated march, and he appointed Innes governor of Fort Cumberland, who remained there. Later, in August, after Braddock had fallen, and his demoralized forces had returned, Col. Dunbar then in command, hastened on to Philadelphia, to go into winter quarters, and left Innes with 400 sick and wounded to care for at Fort Cumberland, and to defend the frontier. In September, 1755, Col. Innes returned to North Carolina, where on September 5, 1759, he died at Wilmington. In his will, made in 1754, he left his plantation and considerable personal property "for the use of a free school for the benefit of the youth of North Carolina."

JOSEPHUS DANIELS,

son of Josephus and Mary Seabrook, was born in Washington, N. C., May 18, 1862. He was educated in Wilson collegiate institute, a high school in Wilson. When about eighteen years of age he quit school to engage as local editor of the *Wilson Advance*. The year after he became editor-in-chief of the same paper, and continued in the capacity of editor and proprietor until 1885. During that year he read law at the University of North Carolina, and in October, 1885, was licensed by the supreme court of the state to practice. Mr. Daniels never practiced, however, but in the same month purchased a controlling interest in the *Raleigh State Chronicle*, succeeding the late Capt. Randolph A. Shotwell. Under his superior management and control, the paper has prospered and has now the largest daily and weekly circulation of any paper at the capital. In January, 1887, Mr. Daniels was elected state printer; was re-elected in January, 1889, and in January, 1890, he was re-elected unanimously by acclamation. May 2, 1888, he was united in marriage with Miss Addie Worth Bagley, daughter of Maj. William H. Bagley, clerk of the supreme court of North Carolina.

CAPT. RANDALL A. SHOTWELL

was born in West Liberty, Va., December 13, 1844. He was the eldest of three brothers, sons of Nathan Shotwell, of Virginia. His mother's maiden name was Martha Abbott, a native of Massachusetts. At an early age Capt. Shotwell entered Media college, Pennsylvania, where he pursued a three years' course of study, his father's intention being to prepare him for the senior class at Princeton. About the time he was ready to enter Princeton, his father's *alma mater*, the Civil war came on, and he immediately left his studies to join in the defense of his southern home. On his way to Virginia he encountered numerous adventures. He met the Virginia volunteers just in time to participate in the battle of Leesburg. Though a mere boy he joined the Confederate volunteers and followed the flag through seventeen hard-fought battles. He led the sharpshooters of a brigade—Pickett's division—in the fatal charge at Gettysburg, and, for his valor and excellent tactics, was tendered a special commission from Secretary Seddon, by order of President Davis. Toward the last of the war he was captured as a spy. He escaped from his captors, but was taken by another party of Federals to Fort Delaware, and there confined as a prisoner of war until three months after the southern flag had been furled at Appomatox. He came to North Carolina in 1866, his father's family having preceded him. They had removed to Rutherfordton in 1858. Capt. Shotwell then discarded the military habiliments he had worn with so much honor and bravery, exchanging the sword for the pen, the mightier weapon of the two. With the latter he has not ceased to defend the principles he deemed sound and right. He went to Newbern, N. C., and with Con. Stephen D. Pool established the Newbern *Journal of Commerce.* After two years here he removed to Rutherfordton and started the *Vindicator,* through which he denounced in scathing terms the Red Strings and Renegades of that region, and thence began the political warfare that ended only after he had suffered all the persecution that could be heaped upon him by his political enemies. Before his arrest, his friends advised him to follow the example of others, but he said: "No, I have done or said nothing but what I believed to be for the best interest of my people, and I shall stay and defend my course and maintain my honor with my life, if need be."

Without capias or warrant Capt. Shotwell was arrested, in July, 1870, and was subjected to rough and inhuman treatment. He was tried at Raleigh and convicted by a partisan judge. Before the assemblage in the senate chamber, where he was tried, his arms were pinioned with ropes and he was remanded to jail. October 5th he was again handcuffed and taken to Albany, N. Y., to serve in the penitentiary a term of six years' imprisonment and to pay a fine of $15,000. He quietly outlived the severe treatment to which he was subjected. He was repeatedly offered his freedom if he would implicate other prominent North Carolinians, which he as often refused to do. Finally, in obedience to an almost unanimous appeal from North Carolina, President Grant accorded him an unconditional pardon. Returning to North Carolina he went to Charlotte and engaged with Col. Hill in the editorial management of *The Southern Home*. A few years later the people of Mecklenburg county nominated and elected him a member of the legislature. He took his seat in the session of 1876 and boldly struck out for the people's rights. In 1878 Capt. Shotwell went to Raleigh, and associating himself with Mr. John W. Dowd, bought out *The Farmer and Mechanic*, a paper up to that time published in the interest of the North Carolina Patrons of Husbandry. The paper at once began to exhibit the evidences of his individuality and independence as an editor. A few months later he became sole proprietor of the concern. Six weeks before his death *The State Chronicle* and *Farmer and Mechanic* were merged under the name of the *State Chronicle*, retained as the title of the consolidated paper. Capt. Shotwell assumed the editorship in chief. Having been appointed by Gov. Scales as state librarian, after long years of struggle, Mr. Shotwell began to enjoy the dawn of an era of success. At length few men in North Carolina had before them so promising a future as Capt. Shotwell and it is well understood that he would have been the next governor of the state had his eventful life been spared, a fit vindication from the aspersions which had been cast upon him in the earlier part of his career.

THOMAS POLLOCK.

The first mention made in the colonial records of Thomas Pollock who took such a high position in the colony of North Carolina is that at the assembly of November 12, 1701, he was appointed on the vestry of Chowan precinct, his name being next to that of President Walker. From that time onward he resided on the Chowan near where Edenton was subsequently built, and at his house, for many years, the council was regularly held, he representing, as deputy, Lord Carteret. He was among the wealthiest men in the province, and, besides cultivating his plantation, doubtless was engaged in traffic with the Indians — which was very lucrative. When the troubles that had their origin in the enforcement of the British act of parliament in reference to oaths of office disturbed the quiet of the colony, Col. Pollock sided with the government and was a supporter of the faction that insisted upon obeying the act. He therefore sustained Glover, and when the assembly of 1708 decided adversely to that side, Col. Pollock fled with Glover to Virginia, where he remained until 1710, being unwilling as he expressed, to live under an illegal government. He was a strong churchman, a man of strong characteristics, educated and self-respecting. He would not give countenance to Carey's government by residing in the colony under his administration. For the want of decision and because of the vacillating course of the lords proprietors, he expressed a low opinion; and when on Hyde's acces-

sion to the administration, he, himself, became the power behind the
throne, he pressed his views to their logical conclusion.   He caused all
the acts of the government for the two years of Carey's administration to be annulled as illegal, and pushed measures against Carey
and Porter and Moseley to such an extremity that in the ensuing
hostile demonstration Carey's force made a descent on his premises,
which were the seat of the new government.

Soon after Hyde's administration began, the Indian massacre occurred, and the governor dying of fever, September 12, 1712, Pollock
as president of the council, succeeded to the administration.   He took
the most active measures that he could to bring the war to an early
close, and although Moseley again controlled the assembly, and the
feeling between them was still bitter, the danger compelled co-operation among all.   He, however, charged Moseley with the purpose of
having him displaced and securing the administration either for Col.
Barnwell or himself.   On the other hand, Moseley obtained from the
assembly resolutions remonstrating against Pollock's acts in the conduct of the war.   On the 28th of May, 1714, Gov. Eden, having
arrived, took the oaths of office, and during his administration Col.
Pollock continued to be the chief adviser of the governor in public
matters.   And notably he had the satisfaction of seeing Moseley punished for "seditious conduct," relative to the Teach affair, and declared incapable of holding office for three years.   In March, 1722,
Gov. Eden dying, Col. Pollock was again elected president of the
council, but his own life was now drawing to a close, and after a second
administration of five months he died, August 30, 1722.   Col. Pollock
kept, during his residence in the colony, a letter-book, which has fortunately been preserved, and which throws much light upon that
early period of colonial history.   He was a man whose excellence of
character and integrity are acknowledged by all, even though his an-
tagonisms may have led him to express at times too harsh an opinion of those who differed with him.   The descendants of Col. Pollock
have been among the most cultured, refined and wealthiest of the
citizens of North Carolina.

ALEXANDER BOYD ANDREWS.

North Carolina has no son who has attained greater prominence
in the important field of transportation and railway management
than the subject of this sketch, nor any, the story of whose life so
forcibly illustrates the truth of the homely maxim that "blood will
tell."   His paternal grandfather was an English gentleman who
made his home in Edgecombe county where, after a life of useful energy, he died in 1810.   He married a daughter of Col. Jonas Johnston, a Revolutionary hero, who was wounded at the battle of Moore's
Creek, and finally sealed his devotion to the cause of his country,
dying from wounds received at the battle of Stono, in June, 1779.
William J. Andrews, a son of the marriage, was born in Edgecombe
county in 1802, and was a leading merchant at Sparta and at Hender-

son. In 1833 he was united in marriage to Miss Virginia Hawkins, a daughter of Col. John D. Hawkins, of Franklin county, and his wife, Jane, who was a daughter of Alexander Boyd, a gentleman of Scotch descent, then residing in Mecklenburg county, Va. They had ten children, of whom, however, but eight reached maturity: Bettie A., the wife of Col. John W. Atkinson, of Wilmington; Alexander Boyd; Ann S., the wife of William J. Robards, of Henderson; Lucy D., the wife of Dr. J. B. Clifton, of Louisburg; Ella H., the wife of Thomas H. Haughton, of Charlotte, and Phil H. Andrews, Esq., of Raleigh. In 1852 these young children were called on to mourn the loss of their mother, and within a year were bereft of their father. The orphaned household thus became the object of the tender care of their grandparents, Col. and Mrs. Hawkins, and never were orphans more fortunate in their lot.

The eldest boy, Alexander Boyd, was born July 23, 1841, and was but eleven years old when he was committed to Col. Hawkins' parental direction and guidance, and in his after career one discerns how much he was benefited by the admirable training then received. For five years he attended school, exhibiting unusual aptitude for his studies, particularly that of mathematics. When he had finished his course, he was already trained in self-command, and to habits of diligence and promptness, and in the spirit of obedience, industry and application. With these qualifications early discovered, his uncle, Gen. Phil. B. Hawkins, who had a large railroad contract in South Carolina, employed him, when less than eighteen years of age, as general superintendent, purchasing agent, and paymaster. The young man soon proved himself equal to the many intricate duties of his responsible position, and here took his first lessons in the work of railway construction, which in after years was to engage his mature powers and make him an instrument in upbuilding the prosperity and material interests of his native state. While thus employed, the alarm was sounded that called the sons of North Carolina to her defense, and young Andrews, not yet of age, enlisted as a private in the First North Carolina regiment of cavalry, commanded by Col. Robert Ransom, who subsequently became, by merited promotion, major-general in the army of Virginia. Soon appointed a lieutenant, the young soldier, during the first year of his service, attained, step by step, to the post of captain of Company B, of his regiment. It was his fortune to participate in all the memorable campaigns of that dashing leader, J. E. B. Stuart, and when Stuart fell, Wade Hampton became his commander. As gallant as were the spirits of that fine command, there were none who displayed more devotion, a more unflinching courage, than Capt. A. B. Andrews. On September 22, 1863, at Jack's shop, near Gordonsville, there was a bloody fight between 2,000 Confederate cavalry and Kilpatrick's corps, 6,000 strong. The Confederate regiments had been greatly depleted by their recent engagments and heavy marching. That to which Capt. Andrews belonged carried into the battle but 130 men, but every man was a veteran. It was a hard-fought field. The adjutant of the reg-

B—30

iment, wrote to the Fayetteville *Observer* a short while after the battle, as follows: "While cheering on his men, the gallant captain Andrews fell, shot through the lungs. No braver or better man has fallen during the war. He was universally beloved."

And such indeed would have been a fitting epitaph, penned by the adjutant of the command, had the colonel then expired. But though Capt. Andrews was mourned as dead, his life was spared for works of greater usefulness in other fields. The wound was truly a desperate one, the ball having passed directly through the left lung and in its exit having injured the spine. Others despaired of his life, but by the exercise of indomitable pluck and will, he maintained his own hope and eventually rallied from the shock. Then followed weary months of suffering and convalesence. Twice in the following year he essayed to return to duty, but his strength proved unequal to the exertion. At last, when Lee surrendered, he hastened to join Gen. Johnston's army, and shared its fortunes in the last days of the war, and was paroled along with the veterans of that army.

The first work that engaged his attention was in the line of his former business. The bridge at Gaston had been destroyed, and in connection with the railway companies where communication had been thus interrupted he established a ferry across the Roanoke at that point, which proved a profitable venture. In July, 1867, Dr. William J. Hawkins, then the president of the Raleigh & Gaston railroad, appreciating the fine capacity of his young kinsman, secured his appointment as superintendent of that line. The duties were comprehensive and embraced not only the department of transportation but also that of construction; but with ease Capt. Andrews fitted himself to the work, and during his eight years of service, not only was that road greatly improved, but many miles of the Raleigh & Augusta Air Line were built.

The Richmond & Danville R. R. Co. had, in 1871, leased the North Carolina road, and thus became a competitor with the Seaboard line. Recognizing the ability of Capt. Andrews, in 1875, that road obtained him as superintendent of its North Carolina division. In this position he exhibited still greater capacity, and with a broader field and enlarged duties won still higher reputation. Particularly did he address himself to identifying the interests of the company with the growth and development of the towns and industries along the lines controlled by his system. His administration was wise and efficient. The lease of the North Carolina Central road to a foreign corporation had been a source of much irritation among the people of the state, and no one could have succeeded better than Capt. Andrews in allaying this feeling and establishing pleasant relations between the people and his company. Of his loyalty to his state he had given indisputable proof, and by his wise management he largely reconciled the people to the existence of the lease, and even those who remained hostile never questioned that the officer, while true to the company, remained true to the interests of his state.

When Z. B. Vance was elected governor, in 1876, he asked Capt

Andrews to become a member of his staff with the rank of colonel, and this position he continued to hold under Gov. Jarvis' administration. Thus he was thrown in close relations with the governors of the state, and he has exerted a quiet but effective influence on public matters that has redounded to the advantage of the democratic party and to the benefit of the public. In recognition of the ability and services of Col. Andrews, in addition to his duties as superintendent of the North Carolina division, he was appointed assistant to the president of the Richmond & Danville system; and he sat at the council board of the Richmond & Danville by successive steps; through the acquirement of other properties, the road reached from Charlotte to Atlanta, to Augusta, Birmingham and remote points at the south, and from Richmond to West Point; from Danville to Washington and other points at the north, until it has become among the greatest systems of the world, controlling about 6,000 miles of road. Of this great system he became third vice-president in 1886, and second vice-president in January, 1890. He is also president of several of the Richmond & Danville roads, Piedmont railroad, the Charlotte, Columbia & Augusta railroad, the Columbia, Greenville, Danville & Western, with the Winston, N. C., railroad, now extended to Wilkesboro; the Oxford & Henderson, the Oxford & Clarkesville, and the Western North Carolina railroad. This latter road, begun by the state before the war, had come to such a pass that in 1880 the legislature sold it to the Best syndicate. Mr. Best's associates, when they came to examine the property, flew the bargain and the contract was about to be forfeited. To prevent a failure of the work, Col. Andrews, associating with himself Col. Buford, Gen. Logan and Mr. Clyde, of the Danville system, advanced $50,000 in cash, and began the construction of the road westward. Shortly afterward he induced the Richmond & Danville syndicate to purchase the contract. This was done and the company was re-organized. Col. Andrews became its president, and at the cost of more than $3,000,000 completed the branch to Paint Rock, and then over the Balsam to Murphy, its extreme western terminus. Thus has been realized the dream of our statesmen, and the people of the western counties have enjoyed the fruition of their hopes.

At one time Col. Andrews was also superintendent of the A. & N. C. R. R., which he ran in connection with the interior lines, thus making a continuous line, operated practically as one road, from the mountains to the sea. As busy as Col. Andrews has been all through life, he has not been devoted exclusively to railroad work. For a number of years the city of Raleigh had his services as alderman, and he has been an active promoter of industrial enterprises, and is a director in various insurance and manufacturing companies, and is also vice-president of the Citizens' national bank, at Raleigh; he is one of the vice-presidents of the World's Columbian Exposition, and is on several important committees. In September, 1869, he was happily married to Julia, a daughter of Col. William Johnston, of Charlotte, by whom he has five children. In 1874 he moved to Raleigh, where he has since resided, bringing with him the aged grandmother, who had so lovingly replaced his sainted mother in the years of his youth. Col. Andrews has never sought political preferment. He has found congenial occupation in his work as a railroad manager, and indeed by his railway construction, he has conferred more benefit on the people of his native state than he could possibly have done as a politician.

WILLIAM SMITH,

general superintendent of the Raleigh & Gaston and Raleigh & Augusta Air Line railroads, with their branches, is one of the most successful railroad men in North Carolina. He was born at Smithville, now Southport, Brunswick county, August 1, 1834, and after receiving his education at the Odd Fellows' academy in Wilmington, N. C., at the age of nineteen entered life as a civil engineer. He found employment on the line of the road now known as the Cape Fear & Yadkin Valley, and was engaged there until, at the age of about twenty-one, he was appointed clerk of the superior court of Brunswick, which office he held for two years. He then purchased a coasting vessel and traded along the coast, but finally, about 1857, he entered the transportation department of the Wilmington & Weldon Railroad company at Wilmington, serving as ticket agent and yard master until April, 1861. When hostilities broke out, Capt. Smith joined the Wilmington light infantry, of which John L. Cantwell was then captain, and was soon elected a lieutenant and was put on duty as acting commissary. At the same time he had displayed such capacity as a railroad man, that the president of the road, Mr. William S. Ashe, promoted him to be master of transportation of the entire line, and for the entire period of the war he discharged with acceptability the onerous and exacting duties of that post, dispatching troops and provisions over the line, when all the material and equipment of the road were exhausted in the heavy and long continued service. Just before the evacuation of Wilmington, he was again promoted to be assistant general superintendent of the road, and he established the shops of the company at Magnolia and Enfield, and had charge of them, and virtually he had charge of the road during the period of 1864-65.

On the return of peace, and when the company's affairs were reorganized, he was again elected master of transportation, and served as such for five years, when he was employed to build a part of the road from Columbia to Sumter, and on the completion of that line, he was employed on the Carolina Central road between the Pee Dee river and Monroe, and he remained with that company until 1882, when he was appointed superintendent of the Raleigh & Gaston R. R., and of the Raleigh & Augusta Air Line R. R. and its branches, which position he has filled to the eminent satisfaction of the railroad authorities. By his energy, sagacity and watchfulness, he has steadily risen as a railroad man to the high position he occupies in the confidence

of his company. Capt. Smith was married in 1857 to Miss Abbe C·
Smith, daughter of John Smith, of Middletown, Conn., and to them
were born four children, of whom there now survives but one, Abbe,
wife of Mr. Cam. Gales. Mrs. Abbe Smith dying in 1867, Capt.
Smith, in 1870, was united in marriage to Miss Josephine Macon, of
Richmond, Va., by whom he has had five children, three of whom are
yet living: Josephine, Roberta and William M. C. Smith. Capt.
Smith's father, Isaac Baker Smith, was a native of Brunswick county,
N. C where he was born in 1806. In early life he was a farmer; then
he went into merchandise, but in after life he was commodore of the
steamship "Gladiator," which plied between Wilmington and Charleston, S. C., and he was so engaged at the time of his death in 1852.
His grandfather, Elias Smith, came to North Carolina from New
York, where he was born, and in early manhood settled in Brunswick
county, where the family have long resided, being ever held in high
esteem by the people of that county.

EDWARD MOSELEY.

But few men have left a deeper impress upon a state when its
institutions were in a formative period than Edward Moseley made
on the colony of North Carolina. Of his history prior to 1705 we
know nothing. In that year he was a householder in Albemarle and
living in Chowan precinct. The council of which he was a member
then met at his house. The next year, 1706, the boundary line between the colony and Virginia came into dispute and Moseley was
designated, together with John Lawson, to run the line on the part
of the lords proprietors. In 1707 he was appointed chief-justice of
the colony. About that time the troubles between the church of
England adherents and the Dissenters began, and Moseley, although
a strong churchman, threw himself on the side of the latter, who
sought to maintain their old privileges under the charter and constitution of the colony. He was elected to the assembly from Chowan
in 1708, but his election was disputed. The assembly, however, admitted him and chose him speaker. He and the body decided in
favor of Carey and after that the Glover and Pollock party fiercely
denounced him. He was a member of the succeeding assemblies
and opposed Col. Pollock's administration in some of his measures
taken during the Indian war. Indeed it was alleged that he was arranging with Col. Moore to have a new administration — perhaps
with Moore for governor. Notwithstanding the failure of the Carey
movement, which involved Moseley so deeply, he maintained a strong
hold upon the people, and was made treasurer by the assembly and
entrusted with the issuing of the government notes for the expenses
of the war. This office of treasurer he continued to hold until the
close of his life. Having married the widow of Gov. Henderson
Walker, a daughter of Gov. Lillington, he became closely connected
with the Porters, Maurice Moore, the Swanns, John Baptista Ashe,

and the Lillingtons; and he sought to preserve the fame of the colony untarnished.

In Gov. Eden's time, he believed that the administration was conniving with the pirate, Teach, and to obtain evidence of it, he held forcible possession of the secretary's room and examined the papers; this led to a conflict between him and Gov. Eden. He was found guilty of seditious conduct and debarred from holding office for three years. As soon as the disability ceased, he was again elected to the assembly and chosen speaker. He was surveyor-general of the colony, and was one of the commissioners who in 1728 ran the Virginia line. He was always employed in such matters. Circumstances show him to have been a very accomplished surveyor, and his familiarity with instruments, together with his scholarly attainments, indicate that he had been trained in the best schools in England. During Burrington's second administration he was speaker of the house, and strongly opposed Burrington's measures. Indeed he was then as before at the head of the people's party. When Gov. Johnston came, in 1734, he brought a commission transferring Moseley to the upper house, and he remained in that body until his death, in 1749. But this did not change his principles. He still co-operated with Swann and the other popular leaders. The assembly continued him in the position of general treasurer of the province, which he held to his death. Toward the close of his life he was also the agent of Lord Granville, and chief-justice of the province. The laws of the state had never been printed, and the few manuscript copies were very imperfect. In 1746 he and Swann were appointed to revise and print them; he reported to the assembly, 1749, that the revisal was completed, but he died before they were printed. About 1735 he removed from Chowan to Rocky Point, where many of his friends had preceded him.

By his first wife Mr. Moseley had two sons, Col. Sampson Moseley of the Revolution and Edward; and by a second wife, Ann Hazell, sister of James Hazell, acting governor in 1771, he had a large family of sons and daughters. Of this distinguished patriot, to whom North Carolina is so much indebted, Dr. Hawks says: "Gale, Little, Moseley and Swann were all men who would have been deemed fit associates for the most intelligent men to be found in any of the English colonies of their day." "Among our old ecclesiastical documents we find Mr. Moseley in another aspect than that of lawyer and politician. We find him in communication with the Missionary society, informing them of the true state of religion among the people and begging them to send missionaries of the proper kind. He sent to England and purchased prayer books as well as works of practical religion for gratuitous distribution in Carolina. He bought also quite a library and presented it to the society for propagating the gospel, as a foundation of a provincial library to be deposited in Edenton for general use. Most of these books were well selected and costly."

And of him, Mr. Geo. Davis has written: "Of all the men who watched and guided the tottering footsteps of our infant state, there

was not one who, in intellectual ability, in scholarly cultivation and refinement, in solid and polite learning, in courage and endurance, in high Christian morality, in generous consideration for the welfare of others, in all the true merit, in fine, which makes a man among men, could equal Edward Moseley."

MAJ. W. W. VASS.

North Carolina has produced few greater railroad men than Maj. W. W. Vass. For nearly half a century he has held the highest positions in the management of railroads, and is to-day one of the best known railroad financiers and managers in the south. Maj. Vass was born in Granville county, N. C., February 19, 1821. He was given a good preliminary schooling in the common schools of his native county. He began active business life as a clerk in the store of Maj. John S. Eaton, with whom he remained for about eight years, the last two years of which time he was a partner in the concern. January 1, 1845, he was elected treasurer of the original Raleigh & Gaston railroad, and held that office until 1848. In the latter year the state of North Carolina became the owner of the road, and it was managed by the governor and a board of commissioners. They elected Maj. Vass president of the corporation, and he continued to discharge the duties of that responsible office until the state disposed of the road to a new company under a new organization. This was consummated September 18, 1851, and the company retained the same name. At the first meeting of the directors Mr. Vass was elected treasurer, and he has since continuously held that office. In October, 1862, he was made treasurer of the Chatham railroad company, known since 1872 as the Raleigh & Augusta Air Line railroad company. and still holds that position. For over fifty years Maj. Vass has been an earnest and consistent communicant of the Baptist church, and has ever carried his religion into his every-day business life. His name is held in the warmest esteem and confidence wherever known. His ability is great, his honesty crystal. He has been twice married, his first marriage having been to Miss Freeman, of Granville county, N. C., who died about a year afterward without issue, and in 1866 he was married to his present wife, Miss Lillie, daughter of Rev. James McDaniel, D. D., of Fayettville, N. C. Three children survive to bless their union: William W., Jr., Eleanor and Lilla May. It will be of interest to insert here the following extracts from the *State Chronicle*, in regard to the fortieth anniversary of Maj. Vass as treasurer of the Raleigh & Gaston railroad company. The following letter explains itself:

President's Office, Seaboard Line, Baltimore, January 16, 1886.

MAJ. W. W. VASS: *My Dear Sir*—The board of directors of the Raleigh & Gaston railroad company have commissioned Mr. Hoffman and myself to select a piece of silverware to be presented to you on the part of the company as evidence of the esteem which they believe is entertained for you by every stockholder. It seems fitting that the opportunity of acknowledging in some way your long period of service should not be lost on the ending of its fortieth anniversary. In sending you a silver pitcher and stand, I beg to express to you, on the part of the board, their sincere and affectionate regard.

I am, yours very respectfully,

JOHN M. ROBINSON, *President.*

The reply reads as follows:

RALEIGH, N. C., January 19.

JOHN M. ROBINSON: *Dear Sir*—You may imagine my surprise, but not my gratification, on receiving this morning by express a box containing the superb silver pitcher and stand, selected with such elegant taste by yourself and Mr. Hoffman, and presented on behalf of the board of directors and stockholders of the Raleigh & Gaston railroad company as a testimonial of personal regard and recognition of official duty for an uninterrupted term of forty years. The gift, costly and beautiful in itself, and bearing as it does a suggestive inscription, is greatly enhanced in value to me by the kind and generous tone of your letter of presentation accompanying the same. I beg to return to you and Mr. Hoffman, and to each member in particular of the board of directors, my warmest thanks and acknowledgment for the honor done me, and to signify my entire willingness to serve the company in the same capacity for the next forty years, if you will be pleased to pardon the very modest intimation of my growing appetite for even greater official longevity. Again thanking you, Mr. President, permit me to express the wish that your beautiful gift in its solid, sterling purity may ever fitly represent the company's financial condition, as it does to-day under your able and wise administration, as evidenced by my official balance-sheet, showing no bills payable outstanding, while its bonds command in the public market twenty-five per cent. above par.

I am, gratefully and sincerely,

W. W. VASS, *Treasurer.*

Thomas Vass, the father of the distinguished subject, was born in King and Queen county, Va., and was a descendant of the Huguenots who fled from France after the revocation of the edict of Nantes. Thomas was born in 1776, and came with his father to North Carolina when a boy. They settled in Granville county, and there Thomas followed farming all his life. He died in 1849, and his wife in 1856. He was the son of Thomas, also a Virginian. He was a pioneer Baptist preacher, and settled in North Carolina in 1790, where he died.

J. R. KENLY,

the general manager of the Atlantic Coast line, was born in Baltimore, January 21, 1847. He spent his early life in that city, and when but sixteen years of age he enlisted, in 1863, in Company A, First Maryland cavalry, Confederate States army, as a private and remained with that regiment until the surrender of Gen. Lee's army at Appomatox Court House in 1865. He participated in the battle of Gettysburg and the battles around Richmond. At the close of the war he entered railroad service, in West Virginia, as rodman in an engineering corps and continued in this position and as assistant engineer until the summer of 1868. He then entered the service of the Baltimore & Ohio railroad, at Pittsburg, Penn., as resident engineer on construction of the Pittsburg & Connellsville railroad. On January 1, 1871, he entered the service of the Union railroad of Baltimore, as resident engineer on construction of the Union railroad tunnel, From November 25, 1871, until April 5, 1872, he was engineer and superintendent in the employ of that road. On April 5, 1872, he entered the service of the Richmond & Petersburg railroad as superintendent with headquarters at Richmond, Va. On January 1, 1875, he was made superintendent of transportation of the Atlantic Coast line, with headquarters at Wilmington, N. C. On January 1, 1889, he was promoted to the position of assistant general manager, and on July 1, 1891, he was promoted to the position of general manager of the Atlantic Coast line, with headquarters at Wilmington, N. C.

J. R. NOLAN,

general manager of the Western South Carolina line, was born in Baltimore, Md., July 19, 1851, and was educated in the schools of that city. When quite a boy he learned telegraphy, and when but seventeen years of age he was given an office on the Pennsylvania railroad. From 1870 to 1872 he was in the employ of the Western Union company, and during these years was stationed at Chicago. From that time until 1881 or 1882 he filled the position of chief dispatcher of the Union Station at Baltimore on the P. R. R. R. R. In that year he accepted a position as train dispatcher and depot master at Roanoke, Va., for the Shenandoah Valley railroad, and remained there for three years. In 1883 Mr. Nolan acted as chief dispatcher with the Atlantic Coast line on the Charleston & Columbia division. This position he held about three years, when he was promoted to the position of assistant superintendent of transportation on the line south of Weldon, where he stayed until April, 1889. At this time he was appointed to the position he now holds, and is acceptably filling the same. Mr. Nolan was married in 1875, and is the father of one son and two daughters. He has never taken any active interest in the political affairs of his county and state, preferring to devote his attention to the railroad business, and it is owing to this fact that he now occupies the prominent position held by him.

THOMAS W. WHISNANT,

the subject of this notice, was born at Shelby, in the county of Cleveland, N. C., July 3, 1847. His parents were natives of that section of the state and were among its most highly respected citizens. His father was a merchant and mill owner who was possessed of indomitable energy and one of character. His father, P. S. Whisnant, was at the time of his death, on his way to his mill on the Atlanta railroad when by a collision of trains, he lost his life. Thomas W. Whisnant first came into notice in the C. C. railroad, as foreman of its night force, on the 11th of April, 1878. In 1880 he was promoted to the position of roadmaster of the second or western division, where he showed great aptness and developed a general knowledge of his business, which made him the rising man of the system. When the lamented L. C. Jones died, July 12, 1889, Capt. T. W. Whisnant was designated by the officers of the road, by the employers, and the public and patrons of the road as the man to succeed to the superintending of the C. C. railroad. Before the close of that month he was tendered the position and he immediately entered upon its duties. Since his induction into this office he has fulfilled every expectation of his most ardent admirers and is recognized among railroad men as a very superior and efficient officer, while his popularity with the public has suffered no diminution. He is a practical and superior business man and with such a history, at his time of life, it is reasonable to expect that the future has much in store for him in the line of the profession he has chosen.

JAMES FRANCIS POST, JR.,

secretary and treasurer of the Atlantic Coast line, was born in Wilmington, N. C., February 24, 1850. His father, James F. Post, a descendant of the old Dutch settlers, was born in New Jersey in 1818, studied architecture in New York city, removed to Petersburg, Va., about 1843, where he married Mary A. Russell, and finally settled in Wilmington, N. C., in 1849, of which city he has been a resident for the last forty-two years. He is skilled in his profession, and has planned and executed many of the finest buildings in this and neighboring cities. The subject of this notice was the third son, and received his education in the grammar schools of Wilmington. When but a mere boy he entered the service of the Wilmington & Weldon railroad company, as freight clerk. In 1873 he was made cashier of that road and of the Wilmington, Columbia & Augusta railroad, which position he held for four years. In 1877 he was appointed through freight agent of those two roads, which position he held for nine years, and the duties of which he discharged to the entire satisfaction of his employers and the general public. In 1886 he was promoted to the position of assistant treasurer of the W. & W., W. C. & A., the Central and A. & R. railroad Co.'s, and served as such until July 1, 1887, when he was elected treasurer of the Atlantic Coast line, composed of the following roads: Wilmington & Weldon, Wilmington, Columbia & Augusta, A. & R., M. & A., Florence, Central of S. C., Wilson & Summerton, and Hartsville railroads. He has been re-elected at every annual meeting of the directors since 1887, and that fact alone is sufficient evidence of his trustfulness and capacity. Beside attending to the arduous duties of his responsible office, he has also been interested in various institutions as president, stockholder and director, serving for a number of years as secretary of a life insurance company.

Mr. Post is a member of the Knights of Pythias, Knights of Honor, and the Masonic fraternity. In 1889 he was elected a member of the board of aldermen of the city of Wilmington, and was re-elected in 1891, and is now serving as such, and has served repeatedly as acting mayor, and justice of the police court, chairman of the sanitary and fire committees, and has done much to improve the condition of the city in these departments. He is an official member of Grace Methodist Episcopal church, and takes great interest in the Sunday-school work of that denomination, and of which he is at present the active and energetic superintendent. He is also president of the Sunday-school union society of his city and county. He was married, in 1876, to Miss Sarah V. Jacobs, of this city, and has been blessed with five children, two sons and three daughters, all of whom are living. Mr. Post entered upon the active duties of life a poor boy, but by his energy, his industry and strict integrity, has won positions of trust and of honor, and has been equal to the requirements of every situation which he has been called upon to fill.

JESSE FRANKLIN

was born in Orange county, Va., March 24, 1760. This was a time, just on the eve of the beginning of the Revolution, when the opportunities for acquiring an education at home were meager, and young Franklin's education was therefore limited. While he was young, his father removed to Surry county, N. C., just before hostilities were opened against the mother country. There was a large element in the state hostile to the war — men who anxiously desired to maintain their loyalty to the British crown. These were the tories of the Revolution and they became so intolerant and hostile to the Revolutionary party as to seriously endanger their lives and property. This party spirit ran so high that the whigs were compelled to erect forts and raise forces to defend themselves and families and preserve their property from spoliation. It also became necessary to raise troops, and young Franklin was among the number to volunteer, under Col. Cleveland, his maternal uncle, for protection against the tories, and, if need be, to take up the offensive against them. Col. Cleveland entered upon his duties with great zeal and with not a little rashness and severity. At the memorable battle of Kings Mountain, in which Col. Cleveland played so conspicuous a part, Franklin was his adjutant and bore himself with such gallantry that he won high praise from his commander. At the battle of Guilford Court House he took an equally courageous part, and was particularly serviceable in the bitter warfare which was kept up by the tories, until those troublesome persons were driven from this part of the state.

After the war was over the country had need of statesmen, not only to inaugurate, but year by year to strengthen, the new government, and in 1792 Mr. Franklin was elected to the house of commons, to take part in the legislation of the state. He was the next year re-elected, and on the completion of this legislative term he was sent to congress to represent the Surry district in that body. At the close of his congressional term, he returned home and was again elected to the state legislature. In 1799 he was elected to the United States senate, and served the full term of six years. During his last year in the senate, he was chosen its president. While he was thus presiding in the senate, Hon. Nathaniel Macon, another distinguished North Carolinian, was speaker of the house of representatives. No sooner was Mr. Franklin's senatorial term finished than he was elected to his own state senate for a term of two years. He was then, in 1807, sent back to the United States senate, where he remained until March 3, 1813. His frequent elections and re-elections were some indication of the esteem in which he was held by his fellow-citizens, and his occupancy of the presidential chair and of high places in the most important committees of the United States senate, demonstrated that he was equally appreciated in that illustrious body. When his term closed in the senate, he was offered a re-election, but he declined and retired to the more restful scenes of private life. But his state had not yet paid him its highest honor, and in 1820, he was elected its chief magistrate, by the legislature, as the successor of Gov. John Branch. The completion of his gubernatorial term was the close of one of the most brilliant and honorable official careers of which the history of North Carolina contains any record. The final end came in 1824, when he had reached the sixty-fifth year of his eventful life.

HON. PHILEMON BENJAMIN HAWKINS.

Among North Carolina's most enterprising and patriotic sons may be found the name of the Hon. Philemon Benjamin Hawkins, who, for many years, was as actively identified with the growth and advancement of the state as any other one man. Born in Franklin county on the 23rd of May, 1823, from that time until his death on the 2nd of January, 1891, his life was spent in his native state. Mr. Hawkins was given a liberal education, having been graduated from the University of North Carolina. After the completion of his collegiate course he turned his attention to railroad building, his first contract having been in South Carolina. Some time later he held the contract for extensive work around Old Point, Va., and during the Civil war had large contracts from the Confederate government for salt. After the close of hostilities between the north and south, Mr. Hawkins resumed railroad contracting, and remained in that business until about the year 1875, when he retired from active life to his plantation in Franklin county, N. C., where he lived at the time of his death. He was a member of the upper house of the state legislature for several terms, both before and after the war, and for a number of years was a county commissioner of Franklin county. A director in the North Carolina railroad for an extended period, he ever evinced the greatest interest in every movement looking toward the development of his native state. President Harrison made him a deputy collector of internal revenue at the beginning of his term, and on Mr. Hawkins' death, which occurred January 2, 1891, William J. Hawkins, his son, was appointed to fill the vacancy in the fourth district. A prominent Mason for a number of years, he was also a member of the Episcopal church. Mr. Hawkins' marriage to Miss Fannie M. Hawkins, daughter of Philemon Hawkins, of Louisburg, N. C., was solemnized in May, 1863, and resulted in the birth of two children, named: Bettie, wife of Walter B. Boyd, of Warrenton, N. C., and William J. Hawkins, who survived his father only a few months, having been taken with a congestive chill, and died after a few days' illness the 21st of April, 1891. The death of this young man was peculiarly sad and greatly lamented by his many close friends and his grief-stricken mother and sister, who almost idolized him.

ROBERT R. BRIDGERS,

one of the prominent railroad men of North Carolina, was born in Tarboro, N. C., December 1, 1854. He received his education at Troy institute, Troy, N. Y., at the Polytecnic institute, and at Princeton, Mass. His course of instruction was thorough and he was twenty-five years of age before he finished his education. Leaving college, he went into the service of the Western Atlantic railroad, with headquarters at Atlanta, in the capacity of assistant engineer, and he remained in that position two years. His next employment was as surveyor on the extension of the Richmond & Alleghany railroad. For one year he was in charge of the Roanoke machine shops, at Roanoke, Va., and then he was employed on the East Tennessee, Virginia & Georgia R. R., in building the railroad shops and terminal facilities of that line, at Atlanta. This important work was completed in nine months, when Mr. Bridgers accepted a position in the office of engineer of maintenance of way of the Pennsylvania railroad, at Altoona, Penn. Here he remained six months, and then was appointed assistant superintendent of the Pennsylvania railroad, with headquarters at Wall, Penn. Later, he was employed as supervisor of the same road, with headquarters at Trenton, N. J. In these two positions he spent two years and a half, and gained most valuable experience, and exhibited a high capacity for the exacting duties of railroad supervision. He was then tendered the position of engineer of maintenance of way of the Western North Carolina railroad, with headquarters at Asheville, N. C., and was so employed for eighteen months, at the end of which time, August, 1888, he was transferred in the same capacity to the Virginia Midland railroad, where he remained until March, 1889.

Thus far Mr. Bridgers had exhibited all the elements of a successful railroad man; cautious, painstaking and energetic, while his judgment had ripened with maturing years, and his scholastic acquirements and training at the institutions of learning had found ready application in the school of experience. He had been practiced in every department, and railroad work of all kinds was practically familiar to him, and he made himself master of every detail of the business. When he had performed the work desired on the Virginia Midland, the management asked his services as superintendent of the North Carolina division of the Richmond & Danville R. R., with headquarters at Durham, and he was engaged in the construction of the new lines then building. On June 1, 1890, his headquarters were transferred to Raleigh, and after a year's service there he was again transferred to the Western North Carolina R. R., with headquarters at Asheville, in the capacity of general manager. Thus, step by step, each year making an advance, Mr. Bridgers has gone forward in his profession, winning new honors and establishing his reputation on a firm foundation as one of the most efficient and valuable railroad men in the south. Indeed, when we consider his thorough preparation, his

aptitude, capacity, judgment and practical experience, we may anticipate that with the passing years he will attain a reputation second to
none in his line in the United States.

On June 1, 1890, Mr. Bridgers was married to Anna King, daughter
of Dr. James F. King, of Durham, N. C. Mr. Bridgers' social position is of the highest. His family have long been among the most
esteemed citizens of Edgecombe county, N. C., where his father,
Hon. Robert R. Bridgers was born, November 23, 1819. Mr. Robert
Bridgers was prepared for college by Benjamin Sumner, and graduated at the University of North Carolina, in 1841, with honors in a
class with Gov. Ellis, Samuel F. Phillips, Dr. Charles Phillips, John F.
Hoke and others of equal merit. He read law at the university
with Gov. Swain, and obtaining his license in 1841 began the practice
in Edgecombe, where he soon established a lucrative business. He
was elected to the legislature as a democrat in 1844, and again in
1856–58–60. But during these years he also was engaged in farming, and together with his brother, Mr. John L. Bridgers, he enjoyed
the reputation of being one of the best and most practical and
progressive planters in the state. On the breaking out of the war,
he was elected a member of the Confederate congress, and there
took rank among the first men of the south for high capacity. After
the war ended, he was elected president of the Wilmington & Weldon
railroad company and here he found an ample field for the exercise
of his fine powers. Taking the road, when a perfect wreck, he built
it up until it became without doubt the best line in the south, and by
his business combinations and management, the value of the property
has been more than doubled. It is to-day a monument to his practical wisdom and splendid management. Soon after his election to
this office Mr. Bridgers removed to Wilmington, where he was residing at the time of his death, in 1888. He was married, in 1848, to
Margaret E. Johnston, daughter of Henry Johnston, of Tarboro, N. C.,
and to them were born ten children, of whom six now survive:
Emily, Robert R., Preston L., George J., Mary and Frank W.
Bridgers.

GEORGE HENDERSON,

the efficient agent of the Southern Express company, and also for
the Eastern Carolina Dispatch line, was born in Quebec, Canada,
September 11, 1840, his parents being Alexander and Mary (Chip-
chase) Henderson, of Scotch and Irish descent, respectively. He
was reared in his native country and educated in the public schools.
In 1860 he came to the United States, and three years later located
in Washington, D. C., where he entered the service of the American
telegraph company. In 1863 he entered the service of the United
States military telegraph line and accompanied the Federal army
through Virginia. After the war he followed telegraphy in Petersburg, Va., and later in Wilmington, N. C. In 1866 he came to Newbern and took charge of the Western Union telegraph office at that

place. In 1869 he was tendered the position of agent for the Southern express company, and has since held that office. When the Eastern Carolina Dispatch line was organized in 1887, Mr. Henderson became its agent, and has since continued as such. For the past eighteen years he has held the agency for several different insurance companies. He has been prominently identified with the public improvements of Newbern, and has done much to assist in the growth and prosperity of the town, being considered a leading citizen and a business man of much ability. He is a member of St. John's lodge A. F. & A. M. In 1871 he was married to Miss Lisette Bell, daughter of David W. Bell, of Newbern. Two children have blessed this happy union, named, Emma and George. Both Mr. and Mrs. Henderson are valued members of the Methodist Episcopal church, and he at present holds the office of steward in the church at Newbern.

MAJ. GRIFFITH JOHN McREE,

a Revolutionary officer of distinction, was born in Bladen county, N. C., February 1, 1758, his father, Samuel McRee, having emigrated from Ireland and settled in that county about 1740. In the early days of the Revolution, young McRee ardently espoused the cause of liberty, and was elected a captain of the Wilmington district, and was, April 16, 1776, commissioned a captain in the Sixth North Carolina continentals. He was at the battle of Fort Moultrie, and later at the battles of Brandywine, Germantown and Monmouth. Early in March, 1779, he was transferred to the First North Carolina continentals, and in the fall of that year marched again to South Carolina, where he endured the hardships of the protracted siege of Charleston, and became a prisoner. For many months he was confined with the other prisoners of Lincoln's army at Charleston, being exchanged February 27, 1781. He hastened to join Gen. Greene, and fought at Guilford Court House, and later at Hobkirk's Hill and Eutaw Springs. For his gallantry in this last battle he was promoted to be major, and breveted lieutenant-colonel. When Gen. Greene entered Charleston upon its evacuation he designed to give precedence to the South Carolina troops, but Maj. McRee protested so vigorously that Gen. Greene was forced to yield to the superior claims of the North Carolina line. In 1784 Maj. McRee was appointed a commissioner to sell the confiscated property of the tories, and rendered satisfactory accounts of the proceeds. He married, in 1785, Miss Ann Fergus, of Wilmington, and cultivated rice on his plantation, Lilliput, below Wilmington. He was appointed captain in the corps of artillerists and engineers, December 26, 1794, by President Washington, and he qualified at West Point, N. Y. He was placed in command of Fort Johnson, and while so employed, March 30, 1798, he was appointed collector of customs for the Wilmington district. He died at Smithville, October 30, 1801—a faithful Christian at a time of great infidelity. He was a member of the society of Cincinnati, and was a delegate to the general convention of the order in

1784. Of his ten children only five attained maturity: Dr. Griffith John McRee, who was a physician in Wilmington, and died in 1831; William, Dr. James Fergus, Samuel, and Margaret, who married Dr. Morrison, of Kentucky, a surgeon in the navy, and died in 1822.

Col. William McRee, the eldest son of Maj. Griffith McRee, was born December 13, 1787. He entered West Point at an early age and graduated in 1805 with the highest honors, being assigned to the engineer corps. He was a brilliant officer, and served with Gen. Scott in the Lundy Lane campaign, which Gen. Swift, in his history of New York, says he planned, attributing to Col. McRee the merit of having brought success to the American arms by his genius. He rose rapidly in his corps and was esteemed the best engineer officer in the army. He was chief engineer of the United States army commanded by Gen. Brown in 1814; was breveted lieutenant-colonel "for gallant conduct in battle of Niagara;" and also "for distinguished and meritorious service in defense of Fort Erie." He was appointed lieutenant-colonel of engineers in 1818. He resigned in 1819. He was United States surveyor of public lands in Illinois, Missouri and Arkansas from 1825 to 1832. He died in St. Louis, May, 1833, unmarried .

Col. Samuel McRee, the youngest son of Maj. Griffith McRee, was born October 6, 1801. He entered West Point at the age of fifteen and graduated, with credit, July, 1820. He was appointed lieutenant of the Eighth infantry, but was transferred to the First infantry. In 1831 he was promoted to be captain and served in the Black Hawk war. In 1839 he was made major and quartermaster. On the breaking out of the Mexican war, he was at New Orleans, and applied to be assigned to the line, but was ordered to report to Gen. Taylor as chief quartermaster, with whom he served until detached to assume charge of the important post at Point Isabel. Here his efficiency won unstinted commendation. Later he served as chief quartermaster of Gen. Scott's army. In May, 1848, he was breveted lieutenant-colonel "for meritorious conduct while serving in the enemy's country." He died at St. Louis, July 18, 1849. His services in the Mexican war were of unestimable value to the American army. He married Mrs. Mary Wheaton. who was a Miss Urquahart, of Wilmington, N. C., and left two sons.

Dr. James Fergus McRee was another son of Col. Griffith McRee. He was born November 18, 1794. His mother being in straitened circumstances, James Fergus was denied the highest educational advantages. He was put to school at Wilmington, and taught the younger boys in school to pay for his own education. Having perfected himself in mathematics and Latin, he studied medicine with Dr. Nat Hill, and after serving several years with him was finally admitted into partnership. He perfected himself in the French language, and thus obtained the practice of the French sailors who frequented that port. When the yellow fever became epidemic at Wilmington in 1822 and depopulated the town, Dr. McRee faced the pestilence and was very successful in his treatment. His practice

Julius Lewis

then became general and extensive, and he steadily gained eminence in his profession until he came to be regarded, at the north as well as at the south, as one of the most eminent physicians of his day. He became a man of rare scholarly attainments, wrote with ease and elegance, was fond of the classics, was equally at home in the researches of philosophy, the mazes of metaphysics, the natural sciences and the polite literature of the day. He was one of the first botanists of his time; was a skilled entomologist, and an expert conchologist. When Lyell, the celebrated geologist, visited America, he and Mrs. Lyell made Dr. McRee a visit at his country residence at Rocky Point, as did also other distinguished savants of Europe. He was a correspondent of the royal society, and obtained a European reputation. His house was a seat of elegance, refinement and culture. To his great learning he united the loftiest virtue, and the noble characteristics of mankind. He was a devoted Christian and stainless gentleman—an ornament of his generation. He married Mary Hill, a granddaughter of Gen. John Ashe, by whom he had two sons: Dr. James F. McRee, Jr., and Griffith J. McRee. He died August 9, 1869, in the seventy-fifth year of age. His son, Dr. James F. McRee, was a physician of fine reputation—served as a surgeon in the Confederate army and died at Asheville, N. C.

Griffith J. McRee graduated with distinction at Princeton, studied law, and became one of the finest belle lettre scholars of his day in North Carolina. He was the author of "The Life and Letters of Justice Iredell, of the United States supreme court." He married Miss Penelope Iredell, and died in 1871, in the fifty-second year of his age.

JULIUS LEWIS.

The name of Julius Lewis is one that is emblematical of what may be accomplished by unrelaxing industry and unswerving integrity. Of New England birth, he early imbibed those qualities which have rendered the Yankee nation famous the world around for their ingenuity, thrift and perseverance. He was born in Southington, Conn., November 9, 1829. His education was somewhat limited, and he abandoned school at the age of fifteen. At that time of life he began the active duties which are usually taken up by men at a much later age. Engaging for a while in a machine shop in his native town, he continued there until 1857. In that year he left his boyhood home and took his way to Newbern, N. C. At the latter place he followed the business of a tradesman for eleven years, establishing in that time a high reputation for fair dealing. At the end of that period he located in Raleigh, where he engaged in the hardware business on an extensive scale, and from that time to this has turned his attention to his constantly increasing trade in this line. In 1862, while a resident of Newbern, he was a member of the militia in that place, and there, on the 14th of April of that year, he was engaged in battle. His broad-minded and liberal ideas concerning the transaction of business, have enabled him to accumulate a comfortable competence. He is now president of the Raleigh Water-works company and of the North Carolina Car works and of the Raleigh Cotton factory, and is director of the Raleigh National bank. Mr. Lewis' parents were Timothy and Sallie (Teasdale) Lewis. The former was also a native of Southington, of which he was for several years its mayor. In early life he was a farmer. Their marriage occurred in 1814, and to them were born eight children, these four surviving: Francis, Harriet, Julius and Billings. Timothy Lewis departed this life about the year 1845, and his wife in 1855. Julius Lewis was united in marriage with Abigail Hart in 1850, who was also born in Southington, Conn., a daughter of Julius Hart.

JOSEPH GRAHAM.

Gen. Joseph Graham, one of the patriots of the Revolution, and the progenitor of the Graham family in North Carolina, was born in Chester county, Penn., October 13, 1759. His father died when he was quite young, leaving his mother to care for a family of six children, with but slender means for her and their support. She removed to North Carolina when Joseph was only ten years of age and settled in the vicinity of Charlotte, Mecklenburg county. Young Graham attended the academy in Charlotte, and there distinguished himself by his mannerly bearing and good scholarship. He was an apt student in history. The study of Cæsar's Commentaries and other histories of battles in the old world gave him some idea of the conflicts of armies such as he was destined soon to be engaged in. He was in Charlotte when, on the 20th day of May, 1775, some of the leading citizens of Mecklenburg county, through a committee appointed for the purpose made a declaration of independence, more than a year anterior to the signing of that immortal instrument whose signing we year by year celebrate. At the age of nineteen, Mr. Graham enlisted in the Fourth regiment of North Carolina troops, commanded by Col. Archibald Lytle. The regiment was ordered to Bladensburg, Md., but on arriving at that place the events of the war had so changed that their services were not needed at that historic point. Mr. Graham was granted a furlough, and returned to his home.

In 1778 he was again called to serve in the defense of his country under Gen. Rutherford, and participated in the battle of Stono, which occurred J n 20, 1779. The next year he was discharged on account of illhealth, having been seized with a fever, and again returned to his home. His health being restored and the British troops having come uncomfortably near to his mother's farm when he was engaged tilling a field for her, he joined the Mecklenburg regiment, of which he was appointed adjutant. The regiment was ordered to Charlotte, there to join Gen. Davis. When the British troops entered Charlotte, September 26, 1780, Gen. Graham was detailed to cover the retreat of Gen. Davis. A sharp conflict took place not far from

Salisbury, in which Col. Locke was killed and Gen. Graham received several severe wounds, the marks of which were honorable mementoes of his gallant conduct, which he carried with him through the remainder of his days. After recovering from the effects of these wounds, Gen. Graham raised a company of mounted riflemen, and joined Gen. Davidson's command, whose army was disputing the progress of Lord Cornwallis toward Cowan's Ford on the Catawba. While the British forces were crossing the ford, Gen. Graham's riflemen kept up a galling fire. In this fight Gen. Davidson was mortally wounded, and the command of the North Carolina troops fell to Gen. Graham, who, with his riflemen and other troops, followed up the British forces on their route to Virginia, constantly harassing their outposts. He soon united his forces with those of Gen. Lee, and attacked and defeated a large body of tories near Hillsboro.

When the British retired to Wilmington, Gen. Graham raised a cavalry force, of which he was appointed major, and near Fayetteville defeated a large force of tories; the fight taking place at Mc-Fall's Mill. He had other encounters with the tories, in which he was generally victorious. At the close of this campaign, Gen. Graham retired from the service in which for so long he had been engaged, and in which he had rendered such important aid in his country's cause. In 1788 he was elected to the state senate from Mecklenburg county, and was several times re-elected. He was again called into the military service in 1814, in the fight with the Creek Indians, being in the command of a brigade at the battle of the Horse Shoe, which ended the war. He was afterward appointed major-general of the Fifth division of the state militia. In later years he removed to Lincoln county and became interested in an iron foundry, which he conducted with great success for many years. He died November 12, 1836, in the seventy-eighth year of his age. Upon the stone which marks the place of his burial in the graveyard at McFall's Mill, is an inscription recounting his bravery and his distinguished services to his country, which closes with these eulogistic words: "His life was a bright and illustrious pattern of domestic, social and public virtue; modest, amiable, upright and pious, he lived a noble ornament to his country and a rich blessing to his family, and died with the hope of a blessed immortality."

COL. WILLIAM L. DeROSSET.

This gentleman is a native of Wilmington, N. C., the eldest son of Dr. A. J. and Eliza J. DeRosset, and was born in the year 1832. He was prepared for college at St. Timothy's Hall, Md., and entered the university of the state in June, 1849, but his stay there was quite brief, as he left the college in December, 1850. He soon afterward engaged in business in New York in his father's office, but having a turn for mechanics he entered a machine shop in Massachusetts, and served an apprenticeship in that business until his health compelled him to abandon it. He returned to his home in Wilmington, and again entered into the commission business, in which he remained until the breaking out of the war. In 1854 he was elected captain of the Wilmington light infantry, and was serving in that position when his company, with others, was ordered by the governor to occupy Fort Caswell in 1861. He was soon afterward sent with his company to Federal Point, which afterward became known as Fort Fisher, and commanded that fort for some time. When the legislature authorized the raising of ten regiments to serve during the war, he was appointed major of the Third regiment, and served as such until May, 1862, when he was promoted to lieutenant-colonel, upon the resignation of Lieut-Col. Cowan, and upon the death of Col. Meares, who fell upon the bloody field of Malvern Hill, in 1862, he was promoted to the colonelcy of the regiment, and served with distinction in that capacity. At the battle of Sharpsburg, while gallantly leading his regiment, he received a wound which incapacitated him for active service in the field, and compelled him to resign, greatly to his regret, for the cause in which he was engaged and for which he perilled his life and limb was very near his heart. At the close of the war he again resumed business, in connection with his father and brother, under the firm name of DeRosset & Co., but in 1877 he withdrew from the firm, and connected himself with the Navassa Guano company, as superintendent of agencies, which position he still holds. He never sought public office nor took any active part in politics, but served one term as alderman of the city. He is a gentleman of high character, frank and manly in his intercourse with the world, sincere and upright in all of his actions, and a worthy representative of one of the oldest and most prominent families of the lower Cape Fear.

MONTFORD STOKES.

Montford Stokes, senator, was born in Wilkes county, N. C., in 1760. In early life he was a seafaring man, in the merchant service. When our Revolutionary struggle began, however, he went into the naval service under the distinguished Commodore Stephen Decatur. In 1776, during one of his cruises, he was captured near Norfolk by the British, and imprisoned on ship board in New York harbor. The war over, he abandoned sea-going and was elected clerk of the superior court, residing at Salisbury. He held this office for a long series of years, discharging its duties with much ability and to the satisfaction of all parties concerned. This was a good training school for more general clerical work, and he was chosen chief clerk of the state senate, for which office he was abundantly equipped. From this he was elected to the senate itself, in which he wielded a powerful influence and became one of the leading members of that body. He was elected United States senator, but declined to serve. He was, however, again elected in 1816, and served the full term of six years.

In 1823 Mr. Stokes was elected governor of the state by the legislature. He resigned this office to accept, at the hands of President

Andrew Jackson, the Indian agency in Arkansas, where he remained till his death in 1842. His death was unquestionably hastened by a wound which he received in a duel with Jesse A. Pearson, which took place near Salisbury. He was a type of the chivalry of those days, and was quick to resent an insult. He possessed learning, genius and talents of a high order, but his early habits, acquired upon the "rolling deep" to some extent subordinated the steadier habits of the clerical vocation, and gave him a taste for less sedative employments. He married Miss Irwin, sister of Capt. Henry Irwin, one of the illustrious continental troops, who fought and fell in the historic battle of Germantown in 1777. She died, leaving him one daughter. He married again, his second wife being Rachel, daughter of Hugh Montgomery, who bore him a family of five sons and five daughters.

OSGOOD PIERCE HEATH.

Among the most successful business men of Charlotte, Osgood Pierce Heath holds a prominent place. He is a native of Lancaster county, S. C., and was born on a farm December 26, 1856. His parents, Moses O. and Mary (Morrow) Heath were both natives of South Carolina. Mr. Heath was reared upon the farm owned and cultivated by his father and here learned the lessons of industry, economy and perseverance which have so characterized his business career and contributed to his success in life. He was taught farm work, spending many days in the field while a youth. He attended the "old field" schools of his neighborhood, where he gained his early education, which was broadened by subsequent attendance in the schools of Fort Mills, S.C., and the Rutherford college, of North Carolina. He began life's struggle at the age of twenty-one by following the pursuit of farming in his native county. He also took up merchandising at a country store in which he did a general business, continuing his farming until the fall of 1882, when he removed to the town of Lancaster, S. C., and entered into mercantile co-partnership with his brother, E. J. Heath. With him he continued in business till the fall of 1885, when he bought out the interest of his brother and formed a co-partnership with others, becoming the senior partner of the firm of Heath, Springs & Co. In 1889 he withdrew from this firm and located in Charlotte, where he has since been dealing in cotton and operating a private bank. His cotton business is carried on by O. P. Heath & Co., his brother, B. D. Heath, being his partner. The banking business is conducted under the name of Heath Brothers.

Mr. Heath is a thoroughly practical business man and success has crowned all his business undertakings. He is emphatically self-made and has achieved success through sturdy industry, perseverance and close application. He is a typical business man, and as a citizen enjoys the respect and esteem of a large circle of friends. He is a gentleman of exemplary character, strictly honest and conscientious, moral and religious. He and his wife are members of the Methodist

Episcopal church. In 1878 Mr. Heath was married to Miss Annie Lee Potts, of Lancaster. S. C. Aside from his cotton and banking operations, he is a member of the Charlotte chamber of commerce, a director in the Charlotte Consolidated Construction Co., and in all the best aspects a progressive man.

JOSEPH LENOIR CHAMBERS,

of Charlotte, N. C., is one of the enterprising business men and manufacturers of that city. He is a native of Burke county, N. C., and was born July 15, 1854. His father, Pinckney Brown Chambers, is a prominent farmer in Iredell county, in which county the subject of this sketch was principally reared. The maiden name of Mr. Chambers' mother was Jestina Avery. Both parents are native North Carolinians of early families in the state. Mr. Chambers was but thirteen years of age when he was placed in Bingham's school at Mebanesville, where he was fitted for Davidson college, whence he graduated in 1873, at the age of nineteen years. Immediately after his graduation he began teaching school at Greensboro, N. C., but his taste was not for teaching and he continued in that calling for only one year. Subsequently he held the position of clerk for one year in the office of the auditor of North Carolina railroad company. In August 1876, he came to Charlotte and accepted the position of local editor of the *Chronicle and Observer* newspaper, and in this capacity and that of associate editor he remained on the editorial staff of that journal five years. In the journalistic field, Mr. Chambers gave evidence of ability and adaptability as a writer, but the force of circumstances forced him to leave the profession and embark in a more remunerative pursuit, and thus journalism lost an educated and cultured votary and an able and brilliant writer.

When Mr. Chambers left the newspaper field, he was induced, at the instance of his father-in-law, the late Robert I. McDowell, to invest in the manufacturing business of Lidell & Co., of which company Mr. McDowell was a member. Since that time (1880) he has chiefly been superintendent of the mechanical department of that concern, the business of which consists of the manufacture of engines, boilers, cotton presses and sawmills. The manufactory has been prosperous. Mr. Chambers at various times has been identified with other manufactories. During the present year he has been elected president of the chamber of commerce, the youngest president during the ten years' existence of that body, who has been called to preside over its deliberations. His previous service on the board of directors, combined with his educational and business qualifications, has well fitted him for the higher position, and enabled him to successfully administer the affairs of the organization. He was a member of the first board of directors of the stock company owning and controlling the Charlotte *Daily Chronicle*, and has now served continuously on that board for three years. He is also a director in the Mecklenburg monumental association. Mr. Chambers is one of the originators and founders of the Charlotte Consolidated Construction Co., organized for the purpose of developing and improving the city, and this company owns and operates the Charlotte street car system. He is a director in the company and its secretary. Mr. Chambers may with truth be said to be a progressive and enterprising citizen, a prudent and judicious business man, and a pleasant and intelligent gentleman, a lover of history and literature. He is a member of the Charlotte Literary and Library association and exhibits a warm interest in every department of education. He has been twice married. In 1880 he was united in marriage with Miss Emma McDowell, who died in 1883, leaving him one child, a daughter named Rebecca. In 1887 he was again married, his second wife being Miss Grace Dewey, of Charlotte, by whom he has had one daughter, Elizabeth Chambers.

JAY HIRSHINGER,

proprietor of the Dixie Pants company, of Charlotte, is a native of Bavaria, Germany, born October 25, 1839. His parents were Herman and Babette Hirshinger, both of whom lived and died in Bavaria. They had two daughters and one son, the latter the subject of this sketch. Jay Hirshinger acquired a fair German education in his native country, and at the age of thirteen years began to serve an apprenticeship of three years as clerk and bookkeeper in a mercantile establishment. For several years thereafter he followed that business at various places and for various parties. In 1866 he emigrated to America, landing at New York city. A few weeks later he went to McGregor, Iowa, where he was engaged one year as a clerk and then became a partner in a general merchandise business at Thomasville, Ga. Here he continued until 1883, during which year he located in Charlotte, where he formed a co-partnership with J. Moyer in the shoe business, which continued till 1888, when the partnership was dissolved. Mr. Hirshinger then embarked in the manufacture of pants, and has since conducted an extensive business in that line. He now has facilities for making about 300 pairs of pants daily, employs from forty to fifty hands, and has so extended his operations that he has an annual business of not less than $120,000. The products of his work are sold in both the Carolinas and Georgia. He is a thoroughly practical business man and has met with great success in his undertakings. All his business plans are thoroughly matured and carried out on strictly methodical principles which insure success. In 1873, Mr. Hirshinger was married to Miss Marion Heineman, of Philadelphia, an educated and accomplished lady, a graduate of the Philadelphia normal school. They have three children, whose respective christian names are Herbert, Sadie and Edna. Mr. Hirshinger is a leading member of the K. of H., of the A. O. U. W., of the Royal Arcanum and of the B'nai B'rith. He is also a member of the Charlotte chamber of commerce. Besides being an energetic and progressive business man, he takes a warm interest in educational improvement. In 1889 he was elected a school commissioner, an office for which, both by taste and ability, he is thoroughly qualified to administer.

W. N. HACKNEY,

now deceased, was born in Nash county, N. C., on the the 26th of January, 1823. He learned the trade of a wheel-wright, and located in Wilson, N. C., in the year 1853. A partnership was formed with Pomeroy Clarke, and they engaged in the manufacuring of wagons and carts. Such was the humble beginning of the present extensive carriage factory operated by Messrs. Hackney Bros. & Simpson. Subsequently Mr. Clarke withdrew, and for several years thereafter the business was continued under the firm name of Hackney & Parker. Mr. Parker becoming associated in business with a Mr. Murray, the established business was then conducted under the firm name of Parker, Murray & Co., till Mr. Parker's death, after which date the style of the firm was changed to Hackney & Murray, and remained as such up to 1878, when W. D. Hackney, son of the elder Hackney, was admitted to a partnership; and C. N. Nurney also becoming a partner the style of the firm was again changed to Hackney, Nurney & Co., which was succeeded in turn by W. N. Hackney & Son. Mr. W. N. Hackney's death occurred December 6, 1887, and his sons, Thomas J. and George Hackney, becoming interested in the business with their brother W. D. Hackney, the business was continued under the name of Hackney Bros., until January 1, 1891, when Mr. William P. Simpson purchased an interest, and the present firm of Hackney Bros. & Simpson was established. The business has steadily grown to its present enormous proportions for the past quarter of a century and more. Notwithstanding times of depression, the substantial character of the men who have been at its head has given it an enviable reputation over a wide-spread territory. Buggies, wagons, carts, and, in fact, all kinds of vehicles are turned out in large quantities by this enterprising concern. Hackney Bros. & Simpson carry on one of the finest carriage and wagon factories in the south — probably the most extensive. They employ many skilled laborers and their pay roll each week amounts to a little over $350. They have capacity and turn out about 2,000 buggies, wagons and other vehicles each year. They have a branch business at Rocky Mount, eighteen miles north from Wilson. Their repository, paint, storage, smith, machine and wood shops at Wilson cover an area of two acres, and are well arranged, and here is done the bulk of their work. A specialty is made of light buggies, phaetons and surreys.

This great and stupendous business, now grown to an annual volume of more than $100,000 practically began with no capital, and its founder, W. N. Hackney, deceased, and who is the direct subject of this sketch, may be justly paid the tribute of having placed the enterprise on a safe and sound basis. He was a leading business man and citizen, and was a man of sterling qualities, ever maintaining a strict

character for probity; and in business transactions, fair, punctual and honest. He came of a respected family, as for three generations the Hackney family resided in Nash county, where their name became to be honored and prominent. W. N. Hackney was prominent as a Mason and was a Christian gentleman, holding for years the office of deacon in the Disciples church. He was three times happily married, and his domestic relations were the most pleasant and happy. His children are: Thomas J., of Rocky Mount, born August 17, 1851; George, born September 19, 1854; W. D., born March 21, 1858; Martha Ann, wife of R. T. Stevens, of Wilson; Mary Ellen and Orpha; and with the exception of the first named, all reside in Wilson. Each of the sons have become interested in and identified with the established business of the father, and are the brothers now comprehended in the firm name of Hackney Bros. & Simpson; and to their sagacious and sapient business qualities and excellent management is largely due the upbuilding of the stupendous and important business of the firm, and following in the footsteps of their worthy father it is worthy of them that they have exemplified the excellent character and business principles of their father.

As has been observed, William P. Simpson became associated with the Hackney Brothers January 1, 1891, at which time he purchased a one-fourth interest in the concern of which he is now a member; he managing the financial part of the business. He was born at Greensboro, Guilford county, N. C., September 30, 1851. In 1880 Mr. Simpson accepted a position with the mercantile house of Branch & Co., of Wilson, as bookkeeper. In January, 1886, he became associated with the banking firm of Branch & Co., with whom he remained till becoming a co-partner with the Hackney Bros. Mr. Simpson has become intimately identified with the business interests of Wilson. He has been president of the tobacco board of trade since its organization in 1889; he is a director in the Wilson Cotton mills, of which he was secretary and treasurer for one year; and he is also extensively interested in agriculture in Halifax county. As a democrat he is active and efficient. His wife, who is a valued communicant of the Methodist Episcopal church, of Wilson, became his wife in 1874. She was Miss Anna R. Williams, daughter of Capt. W. T. Williams, of Halifax county, N. C. The home of Mr. and Mrs. Simpson has been blessed by the birth of four children, viz.: Anna Price, Edgar Williams, William Preston and Rezin Burgess.

HUGH WADDELL

was born in Lisburn, county Down, Ireland, in 1734. He came to America and settled in North Carolina in 1753, and was clerk of the council in 1754-5, and in the same year was a lieutenant in Col. James Innes' regiment, and did good service in the Virginia campaign, for which he was promoted to the rank of captain, in 1755. He built Fort Dobbs and commanded there in 1756-7. In 1758 he led the North Carolina detachment with the rank of major in the expedition to Fort DuQuesne, and became colonel the next year. In 1765 Mr. Waddell was selected to lead the armed resistance to the landing of the English sloop of war " Diligence," which contained the government stamps, seized the ship's boat, and forced Gov. Tryon to deliver to the people William Houston, the stamp master, from whom they exacted a pledge, which he signed in the market place, that he would never receive any stamped paper which might arrive from England, nor officiate in any way in the distribution of stamps in the province of North Carolina. This act of patriotism was of no less importance in the revolutionary movements in North Carolina than that of the Boston tea-party in Massachusetts. In 1771 he commanded the expedition against the regulators with the rank of major-general. He served several terms in the legislature and died in April, 1773.

WILLIAM P. SIMPSON,

one of the leading manufacturers of the south, was born at Grans-burgh, Guilford county, N. C., September 30, 1851. James P. and Sarah (Jacobs) Simpson, his parents, were natives of Baltimore, Md. The Rev. James P. Simpson, at one time a prominent member of the Baltimore conference of the Methodist Episcopal church, removed to North Carolina in 1848, and has been stationed in different places in the state as pastor, and is now residing in Halifax county, N. C. The other children born to these parents are F. A., a commercial traveler, of Wilson; William P., James D., and Lizzie. The mother died and Mr. Simpson married a second time, Money Williams, of Pitt county, N. C., becoming his wife. Mr. William P. Simpson was graduated from Trinity college, N. C. In 1869 he began his business career as a clerk in a shoe and hat store at Martinsburg, W. Va. After remaining there for some time he went to Raywood, Halifax county, N. C., and from 1871 to 1880 was engaged in agriculture in Halifax county. In the latter year Mr. Simpson came to Wilson and accepted a position with the mercantile house of Branch & Co., as bookkeeper. In January, 1886, he became associated with the firm of Branch & Co., bankers, and remained with them until January 1, 1891, when he purchased a one-fourth interest in the concern of which he is now a member, Hackney, Bratton & Simpson. Mr. Simpson manages the financial part of the business. This house is the largest carriage and wagon manufacturers south of Baltimore, and its owners are men of sagacity and great business ability. In 1874 Miss Anna R. Williams, daughter of Capt. W. T. Williams, of Halifax county, N. C., became the wife of Mr. Simpson, and their home has been blessed by the birth of four children: Anna Price, Edgar Williams, William Preston and Rezin Burgess. Mr. Simpson has become intimately identified with the business interests of Wilson. He has been president of the tobacco board of trade, since its organization in 1889; is a director in the Wilson cotton mill, of which he was secretary and treasurer for one year, and he is now vice-president of the State bank, of Wilson, and is also very extensively engaged in agriculture in the county. As a democrat he is active and efficient. Both himself and wife are valued communicants of the Methodist Episcopal church, of Wilson, and are held in the highest esteem in the community. Rezin B. Simpson, grandfather of our subject, was at one time one of the leading merchants of Baltimore, Md., and amassed a large fortune.

JAMES F. TAYLOR, .

secretary and treasurer of the Orion knitting mills, of Kinston, N. C., was born in Lenoir county, N. C., on the 8th of September, 1864, and is a son of F. G. and Jane (Hooker) Taylor. The family originated in England, the first of the name to come to this country having settled in Lenoir county,. N. C. Staunton Taylor, the grandfather of Mr. James F. Taylor, was born in Lenoir county, and became one of the most prominent planters in that section of the country. Two of his sons, S. B. and F. G. Taylor, are still living. The last mentioned gentleman was born in 1821, and received a good common school education, after which he went to tilling the soil, and is now one of the successful planters of the community. A leading democrat, he has served as a justice of the peace for many years, and has also taken a deep interest in public education. Both himself and wife are active and valued members of the Methodist Episcopal church, south. Of the eight children born to these parents, seven are now living. James F. Taylor, the next youngest in the family, was given a thorough scholastic training in the township schools, the Kinston collegiate institute, and later in the Kings Mountain high school. For a time he was engaged in keeping books for a firm in Bennettsville, S. C., and for the succeeding five years was a broker in cotton, fertilizers, etc., and for one year was a member of the firm of McRea & Taylor, cracker and confectionery manufacturers, and also of the firm of Taylor & Co. In January, 1890, he retired from that business to organize the Orion knitting mill company, which was incorporated June 16th, 1890, and he is one of its heaviest stockholders, and since its organization has acted as secretary and treasurer. He is also a member of the Southern Pine Chewing Gum company, of Kinston. In giving to the community these new and important industries, Mr. Taylor performed a service which cannot be too highly estimated. He is a man of great business ability and energy, and has the confidence of the people to a marked extent, because he has ever evinced sterling integrity in his every deal. Should life and health be spared him, there can be no doubt of his future success.

EDWARD B. DUDLEY.

Edward Bishop Dudley, governor of North Carolina, was born in Onslow county, N. C., December 15, 1787. Though he was the son of a wealthy planter, his early education was defective, but he made up for this by the force and energy with which he was characterized, and rose to great eminence among his fellow-citizens. When only twenty-three years of age, he was elected to the lower house of the state legislature, and was twice re-elected. In 1814 he was elected to the state senate, a place which his father had held before him. In the legislature he was distinguished by his strong and effective advocacy of internal improvements under state patronage. He was twice afterward elected to the legislature to represent Wilmington. He was a strong advocate for railroad extension, and subscribed a large amount for the construction of the Wilmington & Weldon railroad, of which corporation he was made president. In the politics of the times he was a Jackson democrat, and in 1829 was elected to congress by that party, serving for the full term of two years. He was offered a re-election, but he became disgusted with the intrigues of partisanship and declined. He was elected the first governor under the amendment of the state constitution in 1835 which provided for the election by popular vote instead of by the legislature. His election was the spontaneous act of the people, the office not having been solicited by him, and he was re-elected for a second term.

Gov. Dudley's reputation was that of one of the most liberal, generous and public-spirited men in the state. He was a person of pleasing address; was large and commanding in form and suave in his manner. He was tolerant toward other people's opinions but firmly decided in his own. He was a strong partisan, but believed that political integrity should be as strictly adhered to as personal integrity, and that the latter should be spotless and incorruptible. His public speeches were marked for their strong common sense, for their public spirit and for their comprehensive patriotism. He was the heir of a large estate, but used his means with an almost unbounded generosity, and no worthy person ever applied to him for assistance in vain. His charities were on a grand scale and he fulfilled and illustrated the scriptural idea of neighborly kindness. He married Elizabeth, daughter of William H. Haywood, of Raleigh, by whom he had several sons and daughters. He died at Wilmington, October, 30, 1855.

W. H. WILLIAMS.

The subject of this sketch was born in Morris county, N. J., June 19, 1848. His father was William Williams, and his mother Susan Wortman Wiggins. His father was brought up from a boy in the iron business, the old-fashioned open fireplace forge, and was one of the pioneers in starting this great industry in the south, moving with his family from Rockaway, N. J., to Kings Mountain, N. C., when his son, William H., was five years old. There he started up the extensive Kings Mountain iron works for Mr. Benjamin Breggs, and in 1860 bought the Maiden Creek iron works in Catawba county. This place is seven miles south of Newton, and here the present subject, on account of his restless activity and buoyant spirits, became as distinctly the leader in boyish sports and all undertakings having mischief at their bottom, as he has in maturer years become the leader in all business and public enterprises in his community that require great capacity, nerve and unerring knowledge of human nature to bring them to successful issues. His educational advantages were few, but being blessed with a brilliant mind, and being thrown when young in all classes of society, he largely made up for his lack of school privileges. He was married at the age of eighteen to Miss Martha S. Finger, daughter of Michael Finger and Rachel Warlick, of Lincoln county, and this important event caused him to enter upon an active business career at a correspondingly early age.

After farming two years on rented land, Mr. Williams moved to Newton in 1869, and embarked in the mercantile business. He had but a slender capital, but more than made up this deficiency in pluck and energy, and his tact at adapting himself to circumstances. At the time he set out in business the railroad facilities of Newton were very unsatisfactory, and he took an active part in this improvement. He has been for several years a director in the C. & L. road. He continued in the mercantile business until 1883, and his success was phenomenal. In that year he was the leading spirit in organizing the Newton Cotton Mills company, and was elected president of the same, which position he still holds. Although started on a small scale this plant has been from time to time enlarged until it has become one of the finest mills of its kind in the south. Encouraged by the success of this mill, a company has been organized to build in Newton another mill, the Middlebrooke mill, and Mr. Williams has been elected president of the company. He is also president of the Newton Roller Mill company, and president of the Newton branch of the North Carolina Building and Loan association. He is also quite extensively engaged in farming.

In a political way Mr. Williams has never been a candidate for office, but, always taking an active part in promoting the fortunes of the democratic party, he has had much to do in shaping the politics of his county, district and state. One of the first things done by the late Daniel G. Fowle, after he was inaugurated governor of North Carolina, in 1889, was to appoint Mr. Williams a member of his staff, with the rank of colonel. Along with Gov. Fowle he attended the constitutional centennial in New York, in May, 1889, was one of the military representatives from North Carolina at the funeral of Jefferson Davis, in New Orleans, in December, 1889, and took part in the unveiling ceremonies of the Lee monument, in Richmond, in May, 1890. He attended the funeral of Gov. Fowle, and before leaving Raleigh tendered his resignation to Gov. Holt, who succeeded to the office, but it was not accepted.

Col. Williams is uniformly kind and considerate towards his employes, and never forgets to keep in view their best interests. To many a poor family he has been a real benefactor, and his kindness and generosity are almost without limit. His career is a fine example of a boy starting out in poverty and by energy and integrity rapidly rising to competence, and while he helped himself proved a blessing and a help to the whole community in which he lives.

HENRY FRANKLIN SCHENCK

was born November 29, 1835, near Gardner's Ford, Rutherford county, now Cleveland county, N. C. His paternal ancestors were of Swiss origin. In the early part of the eighteenth century a colony of Mennonite protestants, being driven from Switzerland by the intolerance and cruelty of the Romish hierarchy, settled in Lancaster county, Penn. Among these were the progenitors of the Schenck family. From this county, Michael Schenck, who was an adventurous disposition, emigrated with a small colony into North Carolina and settled in Lincoln county about the year 1790. In this county, near Lincolnton, on a small stream, he built, in the year 1813, the first cotton factory erected south of the Potomac river. Afterward, in 1819, he formed a company and erected a large factory, running about 3,000 spindles, near the same place on the south fork of the Catawba river, and this was the third and largest cotton mill that was built south of the Potomac up to that time. Henry Schenck, eldest son of Michael, like his father, was progressive and enterprising, and assisted his father in building and managing the business of the second mill, but he finally married and settled down to merchandising and farming at Gardner's Ford, now in Cleveland county. He succeeded in accumulating a large amount of property for that section of the county. Henry Franklin Schenck was the only son of Henry Schenck. He received an academic education and was a schoolmate of Gens. R. F. Hoke and S. D. Ramseur, both of military fame in the Confederate army. Afterward he attended school at Cokesburg, S. C., and at Shelby, N. C. While at the latter school, at the age of eighteen, he had a severe attack of pneumonia, from the effects of which he has never fully recovered. He was advised by physicians to abandon the further pursuit of his studies, which advice he followed, and embarked in merchandising in Catawba county. At the age of nineteen he was elected colonel of the militia and held that rank at the beginning of the Civil war. He then raised a company and volunteered in the Confederate service, being assigned to the Fifty-sixth North Carolina regiment, on the organization of which he was elected major. In this capacity he served until 1863, when the condition of his health, which had all along been on the decline, became so critical that he was compelled to resign his commission and quit active service.

The close of the war found Mr. Schenck still in wretched health, and his financial condition nearly as bad. But the exigencies of the hour and the necessities of his family spurred him on to effort, and he established a small merchandising business in Cleveland county, and this, with persistent outdoor work on the farm, gradually improved the condition of his health, and his business being quite successful he soon added to his enterprise a flouring mill and a cotton gin. In 1873 Maj. Schenck erected a small cotton factory in Cleveland county, on a tributary of First Broad river. In connection with his factory he carried on an enlarged mercantile business, and in 1888 joined with a northern firm, the corporation which was established being known as the Cleveland cotton mills, of which he is the president. He erected a new and large factory on First Broad river, about a mile and a half below his other mill. The product of his mills are carpet warp, ball twine and rope. A store was also established in connection with this new mill. In the progress and development of his section, Maj. Schenck has always been ready to take the lead, and the establishment of this mill and of his mercantile business makes a new era in the history of his district. There has been a steady yet rapid improvement in the material interests of the surrounding country ever since he led off in these enterprises, and his policy has been to treat his help with consideration, and as consequence he is never without applications from good county families for work in his factories. Among his operatives he has established the rule of temperance, by which he secures industrious, sober help, and his influence in the community toward the promotion of temperance and good citizenship is most salutary. Maj. Schenck is not a politician, much less an office seeker, and has steadily declined all proffers for office, except in 1886, in the fall of which year he was drawn into a political campaign. He was always a firm democrat, ever desiring the success of that party, and he finally consented to run for the legislature on the democratic ticket. Cleveland county was divided into factions, which endangered the success of his party and to bring about a union if possible, he made a canvass and was elected by a large plurality, in one of the bitterest contests ever known in the county. He has had other important offices thrust upon him, and has performed his public duties in a quiet, undemonstrative manner. From his youth up to 1882 he has been a member of the Protestant Episcopal church, at that period joining the church to which his wife and children were attached, the Missionary Baptist. For eight consecutive years he has been moderator of the Kings Mountain Baptist association. He is a member of the Masonic order and is a Master Mason.

Maj. Schenck was married in 1868, to Miss Lou Lattimore, a member of a prominent family in Cleveland county. Her great-grandfather, John Lattimore was one of the earliest settlers of Cleveland county and was in the battle of Kings Mountain, where he received a British bullet in his thigh which he carried for the remainder of his days. He came from the battle field borne by a horse he had captured from a British trooper. Maj. Schenck and wife have two daughters and one son. Their eldest, Minnie, is now married to Thomas J. Ramsauer, a stockholder and treasurer of the Cleveland cotton mills. The second daughter, Maggie, is the wife of Dr. J. C. Osborn, of Cleveland county. The son and youngest child is John Franklin Schenck, born, April 17, 1865, received his preparatory education at Kings Mountain high school, and in the first year won the medal offered for the best debater. He entered Wake Forest college in 1882 with more than an average standing in the classes. In the elocutionary contest between the literary societies, he won the medal. In the fall of 1884, Mr. Schenck entered the state university in the junior class and graduated in 1886, receiving several honors during his stay in the university. After a rest, made necessary by the state of his health, he studied law and was admitted to practice in 1888. His first field of work was in Shelby, then in Durham, where he practised with fair success for a year. His father finally prevailed upon him to abandon the profession for a livelihood, and he has located permanently at his original home engaging in the more lucrative business of assisting his father in his manufacturing operations. He is and always has been a total abstainer from intoxicants and a thorough advocate of prohibition. He was the leader in an effort which secured local option in Cleveland county.

BENJAMIN WILLIAMS.

Governor Benjamin Williams was born in Moore county, N. C., in 1754. He was elected a member of congress in 1793, for the full term of two years. In 1799 he was elected governor of the state by the legislature thereof, and was again elected to that office in 1809. He was state senator from 1807 to 1809. When Gov. Davie accepted the mission to France by appointment of President John Adams, Benjamin Williams became his successor as chief magistrate. He was not highly educated; was simple and unostentatious in his manners. He was a man of honest intentions and of most exemplary character. He was undemonstrative, and his integrity was above reproach or suspicion. What he lacked in greatness he made up in a pure and honest purpose, in a strict regard for justice and all the proprieties of life. He died at his home in his native county in 1814. He married Miss Mary Eaton Jones, daughter of Robin Jones, of Halifax, who bore him two sons. They were named Allen and William Williams, and both received their education at Eton college, England.

GEN. ROBERT HOWE

was one of the most brilliant men who ever adorned the annals of North Carolina. His grandfather, Job Howe, was an influential planter in South Carolina and married Mary Moore (then widow Clifford), a daughter of Gov. James Moore, by Elizabeth Yeamans, daughter of Sir John Yeamans. Their son, Job Howe, settled on the Cape Fear, where he married Jane Jones, a granddaughter of Col. Sam Swann, by Elizabeth Lillington, and had issue Robert Howe, the subject of this sketch, who was born in 1732. Young Robert was early bereft of his parents, his father dying in 1748. Finely educated, with a handsome fortune greatly increased by an early marriage with an heiress, Miss Grange, and of close kin with the Moores, the Swanns and Ashes, he attained man's estate with brilliant prospects before him.

Having spent two years in England, with his bride, he returned to Carolina in 1766, and was appointed to the command of Fort Johnson and was commissioned baron of the exchequer. When the troubles with the mother country began he warmly espoused the cause of the native country and was an influential leader in the assembly, and he prepared the address to Gov. Martin, in 1774, which is a masterpiece of composition. He was a member of all the provincial congresses until the war called him to the field, and many of the state papers of that period, whose excellence reflects much credit on North Carolina, are attributed to his pen. When the congress, in August, 1775, organized the provincial forces, he was appointed colonel of the Second regiment. His first important service was in Virginia, when Lord Dunmore was ravaging the region around Norfolk.

In December, 1775, Howe arrived with his regiment in the vicinity, two days after the battle of Great Bridge, and being in command made such successful use of his forces as won for him the thanks of both the Virginia and North Carolina assemblies. Writing from the presence of the enemy he said: "They shall have no rest for the soles of their feet." So effective was he that when Clinton's forces lay at Brunswick, they ravaged his plantation, and he was honored by being excluded from the office of pardon. He was, on March 1, 1776, appointed brigadier-general by the continental congress, and marched with his cousin, Gen. James Moore, to aid in the defense of Charleston. After the repulse of the British at Fort Moultrie, he went with Gen. Lee on the expedition to Florida, Moore being left in command at Charleston. Lee soon went north; Gen. Moore was ordered north but died, and Howe was given command of the southern department. He was appointed major-general October 20, 1777, and was active in making defense against the movements of the British who were approaching Savannah from Florida. He led an expedition through the wilderness from Savannah, in the summer of 1778, and drove the enemy back to Fort Tonyn on St. Mary's river, took that fort and caused them to retreat to St. Augustine. In December, the British being largely re-inforced from the north, where operations in the winter were impracticable, again approached Savannah, and after a hard fight succeeded in putting the Americans to rout. Gen. Lincoln who had been sent south reached the Savannah river with re-inforcements, a few days later, and Gen. Howe proceeded to the north to join Washington's army. The South Carolina and the Georgian authorities had both been restless because Howe was in command there, and Gen. Gadsden having made some reflections on Howe, a duel ensued, Howe's bullet brushing Gadsden's ear. They then shook hands. Maj. Andre, one of the most accomplished officers in the British army, wrote an amusing account of the duel to the tune of Yankee Doodle, of which one stanza ran:

" Such honor did they both display
They highly were commended.
And thus, in short, their gallant fray
Without mischance was ended."

At the north, Howe co-operated with Gen. Wayne in 1779 in the attack on Stony Point, and was entrusted by Washington with the command of West Point; but Arnold, who then stood so high in the confidence of all, subsequently secured an appointment to that post. He sought to surrender it and Andre was captured. Howe was detailed on the court-martial that tried Andre on the charge of being a spy and sentenced him to death. Howe was chiefly employed on the Hudson. Washington reposed the utmost confidence in Howe, and in January, 1781, sent him to quell the mutiny among the New Jersey troops, and for his judicious performance of this duty, Howe was thanked in general orders. The Georgia authorities having requested an examination into the conduct of this case while Howe was at the south, Gen. Washington summoned a court-martial of thirteen officers, Baron DeKalb being president, to pass upon the charges, and after a rigid examination of six weeks, the court acquitted Gen. Howe "with the highest honors" and congress approved of the action of the court. Gen. Howe remained in the army after the war, and in July, 1783, congress directed him to quell a mutiny in the Pennsylvania troops, and he again won approbation for his firm conduct. In May, 1785, he was appointed by congress to treat with the western Indians. In the spring of that year he returned home, and was welcomed by public honors at Fayetteville and elsewhere in the state. He was elected to the assembly that summer from Brunswick, but died in November, 1785, greatly lamented. He left a son and a daughter, who never married. Gen. Howe was not only a brave soldier, an accomplished officer, a warm patriot and a man of lofty character, but he was a man of brilliant parts, a man of elegant culture and of noble sentiments.

CALEB B. PRICE,

a representative merchant of Mount Olive, is a North Carolinian by birth, having first seen the light in Duplin county, on the 12th of May, 1837. His parents were Caleb and Olive (Kennedy) Price, both natives of North Carolina. Two of their five children still survive them, namely: Francis M. and Caleb B. The latter was given a common school education and then apprenticed to the carpenter's trade, which he followed for ten years. In 1861 he joined the Confederate army as a member of the Confederate Grays from the Franklin institute, and subsequently was a member of Company C, Second North Carolina state troops, and from a private was promoted to a captaincy. Shortly before the final surrender he was taken prisoner and taken to Hart's Island. His war record is an honorable one. He participated in the battles of Fredricksburg, Sharpsburg, Boonesborough, Cedar Gap, second Bull Run, Gettysburg, Horse-shoe, Spottsylvania, Petersburg, was in the seven days' fight around Richmond, and several other engagements of minor importance. Returning to Wayne county after the close of the struggle, Mr. Price was engaged in teaching during the winter and in farming in the summer season for the next four years, after which he went to South Carolina and entered the mercantile business, in which he was engaged for two years. He then returned to Wayne county and worked at his trade for some time. For five years he was superintendent of a mercantile business at Mount Olive for Mr. Kornegy, and in January, 1885, he estalished the concern which he has since operated. Mr. Price has served as town commissioner for four years, and is an active democrat. In addition to his large mercantile interests he carries on an extensive plantation. In 1866 he was united in marriage to Miss Ada A. Price, daughter of Whitman Price. Mr. and Mrs. Price are valued members of the Methodist Episcopal church, of which he is a steward.

WILLIAM H. HAMPTON,

one of the most successful and extensive merchants of Plymouth, N. C., is a native of that city, having been born there on the 26th of October, 1843, the son of J. H. and Catherine (Salisbury) Hampton. The mother was a native of Virginia, and the father of Currituck county, N. C. In 1830 he removed to Plymouth, and for many years conducted a hotel in that place, and so successful was he that he owned the two principal hotels of the city. In 1854 he retired to his plantation in Washington county, and died there in 1865. Mr. Hampton was one of the largest land and slave owners in the county, and was prominent as a democrat. His wife died in 1862. She was a life-long communicant of the Episcopal church, and lived a most useful and beautiful life, dying in the firm belief of her Saviour's power to save. Four children were born to these parents who reached the years of maturity. They are: J. T. Hampton, M. D., of Philadelphia, Penn.; Patty, wife of A. M. Johnston, of Washington county, N. C.; Catherine and William H. Hampton. Mr. Hampton was reared in Plymouth, and received his education in the excellent schools of the county. May 20, 1861, he enlisted in the Confederate cause as a member of Company H, Seventeenth North Carolina regiment, under Capt. (afterward major) H. A. Gillam, and served until the close of the war, having taken a valiant part in the battles of Richmond, Petersburg and Five Forks, and was wounded in the battle near Richmond and in the trenches of Petersburg. March 8, 1865, at Five Forks, he was again wounded, and this time was captured and confined in prison until June, 1865. After peace was declared he returned to Plymouth, and there engaged in the fishing business. He has since continued in this enterprise, and now owns and operates no fewer than eight different fisheries, being the the largest dealer in eastern North Carolina. His markets are New York and Philadelphia and Richmond. Mr. Hampton is also extensively engaged in the manufacture of shingles, owning several vessels to transport them to northern markets. In 1881 he established his present mercantile business in Plymouth, and in addition to this very extensive establishment he operates a large area of plantation land. Mr. Hampton is a democrat, and has served as a justice of the peace, and also as treasurer of the city. He is a member of the Knights of Honor. In 1886 Miss Lulu Blount, daughter of Mr. Levi Blount, of Plymouth, became his wife, and Roy and Clara are the two children born to their union. The family are communicants of the Episcopal church.

HON. JONAS W. CROWELL,

sheriff of Wilson county, N. C., was born April 22, 1841, in Nash county, N. C., and was one of six children born to William D. and Mary Ellen (Hamilton) Crowell, the other children being: P. J., the eldest, was a dealer in live-stock; he served in the Confederate army, as a member of Capt. Cole's company from Greensboro, and died in Charlotte; he fills an honored soldier's grave; Sally, married W. B. Strickland, and died leaving two children; Mary Ellen, the wife of J. R. Thomas, of Texas, is the twin sister of Jonas W., and they are the only surviving members of the family. The Crowell family has been in this country for many years, and has been intimately identified with its settlement and growth. The connection is directly descended from the Crowell family of England, that family having first settled in Philadelphia, and later removing to Northampton county, Va., they subsequently found a permanent home in Halifax county, N. C. James D. Crowell, the grandfather of our subject, was born in the latter county, and became an extensive planter and slave owner, and also dealt largely in live-stock. He was an ardent democrat, and was prominent in church work. Miss Boshaba Williams, a native of that portion of Edgecombe county, now included in Wilson county, became his wife and bore him five children: Isily, married William Ferrill, of Nash county, and is now deceased; Eveline, married Willis Barbee, and is also deceased; Susan, married Willis Barbee; William and Jonas, the latter having died in Sumter county, Ala. The father died in Wilson county in 1850. Col. Crowell, the brother of James D. Crowell, settled on the Chattahoocha river in Georgia, and for a number of years was Indian agent. William D. was born in Nash county, N. C., in 1812. He was educated in the schools of that section and turned his attention to agriculture. As a loyal southerner he served throughout the Civil war as a member of a Confederate company organized in Nashville. His demise occurred in 1879, his wife having preceded him to rest in 1841.

Jonas W. Crowell was reared in Nash county, and was educated in the schools of the latter and Wilson counties. He learned the tailor's trade and began active life as a clerk. In 1861 he joined Company I, Fifth Alabama regiment, and after a service of two years was transferred to Company I, Thirtieth North Carolina regiment, and was with that command until the close of the war. Although twice offered a commission as an officer, Mr. Crowell declined, the only position he would accept being that of orderly sergeant of his company. At the battle of Seven Pines he was seriously wounded, and for two months thereafter was confined in the hospital. At the battle of Cold Harbor his left thigh was shattered, and as he was totally disabled, a transfer to the commissary department was given him. We find him in the latter position at the surrender of Appomatox. Mr. Crowell fought in the following battles, First Manassas, Seven Pines, Hanover Court House, Gettysburg, both battles of Cold Harbor, Wilderness engagements, Spottsylvania, seven days at Richmond, and Brandy Station. After the close of the war he came to Wilson county and engaged in the mercantile business for one year. For the succeeding few years he conducted a business at Marlboro depot, Pitt county, and for five years was a traveling salesman for Dixon & Brother, of Baltimore, Md. In 1884 he was elected sheriff of Wilson county, and has since retained that office. He served as mayor of Toisnot, and also held the office of justice of the peace. Mr. Crowell is a prominent member of the Masonic fraternity, chapter and commandery, and is also a member of the Knights of Honor and the Royal Arcanum. He is a stockholder in the Wilson tobacco warehouse, and is interested in various different industrial enterprises in the community. As a leading democrat he has rendered efficient service to his party, and is held in the highest esteem wherever known. May 27, 1866, his marriage to Miss Virginia D. Vick, daughter of Col. Asel Vick, of Nash county, N. C., was solemnized, and one child, Elizabeth C. Crowell, has blessed their union. Mr. Crowell is an active and influential communicant of the Methodist Episcopal church, south, and has been a steward of that society for several years.

WILLIAM J. HARRISS,

a prominent merchant of Wilson, N. C., was born in Charlotte county, Va., on the 6th of September, 1839, his parents being John and Rebecca (Dunn) Harriss. The father was a leading planter and slaveholder, and held a high position in the whig party, and was a deacon in the Baptist church. He was born of English parentage, his father having been a native of that country, and a settler of Charlotte county, Va. John Harriss died in 1884. His wife's demise occurred in 1872. She was a daughter of William Benjamin Dunn, a native of Ireland, whence he came to the United States, and took up his residence in Charlotte county, Va. Six children were born to this happy union: Thomas B. joined the Confederate army as a member of an Alabama company, and died in the hospital in Mobile, Ala., in 1862; John D. was aid-de-camp on Gen. Trimball's staff, and served through the entire Civil war, his death occurring in Charlotte county, Va. William J. Harriss was reared in his native county, and was prepared for college in the high schools of that county. In 1859 he went to Henderson, and engaged in a mercantile business, and in 1861 enlisted in a Granville company, and served as adjutant of the Fifty-fourth North Carolina regiment during the Civil war, being with Jackson's and Lee's armies during that time. Mr. Harriss served as a valiant and faithful soldier at Richmond, Gettysburg, Brandy Station, Wilderness, Petersburg, and in several engagements of minor importance. At the evacuation of Petersburg lost his leg. After the close of hostilities, he located at Wilson, and has since conducted a large mercantile establishment there. Mr. Harriss is one of the most successful, able, and public spirited citizens of Wilson county. He was prominent in the organization of the Wilson cotton factory, and for several years was a member of its board of directors, and is a stockholder in the two tobacco warehouses of Wilson, and formerly was interested in the First National bank. He is a Knight Templar, a member of the order of Knights of Honor, and of the Knights of Pythias, and is an ardent democrat. As a true and substantial friend to public education he is greatly interested in all educational matters, and is a director of the Wilson graded school system. Mr. Harriss has been most happy in his domestic relations, he having married Miss Fannie S. Sheppard, a daughter of Thomas Sheppard, of Suffolk, Va., in 1868. Their home has been blessed by the advent of the following named children: William S., Charles T., Annie R., Bessie B., Herbert H., and James B. Mrs. Harriss is an earnest and valued communicant of the Episcopal church, of Wilson.

COL. JOSEPH B. STICKNEY

is among the prominent citizens of Wilson, N. C. Col. Stickney was born in Alabama, in Greene county, March 8, 1827, the son of Joseph B. and Harriet (Grist) Stickney. The father was a native of Massachusetts, and the mother of Beaufort county, N. C. The father was in early life an officer in the United States navy, but retired and settled in Alabama, where he became an extensive planter, his death occurring in that state. The son, Joseph B., was reared in North Carolina from his twelfth year. His scholastic training was received at Bingham's school and at the University of North Carolina. He turned his attention to agriculture, and settled in Pitt county, N. C., where he soon became prominent in public affairs. For several years he served as chairman of the inferior court of Pitt county, and in 1874-5-6-7 represented that county in the state senate, also holding the office of magistrate of the county. As a democrat, he has rendered much service to his party. In 1881 Col. Stickney removed to Wilson, and has since lived in retirement at that place. His marriage to Miss M. A. Satterthwaite, daughter of F. B. Satterthwaite, a prominent attorney of Beaufort county, N. C., in 1857, has resulted in the birth of two children: Annie, wife of Alexander Greene, of Wilson, and F. S. Stickney, of the New York theological seminary. Col. Stickney is a vestryman in the Episcopal church. Harriet (Grist) Stickney was a daughter of Gen. Frederick Grist. He was a distinguished member of the legislature of North Carolina, and died at Raleigh, while representing Beaufort county. His father, Richard Grist, was also a public man of prominence, and served as a member of the legislature, his death occurring at Fayetteville, during his term of office. The maternal grandfather of Col. Stickney was a planter of Beaufort county, and died while in the service of the patriot army of 1812.

CHARLES A. YOUNG,

senior member of the firm of Young Bros., Wilson, N. C., was born in Dinwiddie county, Va., August 9, 1853, and is a son of John T. S. and Mary (Foster) Young, both natives of Dinwiddie county. The father was a leading merchant and planter there, and in 1872 removed to North Carolina, and is now retired from active business. Four sons and four daughters were born to these parents, Charles A.; M. T., of Wilson; W. B., of Fayetteville, E. F., of Dunn, N. C.; Betty, wife of P. C. Seszer, of Wilson; Mirtie, who married C. W. Priddy, of Greenville, N. C.; Nanny, wife of J. T. McCrow, of Wilson, and Rose Young, who resides at home. Charles A. Young educated himself, and in 1876 entered mercantile life as a member of the firm of C. A. Young & Co., merchants at Wilson, N. C. This concern has had a remarkable growth, and now operates stores at Wilson, where both a wholesale and retail business is carried on, and also at Greenville, Fayetteville and Dunn, N. C. Mr. Young took his brother into partnership with him, forming the firm of Young Bros. This house is one of the largest cotton buyers in Wilson, and has one of the largest mercantile trades in the county. Its senior member is a stockholder in the Wilson tobacco warehouse company; is a director and stockholder in the First National bank of Wilson, and is also very extensively interested in agriculture in Halifax county, N. C. He has been active in politics as a democrat, and has served as an alderman and treasurer of Wilson for several years, and is now a member of the Wilson school board. He has been deeply interested in advancing the industries of the town and county, and has done much to enhance the prosperity of the community. In January, 1888, he commenced the manufacture of clothing at Fayetteville, and this venture gives promise of success. Mr. Young has been twice married. Miss Ella Powell, of Halifax county, N. C., became his wife in 1879, and seven years later died, leaving one child, Russel B. In 1891 Mr. Young was united in marriage to Miss Annie Barnes, daughter of Calvin Barnes, of Wilson. Mr. Young is a prominent member of the I. O. O. F. and is an earnest communicant of the Methodist Episcopal church, south.

WILLIE DANIEL.

One of the most public-spirited and progressive agriculturists of Wilson county, N. C., is Willie Daniel, who was born in Wayne county, N. C., on the 20th of March, 1820, his parents being Isaac and Penelope (Barnes) Daniel. Jacob Daniel, the father of Isaac, was also a native of Wayne county, and was a prominent planter and slave owner. He was a son of Isaac and Mollie (Rouse) Daniel. He married a Miss Simms, who bore him four sons and two daughters, all of whom are dead. Isaac, the father of our subject, was the eldest son of that union. He followed in his father's footsteps as a planter and died in 1825 or 1826. His wife was a daughter of John Barnes, who was an influential planter of Wayne county. After the death of her first husband she married James Martin and accompanied him to Alabama, where she died in 1863. The children of her second marriage are Mrs. Theresa Stephens, of Alabama; Mrs. Mary Weed, and Mrs. Martha Canade, both of Alabama. Willie Daniel was the only child of the first marriage. He was reared in his native county, and received but a limited education. In 1844 he embarked in the mercantile business at Black Creek, and in 1850 removed to Wilson, where he became one of the pioneer merchants. He was a member of the firm of Rountree & Daniel at that time, but subsequently engaged in the naval stores business, in which he continued for several years, and also had a concern in South Carolina for some time. Mr. Daniel was ever a staunch friend of the Union, and during the Civil war took no part on either side, though in sympathy with the Federal government. He has done much to advance the industrial growth of Wilson since his settlement there. He has been a director and stockholder in the First National bank, of Wilson, since its organization; and is a stockholder in the Wilson cotton factory, a stockholder and director in the Planters' tobacco warehouse, and is one of the most extensive and successful planters in the county. Formerly he was a republican, but is now an independent in politics. In 1868 he was a delegate to the constitutional convention, and has served as a town commissioner. Mr. Daniel was married in 1847 to Miss Eliza Rountree, daughter of Lewis Rountree, of Edgecombe county, N. C. She died in 1890, after living a useful, Christian life. Mr. Daniel has two children by adoption, Minnie Eliza, wife of Samuel Hodges, of Norfolk, Va.; and Betty, wife of E. F. McDaniel, of Wilson. Mr. Daniel has been a steward in the Methodist Episcopal church, south, for many years, and has been a trustee of the Wilson female seminary.

BAILEY PEYTON WILLIAMSON

was born in Mecklenburg county, Va., on May 19, 1838, and received his education in Samuel Davie's institute, in Halifax county, Va. Leaving school in 1858 when at the age of twenty years, he was appointed agent of the Roanoke Valley railroad at Clarksville, Va., and remained in that capacity about a year, when he was engaged as a drummer for a Baltimore dry-goods house. He was traveling on the road for this firm when the war broke out. Being an ardent southerner, he left Baltimore on the day of the riot there, when the mob stoned the Massachusetts troops as they passed through the city, and he returned to his home in Virginia. In April, 1861, he enlisted as a private in Col. Thomas F. Goode's cavalry company, which was afterward assigned to a regiment of Virginia state troops, of which I. B. Hood, afterward Gen. Hood, was then the major. Mr. Williamson remained in that regiment during the summer of 1861, and was then commissioned as first lieutenant of an infantry company organized at

his home, which was afterward assigned to the Twentieth North Carolina battalion, commanded by Col. Wharton J.   , which battalion was attached to Wise's legion. Mr. Williamson was captured
at Roanoke Island in 1862, in February, by Burnside's command, and
paroled soon after. While on parole, in August, 1862, he was married to Belle Williamson, daughter of George Williamson, of Caswell
county, N. C., and to them were born four children, as follows: Benjamin Robert; Nellie, wife of J. S. Price, of Houston, Tex.; Frank
Potts Williamson and Bailey Finley Williamson. After his parole
and exchange, Mr. Williamson engaged in the manufacture of
ordnance supplies and agricultural equipments, and carried on this
business until the close of the war.

In 1865, with Dr. W. J. Hawkins, J. M. Heck and Kemp P. Battle,
Mr. Williamson engaged in the wholesale and retail grocery and
commission business in Raleigh, N. C., under the firm name of B. P.
Williamson & Co. These gentlemen continued their co-partnership
about a year, and then dissolved by mutual consent. After that Mr.
Williamson, Dr. Hawkins, C. M. Hawkins and Capt. J. J. Thomas
carried on the business, with a branch house in Baltimore, Md., under
the name of Hawkins, Williamson & Co., until 1872, when the firm
dissolved. Soon thereafter, together with Capt. J. J. Thomas and
W. G. Upchurch, Mr. Williamson went into the grocery and commission business in Raleigh, N. C., on a large scale, and this partnership
continued for four years, when Capt. Thomas retired. Since then
Mr. Williamson and W. G. Upchurch have carried on the business
under the name of Williamson & Upchurch. Mr. Williamson is also
a large and well known farmer in North Carolina, holding extensive
and valuable landed interests, owning 2,700 acres of land in Wake
and Johnston counties. He is also extensively engaged in the breeding of standard-bred trotting horses at his farm, so well known as
Fairview farm, situated near Raleigh, N. C.

Mr. Williamson's first wife died in 1875 and in 1877 he was married to Laura S. Williams, daughter of John R. Williams, of Raleigh,
N. C., she died the following year without issue. In 1879 he was
married to Ella S. Mial, daughter of A. T. Mial, of Wake county,
N. C., and to them were born six children, of whom three survive, as
follows: Mial Williamson, Herbert Williamson and Rosalind Williamson. In 1888, Mr. Williamson was elected a member of the board
of county commissioners of Wake county, of which he became chairman, and was re-elected in 1890, again being the chairman of the
board, but in March, 1891, he retired from the board. During his
term he rendered great service to county affairs, especially in the
matter of road making and similar improvements. Mr. Williamson's
father, James Williamson, was born in Mecklenburg county Va., in
1801. His life of sixty-five years was spent as a farmer and stock
breeder. He was highly esteemed in his community and served
many years as magistrate in his native county. He married Sarah
Pool, and to them were born eleven children, of whom three survive,
as follows: Caroline B., widow of Maj. J. J. Thomas, of Franklinton,

N. C., Marstella A., widow of B. D. Paylor, of Leesburg, N. C., and Bailey Peyton Williamson. Mr. Williamson's mother died in 1864. Mr. Williamson's grandfather, Robert Williamson, was also a native of Mecklenburg county Va. He was a farmer and possessed a considerable landed interest and was universally respected in his community.

JAMES J. THOMAS

was born in Franklin county, N. C., July 19, 1831. He received his education in the schools of Oxford and Louisburg, N. C., and after pursuing his studies for some years with much zeal, at the age of nineteen, he, of his own account and desire, selected the mercantile business as a profession, entering the store of R. & R. H. Kingsbury, in Oxford, N. C., with whom he remained for two years, going from Oxford to Clarksville, Va., he was employed by Capt. Robert Y. Overby, being in charge of his books at his store at White House, Va., and charge of his tobacco and banking business in Clarksville, Va. Having served in this capacity for about four years, and desiring to enter a larger field of business, being highly recommended by his former employer, Capt. Overby, he secured a situation with Willingham & Ellett, of Richmond, Va., wholesale dealers in notions and dry goods. After remaining with them two years, he returned to his native state and entered the store of W. H. & R. S. Tucker, of Raleigh, N. C., as bookkeeper and confidential clerk. Mr. Thomas having acquired a pretty thorough knowledge of business, determined to start out on his own account, and embarked in the mercantile business at Franklinton, N. C.; there he remained until the war between the north and the south broke out, when soon after hostilities were declared he volunteered and enlisted in Company F, Forty-seventh North Carolina infantry, and was commissioned first lieutenant of that company by Gov. H. T. Clark. Later during the same year, he was promoted to quartermaster of the regiment commanded by Col. Sion H. Rogers.

When the office of regimental quartermaster was abolished by act of the Confederate congress, Maj. Thomas, on the recommendation of Gen. R. E. Lee, was appointed by the secretary of war assistant division quartermaster, and assigned to Gen. Harry Heth's division, A. P. Hill's corps, army of northern Virginia. Owing to the frequent absence of Maj. Vick of Heth's division, Maj. Thomas acted and assumed the duties of division quartermaster, which position he held until the surrender at Appomatox Court House, in April, 1865, in addition to many skirmishes and minor engagements Maj. Thomas was at the battle of Drury's Bluff, and in the fights around Richmond. He was in and at the battle of Gettysburg, and after three days' fight upon the return of Lee's army, he was, with many other Confederate soldiers, captured at Greencastle, Penn., by the Federal cavalry, but was rescued and recaptured by Gen. Imboden's flying artillery before the day expired, rejoining his division. When peace was declared

Maj. Thomas returned to his home, and for several months was employed in the mercantile business. Finding it difficult to do much business under the almost impoverished condition of our people generally, he, in connection with Dr. W. J. Hawkins, B. P. Williamson and C. M. Hawkins, of Raleigh, N. C., opened a cotton and commission business in the city of Baltimore, Md., which was actively and successfully pursued until 1872, when Maj. Thomas returned to Raleigh, N. C., and together with B. P. Williamson and W. G. Upchurch, entered into the grocery, cotton and commission business, under the name of Williamson, Upchurch & Thomas.

In 1876, Maj. Thomas retired from the firm and established a thriving business on his own account, which he is still carrying on largely and successfully. He was the first president of the Raleigh cotton and grocery exchange, served several years in that capacity, using his large means as well as his talent and energy in building up the cotton business of Raleigh, which has amounted to as much as 74,000 bales a year. He was one of the promoters and first president of the Raleigh Savings bank, which position he held for about a year or more, until his private business grew such as to demand his entire time. He was president of the Oak city mills until its property was sold to a fertilizer company. Maj. Thomas is president of the Raleigh cotton mills which are now in successful operation, employing seventy-five to 100 hands and turning out about one million pounds yarns a year. He has been recently elected a director and vice-president of the Caraleigh cotton mills and president of the Caraleigh phosphate and fertilizer works; these two industries are now in process of construction, and they will employ a large number of hands and a capital of nearly $200,000. Upon the organization of the Commercial & Farmers' bank, of Raleigh, N. C., with a paid up capital of $100,000, he was elected its president, in which capacity he is now acting.

Maj. Thomas is a thorough democrat of the Jeffersonian school, but though always contributing liberally his support to the cause, has never taken any active steps in politics. His religious tendencies are those of a Baptist. He has been married three times. First, in 1860, Victoria, daughter of Xenophon Halbert, of South Carolina, and to them were born five children, of whom two survive: Lottie, widow of B. T. McAden, and Howard C. Thomas. He lost his first wife in Baltimore, in 1872, and on January 13, 1875, was married to Eveline Briggs, daughter of Thomas H. Briggs of Raleigh, N. C., and to them were born two children, of whom, one, Evie, now survives. His second wife died in February, 1879, and he was next married in September, 1880, to Lula O. Felt, daughter of Eli Felt, of Warrenton, N. C., and to them was born one child: James J. Thomas, Jr. The father of Maj. Thomas, James J. Thomas, was born in Alabama in 1806, and settled in Franklin county about the year 1825. He was a farmer and served as engrossing clerk in the legislature of North Carolina for several sessions. In 1829 he married Charlotte E. Howze, and to them were born four children, of whom two survive:

James J. Thomas and Mrs. Sarah L. Harriss. Maj. Thomas's mother died in 1843, but his father survived until 1874. His grandfather was of English descent as was also his grandmother.

MAJ. RUFUS SYLVESTER TUCKER,

the most energetic and influential and wealthy citizen of Raleigh, N. C., was the third son Ruffin Tucker, a merchant of Raleigh, where he was born, April 5, 1829. He was prepared for college at the celebrated Lovejoy academy, and in 1844 entered the University of North Carolina, where he graduated, in 1848. Among those at the university with him were Gen. Johnston Pettigrew, Senator Mat. W. Ransom, Judge Victor C. Barringer, Seaton Gales and others, subsequently distinguished in their various professions. On leaving the university, Maj. Tucker entered the store of his father, as a clerk, and remained with him until his death, in 1851, when the three sons of Mr. Ruffin Tucker succeeded to the business. Maj. Tucker soon established a fine reputation for sound judgment, and as a practical manager; and on the breaking out of the war, Gov. Ellis appointed him quartermaster and commissary for the post of Raleigh, where all the North Carolina companies as formed were concentrated and organized into regiments before being sent to the front. The duties of the position were thus onerous and exacting. In the latter part of 1861, however, he resigned that commission, and having raised an independent company of cavalry, he was commissioned captain of it, and later joined the Third regiment of North Carolina cavalry, and served in eastern Carolina. He served chiefly near Newbern and Washington until the fall of 1862, when he was commissioned major, and assigned to the staff of Adjt.-Gen. Fowle, and later to that of Gen. Richard Gatling. In the following year he was elected chief clerk of the house of commons, and satisfactorily performed the duties of that position. After the war he devoted himself closely to the firm business of W. H. & R. S. Tucker. His brother, William H. Tucker, was a man of large business experience in the mercantile line, and was considered one of the best judges of goods of any merchant of the south, and he was the head of the firm, being the elder; and having moved, in 1866, into a commodious and splendid new store, enlarged the establishment, until it had no equal in the state. Here he and his brother, William, found an ample field for their respective talents. They sold goods at one price and a fair profit, and their stock was complete in all departments. Their establishment was always crowded with customers, and they made a great deal of money. Their success was due in great part to the skill, enterprise and industry of Maj. Tucker, as well as his brother. For many years, embracing the period of the war, Maj. Tucker was a director in the North Carolina railroad company, and later he became a director in the Raleigh & Gaston railroad, and is now a director in the Seaboard Air Line system, a corporation in which he has considerable interest as a stockholder; and he is also interested in the

Atlantic & North Carolina railroad, he being the largest private stockholder in that company. He was for many years a competent and faithful director in the Raleigh National bank, and his connection with that bank was greatly to its advantage; but becoming largely interested in the National bank of Newbern, he resigned his position in the Raleigh bank, and more recently he has disposed of his interest at Newbern.

Maj. Tucker for thirty-one years has been a director of the institution for the deaf, dumb and blind, at Raleigh, and for many years its president. In this position his judgment and business qualities have had a fair field to exhibit themselves, and no institution in the United States has probably been better managed than this. The service he has rendered the state by his continued connection with this institution, and to the hundreds and thousands of unfortunate children whose condition has been ameliorated through this state charity, is inestimable. In addition to these duties Major Tucker, who is a member of the Episcopal church, has for about twenty years been an active member of Christ church vestry, at Raleigh.

Besides being the largest owner of city property in Raleigh, he has landed interests in Wake as well as other counties in the state, and in late years has been occupied with his extensive farm in the vicinity of Raleigh, which was originally very poor land, known as Old Camp Mangum; by a system of fine cultivation, he has brought up to a high state of fertility and productiveness. He rejoices as much in his success at making more than a bale of cotton to the acre, in his fine hay, and beautiful herd of Jerseys and Oxforddown sheep as in any of his other operations. Entering into business at an early age, he contracted business habits thoroughly, and but few men so systematically arrange their work as to accomplish as much as he does in a day. His assiduity, intelligence and sound judgment have brought him successes in all his undertakings, and he attributes his good fortune largely to his having followed the motto that a thing worth doing at all is worth doing well. He does everything thoroughly, and finishes the matter entirely before leaving it. Thus he is enabled to do an immense amount of work with less worry than it would occasion other men.

Maj. Tucker having made a large fortune, has been for years one of the most enterprising men in Raleigh. He seeks to promote the interest of the city by advocating all improvements that will tend to its advantage. He was active in forming the chamber of commerce and industry, an association of all the business men of the place, having for its object the encouragement of new enterprises, and he was, in 1887, chosen the first president of the chamber, and then declined a re-election, thinking it best to change chief officers each year. His reports while president admirably show what the chamber had accomplished for the prosperity of Raleigh, and the record reflects credit on Maj. Tucker and his associates. Maj. Tucker, after the death of his brother William, retired from active business, and has devoted himself chiefly to caring for his large estate, but as he has long been esteemed as the foremost of Raleigh's business men, he is more or less engaged in all the new industries started. Yet he finds time to travel in the various sections of the Union, and he entertains at his beautiful villa with a liberal hospitality.

Maj. Tucker married early in life Miss Florence E. Perkins, daughter of Churchill Perkins, Esq., of Pactolus, Pitt county, N. C., who for many years was a representative of Pitt county, both in the senate and house of commons of North Carolina, and who was one of the largest planters in the eastern section of the state, and who besides was largely engaged in the turpentine industry in North and South Carolina and Florida. To them were born a number of children, of whom six survive: Margaret Perkins, the wife of James Boylan, of the firm of W. H. & R. S. Tucker & Co.; Florence Perkins, wife of John H. Winder, superintendent of the Seaboard & Roanoke R. R. Co.; William Ruffin Tucker, secretary and treasurer of the Graystone Granite & Construction company, and railroad contractor, who married Miss Gertrude Winder, a daughter of Major John C. Winder, general manager of the Seaboard Air Line R. R. system; Bessie Boylan Tucker, Sarah Sanders Tucker and Minnie Fitch Tucker. Lula Sledge Tucker, one of the loveliest of her sex, married Dr. N. O. Harris, of Atlanta, Ga., but died April 23, 1886. No more charming and attractive household has ever added to the pleasures of Raleigh than that presided over so happily and graciously by Mrs. Tucker.

Major Tucker's father, Ruffin Tucker, was born in Wake county in 1795. He entered into mercantile business at Raleigh with his brother, W. C. Tucker in 1818, and in 1828 began on his own account, laying the foundation of the house which has since become so famous in the dry goods line in North Carolina. He married Lucinda Marshall Sledge, a daughter of Joel Sledge, of Franklin county, N. C., and had by her three sons: William H. H. Tucker, who died in 1882; Dr. Joseph J. W. Tucker, who died in 1856, and Rufus S. Tucker, the subject of this sketch, Mr. Ruffin Tucker died in 1851, and his widow survived him until 1867. In 1846 Mr. Ruffin Tucker associated his son, William, in his business, under the firm name of R. Tucker & Son, and the firm continued until his death in 1851, when the three brothers carried on the business under the style of W. H. & R. S. Tucker, Dr. Tucker being a silent partner. After the war, in connection with his brother, William, Maj. R. S. Tucker projected and erected Tucker hall, the first public hall ever built in Raleigh, and for years it was the only place where amusements or entertainments could be held or addresses be delivered. It is now a part of the magnificent establishment of W. H. & R. S. Tucker & Co., now conducted by young men educated to the business by the former proprietors and to these young men he gave aid on retiring. When the building was first opened it was conceded to be one of the finest in the entire south; and thither the business of the firm was at once removed and from across the street, the former place of business of R. S. Tucker, and a great impetus was imparted to its prosperity. Each year saw it increase in volume and value, until at length, in 1882, Col. William H. H. Tucker died, and in 1883 Maj. Tucker retired from the business, which, under the name of W. H. & R. S. Tucker & Co., has since been continued by his son-in-law, Mr. James Boylan and his associates. The firm name perpetuating the business connection of Maj. Tucker with the active business interests of Raleigh will be an enduring monument to the business capacity of Raleigh's most enterising merchant, who, although retired, still exerts a strong influence on whatever will promote the advantage or redound to the interests of his native city.

WYNDHAM E. GARY,

a leading citizen of Henderson, N. C., was born in Manchester, Va., April 30, 1848, and received his schooling at Richmond, Va., where he remained until 1864. In the latter year he entered the Confederate service as a member of Company F, First Virginia militia, and was stationed at Fort Gilmer, near Richmond. In February, 1865, he returned to the capital of the south and remained there until its evacuation, after which he removed to Petersburg, remaining in the latter city until March, 1867. At this time Mr. Gary entered a business college in Richmond as a student, and after being duly graduated, accepted a position as bookkeeper for Gary Brothers (his uncle and father comprising the firm) in Manchester, and until 1879, was connected with them in the tobacco business; he then came to Henderson, N. C., and embarked in the tobacco business, having formed a partnership with his father, Mr. P. H. Gary. Mr. Gary was married in 1872 to Miss Kate Wells, daughter of A. B. Wells, of Richmond, Va., and nine children have blessed the union, named: Alexander, Eugene, Curtis, George, Meredith, Isabella, Charles, Kate and Mariel. Mr. Gary is a prominent member of the Masonic fraternity, and is recognized as one of the most substantial and prominent business men of Henderson.

Patrick H. Gary, father of the above, is a native of Prince George county, Va., where he was born in 1818. In 1841 he married Miss Isabella Muse, daughter of Meredith Muse, a Virginian, and to them six children were born, viz.: Cornelia A., widow of Robert H. Leonard; Sarah E., widow of W. P. Buell; Wyndham E., Irvin B., George E. and Mattie Gary, wife of Hilary Duval. The grandfather on the paternal side was Richard Gary, a native of Virginia. As a soldier in the war of 1812, he served with valor and distinction. He was a planter all his life, and left a name honored and esteemed. Wyndham E. Gary, our subject, has done much toward increasing the great tobacco industry of North Carolina. From 1884 to 1891 he was of the Henderson board of trade, and has served four years as a member of the city council.

J. C. McCASKILL,

who for many years was one of the most prominent and influential business men of Robeson county, N. C., now retired, first saw the light in Cumberland county, N. C., April 18, 1832, his parents being, Daniel and Mary (Campbell) McCaskill. Daniel was a native of Scotland, while his wife was born in North Carolina. At the age of about twenty years Mr. McCaskill sought a broader field for his labors and emigrated to America. He settled in Cumberland county, N. C., and remained there until his death in 1880; both himself and wife lived to the advanced age of ninety years, the latter having died about three months after his demise. He was a successful planter, and a man of much intelligence and native refinement. The father and mother were life-long members of the Presbyterian church. Two sons and two daughters are living of the seven children born to them. Three of the sons fought in the Confederate service, Neill having enlisted in South Carolina in 1861. He served in the army of northern Virginia, and fought as a faithful and valient soldier in several battles. He was one of the heroes who charged at Reams station, and since that time has never been heard from. He fills an honored soldier's grave. The youngest son was Daniel, who enlisted in the southern army in 1861, having fought in Col. Hokes' brigade, of the army of northern Virginia. After participating in many noted battles, he was mortally wounded at Gettysburg, and died three days later. He was twenty-nine years of age at the time of his death, and like his brother died loving the cause he espoused. The second son is Roderick McCaskill, now a prominent citizen of Laurinburg. Sarah, married Mr. Angus McDonald, and until after the death of her parents and husband she resided at Laurinburg. Mary died at the age of forty-two years. Nancy is a resident of Laurinburg.

J. C. McCaskill received a general education in different private schools in Cumberland county, and at the age of twenty-two began his business career in the turpentine business, to which he added agriculture. He was thus engaged in 1861, when he enlisted in the First North Carolina battalion, in the company commanded by Capt. McRae, and served in the army until the fall of Fort Fisher and Wilmington, when he entered the military telegraph service, later serving in Gen. Lee's army, and he surrendered with the great chieftain's forces at Appomatox. After the war Mr. McCaskill resumed turpentine distilling, but a few years subsequent turned his attention to the mercantile business, which he followed for twenty years with much success. In 1887 he disposed of his business interests, and since has been actively engaged in farming. His marriage to Miss Maggie McClaurin, of South Carolina, December 24, 1867, was most happy. Two years later, on the 9th of August, she was called to rest. She was an active and earnest member of the Presbyterian church, and a lady of most estimable qualities. Her demise occurred in her twenty-fourth year. Mr. McCaskill was married a second time May 17, 1877, when Miss Mary C. McLean became his wife. She was the daughter of Mr. John F. McLean, of Robeson county, N. C. Three children, now living, have been born to this union, viz.: Mary Campbell, John C. and Sarah Amanda. Both Mr. and Mrs. McCaskill are communicants of the Presbyterian church, in which he is an elder, and he is also prominently identified with the Masonic order.

JOHN T. POPE.

The oldest living resident of Lumberton, N. C., is John T. Pope, a retired merchant, who was born in Robeson county, N. C., December 25, 1821. His parents were Hardy and Charity (Pitman) Pope, both of whom were born in North Carolina. Hardy Pope was a merchant, and subsequently a planter. For many years he held the office of magistrate. He served as a soldier in the war 1812, being stationed much of the time at Fort Johnston, in the office of the adjutant of the regiment. His death occurred in 1854, when he was sixty-seven years old. His wife died at the age of forty-nine years, in 1848. She was known far and near for her charity and kindly offices to the offices to the sick and afflicted. Of the nine children born to them, four are now living. Henry Pope, the father of Hardy, moved to Robeson county, N. C., prior to the Revolution, and settled four and a half miles south of Lumberton. He fought as a patriot soldier in the Revolution, and was a man of exceeding prominence in the community, and at the time of his death was the wealthiest man in the county. His wife, Delilah, was a daughter of Samuel Williams, of Halifax, N. C., where Henry Pope married her before his removal to Robeson county. His son, Willis Pope, was one of the most eminent physicians in Robeson county. Mr. John T. Pope began business for himself at the age of twenty-six, having held a clerkship for some years before. In 1847 he established a mercantile house in Lumberton, and conducted that without intermission until his final retirement from business life. During the Civil war he was detailed by the war department as tax-collector. He has held the offices of county commissioner, register of deeds, and for several years was a magistrate. In 1841 Mr. Pope married Miss Caroline Council, daughter of Elizabeth Council. Florence, wife of John A. McAllister, of whom mention is made in another place in this work; and Willis H., are the children that have been born to this happy union. Willis H. Pope enlisted in 1861, before his seventeenth year, in the First regiment, North Carolina volunteers, under Col. D. H. Hill, and served in the battles of Bethel, Roanoke Island, siege of Charleston, battles around Petersburg, Richmond, Newbern, Goldsboro, and others, and was shot and killed at Drury's Bluff while charging the breastworks, June 17, 1864. He held the rank of captain of Company E, Fifty-first North Carolina regiment infantry. At the time of his death he was but twenty years old, but through it all he bore himself as a true patriot and soldier, and died with the

B—33

interests of his people at heart. He now fills a soldier's honored grave, than which no greater praise can be given him. Mrs. Pope is a devout member of the Methodist Episcopal church, south.

CAPT. DAVID REID MURCHISON.

In order that future generations should have a correct idea of the life and character of those men who were leaders in business circles and founders of many institutions, the benefit of which they will enjoy in years to come, we have selected for the subject of this mention Capt. David Reid Murchison (deceased). He was born in this state, in Cumberland county, on December 5, 1837, and was the youngest son of Duncan Murchison, who was a man prominent in business circles prior to the war of 1861, having been engaged in the manufacture of cotton goods in the western part of the state and also largely interested in planting. His father was by birth a Scotchman, but became a citizen of the United States about the year 1760 or 1770. Duncan was twice married and was the father of a large family. Three sons were born to his first marriage. The eldest, John R. gave up his life in defense of the cause of the Confederacy. He enlisted early in the war in the Eighth regiment of North Carolina infantry, and by deeds of valor rose to the rank of colonel of his regiment; he was killed at the battle of Cold Harbor, June 6, 1864. The next son, Kenneth M., was born February 18, 1831, and was educated at the University of North Carolina, graduating in 1853. He spent his early life in the vicinity of his home near Fayetteville, and was engaged in business pursuits until the breaking out of the war in 1861, when he joined the Eighth North Carolina infantry, as second lieutenant of a company, and served as such during the early part of the war. This regiment was captured by the Federal forces at Roanoke island, but fortunately he was not with it at the time. After that affair, he returned to Cumberland county, raised a company and enlisted as captain in the Fifty-fourth North Carolina regiment. With this regiment he saw a great deal of active duty in the Virginia campaign and participated in many hard-fought battles. His many gallant acts won for him the love of his regiment and the respect of his superior officers, and he rose rapidly in rank and early became colonel of his regiment. He was taken prisoner of war in 1863 and was held as such until July, 1865.

Prior to the war he was engaged in business in New York with a Mr. Bowman, under the firm name of Bowman & Murchison, but on the secession of his native state from the Union, he disposed of his business in the north, returned home and offered his services in her defense. After the close of hostilities, in 1865, he returned to New York and formed the firm of Murchison & Murry, which also carried on a large business in Wilmington, N. C. That firm existed but a short time, was dissolved in June, 1866, but was succeeded by the firm of Murchison & Co., consisting of David R. Murchison and George W. and John D. Williams, of Wilmington and Fayetteville. The new firm conducted an extensive business, operating three houses, the one in New York being managed by Mr. Murchison. The house at Wilmington was known as Williams & Murchison, and the one at Fayetteville as J. D. Williams & Co., and were conducted by the partners. This extensive business he still controls. Col. Murchison has resided in New York the greater part of his time since the war, but still spends the winter seasons in North Carolina. He has taken an active interest in the city of Wilmington, being largely interested in her, and has lately erected a large hotel (The Orton House) which is a model for beauty and convenience. He is also the owner of the Orton rice plantations, embracing a large body of land near the city of Wilmington, which is one of the most historic spots in North Carolina, having been the site upon which the first St. Philip's church was erected by our forefathers. This has been improved to such an extent until to-day it is one of the most beautiful spots in North Carolina, and is a typical southern home.

The next son, the subject of this mention, received his education at the University of Virginia, after which he spent his early life at his home, near Fayetteville. His first business venture was in 1860, when he became a member of the firm of Eli Murry & Co., doing a general commission business. He continued as a member of that firm until 1861, when he enlisted in the Seventh North Carolina regiment, of the Confederate army. He remained with that command one year, when, on account of failing health, he was transferred to the Fifty-fourth North Carolina infantry, and assigned to duty. He was soon selected by Mr. Davis as inspector-general of the commissary department for North Carolina, having been appointed to fill those positions on account of his executive ability. He continued to serve in that capacity until the close of the war, after which he connected himself with his brother, Col. K. M. Murchison, and Messrs. G. W. & J. D. Williams. He proved himself to be a business man of much tact and ability, and the great success of the firm was due largely to his energy and foresight. In 1880 he was appointed receiver of the Carolina Central railroad, and soon caused a flurry in business circles by purchasing the entire road. It was predicted by many of his friends that it would result disastrously to him, but in that Capt. Murchison proved himself to be a financier of greater ability than even his most intimate friends supposed. He conducted the affairs of the road successfully for a time, until his rapidly failing health caused him to dispose of his business interests, which he did, to Mr. Robinson, of Baltimore, Md. From that time until his death, on February 22, 1882, he was unable to attend to business, and vainly sought to recover health by means of travel. His death occurred in New York city, while there receiving treatment, and his remains were brought to Wilmington, where they were interred. Mr. Murchison was married Juue 11, 1872, to Miss Lucy Wright, daughter of J. G. Wright, an eminent lawyer. His wife and one child, a daughter, survive him. Capt. Murchison never took any active part in politics, and never sought public honors. He, however, took an active interest in all that tended toward the advancement of the city, and aided it by all the means at his command. By his death, Wilmington lost one of her brightest financiers, and the state a most loyal citizen.

JOHN H. CURRIE, Jr.,

member of the firm of Woody & Currie, commission merchants of Wilmington, N. C., was born in Moore county in 1840. He is the son of John M. Currie, also a native of this state. He, in turn, was the son of Malcom Currie, a native of Scotland, who came to the United States about the close of the Revolutionary war, and settled in Moore county, N. C., where he followed farming until his death. John M., his son, also pursued that calling until his death. He married Mary, daughter of John Black, by whom he was the father of three sons. Our subject received his education in the schools of Moore and Cumberland counties. Removing from Moore to Cumberland with his parents he remained with them until 1861, when he enlisted in the First North Carolina (Bethel) regiment, and served out six months, the time the regiment was enlisted for. He then returned home and re-enlisted in 1862 in Company A, Fifth North Carolina cavalry, raised by Rev. James McNeill, of New York, and served with that command until the close of the war in 1865. He was wounded before Petersburg, and again at the battle of Five Forks, the 31st of March, 1685, being shot through the thigh.

After the close of the war he engaged in business near Fayetteville, distilling turpentine, continuing the same until 1875, when he came to Wilmington, and soon formed a co-partnership with Mr. John D. Woody, under the firm name of Woody & Currie, which was dissolved the 19th of September, 1891, by mutual consent, and on the same day a new co-partnership was formed with J. H. Currie and Duncan McEachem as partners, under the firm name of Currie & McEachem. Mr. McEachem was the confidential clerk of Woody & Currie for many years. Mr. Currie is president of the Cape Fear & People's steam boat company, being elected to that office in 1885. He was twice elected president of the Wilmington produce exchange, the leading commercial body in the city. He is a member of the Presbyterian church, and also holds the office of deacon in that church. Mr. Currie was married in 1881 to Miss Lucy Murphy Jackson, a granddaughter of Gov. Worth, of North Carolina. This union has been blessed with four sons and one daughter. He was elected in 1870 to represent Cumberland county in the state legislature, in which he served very acceptably to his constituents during the long memorable sessions of 1870–71 and 1871-2. He has been very successful in business, and is a man of fine presence and graceful manners. He has taken quite an active part in politics, and is a very forcible and effective speaker.

GEORGE READ FRENCH, Sr.,

founder of the house of George R. French & Sons, was born in Troy, now Fall River, Mass., on the 24th of January, 1802. He is a descendant of Ephraim French, a native of England who came to the United States about 1680 and located in Raynham, Mass. One of the descendants of Ephraim French married Elizabeth Presbry in 1775. He had two sons, Ephraim and Enoch, the latter being the father of our subject and born in 1779. He, Enoch French, located in Troy, now Fall River, Mass., and married Sarah Read in 1799 who bore him eight sons and two daughters, our subject being the second son. He began work when young in the shoe factories of his native city, and advanced so rapidly that at the age of seventeen he was made manager of one of the leading factories of Onysville (now a part of Providence, R. I.). That position, however, he held but a short time when his health failed and he was compelled to resign. He soon after accepted a position with the firm of Perry Davis, of Darien, Ga., formerly of Providence, and later the founder of Perry Davis' Pain Killer. Mr. French remained in Georgia about ten months, when returned to his northern home. In the autumn of 1822, he again started south and located in the city of Wilmington, N. C. Here he soon formed a partnership with John Hathaway, under the firm name of Hathaway & French, and carried on a lumber and general merchandise business. He remained in that firm until 1828, when he opened a shoe store in his own name, and then laid the foundation for the immense business that subsequently grew from it. He was married to Sarah C. Weeks, of Wilmington, N. C., on April 5, 1827, and had issue twelve children, five sons and seven daughters, one son and two daughters dying in infancy and youth. His wife died May 19, 1867, and he was next married on August 27, 1872, to Mrs. Sophia M. Sawyer, of Fall River, Mass. There was no issue to this marriage.

Mr. French's business career was an exceptionally bright one. He assumed entire control of his establishment until the breaking out of the war in 1861, and continued an active part in the management until his death in March, 1889, and never, during the many years of financial changes, did he ever allow his commercial paper to go to protest or be dishonored in any way. He was a man of strong character, and where a principle was involved and he felt that he was right, he was unyielding and adhered with great tenacity to his judgment and his conscientious rectitude. With him "one self-approving hour" was of more value than the plaudits and loud huzzas of the multitude, and on this basis all his commercial transactions were conducted: to represent fairly and honestly just what a thing was; to give value received for value taken, so that it became a guarantee to the buyer when his name was placed on goods. Not only in his business life was this trait prominent, but also in his religious character was the same uncompromising spirit in favor of the right and against the wrong, with no swerving for policy or popularity. In politics he he was an adherent to whig principles, as taught by Clay and others. Taught in his early youth to cherish a patriotic adherence to the union his ancestors had aided in establishing, he took a decided stand against the doctrines of secession, and during that great struggle he adhered to his convictions as to the folly of appealing to arms for the settlement of the then existing differences, although his friends and family were of the opposite belief. In his religious belief he was a decided Baptist, and was prominent in all the enterprises of that denomination. During his long residence in Wilmington Mr. French drew to him many warm personal friends, and by his many generous acts, commanded the respect and good will of all who knew him. In his death Wilmington lost one of her brightest business men, and his family a kind and loving father. Before being called to his reward, George Read French erected, by the labor of his own hands, monuments which will ever keep green the memory of his life in the minds of the citizens of his adopted city. He was one of the original subscribers and an ardent supporter in his earlier days of the Wilmington & Weldon railroad, now forming an important link in that great highway of travel, the Atlantic Coast line; was a director in the bank of Cape Fear; director and also president of the Bank of Wilmington; director in the Wilmington Savings bank, also in the Wilmington Gas Light Co.; director and president of the Oakdale cemetery; one of the original subscribers to the Seamen's Friend society, for many years its corresponding secretary, and for many years its president.

George R. French & Sons, dealers in boots and shoes, continue the business established by George R. French, Sr., in 1822, which had been carried on without interruption until the breaking out of hostilities between the north and south in 1861, and which was continued during the struggle as extensively as conditions and circumstances would permit, under the name of George R. French. In the year 1865, the firm name was changed to George R. French & Son, by the admission of William A. French to an interest in the business, and in 1866 the present style of George R. French & Sons, was adopted, two sons, George R., Jr., and James McD. French, having been taken into partnership, and in 1869 the younger brother, Charles E. French, was placed in charge of the retail department. These four continued until 1879, when James retired, and shortly after Charles E. removed to Minneapolis, to engage in the milling business, as a member of the firm of Christian Bros. & Co. The other three still continued to conduct the boot and shoe traffic until the death of the senior George R. French, which occurred March 15, 1889. Since that date to the present time, the surviving members, W. A. and George R. French, have carried on an extensive trade under the old firm name. Thus for the space of sixty-nine years this house has stood in the front rank of the mercantile houses in this state, doing a large and extensive jobbing and retail trade in their line of business, and during this long time have maintained their high character for integrity and honorable dealing. The several heads of this firm have held and now hold positions of trust and honor in local affairs. The firm was influential in the establishment of the present bank of New Hanover, and George R. French, Sr., was one of its board of directors. They have been firm friends and zealous advocates of all matters pertaining to the upbuilding of this city and state, and are largely interested in many of its enterprises. They are large owners in the Wilmington cotton mills, in which corporation William A. French is the president. The firm took an active interest in the establishment of the Wilmington Savings and Trust company, of which George R. French is a director, and also a member of its board of investors. The firm have always been warm friends and supporters of educational and religious institutions and have assisted in their maintenance by donations and in other ways.

⚓ WILLIAM H. McRARY.

No class of men contributes so largely and certainly none so substantially to any community as the thorough-going business men — the men of affairs and dollars — the men who make all the other callings profitable, and give body, strength and tangibility to all the other professions. Such a man was William H. McRary, one of Wilmington's most prominent and trustworthy business men. He was born in Lexington, Davidson county, in the year 1824. His parents, Joseph and Martha (Halgrove) McRary, were both natives of the state. He was educated in the schools of his native city, which in those days, even before the advent of the free school, afforded excellent educational facilities. Our subject was placed under the immediate and personal supervision of Rev. Rankin, a scholarly divine of his day, from which, the biographer infers, that the boy's early moral and intellectual training was of the conventional order of the southern gentleman of the old school, and all that could be desired.

After acquiring such an education as would enable him to meet and successfully combat all the difficulties presenting themselves in the various phases of a mercantile career, Mr. McRary entered a general store as a clerk, and worked in that capacity for a year or two, when he branched out in a general way for himself at Gold Hill, but a short time after he went to Wilmington and engaged in a general brokerage and commission business, which he successfully conducted till within a short time of his death. He was a patriotic and most public spirited citizen, being a director in the First National bank, and the City gas company. Although full of public spirit he took no active part in politics and never presented himself as a candidate for suffrage of his fellow citizens, who at any period of his busy and useful life would have only been too glad to have cast a ballot in his behalf. He was married in 1863 to Miss Wiggins, of Halifax county. No children ever came to them, and his estimable wife still survives him, and she, in honor of the memory of her husband, has not married again. He died in Wilmington in 1882. Mr. McRary was very successful in his business undertakings and during the years of his active business life amassed a large fortune by his prudence, energy and foresight.

COL. ROGER MOORE,

the genial and able manager of the firm of Patterson, Downing & Co., marine merchants and naval warehouse-men, was born near the city of Wilmington, July 19, 1839. He was the son of Roger and Ann Moore, both natives of the old North state. The boy was educated in the common schools of Wilmington. The biographers of this work have had occasion so frequently to revert to the term "common" or "old field" school in this work in an unqualified sense, that it perhaps would be well to give some idea to the uninitiated of the local significance of these terms, before the advent of the free school system in the south. The teacher of such a school was sometimes eccentric, always a bachelor, but never a knave, the unassuming son of some gentleman with quiet habits, without ambition, against whom the current of life had set too strongly for positive aggression in the open field, a man unfitted for the active duties of life by reason of some bodily infirmity, a superannuated and impecunious aristocrat, thoroughly versed in all the essentials of language, classics and the graces of life, always a man of splendid erudition, he was, to his charges, a dancing master, a music teacher, an example of moral excellence and a pedagogue. He could calculate the movements of the heavenly bodies, could recite a Greek ode in the original text, "lands he could measure, terms and titles per sage," could teach his youthful lady charges to bow and bend and courtesy in the stately minuet, or "treat a royal measure with the king," could guide in the chase with the hauteur of a knight of the holy crusade, or brew an after-dinner punch at the cross-road tavern to tempt the nostrils of the deity of high Olympus, so that when we say a man was educated in the common schools, we mean to say that he sat at the feet of a Gamalial, of which the whole school is unhappily extinct.

At the age of fourteen our subject began life as a clerk in a mercantile establishment, and at the early age of twenty years was a partner, the firm being Pittway & Moore. He entered the Confederate army as a private, in 1861, in the Washington light infantry, which became part of the Eighteenth regiment later in the war. In January of that year he formed a company of which he was elected captain. His next promotion was to the rank of major and from that to lieutenant-colonel of the Third cavalry, which office he held with great distinction until the surrender of Lee in 1865. After the war the firm of Pittway & Moore was revived, and existed until 1869. Col. Moore has been a member of the common council, chairman of the county democratic committee, president of the produce exchange and chief of the fire department, in all of which offices he has discharged the duties with conspicuous ability. Col. Moore was married in 1868 to Rebecca S. Smith, who bore him two children, all, mother and children, however, having since died, and a few years later he married again and is the father of nine children, seven of whom are living. Col. Moore, by reason of his great popularity and his known integrity, is one of the most successful merchants of Wilmington and is held in high esteem by all classes.

HENRY CLAY WATSON

was born in Richmond county, N. C., December 4, 1854, his parents being John and Mary (Smith) Watson. The father was a planter, and a leading man in the community. For several years he served as member of the board of county commissioners, and during the war was warden of the county. He was a prominent and active communicant of the Methodist Episcopal church for many years, and died in the faith of his childhood at the age of sixty-seven years; his widow still survives him, and is now seventy-five years of age. Ten children were the issue of this union; John S., the ninth child, served in the Confederate army, and surrendered at Greensboro, N. C., with Johnston's forces. The eighth child is our subject, Henry Clay Watson. Mr. Watson received his scholastic training in Rockingham, and at the age of twenty years entered active business life as a clerk in a dry goods store, where he remained for seven years. In 1881 he engaged in the mercantile business with his brother, Mr. John S. Watson, the firm name being J. S. and H. C. Watson. This connection was dissolved in 1886, when Mr. John Watson retired. August 30, 1883, Miss Jennie C. Ellerbe, daughter of John C. Ellerbe, became his wife, and has borne him two children, viz.: Henry Ellerbe and Mary Elizabeth. Both Mr. and Mrs. Watson are communicants of the Methodist Episcopal church, south, and he is a member of and an officer in the Order of Chosen Friends, and is also a member of the Royal Arcanum. As a business man he is a success, and as a citizen he is progressive and liberal-minded, having the best interests of the community at heart. He is recognized as one of the most substantial and oblest business men of the county. The names of the offspring, in the order of their birth, born to John and Mary Watson, are: William, died in infancy; Anna J.; Elizabeth; John S., married Miss Mollie Smith; Harriet, wife of M. J. Thrower, of Jonesboro, N. C.; Rebecca, wife of William Long, of Rockingham, N. C.; Mary, wife of S. G. Covington, also of Rockingham; Henry Clay; Archie M., married Miss Josie Entwistle, and is a very successful manufacturer of naval stores, and Robert F., who died at the age of thirty years.

GEN. GRIFFITH RUTHERFORD

was one of the most active of the partisan officers in North Carolina. He was an Irishman who had settled west of Salisbury, in Rowan county, and early was associated with the men who were influential in directing public affairs in western Carolina. He was an officer in Gen. Waddell's command in the Tryon army, in the spring of 1771, against the regulators. He was a member of the committee of safety of Rowan county in 1775, and a member of the second provincial congress that assembled April, 1775, and of that held April, 1777. In December, 1775, Col. Rutherford and Col. Polk and Col. Martin marched their militia regiments into South Carolina against the Scovellites, in what is known as the snow camp campaign, and in April, 1776, he was made brigadier-general, and in July he raised 2,400 men in the Salisbury district and crossed the mountains, going down the Pigeon and Tuckasiegie rivers to the Tennessee, where they destroyed the towns of the "Over-hill" Cherokees, and, having severely punished them, he returned to Salisbury, in October. He was elected a member of the senate continuously except when in captivity in 1781, '82, from 1777 to 1786, and when not in the field was rendering service in the senate chamber. In the spring of 1779, he marched with his brigade to the Savannah, where he was with Lincoln, rendering efficient service until the term for which his men had enlisted had expired.

After the fall of Charleston, in May, 1780, Cornwallis pressed on toward North Carolina, and Gen. Rutherford, with 900 men, threw himself near Charlotte, in Tarleton's front. A tory regiment having embodied at Ramsom's Mills (near Lincolnton), he ordered Capt. Locke and others to fall upon it, but learning that the British forces had retired, he himself hurried to aid Locke, arriving after the victory. He then hastened to the forks of the Yadkin and dispersed a tory rising under Col. Sam Bryan, of Wilkes. Early in August he joined Gen. Caswell in the camp at Cheraw Mills, S. C., and on the 16th was engaged with Gen. Gates in the battle of Camden. There he fought with his accustomed bravery, but was taken prisoner, and was sent to Fort Augustine, and there confined by the British. On his exchange, June 22, 1781, he again took the field, and by October had 1,400 men marching to the lower Cape Fear, to keep in check Maj. Craig, who occupied Wilmington and ravaged the surrounding country. He invested Wilmington toward the close of October, and on the 18th of November had the satisfaction of seeing Maj. Craig take his departure by shipping. That was the end of the war in North Carolina. Gen. Rutherford, as we have said, served in the senate until 1786, and soon afterward moved across the mountains to Tennessee, where he rendered distinguished service in civil life, and where he died about the end of the century.

HON. W. I. EVERETT,

one of the most prominent business men of Richmond county, N. C., president of the Great Falls Manufacturing company, is a native of the county, having been born January 3, 1835, the son of C. A. and Ann (Ewing) Everett, both of whom were native of the same county. The father was a planter. He was a man of much force and ability, and led a most useful life. For many years he was a deacon in the Baptist church, while his wife was a devout and consistent communicant of the Methodist Episcopal church. The father died in 1874, aged sixty-seven years, his wife having preceded him to rest in 1872, at the age of sixty-two. W. I. Everett is the second of seven children. His preliminary education was obtained in Rockingham, and later he completed a course in civil engineering at the university of North Carolina. In 1853, at the age of eighteen, he began his business career as a clerk in a mercantile establishment, and after one year turned his attention to photography, which he followed for about the same length of time, when he became a school teacher. As a civil engineer in the employ of W. C. & R. railroad he worked until 1861, and in May of that year enlisted in Company D, Twenty-third regiment North Carolina volunteer infantry, and served until 1863, as an orderly sergeant and member of the engineer corps, and also quartermaster of the Twenty-third North Carolina regiment. In the latter year the war department detailed him to complete the construction of the railroad from Wilmington to Charlotte, and in 1864 he was made roadmaster of that railroad, holding the position until 1866, when he was elected general superintendent and chief engineer. In 1870 he resigned from that office, and for the next two years was engaged in construction as an engineer. At the expiration of that time Mr. Everett embarked in the mercantile business, and since that time has been successfully engaged in operating a large establishment and also in agriculture.

In 1884 Mr. Everett was elected to the state legislature as a senator from the Twenty-sixth senatorial district. and ran ahead of his ticket. From 1878 to 1890 he held the office of county commissioner, and for over ten years was a member of the city council, and for two terms was mayor of Rockingham. His political career has been marked by the same sterling integrity and sagacity as has characterized his private life. As a democrat he firmly believes in the principles of that party, but is not narrow nor bigoted. Progressive and industrious, his abilities have been devoted to the industrial growth of the community in which he lives. In 1887 he was elected president of the Great Falls Manufacturing Co., now one of the most important and successful enterprises of the city; he is also a director in the Pee Dee Manufacturing Co., and the Robert L. Manufacturing Co., being a stockholder in these concerns. As a merchant he has succeeded in building up one of the largest houses of the kind in the county, and is also a partner in the cotton commission house of Everett Brothers, Gibson & Co., of Norfolk, Va. July 15, 1863, Mr. Everett was most happily united in marriage to Miss Fanny H. LeGrand, a daughter of James and Martha LeGrand, of Richmond county, F. C., and nine children have been born to them, the six living being named: William N., married Miss Lena Payne, by whom he has had gone child, William; Minnie L., wife of H. C. Dockery, of Rockingham; Anna, wife of J. P. Little, of Little's Mills, Richmond county, N. C.; James L., John L. and Bessie F. The family are valued members of the Methodist Episcipal church, south, in which Mr. Everett is a trustee and steward; and he is also a member of the

Masonic order, the I. O. O. F., the Chosen Friends, and the K. of H. Mr. Everett's start in life was made most difficult by the want of money. He began with no capital save health and brains, and his success is creditable to him. At this time he is recognized as one of the leading citizens of the state.

JOHN COOPER POE,

deceased, was born in Pittsboro, Chatham county, N. C., in 1826. His parents were Hasten and Nancy (Stedman) Poe, natives of North Carolina. John Cooper Poe was a merchant at Fayetteville, moving there in 1849. He was for years the most prominent merchant in Fayetteville, was enterprising and energetic, and took part in all operations that looked to the general welfare of the community. He was a man of brilliant parts, of fine business qualifications, and was possessed of characteristics which made him a most popular and distinguished citizen. When Fayetteville moved to the front as a business center, he was one of the prime movers to help it up to that eminence. Mr. Poe was the largest dry goods dealer in the town, and served his county as commissioner for several years, looking well to every interest of the county. He was of English descent.g His useful and busy earthly career closed October 22, 1889, at the age of sixty-three years. During the Civil war Mr. Poe lost his property, and at its close he embarked in the plantation or vineyard business; he set out the vineyard known as the Whippoorwill Station, and lived there for two years before his death. The property is now in the hands of his son, E. A. Poe, of Cumberland county. It is a very desirable piece of real estate, located two miles from Fayetteville, on the Cape Fear river and the Yadkin River Valley railroad. Mr. Poe was connected with this railroad, first as conductor, and later as general passenger agent, which position he held until about 1886, after which he lived g retired life.

Mr. Poe was married April 11, 1849, to Miss Margaret McClain, daughter of Hugh and Margaret (Peabody) McClain. Her mother, Margaret Peabody, was first cousin of the celebrated George Peabody, the great London banker and philanthropist. By this marriage there were born sixteen children, nine of whom are still living. Five died in early childhood and eleven came to mature age. Their names were Alice; wife of John B. Harris; Hasten; Margaret, wife of Laban Exline; Nathan S.; Edgar Allen; Hugh Mc.; Annie, Ida and Archie. The mother of this large family died in 1880, aged forty-nine years. She was a life-long and devout member of the Presbyterian church and in her was embodied the truest and purest type of a Christian wife and mother. She exemplified the life and precepts of her Divine Master in her daily walk and conversation. She had her eyes well opened to the opportunities of doing good, to the possibilities of her life, to the joys and hopes of the true Christian and to the fullness of the precious promises of the Holy Word. The father was a member of the Masonic order. Both died in Fayetteville and are sleeping side by side in the Cross Creek cemetery of that city. This Poe family are relatives of the poet, Edgar Allen Poe, and Hasten, the eldest of the sons, seems to have inherited much of the poetic genius of his distinguished kinsman. He has written several poems, which have been published and greatly admired.

HON. D. A. McDONALD.

The present clerk of the superior court of Moore county, N. C., is the Hon. D. A. McDonald. Mr. McDonald was given the best educational advantages at hand, having obtained his preliminary training in the excellent common schools of the county, after which he was graduated from the commercial department of the University of Kentucky, and in 1874 he completed a course in a commercial college. Thus thoroughly equipped, so far as theoretical knowledge is concerned, he spent one year in teaching, and gave the highest satisfaction in that work. His next position was that of county surveyor and day laborer, to which office he was elected by the county commissioners, and afterward by the people. He served as surveyor until 1879, and evinced the same ability and thoroughness as has ever characterized his every act. In the latter year Mr. McDonald embarked in the naval stores business, manufacturing turpentine with Mr. A. McMillan, he purchasing his partner's interest at the end of two years. After one year of successful operation he formed a co-partnership of one year with W. O. Robeson and T. J. Shaw in the mercantile business, then dissolved. From that date until 1886 he was alone, but in the latter years his brother, Mr. Moses C. McDonald, became associated with him, and the firm now exists, being one of the largest in that line in the county. In 1884 Mr. McDonald ran for the sheriff's office, and was defeated by thirty-six votes, but two years later he was elected to his present high position, and at the expiration of the first term his course was vindicated by his re-election. April 20, 1883, he was so fortunate as to form a marriage alliance with Miss Ida A. Martin, daughter of H. H. Martin, of Moore county, and three children have blessed the union, named: Alice G., Kittie M. and Anna L. Both Mr. and Mrs. McDonald are communicants of the Presbyterian church, and Mr. McDonald is an officer in Carthage Presbyterian church, and he is also a member of the I. O. O. F. Mr. McDonald was born in Moore county, N. C., June 13, 1851, the eldest of eight children born to Allen and Mary A. (McIver) McDonald. These parents are both native of North Carolina, and come from old and leading families. Mr. Allen McDonald is an extensive planter, and is an expert agriculturist as well as a prominent citizen. The children of this marriage are: Maggie, wife of Dr. D. A. Curry (Mrs. Curry died in 1879, leaving one child, Victoria); Katie A., wife of G. W. Bruton; Asa, Neill and Owna Ann are their offspring; Euphemia, Mrs. M. A. Monroe, Luna is their offspring; Moses C.; John A., died in 1879, aged twenty-three years; Neill A., a lumber merchant, and Ellen, who is still residing with her parents. At the present writing both parents of Mrs. McDonald are living, and Mr. McDonald's father and mother are also living and well able to do farm and house labor, and are out of debt.

WILLIAM CARSON.

During the first half of the present century, William Carson figured as one of the most successful merchants of Charlotte, N. C. He was a native of Ireland, born in county Antrim in 1782. He received a fair education in his native country, whence he emigrated in 1805, landing in Charleston, S. C., in that year. A year or so later he located in Charlotte, N. C., where he was engaged in merchandising. He had learned the hatter's trade and his first business in Charlotte was manufacturing and dealing in hats, but he soon extended his business to general merchandising, which he successfully followed up to 1842 or '43' covering a period of more than thirty-five years, a period which he would have extended but for failing health, which forced him to retire. For many years prior to this he had also been engaged in farming, in which he took special pride and interest, but which was not his main source of revenue, his income being chiefly derived from his mercantile pursuits. He was a remarkably successful merchant and amassed a handsome fortune, yet setting out in business with little or no capital. His death took place in 1846, when he had arrived at the age of sixty-four years. His resting place is in the old Charlotte cemetery. He was a moral man, temperate in his personal habits, and it may be said further that he was a truly religious man, although he never united with any church. In faith he was a Presbyterian, and to the Presbyterian church of Charlotte he left a bequest, as he also did to Davidson college, and in many other ways he manifested his testamentary beneficence. He was charitable, magnanimous and hospitable to all. In his disposition he was quiet and reserved. Mr. Carson had no aspiration for public office, its honors or emoluments. He was ever highly respected and honored by all who knew him. Mr. Carson was never married, but was ever domestic in his tastes. He cheerfully assumed the responsibility of rearing and educating a nephew, James H. Carson, of whom he took charge when he was only eight years of age, and who had reached the age of sixteen when Mr. Carson died. To Mr. James H. Carson, now a retired citizen of Charlotte, the writer of this sketch is indebted for furnishing, in grateful remembrance of his beloved uncle and foster father, the foregoing facts.

WILLIAM J. DAVIS

is a merchant of Charlotte, whose business reputation is not confined to that city; he is widely known also as a leading merchant throughout the state. He is a Virginian by birth, having been born in Tazewell county, July 5, 1837. His paternal great-grandfather, John Davis, emigrated from Wales more than a century and a quarter ago, and settled in Fairfax county, Va., where he spent the remainder of his days. His son, John Davis, Jr., left his native county and settled on a farm in Tazewell county. He died from the effects of a gun-shot wound received while a soldier in the war of 1812. He was the father of six sons and one daughter. Rees Davis, one of the sons, was the father of William J. Davis, the subject of this sketch. Rees Davis was born and reared in Tazewell county, and married Elizabeth Rice, who is still living and residing in Montgomery county, Ind., where she and her husband removed about the year 1849, and where he died. He always resided upon a farm, but the last forty years of his life were devoted to the ministry of the Baptist church, of which he was a devout and a life-long member. He was an able expounder of the doctrines of his church and was much respected and beloved by his people. William J. Davis was only twelve years of age when his parents removed to Indiana. He was placed in Franklin college, an institution under the patronage of the Baptist denomination, and was graduated in 1858, when twenty years of age. At that age he left the parental home to begin life's struggle for himself. He made a choice of merchandising as a vocation, and began business on a small scale in Montgomery county, Ind., where he remained until 1862.

In his scholastic days he had imbibed the doctrine of the survival of the fittest, and that he who was not thoroughly trained in and adapted to his vocation would finally succumb and become a failure. That he himself might be thoroughly schooled in merchandising, he determined to go to New York city, where he might avail himself of the advantages of learning the intricacies and principles involved in an extensive and complicated system of mercantile trade. Carrying out this determination, he arrived in that gigantic trade emporium in 1862, and was there employed for about a period of twenty-three years, being for part of this time in the employ of C. B. Rouse, an extensive and prosperous dealer in general merchandise—he still recognizing Tazewell county as his home, and at one time spending two years there recuperating his health. His ancestors on both sides were Virginians. Though he spent much of his youth in Indiana, Virginia has always seemed to him as his more cherished home. His sympathy and his loyalty clung to Virginia, his native state, and his fellowship for southern men, and his attachment to southern customs and habits have been of the most cordial nature. It was this disposition of mind which determined him to choose the south as the theatre of his business life and the home of his latter days. Having thoroughly equipped himself for business by a severe and protracted experience in New York, and desiring to set out for himself, Mr. Davis left that city in 1885, and located in Raleigh, N. C., where he at once established himself in a prosperous mercantile trade. Having a chance to sell out advantageously, he remained at Raleigh only six months, whence he removed to Wilmington, where he carried on merchandising for a short time. But the climate there disagreed with him, by which his health became impaired, and he decided to locate in Charlotte. Here, in July, 1886, he fixed himself and opened up the now famous "Racket Store." Here he has built the largest general merchandise business in the city or state. His trade has been increasing in volume from the beginning. The first year in Charlotte his sales aggregated $85,000, and in 1890 his trade ran up to over $250,000. He carries the largest and most complete stock of general merchandise in the state, and is among its most successful merchants.

His wife, who before her marriage was Miss Emma M. Heard, of Ohio, is an equal partner with him in the business, and to her is great credit due as a woman of business talent and energy. She is a close and skillful devotee to business, being in constant attendance at the store, participating in the work, the cares and responsibilities of their immense trade. Both husband and wife are thorough and practical in their business qualifications, and to them the credit is due of establishing what may be looked upon as an ideal mercantile business, which may serve as an example to others throughout the state, and well worthy of general imitation. They furnish employment for a large corps of clerks to whom they pay a generous compensation, for which they exact efficient service. Mr. and Mrs. Davis maintain a high reputation in their social relations, and are as distinguished for their culture and refinement as for their eminent business qualifications.

THOMAS LAFAYETTE SEIGLE.

Thomas L. Seigle was born in Lincoln county, N. C., on the 11th of June, 1832. His father, Daniel Seigle, was a native of Pennsylvania, born in the vicinity of Philadelphia. The latter came to Lincoln county when he was a young man, and here married a Miss Hoover, by whom he had two sons and one daughter. His trade was cabinet-making, which he carried on in connection with farming. His business life was spent wholly in Lincoln county. Here his son, Thomas L., was reared, on the homestead farm; here in the country schools he acquired a fair education, in the meantime availing himself of books and periodical reading, by the means of which he fitted himself for an active business career. Quite early in life he exchanged farming for the mercantile calling. For some time he conducted a store for other parties, in Lincoln county, but afterward became a member of the firm of Templeton & Seigle, and they did a general merchandizing trade at the same place. This business was interrupted by the breaking out of the Civil war, and Mr. Seigle enlisted in the Confederate service, in Light Battery C, of the Tenth North Carolina troops, known as the Charlotte battery, the first guns of which were cast from the bells donated by the churches of Charlotte. This company was under the captaincy of the late Col. T. H. Brem until the summer of 1862, when he resigned, and Capt. Joseph Graham was chosen as his successor. Mr. Seigle was soon promoted

to sergeant and next to first lieutenant, which rank he held till the close of the war. He was a gallant officer, but the assumption of military authority did not in the least quench in him the generous instincts of a noble manhood. He participated in the battle of Newbern and was with the army of northern Virginia in the seven days' fight around Richmond, was at the battles of Bristol Station, Main River, Gettysburg, Spottsylvania Court House and many other hard fought fields. He surrendered at Appomatox with the tattered remnants of the battery, but a few minutes after one of its guns had fired the last cannon shot of the war.

In the midst of the war, in 1862, Mr. Seigle came home on a furlough and was married to Miss H. Lewra Graham, of Iredell county, by whom he had one son, Thaddeus B. Seigle. Mrs. Seigle died and Mr. Seigle married for his second wife, Miss Sarah S. Hendrick, of Salisbury. Soon after his return from the war, Mr. Seigle embarked in the mercantile business, forming a partnership with John C. Hargrave under the firm name of Hargrave & Seigle. Their principal store was at Deep Well and they had branch stores at other places, doing in the aggregate an immense business. In 1878 he came to Charlotte and connected himself with the firm of Brem, Brown & Co., but some time afterward withdrew and became a member of the firm of Alexander, Seigle & Co. Withdrawing also from this firm he set up business by himself in the general dry goods line. Subsequently he associated himself with T. J. Seigle, of Philadelphia, the firm taking the name of T. L. Seigle & Co. But he soon purchased the interest of his partner and for a short time was again alone. Later, W. S. Alexander became a partner with him, but in January, 1888, Mr. Alexander withdrew and Mr. Seigle's son, T. B. Seigle, became associated with him. Mr. Seigle died February 27, 1891, and the son has continued the business established by the firm. As a merchant Mr. Seigle stood in the front rank, not only in the city of Charlotte but in the state at large. His long experience, fine business instincts and faultless taste well fitted him for a successful merchant. Perhaps no other man in the state combined more of the essential qualities that go to constitute a good merchant than were possessed by him. After the war he began business on a very slender capital, but with a credit that was unimpeachable, and he soon won his way to prosperity. Fair, open, honest dealing was his motto and he never resorted to the artifices of trade or speculation by which to further his purposes. He was religiously inclined and embraced the Lutheran faith, in which he was baptized and confirmed in 1856.

Mr. Seigle was for several years a member of St. Mark's Evangelical Lutheran church of Charlotte, and continuously remained a member of the Lutheran church after his confirmation in that church in Lincoln county. The most fitting and lasting monument to his memory is the beautiful structure in which that society worships. To . his good management, liberality and tireless energy is due the construction of that exquisite piece of architecture. It is a triumph of good taste and perfect workmanship in its entire structure and in all

B—34

its adornments. These attributes are distinguishable in the delightful blending of colors in the interior of the edifice, in its handsome furnishing and mosaic windows, the triumphs of his taste and liberality. He was a trustee and director in the Y. M. C. A. building of Charlotte and a member of the association. Though a representative citizen, Mr. Seigle was not ambitious for political preferment. He was best known in the business and mercantile circles where he held high rank. In the church and in his every day pursuits he was a most exemplary citizen and worthy of all imitation.

EDGAR MURCHISON ANDREWS.

Mecklenburg county, N. C., was the birthplace of Edgar M. Andrews, and he was born March 3, 1850. His father was Ezra H. Andrews, a native of the Isle of Wight, in the English Channel, and when he was only three years of age his parents removed with him to Virginia, in which a large grant of land had been awarded his father by King James. His father was Thomas Wills Andrews and subsequent to his settlement in Virginia, after having utilized certain stocks and exhausted certain supplies he brought with him to America, he returned to his native land, purposing to replenish such stocks and supplies, he was taken ill and died on his way home. His wife subsequently lived in South Carolina, in which state she died. When a young man Ezra H. Andrews came from Virginia and settled in Mecklenburg county, N. C., and here married Miss Sarah Ann Bolton, who was born in Philadelphia, Penn., and reared in Mecklenburg county, N. C., where she now resides. Ezra H. Andrews was by profession a surgeon and dentist and for many years followed his profession at Charlotte. He was a gentleman of education and culture and stood high in his social relations. As a scientist he was one of the ablest mineralogists in North Carolina and collected a large and varied cabinet of minerals and other specimens, aggregating over 10,000 pieces. He made an extensive tour through the state and investigated its mineral resources, especially in western North Carolina, in which he collected many valuable specimens. During the Civil war, having property interests in England, his native country, though a child when brought to America, he started on his way to England. Never having taken out naturalization papers, Mr. Andrews fully believed himself to be a British subject and in consequence could leave American ports for England unmolested. On the contrary he was arrested in New York city and in his possession were found certain business letters from parties in Charleston, S. C., and these confirmed the belief in his captors that he was a subject of the Confederate states. He was detained as a prisoner of war first at Washington, D. C., and then at Point Comfort, for twenty-two months, and during that imprisonment he contracted disease, was released and went home to die, his decease occurring shortly after his liberation. He was an active member of the Methodist Episcopal church and of the Free Masons and Odd Fellows' orders.

The boyhood days of Edgar M. Andrews, the immediate subject of this sketch, were mostly spent in Charlotte, the city of his nativity. During the imprisonment of his father the family resided with his uncle, at Union, S. C., and at that place and at Charlotte he acquired a fair English education. When he arrived at the age of fifteen he joined this uncle, who had removed to Brooklyn, N. Y. At the same time his mother removed to Charlotte, where she has since resided. At Brooklyn Mr. Andrews learned the painter's trade, and worked for some time at South Orange, N. J., and then returned to Charlotte, where he continued to work at his trade. He soon began to invest in town lots on which he built tenement houses, and has since dealt more or less in real estate. He is now the owner of several of these houses and lots in the city. In 1881 he quit the painter's trade, and, purchasing a stock of furniture, embarked in this business which has developed into the largest wholesale and retail furniture establishment in North Carolina. Besides his large stock of furniture, he deals largely in pianos and organs. A few years ago he bought out the Charlotte Undertaking company, and has since carried on that business. With his untiring devotion to his business interests and his correct judgment, he has fairly won success, and prosperity has attended all his undertakings. As a citizen he is held in high respect. He is a leading and influential member of the Methodist church, having embraced the faith as taught by that church when he was fifteen years old. In 1882 Mr. Andrews was joined in marriage with Miss Pattie Parker, of Stanley county, N. C., a most estimable and beloved lady. She died in 1889, deeply lamented by all who knew her, leaving to her surviving husband two precious daughters: Grace and Onnie Parker Andrews. Wednesday evening, October 21, 1891, Mr. Andrews was married to Miss Ella, daughter of Mr. and Mrs. B. E. Sergeant, of Greensboro, N. C., an accomplished and highly respected lady.

H. BARUCH.

Throughout a large portion of both North and South 'Carolina the name of H. Baruch is well and most favorably known, and among merchants and business men of Charlotte he holds a conspicuous place, enjoying the respect and esteem of all his fellow-townsmen. He is a native of the kingdom of Prussia, Germany, born November 28, 1844. His parents were Bernard and Theresa Baruch, whose family consisted of four sons and four daughters, all of whom are living at this date. Both parents were natives of Prussia, where they are still living. Bernard Baruch is a lawyer of prominence and a man of wealth and influence. Up to the age of fifteen, H. Baruch, the subject of this sketch, was reared in his native kingdom, where he received a liberal German education. At this point in his life he left the parental home and joined his brother who had preceded him to the United States. This brother is Dr. Simon Baruch, now an eminent physician of New York city. Dr. Baruch received a thorough edu-

cation in Germany. In 1856, at the invitation of several friends who
were about to emigrate to America, Dr. Baruch was induced to ac-
company them simply on his part as a visitor. He had not completed
his college course, intending to return to his native land, but he was
so pleased with this country that he changed his plans and adopted
it as his home. He landed in South Carolina, and subsequently began
the study of medicine, and graduated from the Medical College of
Virginia. Immediately after his graduation he began the practice of
his profession in South Carolina, where he pursued his practice till
the outbreak of the Civil war. He was then appointed a surgeon in
the Confederate army, first under the command of Gen. Beauregard,
then in the army of Virginia. What was remarkable was that at the
close of the war he was only twenty-three years of age, and was the
brigade surgeon of the Parkdale, Miss., brigade of Gen. Lee's army.
He continued the practice of medicine in Camden, S. C., where he
and his brother, the subject of this sketch, just from Germany, had
repaired after joining each other at Charleston. They continued to
make Camden their home till 1881, when Dr. Baruch changed his
location to New York city, where he has become distinguished.

Upon going to Camden with his brother, H. Baruch secured a
position in a store first as errand boy, and subsequently, after acquiring a fair knowledge of the English language, he was employed as
clerk. In this position he found opportunity by persevering study to
perfect himself in the language of the country, enabling him to
speak and write it with fluency. He held his position as clerk till in
September, 1862, when he enlisted as a private in Gary's brigade of
cavalry, Seventh South Carolina regiment, commanded by Gen. Alexander C. Haskell. Mr. Baruch was a gallant soldier and served in
the same cavalry till the close of the war, surrendering with Lee's
army at Appomatox. In the summer of 1864 Mr. Baruch did special
service as field courier to Gens. Lee and Beauregard, during the
campaign around Richmond, and rendered rare service for a strip-
ling of only nineteen, years of age. After the surrender this young
soldier, foot-sore, poorly clad and penniless, set out on foot for his
home in Camden, where he again began the work of a clerk and
salesman. He continued this employment for a few years in the
service of other merchants, but availing himself of a small capital,
he embarked for himself, in 1870, in a general merchandising business
at Camden. His business prospered and in 1879 he removed to
Charlotte and entered into a co-partnership with a Mr. S. Wittkowsky,
under the firm name of Wittkowsky & Baruch. They carried on a
wholesale and retail trade in dry goods, notions, clothing and boots
and shoes. In 1887 this partnership was dissolved, Mr. Baruch retaining the retail trade and Mr. Wittkowsky the wholesale. Mr.
Baruch carries on an extensive and profitable trade not exceeded by
that of any merchant in the state. He possesses a thorough practical knowledge of merchandising, both in buying and selling, and
bears the reputation in New York city as being one of the most
sagacious purchasers who trade in that wholesale emporium. He

Yours truly
John S. Brown

spends nearly half his time there and is thus enabled to take advantage of the market. He has an extensive establishment which during his absence is in charge of his youngest brother, Joseph Baruch. The example of a man like Mr. Baruch, who has wrought his way up from an errand boy to the head of one of the largest mercantile establishments in the south and who conducts his business upon such intelligent and high-minded principles, is well worthy of imitation, and is a rare beneficence in any community. But Mr. Baruch is not only an exceptional business man but he stands high as a worthy member of society and enjoys the highest respect and esteem among his fellow-citizens. He has a family of eight bright and interesting children, and his wife, whose maiden name was Miss Deborah Sampson, is an excellent and accomplished lady, a native of Georgetown, S. C.

WILLIAM BLOUNT.

This distinguished statesman was born in North Carolina in 1744. He was a son of Jacob Blount, who was a member of the provincial assembly in 1775-6. He was a delegate from North Carolina to the old congress of 1782-3 and 1776-7. He was a member of the assembly four years, and was one of the signers of the Federal constitution in 1787. In 1790 he was appointed governor of that vast territory south of the Ohio. As he had been chosen a member of the commission to form the state of Tennessee, he was its spokesman in the United States senate in 1796, but was expelled 1799, he being concerned in a conspiracy to deliver New Orleans to the British, and for having assisted the Creeks and Cherokees in conquering the territory of Louisiana. This unjust treatment increased his popularity in Tennessee. where the people had unwavering faith in his fidelity, and he was elected to the office of state senator, which office he administered with the utmost integrity for many years. He died in Knoxville, Tenn., March 31, 1800.

JOHN L. BROWN.

Upon the 8th day of January, 1829, in Rowan county, N. C., was born John L. Brown, the subject of the following sketch. His parents were Peter M. and Elizabeth (Pool) Brown, both of whom were of German lineage. Peter M. Brown, in early life, devoted his attention exclusively to farming, but removing to Charlotte in 1829, he embarked in the tanning business, which, together with farming. he continued till his death occurred in 1874. It was in the first year of our subject's life that his parents established their home in Charlotte; and hence in this city Mr. Brown was reared; and here he received a thorough English education, such as has fitted him for a practical as well as successful career. Early in life, by reason of circumstances and opportunity, he began a business career. At the age of eighteen he secured, at Charlotte, a position as clerk or salesman, and continued as such until 1852, in which year he first embarked in a business of his own. Embarking in general merchandising he continued till 1862, when he became a candidate for the legislature. He had been a whig in politics, but in 1862 each candidate ran for office upon personal merit, rather than upon a political party ticket. Notwithstanding the fact that he had been an ardent whig, and that Mecklenburg was overwhelmingly democratic, he was elected by a handsome majority in consequence of his personal merit and popularity, and was almost unanimously re-elected in 1864. He served in the lower house of the legislature till 1865, when he returned to Charlotte and resumed his former business pursuits. In 1866, as a director in what is now the Carolina Central railway, he visited the legislature, where he had been an influential member, and was instrumental in securing, under strong opposition, a desirable amendment to the charter for the railroad. From 1865 to 1878 Mr. Brown was continuously in business. In 1867 was added to the general merchandise, hardware, but in a separate store in Charlotte was conducted the hardware trade. In 1874 a co-partnership was entered into with Messrs. T. H. Brem, J. H. Weddington and J. Vanlandingham, under the firm name of Brem, Brown & Co. In 1879 this co-partnership was dissolved, and a new one was entered into with J. H. Weddington, with whom he conducted a hardware business till 1884, when Mr. Brown's son, Peter M. Brown, was admitted as a partner in the business, and since, under the firm name of Brown, Weddington & Co., there it has conducted the largest hardware business in Charlotte and in the state.

In 1878, as a democrat, Mr. Brown was a third time elected to represent his county in the lower house of the legislature. In this year he retired from active business till in the next year when, as aforesaid, he entered into a co-partnership with J. H. Weddington. In 1879, while in the legislature, Mr. Brown introduced in the house a resolution with a view of effecting a compromise settlement of the state debt. In his resolution it was proposed to appoint a joint committee of members from both branches of the legislature, which committee was to devise a plan upon which to effect a compromise settlement of the debt. In Mr. Brown's resolution he recommended a plan of settlement; the resolution as introduced was adopted; Mr. Brown was made chairman of the house committee, and Hon. Giles Mebane of the senate, chairman of the joint committee, which after deliberation, adopted his recommended plan of settling the state debt, and the bill became a law. The manner in which the state debt was settled has reflected great credit on that legislature and state as well. To Mr. Brown is due the honor and credit of originating the bill, the passage of which was largely due to his efforts and influence. In the fall of 1880, the governor called a special session of the legislature for the purpose of contracting with parties to finish the construction of the Western North Carolina Railroad, and with this special session ended the services of Mr. Brown in the legislature. As a legislator he was an incessant worker, and was honest, faithful and conscientious, quick to discern the right and condemn the wrong.

He was far-seeing, and of wise and practical business judgment, and to the wisdom of his financial policy is due the favorable plan upon which was effected the compromise settlement of the state debt, as well as the subsequent prosperity of the state.

As a business man Mr. Brown maintains the strictest confidence of all who known him, and as an evidence of this, he has been called to fill several very important positions of honor and trust, in which positions excellent business qualifications are most essential to secure prosperity, and in which much has been intrusted to his honesty and integrity. No higher compliment can be paid him than to say here that he amply fulfilled the most sanguine expectations of his friends and promoters in all the several positions of honor and trust to which he has been elevated. He has efficiently served for eighteen years on the board of aldermen for Charlotte, and for a number of years on the county board of commissioners, and was a member of this board when working the public roads by convict labor was inaugurated. Since 1881 he has been president of the Mutual Building & Loan association, and for several years has been a director in the First National bank of Charlotte. During the existence of the Bank of North Carolina he was one of its directors. In 1878, when the Charlotte chamber of commerce was organized, he was made its first president, and he has continued a member of the organization. Mr. Brown has for a number of years been a member of the financial committee of the North Carolina, and Atlantic, Tennessee & Ohio railroads. He was a charter member of the Ada Manufacturing company of Charlotte, of which company he was elected first president, and of which he has continued president. In 1885 there was held at Atlanta, Ga., an international commercial convention. Gov. Scales appointed as delegates from North Carolina to this convention Rufus S. Tucker, of Raleigh, and Mr. Brown. Mr. Brown took an active part in this convention, of which he was elected vice-president.

Mr. Brown has been an ardent friend and advocate of church and education. He has been for years a member of the Presbyterian church, and has for over thirty years been chairman of the board of deacons in his church. For years he was treasurer of the Concord presbytery, and upon the creation of the Mecklenburg presbytery he was made its treasurer, remaining as such several years. He is the oldest member of the committee of home missions of the Mecklenburg presbytery. He is also a member of the executive committee of the regions of orphans' home of the Presbyterian synod of North Carolina. To Mr. Brown is due the credit of a wise purchase of the Barium hotel property, at Barium Springs, N.C., which was converted into an excellent home for the region of orphans. For nearly twenty-five years he has been a member, now its president, of the board of trustees of the general assembly of the Presbyterian church of the United States. In June, 1887, he was elected president of the board of trustees for Davidson college. His deep interest in the college and his valuable services as president of the board of trustees received approval and reward by his being re-elected president of the board in June, 1890. Mr. Brown was in August, 1853, united in marriage with Miss Nannie J. Kerr, daughter of Jennings B. Kerr. The union has been blessed in the birth of two sons, namely: William J. and Peter M. The former is deceased, while the latter is associated in business with his father.

The foregoing is a brief sketch of one of the representative business men and worthy citizens of the state. So eventful has been Mr. Brown's life that only the more important ones can be herein given, but let it suffice to say that in the many duties involved upon him his work has been well done; that his life has been an exemplary one; that his character is irreproachable, and that he is a recognized representative man and citizen, whose life has been one of general utility. In disposition of mind he is philosophical, and of excellent judgment; fair-minded and lenient, kind and jovial, and being of a congenial and pleasant disposition, he is a popular member of society. Such is a brief biography of this cultured and honored citizen.

JOHN D. WALTERS,

who is engaged in the mercantile business at La Grange, was born in Lenoir county, N. C., on the 21st of October, 1858. His parents were Haywood and Sally (Rouse) Walters. The family originally resided in Virginia, but, at an early day, removed from that state to Lenoir county, N. C., where Mr. Walters' grandfather was born and where he grew up a prominent planter. Haywood Walters, the father of the subject of this sketch, was educated in the public schools of Lenoir county. He was a member of the democratic party and a communicant of the Baptist church. He died in 1888. Mr. Walters' mother was the daughter of Benjamin Rouse, of Lenoir county, and she is stil living. She has reared three children: Mary H., wife of Alexander Sutton, of La Grange; David, a farmer of Lenoir county, and John D., the subject of this sketch. He was educated in the country schools and took up farming as his occupation. In 1882, however, he established a mercantile business at La Grange, which he carried on for two years, at the same time supervising his farm and running a cotton gin. He was also a member of the firm of Sutton & Walters, manufacturers of lumber. In 1889, Mr. Walters again resumed the mercantile trade, which he has since continued to prosecute. He is a member of the Masonic fraternity. On the 15th of November, 1877, Mr. Walters was united in marriage with Miss Julia E. Hardy, daughter of Porrott Hardy, of Lenoir county. She died in 1885, leaving him four children, whose respective names are Willie H., John P., Milton L. and Sallie C. Walters. Mr. Walters was next married in 1886 to Miss Kate E. Woollard, daughter of John Woollard, of Lenoir county, by whom he has had three children: Julia E., Cassie R. and Daniel H. Walters. Mr. Walters is a member of the Methodist Episcopal church, south. Though an active politician, he adheres to independent action.

HENRY E. DILLON,

a prominent merchant of La Grange, N. C., is a native of Tyrrell county, N. C., where he was born November 25, 1842. He is the son of Alexander and Sarah (Wynne) Dillon, both natives of the above named county. The paternal ancestors of the family were of Irish nativity. John Dillon was the first of the family to settle in North Carolina, emigrating from his native Ireland at an early day. He first settled in Tennessee but afterward removed to North Carolina. His children settled in various portions of the Union. John Dillon, Jr., the great-grandfather of the subject of this sketch, was born in Tyrrell county and was a planter by occupation. In early life he removed to East Tennessee, where he still continued to carry on farming operations. They reared a large family of children. Alexander Dillon, the father of Henry E. Dillon, was born in Tyrrell county in 1788 and died in 1845. He acquired a good education and followed the occupation of a farmer. He was a man of prominence, and was a leading member of the old line whig party. His wife was a daughter of Robert Wynne, one of the oldest and most respectable of the citizens of Tyrrell county — a Jeffersonian democrat and clerk of the court for many years. He was a member of the Baptist church. The wife died in 1850. She was the mother of nine children named as follows: William J., member of Cowan's regiment and died from the effects of a wound received at the battle of Gettysburg; Silas W., a member of the same company, died in Virginia while in the service; James R., an extensive farmer in Washington county; Henry E., the subject of this sketch; Mrs. Mary Normans, of Washington county; and Caroline E., (deceased), wife of James M. Alexander, of Tyrrell county. Henry E. Dillon was brought up under the care of a guardian, and early taken to Plymouth, Washington county, N. C. He was educated in Dickinson college at Carlisle, Pa., where he remained until the commencement of the Civil war, when he joined the Edenton Bell battery, Third battalion of light artillery as a private. He was soon appointed quartermaster and tithe sergeant for one section and later promoted to ordnance sergeant for one section of the battery, serving until the close of the war. In the early part of the war he was taken prisoner and retained six weeks, when he was exchanged. He participated at the fall of Fort Anderson, was at the battles of Wilmington, Smithfield, Wise's Fork and others. After the close of the war he located at Tarboro, N. C., and engaged in the mercantile trade with his brother, under the firm name of J. R. Dillon & Bro. After a year's trade here, they removed to Stantonsburg, thence to Washington county, and in 1871 to La Grange. Here he established his present business. His is the oldest house and carries on the most extensive trade in the town. In connection with his mercantile trade he is extensively engaged in farming. He is president of the Wilmington Building & Loan association and of the Huntsville (Ala.) Building & Loan association. He was appointed by Gov. Fowle as a member of the southern states inter-state convention, held in Asheville, N. C., in December, 1890. He was also appointed by the governor, January 23, 1891, as a director in the eastern North Carolina insane asylum, to fill the unexpired term of Dr. R. W. King, deceased. He has filled various offices of his adopted town with acceptability. His politics are democratic, and he belongs to the Independent Order of Odd Fellows. In January, 1869, Mr. Dillon was united in marriage with Miss Celestia N., the daughter of Washington Stanton, of Wilson county, N. C., by whom he has four children living, whose respective names are; Lillian M., Celestia, Van Washington and Reginald. Mr. Dillon is an elder in the Presbyterian church and is one of its most active and influential members.

SAMUEL H. ABBOTT.

One of the representative business men of Kinston, is Mr. Samuel H. Abbott, a native of Lenoir county, his birth having taken place there on the 25th of September, 1839. His parents, Thomas J. and Lucinda (Phillips) Abbott, were likewise natives of Lenoir county. The father was born in 1808; he was a coachmaker by trade, but later in life became a planter; he was a captain in the North Carolina militia, and was a prominent whig; his demise occurred in 1853. His wife was a daughter of Peter Phillips, and was born in 1812. Peter Phillips was an extensive planter and served in the war of 1812; he was descended from one of the old and influential families of the county of Lenoir. Mrs. Abbott is still living. Samuel Abbott was the grandfather of our subject. He was born in England, and was a blacksmith and planter. Of the children born to Thomas J. and Lucinda Abbott, seven survive, they are: J. H., Samuel H., Stephen D., Thomas J., Mrs Ella Rouse, Mrs. Susan A. King, of Washington, D. C., and Mrs. Lucinda Abbott, of Lenoir county. Samuel H. Abbott was reared in his native county, where he received but a limited education. In 1862 he enlisted in company A, Fortieth North Carolina artillery regiment, under Col. Lamb, and remained in that command until the close of the war, having rendered faithful and efficient service. In 1866 he located in Kinston, and secured a clerkship in a dry goods establishment. Three years later he had saved about $200, and with that capital opened a general grocery store. At this time he is the leading merchant of the town, and has a large stock. In 1873 he established a brick and tile factory, and also manufactures the Planter's plow, his own patent, and he is one of the original stockholders of the Orion Mill Co., and is largely interested in real estate. Mr. Abbott has served as a town commissioner for several terms, and also as a member of the school board, and is a prominent member of the I. O. O. F. His marriage was solemnized, in 1873, to Miss Nancy Brock, daughter of Daniel and Caroline Brock, of this county. Two children, Ruth and Lunsford, have blessed their home. Mr. and Mrs. Abbott are communicants of the Episcopal church, in which he is a senior warden. He is recognized as one of the substantial and lead-ing men of the town and county.

JAMES C. DOBBIN.

One of the most gifted men of the state of North Carolina was James Cochrane Dobbin, who was born in 1814, at Fayetteville, N. C., where his father, John M. Dobbin, a merchant, had long resided. His mother was Agnes, daughter of Hon. James Cochrane, who rep-resented the Orange district in congress in 1811 and 1813. The sub-ject of this sketch was prepared for college by William Bingham, and entered the University of North Carolina in 1828. At college he formed friendships which lasted through life. His gentle man-ners and fine ability won the hearts of all. He graduated with high honors in a class with Judge Thomas S. Ashe, Senator Thomas L. Clingman, Cadwallader Jones, and other distinguished gentlemen. Having read law with Judge Strange, he was admitted to the bar in 1835. Ten years later, unknown to himself, he was nominated for congress and elected in a doubtful district. In that body he made a fine reputation, his speeches on important questions placing him in the front rank of statesmen. He declined a re-election, but was elected to the assembly in 1848, 1850 and 1852. He was a democrat of the most pronounced faith, but was, like his friend William S. Ashe, of the lower Cape Fear, progressive and in favor of internal improvements by the state. He was speaker of the house in 1848 and 1850, and in the first session warmly advocated with Mr. Ashe the building of the North Carolina railroad from Goldsboro to Char-lotte. He also secured the building by the state of the plank road from Fayetteville to Winston. By his eloquence he secured the building of the insane asylum at Raleigh. In 1852 he was nominated for the senate by the democratic caucus; but the legislature, being about evenly divided, Judge Saunders did not support the nominee, but with some friends prevented an election. At the succeeding democratic national convention, Mr. Dobbin was chairman of the North Carolina delegation. There had been an animated canvass over the chief democratic leaders — Buchanan, Marcy, Cass and Doug-las. It was apprehended that no nomination could be reached. Mr. Dobbin had served in congress with Franklin Pierce of New Hamp-shire, and knew his worth. At a crisis in the convention, he made a short but eloquent appeal and presented with such force the name of Mr. Pierce that he was nominated.

Hon. William A. Graham was then secretary of the navy, and John Branch and Mr. Badger had both held the same cabinet place. Early in the winter Mr. William S. Ashe went to see Mr. Pierce and presented Mr. Dobbin's name for that position and later Mr. Pierce tendered the portfolio to him. As secretary of the navy, Mr. Dobbin rendered his country a great service and made for himself a brilliant reputation. Under his administration the navy attained the highest state of efficiency; the naval academy was put on a proper basis; the inefficient officers of the service were retired and the most splendid war vessels of the time were built — the Niagara, the Merrimac, Wabash, Minnesota, etc., added to the fame of America and won the plaudits of all maritime nations. In the ordnance the Dahlgren gun was adopted; and cannon of the largest caliber of the day were brought into use. No career in the navy department has ever been so full of luster as that of Mr. Dobbin. While in the cabinet he used his influence with effect to have the president sign the bill for the improvement of the Cape Fear river, which Mr. Ashe had pressed successfully in the democratic house. This was one of the first bills for internal improvements ever signed by a democratic president. At this period Mr. Dobbin had lost his wife; his family of young children were at his home in Fayetteville, and his own health was feeble. His brother, John Dobbin, had perished at sea, and he himself felt that his end was approaching. He returned to Fayetteville, where, on August 4, 1857, he expired, his last words being: "Praise the Lord, oh my soul!" No finer character has ever adorned the annals of his native state. Mr. Dobbin married Louisa Holmes, daughter of Mr. Gabriel Holmes, of Sampson, by whom he had two sons, James and John, who left no issue, and Louisa, who married Mr. John Anderson, of Fayetteville, N. C. His father had by his mother, besides himself, a daughter, Anise, who married Mr. John Huske, of Fayetteville; and after the death of Mrs. Dobbin his father married Miss McQueen and had born to him John Dobbin, who served at sea on board the San Francisco; and Kate, who became the wife of Judge Shepherd, of Fayetteville.

W. C. BROWN.

The late William Carter Brown, M. D., was born in Caswell county, N. C. He was graduated from Jefferson medical college, at Philadelphia, and began practicing in Davie county, N. C., where he was residing at the time of his death, in 1865. Among the very first to enlist in the cause of the south in 1861, he was assigned as surgeon of the Forty-third North Carolina regiment, volunteer infantry, and served as such until a short time prior to the surrender at Appomatox. His health was completely shattered by his patriotic devotion to his people's welfare, and he returned home to die. Never absent from the post of duty, with a strong, tender hand he administered to the sick, and gave the best energies of his being to the relief of the southern soldier. Honored and beloved, he now fills a soldier's grave, but the memory of his services will long linger with those whom he visited on the battle-field. He was married, in 1852, to Ann Payne Carter, daughter of Archibald Carter, of the Oaks, Davie county, N. C. Seven children blessed their union, those living being: John A., of Winston, N. C.; Frank Carter, also of Winston; William Carter, of Winston, and Bessie, the wife of E. C. Clinard, a resident of Salem, N. C., and Willie Ann, wife of W. H. LeGrand, of Richmond county, N. C. The grandfather of these children was John E. Brown, M. D., who was born in Caswell county, N. C., in 1800. William Carter Brown, Jr., is a native of Davie county, N. C., where he was born on the 11th of October, 1859. His education was received at Mocksville, N. C., and later in the schools of Salem, N. C. At the age of sixteen he secured a clerkship in a dry goods store at Winston, N. C., and continued in that capacity until 1882. In the latter year he was associated with his brother, Frank Brown, in the establishment of a dry goods business at Winston. This concern has come to be one of the largest of the kind in the county, and its proprietors are regarded as among the ablest and most substantial business men in the community. A more extended mention of the family will be found elsewhere in this volume.

D. S. REED.

Years prior to the Revolution the Reed family settled in Rockingham, N. C., having emigrated from Scotland. John Reed was born in Baltimore county, Md., on June 10, 1777, where he followed the life of a planter. As a soldier in the Revolution he distinguished himself for valor and faithfulness, and left a name of good repute as a heritage to his descendants. One of his sons was Anselm Reed, who was born on the paternal plantation in Rockingham county in 1813. He followed in the footsteps of his father as an agriculturist, and also for many years carried on a large mercantile business in Rockingham, N. C., to which place he removed in 1872. In 1883 he retired from active business. He served as a magistrate in Rockingham and Guilford counties for about forty years. In 1837 he married Miss Martha Winchester, daughter of Jackson Winchester, of Rockingham county, N. C. Two of their seven children survive their parents; they are: John Whitfield Reed, of Greensboro, N. C., and David Settle Reed, of Winston, N. C. The mother died in 1857. It is of one of the last mentioned sons that we will now write. David Settle Reed, one of the leading merchants of Winston, N. C., was born in Rockingham county, April 28, 1847. In very early youth he enlisted in Company A, Second regiment of North Carolina junior reserves, as orderly sergeant, which was first assigned to the Second battalion, and later to the Third regiment North Carolina state troops, and elected first lieutenant of Company A. He fought at Fort Fisher, Bellefield raid, Kingston, Newbern and Smithfield, and none in the Confederate service were more loyal than he. After the war he entered Trinity college, and was graduated in 1867, when he returned home and embarked in the tobacco business, and after a year and a half turned his attention to planting for two years. In 1876 he located at Winston and established a mercantile business, which he has since most successfully conducted. He is a stockholder in the Roanoke & Southern railroad, and is interested in various enterprises of the community. In September, 1871, Mr. Reed was united in marriage with Miss Mary Banks Traynham, daughter of J.

P. Traynham, of Halifax county, Va. Of their six children three are living, named: Frank L., Harry P. and David S. Reed. Mr. Reed is a communicant of the Missionary Baptist church, and is regarded as one of the most substantial and honorable business men of the county.

R. R. CRAWFORD.

Among the honored names of the past may be found that of the Hon. William D. Crawford, who, during his life, was a distinguished lawyer and legislator of North Carolina. He was a native of South Carolina, having been born in Lancaster district, that state, in 1806. When a lad he came to North Carolina, and in 1825 was graduated from the University of North Carolina. He then began the study of the law under the tutelage of the eminent Chief-Justice Pearson, of the supreme court, and was admitted to the bar in 1827. He chose Salisbury as his home, and there entered upon his professional duties. He practiced law with distinguished success until his death in 1838. Although his life was terminated in its first bloom, yet he had made a name for himself of which many an older man might well be proud. Brilliant and able, had life been spared, there can be little doubt but that he would have reached the very pinnacle of fame in his profession. He was a member for several terms of both branches of the state legislature, and his course in both senate and house was dignified and able. In 1828 he married Miss Christina Mull, daughter of Thomas Mull, of Rowan county, N. C., and six children were born to them, of whom four survive, named: Thomas M., James R., R. R. Crawford, Rev. L. W. Crawford, professor of moral science in Trinity college, Durham, N. C. The mother died in 1879.

We have chosen as our immediate subject Mr. R. R. Crawford, the representative merchant of Winston, N. C. Mr. Crawford was born in Rowan county, N. C., October 14, 1839. His scholastic training was obtained at Olin high school. At the age of twenty-one, in 1861, he left his home, Charlotte, N. C., to enlist in Company B, First North Carolina regiment volunteer infantry, Confederate army, commanded by Col. (later general) D. H. Hill. After a six months' term of service expired, private Crawford left the battle-field stricken with typhoid fever and paralysis; after recovering for a time he assisted in organizing a company and regiment at Salisbury, of which he was subsequently elected captain. This command was assigned to the Forty-second regiment North Carolina state troops as Company D. Until December, 1864, Capt. Crawford commanded this company, and at that time was honorably retired on account of physical disability. He served with valor and faithfulness in the following mentioned engagements: Bethel, Shepardsville, Newbern, Cold Harbor, battles around Richmond, Bermuda Hundred, around Petersburg, and, beside, several battles of minor importance. He was wounded at Bermuda Hundred. Leaving the army Mr. Crawford settled at Salisbury and engaged in mercantile pursuits until 1882, when he removed to Winston, and embarked in the hardware business. He has made a marked success as a business man, is keen and progressive, and of undoubted integrity. He is a director in the People's National bank, and is interested in the Roanoke & Southern railroad, as well as in the West End Land Improvement company, and the North Winston·Mechanical works, of which he is a director. He is a prominent member of the Knights of Honor, the A. O. U. W. and the Royal Arcanum. Mr. Crawford was married, in 1866, to Miss Caroline Crawford, a daughter of Thomas Crawford, of Washington, N. C., and to them eight children were born, the surviving ones being: Thomas B., Robert R., Jr., and Christina Crawford. Mrs. Crawford died March 17, 1887, and on April 24, 1889, he was married to Miss Ada W. Dudley, of Kansas City, Mo., and to them one child has been born, John Dudley Crawford.

ALEXANDER C. VOGLER,

one of the leading merchants of Salem, N. C., was born on the 13th of March, 1832, at that place, and was given a fair education in the common schools of his native town. When about thirteen years of age he began working on his father's plantation, and at the expiration of two and one-half years was apprenticed to the cabinet-maker's trade with John D. Siewers, of Salem, with whom he remained for about five and one-half years. It was in the year 1853 that he completed his apprenticeship, and he then traveled as a journeyman for four years, when he returned to Salem and opened a shop of his own. Since that time Mr. Vogler has built up a large and constantly increasing business, and in 1889 took his son, Frank H., into partnership with him, the firm name being A. C. Vogler & Son. In 1859 Mr. Vogler happily married Miss Antoinette S. Hauser, daughter of William Hauser, and to them have been born three children, two of whom survive, named: Mary A., wife of Jacob F. Crouse, and Francis H. Vogler. In May, 1888, Mr. Vogler was elected commissioner of Salem, and so efficient was his discharge of the duties of that office that he was re-elected in 1890 and 1891. He is a leading member of the Masonic order, and also of the Knights of Honor, and Knights and Ladies of Honor, and is a consistent member of the Moravian church. He is quite extensively interested in the Salem water works, and various other enterprises of the town. Mr. Vogler is the son of Nathaniel Vogler, who was born in Salem, N. C., in 1804. He was a gunsmith and planter, and in 1827 married Miss Mary A. Fishel, daughter of Conrad Fishel, of Davidson county, N. C. They were the parents of nine children, of whom seven survive, as follows: Laura C., wife of William Beck; Alexander C.; Mortimer N.; Maria E.; Martha V., wife of Edward Peterson; Regina A., and William T. Vogler. The father died in 1872, and the mother in 1889. Nathaniel Vogler was a son of Christopher Vogler, whose father was a native of Germany, where he was born in 1725. He came to America in his early manhood, and settled in North Carolina, where he died in 1828. He was a gunsmith.

HON. WILLIAM B. CARTER.

The Carter family has long been intimately connected with the growth and advancement of the state of North Carolina. The original founder of the American branch came to this country prior to the Revolution from Bedfordshire, England. The Hon. William B. Carter was born in Caswell county, N. C., in 1814. In early manhood he chose the life of a planter and remained in that calling all his days. He was graduated from the University of North Carolina, and then completed a law course at the University of Virginia, but did not practice. For some time he served as chairman of the Rockingham county court, and was a man of much ability and influence. He married Elizabeth Gallaway, daughter of Robert Gallaway, a native of Scotland, who settled in Rockingham county, N. C., in 1837, and six children were born to them, named: Mary G., Sallie B., William B., Jesse, Bettie G. and Thomas F. Carter. The mother of these children died in April, 1853, and the father, March 8, 1888. The latter was a son of Jesse Carter, who was born in Pittsylvania county, N. C., and in early manhood moved to Caswell county, N. C. He was a planter and merchant all his life. William Brown Carter, son of the Hon. William B. Carter above mentioned, first saw the light in Rockingham county, N. C., September 8, 1845. His scholastic training was obtained at Dr. Alexander Wilson's excellent school, in Alamance county, N. C. In the fall of 1863 he abandoned his studies to take up arms in defense of the Confederate government, and enlisted in the Thirteenth North Carolina volunteer regiment as a private, and served through the remaining years of the war, having surrendered at Appomatox. In 1866 he entered the University of Virginia, and remained there for one year, when he went to Madison, N. C., and until 1874 was engaged in a mercantile business at that place. In the latter year Mr. Carter removed to Winston and embarked in the tobacco business with Maj. Brown, the firm being Brown & Carter. Mr. Carter is also extensively interested in many local enterprises, and is a stockholder in the Roanoke & Southern railroad. He is a man of progressive mind, keen business perception, and of undoubted integrity. In December, 1872, he was most happily united in marriage to Miss Etta Hall, daughter of Daniel E. Hall, of Mobile, Ala., and five children are the offspring born to them, the four living ones being Delphine H., Elizabeth G., Etta and Mary G.

GEORGE W. HINSHAW

was born in Chatham county, N. C., April 22, 1847. He is the son of Zimri and Martha Hinshaw. The family of Hinshaws have for years been prominent members of the Society of Friends, and are distinguished for their honesty and integrity. They are of Scotch-Irish descent. Mr. Hinshaw's father was a tanner by trade and the youth soon made himself master of the trade. His opportunities were poor for acquiring an education, but when quite young he exhibited a fondness for books, and pursued his studies at home as opportunity offered. When he was seventeen years of age he went into the Confederate army, joining the Sixth battalion, afterward the First regiment of junior reserves, in which he served until November, 1864. He was then detailed for service in eastern North Carolina and southeastern Virginia. Here he was complimented by the major-general of the army for gallant conduct in front of the enemy. Though under age he was entitled to a commission and would have had one but for the surrender which soon after took place. May 21, 1865, he was paroled at Greensboro, N. C.; he returned to his home and resumed work on his father's farm. In the fall of 1865, he entered New Garden boarding school, now Guilford college, under Dr. Nereus Mendenhall, one of the most distinguished educators in the country. He made rapid progress, but the condition of his finances and failure in his eye-sight compelled him soon to relinquish his studies. He engaged in selling goods, in 1866, for Worth & McAlister, at Company Shops, where he remained about a year. He then entered Sylvan academy until the close of the session; then attended the Deep River normal school. While there he was employed by the Baltimore Association of Friends to teach an eight months' school. He was eminently successful and built up a large school, but in the midst of his successful career he was attacked by typhoid fever. On his way home he stopped at Winston and saw such indications of the future growth and prosperity of the place, that he determined to locate there.

In 1868 he entered the store of Hodgitt & Sullivan, as a salesman, at a low salary. Here he remained until January, 1870, when he started business on his own account. In 1873 he became a partner with his old employers, and the firm was known as Hodgitt, Hinshaw & Co. For three years the firm were successful, but in 1876 they invested in a patent brick machine, by which they lost heavily. Mr. Hinshaw sold out his interest, and the next year began business again under the firm name of Hinshaw & Bro., with Allison & Addison, of Richmond, as special partners. The firm has now become Hinshaw & Medearis, with the above named gentlemen as special partners, and does mostly a wholesale business upon a heavy scale. In 1870 Mr. Hinshaw was married to Emily A. Miller, of Winston, and they have a bright, intelligent and interesting family of four children. Mr. Hinshaw has always taken great interest in railroad enterprises, which tended to the development of the country. In 1868 he was active in procuring a subscription, by Forsyth county, of $100,000, to the Northwestern North Carolina railroad; in 1878, he was largely instrumental in organizing the Salem, Winston & Mooresville railroad, and later on, the Salem, Winston & Madison railroad, afterward consolidated into the North Carolina Midland road. Other important roads are indebted to him for existence, and he has become an authority in railroad matters. He is a director in the

Northwestern North Carolina, the North Carolina Midland, and the Roanoke & Southern railroads.

Mr. Hinshaw was one of the first to suggest the graded school system for the state, and took a leading part in establishing the school in Winston. He has closely identified himself with city improvements, led off in establishing city water works, was the first to move in organizing the People's National bank, of which he is a director and vice-president; obtained a charter for the Winston Land & Improvement company, of which he is president and the largest stockholder; has several times served as town commissioner and town treasurer, and is now trustee for a company owning about 60,-000 acres of valuable mineral lands, in which he also is a large stockholder. He has taken a lively hand in promoting the interests of the farming community, by instituting fairs and expositions which have proved successful. He possesses every quality for a first-class business man, is quiet and unassuming, devoted to his family and is a general favorite in society. No man takes a deeper interest in the growth and development of his town or in the education, culture and improvement of the society in which he moves.

J. A. VANCE.

Joseph Addison Vance was born in Forsyth county, N. C., December 4, 1851. Having received a fair schooling in his native county, at the age of eighteen he left his native town and removed to Winston, where he learned the carpenter's trade, and followed it for about ten years. In 1880 he established a foundry and machine shop, and in August, 1890, Mr. W. F. Shaffner became associated with him in the concern. They are among the most extensive manufacturers of machinery in the county. Mr. Vance is a member of the I. O. O. F. In April, 1879, he married Miss Adelaide J. Fogle, a daughter of Augustus Fogle, of Salem, N. C., and three children, named as follows, have been born to them: Clara R., Lucy L., and Horace H. Vance. Joseph A. Vance is the son of William M. Vance, who was born in Forsyth county, N. C., in 1819. He has always been engaged in planting, and is an upright and honored citizen. For a number of years just after the late Civil war he held the office of magistrate. In 1841 he married Miss Heptsa J. Smith, daughter of Adam Smith, of Nantucket Island, and seven children have blessed their union, named: John S., Laura A., wife of W. W. Fulp; Virgil P., Joseph A., Mary L., wife of W. S. Linville; Dewitt M., and Alice, wife of F. H. Morris. All these children reside in Forsyth county. The mother passed away in August, 1889. The father of William M. Vance was John Vance, who was born in Forsyth county,, N. C., in 1795. He was an extensive planter and tobacco manufacturer, and lived a life of usefulness and honor. His demise occurred in 1879. His father was born in Ireland, and came to America in his early manhood. He became a farmer. Two of his sons settled in North Carolina and one went west. One of the sons who came to North Carolina located in Mecklenburg county, and was the grandfather of the Hon. Zebulon B. Vance, United States senator, and ex-governor of the state .

C. A. HEGE.

Constantine Alexander Hege was born near Friedburg (Moravian church), in Davidson county, N. C., on March 13, 1843. His early life was spent on the farm, going to school during a portion of the winter months. In the spring of 1857, he attended the Moravian boy's school, at Salem, N. C., and a portion of the years of 1859 and 1860, went to school at the Yadkin institute, in Davidson county N. C. Soon after this the Civil war broke out, and he being a Moravian (and from principle averse from going to war), took no active part in the strife. However, in the summer of 1862, he, with many more of the Moravians of his neighborhood, was forced to take up arms and serve in the Confederate army, and was assigned to Company H, Forty-eighth regiment, North Carolina infantry, where he served for fourteen months, during which time he, with his regiment, was in some of the hard-fought battles, among which were South Mountain, Va., Sharpsburg or Antietam, Md., and a number of skirmishes. Yet he came through it all without a single wound, although many of his comrades were killed and wounded all around him. While in the hottest of the battle at Bristow Station, Va., on October 14, 1863, he was taken prisoner of war by the Federal troops, and then sent to the Old Capitol prison, at Washington, D. C., where he was held a prisoner of war for five months, during which time he was visited by some former residents of his native county, and members of the Moravian church, but then residing in Washington. Among them were A. N. Zevely, the third assistant postmaster-general, and Prof. Hedrick, who was then in the patent office. In consultation with these friends, he decided to take the oath of allegiance to the United States, and go to Bethlehem, Penn., it being a Moravian town. Therefore, on the 14th of March, 1864, he was released from prison and at once proceeded to Bethlehem, Penn., where he met many warm friends, and at once sought employment. He worked in various capacities in the Bethlehem Iron works, which laid the foundation for his business in after life. He thus remained in Bethlehem, Penn., until after the war closed, and in August, 1865, he again returned to his home in North Carolina. In May, 1866, he went to Philadelphia, Penn., and entered the Bryant & Stratton Commercial college. After completing a commercial course, he accepted a posision with Messrs. Weikle & Smith, of 133 North Front street, Philadelphia, Penn., where he remained until the following winter, then returned home to start in the mercantile business himself. In the spring of 1867 he started a small country store, with a cousin of his, near his former home at Friedburg, N. C., but being of a decided mechanical turn of mind, after some years of mercantile life he decided to quit this business. He then moved to Salem, N. C. There, in the spring of 1873, he started a small foundry, but having lost all his capital in his mercantile venture, he had hard struggling, but as he was now in his natural element, by hard work, close attention to business, and determinedly sticking to it, he was soon able to buy a small iron lathe and drill which he operated for nearly a year, by a one horse power lever. Then he obtained a small steam engine and boiler, bought another lathe, and erected a small machine shop. In 1877 he obtained a patent on an improved set works for circular saw mills, and at once began the manufacture of saw mills, for which an extensive trade was built up in a few years. From this time his success has exceeded his then most sanguine expectations, as now (1891), his manufacture of wood working machinery, and more especially the Hege saw mills, are well and favorably known and extensively sold in over twenty-five states of the United States, and several foreign countries. His shop, known as the Salem Iron works, Salem, N. C., is now one of the best equipped works of its kind in the state of North Carolina.

C. A. Hege was married March 10, 1870, to Frances Mary Spaugh, daughter of Thomas and Melvina Spaugh, then residing near New Philadelphia Moravian church, some five miles west of Salem, N. C. To them were born three children, as follows: Walter Julius Hege, October 28, 1873; Ella Florence Hege, March 1, 1875, and Rosa Estelle Hege, December 6, 1883. Our subject's father's name was Solomon Hege, who was born in Davidson county, N. C., near Friedburg Church, on November 6, 1813. He was a farmer by occupation, and was married on the 28th of December, 1841, to Catherine Guinther, who was born August 18, 1813. They had five children, viz.: Constantine Alexander Hege, born March 13, 1843; Julia Elizabeth Hege, December 6, 1845, died October 11, 1846; Mary Louisa Hege, March 25, 1848; Susan Celest Hege, August 28, 1850; Julius Augustus Hege, February 4, 1854. Mr. Hege's father died August 24, 1875, and his mother June 8, 1874. The grandfather of the subject of this sketch was David Hege, who was born at Bethania, N. C. (then in Stokes county), on July 21, 1777. His occupation was farming. On December 1, 1801, he married Elizabeth Hoens, by whom he had five children, viz.: Thomas, born October 12, 1803; John, August 28, 1805; David, February 6, 1809; Catherine, August 18, 1811, and Solomon, December 14, 1813. Our subject's great-grandfather's name was John Belthaser Hege. He was born in Hausen, in Wurtemburg, October 31, 1714, and in 1757 was married to Maria Julian Fry, who was born February 17, 1735. They had the following children, viz.: Juliana, born May 6, 1761; Martha Elizabeth, November 12, 1763; Lazarus John, August 19, 1766; Anna Rosina, July 2, 1769; Christian, December 30, 1771; Sarah, October 14, 1774, and David, July 21, 1777. Mr. Hege's father's ancestors were of German, and his mother of English, extraction.

HERMON HUSBANDS.

The subject of this sketch figured largely in North Carolina as the chief leader of the regulation. He came to this colony probably from Pennsylvania about 1756, and finally settled on Sandy creek, now in Randolph county, where he had a good farm of some 3,000 acres, and cultivated it with industry and intelligent skill. He was a man of integrity, and good morals in his daily life. He was of Quaker raising, and was a public speaker of high standing in that society when he came to Carolina. Though not well educated, he appears to have joined a plain, practical education to a robust mind and habits of observation. In 1766 the regulation movement began in Granville county, and soon afterward Husbands became a leader in it. He drew up all the papers and resolutions of the regulators, and was very active, and became extremely obnoxious to the government. Among his principal coadjutors was Rednap Howell, who is said to have come from New Jersey, and who taught a common school on Deep river. Howell was a poet, and his songs and ditties contributed largely to stir the popular heart, while he himself moved about with rapidity organizing and preparing the people for such action as was desired. In 1768 Husbands and Howell and others raised a riot in Hillsboro; Husbands was arrested for it, but on the trial was acquitted. The agitation continued with increasing violence, and in September, 1770, the court at Hillsboro was broken up, and Husbands and others severely whipped lawyer Williams, afterward the judge of the supreme court of the state. They whipped Col. Fanning, the clerk, and demolished his house and furniture.

The regulators had earnestly requested Gov. Tryon to call a new assembly, and in 1770 he ordered the election of a new house. Husbands was returned as a member from Orange. When the body met at Newbern in December, 1770, he attended and caused to be published in the *Gazette* a statement signed by James Hunter, which was a libel on Judge Moore. He was examined on the matter, and the house found him guilty of falsehood in his testimony. There was some talk about his being put in contempt of the house and confined by its order. He asserted that if the house should confine him the people would march to Newbern and release him. This threat was taken as an insult and the house, December 20th, 1770, expelled him. He was thereupon arrested on court process for his libel on Judge Moore, but eventually the court released him. In the meantime the regulators, hearing of his arrest, embodied and marched toward Newbern to release him by force. They crossed Haw river below Pittsboro, but had not proceeded far when Husbands, returning home, met them. That assembly passed stringent laws against the regulators, and Husbands, Howell and others were indicted at Newbern for their riot at Hillsboro. This set the county in a roar, and Gov. Tryon marched into the upper country, where the battle of Alamance took place. Husbands fled, and a proclamation of outlawry was issued for him and Rednap Howell. Tryon moved his army to Sandy creek and destroyed Husbands' fine fields of clover and wheat. Husbands was next heard of with a dozen of his followers in upper Maryland, where an attempt was made to capture him; and then he located not far from Pittsburg, Penn. Two of his sons settled on Deep river, near Buffalo Ford; and a daughter, who married a man named Wright, also lived in the same neighborhood. Husbands died in Pennsylvania in 1795.

RICHARD J. REYNOLDS.

The place which the state of North Carolina holds among the tobacco raising states of the Union has only been gained by enterprise and persevering industry. As this is the great industry of the community, the credit for this great prosperity lies with those who have made it their life work to advance their state in this particular. Among the largest and most important concerns in the business is the R. J. Reynolds Tobacco company, of which Richard J. Reynolds is the chief. Mr. Reynolds comes of an old and influential southern family, and was born in Patrick county, Va., July 20, 1853. His father, H. W. Reynolds, was born in Patrick county, Va., in 1812, and prior to the late war was one of the largest, if not the largest, tobacco planter in the Old Dominion. He was also a large slaveholder, and in the early days of his state was a captain in her militia service. In 1841 he married Nancy J. Cox, a daughter of Joshua Cox, who was the son of Joshua Cox, a distinguished captain in the Revolution, and whose history is known to the biographers of that trying time. To this marriage fifteen children were born, the six living ones being Abram D., who was a captain in the Confederate service when but sixteen years of age; and before his seventeenth year was given the rank of major. He now resides at Bristol, Tenn; Richard J., of Winston, N. C.; Hardin H., also of Winston; Lucy B., wife of Robert Critz, of Bristol, Tenn; William N., of Winston, and Walter R. Reynolds, a resident of Bristol, Tenn. The father died in 1885, his widow still surviving him. H. W. Reynolds was the son of Abram Reynolds, who was a Pennsylvanian by birth, having emigrated to Virginia in his youth. He was a planter. His father was a native of Ireland, and soon after the Revolution came to the new world.

Mr. Richard J. Reynolds, of whom we will now write more particularly, was educated in the Emory and Henry college, in Virginia, and then completed a course in Bryant & Stratton's business college at Baltimore. Leaving the latter institution in 1874, he then went to Patrick county, Va., and there engaged in the manufacture of tobacco for one year. In 1875 he came to Winston, N. C., where he established the house of R. J. Reynolds, and in 1888 he took his brother, Mr. W. N. Reynolds, into partnership, and about this time Mr. Henry Roan also being received as a partner, the firm name became R. J. Reynolds Tobacco company. This extensive company has a very large trade, and is considered as one of the leading firms in the business. Its head, Mr. R. J. Reynolds, is possessed of unusual business ability, is progressive and keen, and his integrity is unimpeachable. Although he has from early manhood been a stanch and prominent supporter of the democratic party, he has never sought office, being content to lend his influence and strength to the elevation of others. He is a member of the Masonic fraternity.

ABEL PETERSON RHYNE

is the second son and third child of Moses H. and Margaret (Hoffman) Rhyne. He was born in Gaston county, N. C., thirteen miles from Charlotte, February 29, 1844. Attending the schools of the neighborhood, he worked on the farm with his father until the breaking out of the war, when he, at the age of eighteen, enlisted in Company H, Forty-ninth North Carolina regiment. This regiment did active service in the state of North Carolina during the first year of the war, and later went to Virginia. With his regiment, Mr. Rhyne took part in the battles of Harper's Ferry, Antietam, Sharpsburg, Culpeper Court House, first fight at Fredericksburg, Boone's Mills, Gum Swamps, Deep Gully and others. At Gettysburg, on account of sickness, Mr. Rhyne was given a furlough, and while at home was taken a prisoner and carried to Dallas, where he was subsequently paroled. After the war, Mr. Rhyne resumed his work on the farm with his father. Later he entered the Mount Holly high school, taught by A. J. Harrison, and after one year's attendance at this institution, taught school for five months. He then purchased the Hoffman plantation, and at the same time conducted a mercantile establishment at Mount Holly. He continued merchandising until 1870, in which year he became interested in the manufacture of cotton. He purchased a one-fourth interest in the Woodlawn mills, and taking charge of these, acted as manager until 1873, when he sold his share and purchased the Rankin plantation at Mount Holly. In the latter part of 1874, Mr. Rhyne bought Rudisel Shoal on Dutchman's creek near Mount Holly, and here in 1875 began the erection of a cotton mill, which was completed in April, 1876, and which bears the name of Mount Holly mills. The Tuckaseege mills were constructed on the Catawba in 1883, and in 1890 the Albion mills at Mount Holly were built. All these mills are in operation and are prosperous institutions, run by A. P. Rhyne, warps and yarns being the articles manufactured. Over 300 laborers are given employment. In connection with his milling, Mr. Rhyne conducts a large mercantile establishment. As a business man he is practical and successful, full of energy and pluck. He began life with limited capital and his success has been phenomenal. He has never aspired to political honors, preferring to lead the life of the prosperous and useful citizen. Mr. Rhyne is identified with the Lutheran church. October 22, 1872, he was married to Miss Martha J., daughter of Ambrose Costner, of Lincoln county, N. C. Unto this union six children have been born, namely: Augusta G.,

Walter G., Henry A., Lillie C., Susan M. and Helen A. Mr. Rhyne
is a self-made man, and his success in life is largely due to his excellent qualities as a man of culture and a high sense of honor.

HENRY W. COBB,

one of the leading tobacco dealers of Guilford county, N. C., was
born in Caswell county, N. C., January 21, 1866. He was educated in
the common schools of Caswell county and at the Eastman business
college at Poughkeepsie, N. Y. In 1879 he went to Danville, Va., and
until 1883 was employed in a mercantile establishment in that city.
In 1884 he accepted the management of Mr. O. W. Dudley's tobacco
warehouse, and held that position for one year. In 1885 he removed
to Greensboro, N. C., and embarked in the leaf-tobacco business on
his own account. He started in a modest way, but such has been his
success that he has been obliged to increase the capacity of his warehouses four times since he first started in the trade. Miss Jennie B.
Scales, a daughter of Col. J. I. Scales, now deceased, but during his
life a prominent attorney of Greensboro, N. C., and during the late
war a colonel of a Mississippi regiment, became his wife in 1887.
Mrs. Cobb is the niece of ex-Gov. A. M. Scales, of North Carolina.
One child, Effie, is the issue of this happy marriage. Henry W.
Cobb was the father of our subject. He was born in Caswell county,
N. C., June 13, 1822. He was a prominent planter of Caswell county,
and died there in 1876.

B. L. JONES.

One of the great industies of the thriving city of Beaufort, N. C.,
is that of shipping fish and oysters to northern markets. This enterprise gives employment to a large number of men, as large factories
have been erected there for the canning of oysters and manufacture
of fish scraps and oil. Of the few progressive men who have by their
energy and business foresight made this happy state of affairs possible
is Mr. Benjamin L. Jones, who, in connection with Mr. W. S. Chadwick and J. S. Caffrey, is extensively interested in this business. Mr.
Jones is a native of Beaufort, having first seen the light there on the
18th of June, 1838. His parents, John and Susan Jane (Bell) Jones,
were also natives of Carteret county, N. C. John Jones was the son
and namesake of John Jones, a Virginian, who removed to Beaufort
in his early manhood. He was a sea captain for many years, and in
later life was engaged in agriculture. His son, John, was born in
1810. His scholastic training was obtained in the schools of his native state. He entered the ministry of the Methodist Episcopal
church in early life and labored in his honored calling for many years
with signal success. In 1879 he was called home to his Master, and
his life and influence is left as a noble heritage to those who shall
come after. His first wife died in early life, leaving seven children,
one other having preceded her in death, five of the seven children

are living, viz.: William C., Benjamin L., Michael F., Susan I. and Sarah E. The father was married a second time, Sarah C. Davis becoming his wife. Mrs. Mary A. Davis, of Florida, and a deceased daughter, Emily C., by name, who died in early life, were the issue of this union. Benjamin L. Jones was given a practical education in the common schools of his native town. In 1862 he enlisted in the Confederate army a member of Company D, Sixty-seventh North Carolina infantry, and served until the close of the war, leaving the service with the rank of quartermaster-sergeant.

Peace having been declared between north and south, Mr. Jones settled in Beaufort, as a clerk in the mercantile establishment of Capt. Thomas Duncan, with whom he remained until 1871, when he established a business of his own. Two years later Mr. Jones became associated with Mr. W. S. Chadwick in the mercantile business, under the firm name of Chadwick & Jones, and this partnership existed until 1890, in which year they dissolved co-partnership. During this time Chadwick & Jones had become very extensively interested in the fish business, and they formed a company known as the Carteret County Fish Oil and Guano company. These gentlemen are still interested together in this and other ventures. By the exercise of his undoubted business abilities and the most rigid integrity, Mr. Jones has become prosperous, and he has done much to the building up of the community in which he lives. The beautiful building known as the Beaufort high school stands as a monument to the generosity and public spirit of Mr. Jones and others. Mr. Jones is a member of the democratic party in his section of the state, and has been treasurer of Carteret county. He is also a prominent communicant of the Methodist Episcopal church, south, and is a steward in the Beaufort church of that denomination. His domestic life has been most happy, he having married Miss Orpha Neal Gibbs, a daughter of Mr. Lockhert Gibbs, of Carteret county, in 1868. John L., Hugh C., William H. and Mary G. were the children born to this union. H. C., the only child living, is now connected with his father in mercantile business. As one who has done much to enchance the industrial growth of his town, elevate the people by making a more extended education possible, and who has furnished to the young men of the community an example worthy of their following, it is eminently proper that a sketch of Benjamin L. Jones should appear in this volume.

BENJAMIN L. PERRY,

manager of the Carteret Oyster company, of Beaufort, N. C., was born in that city November 7, 1841, the son of B. L. and Elizabeth (Manney) Perry. The parents were natives of Beaufort, and were prominent and highly esteemed residents of that city. The father for many years held an influential position in the community as clerk and master in equity, and for more than thirty years was agent for the board of underwriters. He died in 1868. He was a steward and trustee of the Methodist Episcopal church, south, and was also a member of the I. O. O. F. His wife survived him until 1879. The six children born to this marriage were all reared to maturity, and three of them are now living, viz.:   Edward, a merchant at Newbern; Frederick, proprietor of the Newbern House, at Morehead city, and Benjamin L. The latter was graduated from the University at Chapel Hill, and in 1868 became the proprietor of the Atlantic hotel, at Beaufort, which he conducted successfully for three years, after which he removed to Wilmington, and took charge of the Purcell house there. For six years he was connected with the latter house, and for one year operated a hotel at Carolina Beach, a leading summer resort. After the death of his father, Mr. Perry acted as agent for the underwriters' exchange for several years, and in 1890 accepted the position he now occupies, as general manager of the Carteret Oyster company. Mr. Perry enlisted in Company H, Second North Carolina regiment, in May, 1861, and subsequently was transferred to the Fifty-eighth North Carolina, and served until the close of the war. In 1868 Miss Etta Duncan, daughter of Thomas Duncan, Esq., became his wife, and their children are: Frank, a civil engineer now engaged on the United States River & Harbor Improvement survey corps; John and Etta. Mr. Perry is a prominent Mason, and himself and family are communicants of the Episcopal church, in which he is a vestryman.

EDWARD C. DUNCAN.

One of the leading connections of Beaufort, N. C., is the Duncan family. Mr. Edward C. Duncan, the present collector of customs at the port of Beaufort, was born in that city, March 28, 1862, and is a son of William B. Duncan, who first saw the light in Beaufort on the 13th of June, 1836. The latter was a grandson of Thomas Duncan, who was born of Scotch parentage, and was one of the early settlers of Beaufort. Thomas Duncan, Jr., son of Thomas, and father of William B. Duncan, was born in Beaufort. He was a sea captain for several years, and later entered mercantile life in his native city, and also engaged as a vessel builder. He was a very influential man in the community and was a prominent member of the whig party. He married Miss Eliscia Howland, and they had a large family of children. William B. Duncan married Miss Sarah A. Ramsey, by whom he had six children, the three now living being: William E., Thomas and Edward C., all residents of Beaufort. His first wife dying, he married, sometime later, Miss Emily F. Jones, and their five living children are: David J., Emily E., Julius F., James E. and Lillian. The father was a leading merchant of Beaufort for many years, and for a long time was a director of the A. & N. C. R. R., and was at one time station agent for that road at Morehead City, and also agent for the Clyde line of steamers. He was treasurer of Carteret county for a term, and was elected the first mayor of Beaufort after the close of the Civil war. He is now retired from active business life, and resides in Beaufort. He has been prominent in church work since early manhood, and is now secretary of the board of stewards of the Methodist Episcopal church, south, and also president of the missionary society, and treasurer of the Sabbath-school of the Beaufort church. Edward C. Duncan was educated in the public schools. He entered upon his business career as a member of the firm of Thomas & E. C. Duncan, merchants, and has since been quite extensively engaged in agriculture and cotton speculation. In 1880 he established the first steam cotton-gin ever in Carteret county, and operated the same until 1888. For a time he served as captain of the steamer "Margerie," which plys between Beaufort and points on the New river. March 28, 1890, President Harrison appointed him collector of customs for the port of Beaufort, and he now holds that office. Mr. Duncan has been most active and efficient in the republican party, and is recognized as a leader in that political body in his section of the state. He resigned the office of commissioner of navigation to accept the one he now holds, and his discharge of the duties of this most important office has been as satisfactory as well as his incumbency of the former position.

DANIEL BELL.

One of the prominent merchants of Morehead City, N. C., is Daniel Bell, who was born in the village of Bear Banks, Onslow county, N. C., on the 24th of February, 1846. His parents were William B. and Hannah (Wade) Bell, both natives of Carteret county, N. C. The father was captain of a sailing vessel, and followed the sea all his life. He died in Carteret county in 1851, his wife surviving him until 1882. The son, Daniel, was reared in Carteret county, where he received a very limited education, as, upon the death of his father, his services were required to help support his mother and two smaller brothers. The boy was not daunted by the thought of hard work, and started his business career as a fisherman. He saved enough money to enable him to establish a very small business, and in 1867 he embarked in the fish and oyster trade at Morehead City, and shipped his goods to Goldsboro, and points along the line of the A. & N. C. railroad. His thrift and enterprise were rewarded from the start by success, and the business steadily grew, until it is now one of the largest in the eastern portion of the state. In 1883, he erected a menhaden fish factory and now has two of these factories in operation, and besides he is engaged as a catcher of porpoises. In 1887 Mr. Bell opened his present mercantile house, which is very extensive at this time. In January, 1874, he was so fortunate as to secure Miss Julia W. Gaskill, daughter of Gilford Gaskill, of North Carolina, as his wife, and their union has been blessed by the birth of five children, viz.: Lillie, Mary, Olive, Daniel, Jr., and John. Mr. Bell is an ardent democrat, and has served on the board of town commissioners, and also as a member of the school board. He is a prominent member of the Baptist church, being a member of the finance committee of the Morehead society. As a self-made man who has grasped opportunity and turned it into possession, he is entitled to respect, and his name is held in the highest esteem throughout the community. As a citizen he has shown himself liberal minded and progressive.

HON. ROBERT T. HODGES,

sheriff of Beaufort county, was born in that county on the 20th of September, 1834, and is a son of John and Sally (Perry) Hodges, natives of Beaufort and Martin counties, respectively. The father was a prominent citizen, and for many years was a deacon in the Primitive Baptist church. His demise occurred in 1880, and his wife died in the same year. Their eight children were, Henry, deceased; Francis P., of Beaufort county; John G., deceased ; Edwin G., deceased; Noah B. (deceased) was second lieutenant in Captain Triff's company in the Confederate army; Louisa, wife of John Wood, of Martin county, N. C.; Robert T., and James W., a resident of Beaufort county. Robert T. Hodges received a competent education in the schools of his native county. He remained on the homestead for several years, and was engaged in agriculture, and was also extensively interested in the manufacture of lumber. In 1882 he was elected sheriff of Beaufort county, and in the same year was made treasurer of the county. For six years he served as a commissioner of the county, and was the first democratic justice of the peace ever elected in his native township, and the only man on the ticket who was successful. He is a member of the Masonic fraternity, and also of the I. O. O. F. His marriage to Miss Annie E. Latham, daughter of Dempsey Latham, of the county, was solemnized in 1855, and has resulted in the birth of three children, named as follows: Helen, wife of Walter Jones, of Washington, N. C.; Jimmie and Jennie Gray Hodges. The family are communicants of the Christian church. Mr. Hodges has been a most successful and efficient official, and his continued retention in the important offices he has held speaks for his popularity with the people. He is able, progressive and upright, and his name is honored wherever known.

HON. GOETHE WILKENS,

clerk of the circuit and superior courts of Beaufort county, N. C., is a native of Sweden, his birth having taken place at Carlscrona, on the 2nd of September, 1851, his parents being Rudolph and Charlotte (Thomel) Wilkens. Mr. Wilkens was reared and educated in his native country, having been a student in the military academy of Carlsbere, near Stockholm, and was graduated from that institution before attaining his eighteenth year. In 1870 he sought a wider field for his life work in America, and at that time located at Bath, Beaufort county, N. C., where, in June of the following year, he married

Miss Hattie Harvey, a daughter of W. L. Harvey, of Beaufort county. For several years after his removal to the United States Mr. Wilkens was engaged in agriculture and merchandising. In 1882 he was elected to the office he now holds, having been retained in the office ever since. President Grant appointed him postmaster of Bath in 1871, and for several years he was a justice of the peace. He is a prominent member of the I. O. O. F., Excelsior lodge of the Golden Chain, and is a leading democrat. His marriage has been blessed by the birth of four children, viz.: Annie Thaimee, Henry Theodore, John Harvey and Charlotte D. As a member of the Lutheran church he is active and consistent, and his wife is a communicant of the Episcopal denomination. Mr. Wilkens has proven himself a man well fitted for public office, and the satisfaction he has rendered to the people is amply proven by his continued re-election to so important an office. Intelligent and upright, he is eminently qualified for the highest citizenship.

WILLIAM Z. MORTON,

one of the leading merchants of Washington, N. C., was born in that place on the 15th of June, 1825, and is a son of Winslow B. and Ann Maria (Christ) Morton, the former a native of Lubec, Me., and the mother of eastern Virginia. Winslow Morton came to North Carolina as a captain of a vessel in 1823. He married and located in Washington, though still interested in vessels, he owning one in the West India trade, and at one time he commanded a vessel which sailed from Washington to South America. His death occurred in Havana in 1837. He was a member of the Masonic fraternity. His widow subsequently married Benjamin Meekins, and died in 1842. Three sons and one daughter were born to Winslow and Ann M. Morton, viz.: William Z.; George went to California in 1847, and died there; Valentine was a member of the Washington Grays during the Civil war; in 1865 he settled in Virginia, but two years later went to California, where he died in 1871; and Mary Catherine, who died in infancy. Martha Meekins, the offspring of Mrs. Morton by her second husband, married Charles Huddler, and is now deceased. William Z. Morton, the subject of this mention, spent his boyhood in Washington until his fourteenth year, when he went to Portland, Me., and there learned the trade of a pump and block maker. In 1846 he returned to his native town, and for fourteen years thereafter was engaged in the manufacture of pumps and blocks at that place, and from 1850 to 1862, carried on a large fruit and confectionery business in connection with his other interests. As a member of the Home guards, commanded by Gov. Vance, Mr. Morton served during the Civil war in the state service, having been honorably discharged after the evacuation of Newbern, at which time the company was disbanded. In 1866 he established his present mercantile business, and has since conducted that with marked success. He is also quite ex-

tensively engaged in agriculture.   In 1847 he joined the I. O. O. F.,
and is now a dimitted member.

Formerly a whig, Mr. Morton is now an ardent democrat, and has
served as a town commissioner, and for several years held the office
of justice of the peace.   He was largely instrumental in organizing
the present fire department of Washington, having been for ten years
captain of the old department; and he is also a member of the school
committee, of which he has been a member for ten years.   He was
the one to inaugurate the movement having for its object the erection of the present public school building, and did much toward securing its erection.   In 1847, Mr. Morton married Miss Melissa A. Darden, daughter of George F. Darden, of Virginia, and these children
have been born to them: Mary, wife of Col. D. M. Bogart; Winslow B., William Z., attorney-at-law; James C., Alice, wife of B. M.
Bell, of Chattanooga, Tenn.; Lucy D., wife of David P. Blount, of
Memphis, Tenn., and George O. Morton.   The family are communicants of the Episcopal church, and Mr. Morton is treasurer of the
same, and for fifteen years he has been a vestryman.   As a business
man he is held in the highest respect and esteem by the community
at large, and as a citizen he is regarded as among the most progressive and intelligent.   Winslow B. Morton married Miss Matilda
Lamb, of Martin county, N. C., and their children are: Charles,
Melissa, Irene and Matilda.   William Z. Morton, Jr. was happily
united in marriage with Miss Carrie Hardeson, of Martin county,
and five children have blessed their home, viz.:   Mary, Corney, Irene,
William and Hubert.   By his marriage to Miss Emma Dobbins, of
Baltimore, M. D., Mr. James C. Morton has had three children,
named as follows: Catherine Lee, James and Emma, and Mrs. Alice
Morton Bell is the mother of Mary, Bryant and Douglas Bell.   To the
union of Miss Mary Morton and Col. D. M. Bogart, seven children
have been born, their names being: Isabella, Alice, Malcolm, William, Robert, Gilbert and Mary C. Bogart.

JESSE RUSSELL STARNES,

a representative merchant and business man of Asheville, N. C., was
born in Buncombe county, May 26, 1856.   He is a son of Thomas A.
Starnes, also a native of Buncombe county, N. C., and a farmer by
occupation.   At the age of seventy-eight years, Mr. Starnes still
lives on the old Starnes' homestead in his native county.   He served
in the Confederate army during the entire Civil war.   He is the
son of John A. Starnes, one of the earliest settlers of Buncombe
county, but a native of Burke county.   The mother of Jesse R.
Starnes was Elizabeth Morgan, a native of McDowell county,
N. C., and the daughter of Jesse Morgan, a native of North Carolina.   Mr. Starnes' maternal grandmother, Morgan, was from England.
Mrs. Starnes is also living, and is about sixty-eight years of age.
Jessie R. Starnes was reared on the homestead farm until he reached

the age of eighteen, and he received a good education in the Sand Hill academy, taught by Jacob Hood, a well known educator. He entered Candler college at the age of nineteen, where he remained three years, missing a portion of each year, however, in order to teach school and secure the necessary means with which to keep him in school during the balance of the year. In 1878 Mr. Starnes entered Waversville college and there spent one year. On account of ill health he was compelled to leave the college, but four months before graduation. Prior to leaving the last named college, Mr. Starnes taught for eight months, having a school of 180 pupils, and one assistant. While engaged in this pursuit he devoted his leisure time to the study of law under James H. Merrimon. In 1880 he abandoned the study of law, and engaged as a clerk with Smith, Cheesborough & Co., of Asheville, general merchants. On the 1st of September, 1881, Mr. Starnes embarked in the grocery business, in Asheville, upon his own responsibility, and followed the same for six years. His entire capital, when he began, was $180. In 1887 he sold his stock and went into the undertaking business, with which he has ever since been identified. He was for some time the only undertaker in Asheville, and at present is the leading one in his profession at that place. Mr. Starnes engaged in the dry goods traffic in 1888, and since that year has been identified with the leading merchants of Asheville. Aside from his undertaking and merchandising affairs, Mr. Starnes has given much attention to real estate, not as an agent, but upon his own account. Politically he is a democrat and an official member of the Baptist church. Fraternally he belongs to the K. of H., the A. O. U. W., and the Royal Arcanum. Mr. Starnes was married, in 1885, to Miss Maggie Brand, daughter of Xenophon Brand, late of Asheville. They have an only son, X., who is in his sixth year. Mr. Starnes is now worth from $75,000 to $100,000, and is a strong, healthy man; weighs 152 pounds, and is five feet eleven inches high; square built and level-headed. The young man has been in business for himself only ten years, and can always be found at his place of business at No. 27 North Main street, Asheville, N. C.

ROBERT BURTON MILLER

was born January 29, 1852, at Shelby, N. C. He is the ninth child in order of birth and the youngest son of Dr. W. J. T. Miller and Elizabeth (Fullenwider) Miller, and received his early education at Shelby, which included an academical and a classical course. He showed an early fondness for literature, and after leaving the schools of Shelby at the age of eighteen, he completed his education without the aid of instruction, relying upon his own resources for his mental training. About the year 1870 Mr. Miller entered the mercantile establishment of his uncle, Mr. Fullenwider, as clerk, remaining in this business over two years. He then went to Georgia, where he engaged in business for a year. On his return in the fall of 1873 he embarked in the mercantile trade with his brother at Shelby, under the firm name of Miller Brothers, which firm still exists. In his social relations Mr. Miller is a liberal and public-spirited citizen, and in 1887 he was the prime mover in organizing the Belmont Cotton Mills company. These mills have been in successful operation in Shelby ever since and Mr. Miller is president of the corporation. Two years later he built on his own responsibility the Laural Cotton mills, located on Broad river three miles from Shelby. These mills are now doing a thriving business, and are a source of profit to their owner and to the surrounding inhabitants, who furnish supplies for their operation. The two sets of mills have each over 4,000 spindles. Beside his mercantile and manufacturing interests Mr. Miller is extensively engaged in agricultural pursuits which help to swell his income. Politically Mr. Miller is a staunch democrat, but not one of the demonstrative kind of politicians, and is not in any sense an office-seeker. He has been a member of the executive committee of his party, and in 1880 acted as chairman of the Cleveland county prohibition party. Under his management the party polled the largest vote of any county in the state. He made a personal canvass of his county in this campaign, and the effects of his efforts were obvious in the result. In several conventions he has acted as delegate.

In the development and promotion of the material interests of his town and county, Mr. Miller has both eyes open and is looked upon as a live, energetic and pushing man. In every movement for the progress and prosperity of the industrial and social interests of the community, he is ready to lead off in the expenditure of money and personal effort for the accomplishment of the desired end. Mr. Miller is a member of the Cleveland lodge of Free Masons, and is a devout communicant of the Methodist Episcopal church, south, holding therein high official positions. To that church he attached himself in early manhood, and he has steadfastly kept the faith. October 7, 1885, Mr. Miller was joined in marriage with Miss Laura Glenn, daughter of Hon. James McCants, of Winnsboro, one of the most prominet lawyers in South Carolina. Mr. and Mrs. Miller have had two children, but only one, Laura Burton, is now living. Mr. Miller has a large and well selected library in which to indulge his literary tastes. The ravages of the war swallowed up the estate of Mr. Miller's father, and in the outset he was thrown upon his own resources. But energy, force of character, honesty and integrity of purpose have more than supplied the place of patrimony, the lack of which has served all the more to develop character and give zest to the enjoyment of his own accomplishments. Besides his connection with the church, Mr. Miller is an active member of the Y. M. C. A. He was for many year a member of the Philologian literary society, in the exercises of which he took an active part, and to the training and discipline of which he attributes his qualities as a public speaker. Maj. Miller served several years as a staff officer of his state militia, with rank of major, having been commissioned by Gov. Thomas J. Jarvis.

MAJ. THOMAS J. BROWN,

the pioneer wholesale tobacco dealer of Winston, N. C., and one of the most extensive dealers in the state, was born in Caswell county, N. C., in August, 1833. The family is one of the oldest and most prominent in the state, and its members have at different times held high offices in both the commonwealth and national government. Maj. Brown was prepared for college at the Dan River institute. His mother then removed with her family to Davie county, in the Yadkin valley, where he engaged in agriculture until the breaking out of the Civil war, when he enlisted in Capt. Kelley's company as a private, but was at once elected lieutenant. This company was organized in Davie county, and afterward assigned to the Fourth North Carolina volunteer infantry. Lieut. Brown served with this command until prior to the battle of Culpeper Court House, and while the same was in camp at that point he was given a permit to return home and raise a new company, which he did, and of which he was elected captain. This company was assigned to the Forty-second regiment North Carolina volunteer infantry. The close of hostilities found him still in the field as a member of the last mentioned regiment with the rank of major, which office he had won by his faithfulness and valor on the following battle-fields: Cold Harbor, all the fights around Petersburg, Fort Fisher, two battles below Kinston, and at Bentonsville, and various skirmishes and engagements of minor importance.

Major Brown returned to North Carolina after the war and was engaged in the manufacture of tobacco for a short time, subsequently removing to Winston, where he established the first tobacco warehouse, and where he sold the first tobacco ever brought to that market, in February, 1872. This industry has since grown to enormous proportions in Winston, and forms one of its most important enterprises, the sales from Major Brown's establishment alone amounting to between four and five million pounds annually. This progressive gentleman is also a member of the extensive hardware firm of Brown, Rogers & Co., of Winston; is a partner in one of the largest dry goods houses in the city; is also a director in the First National bank of Winston, largely interested in three different land companies, and a stockholder in the Roanoke & Southern railroad company. Major Brown has been an elder in the Presbyterian church for a number of years, as well as superintendent of the Sunday-school. Major Brown was happily married in 1868 to Miss Delphine Hall, of Mobile, Ala. This estimable lady died on the 8th of August, 1889, leaving no children. Her father was Daniel Emerson Hall, a native of Middle Granville, N. Y., who graduated at Yale in the class of 1834. Subsequently he read law with his brother, Willis Hall, a prominent lawyer and politician and at one time attorney-general of New York state, and then removed to Mobile, Ala., where he soon rose to eminence in his profession, and

B—36

married a descendant of Louis D'Olive, a French officer sent out by his government.

Major Brown is the son of John E. Brown, M. D., who was born in Caswell county, N. C., in 1800 and died in 1846. He was an eminent physician of his day, having prepared for his professional career in the old University of Pennsylvania, at Philadelphia. He served as a member of the legislature of his state, and for many years was chairman of the county board in Caswell county. In 1826 he married Miss Elizabeth B., daughter of Mr. Jesse Carter, and five children blessed their union, the four surviving ones being Col. John Edmunds Brown, of Charlotte, N. C., a prominent lawyer and an elder in the Presbyterian church; Major Thomas J. Brown, Sallie C., widow of Mr. W. E. Hall, and Miss Jessie E. Brown. The eldest child was William Carter Brown, M. D., who was a surgeon in the Confederate service and died from illness contracted in camp in 1862. The Hon. Bedford Brown, who served as United States senator for many years, was an elder brother of John E. Brown, and they were sons of Jethro Brown, a Virginian, who spent his active life in Caswell county, N. C., as a planter and merchant. When a young man he removed to North Carolina, where, for several terms, he served as chairman of the county court of Caswell county, N. C., and died leaving the family name stainless. His father was John Brown, who was born in Virginia, and came to North Carolina during the Revolutionary war, and died in this state. This branch of the Brown family originated in Bedfordshire, England, having emigrated to America many years prior to the Revolution. Elizabeth Brown Carter, who became the wife of the Hon. John E. Brown, M. D., was a descendant of the Shirley Carter family, of Virginia. This proud old family furnished one of the signers of the Declaration of Independence.

GEORGE N. IVES,

a prominent business man of Newbern, N. C., is a native of Connecticut, having been born in New Haven county on the 6th of March, 1843. His parents, Luther and Laura (Barnes) Ives, were of Welsh descent. John Ives, the oldest known ancestor of the Ives family, was the first settler of the town of Cheshire, Conn., he having located there about the year 1640. Stephen Ives, the grandfather of our subject, was a representative man of New Haven county, a large land owner and a respected citizen. At his demise he left a large estate in New Haven and adjoining counties. The father of our subject was the youngest of a large family of children, and became a prominent agriculturist of the section. In 1874 he came to North Carolina, and two years later died in Beaufort, Carteret county. He was a leading politician, having been a member of the Connecticut senate and legislature for a number of years as a republican. For many years he was a deacon in the First Congregational church of Fair Haven, Conn., and was a life member of the American missionary society. His wife still survives him, having taken up her residence at Newbern. Their family consists of three children: George N., Charles, superintendent of the lumber concern of D. Congden & Sons, and Ella, wife of Clarence E. Gipe, of Nevada, Mo. The latter is a musician of rare ability, having at one time been one of the most noted vocalists of North Carolina.

George N. Ives received his early schooling in the Cheshire public schools and later in the Episcopal academy at Cheshire, Conn., completing his studies in the West Haven seminary. He then secured a position as book-keeper for an uncle in New Haven, and after remaining with him for a number of years, engaged in the manufacture of wooden ware, under the firm name of Kellogg & Ives. In 1872 their extensive plant was destroyed by fire, and two years later Mr. Ives removed to North Carolina. He embarked in the fish and oyster business at Morehead City, and in 1877 located in Newbern, still retaining a branch house in the latter place and at Beaufort. He carries on the largest concern of the kind in that section, his business in 1890 amounting to $75,000. In the year 1875, Mr. Ives introduced in navigation on the eastern shore of North Carolina, the "Sharpie" boat, which is much better adapted to successful navigation, than the class of boats formerly used, and to-day a most excellent fleet of boats is in use, and has been a useful reform. In 1863 he married Miss Lucia A. Burnham, of West Haven, Conn., a stepdaughter of the Rev. Dr. Jason Atwater, a distinguished clergyman of the state. John B., an employe in the office of the United States river and harbor surveyor, at Wilmington, N. C., and Lucia E. Ives, are the children of this marriage. Mr. Ives was one of the prime movers in the organization of the Eastern North Carolina Fish, Oyster and Game association, of which he is a director; and he has charge of the fish and oyster exhibit, which is the principal attraction of the annual fair held at Newbern, attracting much attention and winning wide and well deserved reputation. Both himself and wife are valued communicants of the Presbyterian church of Newbern, of which he is a deacon. As a progressive, intelligent business man, Mr. Ives is an honor to the town in which he lives. He is prominent in the democratic party, yet he has never sought nor wanted political preferment.

THE ARENDELL FAMILY

has been most prominently and actively identified with the settlement and growth of eastern North Carolina, and from time to time its members have held offices of trust and honor in the state and national governments. One of the most conspicuous of this connection is Michael F. Arendell, M. D., who was born at Shepperd's Point, now Morehead City, N. C., January 26, 1819, and is a son of Bridges and Sarah (Fisher) Arendell. His paternal grandfather was Thomas Arendell, who was a native of Franklin county, N. C., and was of

English descent. He was a planter and general trader, and amassed a large fortune, and was very influential in the community. His son, Bridges, was born in 1781 and died in 1850. In early life he became identified with the North Carolina Methodist Episcopal conference, and after having completed his education in Franklin county, he was ordained as a minister in that church, and for many years rode what was known as the "Trent" circuit. After his retirement from the ministry he held the office of collector of customs at Beaufort for several years, and subsequently engaged in planting and the manufacture of lumber at Newport on Black creek. Through his wife he became the owner of Shepperd's point, having 600 hundred acres of the land under cultivation, and about 3,000 acres on Black creek. He was a Jacksonian democrat in early life, and afterward a stanch whig. He was chairman of the county court for many years. His wife was a daughter of William Fisher, of Accomack county, Va. William Fisher first moved to Beaufort, and later to Newport, N. C., where he conducted a large general store, and he was also a very extensive land owner. The children born to this union were: Caroline, deceased; William, deceased; Michael F.; Sarah, now Mrs. William N. Dennis; Matilda, Polly and Bridges are deceased, and Thomas Arendell, of Carteret county. Michael received his scholastic training in the schools of his native county, and began the study of medicine under the direction of Dr. James L. Manney, of Beaufort, and later under Dr. G. S. Bedford, of New York city. In March, 1843, he was graduated from the medical department of the University of New York city, and the same year began the active practice of his profession at Beaufort, and continued with marked success until the breaking out of the late war. He was opposed to the disruption of the Union, but when the state declared for secession, he stood with his people and remained true to the southland. He was appointed regimental surgeon, and was detailed for duty in the surgeon-general's office at Raleigh, and later was sent by Gov. Vance to settle a serious difference which had arisen among the soldiers at Charleston, S. C. Dr. Arendell was long before the voters as a leading politician. His first important office was that of state senator, he having been nominated for that position by the people of Jones county, and his nomination confirmed by the voters of Carteret county. He was elected, in 1850, on the whig ticket, and served four conservative years thereafter, and in 1860 was again nominated for the senate and elected, having been opposed by Dr. Laffers. He served in that body during the entire war, and was chairman of the committee on the deaf, dumb and blind, and insane, and on propositions and grievances, and was chairman of the committee on corporations. He was appointed by the legislature one of a committee to confer with President Davis, in regard to the defense of eastern North Carolina, and in his every capacity rendered the highest satisfaction to the people. After the war, Dr. Arendell resumed his practice at Morehead City, and for a number of years was chairman of the court of Carteret county, and also a member of the state board

Yours Truly
W. Duke

of health. He was one of the leading organizers of the Carteret county medical society and was president of the same, and also a member of the State medical society, and of the Royal Arch and Scottish Rite Masons, and the I. O. O. F., having been the first noble grand of Concordia lodge, of Beaufort. Dr. Arendell was intimately connected with the organization of the A. & N. C. railroad company, having been active in securing its charter, and also one of its original stockholders, and a director for many years. At one time he was elected president of the road, but declined to accept the office. He was one of the first to hold the stock of the Shepperd's Point Land company, and was also largely interested in the building of the New Atlantic hotel, at Morehead City. He is prominent as a democrat. By his marriage to Miss Zelphia Ann Lee Craft, of Beaufort, which was solemnized in 1843, two children were born. The mother died in 1848. Mary B. and William L. Arendell are the offspring.

William L. Arendell was born in Carteret, N. C., on the 22d day of January, 1848. After completing the excellent course at Bingham's school, he entered West Point, where he remained for two years, having been prevented from graduating by rheumatism. In October, 1868, he was discharged from the National academy, and at that time returned to his native city. Mr. Arendell became a surveyor, and for the past few years has held the office of surveyor of Carteret county. In 1870 he removed to Morehead City, and has since been extensively interested in the fish and oyster business, having built up a large shipping house. He is prominently identified with the Shepperd's Point Land company, and since 1870 has been one of its directors. Democratic in politics, he has held the office of justice of the peace for the past ten years, and for the same length of time was mayor of Morehead City, and in 1884 was elected a county commissioner, and is the present chairman of the board. Mr. Arendell is a member of the I. O. G. T., and was deputy grand worthy chief templar of the same. In 1870 he was united in marriage to Miss Sarah C. Davis. A leading and influential communicant of the Methodist Episcopal church, south, Mr. Arendell is superintendent of the Sabbath-school, and also a trustee of the church at Morehead City. He is regarded as one of the ablest and most substantial business men of eastern North Carolina.

WASHINGTON DUKE

was born on the 20th of December, 1820, in the then county of Orange, now Durham, N. C. His parents were Taylor and Dicie (Jones) Duke. The father was a native of Orange and the mother a native of Granville county, N. C.; the former was of English and Scotch-Irish ancestry, while the latter was of Welsh lineage. Taylor Duke was a successful farmer by occupation, and was a well respected citizen, and held several county official positions, which he filled with much credit to himself and satisfaction to the people. He was a deputy sheriff of Orange county and was a captain of militia. He was a man of sterling qualities and of strong mind, and enjoyed the esteem and confidence of all who knew him. Of his ten children, we are, in this biographical mention, more directly interested in the career of Washington Duke, whom we have introduced as the subject of our sketch. Reared upon a farm, Mr. Duke early in life chose farming for an occupation, but his career as a business man and manufacturer will prove of special interest, for as such his success in life has been phenomenal. Like so many of the distinguished men of the country, the mental and moral fibre of his nature was hardened and invigorated in the school of adversity. His pathway to fame and fortune was strewn with thorns, not with roses. The educational advantages afforded him in youth were meager, and not more than six months of his life were spent at school, but through the avenues of subsequent years of wide business experience, and being naturally of strong intellect, keen discerning powers, he has become possessed of a well informed mind, recognized wisdom and sound judgment. He labored at farm work on the paternal homestead till he became of age, and at the age of twenty-one began life for himself, beginning as a farmer, farming on rented land for four years with such success as enabled him to then purchase a small farm upon which he continued to farm, and, being successful, he purchased one small tract after another until he had acquired a farm of three hundred acres, and at farming he continued until 1863, when he enlisted in the Confederate army as a private, and being assigned duty at Camp Holmes, as guard, he remained here for a few months when he was transferred to the navy and sent to Charleston, S. C. Six months later he was transferred to Richmond and assigned duty at Battery Brook, where he remained until the army retreated to Appomatox, where he was captured and for a few weeks confined in Libby prison. For his expert management of artillery he was distinguished, and at Battery Brook he was promoted to the rank of orderly sergeant. After the surrender and the establishment of peace, Mr. Duke was given transportation as far as Newbern, N. C., whence he walked home, a distance of 134 miles, "and, accepting the situation in good faith, applied himself once more to tilling the soil."

In 1844 Mr. Duke was united in marriage with Miss Mary C., daughter of Jesse and Rachael (Vickers) Clinton, of Orange county, N. C. To the happy union were born two children, namely, Sydney T., who died at the age of fourteen, and Brodie L. The mother of these children died on the 18th of November, 1847, and on December 9, 1852, Mr. Duke was married to Miss Artelia, daughter of John and Mary Roney, of Alamance county, N. C. To this marriage were born one daughter, and two sons, viz.: Mary E., Benjamin N. and James B. Mr. Duke's second wife died August 20, 1858. When Mr. Duke entered the Confederate army service, he had placed his elde rson, Brodie L., in the care of Major Gee, superintendent of the Salisbury prison, and had placed his three children by his second wife in the home of their maternal grandfather, Mr. Roney. Arriving home from the war, Mr. Duke gathered together his scattered family, and returning to the farm began life anew. He had no capital other than his land, and a determination to succeed. With but 50 cents in silver, received in exchange from a Federal soldier for five dollar Confederate note, and with a pair of blind mules, which he had obtained from the army of Gen. Sherman, Mr. Duke set out to support his family of four motherless children and to repair his shattered estate. He had pluck, character, persistence and courage, and success attended his labors. His daughter, then but twelve years of age, applied herself with remarkable tact and industry to the duties of housekeeping, and he and his sons were left to give their united attention to the farm and factory. The factory was a log cabin 16x18 feet, in which was begun, in 1865, the manufacture of smoking tobacco, in which business Mr. Duke, aided by his sons, has achieved phenomenal success and wide-spread fame. In consequence of a largely increased business he removed to Durham in 1873, and erected a factory with floorage capacity 40x70 feet, three stories high, and fifteen hands were employed. In 1875 another building was added, and in the meantime he had consolidated his business with that of his son, B. L. Duke, who had been engaged in the same business at Durham for three years. From time to time as their business still increased in volume they enlarged their facilities, and the manufacture of cigarettes had been added to the manufacture of smoking tobacco, and now they operate the largest cigarette and smoking tobacco establishment in the world, and are doing an annual business of over four and a half million dollars, employing near 900 hands. In addition to the stupendous establishment at Durham, they operate a branch factory at New York, in which over 500 hands are employed. Their cigarettes and smoking tobacco are sold all over the United States, Canada, and in foreign lands, and the name Duke is one familiar not only to thousands but millions. It is the founder of this great and stupendous business, whom we have introduced as the subject of this sketch.

Mr. Duke is recognized throughout the land and even abroad, as a business man of superior endowment, and to his sons, who have been faithful and instrumental in aiding their father to establish such a stupendous business, is due much credit. Mr. Duke has had abundant cause to feel proud of his family; and his domestic relations are the most happy. The distinguished subject of our sketch is a Christian gentleman, and is an influential member of the Methodist Episcopal church at Durham. He has given largely of his means to church, education and charity. He was instrumental in the building and organization of the Main Street Methodist Episcopal church of Durham, to which he gave abundantly of his means, and of which he is a valuable member. At a very early age he became a member of the Methodist Episcopal church, and through the course of many years he has lead the life of a consistent Christian. When a new building was proposed for Trinity college of North Carolina, Mr. Duke donated to the college $85,000; it being the largest sum ever given by any one man for any purpose in the state. In consequence of his donation, there is building at Durham a magnificent structure for Trinity college, and the same will stand a monument to his memory, and an evidence of his estimate placed upon education. Recently, Mr. Duke purchased, for $5,000, the Louisburg female college, and placed it under the auspices of the Methodist Episcopal church for educational purposes, and, in doing so, again gave impetus to the cause of education, and especially to this particular college, which was about to collapse, but his purchase of the property lifted a long standing indebtedness over the college, and now this barrier to its progress has been happily removed.

Mr. Duke has watched closely the course of public events, and has kept pace with public policy and with the conduct of public men, yet he has never aspired to public political honors. In his views in regard to political science, it may be truthfully said that he has been somewhat in the advance of many of his contemporaries. He foresaw the inexpediency of the passage of an ordinance of secession by his state in 1860, and argued against it; but when it came he went with his people in their choice, and when peace came and found the country in its new and changed condition, he felt and believed the principles of the national republican party to be safer for the country, and fell in line with that party, to which he has since adhered, yet it cannot be said that Mr. Duke is active in politics, nor is it to be understood that he has played a prominent part in the political history of his state, for his time and attention have been given largely to his business interests. And in business relations and affairs he has excelled. From adversity he has surmounted the many obstacles that have fallen in his way to fortune and fame, and having amassed an unusual fortune, established, too, an unusually voluminous business, and having attained to high social standing, and established an unblemished character, he is justly held in high esteem and confidence. For well on to a half century he has displayed business qualifications unrivaled, and his course would secure honor in any field of action. Maintaining a strict character for probity, being mindful of the rights of others, and being kind, courteous and charitable in bearing and disposition, he has become not only highly respected but popular wherever he has extended his acquaintance. Imbued with the spirit of charity, he has annually given largely of his means to charitable purposes, and as a public benefactor, and as a good man, and worthy citizen, he will long live in affectionate remembrance.

WILLIAM DORSEY PENDER.

William D. Pender, a major-general in the Confederate army, was born in Edgecombe county, N. C., February 6, 1834, at the mansion of his father, Mr. James Pender, whose family had long been residents of that vicinity. Entering West Point, he successfully stood the ordeal of that institution, and took a reputable stand in his class, of which G. W. Custis Lee, Stephen D. Lee, J. E. B. Stuart and

John A. Pegram were members. On graduating he was assigned to the artillery, but on his request he was transferred to the dragoons. For several years he was on duty in New Mexico, and on the breaking out of Indian hostilities on the Pacific coast, he was highly complimented for his action in the battles of Four Lakes and the Spokane Plains, and won his promotion to a first lieutenancy. He married, March 3, 1859, Miss M. F. Shepperd, daughter of Hon. Augustin H. Shepperd, of Salem, N. C., and was glad to be stationed in San Francisco, and at Carlisle, Penn., after that event. On March 3, 1861, he left Washington city for the south, and cast his fortunes with his people. On the secession of North Carolina he was appointed lieutenant-colonel, and put in charge of the camp of instruction at Garysburg, but was soon afterward elected colonel of the Third North Carolina volunteers. Upon the death of the lamented Col. Fisher, who was killed at Manassas, Gov. Clark appointed him to the command of the Sixth regiment North Carolina troops, and he behaved with such conspicuous gallantry at the battle of Seven Pines, that President Davis, who was present, promoted him to brigadier-general on the field of battle. His brigade was composed of the Thirteenth regiment, Col. Scales; Sixteenth regiment, Col. Lee; Twenty-second regiment, Col. Pettigrew; Thirty-fourth regiment, Col. Leaventhorpe, and Thirty-eighth regiment, Col. W. J. Hoke.

Gen. Pender was a fine disciplinarian and was most strenuous in his efforts to bring his brigade to the highest state of efficiency. Whenever opportunity offered he had brigade drill and he practiced his brigade in field evolutions. In the fights around Richmond he again displayed high soldierly conduct, and at Malvern Hill was severely wounded. His brigade was assigned to A. P. Hill's light division and was a part of Stonewall Jackson's corps. He gallantly led it in the hard-fought battle of Cedar Mountain, and advanced that night some distance beyond the battle-field in pursuit. He was with Gen. Jackson in the campaign against Gen. Pope, and won praise for his fine generalship at second Manassas, pursuing the enemy on the last day far from the battle-field and capturing many prisoners. Here too he was wounded. And again at Chantilly. He accompanied Jackson to Harper's Ferry, and not knowing the ground, sent Maj. Cole, of the Twenty-second, to reconnoitre. The major entered the Federal lines, and on his report, Gen. Pender urged such movements as resulted in the speedy fall of the post with a great number of prisoners and munitions. He reached Sharpsburg at a critical juncture and rendered important service there. In the battle of Fredricksburg his brigade suffered severely; and at Chancellorsville, he won his promotion to a major-generalcy. His division was composed of the following brigades: Lane's, Scales', McGowan's and Thomas', and it was assigned to A. P. Hill's corps. At the battle of Gettysburg, he again displayed his high qualities as a general. On the first day he carried Seminary Ridge. While on the right of his command on the afternoon of July 2nd, watching the progress of the fight, wrote Gen. Lane; "Our Christian-division commander, who had won so many laurels on so many hard-fought fields, received his fatal wound." He was conveyed from the field and was carried to Stanton, Va., where, on the 8th of July, he expired.

Gen. Lee said of him: "The confidence and admiration inspired by his courage and capacity as an officer, were only equalled by the esteem and respect entertained by all with whom he was associated for the noble qualities of his modest and unassuming character." It is not invidious to say that Gen. Pender deserves to rank next after Gen. A. P. Hill among Lee's lieutenants. Gen. Pender was publicly baptised in August, 1861, on the field near Manassas, by Rev. A. T. Porter, of Charleston, the ceremony being very impressive. He was confirmed as a member of the Protestant Episcopal church during that summer; and in his camp, or on the march, he regularly retired each night apart from his men and humbled himself in prayer and asked for Divine guidance. Gen. Pender left several children, who yet survive.

JOHN STARKEY.

One of the most strongly delineated characters in the colonial days was John Starkey, of Onslow county. He made his first appearance in the legislature in 1739, and at once took a prominent place among the leaders of that body. In 1746, when the committee on proposi- tions and grievances was first formed to hear any matters calling for redress, he was placed on that committee, and from the beginning of his legislative career he was heart and soul in the struggle against Gov. Johnston's measures. To him belongs the honor of having brought forward the first bill to establish a free school in North Carolina. His bill passed the legislature April 5, 1749, but the gover- nor under instructions did not give it effect. On the death of Treas- urer Eleazer Allen, he was elected by the house one of the two general treasurers of the province. The upper house dissented, and a struggle ensued, but the assembly carried its point, and in 1750 he became treasurer, and held the position until his death, when the same controversy was revived. During Gov. Dobbs' administration he was a thorn in the side of the governor. He held the position of colonel of militia in his county, and of justice of the peace, and he was the local adviser of his vicinage, and settled up large numbers of estates. Being continuously a member of the assembly and the treasurer, he exercised a controlling influence. He was held in high esteem by the people, and was powerful in the assembly. He co- operated always with Col. Sam Swann, and was a leader in every important measure brought before the legislature. He was on the committee of correspondence with the assembly's agent at London, the others being Swann, John Ashe and George Moore; and these formed the junta so roundly denounced by Gov. Dobbs, who ascribed to them a purpose to absorb all executive powers into their own hands, and who understood that they would make his administration easy if he would abdicate the prerogative of the crown for their

benefit. He asserted that Starkey and these associates of his were strong republicans, and that republican principles had a deeper hold in this than in any other colony.

Gov. Dobbs said of Starkey that he had won public confidence "by his capacity and diligence and in some measure from his garb and seeming humility, by wearing shoe-strings, a plain coat, and having a bald head." From this we may infer that Starkey practiced democratic principles and differed from the other gentlemen of the province in not wearing knee-breeches and a wig. And again the governor described him as "a professed, violent republican." At least, he always found him a warm friend to the liberty and freedom of the colony and a hot opponent of any arbitrary purpose of the governor. After being a leading spirit in all public matters for more than a quarter of a century, Mr. Starkey died in the spring of 1765.

JULIAN SHAKESPEARE CARR.

Among the eminent and representative men of the Carolinas we would give emphasis to the name of Julian Shakespeare Carr. No other individual, whose achievements and mental characteristics are outlined in this volume, is more deserving or more widely and favorably known, especially in North Carolina, than Mr. Carr. He was born and reared at Chapel Hill, Orange county, N. C., the date of his birth being October 12, 1845. His father was the late John Wesley Carr, who was for many years a respected citizen and successful merchant of Chapel Hill. John Wesley Carr was a man of more than ordinary business talent; and by means of his practical business tact, his honest endeavor, and his frugality, he acquired a competency for the support of himself and family, and to contribute, as he always did, a liberal share toward every public enterprise or worthy charitable object arising in his community. Eliza Pannel Bullock, who is now past the advanced age of seventy-six years, became the wife of John Wesley Carr. She is of a well-known and respected family of Granville county. Her marriage with Mr. Carr gave issue to several children, of which there are still surviving three sons and three daughters. Of those children, however, we are most interested in that son whose name introduces this sketch. Julian Shakespeare Carr remained under the parental roof till he had reached his majority; and being reared in the quiet village of Chapel Hill, his native place, he was afforded but little opportunity to develop those potentialities that have since distinguished him as a business man; but he was reared under the lasting influence of pious and exemplary Methodist parents, who early instilled into the nature of their son the principles and precepts of morality, Christianity, and ambition; and who imparted to him that gentlemanly instinct which from early life has pre-eminently distinguished his character. His early scholastic training was at Chapel Hill, where he was attending school when he entered the Confederate army.

Mr. Carr did true and manly service as a soldier in Company K, Third North Carolina cavalry, Barringer's brigade of W. H. F. Lee's division. His comrades, as an evidence of their esteem and respect for Mr. Carr, recently elected him to the presidency of the North Carolina Veteran association. Mr. Carr has ever manifested love of country, and devotion to the Union and his native state. It is worthy of him that mention is made of an incident in his life, that occurred in the city of Philadelphia, several years ago. Upon the occasion of his visiting old Independence Hall, and while inspecting the many historic relics in that patriotic collection, Mr. Carr observed that suspended on the walls of one of the rooms were the insignia and coat of arms, handsomely designed and printed, of nearly all the thirteen original states, and with humiliation he noticed that North Carolina was not represented. At once, with commendable state pride, at his own instance and expense, Mr. Carr procured permission and caused North Carolina's patriotic emblems and insignia to be placed side by side with her sister states, in the grand old hall of the Union. In November, 1886, Mr. Carr was chosen chief marshal, and acted as such at the Fayetteville centennial celebration of the ratification, by North Carolina, of the constitution of the United States, and to him was largely due the success of that occasion.

For a brief time after the close of the Civil war, Mr. Carr attended the university at Chapel Hill, which he left to become a partner with his father, in the firm of Carr, Freeland & Co., at Chapel Hill. This was Mr. Carr's first venture in business; and after remaining with this firm three years, he went, in 1869, to Little Rock, Ark., on account of the residence of an uncle in that city, and here he merchandised for about one year, after which he returned, in 1870, to his native state, and at this date became interested in manufacturing tobacco, in which his career has been pre-eminently successful.

In 1870 he purchased a one-third interest in the manufacturing business of W. T. Blackwell & Co., then composed of W. T. Blackwell and J. R. Day, at Durham, N. C., and at once Mr. Carr entered upon a career of an active and successful business life, as a manufacturer. At that time the business of Blackwell & Co. had just begun to grow, and the only need was additional capital and prudent management; these Mr. Carr well supplied, and from that day the business of Blackwell's Durham Tobacco company has continuously grown, until now the Blackwell Durham corporation, as now organized, operates perhaps the largest smoking tobacco establishments in the world—having a capital stock of $4,000,000, and doing annually an immense volume of business. Aside from this business interest, Mr. Carr has many others, and his prominence in business affairs may be inferred from the numerous positions of trust in private corporations which he holds, viz.: President Blackwell's Durham Tobacco company; First National bank, of Durham; Commonwealth Cotton manufacturing company, Durham; Golden Belt manufacturing company, Durham; Jule Carr Home Loan fund, Durham; Durham Electric Lighting company; Durham Street Railway company, Durham; Consolidated Land and

Improvement company, Durham; Board Trustees Methodist female seminary, Durham; Commonwealth Club, Durham; North Carolina Bessemer company, McDowell county; Greensboro female college association, Greensboro; Atlantic Hotel company, Morehead City; North Carolina Veteran association; Association Young Men's Democratic clubs; Southern Manganese company, Kings Mountain, N. C.; vice-president Lynchburg & Durham railroad company; Durham Cotton manufacturing company; Durham Bull Fertilizer company, Durham; Consumers' Phosphate company, Richmond, Va.; North Carolina Steel and Iron company, Greensboro; Kerr Bag machine company, Concord; trustee and member of the executive committee University of North Carolina; trustee of Trinity college; Davenport female college; Kittrell's normal school; trustee American university, Washington D. C.; director of Oxford orphan asylum; Oxford & Clarksville railroad; member of governor's staff (paymaster-general), with the rank of colonel; the executive committee of the National Tobacco association of the United Utates; and of the state democratic committee.

That Mr. Carr is a busy man of affairs these numerous positions would seem to indicate and those about him well know, for his executive ability is everywhere recognized and conceded. But in the midst of all his business affairs and engagements he never seems to be in as great a hurry as many having less to do. In his daily intercourse with his employes he never forgets to be a gentleman, and finds time to advise and help them in their own private matters, which few in his position would, if they could, devote spare time to do. Mr. Carr has, by his superior business talent and management, and together with his most excellent traits of character and commendable works, become not only one of the wealthiest men in the state, but has become deservingly one of the most influential, honored and beloved, as well as popular leader among the public spirits of the state. He has ever been an ardent promoter of industrial enterprises, educative and church, and has given much of his means, time and influence to the welfare of his fellow-man. He has given much financial aid to the churches, schools and colleges of his state; and stands pre-eminently an aid and giver to charity. He is the patron of many poor, struggling men, and has assisted out of difficulty scores of the needy. He has given to the hungry; he has aided the sick; he has educated the poor urchin; he has given home and succor to the poor veteran and maimed Confederate soldier; has supported poor preachers, schools and churches in the neighborhood of the poor; and has given large and material financial aid to the university, to Wake Forest college, to Trinity college and other institutions of learning; and in so many ways has he been a blessing to humanity, that manifold are the voices that called him blessed and give praise to his name and deeds. Were we to mention his many worthy traits of character we would give emphasis to his purity of soul and his magnanimous heart. He is wholly free of affectation and ostentation, and in consequence, as a benefactor, he appears in all his deeds as free of all selfishness.

In the political arena Mr. Carr is prominent and active, and while he has never sought political preferment, his name has several times been prominently and favorably mentioned in connection with offices of high honor. In the popular sense of the term he has never been an office seeker, yet some two years ago he was enthusiastically supported for nomination to the office of lieutenant-governor of North Carolina. He was twice elected a delegate for the state at large to the national convention of the democratic party, and in the convention that nominated Mr. Cleveland for the presidency, he was appointed one of the committee to frame the platform on which Mr. Cleveland was elected. His name is prominently mentioned as a candidate for governor of the state in the approaching campaign of 1892, and strong and enthusiastic would be his support if he would consent to become a candidate.

Mr. Carr married at the age of twenty-seven years, and in the selection of his wife displayed equal, if not better, sound judgment than in his most successful business affairs. He was the fortunate winner of the hand and heart of Miss Nannie G., the youngest daughter of Col. D. C. Parrish, of Durham. Two daughters: Lida and Lallah, and three sons, Julian, Marvin and Claiborne, have blessed their happy union. Mr. Carr's family residence in Durham, is one of the most handsome and expensive ones in the south, and ornamented with suitable surroundings, and there can be found nowhere a home of more ideal and elysian domestic happiness. There is nowhere to be found a more dignified, refined and amiable woman than Mrs. Carr, and she has been, and is, in every true sense a helpmate for her husband, worthy to grace and adorn the family circle around any domestic fireside where female virtues shed their hallowed light and contribute the chief essentials to happiness. Whatever may be the lot in life of their children, they will have no cause to regret their parentage.

RUFUS MURRAY JOHNSTON,

the subject of this sketch, was born on June 5, 1825, at the old homestead of the Johnston family, "Oak Grove" farm, which lies along the fertile banks of the Catawba river, in what was known in colonial times as Tryon county. The name was changed to Lincoln, the large county divided, and this well-known plantation was situated about fifteen miles north of Charlotte, in what now constitutes Gaston county. The Johnston family trace their lineage to the bold, sturdy Scotch-Irish stock. Firm and dauntless, loyal, conservative and honorable, are the characteristics that marked this stalwart race in the mother country; traits that were not lost by emigration and residence in this land of freedom and adventure. After the battle of Culloden, when the claims of the Stuarts and the hopes of their adherents were finally dispelled, in those troublous times when men's hearts were wearied and men's lives burdened with the incessant civil and religious agitations that vexed the old country, a tide of emigration flowed from Scotland to America. Among the families who then settled in this country, whose brave deeds brighten the pages of our early history and whose names are household words, were the Johnstons. Henry Johnston, the great-grandfather of Rufus M. Johnston, attracted by the genial climate, the rich soil and the mineral wealth of this section, made his home on the banks of the Catawba river, and began to build up this "Oak Grove" plantation, which is still in the possession of his descendants. During the Revolution his son Col. James Johnston served his country with honor, both on the field and in the council. The firmness and unflinching courage of his Scotch-Irish ancestry can be recognized in this epitome of his character, given by a contemporary, Maj. John Davidson: "He was a most excellent man and never shrunk from the performance of any duty when the welfare of his country demanded such service." Col. Johnston married Miss Jane Ewart, also of Scotch-Irish descent, her father, Robert Ewart, Jr., being one of the patriots of Mecklenburg county. Robert Johnston, the eldest son of Col. James Johnston, was a successful farmer, an influential member of society, and was for fifty years an elder in Unity church, one of the largest and wealthiest congregations in western North Carolina. He married Miss Mary M. Reid, daughter of Capt. John Reid, a soldier in the Revolution, and a senator from Lincoln county in the legislature of 1810–11, and again of 1817–18. They were the parents of a family of twelve children.

Rufus Murray Johnston was the seventh and youngest son of this family. It was the wish of his father that this son should adopt his own vocation and become a farmer, and to him he designed to leave the homestead, Oak Grove farm; consequently all of his early training and education was with this end in view, and the full collegiate course given to the older sons, he did not receive. Mr. Johnston, however, strenuously opposed this plan. His tastes and his abilities led him to prefer so decidedly a business life that he felt it was impossible to fulfil the expectations of his father. At the age of sixteen Mr. Johnston left his ancestral home and entered, as a clerk, the store of his brother, Robert E. Johnston, Jr., at Lincolnton. After two years spent in this position, a good school for the rudiments and discipline of a business, life, he took a bold step and went to New York, that mighty metropolis, which then, as now, tests a man's powers, bringing out all that is strongest and best in a virile character, while the weak are submerged and lost in the struggle for reputation and fortune. Mr. Johnston obtained a clerkship with L. M. Wylie & Co., but soon after embarked in business on his own capital and formed a partnership under the firm name of Churchill, Johnston & Co., which was changed, upon the retirement of Mr. Churchill, to Johnston, Shepherd & Saunders. They were importers and jobbers of fine dry goods and were in the full tide of successful commercial enterprise when

the Civil war interrupted their career and brought upon them un-
avoidable changes and losses.

On May 29, 1856, Mr. Johnston was married to Miss Cecelia Latta,
daughter of Robert Latta. Esq., of Columbia, S. C., a lady of charming grace and dignity of manner, of varied accomplishments and of
wealth. Soon after his marriage Mr. Johnston was elected to the
presidency of the Exchange bank of Columbia, and established his
residence in that delightful city. The office of president he filled till
the close of the war, and during this period he was chosen for two
terms to represent Richland district in the legislature of the state.
At the close of the war, Mr. Johnston made a short stay in Charlotte,
N. C., where his brother, Col. William Johnston, resided. He then
moved to New York city, and after settling up his mercantile and
banking business, became a traveling salesman in the extreme south.
His first engagement was with John T. Martin's Sons & Co., of New
York, and then he formed a business connection with Longstreet,
Sedgewick & Co., of the same city. As an evidence of the high esteem in which Mr. Johnston's ability was held, he received at this
time an annual salary of $10,000, with the addition of certain com-
missions. He continued to travel for only a few years, when his
health became impaired, and, surrendering active business, he removed with his family to Charlotte, N. C., where he had a large circle
of friends and many relatives.

Not more than a year later, in 1869, he died, leaving a widow and
one son, his only living child. Mrs. Johnston continued to reside in
Charlotte after her husband's death, and survived him for more than
twenty years. She died on the 17th of April, 1891, leaving a hallowed
memory. Her life was beautified by untold acts of charity and un-
forgotten deeds of kindness. She exerted a noble and wide-spread
influence in the church, in society and in her own home, which was
ever the center of a refined and elegant hospitality. Latta C. Johnston, their only son, was born in Columbia, S. C., on the 20th of May,
1857. His youth was spent there and in New York and in Charlotte,
successively, with his parents. He was educated mainly at Spartanburg, S. C., and at Charlotte. His home has been with his mother,
with whom he resided until her recent death. On July 14, 1887,
Latta C. Johnston and Miss Annie Lee Thorne were united in marriage, and their union has been blessed by the birth of a son, who
bears the full name of his paternal grandfather, Rufus Murray Johnston, the principal subject of this sketch.

Rufus Murray Johnston was a thoroughly practical man, careful
and judicious in all his business operations. His transactions were
dictated by sound good sense and a correct judgment that seemed to
be inborn and intuitive. Though he began life with a limited capital, his wonderful zeal and energy, combined with prudence and foresight, were worth more to him than an unlimited inheritance.
Though he was cut off in the prime of life, and his business career
interrupted by a civil war of gigantic proportions, he had accumulated at his death a handsome estate and left to his surviving family

more than a competency. He was generous and chivalrous in all his relations in life, kind and affectionate to his brothers and sisters, and a devoted son to his parents. He was liberal and popular with all his commercial and other acquaintances, and made friends of them. The writer of this sketch well remembers the gentleness and winning courtesy of his manner, and his quick sympathy and prompt response to any appeal of distress. His useful life was closed in his forty-second year, and his death was the first, in a family of twelve, to break the charmed circle of sister and brotherhood.

JUDGE DAVID SCHENCK, LL. D.

No compilation of the biographical sketches of the illustrious sons of North Carolina would be complete that excluded the name of Judge David Schenck. His ancestors came from Switzerland to this country in the early part of the eighteenth century, having first been exiled from their native country to England, on account of their religious convictions—they being Menonites—and in that country receiving an invitation from William Penn, in 1708, to join his colony, then being fitted out for settlement in Pennsylvania. Three brothers, Michael, John and Henry Schenck, accepted the invitation of Penn, and in Pennsylvania, February 28, 1737, was born to the eldest brother, Michael, a son, who was also named Michael, and to this second Michael there was born, on the 15th day of February, 1771, in Lancaster county, a son, who was also named Michael. At the age of eighteen years this third Michael Schenck came to North Carolina and settled in Lincolnton, in the year 1790; here he engaged in mercantile business and also established a cotton mill. To this Michael Schenck there was born at Lincolnton, February 3, 1809, a son, who was named David Warlick Schenck, who became a physician and surgeon of great skill. David Warlick Schenck married Susan Rebecca Bevens, of Charleston, S. C., and to this union there was born, at Lincolnton, N. C., March 24, 1835, David, the subject proper of this sketch. David gained a very fair knowledge of books, and, studying the principles of law under Haywood W. Guion, obtained a license to practice the profession in the county courts in June, 1856. Later in the same year he studied law under Chief-Justice R. M. Pearson, at Richmond Hill, and was duly admitted as a full-fledged practitioner of law in Dallas, Gaston county, N. C., in 1857. Near his birth place, August 25, 1859, he married Sallie Wilfong Ramseur. In 1860, Mr. Schenck, having met with eminent success in his practice, was elected county solicitor, having, however, filled the same position in Gaston, where his transcendent abilities had already been recognized. In 1861 he was elected to the state convention to fill the vacancy caused by the promotion of the Hon. William Lander to a seat in the Confederate congress. In 1869 he was compelled to yield his nomination for the state senate, on account of his political disabilities not having been removed by congress, and until 1874 followed his vocation of lawyer. On the 13th day of May, 1874, he was nominated as a democrat

B—37

for the office of judge of the ninth judicial district, won the victory and was seated upon the bench. There the pure and clean characteristics of his legal mind were fully exhibited and his decisions as judge added new luster to his fame. In 1880 the University of North Carolina voluntarily conferred upon him the degree of LL. D., in recognition of his erudition and his profundity of knowledge of law especially.

In 1881 Judge Schenck resigned his seat on the bench and accepted the office of general counsel of the Richmond & Danville R. R. Co., on account of the demands of a growing family in a pecuniary way, and the compensation afforded by the railway company being greater than that given by the state, and for the same reason he declined to accept a position on the supreme court bench of North Carolina, tendered him by Gov. Jarvis in 1883. Judge Schenck is also counselor for the Charleston, Cincinnati & Chicago railroad company, with office at Greensboro, where he is also engaged in private practice.

Ex-Judge Schenck has long been a member of the Presbyterian church, and at Lincolnton was an elder in that religious denomination. Ever alive to the advancement of his local surroundings, the judge lends his services willingly in aid of any project for the benefit or the prosperity of his fellow-citizens, be the task enjoined ever so humble; and so, in May, 1887, he accepted a position as commissioner on the reform ticket at Goldsboro, and gave valuable aid in restoring to vitality the half-dead city. In 1886 Judge Schenck compiled a history entitled, "North Carolina—1780–81," which is essentially of and for North Carolina, which work has met with universal commendation, and, curiously enough, has proved to be a financial success, a result not always rewarding the historian.

COL. JOHN SOMERVILLE CUNINGHAM.

The subject of this sketch is one of the successful planters of North Carolina, who, inheriting a large estate, has in its management exhibited rare executive ability and a sagacity in business affairs that stamps him as one of the foremost agriculturists of the southern country. Residing in Person county, in the center of the famous Bright Tobacco Belt, whose products are unrivaled in the markets of the world, he has on his splendid plantation so developed the culture of the golden leaf as to be known as the largest tobacco planter in the world. He sets out two million hills of Bright tobacco and obtains the highest prices for his crops. Although his father had long resided in Person, Col. Cuningham was born in Warrenton, N. C., the home of his mother's family. He was born September 5, 1861, and in his youth received all the benefits of a cultured and refined home. After a thorough course at those famous schools, Horner's at Oxford, and Bingham's at Mebane, he entered the University of North Carolina, where he completed his education. He entered upon the activities of life admirably equipped, possessing arge wealth, with a wide circle of friends and inheriting a name that was the synonym of honor, courtesy and liberal hospitality. To these he united quick intelligence, pleasing manners and an agreeable address. He might well have chosen a road to fame through the portals of a professional career, or have entered into the alluring walks of political life. But with discretion and wisdom he resisted such inclinations, and has chosen to serve his state by advancing her agricultural interests and setting an example of successful farming, which all can follow to their advantage. He takes a pride in agriculture and devotes himself industriously to the care of his large property, seeking with diligence to make his farming operations a continued success, and inaugurating improvements and improved methods of culture as experience justifies. Thus he promotes the agricultural interests of the state and advances the prosperity of the farming element. His management indeed affords ample proof of what steady application and unremitting industry will accomplish when joined to fine executive ability and love for the vocation of one's choice.

But although strictly pursuing the business of farming, Col. Cuningham has exhibited on suitable occasions great interest in public matters and zeal for the success of the democratic party, of which he is a leading member in his section of the state. His earnestness has been displayed not merely by his personal exertions, his advice and canvasses, but by liberal contributions of money, and his efforts being appreciated by the democrats of his county, Person, he exerts there a powerful influence. As a public speaker, Col. Cuningham is easy and graceful, speaking directly to the point and presenting his ideas forcibly, without any attempt at artificial effect, beyond the excellence of the sentiments expressed and purity of diction, so that the humblest capacity can comprehend his points. In particular did his address at Oxford, N. C., April 18, 1888, upon the completion of the Oxford & Clarksville railroad, win him praise and encomiums. On February 2, 1888, there was held at Danville, Va., the inter-state farmers' convention, and of that large assembly of prominent agriculturists, Col. Cuningham was elected the president, and he presided with admirable poise over the deliberations of the body. As a presiding officer, he is rapid, fair and impartial, and, while hastening business to an end, courteous and pleasant to the members of the body. Evidently he has learned the rule, that he who would rule others well, must first learn to govern himself. Col. Cuningham was a delegate to the Paris exposition in 1889, and spent some time in attendance at the exposition. During the same trip to Europe, he traveled through France, England, Scotland and Ireland, and availed himself of the occasion, to compare the condition of those European peoples with that of his own countrymen, coming to the conclusion that, in all essentials, Americans were ahead of the world. At the opening of the campaign of 1888, some of the friends of Col. Cuningham brought his name forward for the position of lieutenant-governor of the state, but although not seeking such political honors at this time, he participated actively in the canvass and contributed

largely to securing a fine vote for Gov. Fowle in his section of the
state. As a compliment, Gov. Fowle, upon his inauguration, invited
him to become the senior member of his staff with the rank of colonel, and in that capacity he has at various times attended the governor
of the state upon important occasions. When Gov. Holt succeeded
to the executive office, Col. Cuningham was asked to retain his position on the staff and he is yet a member of the governor's military
family.

Col. Cuningham takes a deep interest, not merely in the advancement of agriculture and the development of the resources of
the state, but also in all those questions of an economic character
tending to the amelioration of the condition of the people. He is a
born democrat, and believes that men should be selected to office for
fitness, and for what they can accomplish for the good of the masses
and of the state. In 1889 Col. Cuningham married Miss Otey M.
Carrington, of Virginia, a beautiful, accomplished and lovely lady,
who adorns his elegant home and presides with grace over his hospitable board. There true southern refinement and culture hold
their sway, and a picture is presented of a typical southern home.
Careful business management, activity and progressive ideas are
united with a fine hospitality and liberal giving toward all proper
objects of bounty. The father of Col. Cuningham was the late Hon.
John W. Cuningham, a gentleman of admirable culture, high character and social standing. For more than forty years he took an
active part in public affairs, and left his impress upon the history of
his state. No man was more cherished by his friends than this distinguished gentleman, and none deserved to be held in higher esteem
for his personal worth and rare excellence. He, like his son, was a
successful planter, and added to his fortune by the skillful and prudent management of his farms. His death, in the year 1887, was
greatly deplored by hosts of friends from the mountains to the seaboard.

HON. JOHN W. CUNINGHAM.

One of the most admirable of the public men of North Carolina of
the generation now rapidly passing away, was the gentleman who is the
subject of this sketch. In every relation of life he was excellent. In
his family he was wise and affectionate; as a planter and merchant,
diligent and sagacious; as a neighbor, kind and given to hospitality;
as a friend, stanch and true, and as a public man he was patriotic,
honest and sincere. There was no blemish on his spotless character,
but he stood among the first men of the state, worthy of their warm
admiration and high esteem. He was descended from the Cuning-
hams of Scotland, and inherited the finest characteristics of his
Scotch descent. His father was a wholesale merchant in Petersburg,
Va., and, in 1796, established a branch store in Person county, N. C.,
at what is now known as "Cuningham's Store," and this mercantile
establishment has ever since been maintained, it being the oldest bus-

J. W. CUNINGHAM.

iness house kept up in unbroken succession by the same family in North Carolina. Their honesty, thrift, enterprise and sagacity have been blended in unison for a century, and through three generations the business has been successfully carried on. John W. Cuningham was born in Petersburg, Va., on the 6th day of February, 1820. He was prepared for college at that thorough school — Bingham's — then in the very meridian of its high fame, and passing thence to the University of North Carolina, easily graduated with credit in the class of 1840. Returning to the plantation in Person county, on which he had been reared, he devoted himself to its cultivation, for agriculture was congenial to his simple tastes and his sincere disposition. He was well adapted to the vocation, possessing a robust constitution, sound judgment and untiring industry. The estate was large and valuable, but his energy prompted him to undertake great improvements. Year after year he added something either in ornamentation or in construction of drains, augmenting the fertility of his fields, or enlarging the clearings, until at last he possessed one of the most productive estates and pleasant homes in the county, and his elegant residence and fine fields largely awoke a spirit of improvement in his section. A man of such merit, so much esteemed and so well equipped for the discharge of public duties, could not be allowed to reside in seclusion. In 1844, when but twenty-four years old, he was elected to the house of commons. And from 1852 to 1859, he served in the senate. He seldom spoke in either body, but whenever there was a great question of public importance, he expressed his views and gave his counsel. His strong sense, his force of character, fine intelligence and high integrity gave great weight to his utterances, and contributed to make him one of the most influential of the members.

In those trying days when the clouds began to gather, he was selected as one of the council of state to advise with Gov. Ellis; and in 1861 he was chosen a member of the convention to decide on the action of the state in view of the grave crisis. That convention remained in session until 1863, and in 1864 and 1865 he was again a member of the house. After the war, when the questions arising from the changed condition of affairs wore the gravest aspect, he was returned to the senate chamber, and to the same body he was continuously sent from 1872 to 1880. Frequently solicited to stand for congress or to allow his name to be used in connection with the nomination for governor of the state, he invariably declined, being averse to holding any office that would for any protracted period separate him from his home. He had married Miss Helen Somerville, a daughter of John Somerville, Esq., of Warren county; a lady who was as lovely in character as she was beautiful in person; gifted by nature and of rare accomplishments; and his home was a seat of elegance and refinement. As much as he loved his state, his home and home life were still dearer to him. But in the winter of 1886–87, Mrs. Cuningham died, and life lost its charm for him, and after a deep grief of eighteen sad months, he followed her to the grave, dying on the 15th of July, 1889.

GEN. ALEXANDER LILLINGTON

was one of the foremost men of his generation in North Carolina. His grandfather, Maj. Alexander Lillington, came to the Albemarle settlement from the Barbadoes, when the colony was in its infancy. He was commissioned a justice of the peace in 1679, and he held the court in Berkeley precinct until 1693, when he was appointed deputy governor. During his administration of the affairs of the colony, the people enjoyed tranquility and prosperity. The lords proprietors abrogated the fundamental constitutions, and the people, at their request, were governed under the charter. Without question Maj. Lillington was the most commanding figure in the colony. One of his daughters, Elizabeth, married Col. Sam Swann, and after his death, Col. Maurice Moore; another, Mary, married Jeremiah Vail; Anna married Gov. Henderson Walker, and after his death, Edward Moseley; Sarah married Col. John Porter. There were three sons, George, Thomas and John. The latter married, about 1690, Sarah Porter, sister of Col. John Porter, and to them were born three girls and one son, Alexander, the subject of this sketch. At an early day he was left an orphan, and fell under the care of his uncle, Edward Moseley, and removed with him, about 1735, to Rocky Point, New Hanover county. •He passed his early years surrounded by his kinsmen, Moseley, the Ashes, Porters, Moores and the Swanns. He possessed a large frame, Herculean strength, and intellectual powers of a high order.

When the people embodied in February, 1766, to force a release of the vessels seized for a violation of the stamp act, they chose Lillington, John Ashe and Lloyd to be their "directors." He was a colonel in the army to subdue the regulators. When the troubles with the mother country grew serious, he raised a company of minute men in New Hanover county and entered actively upon military duties. He was a member of the committee of safety in 1775, and was in that year appointed colonel of the New Hanover militia. He commanded at Moore's creek, where the tories were defeated in February, 1776. In April following he was appointed colonel of the Sixth regiment of continental troops and served with them until the regiments were consolidated in May, 1778. He was later appointed brigadier-general of the Wilmington district, and was active during the remaining years of the war. He fought with his brigade at Camden, and when Craig occupied Wilmington he hovered around with his scanty forces and kept the British somewhat in check. After the war he retired to his beautiful home, "Lillington Hall," and passed his declining years in well-earned repose. He died in 1786. He married Miss Waters, and many of his descendants still reside in North Carolina.

B. Cameron

BENNEHAN CAMERON,

the only surviving son of the late Paul C. Cameron, was born at Fairntosh, the residence of his father, and the home established by his paternal grandfather, Judge Duncan Cameron. Fairntosh is in Durham county, N. C., and here our subject was born on the 9th day of September, 1854. His early schooling was at Cedar Grove, Orange county, under Mr. Samuel Hughes, who conducted an excellent boarding school at this place. He then attended the boarding school of Messrs. Horner & Graves, at Oxford. He was now prepared for college, and after completing a commercial course at Eastman business college, at Poughkeepsie, N. Y., he entered the Virginia military institute at Lexington, Va. It would have been his purpose to enter the University of North Carolina, but at that period in his life, when Mr. Cameron was to enter college for higher education, the University of North Carolina was under a cloud of adversity, and could promise but little of that scholastic training and higher education of which he now stood in need. He entered the Military Institute of Virginia, on the 16th of September, 1871, and, with both academic and military distinction, graduated on the 4th of July, 1875. Upon the day of his graduation he was tendered the position of commandant of the corps of cadets, of professor of tactics, ordnance and gunnery, and military history and strategy, in Bowling Green military institute, at Bowling Green, Ky. This position, however, was declined, as he wished to prepare for the law profession, a vocation quite suited to his taste, his mental character, and one which could afford him a broad and intellectual course, application of a liberal education, and becoming qualification for important and future work, honor and consequence, which one of his station might justly anticipate. He took up the study of law under the guidance of his uncle, Mr. William K. Ruffin, of Hillsboro, who, doubtless, was possessed of a greater legal mind and broader learning than any other of his illustrious family. In 1877 Mr. Cameron was admitted to the bar, under an examination conducted by Chief-Justice Richmond Pearson and his associates.

However, although well prepared and equipped for the profession, Mr. Cameron never practiced the profession of law, and after the performance, for a short time, of office work, in the law office of the distinguished law firm of Messrs. Graham & Ruffin, at Hillsboro, he repaired to Stagville and entered the field of agriculture, in which pleasant, honored and useful vocation he has since continued on the broad acres of his paternal ancestors. In this he has followed the enterprising footsteps of his late father; and to the vocation of agriculture he was called in consequence of necessity; for varied and extensive were the agricultural interests of his father, who at this period was nearing the close of a useful, active and honored career, and who very much needed the aid of his son in the control of such vast estates and varied interests. Assuming control of an important and extensive agriculture and subsequently manifesting zeal and ability, meeting with success as an agriculturist, much credit is due Mr. Cameron. He takes special pride in and conducts one of the best regulated stock farms in his state, breeding Hambletonian and English coach horses, and Jersey cattle. Beside the many and absorbing matters pertaining to his agricultural interests, Mr. Cameron has played a prominent part in his attentions to other affairs of varied importance and consequence, and thus has proven a marked financial ability, wide capacity, executive talent, force of energy and enlightenment. He was instrumental in the organization of the Morehead Banking company, which company organized and now operate banks at Durham and Burlington, in each of which banks Mr. Cameron is director. Mr. Cameron is also interested in phosphate lands and the cultivation of oranges in Florida, being a stockholder and director in certain companies controlling such interests and business. He is also interested in cotton manufacturing, being a director in the cotton mills at Rocky Mount, N. C. As a director of the North Carolina railroad, his services have proven his usefulness in this line of industry; he was a member of the committee on the building of the new union depot at Raleigh, and the construction of a branch road from Raleigh to the Caraleigh mills. Mr. Cameron was an ardent advocate and promoter of the Lynchburg & Durham, of the Oxford & Clarksville, and of the Durham & Northern railroads.

But in his military services and his identity with the state guards has Mr. Cameron especially attained to distinction, and become favorably and well known. A year after his graduation, though a very young man, it was his distinguished privilege to introduce at the centennial exposition at Philadelphia, in 1876, Hon. Samuel J. Randall, then speaker of the house of representatives of congress, to the corps of cadets from the Military Institute of Virginia, whom Mr. Randall welcomed to Pennsylvania soil in a fitting speech. In 1877, while reading law at Hillsboro, Mr. Cameron organized the Orange guards, one of the few volunteer companies of the state. This organization resulted in forming a nucleus of what is now the state guards. Mr. Cameron became captain of the reorganized company, but resigned, on changing his residence to Stagville, but at this juncture, he was appointed assistant-inspector-general by Gov. Z. B. Vance, and continued to hold this appointment through the administrations of Govs. Vance, Jarvis and Scales, but by Gov. Fowle was promoted or commissioned on the governor's staff as inspector-general of rifle practice, which commission he now holds under Gov. Holt, upon whose staff he ranks as colonel. In his military and official capacity, Mr. Cameron has done effectual work, and has represented his state on several occasions with deserving credit. At the Yorktown centennial in his official capacity he represented his state, and during Gov. Scales' administration he represented the state at the constitutional centennial, in 1877, being upon the staff of Gen. Phil. Sheridan, of the United States army, and at which time 80,000 troops were in line. By Gov. Fowle he was appointed as aid, representing North Carolina on the staff of Maj.-Gen. Schofield, of the United States army, at the inauguration centennial at New York, April 30, 1889, when 100,000 troops were in line. Again he bore the honor of the Old North State with becoming grace at the Maryland exposition, at Baltimore, where, in his capacity of representing his state, he was upon the staff of Gen. Clinton Payne, who was commander of the Maryland troops, in the military parade and sham battle and bombardment of Fort McHenry. By Gov. Holt he holds commission to represent North Carolina on the military committee of the Columbian exposition at Chicago. In point of commission, Mr. Cameron is an old military man, and among the oldest of the state guards, and has taken prominence in this respect. Honor is due to him for the first suggestion of the formation by state government of a naval militia or of a naval force in addition to the state's present military service. As a man of military affairs, Mr. Cameron is a man of marked ability, learning, and practical ideas, and his services to the state have been of much value and he is deserving of much credit. He was instrumental in establishing a permanent encampment for the state guards, as was affected at Wilmington.

Politically Mr. Cameron is democratic, and an influential member of the democratic party, and his name has frequently been mentioned in connection with the highest and most honored offices in the gift of the people, but he has never sought political preferment, and has an aversion to politics as such. In all his multifarious relations he has not neglected to give attention and encouragement to education. He is chairman of the North Carolina branch of the society of alumni of Virginia military institute, and as such participated in and arranged for the semi-centennial celebration of the institution in 1889. Mr. Cameron is a trustee of the University of North Carolina, and secured the establishment of ten scholarships by the Paul C. Cameron heirs. He is also manager of property of the St. Mary's school for girls, at Raleigh, managing the property for the owners, who are the Cameron heirs, as he is executor of his father's estate. Mr. Cameron is a man of strong force of character, charitable and kind in disposition, hospitable and a royal entertainer. He is a man, too, of iron will and good nerve, and firm as a rock; such a man could not be other than a good general, an excellent citizen, and a hero in adversity, or at a critical period.

We would fail signally to do our subject justice in this sketch were we not to make mention of his heroism on the night of August 27, 1891, when on the Western North Carolina railroad, near Statesville, N. C., there occurred one of the most fatal railroad wrecks in the history of the south. On this occasion he was the only one of some less than a hundred passengers who were either killed or so wounded that they were helpless. He rendered timely aid, and his coolness and nerve saved many fellow-passengers. He was the hero of the wreck, and the public spoke of his heroism and presence of mind in terms of warm praise, and his course and action on this occasion are but the expressions of the brave, prudent and good man he is. On Wednesday evening, October 28, 1891, there occurred at All Saints church in Richmond, Va., the marriage of Mr. Cameron to Miss Sallie Taliaferro Mayo, daughter of Mr. P. H. Mayo, a prominent and wealthy manufacturer and tobacconist of Richmond. Mrs. Cameron is a lady of rare accomplishments and universal popularity with an extended acquaintance, and comes of an old and highly respected Virginian family, most of whose members have attained distinction in more than one way.

WILLIAM F. KORNEGAY,

a representative agriculturist of Goldsboro, N. C., was born in Wayne county, N. C., June 18, 1832. His parents were James F. and Harriet H. (Whitfield) Kornegay, both natives of Wayne county. The father was a leading farmer and owned many slaves. Although he took no active part during the Civil war, yet his sympathy and support were given to the Confederate cause. He served as chairman of the board of county commissioners, and for many years was a steward and trustee of the Methodist Episcopal church, of which he was a member and liberal supporter, having built a church, mainly by himself, for that denomination at Indian Springs, N. C. He died in 1885. Mr. Kornegay was thrice married, his first wife having died in 1845. Three children were born to this union, of whom two are now living, named: John J., of Goldsboro, and William F. His second marriage was to Mrs. Margaret Kornegay, by whom he had no children. Mrs. Fannie E. Saul became his third wife and bore him two children, Albert U., of Goldsboro, being the one now living. William F. Kornegay, of whom we are now writing, was reared on the homestead farm, and was educated at Randolph-Macon college, and then for some time taught school. Subsequently he turned his attention to agriculture and was thus occupied when the war broke out. He joined the Confederate army and was elected second lieutenant of the First North Carolina cavalry. For two years of the war he was confined to his home with rheumatism, but was at his post of duty when able. At the close of the conflict he exchanged his farm for a mercantile business in Goldsboro, and continued in that for seven years. At this time he formed a partnership with Charles Dewey in the organization of the Goldsboro Machine works. In 1884 the concern was burned out, and at that time Mr. Kornegay sold his interest and returned to farming.

Mr. Kornegay and Mr. Dewey were largely instrumental in introducing steam-power for cotton-gins in the eastern portion of the state, and manufactured a great number of engines for that purpose. His plantation extends for two and a half miles on the line of the W. & W. railroad, and he is one of the largest cotton producers in Wayne county. He is an active supporter of the democratic party, and was its nominee for state senator in 1886, but was defeated. Since June, 1890, he has been the chairman of the board of county commissioners. He was one of the organizers of, and is now a stockholder in, the

Goldsboro Oil company, and for the past thirteen years has been a director of the North Carolina railroad company, of which company he has been president since April, 1891. Mr. Kornegay is a prominent member of Goldsboro chapter, Raleigh commandery of the Masonic order, and is past grand master. He was a prime mover in the establishment of the farmers' alliance in Wayne county, and is its treasurer at the present time. His first marriage was solemnized on the 6th of October, 1857, to Miss Lou Borden, daughter of Mrs. Maria A. Borden, one of the early settlers of Goldsboro. Mrs. Kornegay died in 1883, leaving no children. Two years later Mr. Kornegay was united in marriage to Miss Annie L. Snow, daughter of Theophilus Snow, of Raleigh, N. C. Both himself and wife are earnest communicants of the Methodist Episcopal church, south, and he has been a trustee of the Goldsboro church for some years, and its Sunday-school superintendent for nine years. He was a lay delegate to the general conference of the Methodist Episcopal church, south, in 1877, held in Atlanta, Ga., and has also served as a steward of the church.

BEDFORD BROWN,

farmer and statesman, was born in Caswell county, N. C., in 1795. He embarked early in political life, and in 1815, was elected to the North Carolina house of commons, to represent his native county. In that body he was regarded as one of its ablest members. Again, in 1823, he was elected to the same house, and in 1828, he was elected to the senate, and was chosen its president. When John Branch resigned his seat in the United States senate, to be made secretary of the navy, Mr. Brown was appointed to succeed him, and was afterward re-elected by the legislature. He served in this position until 1840, when he resigned, because he could not conscientiously follow the instructions of the state legislature. In 1842, while a member of the state senate, he was again a candidate for the United States senate, but was beaten in the race by W. H. Haywood, Jr. He then retired from official life for a time, and went to Missouri, but did not long tarry in that state. He returned again to North Carolina, and was elected again to the state senate, from 1858 to 1862, and again in 1868. But he had scarcely completed this last term before death put an end to his long and busy career. He died at his home, December 6, 1870, deeply lamented by both state and nation.

Mr. Brown was a man of firm purpose and of unyielding tenacity to what he deemed sound in principle. His integrity never came in question, and there was no taint to the purity of his character. He was not a person of brilliant parts, but of strong common sense. His political life began when politics were sharply defined; he took his stand with the democratic party, and with that party he preserved his standing through life. He was honest, firm, patriotic and ever true to his highest convictions.

JOHN ROBINSON,

the efficient and distinguished commissioner of agriculture of the state of North Carolina, was born in Marlborough county, S. C., March 20, 1831, and was brought by his parents to North Carolina, when they settled in Anson county, in January, 1835. He attended school in Anson county, and afterward finished his education at Davidson college. He left college, however, in 1850, before graduating, and, returning home, lived on his father's farm until 1853, when he married and began farming on his own account. This has been his vocation in life. His best thought has been bestowed on agriculture and methods of improvement in farm work. Acquainted with the theories of advanced agriculture, he experimented on his own fields, and proved what was good and put it into practice. Success attended his efforts, and in cotton growing especially he won many prizes, the most gratifying being the award made to him at the international cotton exposition, at Atlanta, Ga., for the best bale of cotton exhibited from North Carolina. He served for many years as a magistrate in Anson county, and was highly esteemed throughout the state. At the re-organization of the department of agriculture, in 1883, he was elected by the legislature as a member of the board of agriculture from the Sixth congressional district, and in 1887 he was selected by the state board of agriculture as the fittest man to fill the chair of commissioner of agriculture. In this position his services have been of great advantage to the people. He has the chief honor of originating and organizing the farmers' institutes in the state, and he has delivered many addresses stimulating thought among the farmers in regard to the amelioration of their condition and the advancement of agriculture. Under his direction the department has issued many valuable pamphlets and bulletins, and the information disseminated has had an elevating and beneficial influence on the farm work of North Carolina. He was re-elected to this position in 1889, and in 1891 there was added to his duties the office of commissioner of immigration. In 1891, the legislature passed an act, providing for certain agricultural statistical reports, and under Mr. Robinson's direction, as commissioner of agriculture, a system for gathering statistical reports of farm, garden, orchard products and live stock statistics, was originated, and in 1891, for the first time in the history of the state, were collected and reported these statistics, which reports, when compiled, will comprehend a large volume of valuable information.

Mr. Robinson is a man of fine appearance, agreeable address and of admirable sentiments. For many years he has been an active and zealous member of the Methodist Episcopal church, south, and he has sought to discharge all his religious duties equally with those of a secular nature. In November, 1853, he was married to Araminta J. Watkins, daughter of Dr. Christopher Watkins, of Anson county, and by her had a family of children of whom eight survive, viz.:

T. C., John A., Jennie W., E. C., L. D., Frank P., Percy P. and M. Marie. Mrs. Robinson dying in 1881, Mr. Robinson was married again in October, 1883, to Miss Harriet A. Coleman, of Edgefield county, S. C., and to them has been born one child, Sallie Berry Robinson. Mr. Robinson's father, Thomas Robinson, was born in Cumberland county, England, in 1801, and came to America in 1822, settling first in South Carolina, and then removing to Anson county, where he continued to reside until his death in 1876. The father of Thomas Robinson was John Robinson, who was born and always lived in Cumberland county, England, where he died at the advanced age of eighty-four. Mr. Robinson's mother was Ann E., a daughter of Henry W. Auld, a prominent North Carolinian. She was married to Mr. Thomas Robinson in 1830, and bore him two children, Henry W. Robinson, who died in 1885, and the distinguished subject of this sketch.

NATHANIEL MACON,

patriot and statesman, was born in Warren county, N. C., December 17, 1757. When the Revolutionary war began he was engaged in his studies at Princeton college, but he left his books to engage in the defense of the independence of the colonies. He returned to his home and enlisted as a private in a company of volunteers who joined the regiment of which his brother, John Macon, was colonel. He was offered promotion in the regiment, but persisted in remaining a private. He was present at the surrender of Fort Moultrie, the evacuation of Charleston and the rout at Camden. While in the service and without his knowledge, he had been elected to the general assembly of North Carolina, as a member of the senate to represent the county of Warren; he was in camp on the banks of the Yadkin, when the summons came from the governor of North Carolina to attend a session of the general assembly. At first he declined to obey this civil order, declaring that "his country needed the services of all her sons; that he had seen the faces of the British many times but never their backs; he intended to stay in the army until he did." He was finally persuaded by Gen. Greene, who had great respect for his ability, to recall this determination. That distinguished officer intimated to Macon that "he could do more good as a member of the legislature than as a soldier; that in the army he was only one man, but in the legislature he might induce many to furnish supplies to the army by showing what utter destitution prevailed among the soldiers." He yielded to the evident reasonableness of this appeal and returned to his state. But though this was a most honorable discharge from the military service, he refused pay and could not be prevailed upon to accept a pension. He served in the senate continuously from this time until 1785, and was most effective in securing the adoption of measures for the relief of the army. He held positions on the most important legislative committees in which he could make his influence felt. During this time he settled upon a plantation on the

Roanoke river which became his permanent home. He was opposed
to the adoption of the Federal constitution, but was elected a member
of the second congress under it. He was re-elected without opposition for the next twenty-two years. During this time, he was twice
chosen speaker of the house, and twice during the administration of
President Jefferson was he offered the position of postmaster-general, which honor he declined.

In 1815 Mr. Macon was elected a United States senator, and was
re-elected to that office, serving two senatorial terms, when he declined another election. From 1825 to 1827 he was president of the
senate, and in 1824 he received the twenty-four electoral votes of
Virginia for vice-president. In his long congressional career, he
served in the house during the presidential administrations of Washington, Adams, Jefferson and Madison, and in the senate during those
of Madison, Monroe and John Quincy Adams. He was of the strict
school of Jeffersonian democrats; he would accept no appointive
office; it required the suffrages of the people, or their representatives, to bring him into the public service, and in the exercise of official patronage he would never recommend any of his relatives for
appointments. His speeches were of the laconic order, and Mr.
Benton said of him, "He spoke more good sense while getting in
his chair and getting out of it than many delivered in long and elaborate speeches." John Randolph said of him: "He is the wisest,
the purest and the best man that I ever knew." His political services
were finished up, first as a delegate in the North Carolina constitutional convention, in 1835, and then as presidential elector, in 1836, in
favor of Van Buren and Johnson. Mr. Macon married Miss Hannah
Plummer, by whom he had two daughters. He was a thorough
student of the Bible, and in religious belief inclined to the Baptist
denomination. He died at his home quite suddenly, on the 29th of
June, 1837.

ALGERNON S. PERRY

was born near Louisburg, N. C., in the year 1807. He was graduated
from the Jefferson medical college, at Philadelphia, and was engaged
in the practice of medicine in Franklin county, N. C., from the time
of his graduation until 1865, when he retired. In 1836, Dr. Perry, was
united in marriage with Miss Leah Hillard, daughter of James
Hilliard, of Hilliardston, Nash county, N. C., and to their
union were born nine children, six of whom now survive, as
follows: Stella, Jeremiah, Leah, wife of D. C. Cooper, of Henderson, N. C.; Redding, also a resident of Henderson; Tempie,
wife of A. C. Zollicoffer, of the same place; and Genevieve, who married Dr. W. H. Nicholson, of Louisburg, N. C. The father of these
children died on the 23d of January, 1873, having lived a life of usefulness and honor. Dr. Perry was the son of Jeremiah Perry, a native of the vicinity of Louisburg, where he was born about the year
1785. He followed planting during his active life, and died in the

year 1845. His father was also named Jeremiah, and he was a native of England. With five brothers he emigrated to the American colonies prior to the Revolution. Settling in North Carolina, he turned his attention to agriculture, and followed that vocation for the remainder of his days. Having given a brief outline of the family since its settlement in this country, this sketch may now properly be brought down to the present generation. Henry Perry, the son of Dr. Algernon S. Perry, was born in Louisburg, Franklin county, N. C., on the 3d of December, 1857. He was given ample opportunity for thoroughly laying the foundation of his literary education at McCabe's school, in Petersburg, Va. Subsequently he entered the University of Virginia, and was graduated therefrom in 1879, after which he settled in Henderson, N. C., where he became interested in the tobacco business. For the succeeding five years, or until 1884, Mr. Perry continued in the tobacco business. At the expiration of that time he engaged in agriculture, retaining his home at Henderson, however. From 1885 to 1888, he held the deputy collectorship of internal revenue of his district, under President Cleveland, and in November, 1890, was elected clerk of the superior court, of Vance county, N. C., for a term of four years, and he is now engaged in the discharge of the duties of this honorable office. Mr. Perry was very fortunate in his marriage to Miss Jane L. Hall, a daughter of John G. Hall, now deceased, of Oxford, N. C. This union has resulted in the birth of one child: H. Leslie Perry.

HON. E. A. POWELL.

The Hon. Erastus A. Powell is a North Carolinian by birth, having come into this world in Granville (now Vance) county, July 10, 1846. He obtained his scholastic training in the public schools of his native county. When he was about eight years of age his father, who was a farmer, established a grist-mill, and the boy was employed about the mill until his eleventh year. When he was but thirteen, in company with a younger brother, he operated a very small farm, which he had the charge of for about three years. From 1861 to 1863 he was employed by the government in hauling provisions. From the latter year until the close of the war he held a position on the R. & G. railroad, which he left to embark in the milling business in Granville county, in which he remained for eighteen months. At the expiration of this time he purchased a tan-yard and conducted that enterprise for three years more, after which he turned his attention to agriculture and has since been successfully engaged in this vocation. His first public office was held as a constable of Granville county, to which office he was appointed in 1870. Having held that position for four years, he was appointed magistrate of Granville county in 1876 by the legislature, serving in that capacity for eight years. In 1884 he was made magistrate of Vance county and was serving on the last year of the six years' term at the time of his removal from the township. In 1885 he was appointed deputy sheriff, and in November,

1890, was elected treasurer of Vance county. Mr. Powell is a member of the Kittrell lodge, No. 337, and is a prominent member of the farmers' alliance. October 1, 1868, he was married to Miss Candice E. Falkner, daughter of Noel J. Falkner, of Granville county, N. C., and to them have been born eight children, the surviving ones being: Sadie E., Della E., Robert D. G., Henry, Alice, Jessie P. and Elma Cromwell Powell. Mr. Powell is the son of Henry Powell, who was born in Granville county, N. C., in 1826. He was a farmer in his early manhood, but subsequently became a miller. For a number of years he was constable of Granville county, and was a man of considerable influence in the community. He was married in 1844 to Miss Elizabeth Hayes, a daughter of Presley Hayes, and to their union were born five children, of whom four are now living, as follow 3: Erastus A., Silas, Geneva, wife of J. W. Duke, of Vance county, N. C , and Delia, wife of J. M. Harp, of Vance county, N. C. . The moth..r died in 1862, and the father was again married one year later, Miss Pattie F. Robinson becoming his wife. One daughter was the issue of this marriage, viz.: Lena, wife of W. A. Falkner, of Vance county, N. C. Henry Powell's demise occurred in 1870. He was the son of Robin Powell, a native of England, whence he came to America in his early manhood. He was accompanied by his two brothers, William and Edwin. They all settled in Granville county, N. C., where the family has since been prominently identified with the growth and advancement of the community.

TIMOTHY BLOODWORTH

was one of those early patriots and statesmen of North Carolina, to whom the public records have done but partial justice. He was born in 1736; the place of his birth is not recorded, but it is probable that it was in New Hanover or Moore county. Owing to the straitened circumstances of his father, his education was quite limited, but he had natural endowments which equipped him for high official stations. About 1758 he was chosen a member of the legislative assembly of North Carolina, to represent his native county, and he made his services so valuable that he was retained in the same office for about thirty years. He was a member of the continental congress in 1786-7, and was also a member of the first congress under the Federal constitution. In 1795 he was elected a United States senator, holding that office for the full term of six years. At the end of his congressional service, he was appointed collector of customs at the port of Wilmington. While serving his district in the general assembly, the question of the location of the state capital was at issue, Fayetteville and Raleigh being the chief contending places desiring its location. The members of the general assembly were very nearly equally divided in their preferences between these two places, and it appears that Mr. Bloodworth was the member who held the balance of power. He voted for Raleigh, and thus incurred the displeasure of all of the ardent friends of Fayetteville.

It was for his partiality to Raleigh that the commissioners who platted that city named one of its streets for him, thus perpetuating the memory of his name and official act. He was a man of broad views and charitable instincts. Benevolence towards his fellow-men was one of his distinguishing characteristics. He knew from experience what poverty was, and sympathized with those who were called to endure its trials. Besides serving the state and nation for so many years in a legislative capacity, he tried at different times almost every vocation in life to gain a respectable living. He was politician, farmer, minister of the gospel, smith, physician and wheelwright, but in none of these occupations did money stick to his palms. His versatility of employments was doubtless one cause of his lack of accumulation, but the great cause was probably his open-handed liberality. He held very radical views upon the subject of statesmanship and morals, which carried him quite to the verge of eccentricity. He possessed a will that was unyielding and a determination which no selfish or mercenary considerations could turn aside. Mr. Bloodworth died near Washington, N. C., August 24, 1814.

SPOTSWOOD BURWELL.

Among the leading agriculturists and millers of Vance county, N. C., appears the name of Spotswood Burwell, a native of that county, his birth having occurred on the 7th of January, 1847. Until his eighteenth year he was engaged in acquiring an education, having been a student in the common schools of his native county, and subsequently in the high school at Oxford, Granville county, and the Hillsboro academy. While a cadet in the latter institution he was ordered into the Confederate service, in 1865. The Hillsboro cadets were under the command of Maj. William M. Gordon, of Virginia, doing guard duty for several months. In 1866 Mr. Burwell settled on a plantation in Granville county, and some time later went to Portsmouth, Va., and engaged in the mercantile business with his brother-in-law. After three years spent in in the latter place he removed to Baltimore, Md., and for one year was in business in that city, after which he returned to Granville county, N. C., and has since been conducting a plantation and also operating a milling business there. Mr. Burwell was fortunately married to Miss Mary S. Parker, a daughter of Dr. R. H. Parker, Sr., of Portsmouth, Va., February 28, 1877, and six children resulted, as follows: Emma S., Willis M., Mary Parker, Sarah E., Spotswood. and William Sumner Riddick Burwell. Mr. Burwell is the son of John Spotswood Burwell, who was born in North Carolina in 1811. In his early life he was a merchant in Granville county (now Vance county), and subsequently became a planter and miller. For many years he served as a magistrate of the county. His marriage to Sarah E. Hayes, daughter of William Hayes, of Warren county, N. C., took place in 1834, and was blessed by the birth of these children: Martha H., wife of J. B. Hunter, of Gates county, N. C.; Mary L. (deceased), wife of Dr. R. H.

B—38

Parker, Jr., of Portsmouth, Va.; and Spotswood Burwell. The father's demise occurred in 1889, his wife having died in September, 1865. Spotswood Burwell, the father of John S., was born in Virginia in 1786, and came to North Carolina about 1810, settling in Granville county. He was a planter of prominence. He died in 1856. His father, a captain in the Revolutionary war, was Lewis Burwell, a Virginian, who was also a planter. His first wife was Ann Spotswood; his second wife, Elizabeth Harrison. So in this way the present Spotswood Burwell, of Vance, is connected with the Burwells, Spotswoods and Harrisons, of Virginia.

S. W. BENNETTE.

One of the leading planters of Lumberton, Robeson county, N. C., is Mr. S. W. Bennette, who is a native of this state, having been born in Brunswick county, April 13, 1832, the son of Samuel and Ann (Mintz) Bennette, both North Carolinians. The father was a planter, and was a man of influence and and ability. He fought in the war of 1812, and although he never sought office was deeply interested in public affairs. For many years he was a consistent communicant of the Baptist church, in which he held the office of deacon. At the age of fifty-three years, on the 5th of August, 1845, this worthy citizen died; his wife survived him until 1875, when she too went to rest, having attained to the advanced age of seventy-five years. Of the twelve children born to this union, seven are living: S. W. Bennette was educated in Trinity college, which institution he left, in 1856, to engage in teaching. For more than twenty-five years he held a professorship in different leading academies. Like most educators who love the calling, Mr. Bennette met with distinguished success, and the beauty and strength of his own mind have been deeply impressed upon many students who will, doubtless, rise to eminence in the land. His last teaching was done at Lumberton, where he now lives. For four years he held the office of register of deeds at the latter place, and for two years has been a member of the board of education, and during the last few months has received the appointment of soliciting agent for the Carolina Inter-state Building and Loan association. On the 11th of April, 1861, this man offered his life and services to his state by enlisting in the Thirtieth North Carolina volunteer infantry. He enlisted as a private, was soon after elected a second lieutenant, and subsequently was promoted to the rank of first lieutenant for gallant conduct on the field. He fought in the battle of Fredericksburg, and at Chancellorsville was grievously wounded, May 3, 1863, and incapacitated for further service. May 25, 1870, he was most happily married to Miss Amanda M., daughter of Maj. Giles Williams, of Robeson county, N. C., and three children have been born to them: Henry Leo, the eldest, died at the age of seven years; Cora E. and Mary Cornelia are living. Both Mr. and Mrs. Bennette are active and valued members of the Methodist Episcopal church, south, in which he is recording steward and Sunday-school superintendent. He is also a member of the Masonic order and of the K. of H.

COL. JOHN D. JONES

was the son of David Jones, who was an officer in Gen. Washington's army. He was with Washington at the crossing of the Delaware and the attack on Trenton, where he gained distinction and was promoted to the rank of colonel. He married Annie Morris, a relative of Robert Morris, one of the signers of the Declaration of Independence and distinguished financier of the Revolution. Shortly after his marriage he removed to North Carolina and settled at Love Grove, on the northern confines of the present city of Wilmington, at which place his son, the subject of this sketch, was born in 1790. Col. Jones received a collegiate education and was reared to the practice of the law but soon abandoned it for the more congenial pursuits of literature and agriculture. He held the pen of a ready writer and it was his delight to go back into the past of our history, and, in a style of great purity and infinite humor, record the transactions and traditions of the olden time. His knowledge of events and incidents connected with our early history was full and accurate, for he was a close observer and blessed with a remarkably retentive memory. He loved books and was familiar with the work of the standard authors but had little fancy for the light and ephemeral publications of the day, did not believe in multiplicity of books, but thought if one would study carefully the Bible, Shakespeare and Walter Scott he would be well equipped for the battle of life. They were sufficient, he thought, to constitute as good a library as one could desire.

Mr. Jones entered public life in 1811 as the representative from the county of New Hanover in the state legislature, and was also elected from the borough of Wilmington in 1819-20-21 and 22, and again in 1833; he was also a member of the convention of 1835. He assumed a high position in the councils of the state, was chosen speaker of the house of commons, and presided over its deliberations with dignity and marked ability. He was a skilled debater, quick and pungent at repartee and prompt to take advantage of any exposed point of his adversary, but was uniformly courteous and urbane. He never indulged in personalities, but was always and under all circumstances the courtly gentleman. He could not tolerate prevarication or deceit, for he was one of the most sincere of men. He had the courage of his convictions and never hesitated to express what he thought, not offensively, but with a firmness and with a dignity of manner that commanded respect. Upon his retirement from political life, he accepted the position of naval officer for the post of Wilmington and was subsequently elected president of the Bank of Cape Fear, which position he held for some years, until failing health compelled his resignation. He conducted the affairs of the bank with great skill and prudence, to the entire satisfaction of the directors and the public. He died at Greenville, S. C., while on a visit to his daughter, the wife of the late Hon. Waddy Thompson, of that state, at one time minister to Mexico, and was buried at that place. Col. Jones was a most estimable gentleman, genial in manner, particularly so to the young, a delightful conversationalist, free from guile and always scrupulously regardful of the feelings of others.

DAVID FANNING.

There was born in Johnston county, N. C., in 1756, one of the boldest men, fertile in expedients and quick in execution, that ever sprang from North Carolina parentage. He was a poor boy, obscure, humble and unlettered. He was apprenticed to a Mr. Bryant, from whom, on account of harsh treatment, he ran away when about fifteen years of age. His miserable condition secured him a temporary home with Mr. John O. Deneill, of Haw Field, in Orange county, but in the course of two or three years he went to South Carolina and engaged in trafficking with the Catawba Indians, and settled on Raeburn's creek, a branch of Reedy river, in Laurens district in upper South Carolina. He was but eighteen years of age, when he was made sergeant of Capt. James Lindley's company, and on the 15th day of May, 1775, together with 118 other men of that settlement, refused to sign "the Revolution papers," but signed in July a paper agreeing to fight for the king. They embodied about the post of "Ninety-Six," in upper South Carolina and engaged in an active warfare with their whig neighbors. In July, 1776, he made his way with a body of tories to the Cherokees and came down with them and attacked a whig force, but the attack was unsuccessful. Returning to Raeburn creek, he underwent many vicissitudes, was often captured, escaped, and always engaged in predatory warfare.

On March 1, 1778, orders were received from east Florida for "the loyal militia" to embody. Fanning was chosen by the tories of his section to be their commander. They scoured the country, took prisoners and seized horses, and marched to Savannah river, two miles above Augusta, where they were turned back by a body of whigs and pursued, and the party dispersed. He was again captured, but escaped. Eventually he embodied some 500 men to go to St. Augustine, but was again turned back by superior forces. He was on his way alone to the Holstein river, 140 miles distant over the mountains, when he was again captured and confined, as often before, in the jail at Ninety-six, but again got free. Eventually he made submission to Gov. Rutledge, of South Carolina, and was pardoned on condition of living peaceably at home. He remained a year under those terms, but after Charleston was captured, he and "Bloody Bill" Cunningham began to embody a loyal force, and became very active and daring in their operations. After the battle of Kings Mountain, the whigs grew stronger in that part of South Carolina, and Fanning made his way to Deep River, N. C., where he remained quiet until February, 1781, discovering the disposition of the people. When Cornwallis came into this state Fanning raised the tory standard in the Deep River country, and upon the arrival of the British army at Hillsboro, quite a number of disaffected people joined him. Col. Pyles also had a force of about 300 tories in the same region. This was the beginning of his active operations in central North Carolina.

After Cornwallis withdrew to Wilmington and Greene went into South Carolina leaving North Carolina a free field for Fanning's operations, nearly every day had its incidents. Often with a considerable force, sometimes he was compelled to fight single-handed for his life; fleeing one day through the wilderness; the next saw him pursuing the whig parties that had divided to capture him. Foraging on the country, seizing what he wanted, slaying, slaughtering, burning homes and butchering in cold blood according to his mood, he was a terror and a scourge. On the 5th of July, 1781, he went to Wilmington and obtained from Major Craig an appointment as colonel of the Loyal Militia of Randolph and Chatham counties and on the 12th of July organized at Coxe's Mills the loyalists of Anson, Cumberland, Orange, Chatham and Randolph counties into 22 companies. Hearing that there was a general muster at Pittsboro and a court-martial to try some tories there, he marched seventeen miles that night and by seven o'clock took the village — with fifty-three prisoners — among them the colonel, major and all the milita officers in the county, a captain in the continental army and three members of the legislature. He next attacked Col. Alston's force and took them, patroling the colonel to his residence in Cumberland county. And so he continued fighting, whenever he could with a chance of success, from Wilmington to Hillsboro. In September, finding himself at the head of 950 men, he left Coxe's Mills, marched as if to attack General Butler and Col. Robert Mebane, of the continentals who were near by but avoided them and hastened to Hillsboro, where at seven o'clock on the morning of the 12th of September, 1781, he captured Gov. Burke, the governor's council, Col. Reade, Mr. Hurke, Col. Lyttle, seventy-one continentals with their officers and over a hundred other persons, and opened the jail, turning loose a number of tories and criminals. Leaving Hillsboro at twelve o'clock, by the next morning they were at Lindsey's Mills on Cane creek, and pushing on were attacked by Gen. Butler. The fight lasted four hours and Butler's force was driven off. Fanning lost twenty-seven killed, sixty badly wounded and thirty slightly wounded. He himself was disabled, and he sent his force with the prisoners under Col. McDougal on to Wilmington, Gen. Butler and Col. Mebane being in hot pursuit until Maj. Craig with a force from Wilmington joined the fleeing tories and turned the whig army back. In twenty-four days Fanning was again in the saddle. In November he had intelligence of the surrender of Cornwallis and of the evacuation of Wilmington by Maj. Craig, but this only increased his activity and desperation.

Every day he left his mark. On December 10, Col. Isaacs came from the west with 300 men, to Coxe's Mills, to capture Fanning, who eluded his foes with great address. About the first of January, he offered to make terms with Gov. Martin, and remain neutral thereafter, living with his men within bounds — " from Cumberland twenty miles north and south, and thirty miles east and west; to be totally clear of your Light Horse." But although the proposition was entertained, the truce was not made, and Fanning continued, with but slight intermission, to kill and burn until May 7, 1782, when he started to " a Major Garner's truce land in Pee Dee, S. C., where I had made a truce with the rebels some time before." Here he remained a month with Mrs. Fanning, and his plunder, and then repaired to Charleston. On the 28th of September, he took shipping with other loyalists to St. Augustine, and two years later went to Halifax, Nova Scotia, where he continued to reside in poor circumstances until his death, in 1825.

Fanning's career in the upper Cape Fear region, after Greene went into South Carolina, has no parallel in the history of the colony for audacity, bold enterprise, bloody encounters and remorseless rapine. He refers to having been in thirty-six encounters; but if minor engagements were reckoned the number would be greater. He was one of the three persons excepted from pardon and amnesty, proclaimed by the general assembly of the state after peace was declared.

COL. J. T. ROPER.

One of North Carolina's oldest and most highly respected connections is the Roper family, Col. J. T. Roper, of Richmond county, N. C., being the representative of the family chosen as the subject of this sketch. Col. Roper was born in Richmond county, September 14, 1819, the son of Thomas and Hannah (Hunter) Roper, natives of Virginia and North Carolina respectively. Thomas was a planter. His father, Frederick, and his two brothers, John and James, were patriot soldiers in the Revolution. They were the sons of an itinerant Methodist minister. Thomas died in 1858, and his wife in 1860, aged respectively eighty and seventy-eight years. Two sons and two daughters are the children surviving them, of whom Col. J. T. Roper is the eldest. Col. Roper began active life at the age of twenty years as a planter, in which calling he has continued with much success. In 1844 he married Miss Mary A., daughter of Daniel McBride, of Richmond county, and six children have been born to them, named as follows: Green A., an extensive planter of the county; he married M. Ella Bethea, and Willa and Fanny are the offspring; Sallie, wife of A. F. Bizzell, their children are Frank, John, Drew, Mamie, Albert and Malcom; Fanny, wife of C. E. Smith, a commission merchant of New York city — their two children are Margaret and Roper. Col. and Mrs. Roper have been active and valued communicants of the Methodist Episcopal church for nearly half a century, the former having served as a steward for much of that time. During the Civil war he held the commission of colonel of the militia of the state, it being his duty to protect the homes, and capture deserters from the army. His service in that capacity was most valuable to the community, and brought him much credit.

HON. A. H. McNEILL,

who for thirty-two years served the citizens of Moore county, N. C., as clerk of the county and superior courts, is a native of the county, having been born there in 1831. His parents were John and Fanny (Muse) McNeill, honored residents of the community. The former died in 1840 at the age of thirty years. His father was Daniel McNeill, who married Margaret McLeod, both being natives of Scotland. Daniel was the son of John McNeill, who is mentioned in Caruthers' History of North Carolina; he was known throughout the region as "Strong John." Mrs. John McNeill is living at the advanced age of seventy-seven years, and is a lady of great piety and of true Christian character, being a life-long member of the Methodist Episcopal church. Of the three children born to John and Fanny McNeill, A. H. is the eldest, and Martha is the widow of A. M. Branson, of Carthage, N. C. Our subject began life for himself at the age of fifteen as a clerk, five years later becoming the proprietor of a store in Carthage. In 1855 he was elected clerk of the county court, and later clerk of the superior court, holding these positions for thirty-two years, having served during the administration of the Confederate government. In 1852 he was happily wedded to Miss Margaret, daughter of A. C. and Christian Currie, and it is a strange coincidence that for twenty years Mr. Currie held the same office in which his son-in-law was retained so long, the latter having succeeded him at his death. The children of this marriage are: Eveline, wife of Dr. J. C. Blue; their children are, Ela M. and Alexander; Maggie, wife of George C. Graves, a leading merchant of Carthage; their children are, Lessie, Maggie and George; Charles A., a prominent attorney of Carthage; Robert L., a planter; Mittie, wife of Charles H. Graves; Fannie, Ella and George W. The mother went to her final rest, May 26, 1888, aged fifty-five years. She was a devout member of the Presbyterian church, in which her husband is a deacon. Mr. McNeill is a prominent member of the Masonic order, and of the I. O. O. F.

Mrs. McNeill lived a most beautiful life. For more than forty years she served her Master with ever increasing faith, and died firm in the belief of His supreme power to save. The influence of a godly, virtuous life, such as this woman lived, cannot be estimated; it is widespread, and like the waves of the ocean, never ending. The love in which she was held by the entire community was touchingly illustrated by the last sad services, when rich and poor joined in paying tender tribute to her memory. Mr. McNeill's mother is from a Virginia family, her grandfather being Dr. George Glasscock, who was a first cousin of the great Washington, their mothers being sisters, and their surname Ball. Daniel and Neill McLeod of Cumberland county, the great uncles of our subject, were robbed and murdered by the famous Lowrey gang of Robeson county. Mr. A. H. McNeill is probably more intimately acquainted with the rank and file of the citizens of Moore county than any other man. His close connection with the business interests of the county for so long a period in a high official position, brought him into the closest contact with the community, and the fact that his name is universally honored and esteemed as that of a man of undoubted ability, and the most rigid uprightness, is ample proof of his worth.

HON. SYDENHAM B. ALEXANDER.

Among the many agriculturists of North Carolina, there is none more distinguished or deservedly popular than Hon. Sydenham B. Alexander. He is a resident of Mecklenburg county, N. C., in which he was born December 8, 1840, at Rosedale farm, some nine miles north of Charlotte. His descent is from a distinguished Scotch-Irish family having many representatives among the early settlers of Mecklenburg county. The progenitor of the family in America was James Alexander who emigrated from Armaugh, Ireland, first settling in Chester, Penn., and later in Maryland, where he died. He had twelve children, two of whom, James McKnitt Alexander and Hezekiah Alexander came to Mecklenburg county, as early as 1742. The first named was the secretary of the convention which first passed the Mecklenburg declaration, May 20, 1775. He had several sons and daughters. Among the sons was Dr. Joseph McKnitt Alexander, for many y   a distinguished physician of Mecklenburg. He married Miss Dorey Winslow, and by her had an only son, Dr. Moses Winslow Alexander. He was the father of the subject of this sketch. In his early days he was a practising physician, but later in life followed farming and was a man of distinction and wealth. He lived and died in his native county. He was married to Miss Violet Graham, a daughter of Gen. Joseph Graham, of Revolutionary fame and a sister of Gov. William A. Graham. The issue of this marriage was twelve children, of whom, Sydenham B. Alexander was the youngest but one. He was reared upon a farm and acquired his early education under the instruction of Capt. Silas Lindsley, at Rock River academy, in Cabarrus county, and at Wadesboro institute. In July, 1856 he was admitted to the University of Chapel Hill, whence he was graduated in June, 1860. In April, 1861 he enlisted as a private in the Hornets' Nest military company, of Charlotte, and in the following August was made drill-master as an aid 'to Col. J. H. Lane, of the Twenty-eighth regiment. After the battle of Newbern he was made first lieutenant of Company K, Forty-second regiment. This was in March, 1862, and in the following August he was made captain of the same company. In the latter part of 1864, he was detailed as inspector-general on the staff of Gen. Hoke and held this position till 1865. A while before the close of the war he returned to the captaincy of his company, which surrendered with Johnston's army at Greensboro.

Upon the close of the war, Capt. Alexander returned to his native county, and adopting farming for his occupation, has ever since continued an active and successful prosecutor of that vocation. He was master of the state grange and ex-officio member of the board of agriculture from 1877 to 1879, when he resigned. In politics, Capt. Alexander has been a consistent democrat, and in 1878 was elected by them to the state senate from Mecklenburg county, during his term in the senate acting as chairman of the committee on agriculture. He was also instrumental in securing the passage of a road law, levying a tax to aid in supporting and improving the public roads. The law proved to be very unpopular, especially with his constituency, and in 1880 he was defeated as a candidate for re-nomination. His opponent was nominated and elected, and secured the repeal of the obnoxious law, but in the meantime the wisdom of the law and the advantages it was calculated to secure had been made manifest, and there was a direct reversal of public opinion in its favor. That it might be re-enacted, Capt. Alexander was re-elected as senator in 1882, without opposition. He secured the re-instatement of the act, and as a token of approval of his valuable services he was re-elected in 1884 and 1886. In 1888 his party tendered him the nomination again, but he declined. The same year he was unanimously nominated for lieutenant governor, but declined also this proffered honor. While in the senate, Mr. Alexander during his last three years was chairman of the finance committee, and his invaluable work in this committee earned for him the admiration and applause of his constituents, as well as of the people at large. In 1884 he was appointed chairman of the committee on military affairs.

At the democratic congressional convention of the sixth district in 1890, Capt. Alexander was nominated as the candidate for representation by acclamation, having been the choice of all the delegates at the primary caucuses. The democratic party in the district being largely in the ascendant, he was elected by a handsome and increased majority. As a legislator Capt. Alexander is ever alive to the interests of the state and the people he represents. He is sincere, prudent and conscientious, and is regarded as a safe and reliable exponent of the wants of his section. He is not a demonstrative man, neither is he of an autocratic or dictatorial disposition, but is careful and considerate of the rights of others. He is a citizen of the progressive stamp and is a warm and ardent friend and advocate of the church, of education and the public advancement. His friendships are warm and cordial, devoid of selfishness and permeated with a geniality which makes an intimate acquaintance with a rare beneficence. He has been twice happily married, but unfortunately has lost in death both of his successively chosen companions. His first marriage was in 1872, to Miss Emma P. Nicholson, of Halifax. They had six children, three sons and three daughters. In 1880 the mother died and in 1885 Mr. Alexander married for his second wife Miss Louise Perry, of Franklin, who died in June, 1890, leaving no offspring. Such is a brief sketch of a noble and refined gentleman whose qualities of mind and heart have not only fitted him for the varied and responsible positions he has been called upon to fill, but have endeared him to a large and respectable circle of friends who hold him in the highest esteem.

JAMES TURNER

was a native of Southampton county, Va., and was born December 20, 1766. When he was quite young his father with his family removed to Warren (then Bute) county, N. C. There young Turner received the best education afforded by the common schools of the district. In the Revolutionary war he was a volunteer in a company under the command of Col. John Macon. His public career had its beginning when he was elected to the North Carolina legislature in 1798. He was twice re-elected, serving in the sessions of 1799 and 1800, then elected to the upper house in the sessions of 1801 and 1802. Progressing another step on the ladder of public service, he was elected governor of the state, administering that office until 1805. He was then chosen United States senator, which office he held for two full terms of six years each. Failing health then compelled him to withdraw from official life. His death took place at Bloomsbury, Warren county, N. C., January 13, 1824.

Mr. Turner's colleague in the senate was Gov. David Stone, and between them there was a diversity of political sentiment. Mr. Turner was a democrat of the old school, while Gov. Stone opposed some of the distinctive measures of President Madison's administration, particularly the embargo act, while Gov. Turner supported the most vigorous measures for the prosecution of the war against Great Britain. The personal characteristics of Mr. Turner were of a highly exemplary type. He was a sincere and firm friend, and was faithful to every public and private obligation. He was three times married. First to Mary Anderson, of Warrington, in 1793, by whom he had two sons and two daughters; second to Mrs. Anna Cochran, third to Mrs. Elizabeth Johnson, by whom he had two daughters. One son, Daniel, by his first wife, graduated from West Point military academy, in 1814, and entered the regular army as second lieutenant of artillery. He served in the second war with Great Britain, as acting assistant engineer. Later he resigned his military commission. He was a member of the North Carolina legislature from 1819 to 1823, and a member of congress from 1827 to 1829.

THOMAS LODOWICK VAIL

was born in Wayne county, N. C., September 29, 1827. His father was Benners W. Vail, a native of Washington county, N. C., and his mother before marriage was Susan M. Alford, a daughter of Lodowick Alford. Mr. Vail's father was the son of Thomas Vail, a native of New Jersey, and of Irish and English lineage. Thomas Vail came from his native state to Washington county at an early age. Our subject's father was a farmer by occupation, and leaving Washington county, married and settled on a farm in Wayne county, where he lived and died. He left two sons, of whom the subject of this sketch was the eldest, and two daughters. Thomas L. Vail was sixteen years of age when his father died, and being the eldest of the children, he came to be the head of the family, to whom his minor brother and sisters looked for support. The responsibilities thus devolved upon him took him out of school before he had completed his education, but he had in the meantime in his own county and at Goldsboro gained a fair English education, principally under the instruction of Prof. Cowan, an Irish scholar of much repute. Thomas remained with the family on the farm until 1850. When the Mexican war was at hand he volunteered to go into the military service of his country, but when hostilities actually broke out, he was prevented by the entreaties of his mother from going to the seat of war. Through the intervention of friends, a "substitute" was prevailed upon to take his place, and young Vail was thus induced to stay at home and still look after home interests.

In May, 1850, Mr. Vail was married to Miss Smitha J. Person, of Greene county, and he then removed to Columbus county, where he embarked in the turpentine business, in which he was very successful. He continued his residence in this county until 1859, when he returned to Greene county. While residing in Columbus county he was chosen clerk of the superior court, holding this office from August, 1853, to January, 1859. His removal to Greene county necessitated the resignation of his clerkship, and he located on a farm in that county, where he continued until the breaking out of the Civil war. He then volunteered, and was made first lieutenant of Company H, First North Carolina cavalry. He was in active service, his first engagement being at the battle of Dranesville. Subsequently he participated in the fight around Richmond, and other actions. While in charge of a part of Gen. Hampton's brigade at Winchester, Va., he was relieved from further active work in the field by reason of ill health. Returning to his home in Greene county, he made a visit to Mecklenburg county, where, in Providence, he purchased land, and in January, 1863, removed his family to his new purchase. Soon thereafter he was detailed to collect and supply the Confederate soldiers with necessities, continuing in this service until the close of the war. After that period Mr. Vail continued on his farm at Providence till 1872, in which year he removed to Charlotte. For several years he was cashier of the Farmers' Savings bank at Charlotte. This bank was merged into the Traders' National bank, but Mr. Vail was retained as its cashier. The bank went into liquidation in 1883, and was discontinued. With the intermission of about three years, Mr. Vail has been continuously a member of the Mecklenburg county board of commissioners. In 1868 he was elected and commissioned by Canby a military commandant, and during the long time that Mr. Vail has served as a member of the board he has been its chairman. He is a progressive and representative citizen, a practical and successful farmer, a moral and religious man, whose honesty and integrity are unimpeachable. He has been for many years an active member of the Baptist church. His family, consisting of himself, his wife, one son and four daughters, enjoy a high social standing among the leading society people of Charlotte.

WILLIAM M. VANDEVER,

a farmer by occupation and a resident citizen of Charlotte, is a native of Wilmington, Del., born in that city February 21, 1825. His father, John Vandever, was a native of the same city and was the son of Peter Vandever, a native of New Castle county, Del. The family is of distinguished lineage, having been prominent among the early settlers of Delaware. The progenitor of the family emigrated to America with the Swedes, who, at an early day, took up their residence in this state. The family became wealthy and was highly respected, and for years were worshipers in the Swedish church at Wilmington. Their ancestors adopted the views of Martin Luther, and fled from persecution in the Netherlands to the American wilderness in the sixteenth century, settling in Delaware on the Brandywine, christening their place "Vandever's Island." Such is the paternal lineage of the subject of this sketch. His mother was Sarah Chambers, who, though a native of Delaware, was of English descent. Mr. Vandever is the eldest of ten children, only three brothers and three sisters arriving at maturity. He was reared in Wilmington and there received a fair English education. Early in life he learned locomotive engineering, and, upon reaching his majority, left the parental home and began railroad engineering. This business he followed throughout several states, including Pennsylvania, Ohio, Indiana, Tennessee, Mississippi, Alabama, Georgia and the Carolinas. While running an engine on the Madison & Indianapolis railroad, he enlisted for the Mexican war, but did not reach the seat of actual service before peace was declared. In 1850 he first came to the Carolinas, the occasion being the acceptance of a position as engineer on the Charlotte & Columbia railroad, on which he was employed until 1852. In 1851 he married Mary, the daughter of Dr. A. F. Clifton. She died in the same year, and in 1852 Mr. Vandever married his present wife, Louise A. Cornwell, daughter of Elijah Cornwell, a prominent and wealthy farmer of Chester county, S. C. The issue of this marriage was two children, both of whom died early in life.

In 1858 Mr. Vandever settled on a plantation in Chester county, and quitting the calling of an engineer took up the occupation of farming. During the war between the states, he served the Confederacy as a railroad engineer, operating, among other roads, upon the North Carolina Central, the Western North Carolina, and the Charlotte & Columbia. While on the North Carolina Central railroad he was hauling from Charlotte to Raleigh the Thirteenth South Carolina regiment, and to the train befell the uncontrollable accident of breaking an axle of one of the cars. Some of the soldiers became

A. B. DAVIDSON, Esq

enraged at him, attributing the accident to carelessness and a willful intention to wreck the train. For a time his life was in peril, and he was threatened with death by shooting, but pulling his engine loose from the train he hurried to Salisbury, eleven miles in advance, and thus escaped harm. When the war closed he returned to his plantation, which his faithful wife had continued to operate, keeping the slaves under control. Loaded with debt, Mr. Vandever now began active and zealous work at farming, which he has ever since continued with remarkable and gratifying success. He resided in Chester county, S. C., till 1874, when he removed into Mecklenburg county, N. C., where he has from that time remained. Since January, 1890, he has resided within the city of Charlotte, where he and his wife have a nice home and enjoy the advantages of church and society. He is of the Presbyterian faith, and his wife of the Methodist. Mr. Vandever is a prosperous and practical farmer and a representative citizen.

A. B. DAVIDSON

is one of the oldest descendants of a signer of the Mecklenburg declaration of independence, now living in Charlotte, N. C. He was born in Mecklenburg county, March 13, 1808, and is now just eighty-three years of age. His paternal grandfather was Maj. John Davidson, of Highland Scotch birth, and of Revolutionary fame. Subsequent to the Scotch rebellion, Maj. Davidson came to America with his mother, then a widow, and settled in the Cumberland valley of Pennsylvania. About 1735 he removed to North Carolina, locating a plantation on the Catawba river. Here our subject was born, reared, married and raised his large family, as did his father. Adam Brevard Davidson is one of the best of men, a faithful Christian and a true patriot. He is a plain and unassuming man, but a man whose sterling qualities of heart had elevated to a high plain of moral excellence and to the most cordial respect of all who knew him, and their "name is legion." He is an uneducated man, for in his youth his father was not able to school him. However, he gained a fair knowledge of the rudiments of an education in reading, writing and perhaps arithmetic. But his noble disposition, determined mind and practical qualities, have made him well fitted for his labors. He chose the vocation of a planter at the early age of ten, remaining under the direction of his father. April 20, 1836, he was united in marriage with Mary Laura, the daughter of Hon. John Springs, of York district, S. C. The union was blessed by the birth of fifteen children, all of whom were given thorough educations. In 1876 Mr. Davidson married for a second wife Cornelia C. Elmore, the daughter of Hon. Franklin Elmore of South Carolina. As a farmer, Mr. Davidson was remarkably successful, and is an excellent representative of the noble and honest occupation. Since 1872 he has continued an active improvement of his real estate in Charlotte, for which he has done much to make a city. He was president of the Mecklenburg agricultural society for about fifteen years, until that society was broken up by the Civil war.

In September, 1847, Mr. Davidson was elected one of the twelve of the first board of directors for the C. C. & A. railroad, and has since continued on that board to the present time. For many years he has served as a valuable director of the Granitesville manufacturing company, of South Carolina. He has also served as a director in the Merchants & Farmers' national bank of Charlotte since 1880. Mr. Davidson rendered no military service in the war between the states, as he was beyond sixty years of age at the outbreak of hostilities. He furnished three sons in the defense of their country, named John, Robert and Richard. Mr. Davidson, though not in favor of the war, was a great loser thereby, having at one time bought Confederate bonds to the amount of $30,000 which were payable in gold, every dollar of which was lost, beside a loss of about $70,000 in the same bonds which came into his possession. Mr. Davidson has been an active life-long member of the Presbyterian church. For nearly a half century he was an elder in the Hopewell Presbyterian church, to which he was a large donator when it was organized and constructed, as well as in after years. In 1856 he was a delegate to the old school general assembly which convened at New York city. He served as a trustee of Davidson college for over twenty-five years in which college he has always taken special pride, it having been founded by his ancestors and he having contributed largely to its progress and improvement. In December, 1835, he contracted with Henry C. Owens, for the college, agreeing to furnish 150,000 feet of lumber for the college, all of which he sawed at his own mills and delivered from his plantation by September, 1836. He has been since residing in Charlotte, an active and leading member of the First Presbyterian church of Charlotte, and when the Second Presbyterian church was about to be erected he gave as a donation to that purpose $500. He has donated several thousand dollars to Davidson college, to the Theological Seminary of Columbia, S. C., of which he was trustee for about fifteen years, and the Union Seminary of Virginia, and to other religious and educational institutions. He has lived to see his beneficiaries fruitful and appreciated.

WILLIAM L. KENNEDY.

The Kennedy family has long been intimately identified with the advancement of Lenoir county, N. C. William L. Kennedy was born near Falling Creek, that county, March 18, 1845, the son of Thomas Jefferson and Martha (Allen) Kennedy. The family is of Irish descent. John Kennedy, the great-grandfather of Mr. William L. Kennedy, was a soldier in the Revolutionary war. He was the father of Jesse Kennedy, who was a prominent planter and slave owner of Lenoir county. He reared two sons and four daughters, all now deceased. Sally, the eldest child, who died recently, was the wife of Oliver Parrott, of Darlington, S. C. Thomas J. Kennedy was born in Lenoir county, March 30, 1818, and was educated in the public and private schools of his native county, after which he engaged in planting, and continued in that calling the remainder of his days, having met with much success. He was one of the original stockholders of the A. & N. C. R. R., and for a number of years was a member of the finance committee of the company. During the Civil war he held the office of tax assessor for the Confederate states, and for many years was a justice of the peace. First a whig, he left the party at the organization of know-nothingism, identifying himself with the democratic party, and became a leader in that party. His death occurred in 1885, and his wife's in 1883. Their children are: William L., Alpheus T., of this county; Mrs. Mary Rayner, of Kinston; Mrs. M. H. Wooten; Jesse C., deceased, was born in Lenoir county, December 13, 1841, was educated at Bingham institute, and in 1861 entered the Confederate service as a member of Company H, First North Carolina regiment. After an efficient service of twelve months he was honorably discharged owing to physical disability. Subsequently he re-enlisted in Company D, Thirty-fifth North Carolina infantry, and fought until the close of the war under Gen. Robert Ransom. He returned home and became a leading planter, and was a justice of the peace, and a director in the A. & N. C. R. R.

William L. Kennedy was reared on his father's plantation, and completed his scholastic training at Lexington, N. C., under Prof. Smythe. At the age of sixteen he enlisted in Company D, Thirty-fifth North Carolina regiment, and was attached to Gen. Robert Ransom's staff during the entire war. After the close of hostilities Mr. Kennedy returned home and turned his attention to agriculture, in which he has been most successfully engaged since, owning one of the largest plantations in the county. He has held the office of justice of the peace for many years, and is a stanch and representative democrat. In September, 1890, Gov. Fowle appointed him a director of the A. & N. C. R. R. company, which he now holds. Mr. Kennedy was happily married, in 1874, to Miss Emily Hardee, a daughter of Pinckney Hardee, of Kinston. Both Mr. and Mrs. Kennedy are of the Baptist church faith. He is largely interested in different industrial enterprises, being a stockholder in the Orion Knitting mill company, of Kinston. His plantations are under the highest cultivation, and produce great quantities of cotton and grain, and he owns large herds of fine cattle, his Jersey herd being one of the most noted in the country, and in the breeding of Jersey cattle he is a pioneer in the county.

WILLIAM DUNN

was born in Newbern, N. C., September 7, 1847, his parents being William and Margaret (Oliver) Dunn. For many years the elder Dunn was engaged in the mercantile business at Newbern, and also owned several vessels sailing from Newbern to the West Indies. His father, also named William, was a native of Maryland, and settled in

Newbern, N. C., in the latter part of the year 1790, where he was engaged in merchandising. William Dunn, Jr., father of our subject, died in 1856; his wife and three children still survive him. The names of these children are here given: William, John and Mary. William Dunn, our subject, received his education in the public schools of his native town. At the age of seventeen years he secured a position as clerk on a steamship running into New York city, and was thus employed until 1876, when he became superintendent of the Atlantic & North Carolina railroad, holding that office until 1888. In the latter year Mr. Dunn embarked in agriculture and now ships large quantities of vegetables to northern markets. He was one of the organizers of the eastern North Carolina fair association in 1887, and was made the second president of the same, which position he still holds. Under his management the association has grown to be the largest and most important exhibit in the state. Mr. Dunn is also largely interested in real estate, owning a large tract of land adjacent to Newbern, which he is laying off into town lots. He is past master of St. John's Lodge No. 3, A. F. & A. M., and is a stanch democrat. After retiring from the superintendency of the A. & N. C. railroad, Mr. Dunn formed a partnership with Mr. William C. Willett and purchased a plantation of 1,000 acres and established the first stock farm in the vicinity of Newbern. Some time later he sold his interest in this important enterprise.

THEOPHILUS H. HOLMES

was the senior officer from North Carolina in the war between the states. He was sprung from a family that had for generations been esteemed in North Carolina for virtue and excellence of character. His father was Gov. Gabriel Holmes, a resident of Sampson county, N. C., where the subject of this sketch was born November 11, 1804. He received an ordinary education in the local schools, and in 1825 entered the military academy at West Point, where he graduated in July, 1829, and served in the army with acceptability. He attained the rank of captain, December, 1838. His army life was largely spent on the frontier. He served with distinction in the Seminole war. In the Mexican war he won encomiums for his valor and for gallant and meritorious conduct in several conflicts; at Monterey he was breveted major. In his Rise and Fall of the Confederacy, Jefferson Davis refers to his conduct on that occasion in the following words: " I, who knew him from his school-boy days, who served with him in garrison and in field, and with pride watched him as he gallantly led a storming party up a rocky height at Monterey, and was intimately acquainted with his whole career during our sectional war, bear willing testimony to the purity, self-abnegation, generosity, fidelity and gallantry, which characterized him as a man and a soldier."

For many years Maj. Holmes served in Arkansas and across the Mississippi, but in 1860 he was in command of Governor's Island, in New York harbor. On the breaking out of the war he resigned his

commission and cast his lot with his people. President Davis, who esteemed him most highly as a man and an officer, at once appointed him a brigadier-general in the Confederate army, and he was assigned to duty in North Carolina. Here Gen. Holmes rendered most efficient service in selecting officers for North Carolina regiments, and in organizing them. It was largely due to him that the North Carolina state troops were so finely officered; their excellence being rarely equaled. Soon afterward he was promoted to be major-general, and assigned to the command of the district of Fredericksburg, Va., and he was in command of the forces that held the Potomac during the winter of 1861–62. In 1862 he was transferred to the district of North Carolina, and in the fall of that year was tendered the rank of lieutenant-general, and ordered across the Mississippi, where it was supposed that he would be particularly useful, because he had served so long in that region and possessed the confidence of the people there so thoroughly. He declined the promotion, but accepted the duty. The condition of affairs in the trans-Mississippi department was at that time very embarrassing, and Gen. Holmes' service was very acceptable. He was again tendered the rank of lieutenant-general, and did not decline it. In 1864, his health becoming infirm, he was placed in command of the reserves of North Carolina, which he organized and put on an effective footing.

At the end of the war Mr. Holmes returned to Fayetteville, and resided on a small farm near that place, which he cultivated with his own hands. He accepted the results of the war with manly fortitude. His patriotic heart was deeply touched for the sorrows of the people, and we remember to have heard him lament that a particular person, who had not survived the war, had not been spared—"because he could have done more than any one else to lead the people to accept their changed situation without undue repining." He was a gentle, Christian gentleman; without guile, but with a stern Roman virtue. No finer spectacle has been presented in the annals of the world than that of this old hero—without a murmur of discontent, after so many years of distinguished service, enjoying the esteem and high regard of so many men notable in the history of his country—retiring to a secluded spot and plowing his own fields and setting an example of personal labor and industry and frugality to his unfortunate countrymen. He survived the war fifteen years, and died in 1880, in the seventy-sixth year of his age, and was interred at MacPherson church, near Fayetteville, N. C. In 1841, Gen. Holmes married Miss Laura Wetmore, by whom he had eight children, four of whom still survive. His eldest son, Lieut. T. H. Holmes, fell at Malvern Hill.

RICHARD BEVERLY RANEY,

the well known and successful proprietor of the Yarborough House, Raleigh, N. C., is a native of Granville county, being born at "Retreat," that county, February 7, 1860. His paternal great-grandfather was William Raney, a native of Sussex county, Va.; he married Cath-

B—39

erine Vaughan, by whom he had several children, one of whom, Hall Raney, married Mary Hall, and became the father of Thomas Hall Raney, the father of the subject of this sketch. Thomas Hall Raney was born in 1814, and in 1844 removed to North Carolina, settling in Granville county, where he purchased and subsequently cultivated a large estate. In 1836 he was united in marriage with Miss Eliza Partridge Baird, daughter of Rev. Charles William Baird, of Mecklenburg county, Va. This union was blessed by the birth of nine children, namely: Mary Archer, Charles William, Lucy Speed (who died in 1878, aged thirty-seven years); George Hall (who died in 1861, of fever contracted while in the Confederate army, aged eighteen years); Elizabeth Harriet, Ann Eliza, Rose Virginia, Thomas Hanserd, Cora Partridge (who died July 19, 1880, aged twenty-three years), and Richard Beverly. August 7, 1872, the death of the father of these children occurred. The maternal grandfather of our subject was Rev. Charles William Baird, a native of Mecklenburg county, Va., born in 1790. His father was William Baird, a native of Scotland, whence he came to this country at an early age. The great-great-grandfather of the mother of our subject was James Speed, who was a descendant of John Speed, of Cheshire, England, a distinguished historian of the sixteenth contury.

Richard Beverly Raney was educated at Fetter school, in Kittrell, Vance county, N. C. At the age of sixteen years he left school and went to Norfolk, Va., where he spent a year in the employment of Tredwell & Mallory, cotton factors. In March, 1878, Mr. Raney removed to Raleigh, and entered the Yarborough house as clerk, in which capacity he acted for four years, then going to Atlanta, Ga., where he became cashier of the Kimball house, of that city. His connection with this house was severed in 1883, when the famous old hostelry was destroyed by fire. Returning to Raleigh in December, 1883, Mr. Raney leased the Yarborough house, since which time he has continued its proprietor. In 1884 he formed a partnership with Mr. John Gatling, of Raleigh, and Hon. F. M. Simmons, of Newbern, and the firm leased the Atlantic hotel at Morehead City, N. C. In 1885 Mr. Gatling retired from the firm, and his place was filled by Mr. J. A. Kennedy, of Norfolk, Va. One year later this partnership was dissolved. In 1889 Mr. Raney assumed the management of the Atlantic hotel for the present owners. Mr. Raney is also interested in agriculture, operating a farm in Wake county, and has recently purchased a plantation in Warren county, N. C. Desiring to promote the interests of Raleigh, Mr. Raney became a subscriber to the stock of nearly all of its manufacturing enterprises, among them the North Carolina wagon factory, the Raleigh cotton mills, the Caraleigh cotton mills, and the Caraleigh phosphate mills. He is a director of the South Piedmont land and manufacturing company, of Greensboro, N. C.; director of the West End hotel and land company, of Winston, N. C., and also a director of the Commercial & Farmers' bank, of Raleigh, N. C. Mr. Raney is a progressive and successful business man, and is a valued citizen of the town of his adoption.

HON. JAMES J. McKAY.

Among the distinguished men who have represented North Carolina with high credit in the Federal congress was James J. McKay, of Bladen county. He was born in Bladen in 1793, studied law, and at the early age of twenty-two was elected to the state senate, and served almost continuously from 1815 to 1826. He was appointed district attorney for the United States for North Carolina and shone conspicuously in that office. In 1830 he was elected a member of congress and served for nine consecutive terms — until 1849. His long term of service, united with his fine abilities and learning, made him a leader in the house, and he served for several years with great acceptability and credit as chairman of the committee on ways and means, a position second in importance only to that of speaker. He was an ardent democrat, and in the national democratic convention of 1848 he received the vote of his state for vice-president. "As a statesman he was of unquestioned ability, of stern integrity, capable of great labor and patient investigation." He died suddenly at Goldsboro, N. C., in 1853.

P. A. FRERCKS.

The gentleman to whom reference is made has certainly had a varied business career, of which an outline may be of more than ordinary interest. Mr. Frercks is a native of Schleswig-Holstein, and was born March 27, 1825. He was given a thorough education in his native town, Heiligenstadten, and subsequently completed his course at the Polytechnical institute of Copenhagen, Denmark. He came to the United States in 1851, landing in New York city, where he made his home for the first four years, his employment being in a tool or machine shop. Upon leaving New York, he went to Savannah, Ga., and for two years did locomotive engineering on the Central Georgia railroad. In 1856 he returned to New York, and was employed as marine engineer in the Novelty yard there. In 1857 he located in Salisbury, N. C., where he accepted a position with Bayden & Son, who were carrying on a machine shop. One year later he entered into partnership with Mr. William Raeder and bought the machine shops of Bayden & Son, and operated the same until the outbreak of the war. Raeder absconded and fled to the north in 1861, leaving Mr. Frercks to pay heavy debts contracted by the concern, which he honestly and punctually did. In 1862 Mr. Frercks disposed of the property and the Confederate government rented it, using it as a manufactory of shot, shell, percussion caps, etc., Mr. Frercks being retained in charge. In the spring of 1863 he was made chief engineer of the High Shoal Iron works, of Gaston county, N. C., owned by Bridges & Co., holding that position until the close of the war. Also soon after was made master machinist of the Western North Carolina railroad, then running to Morganton. In

November, 1863, he left the railroad and moved to Wilmington to rebuild a large steam cotton press for the government and was made the superintendent of the Hart & Bailey Iron works.

When the Federal forces captured Wilmington, Mr. Frercks was offered employment under their direction if he would serve them as well as he had served the Confederacy, and so remained until the close of the war, returning to Salisbury in September, 1865. He was then appointed revenue inspector and gauger, and subsequently became connected with mining operations, putting in the chlorination works in the Reimer and Yadkin mines. In the meantime he opened at Salisbury, machine shops which grew in importance until they consumed most of his time. In consequence of other growing business interests, Mr. Frercks has reduced his shops almost exclusively to a place of repair work, and here he is prepared to model tools and conveniences, and can do almost any form of work, being one of the most skilled of mechanics, and having a varied knowledge of, and experience in, all forms of mechanism, physics, geometry, mathematics and other sciences. In 1880, Mr. Frercks, realizing the necessity which existed at Salisbury for better hotel accommodations, built the "Mount Vernon" hotel, one of the best equipped and kept establishments in the state. The manner in which it is kept reflects great credit upon its proprietor and the town, and guests who stop beneath its shelter go away bearing pleasant impressions with them. Mr. Frercks is not only a man of varied business experiences, but has seen and traveled much. He served from 1848 to 1851 in the struggle of the Duches against Denmark. He volunteered in Gen. Van Der Tan's Free corps, and afterward served in the Ninth battalion, in Holstein. On the close of his service he came to America, and at New York city declared his allegiance to the government of the United States by taking out his naturalization papers in 1853 and 1857. He has since been a faithful and worthy citizen of this vast country. In 1885 Mr. Frercks married Miss Fannie E. Kelly, a lady of excellent family and culture, being a native of North Carolina, and of Scotch lineage. The marriage of Mr. Frercks and wife has been blessed by the birth of a son, Francis. The parents are valued communicants of the Episcopal church. In 1854 Mr. Frercks became a Master Mason, and in 1860 was made a Royal Arch Mason, of chapter 20, of Salisbury.

SAMUEL JOHNSTON,

early a leading citizen of North Carolina, was born in Dundee, Scotland, in 1733. He was the son of John Johnston, his mother's maiden name being Helen Scrymsour. In 1736 John Johnston came with his family to North Carolina. A brother, Gabriel Johnston, had preceded John, and settled in what is now Johnston county, which took its name from him. Samuel Johnston was a man of broad and liberal views and of fine education. He was a friend of the rights of the people against the encroachments of the British government, and, in 1775, was suspended from the position of deputy naval officer at Edenton, N. C., on account of his political sentiments. In reply to the notification of his suspension, he wrote a manly letter to Gov. Martin, traversing many of the points in the accusations brought against him, but in no way receding from the position he had taken in politics. He was a member of the provincial congress in 1775, to represent the Chowan district, and was chosen presiding officer of that body to succeed John Harvey, who died while holding that position. From 1780 to 1782 Mr. Johnston was a member of the continental congress, and was chosen president of that body. He was, however, obliged to forego that distinction on account of the low condition of his finances. He was elected governor of the state in 1787. He was a firm supporter of the Federal constitution, and was president of the North Carolina state convention which met, in 1788, to consider and ratify that instrument. He was elected, on the adoption of the constitution, to the United States senate in the first congress, Benjamin Hawkins being his colleague from North Carolina. He was appointed a judge of the superior courts of law and equity of North Carolina in 1800, an office which he administered with great ability, discretion and impartiality. He resigned this office in the fall of 1803.

Governor Johnston was a fine type of a man, both physically and mentally. He had a stalwart frame, well formed and imposing, erect in stature, and virile in all his movements. He possessed a severely disciplined and highly cultured intellect. He had a will which was unbending, but he was always open to the voice of sound reason and true philosophy. Mr. Johnston was a Mason of high degree, and, in 1778, was grand master of the grand lodge of the state. Mr. Johnston died in 1816. He married Frances Cathcart, by whom he had several children. One of his sons, James C. Johnston, of Edenton, was a prosperous planter and accumulated a large estate, amounting to several millions of dollars. He was strongly opposed to the secession of the states, in which he appeared to be alone among his relatives, they being advocates of that measure. For this reason he disinherited them in his will, bequeathing his large property to his personal friends. He was an ardent admirer of Henry Clay, generously discharging the debts of that great statesman, without his knowledge and as a gratuity. At the opening of the Civil war he set his slaves free, but did not live to see the close of the war which he so earnestly opposed. He died in 1864.

MICHAEL CRONLY,

senior member of the firm of Cronly & Morris, real estate agents of Wilmington, was born in New York city in 1828, the son of James and Sarah L. Cronly, natives of New York. His grandfather, John Cronly, was a native of Ireland and emigrated to the United States in 1780, settling in New York. James Cronly was for many years engaged in mercantile pursuits on Park Row, New York city. He died and left but one heir, the subject of this sketch, who was brought by his mother to Wilmington, N. C., when he was an infant. He spent his early life with Mr. John A. Taylor, his mother's brother, and received his education at the Donaldson academy, of Fayetteville, N. C. Mr. Cronly entered the stock brokerage and real estate business when but twenty-one years old, in connection with Messrs. John Walker and Eli W. Hall, under the firm name of Cronly, Walker & Hall, the same existing about two years, when Mr. Walker removed to California and Mr. Hall began the study of law and became a prominent attorney. Mr. Cronly continued the business until 1865, when he formed a partnership with Mr. Wilkes Morris, which still exists. The firm disposed of all brokeraged goods, sales often amounting to $1,000 per day. Mr Cronly was married, in 1848, to Miss Margaret McLaurin, of Wilmington, who bore him four sons and five daughters. He is a member of the Masonic order, K. T. degree. He has never taken any active part in politics, but has attended strictly to his business. He is regarded as a man of intelligence, good judgment and the strictest probity.

TODD R. CALDWELL

was born at Morganton, Burke county, N. C., February 19, 1818. He was of Irish descent, his father, John Caldwell, having emigrated from Ireland in 1800, and settled in Morganton, where he carried on an extensive mercantile business. Todd R. Caldwell was educated at the schools in the neighborhood, entered North Carolina university, from which he graduated in 1840, with honor. He read law with Judge David Lowry Swain, was admitted to the bar and began practice, in which he was eminently successful. But the natural tendency of the legal profession soon drew him into the arena of politics, whose ever changing fortunes he followed through life. He entered upon this course when his party, the old line whig, had succeeded to power as the result of the political revolution of 1840, and though its tenure at that time was brief, owing to the differences which sprung up between its principal leaders and Mr. Tyler, who had succeeded to the presidency by the untimely death of Gen. Harrison, we find Mr. Caldwell one of the successful presidential electors in the campaign of 1848. His vote in the electoral college was cast for Zachary Taylor and Millard Fillmore, but he does not seem to have figured largely as an office holder till later in life.

In the great civil strife, which culminated in hostilities in 1861, Mr. Caldwell's political antecedents prompted him to take the side of the Unionists in strong opposition to the secession movement. When the catastrophe of the war was concluded, Mr. Caldwell was elected a delegate to the state convention which immediately followed the close. In 1868 he was elected lieutenant governor, upon the ticket headed by Gov. W. W. Holden, whom he succeeded as governor, when that functionary was removed by impeachment in 1871. In 1872, Mr. Caldwell received the nomination for governor in opposition to Hon. Augustus S. Merriman. The contest was a warm one, and each candidate, in his own behalf, made a lively canvass. Mr. Caldwell was elected, but he did not live to administer his full term. He died at Hillsboro, February 11, 1874. He was regarded as one of the ablest criminal lawyers in the state, and was a public speaker of much force and eloquence, which gave him great advantage in his political campaigns. He married Miss Cain, daughter of William Cain and a niece of Judge Thomas Ruffin.

THOMAS A. RÒBBINS,

proprietor of Long's hotel, at Rockingham, N. C., was born in Brunswick county, N. C., August 27, 1841, the son of Enoch and Charlotte G. (Hankins) Robbins, both North Carolinians by birth. The father was a merchant and planter, and also dealt extensively in turpentine. He was a successful business man, and esteemed throughout the community as one of rigid uprightness and of ability. His death occurred January 6, 1860, when he was but fifty-seven years old; his wife survived him until her eightieth year. Both parents were active and earnest members of the Methodist Episcopal church, and brought their twelve children up in that faith. Five of these offspring are living. The son, Thomas A., was educated in the academy at South Port, and later attended Trinity college, where he remained three years. He was one of sixty in the state who first offered their services to the Confederacy, this force having taken possession of Fort Caswell, at the mouth of Cape Fear river, the day succeeding the one the Star of the West was repulsed in her attempt to re-inforce Major Anderson at Fort Sumter. April 16, 1861, the governor of the state called for volunteers to assist in capturing this fort, which had been relinquished on the request of the governor that he might keep his oath of office and not allow the property of the United States to be destroyed before formal action had been taken by the southern states. Mr. Robbins enlisted at this time in the Cape Fear artillery, and after a short time was assigned to ordnance duty. He surrendered at Greensboro, N. C., with Johnston, after a faithful and efficient service of four years and sixteen days, having served longer by a month or so than any other man in Richmond county. After the declaration of peace Mr. Robbins turned his attention to planting, and after several years purchased a steamboat, and operated that in connection with a mercantile business until 1872, when he sold out, and for the succeeding seven years was engaged as a traveling agent for the Wheeler & Wilson manufacturing company. At the expiration of this time he removed to Rockingham and embarked in the hotel business, in which he has since continued with the most happy results. December 29, 1876, Mr. Robbins married Miss M. Long, daughter of Hon. R. T. Long, late of Richmond county, and two children, Wm. A. and Charlotte G., have been born to them. Mrs. Robbins is a communicant of the Presbyterian church and he is a member of the K. of H.

STUART W. CRAMER, M. E.,

is the assayer in charge of the United States assay office at Charlotte,
N. C. He was born in Thomasville, Davidson county, N. C., March 31,
1868, the son of John T. Cramer, M. E., president of the Thomasville,
Silver Valley & Pee Dee railroad company. S. W. Cramer's mother,
before marriage, was Jennie Thomas, whose father is one of the
wealthiest and most prominent men in Davidson county. The subject
of this sketch is the second of three children and was reared in his
native village, where he received his early education. In June, 1888,
he was graduated from the United States naval academy at Annapolis, Md. September 15, 1888, he resigned from the United States naval
service and then took a post-graduate course during 1888–9 in the
school of mines, Columbia college, New York city. June 24, 1889, he
married Miss Bertha Hobart Berry, an accomplished lady of Portland, Me. On the 1st of July, 1889, being recommended by Mr.
Windom, the late secretary of the United States treasury, Mr. Cramer
was appointed assayer in charge of the United States assay office at
Charlotte, which position he has since filled. During the year 1890,
while taking his vacation, he compiled, for the United States census
bureau, a report on the gold and silver mines of the south. Mr.
Cramer is a special contributor, for the south, to the *Engineering and
Mining Journal* of New York, and an enthusiastic and thorough investigator and student of mining engineering. At the age of twenty-
three years he is holding one of the most important positions in the
United States mint service. He is a member of the American institute of mining engineers, also of the United States naval institute.
Mr. Cramer is a highly energetic young man, possessing a strict sense
of duty and a special ability and adaptation for the performance of
his official functions. He is one of the brightest and best qualified of
the members of his profession — that of a mining engineer.

GEN. JETHRO SUMNER

was a patriot and hero during the Revolutionary war. His
grandfather was William Sumner, who emigrated from England and
settled, in 1690, near Suffolk, Va., where he raised five sons, namely:
Jethro, the father of the subject of this sketch; John, whose daughter
married Elisha Battle, who removed to Edgecombe county, N. C.,
and from whom is descended the distinguished Battle family of
North Carolina; James, whose sons, Luke, David and Thomas, were
prominent in civil life; Damsey, the ancestor of Col. Thomas Jethro
Sumner, of Rowan county, and another son, William. Jethro, the
younger, was born near Suffolk, in 1732. During the French and Indian wars he was appointed lieutenant, and then captain, in the Virginia forces and served under Col. George Washington, and was at
the taking of Fort DuQuense. After the cessation of hostilities, he
moved to North Carolina, settling in Bute county, now Warren,

where, in 1772, he was appointed high sheriff. The troubles coming on with the mother country he ardently espoused the cause of the colonies, and was a member of the first provincial congress, which met in August, 1774. He was appointed major of the minute men, of Bute, and served under Gen. Howe in the winter of 1775-6, near Norfolk, Va. In April, 1776, he was appointed colonel of the Third regiment of North Carolina continentals, and with his command was at the battle of Fort Moultrie, when the North Carolina troops won such high praise from Gen. Charles Lee.

Col. Sumner went with Gen. Lee in July, 1776, on the expedition against Florida, returning to Charleston in September. The North Carolina troops were then ordered north, and the six regiments of continentals spent the month of November in camp at Wilmington, but later returned to Charleston. On March 9, 1777, Gen. Francis Nash being in command, the entire brigade set out on their long march to the north, and reached Middlebrook, N. J., in June, but spent the dreadful winter at Valley Forge, Penn. Col. Sumner fought gallantly at Brandywine, Germantown and Monmouth, and when, in the summer of 1778, the six regiments were compressed into three, he was retained as colonel of the third regiment, and on January 9, 1779, he was promoted to be brigadier-general, and ordered to the south. He was with Gen. Lincoln on the Savannah river with 700 North Carolina continentals, April 19, 1779, and at the battle of Stono, June 19, he commanded a North Carolina brigade on the left of the line. A few weeks later, he returned to North Carolina to recruit. The continental troops were entirely distinct from those under the state authorities, the officers being commissioned by the continental congress and the troops being paid by congress. Being an officer in the continental line, after the fall of Charleston, where his brigade was captured, he himself being absent, he had no other forces and remained in North Carolina.

In August, when Gates and Caswell fled from Camden, he was assigned to the command of the militia from the counties of Guilford, Cornell and Orange and hastened to Salisbury, and on toward Charlotte, where he and Col. Davidson hedged in Cornwallis, who had taken post at Charlotte. Gen. Sumner was at Alexander's Mills, on Rocky river, on October 9, 1780, when Cornwallis retreated. About that time the legislature appointed Gen. Smallwood, of New Jersey, to the command of the North Carolina militia, and Gen. Sumner withdrew. On December 3, 1780, however, Gen. Greene arrived at Charlotte and called on Gen. Sumner to take immediate steps to reorganize the continental line, and to this Gen. Sumner was addressing himself when the battle of Cowpens occurred and the state was thrown into great perturbation by the movements of Greene and Cornwallis. Greene, on February 10, wrote to Sumner, suggesting that he should take command of the North Carolina troops that were to join him, and Sumner offered his services to Gen. Caswell, who had charge of the military affairs of the state, and hoped at least to have a brigade of militia, but was repelled, notwithstanding Gov. Nash also desired his services. After that he continued his efforts to form new regiments for the continental line. The process was very slow, notwithstanding the militia that had behaved badly at Guilford Court House was drafted for that purpose. He established military camps at different points in the state and soon had his officers at work disciplining the recruits. The chief camp was at Salisbury, where Maj. Blount was in charge, and as soon as a sufficient number were organized they were sent to the front. Arms were very scarce and it was with the utmost difficulty that a supply could be obtained from Virginia. Eventually, however, during the summer, Gen. Sumner succeeded in getting the last detatchment of his brigade in the field and joined Gen. Greene with a well drilled corps, who behaved with a steadiness and intrepidity worthy of the stanchest veterans. At the bloody battle of Eutaw Springs they won imperishable laurels, and under the command of Sumner, Ashe, Armstrong and Blount reflected honor upon the military fame of their native state.

While Greene was in South Carolina, some bold royalists captured Col. Burke, the governor of the state, at Hillsboro, and hurried him off into captivity. The loss of the governor disorganized the government and disturbed the patriots in the state to such a degree that Gen. Greene sent Sumner back to North Carolina to quiet apprehensions and restore confidence. Thus the last months of the war found him again separated from his command. At the close of hostilities he settled on his plantation in Warren county, but took no active part in political life. He was elected, in 1784, president of the society of Cincinnati for North Carolina, and received other tokens of public approbation. But his health was impaired, and in March, 1785, he died at his residence in Warren, where his remains were interred. A century later, in 1891, the legislature of the state made an appropriation to remove his remains to the Battle Park, the scene of the battle of Guilford Court House, and a monument has been erected there to his memory. Gen. Sumner married "the widow Heiss," a lady of wealth, a resident at Newbern, and left three children, two boys who died unmarried, and a daughter, "Jocky Sullivan," who married Hon. Thomas Blount, a member of congress, changing her name to Mary Sumner Blount, but she also died childless in 1822.

GEORGE B. HANNA,

the subject of this sketch, is a native of Massachusetts, born in 1835. His father, A. G. Hanna, carried on a successful business in the manufacture of shoes. Mr. Hanna graduated from Brown university, Providence, R. I., in 1865, and took a post-graduate course at Columbia college, New York city, in the School of Mines. In 1869 he accepted a call to Raleigh, N. C., and subsequently assisted Prof. W. C. Kerr, in making a geological survey of North Carolina, taking the position of chief chemist. In 1870 Mr. Hanna was appointed assistant assayer in the United States mint, at Charlotte, N. C. Prof. Hanna has since continued in the assay office, his position from time to time being variously designated as melter, clerk, etc., but substantially continuing as assistant assayer. In this capacity he has made to the United States bureau of mints numerous mineralogical reports of the Apalachian gold field. He has investigated the geology and mineralogy of North Carolina, and published several monographs on the resources of the state. In 1888 he took up the unfinished work of Prof. Kerr, then deceased, and, in connection with Prof. J. A. Holmes, compiled the last geological survey of North Carolina under the title of "Ores of North Carolina." Perhaps Prof. Hanna has given more attention to the investigation of the mining resources of North Carolina than any other mining engineer. In connection with his official work he has found it necessary to give much attention to the science of numismatics. It is worthy of note that, notwithstanding political influences and the appointments in the assay office, Prof. Hanna has, under all changes in the administrations, been continuously retained, and has been relied upon as a skillful and well qualified man for the important work done by him in his official capacity. His long continuance in the mint office is high complimentary to him.

Besides being a student in the sciences, Prof. Hanna is a lover of history, both sacred and profane. He is a member of the Mecklenburg county Bible society and of the First Presbyterian church of Charlotte, of the Y. M. C. A., and of the Charlotte chamber of commerce. In 1879, Prof. Hanna was united in marriage with Miss Nina C. Trotter, of Charlotte, of whom he was bereft in October, 1891. She was a devout member of the Presbyterian church. For several years Prof. Hanna has been superintendent of the Sunday-school. In he was 1876, made president of the Y. M. C. A., and with the exception of six months' relief from the position, he has continued since 1876 up to the present time to preside over that body. His administration of its presidency has been marked by its rapid progress and prosperity. He has done much profitable and important work for this association and is vice-chairman of the state committee for the same. The professor is, as was his wife, a member of the Presbyterian church.

HON. JOHN STEELE HENDERSON,

of Salisbury, N. C., representative in the forty-ninth, fiftieth, fifty-first and fifty-second congresses, was born in Rowan county, N. C., January 6, 1846; and is distinguished no less for his own high character and shining qualities than for his descent from a host of patriotic forefathers, eminent in their generation, and who contributed largely to the formation and development of his native state. Indeed we hazard but little in saying that there are few Americans, themselves of such sterling worth as Mr. Henderson, who have sprung from such an illustrious ancestry. He is the son of Archibald and Mary Steele Ferrand Henderson. Archibald Henderson (1811–1880) was, for many years, a member of the council of state of North Carolina. A planter with an ample income, endowed with unusual native ability, and highly cultured and refined, he exerted great influence and impressed himself upon his generation. His knowledge of men and his political acumen were wonderfully accurate and discriminating. He solved as if by intuition the most difficult political problems, and came to be regarded by his party friends as a democratic oracle, almost infallible in his judgment. He was the son of Archibald and Sarah Alexander Henderson. This Archibald Henderson (1768–1822) was one of the most distinguished lawyers that North Carolina has ever produced, and his characteristics strikingly re-appear in the grandson, the subject of this sketch. He was a member of the sixth and seventh congresses, taking a prominent part on the floor, and particularly may it be mentioned that he made an exhaustive and memorable speech on the subject of the judiciary bill. The father of this gentleman was Judge Richard Henderson who married Elizabeth Keeling.

Judge Henderson (1734–1785), resided in Granville county, and was one of the three judges in colonial times. He was president and founder of the colony of Transylvania, including a large portion of the present state of Tennessee and Kentucky, which he organized in 1775, with a representative government and on the basis of entire religious liberty. He and his legislature, which met April 23, 1775, virtually declared their independence of the British crown. Lord Dunmore, the royal governor of Virginia, was greatly scandalized by this proceeding and denounced the Transylvania proprietors by proclamation, as "one Richard Henderson and other disorderly persons, his associates." Daniel Boone was in the employment of Judge Henderson and made trips into "the dark and bloody ground" in his interests; and the judge's colored servant Dan, who lived until about 1825, used to boast that he "was the first black man who ever set his foot upon the banks of the Ohio." One of the sons of Judge Richard Henderson was Chief-Justice Leonard Henderson (1772–1833). His younger brother, Maj. Pleasant Henderson (1736–1842), who attained a great age, was in the North Carolina military service during the Revolution (1775–1781), and was major in Malmedy's mounted corps of North Carolina state troops. His cousin, Col. John P. Williams, was colonel of the Ninth regiment North Carolina continental troops, and his wife's uncle, Col. James Williams, commanded at the victory of Mulgrove's Mill, and fell while gallantly leading his column at King's Mountain, with the shouts of victory ringing in his ears.

Judge Henderson was the son of Samuel and Elizabeth Williams Henderson, who thus were the great-great-grandparents of the subject of this sketch. Samuel Henderson, the founder of the Henderson family in North Carolina, removed from Hanover county, Va., to Granville county, N. C., in 1745, bringing with him his two sons, Judge Richard and Maj. Pleasant. He was·greatly esteemed and wielded a strong influence, not only among the people, but with the colonial government, holding by appointment the commission of high sheriff of his county. He had the satisfaction of seeing his son, Richard, and his connection, Judge John Williams, both upon the bench, which in after years was so highly adorned by his grandson, Chief-Justice Leonard Henderson.

As distinguished by eminent worth and high station as have been Hon. John S. Henderson's ancestors in the paternal line, on the maternal side are to be found memoirs and traditions equally patriotic and inspiring to one who aims to do his whole duty to the people of his native state. He is a great-grandson of Moses Alexander, whose son, Nathaniel Alexander (1756–1808), was a soldier in the Revolutionary war, a member of congress and governor of the state; is a great-grandson of William Ferrand, and Mary Williams, a sister of Hon. Benjamin Williams, who was a captain in the Second regiment of North Carolina continentals; member of the second congress, and after having served three terms as governor of the state, he was again elected governor on the expiration of the constitutional inhibition.

Mr. Henderson is also a great-grandson of John and Mary Nesfield Steele. Gen. John Steele (1764–1815) was member of the constitutional convention of 1788, and was a member of the first and second congresses. He was a personal friend of Washington and Jefferson, and was greatly honored and beloved by all who knew him. He is likewise the great-great-grandson of William and Elizabeth Maxwell Steele· Mrs. Elizabeth Steele resided at Salisbury, and in February, 1781, she gave needed aid to Gen. Nathaniel Greene, then in command of the patriot army, and hard pressed for necessaries, by presenting to him two bags of specie, all of the money she had saved. " Never," declares Greene's biographer, " did relief come at a more opportune moment." And he is a grandson of Dr. Stephen Lee and Margaret Steele Ferrand.

Sprung from a lineage so devoted to patriotic purposes and so associated with the great events in the history of his native state, Mr. Henderson inherited noble impulses and patriotic resolves; nor has the example of gallant and enterprising spirits of earlier generations been without legitimate influence. Mr. Hendrson's brother, Leonard Alexander Henderson, was captain of company F, Eighth regiment, North Carolina troops, in the Confederate service, and when in his twenty-third year, was killed June 1, 1864, at Cold Harbor, while leading with splendid dash and elan his regiment in a desperate charge. Another brother, Richard Henderson, is now a lieutenant in the United States navy, and is esteemed as a very efficient officer of distinguished promise. He was present at the bombardment of Alexandria, Egypt, and has seen much service abroad.

Mr. Henderson was prepared for college at Dr. Alexander Wilson's celebrated school in Alamance county, and entered the University of North Carolina in January, 1862, remaining there until November, 1864, when, at the age of eighteen, he entered the army as a private in Company B, Tenth regiment North Carolina troops, and served until the war ended at Appomatox. He then read law with Chief-Justice Pearson, and obtained his first license in June, 1866, and his superior court license in June, 1867. He applied himself zealously to the practice of his profession, and soon gained an eminent position at the bar. But few men in the state have as fine a reputation as a thorough lawyer as Mr. Henderson. In addition to his diligence and laborious study, he is gifted with an acute intellect, and a clearness of view that distinguish him from many others of the profession. Besides, he is a man of unspotted character. A member of the Protestant Episcopal church, he is esteemed as one of the most sterling laymen of that communion in the state, and his views exert great weight in their councils. In 1874 Mr. Henderson was happily married to Miss Bessie B. Cain, of Asheville, N. C., and in his home domestic life exemplifies the many charms of culture and refinement.

Mr. Henderson, in his earlier days, did not desire political preferment, but addressed himself to the more exacting duties of his laborious profession. However, in 1871, he was brought out as a candidate for the proposed constitutional convention, and led his distinguished competitor, Dr. James G. Ramsay, 497 votes, indeed running 102 votes ahead of the general democratic ticket. The next year he declined the nomination for the legislature, but when the constitutional convention of 1875 was called, his friends in Rowan county again desired to avail themselves of his legal ability in that body, and elected him a member. He proved to be one of the most useful members, and was a recognized leader, drafting many of the most important amendments and in a large measure giving direction to the work. The next year Rowan county sent him to the house, where he was again a leading and valuable member, being the author and draughtsman of many of the most important statutes passed at that session. His popularity and the hold he had on the confidence of the people may be estimated when it is stated that though Gov. Vance's majority in Rowan county was 862, and Tilden's 868, his was 1,066. At the next session he was elected to the state senate, running 475 votes ahead of his ticket; and again did he display that fine legal acumen which which gave him a title to leadership, and his services were recognized as most valuable to the state. Two years later, along with Hon. W. P. Dortch and Hon. John Manning, he was appointed to codify the laws, a position won by his conspicuous merit and painstaking exactness. His discharge of this important duty enhanced his reputation, which now extended all over the state.

On September 9, 1884, he was nominated for congress in the Rowan district, and was again opposed by his former competitor, Dr. J. G. Ramsay, one of the shrewdest and best posted politicans of the state, and whose standing was high, since he had never been connected with the unpopular proceedings of the republican party, of which he was a member. Mr. Henderson made a strong and able canvass and was triumphantly elected by a majority of 3,411. He was re-elected in 1886, virtually without opposition, his plurality being about 10,000; and elected a third time in 1888; and in 1890, notwithstanding he boldly took ground against the sub-treasury bill, the foundation stone of the alliance organization, he was successful by 4,166 majority. Indeed, it may be said that much of the personal strength of Mr. Henderson

Rufus Barringer
Brig. Genl. C. S. A.

before the people is found in his open candor. He never evades an issue. He has the manhood to express his convictions, and the ability to so present his views that those who disagree with him, yet recognize the honesty of his purpose and the sincerity of principles. He commands respect even where he may not receive support. In congress he has made for himself an enviable reputation. He is an indefatigable worker, and has labored both in the committee rooms and on the floor of the house to advance the measures he has advocated. Many of his speeches have attracted much attention, especially one in favor of seating Hon. Frank Hurd, and others made in support of tariff reform and on the subject of the internal revenue system. He has been a member of the judiciary and other important committees, and is now chairman of the committee on postoffices and postroads. While he is a statesman, and considers public measures in a broad and liberal spirit, his genius is particularly evinced in the excellence of his work as a draughtsman of laws. In this respect he ranks very high among his associates in congress. Indeed, it is conceded that he is the ablest and most useful representative that North Carolina has sent to congress since the war.

GEN. RUFUS BARRINGER.

This distinguished soldier, whose valor, intrepidity and skill have won for him the admiration of his fellow-citizens, is a resident of Charlotte, Mecklenburg county, N. C., but is a native of the adjoining county of Cabarrus, where the Barringer family has long been settled. His grandfather, John Paul Barringer, was born in Wurtemburg, Germany, in 1721. Coming to America, he first settled in Pennsylvania, but soon afterward removed to North Carolina. He was an ardent whig during the Revolution, and having been captured by the tories, suffered a long and tedious confinement. He died at the homestead, in Cabarrus county, January 1, 1807. One of his sons, Gen. Paul Barringer (born 1778, died 1844), was the father of the subject of this sketch. He was a man of influence in his section, was elected to the legislature ten times consecutively from Cabarrus county, and was greatly esteemed for his high character and abilities. He married Elizabeth, a daughter of Matthew Brandon, a soldier of the Revolution, whose family were distinguished for their love of liberty. His eldest son was Hon. Daniel Moreau Barringer, who was born in 1806, and after graduating at the University of North Carolina, studied law under Chief-Justice Ruffin. He served several years in the legislature, and was a representative in congress continuously from 1843 to 1849, when President Taylor appointed him minister to Spain, and on his return to North Carolina he was during the remainder of his life a conspicuous and highly esteemed citizen.

Gen. Rufus Barringer was a younger son. He was born in Cabarrus county, December 2, 1821. Having received a preparatory education at Sugar Creek academy, Mecklenburg county, he entered the university of North Carolina, where he graduated in 1842. He studied law with his brother, Hon. D. M. Barringer, at Concord, and finished his legal training under Hon. Richmond Pearson, the distinguished chief-justice of the state. Opening a law office at Concord, he soon gained a lucrative practice and won a high place at the bar. He was a whig in politics, and in 1848 was elected to the house of commons, where he urged with intelligent discrimination the construction of a railroad from Charlotte to Danville, and otherwise advocated a progressive system of internal improvements, including the North Carolina railroad. The following session he represented his district in the state senate, and displayed unusual ability in that body. His growing practice claimed his entire attention until the great questions involved in the political campaign of 1860 drew him again into active politics. He was in that year a whig elector and made an earnest canvass in behalf of Bell and Everett. Momentous events then crowded fast upon each other, and the question of secession soon became a living issue. A whig from early life, ardently attached to the Union and full of devotion to the constitution of his country, Mr. Barringer was no indifferent spectator to passing events. With rare discernment he foresaw the consequences of the movement in which the more southern states were engaged, and he took a strong stand against secession, urging that secession would be accompanied by war, and if war came it would prove the fiercest and bloodiest of modern times, and would involve not only the continuance of slavery but the entire structure of southern society itself. These sentiments were so unpopular that, for boldly urging them, he was once caricatured in the streets of Charlotte. But even before the final step was taken by North Carolina and before the ordinance of secession was passed, he sought "to pluck the flower safety from the nettle danger," and advocated immediate preparation for the war that he saw was inevitable. He urged the legislature then in session to arm the state and warned the people that now they must prepare to fight. He awaited no overt acts of war to decide his course, nor did he beguile his people with hopes of peaceable secession or of compromise. He believed that the only hope of success lay in aggressive action, and that delay meant destruction.

When the first gun was fired on Fort Sumter, he knew it was the signal to arms, and he was among the first to volunteer for the service. He at once raised a company of cavalry in his native county, which was afterwards assigned, as Company F, to the First North Carolina cavalry, his commission as captain bearing date May 16, 1861. Of this regiment Robert Ransom became the first colonel, and he so drilled and disciplined the fine material of which it was composed that it became widely known as the best cavalry regiment in the Confederate service. Assigned in Virginia, first to Gen. Hampton's brigade, and afterward to the North Carolina cavalry brigade in Hampton's division, its history was glorious in every campaign until the chapter of war was fully closed. Throughout its whole career Gen. Barringer was associated with it. On August 26,

1863, he became major of the regiment, and three months later he was again promoted to be its lieutenant-colonel. On the death of Gen. J. B. Gordon, in June, 1864, he was commissioned brigadier-general, and succeeded to the command of the North Carolina brigade of cavalry, consisting of the First, Second, Third and Fifth regiments. This brigade was one of the most efficient cavalry corps in the army. Its record is a succession of splendid achievements. It was often complimented, and especially by Gen. R. E. Lee, for gallant and meritorious conduct at Ream's Station, but its most heroic achievement was at Chamberlain Run, March 31, 1865, where it forded a stream a hundred yards wide, and saddle-girth deep, under a galling fire, and attacked a division of Federal cavalry, driving them from behind their breastworks. This was the last decisive Confederate victory of the war, and was attended with a loss of over two hundred officers and men.

General Barringer was in seventy-six actions, received three wounds and had two horses struck under him. He was conspicuous in the battles at Willis Church, at Brandy station, where he was severely wounded; Auburn Mills and Buckland Races, where he led the charge; Davis Farm, where he was sole commander; and he was in command of the division at Ream's Station. He was an able and enterprising officer, efficient in the discharge of his duties, and having both the confidence of his superiors and the esteem and affection of his soldiers. His courage, his gallantry and military services establish his fame and place him alongside of the renowned cavalry leaders of the Confederate cause. He was a fine disciplinarian, but was so careful of his men that they were attached to him, and he, in like manner, was attached to his command. In 1862 Gen. Jackson proposed to organize some columns of light troops for offensive action and offered him the position of quarter-master general, on his staff, but he preferred to remain with his men and declined. On April 3, 1865, while making an effort to extricate one of his regiments from a perilous position at Namozine Church, Va., he was captured and taken to City Point, of which port Gen. Collis was in command. Gen. Ewell and Gen. Custis Lee had also been taken, and along with Gen. Barringer (to use the language of Gen. Collis), "became his guests."

President Lincoln was then at City Point, and requested that Gen. Barringer be presented to him at the tent of Col. Bowers (Gen. Grant's adjutant), jocosely adding, "Do you know I have never seen a live rebel general in uniform?" Gen. Barringer was thereupon formally presented to him, and the president shook hands with him warmly and became much interested when, on inquiry, he elicited the fact that Gen. Barringer was the brother of Hon. D. M. Barringer, who, he said, had served with him in congress and had been a warm friend. The president, with his accustomed good nature and sympathy, expressed himself as desiring to render some friendly service to the general, and on his rising to depart, asked, "Do you think I can be of any service to you?" To which Gen. Barringer promptly

B—40

replied, "If any one can be of service to a fellow in my situation, I suppose you are the man."

Expecting to be detained as a prisoner of war, and desiring to be confined in some prison where he could communicate readily with northern friends, he so expressed himself to the president, who, taking a card from his pocket, wrote a note on it to Secretary Stanton. Gen. Barringer was at first confined at the old capttol prison, Washington City, but finding the quarters inconvenient and uncomfortable, he forwarded the note the president had given him to the secretary of war, who transferred him at once to Fort Delaware, where he remained until August, 1865. While there he had an opportunity of ascertaining the current of public sentiment among the northern people in regard to the results of the war, and he foresaw that negro suffrage was one of the requirements of northern opinion.

On his return home he urged that the white men of the south should voluntarily concede it and he warmly urged the measure. He also regarded it as indispensably necessary for the welfare of the people that the states of the south should be speedily re-habilitated in the union; and when some spoke of expatriation, he denounced the idea as base ingratitude to the masses of the people. Because of his position on these political matters, he was by some stigmatized as a traitor to his race and section, but such charges fell harmless at his feet. He accepted the reconstruction acts of 1867 and stood forth as a bold and able champion of the measures and principles of the republican leaders in congress. Since the settlement of those questions he has mainly co-operated with the national republican party, whose policy and principles he believed were best suited to the country in its new and changed condition. But during the most violent and bitter struggles in the state, political differences detracted nothing, in the public estimation, from the substantial worth of his personal character, and when, in 1875, the state convention was held to amend the constitution, he was elected as a republican from the democratic county of Mecklenburg. He has not however sought political preferment, although, in 1880, he accepted the republican nomination for lieutenant-governor and by his strong canvass in his section, made great gains for his party. Gen. Barringer is a man of culture and is fond of literature and history. He takes a pride in the heroism displayed by the southern soldiers during the war, and has ably written for the press, perpetuating accounts of their noble deeds and maintaining the propriety of their action. He has also been liberal and generous to the war-worn veterans.

A student by long habit, he has in recent years devoted much attention to political economy. He believes in the largest individual liberty, properly regulated and restrained by church, state and family. He has ardently advocated temperance reform and industrial education, and has been a trustee in the North Carolina college of agriculture and mechanics. He has also been influential in establishing an industrial school at Charlotte, and also the literary and historical library in that city, to which he has made valuable donations. He

NORTH CAROLINA.   627

removed to Charlotte in 1866, and practiced his profession there until 1884, when he retired and devoted himself to farming, in which he
has been largely interested. He has long been an active member of
and liberal contributor to the Presbyterian church at Charlotte. He
has traveled much, and his ripe judgment and progressive ideas have
been turned to the advantage of the community in which he lives.
No citizen has done more for the material improvement of Charlotte
than Gen. Barringer. In his domestic life Gen. Barringer is esteemed
and admired. He has been thrice happily married, and is the father
of three sons who worthily bear his name.

WALTER CLARK.

Judge Walter Clark is a native of Halifax county, N. C., being
born in that county on the 19th day of August, 1846. He was a student at Col. Tew's military academy, at Hillsboro, when the Civil
war came on, and as early as in the spring of 1861, at the age of fourteen years, he entered the Confederate army as drill master in Gen.
Pettigrew's regiment, the Twenty-second North Carolina, and which
proceeded to Richmond and to Evansport, on the Potomac. The
next year he was made adjutant of the Thirty-fifth North Carolina,
under the command of Col. M. W. Ransom. With this regiment,
and in this rank, he participated with gallantry in the first campaign
of Maryland; in the capture of Harper's Ferry, the battle of Sharpsburg (Antietam) and Fredericksburg. At the last two named battles he was especially complimented for gallantry. In the spring his
brigade returned to North Carolina for recruits; he resigned and
entered the University of North Carolina in July of 1863, joining the
senior class. In the camp he had kept up his studies, carrying his
Homer and Virgil, which, too, received study. He graduated from
the university with first honor, on June 2, 1864; and the next day
again entered the army, being made major of the Sixth battalion of
junior reserves, and a few days later (then but seventeen years of
age) was commissioned lieutenant-colonel of the Sixty-ninth North
Carolina regiment, which was attached to Hoke's division. After
participating in the battle of Southwest Creek (near Kinston) and at
Bentonsville, he surrendered, and was paroled with the army of
Johnston at High Point, N. C., May 2, 1865. After the close of hostilities, he studied law under Judge Battle, at a law office in Wall
street, New York, and at Columbia law college, Washington, D. C.,
obtaining license to practice in January, 1868. He located first at
Scotland Neck, N. C., but subsequently removed to Halifax, N. C.,
where he entered into a co-partnership with Hon. J. M. Mullen, under the law firm of Clark & Mullen. While practicing in Halifax,
he was twice a candidate for the legislature, and though the usual
republican majority in Halifax county was over 2,500, he was defeated by small majorities.

In January of 1874, he married the only daughter of Hon. Wil-
iam A. Graham, and removed to Raleigh, in which city he has since

continued. He was sent as a lay delegate for North Carolina to the Methodist Ecumenical council in London, in 1881, and profited by the occasion to travel extensively in Europe. In April of 1885, Gov. Scales appointed him judge of the superior court, and in August of 1886, he was renominated by acclamation by the convention at Smithfield, and at the November election was elected, leading the rest of the superior court ticket. When Associate Judge Merrimon, of the supreme court, was elevated to chief-justice of the tribunal, the governor of the state appointed Judge Clark to fill the vacancy occasioned by the promotion of Chief-Justice Merrimon, and at the regular fall election of 1888, the people elected him to succeed himself on the supreme bench. Judge Clark has done much to instill into the courts business principles, and is deservedly popular. He is an able judge, a man of profound learning, and a diligent student, and a zealous and active worker. He is author of "Overruled Cases," of "Laws for Business Men" and of "Clark's Annotated Code of Civil Procedure." In 1871, while on a tour to California and the west, he wrote a series of articles, "From Ocean to Ocean," which attracted favorable attention from the press and public.

JOSEPH B. BATCHELOR

was born in Halifax county, N. C., February 5, 1825, received his preliminary education in the schools of his native county, and afterward attended the University of North Carolina, from which he graduated with first honors in 1845, and delivered the valedictory. Leaving college, our subject commenced to read law at home, was admitted to the bar in 1846, and opened a law office in Heathsville, N. C., where he practiced until 1850. Then he went to Halifax, N. C., where his superior abilities were at once recognized, and where he was elected county attorney, and served four years. In 1854, in the fall, he moved to Warrenton, N. C., where he quickly became popular, was elected county attorney, and in 1855 was appointed attorney-general by Gov. Thomas Bragg, and served two years. He was re-elected county attorney of Warren county during the war, and served several years. In 1866 he removed to Raleigh, N. C., where he opened a law office, and here he has conducted a successful practice ever since. In 1870 he was appointed by the legislature one of three commissioners— Gen. William M. Shipp and Gen. James G. Martin being the other two—to investigate alleged corruption in the conduct of the affairs of the state. Our subject is a democrat, and while not an office seeker, has always taken an active interest in the welfare of his party, and has cheerfully served it when called upon. He is a member of the Masonic fraternity, having served as senior grand warden and deputy grand master, and is also a member of the Episcopal church. Mr. Batchelor was married, in 1850, to Mary C. Plummer, the accomplished daughter of William Plummer, of Warren county, N. C., and to them have been born thirteen children, of whom six still survive, as follows: William P. Batchelor, Wake county, N. C.; Joseph B. Batch-

HON. ZEBULON VANCE.

elor, lieutenant in the United States regular army, and located at Ft. Leavenworth; Stark S. Batchelor, of Raleigh, N. C.; Eliza A., wife of Harry Loeb, of Waymanville, Ga.; Dr. Kemp B. Batchelor, of Baltimore, Md., and Frank H. Batchelor, of Raleigh, N. C.

James W. Batchelor, the father of our subject, was born in Halifax county, N. C., April 7, 1793, and received a common school education in his native county. He was a farmer and merchant all his life, and died in 1850. He was a prominent man in his county, held several county offices, and served as county treasurer for twenty years, without making a mistake in his accounts. He was married October 26, 1816, to Mary Shelton, daughter of Burwell Shelton of Halifax county, N. C., and on her mother's side was a descendant of the Lane family. To Mr. and Mrs. Batchelor were born five children, named as follows: William B., who died in infancy; Littleburg W., whose death took place in 1886; Joseph B., now residing in Raleigh, N. C.; Martha, widow of Dr. Thomas Davis, of Franklin, N. C., and Mary F., who died in 1842, aged twelve years. Mrs. Mary (Shelton) Batchelor died in 1852, sincerely mourned by her surviving children and friends. William Batchelor, grandfather of the subject proper of this sketch, was born in North Carolina about 1750, and was in the Continental army. He died about 1820. Our subject's paternal grandmother's maiden name was Elizabeth Bradford, of the influential family of Bradford, in Halifax county, N. C. The social standing of Mr. and Mrs. Joseph B. Batchelor is of the highest, while in his profession Mr. Batchelor stands in the front rank, and no stigma has ever been attached to his honorable name.

ZEBULON B. VANCE,

present United States senator from North Carolina, and the colleague of Hon. Matt. W. Ransom, and who also served his native state three times as its governor, was born in Buncombe county, N. C., May 13, 1830, and probably no native of the state has had a more eventful and brilliant career as a statesman and soldier than he. Descended from revolutionary ancestry, and born in the mountain district of his section, he carries the best blood of the country in his veins, and is charged with animal magnetism. His father was David Vance, a son of Col. David Vance, who was wounded at King's Mountain, and his maternal grandfather was Zebulon Baird, of Buncombe, after whom he was named. Our subject received his first lesson in law at the University of North Carolina, in which he passed the year 1851, and soon afterward was admitted to the bar. Being possessed of a tenacious or retentive memory, and a mind of comprehensive receptivity, he met with phenomenal success in the practice at Asheville; but he was a natural born statesman, and political ambition imbued his whole nature. In 1854 he was elected by a handsome majority to the state legislature on the whig ticket, and from that time on his political career has been a series of brilliant triumphs. In 1856 he canvassed the mountain district against Col. David Coleman for the state senate, but met with defeat.

In 1858, Gen. Thomas L. Clingman, then a democrat and holding a seat in the United States house of representatives, was appointed by Gov. Bragg to fill a vacancy in the United States senate, caused by the resignation of Hon. Asa Biggs. Col. Coleman and W. W. Avery, of Burke, both democrats, entered the field as candidates for Clingman's late position, and both [were strong men. Just then young Vance, at the age of twenty-eight years, sprang into the arena, when Col. Coleman withdrew, leaving the struggle to Avery and Vance, the latter gallantly carrying off the trophy by overcoming a democratic majority of over 2,000, although prior to that time the democratic majority in the district had been 2,500. In 1859 Mr. Vance was re-elected to the house, defeating his old opponent, Col. Coleman, and served until March, 1861. In congress Mr. Vance pursued a conservative course, and was strongly opposed to secession, but, true to his state, he hastened to her aid when he saw that she would pass an ordinance of withdrawal from the union, and on the very day that ordinance was passed, in May, 1861, he was Capt. Vance and had his company of North Carolina troops in camp at Raleigh. His company was attached to the Fourteenth regiment, with which he served in Virginia until August, 1861, when he was elected colonel of the Twenty-sixth regiment, which he led at the battle of Newbern and in the fights around Richmond. His gallantry and faithfulness won for him the admiration of soldiers and civilians, and the voices of both classes went up in a demand that he become the governor of the state, and in August, 1862, he was elected to that high office by an overwhelming majority, and was inaugurated in September; in 1864 he was re-elected governor and was inaugurated January 1, 1865. This was indeed a stormy period, and the Old North state was a veritable ship of war, but she had at her helm the steady hand of Zeb. Vance. It was the duty of the governor to secure and maintain the military contingent of the state in aid of the Confederate government, and this he did with a masterly hand, but ever subordinated the military to the civil power, and never did he permit throughout the desperate struggle, the suppression of the precious writ of *habeas corpus*.

In April, 1865, Gov. Vance left Raleigh with Gen. Joseph E. Johnston's army for Greensboro, and thence went to Charlotte, where he joined President Davis; thence he went to Statesville, Iredell county, where he had placed his family for safety. There, in May, 1865, he was arrested and taken to Washington, D. C., and for many months was confined in the old capitol prison. At the close of the year the governor returned to Charlotte and resumed the practice of his profession. During the period of reconstruction, however, he took an active part in upholding the rights of his people and of the state, and, although his political disabilities had not been removed his voice was everywhere heard in support of right and justice. When political rights had been partially restored to the citizens of the state, Mr.

Vance was elected, in 1870, to the United States senate, but, as he had not been fully purged of his disabilities, he was denied his seat. In 1872 he was the nominee of the democratic party in the legislature for the same high office, but by a coalition was defeated. In 1876 he was nominated by the democrats for governor and was elected by a large majority over Judge Settle. January 1, 1877, Mr. Vance for the third time took the oath of office as governor, and resumed the seat from which he had been ejected by Federal bayonets to make room for W. W. Holden. In 1878 Mr. Vance was again the nominee of the democrats of the legislature for the office of United States senator, and, his disabilities having been fully removed, he was allowed to take the seat, which, by repeated re-elections, he still holds, his last term expiring March 3, 1891.

In August, 1863, Zebulon B. Vance married Miss Harriet Newell Espy, daughter of the Rev. Thomas Espy, a Presbyterian clergyman, of Allegheny county, Penn., who came to South Carolina in 1828, and married Miss Louisa Tate, of Burke county, and died in 1830. To the felicitous union of Mr. and Mrs Vance, have been born four sons. To speak of the social standing of Mr. Vance and his family would be a work of supererogation. We have given but a brief sketch of this gentleman's political career, which has not been that of an ephemeral meteor, lighting for a brief moment the horizon of politics, but that of an effulgent sun, whose fervid rays still brighten and ripen the fields of statesmanship. His name stands as one graven on a monument of brass, which shall endure as long as his native state of North Carolina shall bear a history.

L. BANKS HOLT,

one of the leading business men of Graham, Alamance county, is a native of North Carolina, born in the above named county January 28, 1842. His parents are Edwin L. and Emily (Farish) Holt, both natives of North Carolina. Mr. Holt attended school in Alamance county, under the tutelage of Dr. Wilson, an educator of distinction. He entered the military academy at Hillsboro in 1859, and enlisted from this institution in 1861, tendering his services to the governor of the state. They were accepted, and he was assigned to duty in the Orange guard. This company at once entered the service and captured Fort Macon, N. C. Later Mr. Holt joined Col. Fisher's regiment of infantry, as drill master, and served in this position until after the battle of Manassas, when he was transferred to the Eighth North Carolina infantry, and remained with this regiment until the close of the war. In the early part of the struggle he was promoted to the rank of first lieutenant, which he held until the close of hostilities. He participated in some of the most hotly contested conflicts of the war, and was severely wounded at Petersburg, Va., and at the battle of Fort Harrison, where he was taken prisoner. After spending four months in the hospital he was confined in Fort Delaware until 1865. Returning home, he engaged in farming and cotton manufacturing.

He worked in the Alamance cotton mill for a time, which was owned by his father. In 1868 the Carolina cotton factory, in which Mr. Holt holds a large interest, was erected. He and his brother, Lawrence Holt, built, in 1880, the celebrated Bellemont cotton mills, which they still own. He is also a partner in the E. M. Holt plaid mills, located at Burlington, N. C., and is sole proprietor of the Oneida mills, located at Graham, N. C., in which he employs nearly 200 operators. Mr. Holt is a stockholder in the Atamahaw cotton mills, and owns stock in the Commercial National bank and of the Merchants & Farmers' National bank of Charlotte. His varied and extensive experience in the manufacture of cotton fabrics, together with his native skill and industry, have elevated him to the top round of excellence and prosperity in his products and patronage. Enterprising and public-spirited, courteous and honorable in all his dealings, an exemplary in Christian morals, just and humane to his employes, he is esteemed by all who know him.

Mr. Holt is one of the most prominent and successful farmers in the state, his Oak Grove stock farm consisting of 1,400 acres of land, being one of the best cultivated farms in the south. On this farm he keeps a herd of pure-bred and registered Devon cattle numbering one hundred head, and aside from this he raises pure-bred Shropshire sheep and Poland China swine. The records of state fairs show that he has been foremost in winning premiums on field crops and cattle for several years. Mr. Holt was married in October, 1865, to Miss Mary C., the daughter of Hon. Giles and Mary C. Mebane, of Caswell county, N. C. They have seven children, namely: Mary V., wife of Dr. Geo. A. Mevine; Kate M., Fanny Y., Carrie B., Cora A., Emily L. and Mattie. Mr. Holt is a member of the Presbyterian church, and for many years has been deacon in the same. The amount of good done by the Holts can be scarcely estimated in this life. There is no miserly spirit about any of them. They have, through their superior business abilities, industry and economy, accumulated considerable wealth, but they have not hoarded. On the contrary, they invested their means with an eye single to evolving the greatest and most permanent amount of good to humanity. Hundreds of families to-day are living in comfort and happiness through their philanthropic hospitality. Their employes are comfortably provided for in cheerful homes, near neat and commodious churches and well furnished school houses. Such men are a great blessing to any community. Mr. Holt took part in the battles of Manassas, Roanoke Island, was at Charleston during the siege of Charleston; at the battle of Drury's Bluff, Cold Harbor, around Petersburg, and many other sharply contested and dangerous engagements. At Petersburg, Mr. Holt received a flesh wound in his face, the scar of which he will carry to the grave. He was furloughed in consequence of it. His second wound was received at Fort Harrison, where he was shot through the thigh and fell into the hands of the enemy. He was carried to Fortress Monroe and was placed in the Chesapeake hospital, where he remained for four months. He was then sent to Fort Delaware, from which place he was released June 16, 1865.

HON. JOHN McCLINTOCK DICK.

Hon. John McClintock Dick was born in Guilford county, N. C., on the 6th of January, 1790. He was descended from Scotch-Irish stock. His classical education was acquired in the celebrated school of Rev. Daniel Caldwell, D. D., a distinguished patriot of the Revolution, an eminent scholar and a pious and eloquent preacher. He was admitted to the bar in 1816, and settled in Greensboro, where he always had his home. He was successful in the practice of the law, and acquired considerable property. In 1821 he was married to Miss Parthenia P. Williamson, of the county of Person, N. C., and had by her ten children. He was twice elected a senator of the state for his native county, and his services received the approval of his constituents. In 1835 he was elected, by the legislature, a superior court judge, and held this office until the time of his death, on the 15th of October, 1861. He possessed in a high degree the qualities and virtues that adorn and benefit individual, domestic and social live. In public life he gained and always retained the sincere esteem and confidence of his fellow-citizens. As a judge, he was honest, patient and faithful in the discharge of official duties. His highly respectable knowledge of the law; his wisdom matured by long experience and careful reflection; and his purity of character and conscientious regard for the rights of all men, enabled him to administer justice with intelligence and impartiality, and to the satisfaction of all good citizens. His example exerted a beneficial influence upon the society in which he mingled, and his advice and efforts contributed to the moral, educational and material progress of the state. He was a good man and his memory is honored and cherished by his loving and numerous friends.

ROBERT PAINE DICK, LL. D.,

judge of the United States district court, is the son of John McClintock Dick, a judge of the supreme court of North Carolina for twenty years. The maiden name of his mother was Parthenia P. Williamson, of Person county. Robert, who is the second of ten children, was born October 5, 1823. He was prepared for college at the Caldwell institute, in Greensboro, under that eminent educator, Rev. Dr. Alexander. He made such proficiency at this institute that he was enabled to enter the sophomore class of the North Carolina university, from which he graduated with distinction in 1843. He was a faithful student and was celebrated in his class for being an elegant writer and a fine speaker. To prosecute his studies with greater facility, he often retired to the university forest, where he erected a rustic seat, and there, by a lovely spring in the grateful shade, on pleasant days, he was accustomed to peruse his text books and occasionally to make the forest ring with his declamations. He was a member of the dialectic society, and was one of its most diligent members. He was an honor graduate and therefore entitled to be among the orators of the graduating class. He chose for his theme, "The Resources of North Carolina," and his treatment of the subject showed that he began life with the enthusiastic love of his native state which he still possesses. Mr. Dick chose law as his profession, preparing with ardor under his father and Mr. George C. Mendenhall, a noted practitioner of that day. He obtained his law license in 1845, and began the practice at the county seat of Rockingham, called Wentworth. He attended, as his regular circuit, that county, with Guilford and Randolph, and afterward for several years, Surry, Stokes, Forsyth, Alamance and Caswell. There were many lawyers of uncommon strength with whom young Dick had to cope, but by faithfulness to the interests of his clients, by thorough preparation of his cases, and zealous and intelligent handling of them in court, he soon received a fair share of business.

In 1848 he married Mary E. Adams, of Pittsylvania county, Va., and soon afterward removed to Greensboro, Guilford county, where he has since resided. They have five children. Mr. Dick, like nearly all ambitious young lawyers, soon entered political life as a member of the democratic party. He did not run for any office, but made many political speeches on the tariff, internal improvements and state rights, always opposing secession. His party friends sent him to the democratic national convention at Baltimore in 1852, at which Pierce and King were nominated. Mr. Dick did effective service in the campaign, and President Pierce, recognizing his intelligent labors for his party, conferred on him the office of United States district attorney. In this office he was exceedingly zealous and no professional trick was ever imputed to him. He held the office until February, 1861, when he sent in his resignation. Although a firm believer in the old democracy, Mr. Dick attached himself to Stephen A. Douglas, and in the Charleston democratic convention struggled for the nomination of that gentleman. When the adjourned convention met at Baltimore he had the moral courage to refuse to join all the other members of the North Carolina delegation in their secession and nomination of Breckinridge at Richmond, and so heated was the feeling that all who declined to sanction the action of the Richmond convention were freely denounced as traitors to the cause of the south.

When the war began and the Union men were forced to decide between fighting for the southern states or against them, Mr. Dick followed his party. He accepted a seat in the convention of 1861, to which he was elected without opposition. He was a worthy member of this body and acted with the party headed by Graham and Badger. He voted for Badger's declaration of independence, but when this failed to pass, he, in common with all the other members of the convention, gave his voice for secession. Until 1864 he acted with the conservative party of which Gov. Vance was the leader. His prominence during those trying times led to the request of President Johnson that he with others should proceed to the seat of government and advise with him as to the best mode of restoring the state government. Mr. Dick earnestly advised the restoration of the state under its old constitution and form of government, with some necessary amendments, and he also urged a general amnesty. The substance of this plan had been approved by President Lincoln and granted by Gen. Sherman in the articles of capitulation of Gen. Johnston's army, but President Johnson, after Lincoln's assassination, declined to ratify it. He, however, tendered to Mr. Dick the office of United States district judge, which he accepted, but resigned when he found that he could not retain it without taking the test oath. He returned to the practice of law and soon gained a large business. He was a member of the convention of 1865–66 called by President Johnson.

Being convinced that the restoration of the state to its normal relations with the Federal government belonged to the legislative and not the executive branch of the government, Mr. Dick advocated with zeal and ability the acceptance of the "Howard amendment" as containing the best terms of re-construction which congress was likely to grant. Judge Dick was elected in April, 1868, a justice of the supreme court. This position he held until 1872, when he resigned in order to accept the judgeship of the United States district court for the western district of North Carolina, tendered him by President Grant. As a member of the supreme court, Judge Dick was called to aid in deciding many delicate and difficult questions growing out of conflicting legislation, the constitution of 1868 and the code of civil procedure. As judge of the district court he has been distinguished for his kindly temper in administering the internal revenue laws of the United States. He presides with impartial courtesy and patience, and studies the cases before him with the utmost care. His rulings have been generally sustained by the appellate courts. Judge Dick has not only devoted attention to the law and history, but he has specially studied Biblical literature. In Sunday afternoon lectures to his law classes he has treated with singular beauty of language and wealth of illustration, "The Influences of Poetry and the Bible of Modern Civilization;" "The Education, Character and Laws of the Hebrews;" "The Style of Hebrew Poetry;" "Messianic Hopes;" "The Age of David and Solomon;" "The Prophets," and "The Jews in History and Their Return to the Promised Land." These topics, with others, are discussed in sixteen lectures, making a volume of over 200 pages, written in a most loving and reverent spirit, and in beautiful, often exceedingly eloquent language. Judge Dick's powers as a writer and orator are frequently called upon, and he has delivered literary addresses at the state university, at Davidson college, and many academies and schools. He has been for years an ardent advocate of temperance reform, and has delivered strong addresses for its furtherance. Judge Dick is an active and useful member of the

Presbyterian church, being one of the congregational officers — ruling elder. He takes much interest in Sunday-school instruction, being superintendent of that connected with his church.

DR. GEORGE W. PUREFOY,

a prominent and popular young physician of Asheville, N. C., was born at Chapel Hill, Orange county, N. C., January 31, 1851, and is the son of Rev. George W. Purefoy, D. D., a prominent Baptist divine who died in 1880. Rev. George W. Purefoy was the son of Rev. John Purefoy, also a Baptist minister, and who, besides the Rev. George W. Purefoy, had two other sons in the Baptist ministry. Rev. John Purefoy was a native North Carolinian, and the grandson of a French Huguenot who came to America from France at the time of the revocation of the edict of Nantes. The mother of the subject of this sketch was Lucy C., the daughter of Rev. William H. Merritt, a Baptist minister. She was born in North Carolina, and is still living. Dr. George W. Purefoy was reared on a farm adjoining Chapel Hill. He was prepared for college by Prof. M. Fetter, a well-known educator of that day, and after spending one year in the University of North Carolina, he, in 1870, on account of the suspension of that institution, entered Wake Forest college, from which he was graduated in 1874 as a bachelor of science. He at once entered upon the study of medicine, and in the fall of 1874 entered the Jefferson medical college of Philadelphia, from which he graduated in 1876. He began his professional career at once in his old home, Chapel Hill, and soon secured the confidence of the community, and won a lucrative practice there, to which he devoted himself until 1885. In that year, Dr. Purefoy, desiring a broader field of labor, removed to Asheville, where he has successfully and actively practiced his profession ever since, and of which city he is a prominent physician. In order to better equip himself for his profession, Dr. Purefoy has frequently taken post-graduate courses. In May, 1890, he was elected a member of the North Carolina state board of medical examiners and was placed in charge of the department of obstetrics and gynecology. He is a member of the North Carolina state medical society and of the Buncombe county medical society. Dr. Purefoy is a member of the Baptist church, and in politics he is a democrat, but takes no active part in partisan contests. He was married in 1880, at which time Miss Lizzie, the daughter of John Watson, a wealthy planter of Warren county, N. C., became his wife. They are the parents of four children, two sons and two daughters. The doctor is universally recognized as a man of great force of character, intrinsic worth and strong moral tendencies. He is studious, well-read and fluent in speech, and accurate in composition, as well as a close investigator of science. Having ever been conscientious in the performance of his professional duties, he has reached the front rank as a physician, and his social standing is co-equal with his professional position.

Yours Sincerely

E.W. Puncifoy

HON. JAMES A. LOCKHART

is a native of North Carolina, having been born in Anson county, that state, June 2, 1850. His father, Adam Lockhart, was born in North Carolina, and in early life turned his attention to agriculture, in which he has been most successful. He married Miss Ann McDiermid, a daughter of Martin and Mary McDiermid. She died at the age of thirty-eight years, in 1858, and was a woman of culture and exemplary life. Martin and Mary McDiermid came to this country from Scotland in 1820, and settled in the Cape Fear section, subsequently removing to Anson county. The latter's mother was descended from the Ferguson family, of which the famous Col. Ferguson was a member. Col. Ferguson commanded the British forces at King's Mountain. James A. Lockhart was the eldest of four children born to his parents. In June, 1873, he was graduated from Trinity college, and immediately thereafter began the study of law under the direction of Col. Clement Dawd, of Charlotte, N. C., and in June, 1874, was admitted to the bar. Having received his license to practice, Mr. Lockhart decided to take up his residence at Wadesboro, and he has since been most happily situated there, having succeeded in building up an extended practice. Soon after his removal to Wadesboro he was elected to the office of mayor of the city, and served one term. In 1878 he was chosen to represent the county in the house of representatives of North Carolina, and in 1880 was elected to the state senate. While a member of the legislature he was appointed to some of the most important committees of that body, and his course was both dignified and able. He was married on the 6th of February, 1878, to Miss Caroline, the youngest daughter of Judge Thomas S. Ashe, of the state supreme bench. That gentleman was a member of the Confederate house of representatives, and later was a senator under the Confederate government. After the close of the Civil war he represented his district in the United States congress for several years, and was twice elected to the supreme court of North Carolina. He died in February, 1887, during his last term as a judge of the supreme court. He married a Miss Burgwyn, of North Carolina, who still survives him. Mr. and Mrs. Lockhart are the parents of five children, named Margie A., George B., James A., Sebor S., and Ashe.

HON. JOHN L. CURRIE,

sheriff of Moore county, N. C., was born in Moore county, November 4, 1861, and is a son of N. R. and Jennette (Leach) Currie. Both parents were born in North Carolina, where for many years the father was extensively engaged in agriculture. He served as captain of a home company during the Civil war, and was a man of influence in the community. For many years he was an active and valued member of the Presbyterian church, as was his wife. Seven children were born to them, viz.: Angus M., who is engaged in railroading in Texas; Sarah and Mary; Murd, who married Miss Robinson, a sister of Dr. Robinson, of Guilford college; Maggie, wife of C. Cole (their two children are Nettie and John W. Cole); William A. and John L. The latter was prepared for college at Union Home school, then under the management of Prof. John E. Kelley. At the age of twenty-two years, in 1884, Mr. Currie was elected surveyor of the county, and two years later was the nominee of his party for sheriff, but was defeated by a small majority. His opponent was one of the most popular men in the county. Mr. Currie was again nominated for that office in 1888, being pitted against the same candidate as before, and this time was elected by a handsome majority, and in 1890 was re-elected without opposition. Mr. Currie is an active member of the Presbyterian church, and is also prominently connected with the farmers' alliance. It is seldom that one so young as he, when first placed in public office, is brought before the people in an official capacity. It is a proof of unusual ability that he has not only been successful in running for office, but that his administration of the affairs of his important trust has been so satisfactory to the people, and so free from unhappy occurrences. It is safe to say that, should life and health be spared him, a bright and useful career awaits him.

JOHN SHAW, M. D.

One of the most prominent physicians and citizens of Moore county, N. C., is John Shaw, M. D., who was born in Moore county, the son of Charles C. and Mary (Ray) Shaw, October 10, 1824. The parents were natives of Cumberland county, N. C., and both were of Scotch parentage. Charles Shaw was an intelligent planter, and served as a soldier in the war of 1812. He was an elder in the Presbyterian church, his wife also being a devout member of that denomination. John Shaw was the second of the ten children born to these parents, of whom seven still survive. He was graduated from the medical college of Philadelphia, after having obtained a thorough scholastic training, and in 1848 began the active practice of his profession at Carthage, where he has since continued. For twenty years the firm of Shaw & Turner was in existence, and after the dissolution of that connection the senior partner continued alone for seven or eight years; at the expiration of that time, Dr. G. McLeod became associated with him, this partnership still being in force. In 1858 Dr. Shaw was elected to the state legislature, and in 1872 was again the successful democratic candidate for that position. At the present time he is serving as chairman of the board of county commissioners of Moore county, he having held that office once before, when appointed by Gov. Vance to fill an unexpired term. Before the Civil war Dr. Shaw was for many years an efficient member of the county court. One of the happiest events of his life was his marriage, in 1852, to Miss Catherine J. Jackson, daughter of William Jackson, of

Moore county, and their children are: Charles J., proprietor of the Central hotel at Carthage; John B., secretary and treasurer of the Carthage carriage manufactory; Mary J., wife of Jesse J. Wicker; Florence, who married Rev. W. F. Watson; Maggie, deceased, at the age of sixteen years, and Hattie, wife of Rev. M. G. Shields. Dr. and Mrs. Shaw are earnest and leading members of the Presbyterian church, and he is a ruling elder in the same. Dr. Shaw stands in the front rank of the medical profession in the state.

H. TURNER, M. D.

The oldest physician of Moore county, N. C., is the Hon. H. Turner, M. D., who is a native of the Highlands, Scotland, where he was born in 1820. His parents, Malcomb and Isabella (Currie) Turner, came to America one year after the birth of their son, in 1821, and settled in Moore county on a plantation, where they continued to reside until called to their final rest, the father at the age of sixty-nine, in 1853, and the mother in 1852, when she was in her sixty-fifth year. Both were devout members of the Scotch Presbyterian church, and were most worthy and respected people. Their children were Daniel, who married Lydia Blue, and died in 1853, aged thirty-five years, and H., our subject, and Alexander Turner. Alexander resides on a plantation in Alabama, and is a prominent physician, being a graduate of the Charleston medical college; he married Miss Lottie Carlton, who was a native of Vermont. Dr. H. Turner received the greater part of his literary training in the Fayetteville high school, and in 1847 was graduated from the University of New York. After practicing for a short time alone, he became associated with Dr. John Shaw, this connection being sustained for nearly twenty years. During the Civil war Dr. Turner served as surgeon of the Twenty-seventh North Carolina regiment, and also as a brigade surgeon. Remaining in the army until the last surrender, he then returned home and resumed his practice at Carthage, at the same time turning his attention to agriculture. Subsequently he removed to Cameron. In 1881 he was elected to the state legislature, and again, in 1883, was returned to that assembly. He was a member of the state secession convention in 1861, and cast his vote in favor of that measure. In 1866 Dr. Turner was united in marriage with Mrs. Kate (Ferguson) Leach, a daughter of Norman Ferguson, who was a native of Scotland. Two children have blessed this happy union, viz.: Alexander, who was educated at the Bingham military academy, now operating a drug business for his father, and Lulu, who is a leading teacher of the county, having graduated from Peace institute, at Raleigh, and from the Salem female academy. The family are communicants of the Presbyterian church, and are held in the highest esteem throughout the community. Dr. Turner is one of the ablest physicians in that portion of the state, and his name is beloved as that of a man of unbending integrity and of charitable heart.

MATT. W. RANSOM,

the colleague of Zebulon B. Vance, as United States senator from North Carolina, was born in Warren county, N. C., 1826. He graduated from the University of North Carolina, at Chapel Hill, in 1847, was admitted to the bar, and five years later, in recognition of his erudition and practical business ability, was elected attorney-general of the state, which office he resigned in 1855, resuming his law practice. In 1858, however, he re-appeared in politics, and was elected to represent his district in the state legislature, and was re-elected and served in the same body during the sessions of 1859 and 1860. In 1861 he was sent as a peace commissioner from the state of North Carolina to the congress of southern states at Montgomery, Ala. At the opening of the late Civil war he took up arms for the Confederate cause and was advanced in rank to lieutenant-colonel, colonel, brigadier-general and major-general, and served until the close of the war, surrendering with General Lee at Appomatox. At the close of hostilities he resumed the practice of the law, and at the same time engaged extensively in planting, pursuing these peaceful occupations until 1872, when he again entered public life, and in January of that year was elected as United States senator by the democrats of the state legislature, and took his seat April 24; three times since then, he has been re-elected to the same high office, viz.: In 1876, 1883 and 1889, and will hold until March 3, 1895 — a continuous period of twenty-four years, a record of which he may well feel proud. Senator Ransom is not aggressive and seldom indulges in set speeches, but he has a keen insight into everything that comes before the august body in which he serves, and his vote is cast without hesitation either for or against any measure that his judgment approves or disapproves. Although somewhat reticent while in Washington, Mr. Ransom is an eloquent speaker at the hustings and is a power in his state. He has a clear, resonant, far-reaching voice and his gestures are exceptionally graceful. His language is chaste and forcible, and his style, while not ornate, is filled with apt illustrations. He is tall in stature, is erect, and he has a large, well-shaped head. His eyes are black and piercing, but usually assume a mild and kindly expression. Mr. Ransom is personally as well known as any inhabitant of the state, and his popularity is co-extensive with its boundaries, while his national fame is as enviable as his local reputation.

REV. BAYLUS CADE,

a prominent citizen of Raleigh, was born in Barker's settlement, Va. (now West Virginia), September 3, 1844. His father was John Cade, who was a grandson of a Revolutionary soldier who came to this country with Gen. LaFayette. His mother's maiden name was Margaret Wright, granddaughter of a Revolutionary soldier, whose parents

sincerely yours
Wm Johnston

came from England, in 1767. Baylus Cade was taught the primary branches of education by eleven months' of " old field " schooling. In the spring of 1862 he joined Company G, of the Eleventh Virginia cavalry, and surrendered with Lee, in 1865. His early education was supplemented at Richmond (Va.) college, by his entering that institution in October, 1866, and leaving it July 1, 1869. He had previously, in March, 1868, been ordained to the Baptist ministry. January 19, 1870, Mr. Cade was united in marriage with Nannie, daughter of William A. and Elizabeth J. Love. He has been engaged in the ministration of the gospel, and in teaching at intervals, for twenty-four years. The field of his labor has been in the states of Virginia, Ohio, West Virginia and North Carolina, and in every instance he proved himself to be an efficient instructor. Rev. Cade is, at this time, pastor of the Baptist church at Lewisburg, N. C., and editor of the *Progressive Farmer*, published at Raleigh. This paper is the organ of the state alliance of North Carolina, has an extensive circulation and wields a powerful influence over the politics of the state. The editorials are able and pungent and it has an advertising patronage commensurate with its circulation.

COL. WILLIAM JOHNSTON

was born in Gaston (formerly Lincoln) county, N. C., near Cowan's ford, on the Catawba river, and is a son of Robert and Mary (Reid) Johnston—the latter a daughter of Dr. John Reid, an officer of the Revolution. Henry Johnston, the father of Robert, was of Scotch extraction, and settled in North Carolina about the year 1740, and also served in the Revolutionary war, with the rank of colonel. Both grandfathers served in the upper house of the state legislature, and were equally renowned as statesmen as well as warriors. To Robert and Mary (Reid) Johnston were born twelve children—seven sons and five daughters—and of these there still survive: William, the subject of this sketch; Mrs. Mary E. Davidson and Mrs. Martha M. Rankin.

After William Johnston had acquired a sufficient preliminary education, he entered the University of North Carolina, and was later prepared for the bar by Hon. Richmond M. Pearson, late chief-justice, and entered upon the active practice of his chosen profession at Charlotte, in 1842, and here he has ever since made his residence. He continued in practice until 1856, when he assumed the presidency of the Charlotte & South Carolina railroad company, and rescued the road from a state of dilapidation to a prosperous condition. This road proved to be of immense benefit to the Confederate government during the Civil war until its destruction by Sherman, in February, 1865. In 1859 Mr. Johnston inaugurated the Atlantic, Tennessee & Ohio railroad, and completed forty-six miles of construction, when the oncoming of the war of course led to its abandonment.

Mr. Johnston was an ardent supporter of the southern cause, and heartily endorsed the scheme of secession, and was sent by the people

B—41

of Mecklenburg to the convention called by the legislature, in February, 1861, to consider Federal relations. His response to a letter which had been submitted by the county convention to a committee of citizens will fully disclose Mr. Johnston's position on this momentous question:

COLUMBIA, February 7, 1861.

GENTLEMEN — I am in receipt of your favor of the 4th inst., propounding the following interrogations: "Are you in favor of withdrawing the state of North Carolina from the present confederation, on the assembling of the state convention? Are you in favor of a southern confederacy, and that North Carolina take prompt steps to form one of its members."

Without hesitation I reply in the affirmative to both of the foregoing queries. It is my deliberate conviction that the true policy of North Carolina is to sunder connection with the Federal government as early as practicable. In the present juncture of affairs this course appears to be dictated by the highest considerations of peace, security and honor. Having taken this step, I believe that it will be her interest and duty to unite as speedily as possible in a southern confederacy.

These, gentlemen, are briefly my views, given in the midst of other engagements. I have no reserve on the momentous issues now convulsing the country. For five years I have taken no part in politics, and am frank in stating that I desire none. It is admitted that there may be times in the affairs of state when no man should feel at liberty to withhold his services from the country. But when it is recollected that Mecklenburg is not without her "jewels," and that "Sparta hath many a worthier son than he" who addresses you, you will admit the propriety of my course.

With acknowledgement for the kind motive which prompted your letter, and with every feeling to support cordially the nominees for your convention, I remain very truly,

Your friend and fellow citizen,
WILLIAM JOHNSTON.

In this convention Mr. Johnston strongly advocated the propriety of North Carolina's standing by her sister states of the south. A second convention was called for May 20, 1861, and Mr. Johnston was again elected a delegate, receiving every vote cast in Mecklenburg. He again was fervent in his advocacy of secession, and the ordinance was passed the first day of the meeting. He was then induced by Governor Ellis to accept the position of commissary-general, which position, indeed, had been previously tendered him, but which he had declined, with the rank of colonel, but he discharged the duties of the office until the following September only, when he was compelled to resign to give personal supervision to his railroad companies. Later, President Davis offered him a similar position under the Confederate government, but his transportation duties he thought to be of more value to the country. In March, 1862, Mr. Johnston was called upon to run for the office of governor of the state, and at a meeting of the people, without regard to party, was put forward as a candidate through the following resolutions:

WHEREAS, The people of North Carolina will be called upon in August next to make choice of a suitable man to fill the office of governor, and believing that the only motive which should influence us in making that selection is a desire to secure the services of one who possesses capability, integrity and industry.

Resolved, That we pledge ourselves to eschew old party preferences, and to support any man who we have reason to believe will faithfully and fearlessly discharge his duties and favor a vigorous prosecution of the war until our complete independence is fully acknowledged.

Resolved, That we have seen the name of our fellow citizen, William Johnston, Esq., mentioned in several of the public prints of the state as a suitable person for the office of governor, and that we heartily join in the recommendation, and suggest him as a candidate who will bring to his aid, in discharging the duties of governor, a varied experience, great industry and unimpeachable integrity.

Resolved, That while we are engaged in a struggle for independence — for our existence as a free people —we think that a canvass of the state by candidates would prove injurious to our cause, and, therefore, express the hope that if there is more than one candidate for the office of governor they will remain at home and allow the voters of the state to decide matter in a quiet way.

But Mr. Johnston had for an opponent a most powerful rival in the person of Zebulon B. Vance, then a colonel in the Confederate army, whose speeches in the field, among the soldiers, carried the day for him. The greatest service that any one man could render the Confederacy throughout the war, however, was that rendered by Mr. Johnston in the transportation of men and munitions of war, for without this aid the government would have been powerless. Before the close of the war, Col. Johnston made an effort to extend his line from Columbia to Augusta, but no great progress had been made in this enterprise before hostilities ceased; after the close of the war, however, the road was pushed through by Col. Johnston, regardless of great opposition from rival corporations, and a "plentiful lack" of capital. In 1873 the colonel retired from active business, and has since devoted his time solely to his private affairs.

Just after peace had been declared, President Davis arrived in Charlotte, April 18, 1865, and was there met by Col. Johnston. As there has been a statement made by one Bates that Mr. Davis spoke exultingly on hearing of the assassination of President Lincoln, it may be well here to contradict that slander, and give the facts in the case: A small crowd had gathered on the streets of Charlotte, on the day mentioned above, to greet Mr. Davis, and while that gentleman was engaged in making a brief address a telegram was passed to him; having read it, his face assumed a serious expression, and, passing the dispatch to Col. Johnston, Mr. Davis immediately retired to privacy. Subsequently Col. Johnston volunteered, when President Davis was under arraignment by the United States government, to go to New York and furnish the facts to Charles O'Conor, counsel for Davis, as evidence.

Colonel Johnston was married, in 1846, to Miss Ann Eliza Graham, daughter of Dr. George F. Graham, the brother of William A. Graham, and to this union were born four children, viz.: Julia M., wife of A. B. Andrews, of Raleigh; Frank G., of Mecklenburg; Cora J., wife of T. R. Robertson, of Charlotte, and William R., of Richmond. Mrs. Eliza Johnston departed this life in 1881. ˙

HON. HAMILTON GLOVER EWART

was born in Columbia, S. C., on the 23rd day of October, in the year 1849. His father was James B. Ewart, who was born in Kershaw county, S. C., the son of James, who was the son of James Beckett Ewart, a native of Ireland. The latter immigrated to America and first located in New York, but subsequently came to South Carolina and for many years was a leading merchant of Columbia. He was an extensive land owner, and in his day was prominently identified with the development of his adopted state. James B. Ewart, the father of the subject of this biographical mention, was a lawyer, and although he died before reaching his thirtieth year, he came to be one of the leading jurists of the state. He married Miss Mary A. McMahon, whose family for several generations had been active in the onward career of South Carolina. Hamilton G. Ewart attended the schools of Columbia during his boyhood, and after due prepara- tion, entered the University of South Carolina and soon evinced the same energy and brilliancy that have characterized his whole life. As a student he excelled, having carried the double courses of law and the regular classical studies at the same time. In 1872 he was gradu- ated with the highest honors of his class, having been valedictorian, and was also given the degree of bachelor of laws. In 1872 Mr. Ewart began the practice of his chosen profession at Hendersonville, N. C. We first find him in public life as the register in the office of Chief-Justice Waite in 1874. He ably discharged the duties of this important trust until the abolishment of the office in 1880. During the years of 1873-74 he was honored by his townsmen by being chosen as their mayor, and the fact of his having served two terms makes it probable that he administered the affairs of that position as honorably and satisfactorily as he has since discharged other and greater trusts to which he has been elected by the people. Mr. Ewart was reared among a people who are almost universally demo- crats. He was brought up in the beliefs of that party, but his inde- pendent character asserted itself in 1876, when he utterly refused to vote for Horace Greeley as president of the United States. He rather preferred to cast his vote for a soldier who had at all times shown himself honorable, therefore his vote was cast for Ulysses S. Grant.

In 1876 Mr. Ewart was an elector on the Hayes and Wheeler ticket. In the year 1884 he was nominated for congress, but was de- feated by Thomas D. Johnson. In 1886 he was chosen representative in the state legislature, and during his term of service in that body was chairman of the committee on corporations, and also a member of the committee on judiciary. He was the successful candidate for congress in 1888, and in the fifty-first congress Mr. Ewart has made a record for himself, and brought honor on the constituency that sup- ported him. As a member of the committee on claims he has shown himself worthy to deal with great subjects. He was also a member of the committees on the merchant marine and private land claims. The crowning act of his public career was his prominent relation to the investigation of the civil service commission. He drafted and introduced the resolution which led to the memorable investigation of that department of the government service, and handled the sub- ject with such skill as to win for him notice from the entire newspaper press of the country. The friends and foes of the measure alike re- spected the ability and seeming sincerity of the author of the resolu- tion. Although at all times a loyal and earnest champion of the republican party, Mr. Ewart made a telling speech against the pass- age of the famous Federal election bill, taking the ground that the bill would unneccessarily engender renewed animosity between the north and south. He made an eloquent appeal for the passage of educational laws suitable to reach the ignorant and degraded of the south of both colors, and also urged the repealing of internal revenue laws, as by these measures the north would show to the south that she was sincere in her expressions of good-will.

May 6th, 1874, Mr. Ewart was so fortunate as to form a marriage alliance with Miss Sarah C. Ripley, the daughter of Col. Valentine Ripley, a prominent merchant and planter of North Carolina. Seven children have been born of this union, named: Mary D., Eliza Adger, Hamilton Gustavus, Sarah Cordelia, Valentine, James Beckett and Matthew Quay Ewart. Mr. Ewart is considerably interested in agriculture and owns and operates a fine plantation a few miles from Hendersonville. He is a member of the farmers' alliance, and has always shown himself the friend of the people. Although still a young man, Mr. Ewart has accomplished much more than ordinarily falls to the lot of man. He brought to his life work a mind of keen, receptive qualities, and as a lawyer excels. He has never sought political office. Honor has sought him. His record in both public and private life is above reproach, although at times he has done things which he knew would not add to his own aggrandizement. His life has been measured up to a high standard, and the outcome thus far proves how well he has succeeded in following the dictates of his conscience.

DR. WILLIAM R. WOOD,

superintendent of the state insane asylum at Raleigh, was born near Plymouth, Washington county, N. C., November 23, 1834. His father, Richard Wood, also a native of the state, was born September 25, 1807, and, January 26, 1832, married Miss Emily Bozeman, and to this happy union were born six children, of whom three survive, viz.: William R., Mirabeau L. (a member of the legislature from Bertie county) and Josephine, widow of J. N. Gammon, of Durham, N. C. Early in his business life Richard Wood was engaged in mercantile pursuits, but in 1836 he relinquished merchandising and moved to Tennessee, where he remained for several years, engaged in farming and dealing in real estate. In 1848, however, he returned to North Carolina, and settled in Halifax county, where he passed away in 1865. Mrs. Emily (Bozeman) Wood was a daughter of Capt. Levin Bozeman, a soldier of the war of the Revolution and a wealthy planter and ship owner, as well as a member of the North Carolina legislature.

William R. Wood was educated at an academy until seventeen years old, when he entered upon the study of medicine under Dr. Warren W. Ward, of Plymouth, and subsequently attended the university of Pennsylvania, Philadelphia, from which he graduated with distinction before he had reached his twenty-first year, in 1855. Soon after graduation, the young physician was united in wedlock with Miss Mary E. Daughtry, of Gates county, N. C., but this lady died a short time after the marriage ceremony, leaving no children. The second marriage of the doctor was in 1862, to Miss Henrietta Anthony, daughter of Col. Whitmil H. Anthony, of Scotland Neck, and of the family born to this felicitous union there lives only one son, Capt. John W. Wood, assistant adjutant-general of the state guard, and a lawyer of prominence in Bertie county.

In 1858 Dr. Wood located in Halifax county and entered upon the discharge of the duties of his profession. His success was complete, and in it he was kept busy until the breaking out of the Civil war, when he entered the Confederate service, and during the first year served on picket duty along the Potomac, between Centerville and Fairfax C. H., under Gen. J. E. B. Stuart. In 1862 he fought gallantly at Newbern, and in defense of Richmond under Gen. Robert E. Lee, and at the advance on Gettysburg was severely wounded, which wound caused his resignation as captain and his temporary retirement from the service. In 1864 he was promoted to be major of the First cavalry, but, on account of his old wound, was again compelled to resign. He then resumed his private practice, in which he continued until appointed to his present office of superintendent of the North Carolina insane asylum, a position for which he is peculiarly well fitted. For many years the doctor has been an active and prominent member of the state medical society, and in 1884 was elected president of the state board of medical examiners for six years — a position he filled with dignity and great ability. A descendant of one of the oldest families of the state, he naturally takes great interest in her progress, and none better than he is aware of the immense wealth hidden within her bosom, or takes a greater pride in its development. The social standing of the doctor is one of undisputed prominence and the efficiency with which he discharges his official duties is the admiration, not only of his innumerable personal friends, but of the citizens of the state at large.

JAMES DODGE GLENN

was born October 20, 1852, in Rockingham county, N. C., and is the son of Chalmers Glenn, who was related to Thomas Chalmers, the great Scotch divine. Chalmers Glenn was born in North Carolina in 1830. Graduating from Judge Pearson's law school in Yadkin county, N. C., he then began the practice of his chosen profession, and rose to eminence. He was a whig, and strongly opposed to the disruption of the Union in 1860, but when the south seceded as a body he cast his fortunes with the new government, and in April, 1861, enlisted in Company I, Thirteenth North Carolina regiment volunteer infantry, and was elected first lieutenant, subsequently being promoted to the rank of captain. He was killed at the battle of South Mountain, September 14, 1862. None fought better, and had he lived there can be no question but that he would have risen to still greater rank in the army. In December, 1851, Captain Glenn married Miss Anna Dodge, a daughter of Col. James R. Dodge, of Yadkin county, N. C., and to them were born five children of whom three are now living, viz.: James Dodge Glenn, of Greensboro, N. C.; Robert B. Glenn, of Winston, N. C., and Edward Travis B. Glenn, of

Macon, Ga. Chalmers Glenn was brought up in the family of Dr. E. T. Brodnax, of Rockingham county, N. C., as his mother died in giving him birth. He was a man of great ability, and his integrity was unimpeachable. His father was John W. Glenn, a native of North Carolina, whose death occurred in 1850. John W. Glenn was the son of James Anderson Glenn, who was a native of Scotland, whence he came to America in his early manhood. He settled in Pittsylvania county, Va., and there married Miss Wilson, a descendant of a prominent old Virginia connection. James D. Glenn is descended from a family of noble heritage on the maternal as well as the paternal side. His mother, Anna Dodge Glenn, was a granddaughter of Gen. Richard Dodge, of New York, who was a brigadier-general in the United States army, and was in command of Sackett's Harbor during the war of 1812. He married Miss Ann S. Irving, who was a sister of Washington Irving. James R. Dodge, the father of Anna Dodge Glenn, was born in New York, and left his native state to settle in the western portion of North Carolina, where he married a Miss Williams, daughter of Col. Joseph Williams, of Surrey county, N. C., and a niece of Nicholas Williams. She is a sister of Richard Irving Dodge, a colonel in the United States army.

After the death of his father, James D. was adopted by his uncle, Dr. E. T. Brodnax, of Rockingham county, and attended the Virginia military institute at Lexington, Va., and graduated with distinction in 1871. Upon leaving school he adopted the profession of civil engineering, and followed the same for two years. Owing to the declining health of his uncle, Dr. Brodnax, he gave up civil engineering, and took charge of his uncle's farm in Rockingham county, which he successfully managed from 1873 until 1885. In 1880 he was elected to the legislature, as a representative from Rockingham county, making one of the most dignified and brilliant canvasses in the history of that county. His course in the legislature was so entirely in consonance with the best interests of the people, so able, conscientious and faithful, that he was re-elected in 1882 and in 1884, serving in that honorable position three terms, or six years. In 1881 he was elected as captain of Company H, Third regiment North Carolina state guard. In 1882 he was elected lieutenant-colonel of the Third regiment, and in 1884 elected colonel. He was re-elected in 1886 and 1888, and appointed adjutant-general by Gov. Fowle in 1889. In commenting upon the appointment of Gen. Glenn, the *State Chronicle* very justly remarks: "Gov. Fowle could not have made a wiser selection of an adjutant-general than he made in the appointment of Col. James D. Glenn. His appointment has been received with pleasure and satisfaction throughout the state." And Gen. Glenn, by his courteous, soldierly bearing, his skill as a military leader, and his devotion to the highest interests of the state, has abundantly proven the wisdom of Gov. Fowle's selection. Endowed with brilliant intellectual powers, and actuated by a noble ambition to be useful in the accomplishment of good in his day and generation, a bright future is opening before him.

General Glenn was married in June, 1877, to Miss Mary, the accomplished daughter of Dr. John G. Brodnax. Four children have been born to this union, but only the younger two are now living. Gen. Glenn is a Knight Templar Mason, and has been honored with the highest local offices of that ancient and honorable fraternity, being a past master of the lodge and eminent past commander of the commandery of which he is a member. He is also a consistent and active member of the Protestant Episcopal church. For four years Gen. James D. Glenn was a member of the state board of agriculture from the fifth congressional district, and only resigned that office to accept a position in the United States marshal's office, at Greensboro, N. C., having been appointed thereto by Gov. Vance.

WILLIAM H. HARRELL, M. D.,

is descended from an old and honorable connection. He is a son of William H. and Annie (Long) Harrell, both parents having been born in Martin county. William H. Harrell, Sr., was a man of ability and standing in the community. At the age of eighteen, having completed a thorough academic training, he was made a deputy sheriff of the county, and subsequently was elected sheriff, having filled that office for many years. At the time of his death, in 1867, he was clerk of the superior court. His wife survived him until 1890, when she, too, went to rest. The son and namesake was born in Martin county, on the family estate, on the 23rd of September, 1864. His literary training was obtained in the Williamston academy, and after completing the course there he took up the study of medicine with Dr. T. S. Burbank, of Wilmington, N. C., and was graduated from the medical college of Virginia, at Richmond, with the class of 1885, and in the same year received a diploma from the New York Polyclinical institute. At this time Dr. Harrell opened an office at Williamston, and he is now the oldest practitioner of the town. He is a prominent member of the state medical society, and is chairman of one branch of that organization, and is also a member of the Martin county medical society, at the present time holding the office of county superintendent of health. As a Mason he is active and esteemed, being master of the Williamston lodge, Canaba chapter, and he is also a member of Hassell encampment of the I. O. O. F. Dr. Harrell is an original stockholder in the Williamston furniture factory, and takes a deep interest in every movement calculated to increase the prosperity of the town. He is active in local politics, and is an ardent supporter of the democratic party.

EDWARD CHANCEY REGISTER, M. D.

The subject whose name heads this sketch is one of the most skillful and successful physicians now in the practice of medicine in North Carolina, of which state he is a native, having been born in Duplin county, October 20, 1860. His parents are Dixon Sloan Register and

Sarah (Wilkins) Register. The father is also a native of Duplin county, of which county he has long been an extensive and wealthy planter of prominence. He is of English ancestors, who, in an early day, settled in Duplin county, and all of whom were farmers by vocation. Sarah, the mother of our subject, was also born in Duplin county, unto English parentage. To her marriage with Mr. Register were born four children, a daughter and three sons.

The subject of this sketch was reared upon a plantation, but early in his youth was sent from home and placed in school — first in a private school at Warsaw, N. C., and two years later was admitted to the university at Chapel Hill, where he completed a two years' course in the classics. Then, desiring to take up the study of medicine, he entered the medical department of the university under the instruction of T. W. Harris, M. D., graduating from the department in June, 1883. During the winters of 1883-4 and 1884-5 he spent sixteen months in medicine at the university of New York city, receiving the degree of M. D., in March of 1885. He had begun the practice of medicine in 1883, after his graduation in medicine at Chapel Hill, but suspended it to attend the university at New York city, and after his graduation there he located at Enochville, N. C., and began practicing in his chosen profession, continuing till December, 1887, when he located in Charlotte, where from the first he has conducted a large and lucrative practice. He has rapidly risen in the profession, and at the early age of thirty years ranks among the foremost physicians of his state. He is a member of the state medical association and is a leading member of the Charlotte academy of medicine. He maintains a general practice and is a thoroughly posted man in every branch of his profession. He is a close attendant to his work, and is thorough and cautious in diagnosis; and is of a kind and tender disposition; free of all bigotry, and in bearing manifests refinement and culture. He is of tall and striking physique, neat and attractive in appearance. He is progressive as a citizen, respected and honored as a moral and religious man. He is a member of the Methodist Episcopal church, and is also a member of the fraternity of Free Masons. In 1887 he was wedded to Miss Lavenia C. Montgomery, an accomplished lady of Concord, N. C.

ALBERT D. PARROTT

was born in Lenoir county, N. C., on the 24th day of January, 1853, the son of James M. and Elizabeth (Waters) Parrott. The great-grandfather of our subject was Simon Parrott, who was a native of Ireland. In his early manhood he settled in Virginia, and there died. His son, Jacob, was born in Virginia in 1793, and came to North Carolina in 1810. He married Miss Percy Arendell, a highly educated and refined woman, who gave him an education. She was a great-granddaughter of the Earl of Arendell, of Scotland. Jacob began life as a day laborer, and saved sufficient money to purchase a small plantation, and finally became a very wealthy man, and an ex-

tensive land owner. He reared a family of four sons and five daughters. James M. was the youngest son. His birth occurred in Lenoir
county in 1824, on the homestead which had been patented by
William Arendell, and since come into the possession of the Parrott
family. He became a planter; served as a captain in the state
militia, and was one of the first and largest stockholders in the
A. & N. C. railroad company, and was a director in that organization
until his death. For many years he was a member of the board of
internal improvements, and was one of Gov. Worth's council, and a
director in the State bank, at Newbern. Prominent in church work,
he was for many years identified with the Disciples church; was a
leading Mason and a stanch friend to public education. He died in 1878,
his wife still surviving him. Albert D., George F., James M., Susan M.,
and Thomas W. are the children born to them. Albert D. Parrott
was graduated from the University of Virginia, and became a civil
engineer, and was the youngest man to graduate from that institution with the degree of C. E., he being but eighteen years of age.
After completing the course there Mr. Parrott was employed in the
government survey of West Virginia for six months, and then returned home and turned his attention to agriculture, being a part
owner in the homestead plantation of 1,000 acres. He is a stockholder in the A. & N. C. railroad; a member of the Masonic fraternity; a member of the school board, and president of the graded
schools of Kingston; has served as a justice of the peace for many
years, and also as a member of the special court of the county. In
1876 he was married to Miss Elizabeth M. Karnegy, daughter of
John M. Karnegy, and their children are: John L., Robert D., and
Charlotte M. Mr. Parrott is a prominent and influential member of
the Episcopal church.

DR. GEORGE G. THOMAS,

one of the leading physicians of Wilmington, was born in Edgecomb,
in 1848, and is the son of Dr. William G. Thomas, who died on the
18th of February, 1890. Dr. George G. Thomas removed with his
parents to Wilmington when he was but three years old. He received his early education in the schools of this city, and, in 1864, entered the University of North Carolina, remaining there until he entered the sophomore class, when he began a course of study at the
University of Virginia. He studied there for three years, but was
compelled to abandon it on account of ill health. He afterward completed a medical course in the University of Maryland, at Baltimore,
graduating from the institution in 1871. He began the duties of his
profession the following year at Wilmington, and has remained here
since in the enjoyment of a successful and lucrative practice. At first
he was in partnership with his father, a renowned physician of the
south, and at the death of that gentleman remained alone in the
practice. He is a member of the state medical society, of which he
has served as president, and is now a member of the board of medi-

cal examiners. Dr. Thomas was married, in 1873, to Miss James, a native of Orange county and the daughter of Dr. P. James. The union has been blessed by the birth of two sons. Dr. Thomas is associate editor of the North Carolina *Medical Journal*, and during the sickness of Dr. Wood, in 1886, he acted as its editor. He is a member of the Church of England and fraternally belongs to the K. of P. lodge.

DENNIS SIMMONS.

One of the extensive lumber manufacturers of the state of North Carolina is Dennis Simmons, a resident of Williamston, N. C. Mr. Simmons was born in Carrituck county, N. C., on the 27th of December, 1826, his parents being Thomas and Martha (Duncan) Simmons, natives of the same county. These parents died before the son had reached the years of manhood. Ashel Simmons, the paternal grandfather, was a major in the Revolutionary war, and was a man of much prominence. Mr. Dennis Simmons was engaged until his nineteenth year in gaining an education. At the latter year he embarked in the lumber business, and in 1857 settled in Martin county. In 1865 he removed to Williamston, and has since resided there. At the time of his settlement in Martin county, in 1857, Mr. Simmons began the manufacture of shingles, and in 1877 he erected a large mill on Roanoke river, near Astoria, for the manufacture of shingles and lumber. This property was destroyed by fire in 1884, and was rebuilt in 1887 on a much larger scale. Since that time another extensive plant has been erected on the Tar river, and with the combined capacity of these plants Mr. Simmons has built up one of the most important industries in the state. Within the past few years Mr. D. D. Simmons and Mr. D. W. Tillman have been associated with him in business, and now have the management. At one time Mr. Simmons was an extensive stockholder in the Roanoke, Norfolk & Baltimore steamboat company, serving as president of that corporation for some time. From 1870 to 1884 he was a member of the firm of John D. Biggs & Co., the leading merchants of Williamston, and at the present time he is one of the large and successful planters of the county. During the Civil war he was tax assessor of Martin county and Williamston, and has rendered efficient service as a democrat. His marriage was solemnized with Miss Martha Alexander, daughter of Joseph Alexander, of Tyrell county, N. C., in 1857. Both Mr. and Mrs. Simmons are earnest members of the Missionary Baptist church, and he is superintendent of the Sunday-school of the society of Williamston. He is a man of much influence, and is known with great favor throughout the county and state.

HON. CALEB B. GREEN,

one of the prominent citizens of Durham county and clerk of the superior court, was born in Person county, in 1848. His parents were

Mager and Anna (Brooks) Green, both natives of North Carolina. The father was a farmer and took but little interest in politics, though he served a term in the legislature. He was a quiet, unassuming man, and took his greatest pleasure in the bosom of his family, yet he was quite well known in his county and was highly respected as an honest, square business man. He and his wife were devout members of the Baptist church. They went from labor to reward, the father in 1878, aged seventy-two; the mother in 1867, aged fifty-nine. These parents had eight chiidren, our subject being the only one now living; all the other members of the family died with the consumption except the father. Our subject began for himself at the age of seventeen years, and learned the printing business, which he followed about sixteen years. He established the Durham *Tobacco Plant* in January, 1872, and this was the first paper ever published in Durham. He edited and owned this paper until September, 1886, when he sold it. After this, its name was changed to the *Globe.* In 1874 he was elected county commissioner of Orange county, and served two years. In 1880 he was elected to the legislature from Orange county, and in that election he defeated Hon. Josiah Turner, a man of state reputation. The session of 1881 he introduced and secured the passage of the bill making Durham a county. This was one of the most hotly contested measures that were ever enacted by a legislative body in North Carolina. In 1883, he was elected a county commissioner of Durham county, resigning in the fall of 1884 to accept a seat in the state legislature from Durham county. In November, 1890, he was elected clerk of the superior court of Durham county, the office holding for four years. It will thus be seen that he has been ardent, honorable, prudent and persevering in taking care of the interests of those who intrusted their rights in his keeping. He generally takes part in all such measures as look to the advancement of the general welfare of the community, county and state. In 1887 and 1889 he was county proxy for the county of Durham, representing $100,000 worth of stock in the Lynchburg & Durham railroad. Mr. Green was married in 1870 to Miss Kate, daughter Robert F. and Caroline Morris, of Durham county. Mr. and Mrs. Green were the first couple ever married in a church in the town of Durham. Three children have blessed this union, viz.: Freddie A., who is a graduate of Durham high school, Oak Ridge institute, and who attended the University of North Carolina for two years. He is now deputy clerk in his father's office. Ernest J. and Rosa E. are the names of the other two. All the family, save one, are members of the Trinity Methodist Episcopal church. Our subject is a member of the Masonic order and a worthy citizen.

HON. T. D. McCAULEY.

Among the most prominent and influential families of Union county, N. C., we find the name of McCauley. The Hon. Thomas D. McCauley, a leading attorney, and superintendent of public instruction in Union county, was born January 22, 1846, in that county, his parents being the Hon. C. M. T. and Henrietta (Dillon) McCauley, both natives of North Carolina, and both descended from honorable connections. Hon. C. M. T. McCauley is one of the oldest and ablest attorneys at the Union county bar, and for many years has been a respected citizen of Monroe. For many years prior to the Civil war he held the offices of clerk and master in equity of the county; and during the war served the Confederate government as captain of Company C, Tenth regiment North Carolina volunteer artillery, his service extending over the greater part of the war. After the close of hostilities he was several times elected to both branches of the state legislature, in which he conducted himself with ability and dignity. Six children have been born to his marriage with Miss Henrietta Dillon, named, in the order of their birth: Thomas D., Anna, wife of G. W. Redfearn; William, who served for several terms as county surveyor—now a planter; Emma, wife of W F. Askew; Maurice E., a druggist, and Matthew McCauley, a physician. Thomas D. McCauley was given exceptional educational advantages, having completed the full course in that noted institution of learning known as Horner's academy, at Oxford, N. C. After leaving the academy he entered his father's law office as a student, and in 1870 successfully stood an examination for admission to the bar. Six years later he was elected mayor of the city of Monroe, and in July, 1890, he was called to his present responsible office as superintendent of public instruction for the county of Union. Mr. McCauley is a communicant of the Episcopal church, and is a prominent member of the Masonic order, having served as W. M. of lodge 244, at Monroe, and before that as S. W. of the same lodge. He holds the office of adjutant of the Union County Confederate veterans' association, an organization that embraces all the living ex-Confederate soldiers of the county. Mr. McCauley enlisted in December, 1863, in the Confederate army, and supported his people's cause until Johnston's surrender in 1865. He fought at Averysboro, Bentonsville, and in several dangerous skirmishes, but the greater portion of the time was on detached duty as a clerk to the adjutant-general.

ERNEST S. FOSTER, M. D.,

one of the leading physicians of Franklin county, N. C., was born in that county and state on the 10th of November, 1846. He received his early schooling at the academy in Louisburg, N. C. In May, 1864, he enlisted in Company A, First North Carolina regiment of junior reserves, acted as brigade ordnance officer for that brigade until the close of the war, and was in the battles of Kinston and Bentonville. After the war he returned to Franklin county, and for two years following was engaged in teaching school, meanwhile applying himself to the study of medicine. Subsequently he entered Washington university at Baltimore, from which he was graduated March 1, 1869. Until January, 1879, he practiced in his native place, but at the latter date removed to Louisburg, N. C., where he has since resided. He is the superintendent of the board of health of Franklin county, and, since 1878, has been a member of the medical society of North Carolina. Miss Mary Cooke, daughter of Thomas B. Cooke, of Franklin county, became his wife in 1872, and to their union have been born three children, named as follows: Lucy K., Matilda K. and Virginia C. Dr. Foster is the son of Peter S. Foster, who was also born in Franklin county, the date of his birth being 1823. He was an eminent physician, and practiced in his native county during his active professional career. In 1844 he married Miss Matilda K. Williams, daughter of Joseph J. Williams, of Warren county, N. C., and a large family of thirteen children were born to them. The six who survive are: Ernest S., Peter, Edward, Junius, Martha, wife of Rev. Paul J. Caroway, and Matilda, wife of George W. Brown, of Louisburg, N. C. The mother died in 1868. Peter Foster, Sr., the grandfather of our subject, was born in Matthews county, Va., in 1797, and came to North Carolina after reaching the years of manhood. He settled in Franklin county, where, for many years, he was an extensive farmer and merchant. For a number of years he held the office of magistrate. He was a captain in the war of 1812, and died in 1844, full of years. His father was also named Peter, and he was a Virginian. Ernest S. Foster is of English descent on the paternal side, and of Welsh-Irish parentage on the maternal side. The Foster family has been held in high esteem in Virginia for many years, and the North Carolina branch is equally honored in this state.

J. B. CLIFTON.

For almost 200 years the Clifton family has been identified with North Carolina. From time to time its members have been honored by public offices within the gift of the people, and their best efforts have been directed toward the building up of the grand commonwealth. From the time Thomas Clifton came from England, where he was born, and settled in North Carolina, early in the year 1700, the family escutcheon has remained unstained. Wiley Clifton was born in North Carolina, in 1777, was a planter, and died April 20th, 1847. His son, Thomas Turner Clifton, was born in Wake county, N. C., August 10, 1810. He also followed agriculture, and during the war held the office of magistrate in Franklin county, he having removed to that county with his parents in early boyhood. He was married, in September, 1834, to Nancy Pippin, daughter of John Pippin, a native of England, who came to America in early manhood, settling in Virginia. He served as a soldier in the Revolution, and was at Yorktown when Cornwallis surrendered. After the war he settled in Franklin county, N. C., where he died about 1840. To Thomas Turner and Nancy (Pippin) Clifton were born nine children, eight of whom survive, viz.: James Beverley, of Louisburg, N. C.; John Thomas, of Franklin county, N. C.; Virginia N., of Franklin county, N. C.; Joseph Allison, of Waco, Texas; Sarah E., wife of A. J. P. Harris, of Franklin county; Ella F., wife of John R. Mitchner, of Franklin county; Robert Turner, of Franklin county, and William Ridley Clifton, a resident of Waco, Texas. The father of these children died July 13, 1882, the mother having preceded him to rest May 12, 1875. The principal of this biographical mention is Dr. James B. Clifton, who was born in Franklin county, N. C., April 27, 1836. Having obtained an excellent preparatory education at the Louisburg academy, he entered the University of Virginia, and subsequently was graduated from the medical department of the University of New York, in the class of 1857. He then located in his native county and continued to practice there for two years, after which he moved to Louisburg, N. C., where he has since been engaged in the practice of his chosen profession with marked success. During the Civil war Dr. Clifton enlisted in the Confederate army, in June, 1861, as a member of the Franklin regiment, which was organized at Louisburg. The organization was later changed to the Fifth regiment North Carolina volunteers, and was known as Company K. In June, 1861, our subject was commissioned assistant surgeon of the regiment, and after a service of six months was assigned to various hospitals, and in December, 1861, he was made surgeon of the post at Jamestown Island, Va., where he remained until the evacution of the peninsula, about five months later. During the succeeding year Surgeon Clifton was in charge of the Richmond defenses, and was then ordered into the field near Fredericksburg and assigned to McCaw's division, Longstreet's corps, army of northern Virginia. From that time until the close of the war he served as surgeon of the brigade. Peace having been declared, Surgeon Clifton returned to Louisburg, and once more took up his professional duties. As a physician he has risen to eminence, being recognized as one of the most skillful practitioners in the state. Dr. Clifton has been twice married. His first union was to Miss Ann R. Smith, daughter of S. W. Smith, of Granville county, N. C., to whom he was married November 6, 1867. Of the eleven children born to them, six now survive: William Thomas, Mary G., Maurice S., Fannie N., Lucy B. and Kate D. Mrs. Clifton died November 29, 1885. June 4, 1890, Mrs. Lucy D. Clifton, widow of B. P. Clifton, and a daughter of William Andrews, of Granville county, N. C., became his wife. Dr. Clifton is a member of the Masonic order, and is a communicant of the Episcopal church.

WINFIELD S. CHADWICK.

One of the most progressive and successful business men of Carteret county, N. C., is Winfield S. Chadwick, president of the Atlantic & Northern R. R. Co. He was born March 18, 1848, in Beaufort, N. C., his parents being Barnabas and Mary (Bell) Chadwick, both of English parentage. Three brothers by the name of Chadwick immigrated to America from England, and settled in Carteret county, N. C., one of them being Barnabas, the grandfather of our immediate subject. He was an influential planter and a large slave owner. His son, Barnabas Chadwick, Jr., was for many years a sea captain in the Beaufort and West Indies trade. He commanded his own vessel and accumulated considerable property. During the war, and until 1875, he was a pilot off the coast of Beaufort, and now resides in that town, having retired from active life. Winfield S. Chadwick was educated in the public schools of Beaufort, and at the age of fifteen ran away from home to enter the Confederate service, and joined Company G, Tenth North Carolina regiment He remained with that regiment until the close of hostilities, having participated in the battles of Newbern, Plymouth and Petersburg, and for ten months he was stationed at Fort Clifton. After the war he returned to his home and for the succeeding two years was engaged as a clerk in a mercantile establishment at Beaufort. At the expiration of this time Mr. Chadwick embarked in the mercantile business for himself on a capital of $83, pluck and brains. He continued in this alone until 1871, when he formed a partnership with Mr. Benjamin F. Jones, the firm name being Chadwick & Jones. This concern existed until 1890, when Mr. Jones retired. In 1885, the firm purchased a two-thirds interest in the Carteret County Fish Oil & Guano company, this company owning several vessels which ply between Beaufort and northern markets, besides many boats engaged in the fish and oyster trade.

Mr. Chadwick was the founder of the oyster industry of Beaufort, and was largely instrumental in locating the large canning factories at that place. For four years this enterprising gentleman served as a member of the board of directors of the Atlantic & North Carolina railroad company, and at the expiration of that time, in 1889, was elected president of the same. Since his assumption of the management of the road it has been placed on a paying basis, new equipment has been added, and the rolling stock greatly improved. He was active in the organization of the Farmers & Merchants' Bank of Beaufort, and now holds the office of first vice-president of that institution. As a democrat he has held the office of chairman of the county democratic executive committee for six years. On the 27th of January, 1875, Mr. Chadwick was so fortunate as to form a marriage alliance with Miss Mary F. Thompson, daughter of Frank Thompson, Esq., of Wilmington, Dela., and four children have been born to them, viz.: Mabel, Corinne, Carl and Walter. Both Mr. and Mrs. Chadwick are active members of the Methodist Episcopal church, south.

ROBERT IRWIN McDOWELL,

whose name introduces the following biographical sketch, was for many years a prominent and well-known citizen of Charlotte, N. C He was a native of Mecklenburg county, and was born in the year 1813. His ancestors were among the illustrious Revolutionary characters of Mecklenburg, Gen. Irwin, his maternal grandfather, having been a signer of the famous Mecklenburg declaration of independence. Robert I. McDowell was educated at the Hampton–Sydney college, of Virginia, where he graduated in 1832, at the age of twenty years. In early life he taught school, but, marrying, settled down in life upon a farm in Iredell county, and took up agricultural pursuits. Mr. McDowell married Miss Rebecca Brevard—a grand-niece of Dr. Ephraim Brevard, the acknowledged author of the immortal Mecklenburg declaration of independence, May 20, 1775. The ancestors of the Brevard family were French Huguenots. The marriage of our subject and wife gave issue to the following offspring: William H., who was a cadet of the Virginia military institute, and was killed at the battle of New Market, Va.; Franklin B., whose sketch appears elsewhere in this volume; Maggie C., recently wedded by Baron Van Maltzahn, of Berlin, Germany; Emma, deceased, who was wedded by J. L. Chambers, of Charlotte; and Rena, the wife of Dr. E. W. Roach, of Charlotte.

As above stated, Mr. McDowell located on a farm in Iredell county, soon after the consummation of his marriage. Here he continued at farming till 1872, in which year he removed with his family and located in Charlotte, where he continued to reside till his death occurred in 1885. On coming to Charlotte, Mr. McDowell became interested in the Traders' National bank of Charlotte, and continued in the banking business until that bank went into voluntary liquidation and was discontinued. For several years prior to his death, Mr. McDowell was also a member of the firm of Liddell & Co., operators of a foundry and machine shop at Charlotte. As a business man he was possessed of remarked ability. He began in life with a limited capital and at the time of his death had amassed an estate of large wealth. Being, in all things, a careful and scrutinizing observer and being of excellent judgment and foresight, success attended all his undertakings. Mr. McDowell was a considerate man, and was calm and deliberate in thought and action. He never desired political preferment, as he had no special liking for political life. However, while residing in Iredell county, the people of that county elected him to the lower house of the legislature, in which he served one term, and then withdrew from the field of public life and politics. Being a close observer and student of public events and political history, Mr. McDowell was regarded as a man of learning and excellent judgment, and his expressed opinion in all phases of life was sought and appreciated by many confiding friends and admirers. In disposition, Mr. McDowell was retired, modest, and cultured; but when duty prompted him to action, he directed his efforts, with zeal, confidence and ability. In colloquy, and from the rostrum he was pleasing, instructive and eloquent. As a citizen, progressiveness ever characterized his course.

To public improvement, church and education, Mr. McDowell was an ardent friend and supporter. He was a life-long member of the Presbyterian church, and was for many years an elder. A lasting monument to his memory and generosity is the Second Presbyterian church of Charlotte, of which he was founder, and for years a liberal supporter. For as many as twenty-five years Mr. McDowell was

B—42

treasurer of the board of trustees for Davidson college, of which college he was a trustee at the time of his death. On the close of the Civil war this college was in an unpromising condition of finances, and might have collapsed but for his aid. Advancing his own money, Mr. McDowell continued, for several years, the main financial support of the college, and in subsequent years he remained a liberal contributor to the institution, taking special pride in its progress. At the time of his death, Mr. McDowell had been for several years a trustee of the Union Theological seminary of Virginia. Such is a brief review of the career of Robert Irwin McDowell. No more worthy character ever graced the varied circles of society; no truer patriot ever spoke in defense of his native land; no more faithful friend ever gave a helping hand; no more devoted father graced a family, and no nobler spirit ever took its flight above than he whose name heads this sketch.   .   .

FRANKLIN BREVARD McDOWELL,

the subject of the following biography, is one of the best and most favorably known citizens of Charlotte, N. C. He is a native of Iredell county, and was born December 31, 1849. His father was the late Robert Irwin McDowell, of Charlotte. Our subject's youth was spent on the farm of his father in Iredell, and he was taught the precepts of industry, perseverance and other like virtues, such as have characterized his brilliant career. Mr. McDowell's scholastic training began in the "old-field" schools in the neighborhood of his home; subsequently, by attending the Finley high schools, he was prepared for college under the instructions of Mr. E. W. Faucett. Entering Davidson college, Mr. McDowell graduated in 1869, at the age of nineteen. He then attended the University of Virginia, and completed a two years' course in the law. After being duly examined and admitted to the bar by the supreme court of North Carolina, Mr. McDowell began the practice of law at Statesville, the county seat of his native county. Early in life Mr. McDowell entered politics, and in 1872 was nominated the Greeley presidential elector for the Seventh congressional district of North Carolina. This district was composed of eleven mountain counties of western North Carolina, and in each of these counties Mr. McDowell, notwithstanding his early age, made an able canvass in joint debate with the Grant presidential nominee as elector, who was Hon. J. G. Ramsay, one of the ablest speakers and campaigners of the republican party.

In the fall of 1872, Mr. McDowell located in Charlotte, where he has since resided. At this date he left the forum and entered the journalistic field. Accepting a position on the editorial staff of the Charlotte *Daily Observer*, Mr. McDowell was connected with this journal for three years. Subsequently, for two years he conducted the *Southern Home*, succeeding, in this work, the late Gen. D. H. Hill. During his college days, Mr. McDowell developed marked talent as a speaker and writer; and having made extensive travels in Europe, was by reason of natural taste, by education and culture, well fitted for newspaper pursuits. However, after becoming interested in several important business enterprises, and in consequence of being elected mayor of Charlotte, and being made executor of his father's large estate, Mr. McDowell was compelled to abandon newspaper work. Yet he has never been wholly free from such work, being at this date vice president of the Charlotte *Chronicle* publishing company. His first public office in Charlotte was that of alderman, and as such he made an excellent official. Winning the admiration of his party and fellow citizens, Mr. McDowell was urged to become a candidate for mayor of Charlotte, to which office, as a democrat, he was elected in 1877, by an unprecedently large majority. Two years later, as an evidence of the people's approval of his administration as their mayor, Mr. McDowell was elected for a second term. His administration continued for four years, during which was observed rapid progress of the city. Several desirable reforms were wrought and prosperity and confidence in the progress of Charlotte were fixed. Streets were appropriately lettered as well as materially improved; houses were numbered, and free postal delivery inaugurated; a competent police and detective force employed, and the heart of the city cleared of disreputable houses and desperate characters. Mr. McDowell has ever been alive to whatsoever measures tend to advance the good and welfare of the city and its people. He is a director in the Charlotte Consolidated Construction company, which company was organized to improve and develop Charlotte, and which company are owners and operators of the Charlotte street car railway on the electric system. Mr. McDowell is vice-president of the Liddell & Co. foundry and machine shops, an important industrial enterprise of Charlotte. In 1884 Mr. McDowell was united in marriage with Miss May Flora King, an accomplished lady of New Orleans. Her father was the late Hon. William W. King, who was an eminent lawyer of New Orleans. Mrs McDowell is a sister of Miss Grace King, an authoress, and of Judge F. D. King of the civil district court of Louisiana. Mr. McDowell is an excellent and representative citizen; a man of education and culture; a ready conversationalist and speaker. His writings and speeches are highly enjoyed on account of their spontaneous humor and turn of thought. His generousness of heart and fidelity as a friend have won for him many friends, and no other citizen of Charlotte enjoys a higher esteem and more implicit confidence of his fellow-citizens than does Franklin B. McDowell.

HON. ROBERT PAYNE WARING,

of Charlotte. The subject of this sketch was born in King and Queen county, Va., on the 1st day of February, 1827, at the family seat of the Roanes. His mother, Miss Roane, was a daughter of that historic family. In his earliest school days he was under the tuition of H. J. Christian, afterward professor of ancient languages in Richmond college. At the age of sixteen he entered the junior class at Richmond college, where he remained two years. In 1845 he matriculated at the University of Virginia, and took an irregular course, graduating in 1847 in the school of law. In 1848 he married Augusta, the third daughter of Hon. Louis D. Henry, and settled in Charlotte, N. C., in 1850, and entered upon the practice of law. In 1854 he was elected county attorney, and after serving four years was unanimously re-elected, but resigned the same week to accept the United States con-sulship to St. Thomas, Danish West Indies. Wheeler's Reminiscences say he filled this responsible and honorable position with signal abil-ity, reflecting great credit upon the government. In April, 1861, he promptly tendered his resignation, preferring to throw his fortune in with the struggling south than to live in ease in the service of her then oppressors. In June, 1861, he returned to the United States and was arrested on his arrival and held a prisoner until October. For-tunately a letter of introduction, which he bore from a prominent captain of the merchant marine to the owners of his ship, secured him his release on parole, and thus he escaped imprisonment in Fort La Fayette. After the most thorough investigation, no charge could be established against him. He had only, with his usual urbanity, lifted his cap in passing a vessel on the water which bore the emblem of the infant Confederacy. On his release he returned to North Carolina, and in 1861 raised a company and served until January, 1864, when, from disability from wounds and rheumatism, he was retired. In the fall of the same year, at the request of Gen. Holmes, he took a position in a regiment of senior reserves, and was stationed at Salisbury, where, in 1865, he was captured by Gen. Stoneman and taken to Camp Chase. When released in July of the same year, he returned to Charlotte and became the editor of the *Daily Times.* Wheeler says so fearless and outspoken was his condemnation of the politico-military administration, that he was arrested by the military commandant in the time of peace and tried before a court martial, where he was defended by Hon. B. F. Moore and Col. E. G. Haywood. Conviction was a foregone conclusion, and he was offered the alter-native of paying a fine of $300 in five days, or suffering six months' imprisonment in Fort Macon.

Such treatment gave him notoriety and his paper a wider circula-tion. It was by his able editorials he contributed largely to the change of administration at the ballot-box. Mr. Waring had been elector on the Buchanan ticket. " In 1870 he was sent to the legisla-ture (we again quote from Wheeler), where an important and novel question met him at the threshold — should North Carolina place her-self on record as the first American state to exercise the power of impeaching a governor? Troops had been raised by this governor, ostensibly to ferret out the perpetrators of two mysterious murders, but without a resort first to the *posse comitatus* — worst of all, this was done on the eve of a general election. The best citizens of the state in two counties had been arrested without the pretense of indictment or information and incarcerated as common felons, to await trial by a contemptible *militia* court martial, and this, too, in a time of profound peace. The great writ of *habeas corpus* had been suspended, and a band of cut-throats were here, under command of the notorious Kirk, to enforce the lawless orders of this petty usurper. Should such conduct, at the suggestion of probable Federal interference, be overlooked or patiently borne, or should an example be made for posterity? Mr. Waring's position was not doubtful. Liberty is more valuable than money, and eternal vigilance is its price. His influence was acknowledged in appointing him on the committee which prepared the articles of impeachment." In 1872 he was unanimously nominated for the senate, and after a most exciting and able canvass, in which Gen. Barringer was his opponent, he was elected. He was re-elected in 1874, and served as the chairman of the committee on internal improvements; chairman of the joint committee to compromise, commute and settle the public debt, and was also a member of several other committees, among them the judiciary.

In 1876 Mr. Waring was elector on the Tilden ticket, and cast the vote of his district for that great statesman, just twenty years after he had voted in the electoral college for Buchanan. The college chose him to take the message to Washington and deliver it to the vice-president. In 1877, on the organization of the inferior court for Mecklenburg county, he was elected chairman, and was regularly re-elected by acclamation until 1884, when he resigned to accept a seat in the house of representatives in the state legislature. He was, of course, elected, for he has never been defeated before the people, though he has served them for the third of a century. He is regarded as a fluent, clear and forcible speaker.

In 1885 he was appointed by President Cleveland assayer, in charge of the United States assay office at Charlotte, N. C., which honorable and responsible position he filled until July, 1889. February 13, 1889, President Cleveland appointed Mr. Waring as a member of the committee to weigh and assay the United States coins, as a representative of North Carolina. Such a committee is annually appointed for such work in keeping with a law of congress. He served on this committee through 1889. He is still vigorous, and takes a deep interest in the politics and material and educational development of the state he has served so long and so faithfully.

JOHN MOTLEY MOREHEAD,

ex-governor of North Carolina, was born in Pittsylvania county, Va., July 4, 1796, and died in Rockbridge Alum Springs, Va., August 28, 1866. He was graduated at the University of North Carolina in 1817; studied law; was admitted to the bar in 1819, and acquired a large practice. He was a whig in politics; was a warm friend of Henry Clay, and served in the North Carolina legislature. From 1841 till 1845, he was governor of the state, and in 1848 president of the national whig convention that nominated Zachary Taylor for president.